Third Edition
CORRECTIONAL COUNSELING & TREATMENT

Peter C. Kratcoski
Kent State University

**WAVELAND
PRESS, INC.**

Prospect Heights, Illinois

This book is dedicated to the memory of my brother,
John E. Kratcoski.

For information about this book, write or call:
Waveland Press, Inc.
P.O. Box 400
Prospect Heights, Illinois 60070
(847) 634-0081

Contents

iii

Preface

Correctional Counseling and Treatment, Third Edition, is designed
to provide information on a number of treatment techniques
currently being used in American corrections and to describe and
demonstrate the applicability of these treatment techniques in
correctional settings.

No attempt was made to include every counseling and treatment
method currently in use. Rather, the selections in this book concentrate on the most widely used techniques, those that can be
applied to juveniles and adults in both institutional and community
settings.

The scope and purposes of correctional treatment today and
methods of evaluating correctional treatment are considered in the
introductory pages and in Section I. A key element in the controversy that has arisen over the comparative effectiveness of various
treatment techniques is the fact that the *purpose* of correctional
treatment has come to be regarded as prevention of recidivism.
Many staff members who administer correctional treatment programs maintain that the goals of correctional treatment must be
more broadly defined and that successful treatment should be
measured not only in terms of lack of recidivism, but also by such
factors as improved mental health, ability to perform adequately
in a work situation, successful adjustment in the community, and
appropriate handling of interpersonal relationships.

Section II is devoted to career opportunities in corrections today
and the characteristics and unique problems of people involved in
correctional work. In Section III, "Classification for Correctional
Treatment," the many facets of an offender's case (age, sex, family
history, offense record, results of psychological and educational
testing, physical health, presentence investigation, and reports by
social and correctional workers) that may have a bearing on the type
of treatment chosen are explored. Various classification systems
developed, implemented, and evaluated by experts in the field are
described.

Sections IV, V, VI, and VII are devoted to detailed descriptions
of various treatment techniques, including crisis intervention,

reality therapy and responsibility training, behavior modification, and group counseling.

Section VIII, "Special Areas of Correctional Treatment," focuses on the problems and unique situations that arise when counselors are working with retarded or mentally ill offenders, sex offenders, substance abusers, or older inmates. The selections in this section provide many practical suggestions for working with such problem clients and describe programs that have been applied effectively.

Section IX, "Correctional Treatment: Past, Present, and Future," summarizes the successes and problems of correctional treatment and highlights innovations in correctional supervision and administration, including the use of electronic monitors, privatization of correctional services, development of prison industries, educational programs in prisons, and shock incarceration (the "boot camp" approach).

No attempt is made here to discuss the relative merits of various counseling and treatment techniques or to compare the effectiveness of community and institutional programs. Instead, the techniques are presented in such a manner that they can be applied in either type of correctional setting, with juvenile or adult offenders, or adapted to deal with the adjustment problems of members of the "normal" (noncriminal) population.

Counseling and treatment techniques cannot be considered without reference to those who apply them. A number of selections in this book report the efforts, frustrations, styles, reactions, and learning experiences of correctional personnel engaged in treatment.

Presentation of the wide range of correctional counseling and treatment techniques described here would not have been possible without the cooperation of the many contributing authors and their publishers. In addition, the encouragement and support of Neil Rowe and Carol Rowe of Waveland Press, Steve Dungan, Rights and Permissions Manager, and Jeni Ogilvie, Assistant Editor, helped make this book a reality. Also the suggestions for improvements and additions made by professional colleagues who reviewed the second edition of this book, including John O'Kane, Sean Cassidy, Avlin Zumbrun, Byron T. Robinson, Frank Polk, John Fuller, Johnnie Myers, Alexander Bassin, Jeffrey Rush, Georgia Smith, Ted Marshall, Gail Flint, Tim Goolsby, Robert Morgenstern, Paul R. Thomas, Anthony J. Biondo, James A. Embree, and Allen D. Sapp were invaluable in developing a third edition that will be useful to those in the correctional field. Special thanks to Lucille Dunn Kratcoski, who assisted in all phases of the book's development.

Introduction

The Scope and Purposes of Correctional Treatment

This book is designed to present and describe some of the counseling and treatment techniques that are available to assist correctional workers toward accomplishing the goals they have established for their work. These goals are broadly defined as (1) to assist the offender to establish a lifestyle that is personally satisfying and conforms to the rules and regulations of society and (2) to protect the community from harmful activity by offenders placed under correctional workers' supervision. These dual demands of correctional work—to provide assistance, counseling, and treatment and, at the same time, to act in a manner that will minimize the offender's threat to the community—are present for correctional workers who serve as youth counselors, guards, probation officers, juvenile aftercare supervisors, parole officers, social workers, psychologists, or coordinators of educational or employment programs.

In the view of many, correctional counseling and treatment is associated with employment by a government agency (federal, state or local) which has the responsibility to control offenders. While this description is accurate for the majority of individuals who work with delinquent and criminal offenders, there has been a significant trend in recent years toward contracting correctional or counseling services with private agencies or corporations. As a result, many of the professionals who work with offenders have credentials in fields other than criminal justice and corrections, including psychology, rehabilitation counseling, education, sociology, and social work. Occupations which involve some contact with offenders

1

through counseling or treatment activity also include parole officer, child welfare caseworker, recreation leader, social group worker, academic teacher, vocational instructor, correctional counselor, and psychiatrist.

Traditionally, the correctional worker's role was viewed as one of supportive assistance and surveillance-supervision. The correctional worker had to balance these two facets of the role and decide whether allowing certain behavior to occur was in the best interests of the offender or of the residents of the community. Today, the roles of correctional workers, particularly those who work in community settings, have become more complex. The expertise needed to provide the appropriate types of counseling, therapy, or treatment appropriate for certain offenders may be beyond the scope of a single professional's training. For example, offenders who have problems with alcohol or drug abuse, sexual deviance, mental retardation, or violent behavior may require widely divergent types of counseling and therapy. Thus, a very important function of correctional counseling today is assessment, classification, and referral activity. In many instances, a correctional counselor must be aware of the possibilities for referral and make decisions as to the most appropriate therapy, rather than attempt to personally provide specialized types of counseling to the offenders. The ambiguities and pressures associated with such decision making are documented and discussed by various authors in this book.

Defining Correctional Treatment

When correctional treatment is discussed, terms such as humanitarian reform, corrections, rehabilitation, and treatment are often use interchangeably, creating some confusion as to just what correctional treatment involves. Also at issue is the part played by incarceration and mandatory supervision in the correctional treatment process.

Humanitarian reforms are usually thought of in terms of what directly benefits and affects the physical welfare of the offender. Such initial modifications of the penal system as elimination of long periods of solitary confinement, flogging, or bread-and-water diets obviously fall within this definition, as do more contemporary changes that allow prisoners to wear personal clothing rather than uniforms and provide recreational facilities for inmates. Such liberal practices as allowing attendance at college classes outside the institution, weekend home visits for selected prisoners, or providing opportunities for conjugal visitation within the prisons or social contacts between male and female inmates have caused some critics to observe that humanitarian reforms have gone too far and that the "country club" atmosphere of many institutions has minimized or virtually eliminated the impact of incarceration as punishment. Such thinking ignores or downplays the importance of personal motivation as an important factor in correctional treatment.

As implied in the word itself, "corrections" means to change a condition that is considered to be undesirable or has been a mistake and to bring things back to a state that is considered desirable or appropriate. In the correctional process, measures are taken to change the behavior of the offender to that which conforms with the standards and laws of the society. Corrections involves care, custody, and supervision of convicted offenders who have been sentenced or whose sentences have been suspended. The correctional process can occur in a federal or state correctional institution; as part of parole from such an institution; in a local jail or workhouse; or as part of probation at the federal, state, or local level. With the advent of diversion, pretrial intervention, deferred prosecution, and similar types of programs, it is logical to say that corrections has an opportunity to occur at any stage within the criminal justice process after a contact has been made between the offender and a law enforcement official.

The primary goal of corrections is to change the offensive behavior of the offender to a behavior that is designated appropriate by the laws of society. Before the eighteenth century, punishment was considered the central ingredient of corrections in European countries; thus, the dispensation of justice involved some form of physical torture or mutilation, banishment, or enslavement in galleys or on work farms. Prisons were used almost exclusively for those awaiting trial and for political prisoners. It wasn't until the eighteenth century that Cesare Beccaria (1738–1794) proposed the *pleasure-pain principle*—that is, that punishments should only be severe enough to deter offenders from repeating their unacceptable behavior.[1] At the same time, Jeremy Bentham (1748–1832) expounded his theory of utilitarianism in England. Both Beccaria and Bentham assumed that, given a free choice, a reasonable person would choose to avoid behavior for which he was sure to be punished. Bentham envisioned the prison as a correctional institution, located within the community, where citizens who had chosen to violate the law would be punished, while others would view it as a daily reminder of the penalties or violation of the law.[2] The idea that the punishment should "fit the crime" became an accepted part of correctional practice and various types of prisons and workhouses were built for the express purpose of being correctional centers or "houses of correction."

In the above context "correction" did not include rehabilitation as a key component. As time passed it became apparent that punishment alone did not guarantee a reduction in the criminal behavior of offenders, and there was gradual acceptance of the notion that those who would be eventually returned to society must be given some guidance and opportunities that would lead them toward a socially acceptable future lifestyle. Thus, while present-day "corrections" is not synonymous with "rehabilitation," it is very closely linked to it. Rehabilitation activity is set in motion when an individual comes to the attention of the correctional system after conviction. Such rehabilitation is involuntary in the sense that the offender has not actually sought it, but is rather required to undergo certain therapies, engage in counseling, or follow specified courses of action.

According to Francis A. Allen, the theoretical basis of rehabilitation is a complex of ideas that assumes human behavior to be a product of antecedent causes which are in turn part of the physical-social environment. This idea also presupposes that, given knowledge of the causes of human behavior, it is possible to scientifically control human behavior. Measures designed to treat the convicted offender should therefore serve a therapeutic function and should effect changes in his or her behavior that will be in his own best interests.[3]

The notion of correctional rehabilitation as a return to a point in an individual's development when his or her behavior was satisfactory has been challenged by those who have observed that many offenders never experience anything in their lives resembling satisfactory adjustment, and that such persons are candidates for "habilitation" rather than rehabilitation. "Habilitation" here would refer to familiarity with and adjustment to normal society and the holding of values in line with the norms and laws of the community. Correctional work concerned with "habilitation" could well involve attack on the causes of an individual's poor adjustment to society (family problems, unemployment, lack of education) in addition to guidance toward acceptable behavior.

Correctional treatment, then, can be defined as any planned and monitored program of activity that has the goal of rehabilitating or "habilitating" the offender so that he or she will avoid criminal activity in the future.

The Effectiveness of Correctional Treatment

In *Correctional Counseling and Treatment*, Third Edition, we will explore the many ways in which correctional treatment may be attempted, and note points of disagreement, controversy, or even diametric opposition in the approaches advocated.

No individual type of treatment has proved to be a panacea for reducing criminal activity. During the past twenty years, a debate has raged regarding the possibility that correctional treatment may be ineffective in reducing recidivism (additional criminal behavior) by those who receive it. If this is true, should correctional treatment attempts be abandoned, or is lack of recidivism by offenders the only factor to be considered in assessing treatment success? Is partially successful adjustment of the offender to his or her social environment justification for providing correctional treatment, even if some recidivism does occur? We must also consider another question that has gained considerable attention in recent years— is the application of correctional treatment better or more effective in changing offenders' behavior than doing nothing at all? If the answer is negative, should we revert to a punishment-centered correctional philosophy?

Punishment vs. Treatment

In *We Are the Living Proof*, Fogel noted that two camps developed in regard to the advisability of undertaking rehabilitative correctional treatment with all types of offenders. One side, disillusioned by revelations of the inadequacy of policies in criminal justice and corrections, and buttressed in its arguments by high crime rates, citizens' fear of crime, and the apparent ineffectiveness of correctional treatment in preventing recidivism, advocated a very punitive, severe sentencing approach. The opposite camp had not given up on the possibilities of effective correctional rehabilitative treatment, but contended that the failure of correctional policies and programs was linked to inadequate resources, poorly trained personnel, political interference, and the existence of huge, brutalizing and dehumanizing prisons, which were schools for crime. This group was convinced that, with improvements in these areas, attempts at rehabilitative correctional treatment could still be successful.

Between these two points of view, Fogel saw an approach that would place renewed emphasis on an offender's responsibility and accountability for his or her actions, coupled with an emphasis on rehabilitative treatment that is *available* but not *mandatory*. Fogel termed this the "justice model for corrections." In this model, "justice as fairness should be the goal of all attempts at corrections, and all agencies of criminal law should perform their assigned tasks with offenders lawfully."[4] Fogel addressed the area of the offender's responsibility for his or her actions and noted that restitution might often be substituted for harsh punishment, depending on the nature of the offense. He suggested an alternative to indeterminate sentences. In their place, Fogel advocated a return to "flat time," a set length of time in prison, which could be shortened only by good time (lawful behavior) credit, not by participation in any sort of treatment program.[5]

In applying the justice model to the prison, Fogel noted that time in a prison is an "enforced deprivation of liberty" and that opportunities for self-improvement should be offered but not made a condition of freedom."[6] Those in charge of the prisoners have the obligation to treat them in a lawful and just manner. Being in prison in itself is a form of punishment, and out of humanitarian concerns correctional personnel should avoid adding to the burden of loss of freedom and dignity which the incarcerated person experiences merely by being there.

As Fogel saw the justice model, in order to learn responsibility and be able to accept prison, inmates would be given some degree of self-governance or be part of an inmate-staff governance group. Conflicts within the institution would be resolved through rule of law, and prisoners would be given opportunities for legal aid, while an ombudsman would oversee the activities of both inmates and staff. Counseling and self-help and improvement programs would be available, but not required, and taking part in them would not help determine the inmate's readiness for release. Work programs would involve the inmate being paid for his or her work in wages that would be commensurate with what he or she would receive on the outside. In turn, the inmate would be required to compensate the institution for lodging and food, pay taxes, send allotments to his or her family, and pay restitution to the victims of the crime.[7]

This justice model which emphasizes responsibility under the law, could reasonably be applied in programs outside institutions, including probation, parole, and community residential programs.

Many states and the federal prison system were quick to accept the assumption underlying the "justice model" and proceeded to adopt determinate sentencing policies for all convicted offenders.[8] Other states, while not totally eliminating indeterminate sentencing, instituted measures which tended to reduce the emphasis given to the treatment and rehabilitation of convicted offenders and increased measures to deal more harshly with them (see Moore and Miethe, 1987 and Hamm, 1987).[9]

The enthusiasm for the "justice model" has waned somewhat in recent years as a result of the increasing amount of evidence which shows that determinate sentencing has not led to the results anticipated. For example, Wakefield, who surveyed sentencing reforms for forty-four states, found that, rather than being treated more harshly by being given longer sentences, the lengths of the sentences given to drug traffickers were actually shorter than they were before the sentence reforms were instituted.[10]

It is also apparent that treatment programs for convicted offenders did not disappear. As the evidence accumulated that much criminal activity is directly or indirectly related to such factors as substance abuse, illiteracy, mental illness or unemployment, which must be addressed if there is any hope of the offender becoming a productive person, the number and variety of treatment strategies actually increased. While the "justice model" proposes a "no right to treatment" policy and maintains that convicted offenders under local, state or federal supervision either in institutions or in the community should not be required to become involved in treatment programs, in practice, correctional agencies have not abandoned treatment.

In some instances, the nature of the programs has changed. Many of these programs, such as "boot camp" training, may appear to be punishment rather than treatment oriented. However, they are well-thought-out projects which are geared toward making the offender accept responsibility and become disciplined and self-reliant. No one says treatment has to be pleasurable. The definition of treatment has also been expanded, so that work and educational programs are now encompassed under the treatment label. Many states and the U.S. Bureau of Prisons require prisoners to work, if they are physically able, or to go to school, if they are illiterate. Some forms of treatment are not only provided, but mandatory in these jurisdictions.

Thus, in most community or institutional corrections situations, the matter of choosing or rejecting treatment is not even debatable. Juvenile corrections continues to provide a range of counseling, education, vocational development and treatment services. On the adult level, those on probation, parole, or in community rehabilitation facilities discover that involvement in substance abuse counseling, employment counseling, or family therapy is likely to be required as a condition of placement in this status. Even those serving determinate sentences may elect or are required to take part in correctional counseling or treatment programs. Correctional counseling and treatment continue to be vital aspects of correctional work.

Notes

[1] Edwin H. Sutherland and Donald R. Cressey, *Criminology* (Philadelphia: Lippincott, 1974), p. 50.

8   Introduction

[2] Sue Titus Reid, *Crime and Criminology* (Hinsdale, IL: Dryden Press, 1976), p. 106.

[3] Francis A. Allen, "Legal Values and the Rehabilitative Ideal," in *The Borderland of Criminal Justice* (Chicago: University of Chicago Press, 1964), p. 25–41.

[4] David Fogel, "*. . . We are the Living Proof . . .*" (Cincinnati: Anderson Publishing, 1975), p. 184.

[5] Ibid., p. 47

[6] Ibid., p. 204

[7] Ibid., p. 261

[8] Dean J. Champion, *Probation and Parole in the United States*, (NY: Macmillan Publishing Co., 1990), p. 123.

[9] Charles A. Moore and Terance D. Miethe, 1987, "Can Sentencing Reform Work? A Four-Year Evaluation of Determinate Sentencing in Minnesota." Unpublished paper presented at the American Society of Criminology meeting. Montreal, P.Q., Canada, and Mark S. Hamm, "Determinate Sentencing in Indiana: An Analysis of the Impact of the Justice Model." Unpublished paper presented at the American Society of Criminology meeting, Montreal, P.Q., Canada.

[10] Penny Wakefield, "The Sentencing Process: Redefining Objectives" in *State Laws and Procedures Affecting Drug Trafficking Control*, edited by J. Bentevoglio et al. (Washington, D.C.: National Governors Association, 1985).

Section *I*

Evaluation of Correctional Treatment

In this era of tightening state and federal budgets and emphasis on cost efficiency and fiscal accountability, any treatment program extensive enough to seek state or federal funding must contain some provision for evaluation. Statistical reports, which concentrate on numbers of clients served, hours worked by staff, estimates of the number of community members affected directly or indirectly by the program, and recidivism rates of the clients are familiar to those involved in correctional treatment. It has become very important to examine whether a certain type of treatment works as well as or better than another type and whether clients given a specific mode of therapy or supervision are likely to adjust in the community and remain offense-free more frequently than those given another type of treatment or no treatment at all.

Producing a meaningful and effective evaluation of any type of treatment program is beset with problems. It is difficult and often impractical to establish control groups with which those receiving treatment can be meaningfully compared, and there is concern about the ethics of giving treatment to some offenders and withholding it from others for the sole purpose of comparative research. The short length of time between the initiation of the program and the required evaluation report frequently makes it difficult to establish comparative experimental and control groups. The ideals of random placement of those treated in experimental or control groups, or even matching of offender populations according to age, number of prior offenses, or background characteristics must frequently give way to less meaningful comparisons. For example, the current residents of a halfway house that has a new job-training or employment-education program may be compared with those who resided in the house before the program began, with regard to their ability to get and hold jobs. In such an instance, changes in economic conditions within the community between the two time periods may be so extreme that the results coming from such a comparison may be questionable.

Evaluation may also be colored by the personal biases or characteristics of the evaluators. Internal evaluations, that is, those completed by the administrators of the programs, are particularly prone to this type of problem, since those in charge are anxious to show that the program is succeeding and that they are doing a good job. Outside consultants may also lean toward showing that the program is successful, since payment for their services in the future obviously hinges upon re-funding and continuing the program. The subjects of a treatment program may also behave in such a way as to color its results. If, for example, subjects are aware that they are involved in a new or experimental program, they may do everything in their power to make sure it appears to succeed—or may sabotage it, if they dislike the demands made upon them.

A problem in developing the research design to evaluate a program is the formulation of a definition of "success." The indicator chosen most often to measure the success of correctional treatment is the amount or rate of recidivism (new offenses). Even on this point evaluation cannot be precise, because recidivism statistics are available only for those offenders who have been arrested and do not necessarily include all of the unlawful behavior that has occurred following correctional treatment. The level of supervision given to those who complete treatment is an important consideration in the amount of recidivism reported, particularly if violations tabulated as "new offenses" are probation or parole violations.

Also, the length of time covered by recidivism measurements has a bearing on the effectiveness evaluation. For example, the Highfields experiment in guided group interaction was declared a success because the recidivism rates one year after its completion were much lower for the experimental group than for a comparison group. After two years had passed, however, the variations in levels of recidivism between the two groups were greatly reduced.

If measures other than recidivism rates are used for purposes of evaluation, the problem of bias by the evaluators increases. Such instruments as personal adjustment checklists and case reports by probation or parole officers, which report the offender's readjustment to the community or degree of effort put forth in working on solutions to his or her problems, are obviously colored by the reporter's reaction to the offender. Even when a program has been judged to be successful by what appear to be objective evaluators and firm criteria, the reasons for its success may lie in the dedication or ability of the program's directors or workers or in certain ethnic or environmental characteristics of those being treated, and the likelihood of attaining the same level of success in other settings may be low.

The matters of correctional treatment and the possibilities for rehabilitation of offenders came under scrutiny in the 1970s when Robert Martinson, a sociology professor, wrote a series of articles in *The New Republic* which described and commented on his extensive examination of correctional treatment programs in English-speaking countries in the years 1945 through 1967. While the evidence presented in these articles was grounded in empirical research and eventually published in the book, *The Effectiveness of Correctional Treatment* (1975), by Douglas Lipton, Robert Martinson, and Judith Wilks, their conclusion that "with few and isolated exceptions, the rehabilitative efforts that have been reported so far have no appreciable effect on recidivism,"[1] aroused a furor in correctional circles. Those who felt that the criminal justice system had gone too far in terms of protecting the rights and interests of offenders at the expense of the victims of crime seized upon the study's conclusion, simplified it to contend "nothing works" to change the behavior of criminals, and used this contention as the basis for calls to abandon the efforts to rehabilitate and to focus on harsher punishments.

It is true that Martinson painted a gloomy picture of the possibilities for rehabilitation success. In his article, "What Works?—Questions and Answers About Prison Reform," (1974), he reported the specific types of programs which he had evaluated and found lacking in success in preventing recidivism. The types included academic education, social skill development, vocational education, individual counseling, group counseling, and even milieu therapy, which used every element of the inmate's environment as part of the treatment modality. After reviewing many community treatment programs administered in halfway houses or as part of probation or parole activity, the author stated: "In some, even in the case of treatment programs administered outside penal institutions, we simply cannot say that this treatment in itself has an appreciable effect on offender behavior."[2] On the basis of his examination of more than 200 programs of correctional treatment involving hundreds of thousands of offenders, Martinson stated that, although instances of success or partial success were noted, no pattern emerged to indicate that any method of treatment was effective in reducing recidivism.[3]

There is no doubt that *The Effectiveness of Correctional Treatment*, popularly known as "The Martinson Report," had a strong impact. The trends away from probation and toward sentencing to institutions, calls for determinate sentences and shifts in emphasis in many correctional programs to punishment rather than rehabilitation closely followed circulation of the view that "nothing works"—or that very little can be done to change the behavior or offense patterns of juveniles or adults who have been involved in offenses serious enough to warrant their formal handling by the justice system.

Stuart Adams, in a review and critique of Martinson's research, observed that academicians as well as administrators and politicians may cloud the real issues and findings with rhetoric. He noted that before *The Effectiveness of Correctional Treatment* (the book which detailed the research) appeared, Martinson's articles in *The New Republic* and his appearance on the television program "60 Minutes" created a good deal of public interest in his findings. Efforts to capsulize them for popular consumption resulted in their simplification into what might be termed the "Nothing Works Doctrine," which became a rallying point for those interested in changing the focus and direction of correctional policy.

When Adams systematically compared the evaluations of specific programs cited in *The Effectiveness of Correctional Treatment* with evaluations of the same programs by other researchers, he found considerable variations in the conclusions reached regarding the effectiveness of the programs. For example, Palmer reported that 40% of the 231 program evaluations in *The Effectiveness of Correctional Treatment* showed at least partial positive results, and termed them "partially or fully successful," while Martinson characterized the same programs as "few and isolated" instances of success. In addition, Adams concluded that the key factor in programs that achieved some success was the change agent—the rare individual who could inspire, goad, coax, frighten, or bully an offender enough to make him or her want to change.[4]

Martinson continued to explore the degree of success of correctional treatment programs. In the article, "New Findings, New Views: A Note of Caution Regarding Sentencing Reform," he reported the results of additional research, which included not only evaluative research studies that matched control groups with the experimental groups receiving treatment, but also studies that reported on the progress of groups of more than nine sentenced offenders. Believing that the term "recidivism" was a confusing one,

Martinson developed the notion of "reprocessing" in his later studies, with "reprocessing" defined as "subjecting an offender to further arrest, conviction, or imprisonment." Based on his new information, from 555 studies, Martinson retreated from his earlier conclusion that "with few and isolated exceptions, the rehabilitative effects that have been reported so far have no appreciable effect on recidivism." Instead, he declared that some programs were beneficial, others were neutral (had no impact), and still others were detrimental. He identified the key factor in the success of treatment programs as the "conditions under which the program is delivered."[5]

Gendreau and Ross (1987) reviewed the research pertaining to offender rehabilitation for the period of 1981 through 1987. They assessed the literature that pertained to the effectiveness of a wide variety of treatment programs. They concluded that the "nothing works" statement on the effectiveness of treatment programs was fallacious. They also discovered that many innovative approaches being used in correctional treatment showed great promise. Some of these approaches were not being used during the period when Lipton, Matrinson, and Wilks conducted their research.

Gendreau and Ross summarized their findings by stating: "It is downright ridiculous to say 'Nothing works.' This review attests that much is going on to indicate that offender rehabilitation has been, can be, and will be achieved. The principles underlying effective rehabilitation generalize across far too many intervention strategies and offender samples to be dismissed as trivial" (395).[6]

In selection one, "The 'Effectiveness' Issue Today: An Overview," Ted Palmer reviews the debate sparked by Martinson's findings and concludes that two quite divergent points of view regarding the effectiveness of correctional treatment emerged in the late 1980s. Those who belong to the "skeptical" camp have concluded either that rehabilitation should be given a minor role because it holds little promise or that the research into its effectiveness or the implementation of rehabilitation programs have been so flawed that we still do not know if it can work. In contrast, Palmer's "sanguine" camp holds that some programs have been shown to work with certain offenders, even though many or most offenders will not be positively affected or that the specific approach and external conditions are the key factors which dictate whether offenders will respond positively, neutrally, or negatively to treatment programs. He identifies intensive applications of "multiple modality" approaches, which combine various types of counseling or training and distribution of treatment and counseling according to the needs, interest, and limitations of individual offenders rather than to the total offender population, as areas where both camps agree efforts should be concentrated.

In the second article, "Evaluating Intensive Supervision Probation/Parole: Results of a Nationwide Experiment," the authors report some very recent findings relating to the use of intensive supervision for probationers and parolees. Intensive supervision has been hailed as a very important innovation for the rehabilitation of offenders for various reasons, including the fact that it is much less expensive than institutionalization and, since it is considered a substitute for incarceration, it helps relieve the current serious prison overcrowding problem.

The researchers discovered that those under intensive supervision are likely to be charged with more technical violations than those who receive traditional styles of supervision. However, compared to those supervised in other manners, intensively supervised offenders received more treatment in the forms of drug and alcohol counseling and employment counseling and participated in more community service and restitution programs. Involvement in the treatment components of intensive supervision correlated with a reduction in recidivism in some of the programs studied.

While the debate over the effectiveness of correctional treatment has not resulted in the total demise of treatment programs, it has had the positive effect of making those responsible for administering correctional treatment more selective in the types of treatment offered. The faddishness which was associated with earlier choices of treatment, with many techniques used experimentally because they appeared to offer novel approaches, has disappeared. Administrators and program directors now have to reach some degree of conviction that a treatment technique has long-term merit before it is instituted. Most treatment programs, particularly those that receive outside funding, have an evaluation component built in and must demonstrate that positive results are occurring.

Notes

[1] Robert Martinson, "What Works? Questions and Answers About Prison Reform," *Public Interest* (Spring 1974): 25.

[2] Ibid., 50–51.

[3] Ibid., 54.

[4] Stuart Adams, "Evaluation: A Way Out of Rhetoric," in Robert Martinson, Ted Palmer, and Stuart Adams, *Rehabilitation, Recidivism, and Research,* Washington, D.C., National Council of Crime and Delinquency, 1976, 75–91.

[5] Robert Martinson, "New Findings, New Views: A Note of Caution Regarding Sentencing Reform," *Hofstra Law Review,* 7,2 (Winter 1979): 243–58.

[6] Paul Gendreau and Robert R. Ross, "Revivification of Rehabilitation: Evidence from the 1980s," *Justice Quarterly,* 4,3 (September 1987): 349–408.

1

The *"Effectiveness" Issue Today*
An Overview

Ted Palmer

In 1974, a wide-ranging debate regarding the effectiveness of rehabilitation was launched by Robert Martinson's assertion that nothing or almost nothing works. [18] Since then, rebuttals and counter-rebuttals have been exchanged and, in the process, some light has been shed though considerable heat and haze remain. This process has been difficult but necessary; and though "sides" are still sharply drawn, the justice system may soon reap some benefits from the exchange. What, then, is the current status of this debate, and what are its emerging trends?

The overview that follows derives primarily from several major works conducted during 1966–1980. Chief among these are reviews and evaluations by: Adams; Bailey; Empey; Gendreau and Ross; Greenberg; Lipton, Martinson, and Wilks (*LMW*); Martinson; the National Academy of Sciences Panel; Palmer; Romig; Wilson; Wright and Dixon. [1; 3; 6; 7; 10; 14; 18; 20; 21; 23; 24; 26; 27] These efforts focused on experimental studies of juvenile and adult offenders in institutional as well as community settings. Each such category of offender and setting was well-represented in the studies reviewed, as were the major traditional, rehabilitation methods (individual and group counseling; vocational and educational training; etc.); other less common interventions were also included. Most such methods were implemented under nonvoluntary conditions and—in the case of institutional programs—in an

Source: *Federal Probation*, 47(2) (June 1983): 3–10.

indeterminate-sentence context. Though the studies which were reviewed related to minor as well as serious or multiple offenders, the present overview will emphasize the implications of those reviews for the latter individuals. Throughout, the central question will be: Does rehabilitation work?

To address this question we will focus on programs that were judged successful or unsuccessful because—whatever else they did or did not accomplish with their target group—they either did or did not reduce recidivism. Use of recidivism is consistent with our view that the ultimate goal of rehabilitation is increased public protection. *Clearly*, rehabilitation efforts may also produce successful or desirable outcomes with respect to attitude-change, skill development, and various aspects of community adjustment, and these as well as other outcomes often do—but often do not—relate to recidivism. Nevertheless, for present purposes, the central criterion of success or effectiveness will be the reduction of illegal behavior—arrests, convictions, and related actions. This criterion was also used in the reviews mentioned above.

As discussed in this overview, rehabilitation or habilitation includes a wide range of interventions whose principal as well as ultimate goal is the increased protection of society This, the *socially centered* goal of rehabilitation, is achieved when the offender's behavior is modified so that it conforms to the law. It is promoted but not in itself achieved by modifying given attitudes, by strengthening the offender as an individual, by reducing various external pressures and increasing given supports or opportunities, and/or by helping him or her become more satisfied and self-fulfilled within the context of society's values. Attitude-change, increased coping ability, etc., comprise the secondary or *offender-centered* goal of rehabilitation. Though this goal has absolute value in itself, it is—from the perspective of the overall justice system and this system's function in society—chiefly a "means" to the socially centered "end" of public protection. [20]

Before proceeding, let us briefly indicate what we mean by the phrase "rehabilitation program or approach." The following is not a formal exhaustive identification of rehabilitation or habilitation; however for present purposes, it will suffice.

The primary and secondary goals of rehabilitation are achieved by focusing on such factors and conditions as the offender's present adjustment techniques, his interests and skills, his limitations, and/or his life-circumstances, in ways that affect his future behavior and adjustment. Rehabilitation efforts are thus focused on particular factors or conditions and are directed toward particular future events. Insofar as they involve specific components or inputs (e.g., counseling or skill-development) that are organized, interrelated, and otherwise planned so as to generate changes in those factors and conditions (e.g., skills or life-circumstances) that may *in turn* help generate the desired future events, those efforts can be called rehabilitation programs or approaches. Such efforts—"interventions"—may involve what has been called treatment, external control, or both. Under some conditions, what has been called punishment may be considered an adjunct approach to rehabilitation.[1] However, methods such as electroshock treatment, psycho-surgery, etc., are not included under rehabilitation despite the factors or conditions on which they may focus and despite the specific effects—e.g., reduced illegal behavior—they may produce or be designed to produce.[2]

We now turn to the overview of "effectiveness."

Current Status of "Effectiveness"

Martinson's conclusion that "nothing works," which was widely accepted during the middle and later 1970s, is increasingly seen as a faulty synthesis of the findings from 138 recidivism studies previously described by Lipton, Martinson, and Wilks. [14; 18] Palmer's critique of Martinson's method of synthesizing those findings showed that the latter's conclusion was valid only in the following sense: No single, broadly categorized treatment *method*, e.g., group counseling or vocational training (each of which, of course, has many variations[3]), is guaranteed to reduce the recidivism of its target group. [21] The critique ("Martinson Revisited") showed that several group counseling *programs* (in effect, variations or types of group counseling) did reduce recidivism either for the target group as a whole or for various subgroups within the total target group. This was observed in high-quality and acceptable-quality research studies alike. Because of this and subsequent critiques, Martinson, in 1978 and 1979, explicitly repudiated his highly pessimistic conclusion that nothing or almost nothing works. Instead, he recognized the difference between evaluative statements concerning *individual* programs and those relating to *groups* of programs, i.e., broadly categorized methods. [2; 8; 17; 20]

Though extreme pessimism no longer prevails regarding the effectiveness of rehabilitation or habilitation programs, the pendulum is by no means swinging rapidly toward the opposite extreme. Nor is it even approaching the rather optimistic position that most treatment efforts (broadly categorized or not) have substantially reduced recidivism with many or perhaps most offenders, even in certain settings only (e.g., institutions). Moreover, what might be considered today's officially sanctioned position—that taken by the National Academy of Sciences in 1979—is very guarded: No single correctional program (and, therefore, no broadly categorized method) has been unequivocally proven to reduce the recidivism of its target group; that is, using very strict standards of evidence, none has been shown to work beyond almost all doubt. At any rate, none can be guaranteed to work. [24]

Despite its extreme scientific caution and stringent methodological standards, the NAS Panel indicated the following (these views were based on what it acknowledged as the "suggestions . . . concerning successful rehabilitative efforts" that were reported by *LMW*, and partly on the above and subsequent critiques):

(1) A few approaches may perhaps be working for some subgroups within the total target group; however the quality and especially quantity of evidence do not allow for definite conclusions regarding the subgroup-success of these approaches.

(2) Though no specific approaches have been proven to work, neither have they been disproven; instead, it is simply unclear which approaches have and have not been "given a fair trial." [24]

(3) Many programs might have proven effective if they had been better implemented, if they had operated more intensively (i.e., had more treatment-input per client), etc.

In sum, the NAS Panel's position was very guarded and carefully qualified, but contained some glimmers of hope. In 1981, the Panel reaffirmed its position and further discussed these glimmers. [15]

The Panel's marked caution seemed to closely parallel the position taken by Empey in 1978, both as to the "inconclusive" nature of most research studies and the extreme difficulty of scientifically sorting-out precisely what works. [6] (That is, sorting-out is difficult even when good-quality research designs exist and certainly when program operations are only sketchily described.) Yet Empey was less restrictive than the Panel in one respect. He apparently did not believe that the results from all research studies which, methodologically, had been somewhat less than flawless but which were still relatively strong, should be discounted as a basis for correctional policy recommendations. Rather than insist that the results from any given study be demonstrated with almost absolute certainty, e.g., beyond the shadow of a doubt, he seemed to accept what amounted to a preponderance-of-evidence standard in this regard. As a result, he believed that some programs, though probably not many, *had* been adequately shown to be successful with serious offenders; at least, they seemed promising enough to have positive policy implications. Beyond this, Empey—like the NAS Panel after him—believed that some programs might have produced better results if they had been directed, not at the full range of offenders, but at certain subgroups only. This view reflected the already existing "differential intervention" position, summarized below.

Several researchers and scholars—chiefly Palmer and Warren; Romig; Gendreau and Ross—have expressed a more sanguine view than that offered by the NAS Panel, by Greenberg, and, more recently, by Conrad. [4; 7; 10; 20; 23; 24; 25] To be sure, these individuals, like the Panel and Conrad, believe that *much* criminal justice research has been mediocre and that *most* rehabilitation efforts have probably been unsuccessful thus far, relative to their overall target group. Nevertheless, they believe that many programs, often well-researched programs by *LMW*'s detailed standards and those of others, have been shown to work with specified offenders (subgroups) under specific conditions. Their view—with the partial exception of Romig's—is generally known as the differential intervention (DI) position.[4,5] This view, which mainly grew from the early efforts of Warren, et al., in California's Community Treatment Project [25] goes beyond another well-known view—that which focuses on "amenability" alone.

In contrast to DI (see below), what might be termed the basic treatment-amenability (BTA) position only minimally distinguishes among types of offenders. The BTA position generally asserts that (1) certain offenders (e.g., the "bright, verbal, and anxious") will respond to many treatment approaches, presumably under most conditions or settings, and (2) most remaining offenders will respond to few if any approaches, again, regardless of conditions or settings. In contrast, the differential intervention view suggests that some offenders (BTA's amenables included) will respond positively to given approaches under certain conditions only, and that these individuals may respond *negatively* to other approaches under very similar conditions; other combinations of offender, approach, setting—and resulting outcome—are also implied. Finally, DI also suggests that many offenders who in the BTA view are generally described as nonamenables may in fact respond positively to certain approaches under particular conditions, e.g., close structuring within institutional settings. [7; 20; 25]

> In short, overly simplified, DI asserts that certain categories of offenders (e.g., the Conflicted) but not others (e.g., the Power Oriented) will respond positively to certain approaches only, at least under specified conditions—and that the opposite may

occur in response to other approaches or conditions. There are
no all-around amenables and nonamenables, even though some
individuals do usually perform better than others.

Thus, compared with BTA, the DI view is both more and less
"optimistic" about so-called amenables; it is more optimistic about
offenders who are often considered non-amenables, as well.

The "basic treatment amenability" and "differential
intervention" positions have both been supported by Glaser,
Adams, and others. [1; 8] The *amenability* view has, in addition,
recently been supported by Wilson, a long-time critic of rehabilitation who also accepts the NAS Panel's overall caution regarding the
validity of research findings to date. [26] All in all, there is increasing
agreement among researchers, academicians, and practitioners as
to which offenders are most likely to respond positively to
standard—and, to a lesser extent, more specialized—rehabilitation
approaches. *DI* has further been supported by Jesness, Hunt, Quay
and Parsons, Megargee, et al., Wright and Dixon, and others. [11;
12; 13; 19; 22; 27] By 1979, Martinson himself was essentially
supporting differential intervention:

> . . . no treatment program now used in criminal justice is
> inherently either substantially helpful or harmful. The critical
> fact seems to be the *conditions* under which the program is
> delivered. For example, our results indicate that a widely-used
> program, such as formal education, is detrimental when given
> to juvenile sentenced offenders in a group home, but is beneficial
> (decreases reprocessing rates) when given to juveniles in juvenile
> prisons. Such startling results are found again and again in our
> [recent] study for treatment programs as diverse as individual
> psychotherapy group counseling, intensive supervision, and
> what we have called "individual/help" (aid, advice, counseling).
> [17]

Finally, as indicated, both Empey and the Panel believe there may
be something to this view.

In sum, both the BTA and DI positions have received moderate
but clearly growing support within the justice system community;
quantitatively, this applies to their empirical support as well.
Nevertheless, as the Panel indicated, this evidence—while
suggestive—is neither overwhelming nor entirely consistent.[6] [9; 24]

Whether *many* programs or only a *small percentage* of programs
have reduced recidivism is unclear. (Here, it makes little difference
whether numbers or percentages are considered. However, by
"many" we mean at least 302 of the sample-of-programs reviewed
by such authors as *LMW*, Bailey and Adams, respectively—
recognizing that many programs were included in more than one

such sample.) The many-programs position is found not just among differential intervention proponents but among reviewers who have questioned the effectiveness of rehabilitation efforts. The small-percentage view—with no specific percentage or percentage-range having been stated—is that implied by the Panel, by Empey, and by Greenberg.[7] Though the truth (objective reality) may well lie between these positions, the available evidence favors the former—assuming that "small" means less than 15 percent. More specifically direct counts (Bailey's included, e.g., for "experimental studies") suggest that—conservatively—at least 20–25 percent of all experimental programs reviewed have reduced recidivism for their total target groups, while at least an additional 10–15 percent have done so for one or more subgroups only. [1; 3; 20; 21] However, the exact percentages may not be too important. What may matter in the long-run is whether knowledge has been and can be gathered regarding the nature of (1) those programs which work and (2) offenders whom those programs apparently serve best. Such information could make it possible to reproduce, improve, and more efficiently utilize those and similar programs, and to discard whatever approaches seem to accomplish little for the preponderance of their clients. In this way, the percentage of successful programs could increase—whether from today's small or more substantial level.

Long-range considerations aside, percentages—or at least terms such as "most," "many," and "few"—have nevertheless played a large and often confounding role in the effectiveness literature. For instance, DI proponents believe that many individuals who consider rehabilitation programs ineffective consistently overlook or ignore a basic fact, whether or not recidivism is involved as the sole outcome-measure. Although *most* programs have probably not worked well and *most* research was probably not done well, this still leaves numerous programs—i.e., from among the several hundred that were experimentally studied—that did work well or moderately well, that were researched satisfactorily or both. Moreover, even if only 10 percent of those several hundred were found to work, this would still leave "many."

> In short, proponents feel that, by overlooking this fact, these effectiveness-critics erroneously conclude or at least imply that since most programs—literally hundreds of programs—have not done well, rehabilitation efforts are obviously a failure and claims of effectiveness can be dismissed. Yet, in context, most is far from *all*.

DI proponents also believe that the dozens of programs mentioned above have collectively provided not only very strong evidence that *something*, in fact several things, work, but substantial converging evidence as to what works for many offenders. Thus, given these numerous positive-outcome programs, they consider it immaterial that the *general* quality of research-to-date, and even program-implementation-to-date, may have been far from satisfactory, or perhaps even lamentable. Meanwhile, however, effectiveness-critics suggest that DI and perhaps BTA proponents greatly exaggerate the importance or implications of what they, the critics, consider the *few* programs that may possibly have worked. In any event, effectiveness critics usually emphasize the atypical—and, by implication, the probably-difficult-to-replicate—nature of these few. [4]

Apart from *how many* programs reduce recidivism, there is the question of how sizable that reduction is. *LMW* indicated that although some programs did indeed work, "corrections has not yet found satisfactory ways to reduce recidivism by significant amounts." [14] They neither defined significant nor presented a percentage-reduction figure. In addition, Martinson, in 1976, suggested that the reduction in question was probably trivial—meaning, 5-to-15 percent. [16] (In 1979, however, he stated: ". . . contrary to my previous position, some treatments do have appreciable effect on recidivism." [17] The NAS Panel was silent on this point, and, at present, only one percentage-reduction figure seems to exist: Focusing on all programs reported in LMW which reduced recidivism by at least 10 percent.[8] Palmer found an average reduction of 32 percent, the mean follow-up being 19 months; from a public-protection as well as cost perspective, even half this figure might often be considered important. [20] At any rate, since this is the only available figure, it is perhaps best to conclude that little is presently known regarding the average recidivism-reduction of positive-outcome studies—i.e., of *all* such studies (not just *LMW*'s), and using varying definitions of success. Nevertheless, we suspect that the average reduction is substantial, e.g., over 20 percent. (The problem of defining successful programs is independent of the fact that *LMW* and Martinson may have made their estimates by combining successful and unsuccessful programs. At any rate, much depends on how success is operationally defined.)

The following question is closely related to the issue of percentage reduction in recidivism. For what percentage of the total target group, i.e., all offenders combined, have programs been "appropriate?" That is—in terms of the presently considered criterion—how often have they reduced recidivism? Here, no specific answer is known, and no average figure exists. Despite this absence of information, certain principles and related implications can be stated: Clearly if a program and all its offender-subgroups are matched, the percentage reduction that may result will be larger than if unmatched, in this case "inappropriate," subgroups are included. To date, few programs or even major program components have been designed for defined offender subgroups only—more specifically, for only those individuals who would presumably or theoretically be matched to those particular approaches. However, where program/offender matching *has* been used—as in California Youth Authority institutions during the 1960s—it has shown considerable promise. [12] Of course, the ideal program would perhaps be one that is flexible enough or contains enough relevant components to successfully work with *all* major subgroups, even though that program might not quite maximize the percentage reduction in recidivism for all its offenders combined.

Such programs—in effect, near-panaceas—are nowhere on today's horizon; in fact, as indicated, the NAS Panel believes that no approach has been decisively shown to work even for *specific subgroups*. To be sure, the Panel's view with respect to demonstrated subgroup success is shared by neither differential intervention nor treatment-amenability proponents. Yet, despite this disagreement, both sets of individuals agree as to the existence of two major preconditions to effective rehabilitation or habilitation:

(1) Single-modality approaches may be too narrowly focused to deal with the complex or multiple problems of most serious offenders. Instead, combinations-of-methods, e.g., vocational training *and* individual counseling, may be required.

(2) Program input may have to be considerably greater ("more intense") than it has typically been—that is, if, as in (1) above, one wishes to generate lasting behavioral or other forms of change in most serious offenders.

These preconditions would apply regardless of the program components or specific input involved, provided, of course, that the latter do bear on the particular offenders' problems. As indicated, the Panel believed that—with improved research designs—many approaches might have been shown to work if they had met preconditions such as these.

This agreement among otherwise differing observers is important, particularly in light of their further agreement regarding the value (or, in the case of the Panel, the directly implied value) of matching offenders with programs. Together, these preconditions/principles suggest that concentrated efforts, and perhaps greater individualization than in the past, are needed in order to affect substantial change in serious offenders. These suggestions may comprise some of the more constructive or at least potentially constructive products of the effectiveness-debate thus far. At any rate, they would have policy implications regardless of *how many* programs have been successful, and exactly *how* successful they have been.

Finally it should be added that differential intervention proponents largely agree among themselves on two additional points (here, the Panel took no public stand):

(1) Some offenders probably require, not so much the standard rehabilitation inputs such as counseling, vocational training, etc. They may require—primarily or perhaps on an equal footing—external controls, heavy structuring, and, with respect to community programs, considerable surveillance.

(2) Staff characteristics and staff/offender matching are probably major factors in successfully implementing given approaches, at least for many offenders.

Though the evidence for these points is neither overwhelming (quantitatively) nor entirely consistent, it is by no means insubstantial and has grown considerably in the past several years. At any rate, the present author would add a different and perhaps broader point, one that focuses on likely preconditions to effective rehabilitation and applies across the board:

(3) Fairness or fair treatment by the justice system, and humane interactions overall, can help create a tolerable, believable, sometimes supportive atmosphere for involvement and decision-making by offenders, especially but not exclusively in institutions.

Yet the following might be kept in mind. Fair treatment, etc., like just deserts and standardized dispositions by themselves, do not supply the direction, do not arouse the motivation, and do not provide the feedback or personal reward that probably must exist before realistic satisfying decisions are generated and maintained by those individuals. That is, unlike many rehabilitation efforts, they do not address the specifics or the offenders' future—their concrete needs and opportunities within an often demanding environment. Nor do they address the often complex task of motivating or realistically helping them come to grips with that environment and, in many cases, with themselves. Thus, for many offenders, fairness and humane interactions without programmed assistance can be empty, in a sense blind, and programs without fairness can be futile, even pathetic. [20]

Review and Conclusion

An unsettled atmosphere exists regarding the effectiveness of rehabilitation or habilitation. Neither the global optimism of the 1960s nor the extreme pessimism of the middle and later 1970s seem justified, and neither view in fact prevails. Two slightly more moderate "camps" have replaced them, and a sizable but not entirely unbridged gap exists between these two.

Within the "skeptical" camp, some individuals believe it is clear—based on what they consider enough adequately conducted research—that relatively few rehabilitation programs work; moreover, those which work probably reduce recidivism by fairly small amounts. These individuals feel that rehabilitation, while not a total loss, therefore holds little promise and should be given a minor role. The remaining individuals within this group believe that *very little* is clear: Because of (1) minor or major research flaws in almost all studies, (2) poorly implemented programs, or (3) both, we don't really know whether given approaches do or do not—can or cannot—work, for their target groups as a whole. In this respect, rehabilitation has not been "given a fair trial." Though some approaches may possibly have worked for at least some offenders, the picture is again unclear because the findings are neither ironclad for any one study nor entirely consistent across various studies. These individuals believe that rehabilitation may well have promise—and a major role—but that no specific approaches can be recommended right now, at least not widely.

The more "sanguine" camp agrees that most programs have not been particularly effective thus far, certainly with their overall target groups. However, it believes that many programs and approaches have been shown—with reasonable scientific assurance—to work for specified portions of their target group. Some such proponents believe that certain offenders ("amenables") will respond positively to many approaches under a wide range of conditions and that many or most remaining offenders will probably respond to very few. Other proponents partly accept this view but believe that almost all offenders will respond positively, neutrally, *or* negatively depending on the *specific* approach and the external conditions or setting. The objective evidence, while neither vast in quantity nor flawless in quality, tends to support the latters' position while not negating the formers'. Both groups believe that successful programs often reduce recidivism by substantial amounts; they also feel that various approaches can be recommended right now for some offender-groups, even though these recommendations would reflect knowledge that is still largely "atheoretical" or at least not systematically and explicitly linked to a carefully defined set of underlying mechanisms and principles which have themselves been largely validated or seem quite plausible. Moreover, whether few or many programs have worked thus far (however those terms are defined), those and similar programs can perhaps be built upon and the remaining programs or approaches can eventually be discarded. In addition, whether recidivism reductions are considered moderately large or relatively small within typical programs to date, those reductions—like the percentage of successful programs itself—can probably be increased through program/offender matching, in future rehabilitation efforts.

The differences between the more skeptical and more sanguine individuals are complex and can only partly be traced to technical factors such as differing units of analysis,[9] differing standards of evidence, differing approaches to synthesizing as well as generalizing various findings from within and across studies, etc. They seem to be partly experiential and philosophical as well. For the most part, these differences—especially the latter two—will probably long remain, even though the former (the technically centered) will doubtlessly be narrowed quite a bit. Beyond this, disagreement exists as to when the results from a given study or *group* of studies should be used for various types and levels of policy recommendation, especially if those results are positive. At a more basic yet related level, disagreement has clearly emerged as to what constitutes an adequately or well-researched study, one whose findings—whether positive or negative—can be considered valid and somewhat generalizable.

Given such differences and disagreements, it is significant that certain areas of agreement nonetheless exist: Basically many "skeptics" and "sanguines" seem to believe that, to be effective with serious or multiple offenders, rehabilitation programs must be broader-based and more intensive than in the past. That is, given the often complex and interrelated problems, limitations, and attitudes of most such offenders, future programs will often have to use "multiple modality" approaches, e.g., simultaneous or successive combinations of vocational training, individual counseling, and perhaps others. Moreover, to achieve substantial rather than minimal impact, such approaches will have to be provided on a more intensive basis. One final area of agreement exists or is at least implied: program/offender matching. Here, a program's resources—multiple or otherwise, intensively provided or not—are organized and distributed according to the needs, interests, and limitations of the offender subgroups that are present; they are not applied to the *total* offender group in an indiscriminate, across-the-board manner. Taken together, these areas of agreement suggest that future programs should be more carefully adapted to the life circumstances and personal/interpersonal characteristics of offenders. This view has policy implications regardless of the exact content of those as well as present programs.

The truth regarding "effectiveness" may lie between the skeptical and more sanguine views—in fact, it probably does. Yet however the effectiveness issue may finally devolve, the future of rehabilitation or habilitation programs will be neither dim nor dull; for one thing, not only direction but considerable room for improvement already exists. In any event, the above areas of agreement may reflect one important part of that truth, and future.

And regarding that future, three last points. First, rehabilitation need not be wedded to a medical model; it can proceed on the assumption that offenders, like nonoffenders, have positive potential which they can, should, and usually wish to use. Offenders need not be viewed as defective; and, like most nonoffenders, the vast majority are quite capable of recognizing the potential relevance to their lives of various forms of assistance, e.g., vocational training. To assume that offenders lack this ability or can seldom exercise or sustain it is to consider them defective or highly indifferent indeed—no less so, perhaps, than in a "medical model" itself. Along a related line, the fact that some or perhaps many offenders often play "treatment games" within or outside institutions does not mean that the majority do so or that they do so most of the time. [20]

Secondly, rehabilitation need not be linked to indeterminate sentencing; it can be implemented for—and by—offenders under conditions of determinate sentencing, with or without written contracts.

Finally, rehabilitation or correctional intervention need not demean its participants or interfere with given reform movements. It can disassociate itself from the more questionable or undesirable practices of the past and can be integrated with numerous justice system concerns and legitimate strivings of the present and future. Correctional intervention can operate in a framework of humane interaction and exchange despite the unavoidable need, outside and inside the system, for some degree of social control. By building on its past successes, be these "many" or "few," it can eventually regain its place and recognition (this time on more solid grounds) as one more useful tool—another option for society and offenders alike. [5; 20]

Notes

[1] Though punishment—temporary confinement, withdrawal of privileges, added restrictions, etc.—may well affect future behavior and adjustment, it is not part of a rehabilitation effort if used as an end in itself or as a means to such ends as revenge. However, if used in the context of focused, directed, and organized activities such as the above, e.g., if occasionally used to bolster given components by gaining the individual's attention, it may be considered part of rehabilitation. Nevertheless, the distinguishing features of most rehabilitation programs are those which have been designed to (1) change/modify the offender mainly through positive incentives and rewards, subtle and otherwise, or to (2) change/modify his life-circumstances and social opportunities by various pragmatic means.

[2] Perhaps arbitrarily we are including only those methods whose "humaneness" is not open to serious, certainly widespread, question. At any rate, we are focusing on methods that basically utilize, develop, or redirect the powers and mechanisms of the individual's mind, not reduce, physically traumatize, disorganize, or devastate them, whether or not by mechanical means; the former may be called positive treatment programs (PTP's) the latter, drastic or traumatic rehabilitation approaches (DRA's). We are also excluding various methods—not infrequently used in other times and/or places—such as: mutilation or dismemberment; sterilization or castration; physical stigmatization (e.g., branding); public humiliation (e.g., via stock and pillory).

[3] That is, each *individual program* which is categorized as, say a "group counseling" *method* represents a variation within the method.

[4] These individuals believe that the conclusions which were drawn from several hundred studies conducted during 1945–1978 (mainly 1960–1975) were justified either in terms of a preponderance-of-evidence standard or, somewhat more strongly beyond a reasonable doubt; at least, this applied to the conclusions from numerous studies that yielded positive results. In any event, they regard the latter conclusions as scientifically supportable even though the individual study designs were indeed far from flawless and the conclusions were therefore not justified with almost absolute certainty (as the NAS Panel would have preferred), i.e., virtually beyond the *shadow* of doubt. Moreover, they believe it would be inappropriate and certainly peculiar to dismiss the similar or converging evidence regarding given program approaches and program components that was observed *across* many such positive-outcome studies—studies which they feel had defensible research designs and that involved at least adequate program implementation.

[5] Romig, while accepting this view believes one should go beyond it—to "truly individualized treatment." [23] Thus, he supports but does not identify with DI per se. (It might be noted that individualization is a relative term.)

[6] Regarding the question of (1) which offenders are usually more amenable than others? and (2) which approaches seem to work for whom?, BTA and/or DI proponents and supporters generally believe that results from various studies, i.e., *across* studies, are more consistent than inconsistent and show greater convergence than scatter. At any rate, they believe the consistency and convergence is substantial and revealing, and that it—in some respects, an expression of partial replication—partly compensates for less-than-flawless research designs. On this latter point, "the importance of scientific replication does not negate that of unusually impressive [e.g., the virtually flawless] individual studies. However, the latter value can hardly substitute for the former . . ." Thus, for example, one unusually impressive study which, say, "focused on particular treatment inputs and involved specific operating conditions" would not necessarily be seen, by most DI proponents, as outweighing "several acceptable [or perhaps high-quality] studies

which collectively may have covered a wider range of treatment inputs and operating conditions." [20]

[7] The reason for substantially differing estimates is somewhat unclear. At any rate, the many-programs estimates generally range from 30% to 55% and were obtained not just from reviews which did, but from others which did not, include the following among their sample-of-programs: those for which positive results were reported either for the total target group or only for a major subgroup within the total group. When the latter were included, estimates were only slightly higher than when they were not. An explanation for the differing estimates may partly lie in the fact that the various reviewers seldom focused on an identical or even nearly identical set of programs. Beyond that, they used somewhat different definitions of success.

[8] Included here was 42% of *LMW's* pool of positive- and negative-outcome studies combined. These 42% comprised four-fifths of all programs which—based on a behavioral, not just a policy-related index such as revocation or discharge—had reduced recidivism by *any* amount, i.e., by 1% or more. (Again, programs that reduced recidivism by less than 10%—viz. by 1–9%—were *not* considered positive-outcome studies in this as well as in most reviews and evaluations; if these programs *had* been included in the present analysis, the 32% recidivism-reduction figure would have dropped to 26%.) Most of the 42% showed a statistically significant difference (0.5 level) between the total target group and its control or comparison group. *LMW* had categorized many studies from within this 42% group as high-quality not just adequate-quality [14; 20][9] For example, an emphasis on either (1) broadly categorized treatment methods only (in effect, treatment-*types* or types of individual programs—as in Martinson, pre-1978), (2) overall programs, i.e., individual programs, viewed as undifferentiated entities, (3) program components within the overall program, or (4) similar program components or common factors that are found *across* numerous overall programs.

References

[1] Adams, S. "Evaluation research in corrections: status and prospects." *Federal Probation, 38(1),* (1974): 14–21.

[2] Allinson, R. "Martinson attacks his own earlier work." In: *Criminal Justice Newsletter 9,* (December, 1978): 4.

[3] Bailey W. "Correctional outcome: an evaluation of 100 reports." *J. Crime, Law, Criminology, and Police Science, 57,* (1966): 153–160.

[4] Conrad, J. "Research and developments in corrections: A thought experiment." *Federal Probation, 46(2),* (1982): 66–69.

[5] Cullen, F. and Gilbert, K. *Reaffirming Rehabilitation.* Cincinnati, OH: Anderson Publishing Co. 1982.

[6] Empey, L. *American Delinquency: Its Meaning and Construction.* Homewood, IL: Dorsey. 1978.

[7] Gendreau, P. and Ross, R. *Effective Correctional Treatment.* Toronto: Butterworths. 1980.

[8] Glasser, D. "Achieving better questions: A half century's progress in correctional research." *Federal Probation, 39,* (1975): 3–9.

[9] Gottfredson, M., Mitchell-Hersfeld, S. and Flanagan, T. "Another look at the effectiveness of parole supervision." *J. of Research in Crime and Delinquency 19(2),* (1982): 277–298.

[10] Greenberg, D. "The correctional effects corrections: A survey of evaluations." In: Greenberg, D. (Ed.) *Corrections and Punishment.* Beverly Hills: Sage Publications. 1977. 111–148.

[11] Hunt, D. *Matching Models in Education.* Toronto: Ontario Institute for Studies in Education. 1971.

[12] Jesness, C. *The Preston Typology Study: Final Report.* Sacramento: California Youth Authority 1969.

[13] Johnson. S. "Differential classification and treatment: The case against us." *The Differential View, 11,* (1982): 7–18.

[14] Lipton, D., Martinson, R., and Wilks, J. *The Effectiveness of Correctional Treatment: A Survey of Treatment Evaluation Studies.* New York: Praeger. 1975.

[15] Martin, S., Sechrest, L., and Redner, R. *New Direction in the Rehabilitation of Criminal Offenders.* Washington, D.C.: The National Academy Press. 1981.

[16] Martinson, R., "California research at the crossroads." *Crime and Delinquency, 22,* (1976): 180–191.

[17] _____. "Symposium on sentencing. Part II." *Hofstra Law Review 7(2),* (Winter, 1979): 243–258.

[18] _____. "What works?—questions and answers about prison reform." *The Public Interest 35,* (Spring, 1974): 22–54.

[19] Megargee, E., Bohn, M. Jr., Meyer, J. Jr., and Sink, F. *Classifying Criminal Offenders: A New System Based on the MMPI.* Beverly Hills: Sage Publishers, Inc. 1979.

[20] Palmer, T. *Correctional Intervention and Research: Current Issues and Future Prospects.* Lexington, MA: Lexington Books. 1978.

[21] _____. "Martinson revisited." *J. of Research in Crime and Delinquency 12,* (1975): 133–152.

[22] Quay H. and Parsons, L. *The Differential Behavior Classification of the Juvenile Offender.* Morgantown, WV: Robert F. Kennedy Youth Center. 1970.

[23] Romig, D. *Justice for Our Children.* Lexington, MA: Lexington Books. 1978.

[24] Sechrest, L., White, S., and Brown, E. *The Rehabilitation of Criminal Offenders: Problems and Prospects.* Washington, D.C.: The National Academy of Sciences. 1979.

[25] Warren, M. "Classification of offenders as an aid to efficient management and effective treatment." *J. Crime, Law Criminology, and Police Science, 62,* (1971): 239–258.

[26] Wilson, J. "'What works?' revisited: New findings on criminal rehabilitation." *The Public Interest 61,* (Fall, 1980): 3–17.

[27] Wright, W., and Dixon, M. "Juvenile delinquency prevention: A review of evaluation studies." *J. of Research in Crime and Delinquency 14(1),* (1977): 35–67.

2

Evaluating Intensive Supervision Probation/Parole
Results of a Nationwide Experiment

Joan Petersilia and Susan Turner

Sentencing practices in this country suggest that offenses can be divided into two categories. When the crime is relatively serious, offenders are put behind bars; when it is less so, they are put on probation, often with only perfunctory supervision. This two-fold division disregards the range of severity in crime, and as a result, sentencing can err in one direction or another: either it is too harsh, incarcerating people whose crimes are not serious enough to warrant a sanction this severe, or too lenient, putting on probation people whose crimes call for more severe punishment. This need for more flexible alternatives—punishments that in harshness fall between prison and probation—led many States to experiment with intermediate sanctions, such as intensive supervision probation/parole (ISP).[1]

Intensive supervision probation/parole is a form of release into the community that emphasizes close monitoring of convicted offenders and imposes rigorous conditions on that release. Most ISP's call for:

- Some combination of multiple weekly contacts with a supervising officer.
- Random and unannounced drug testing.
- Stringent enforcement of probation/parole conditions.

Source: *National Institute of Justice: Research in Brief*, U.S. Department of Justice, May 1993: 1–11.

• A requirement to participate in relevant treatment, hold a job, and perhaps perform community service.

Interest in ISP's has been generated in part by the increased proportion of serious offenders among the probation population, a group whose needs and problems may not be effectively addressed by routine probation. Another reason for interest in ISP's is the greater flexibility in sentencing options that they permit. They are better able than the traditional alternatives—prison or probation—to fit the punishment to the crime.

The Problem

The population on probation is a particular focus of ISP's. This population has been growing, increasing 5 to 7 percent each year from 1985 to 1990. At the end of 1990, two-thirds of all people who were under correctional supervision were on probation.[2] More importantly, the type of offender on probation has also changed. More of the current probation population consists of people convicted of felonies than misdemeanors.[3]

As a sentencing option, routine probation was neither intended nor structured to handle this type of offender. One reason is that felons are not good risks for routine probation. A recent report by the Bureau of Justice Statistics revealed that 43 percent of felons on State probation were rearrested for another felony within 3 years.[4] This threat to public safety underscores the need for sentencing alternatives. Moreover, the need is even greater in view of budget cuts at probation agencies.

At the other extreme, reliance on imprisonment has limitations. Prison populations have tripled since 1975. States have responded to the increased need with enormous investments in prison construction. Yet the level of violent crime is now substantially higher than it was a decade ago, indicating that the prospect of imprisonment has not had the deterrent effect that investment in prisons hoped to buy.[5] It has also meant that 36 States are currently operating all or part of their correctional systems under court orders or consent decrees to reduce crowding.[6]

The Rationale for ISP's

Since neither prison nor routine probation can fully respond to the current situation, ISP's have increasingly been viewed as an alternative. Indeed, these programs have been hailed by many as

---

Types of ISP's

ISP's are usually classified as prison diversion, enhanced probation, and enhanced parole. Each has a different goal.

Diversion is commonly referred to as a "front door" program because its goal is to limit the number of offenders entering prison. Prison diversion programs generally identify lower risk, incoming inmates to participate in an ISP in the community as a substitute for a prison term.

Enhancement programs generally select already sentenced probationers and parolees and subject them to closer supervision in the community than regular probation or parole. People placed in ISP enhanced probation or enhanced parole programs show evidence of failure under routine supervision or have committed offenses generally deemed to be too serious for supervision on routine caseloads.

---

the most promising criminal justice innovation in decades. Between 1980 and 1990 every State adopted some form of ISP for adult offenders.[7] The Federal system has not been as aggressive as the States in ISP experiments, although there are a few programs in selected districts.

A growing number of jurisdictions have come to believe that by providing increased supervision of serious offenders in the community, ISP's can both relieve prison crowding and lessen the risks to public safety that such offenders pose—and all at a cost savings. In addition to these practical considerations, many believe ISP's should be adopted as a matter of principle, to meet the need for greater latitude in sentencing and to achieve the sentencing objective of just deserts.

The practical argument is the one advanced most often. ISP's are believed to be cost-effective, either in the short run or the long run. Prison-diversion programs (see "Types of ISP's") are thought to be able to reduce corrections costs because they presumably cost less than prison. Probation-enhancement programs are believed to prevent crime because the close surveillance they provide should deter recidivism. With lower recidivism, the need for imprisonment is also reduced, since fewer offenders will be reprocessed by the system.

Assumptions about the effect of ISP's on crime control involve comparisons of various types of sanctions. Prison is assumed to provide the strongest, and routine supervision the weakest, crime control. ISP's are a middle ground, with more control than routine supervision but less control than prison. Theoretically, offenders in ISP programs are deterred from committing crimes because they are under surveillance, and they are constrained from committing crimes because the conditions of the program limit their opportunities.

Initial Reactions to ISP's

Some of the enthusiasm for ISP's was generated by early reports from programs like that of the Georgia Department of Corrections, which seemed to bear out many of the assumptions and to produce a number of benefits.[8] Many ISP programs claimed to have saved at least $10,000 a year for each offender who otherwise would have been sentenced to prison.[9] Participants in the Georgia program, which served as the model for programs adopted elsewhere, had low recidivism, maintained employment, made restitution, and paid a monthly supervision fee.

In other places where ISP's were adopted, evaluations produced mixed results, with some sites reporting cost savings (Illinois and New Jersey, for example), while others did not (such as Massachusetts and Wisconsin); and some reporting reduced recidivism (Iowa, for example), while others did not (such as Ohio and Wisconsin).

The ambiguous results of these programs indicate that assumptions about the ability of ISP's to produce practical results—relieve prison crowding, lower costs, and control crime—may not have been well-founded. Reservations have been raised by independent agencies (such as the U.S. General Accounting Office), as well as by a number of scholars, including proponents of the ISP concept.[10] It appears not that the ISP's themselves have failed, but that the objectives set for them may have been overly ambitious, raising expectations they have been unable to meet.

The evidence seems better able to support the argument based on principle. That is, because ISP's are more punitive than routine probation and parole and because they provide for greater surveillance, they may be able to achieve the goal of permitting needed flexibility in sentencing.

The Demonstration Project

To test the relative effectiveness of ISP's and traditional sanctions, NIJ evaluated a demonstration project sponsored by the Bureau of Justice Assistance (BJA). The demonstration, which involved 14 programs in 9 States, ran from 1986 to 1991 and involved about

Exhibit 1. **The 14 Demonstration/ Evaluation Sites**

Contra Costa County, California

Los Angeles County, California

Seattle, Washington

Ventura County, California

Atlanta, Georgia

Macon, Georgia

Waycross, Georgia

Santa Fe, New Mexico

Des Moines, Iowa

Winchester, Virginia

Dallas, Texas

Houston, Texas

Marion County, Oregon

Milwaukee, Wisconsin

2,000 offenders. NIJ commissioned the RAND Corporation to evaluate the programs in a project supported by the Institute as well as BJA.

The participating jurisdictions (see exhibit 1) were asked to design an ISP program and were given wide latitude in doing so. Only two sites (Marion County, Oregon, and Milwaukee, Wisconsin) selected prison diversion programs, in which lower risk offenders who would have entered prison were diverted into the community. All others chose either probation enhancement or parole enhancement programs for the more serious offenders who were then under community supervision.

The offenders whom the jurisdictions chose to target had to meet only two criteria: they had to be adults and they could not be currently convicted of a violent crime. Once these criteria were met, the jurisdictions were free to focus on whatever type of offender population they wished: probationers and/or parolees, people currently in jail, or people who were prison bound.

They were also free to tailor their programs to meet local needs. For example, several sites designed their programs specifically for drug offenders. However, for a variety of reasons, the agencies were unable to place many offenders in drug, alcohol, or other such treatment programs. Thus, the ISP's evaluated were not primarily service and treatment programs, but rather were oriented more toward surveillance and supervision. (See "Study Methods.")

Effectiveness of ISP's

The demonstration was intended to answer the question of how participation in an ISP affected offenders' subsequent criminal behavior (that is, its effect on recidivism). The evaluation was intended to bring to light information about cost-effectiveness and extent of offender participation in counseling, work, and training programs. The effect of ISP's on prison crowding was not a study

Study Methods[11]

Program Design

All jurisdictions selected by the Bureau of Justice Assistance for participation in the demonstration and evaluation were asked to design and implement an ISP program that was to be funded for 18 to 24 months. The jurisdictions also were required to receive training and technical assistance, both provided by outside consultants.[12] In addition, they took part in the independent evaluation, which required their gathering data about the program.

The population studied consisted of approximately 2,000 adult offenders who were not currently convicted of a violent crime (homicide, rape, robbery, and assault). The vast majority of the offenders were men in their late 20s and early 30s, and most had long criminal records. In other respects, sites varied. Some, for example, chose offenders with more serious prison records than others. The nature of their offenses varied, as did their racial composition. The proportion of offenders in Dallas had served a prison term, while for Contra Costa the figure was only 5 percent.

Because each site was allowed to design its own ISP, no two programs were identical. They adopted whatever components of the general ISP model they wished (such as random urine testing, curfews, electronic monitoring, and treatment referrals).

Close supervision of offenders was one of the few required program components. It consisted of weekly contacts with the officers, unscheduled drug testing, and stricter enforcement of probation/parole conditions.

Random Assignment

The study was conducted as a randomized experiment. Indeed, the study may well be the largest randomized experiment in corrections ever undertaken in the United States. At each site, along with the experimental group, a control group of offenders was set up to serve as a comparison. The offenders in the control group were not part of the program but instead were given a different sanction (either prison or routine probation or parole, for example).[13] After the jurisdictions selected the pool of offenders they deemed eligible for ISP programs, the researchers assigned them randomly to one or the other of the two groups.

Having a control group with which to compare findings ensured that the results were the product of the manipulated variables of the ISP program rather than of differences among the offenders in the two groups. Previous ISP evaluations lacked matching comparison groups.

Data Collection

For each offender, in both the experimental and the control groups, data collection forms were completed by the participating agency in the respective jurisdictions. A *background assessment* recorded demographic information, prior criminal record, drug dependence status, and similar information. The other forms—*6- and 12-month reviews*—recorded probation and parole services received, participation in treatment and work programs, and recidivism during the 1-year followup. Also recorded on this form were the number of drug tests ordered and taken, the types of drugs for which the offender tested positive, and the sanction imposed.

Measuring Program Effects

Separate calculations were devised for estimating costs and for measuring program implementation, the effect of the ISP's on recidivism, and the effect on social adjustment (percentage of offenders who attended counseling, participated in training, were employed, and the like).

aim, but it has been a major policy interest in all ISP programs. The participating sites had their own objectives and interests. Most wanted to learn whether ISP's are an effective intermediate sanction, in which probation and parole conditions are monitored and enforced more credibly.

Overall, the results revealed what *cannot* be expected of ISP's as much as what *can* be. Most notably, they suggest that the assumptions about the ability of ISP's to meet certain practical goals—reduce prison crowding, save money, and decrease recidivism—may not have been well-founded and that jurisdictions interested in adopting ISP's should define their goals carefully. Other study findings indicate that ISP's were most successful as an intermediate punishment, in providing closer supervision of offenders and in offering a range of sentencing options between prison and routine probation and parole.

The programs were effective as surveillance. The ISP programs were designed to be much more stringent than routine supervision, and in every site they delivered more contacts and monitoring than did the routine supervision provided in the control groups. Most of the ISP's were significantly higher than the control programs in number of face-to-face contacts with supervisors, telephone and collateral contacts, law enforcement checks, employment monitoring, and drug and alcohol testing. (See exhibit 2 for findings on contacts and drug tests.)

The data reveal no straightforward relationship between contact levels and recidivism; that is, it is not clear whether the surveillance aspect of the ISP had a positive effect on offenders' subsequent behavior. For example, although the average number of face-to-face

Exhibit 2. **Number of Monthly Face-to-Face Contacts and Drug Tests During 1-Year Followup**

	Face-to Face Contacts		Drug Tests	
	ISP	Controls	ISP	Controls
Contra Costa County, California	2.7	0.5*	1.7	0.2*
Los Angeles County, California	4.1	0.6*	0.5	0.2*
Seattle, Washington	3.4	0.8*	0.4	0.1*
Ventura County, California	7.4	3.0*	2.7	1.3*
Atlanta, Georgia	12.5	14.9	4.8	4.9
Macon, Georgia	16.1	17.7	5.8	3.7*
Waycross, Georgia	22.8	22.4	14.2	1.6*
Santa Fe, New Mexico	10.6	2.8*	2.9	1.1*
Des Moines, Iowa	5.8	3.8*	2.8	1.0*
Winchester, Virginia	8.1	1.9*	1.5	0.4*
Dallas, Texas	3.3	1.5*	0.1	0.0*
Houston, Texas	4.0	1.9*	0.7	0.0*
Marion County, Oregon**	12.2	n/a	2.2	n/a
Milwaukee, Wisconsin	8.8	n/a	0.7	n/a
AVERAGE	5.8 [a]	1.6 [b]	1.4 [a]	0.2 [b]

* Indicates that ISP and control are significantly different, $p < .05$.

** Based on 6-month followup only.

[a] Weighted average of ISP in all sites.
[b] Weighted average of routine probation in Contra Costa, Los Angeles, Seattle; routine probation/parole in Santa Fe, Des Moines, Winchester; routine parole in Dallas and Houston.

contacts in Seattle was 3.4 per month and the average in Macon was much higher at 16.1, the percentage of ISP offenders arrested at both sites was about the same—46 percent in Seattle and 42 percent in Macon.

This finding must, however, be qualified by the nature of the data. The ISP programs were "packages" of contacts and services, and for this reason it is difficult to distinguish the specific effect of individual components of a package (such as contact level, drug testing, and electronic monitoring) on recidivism.

The programs were effective as intermediate sanctions.   In a sense, this issue is the same as the preceding one if more frequent contacts and drug testing are viewed as punishment. Most of the ISP's had significantly higher levels of the features that curtail freedom.[14] Both coercion and enforced diminution of freedom were higher for most ISP's than for the control group when measured by the criminal justice system response to offenders' technical violations.[15] In fact, the response to this type of violation gives ISP's their greatest punitive value. The rate of technical violations was high, making the resultant coercion and diminution of freedom experienced by the offenders an added punitive sanction as well as creating a public safety benefit.

The General Accounting Office, in its report on intermediate punishments, noted that if judged by a standard of zero risk, all ISP programs fail to protect public safety.[16] However, what most of these programs try to achieve is a more stringent punishment for at least some of the serious offenders who now receive only nominal supervision. Judged by that criterion, virtually all of the sites succeeded. It is also possible that the closer surveillance imposed on ISP participants may increase the probability that they are caught for a larger percentage of the crimes they commit.

To test this effect, researchers conducted interviews with ISP participants in the Contra Costa site to discuss their perceptions of the harshness of the program. The interview findings confirmed that these offenders viewed the likelihood of their being caught for probation violations to be higher than for offenders who were on routine probation. They felt this to be particularly true when the violations involved drugs. In addition, the ISP offenders believed they would be treated more harshly for most types of violations than would their counterparts who were on routine supervision.

Evidence also suggests that some offenders may view ISP's as even more punitive and restrictive of freedom than prison. Among offenders at the Oregon site, 25 percent who were eligible for prison diversion chose not to participate. The reason may be that Oregon's crowded prisons made it unlikely that anyone sentenced to a year would serve the full term, while offenders assigned to ISP's could be certain of a full year of surveillance in the program. As prisons become more crowded and length of sentence served decreases, ISP's may come to seem increasingly punitive to offenders.

The Effect on Recidivism

The major recidivism outcome measures were officially recorded arrests and technical violations. On these measures, the ISP programs were not as successful as on others.

ISP participants were not subsequently arrested less often, did not have a longer time to failure, and were not arrested for less serious offenses than control group members. The findings reveal that in 11 of the 14 sites, arrest rates during the 1-year followup were in fact higher for ISP participants than for the control group (although not significantly so). At the end of the 1-year period, about 37 percent of the ISP participants and 33 percent of control offenders had been arrested. (See exhibit 3.)

These findings should be interpreted with caution, because officially recorded recidivism may not be as accurate an indicator of an individual's criminality as it is a measure of the impact of the ISP program on the criminal justice system. That is, officially recorded recidivism measures enforcement—the system's ability to detect crime and act on it (through arrests).

As noted earlier, with an ISP program, surveillance may be so stringent as to increase the probability that crimes (and technical violations) will be detected and an arrest made. In this way ISP's may increase officially recorded recidivism. Thus, it may be that an ISP offender is committing the same number or fewer crimes than someone on routine supervision, who has a lower probability of being arrested for them. The ISP offender, whose behavior is more closely monitored, may be caught in the enforcement net, while the offender on routine probation or parole may escape it.

Effect of technical violations. If technical violations are interpreted as another measure of recidivism, the findings are also less positive for the ISP's than the controls. An average of 65 percent of the ISP clients had a technical violation compared with 38 percent for the controls. (See exhibit 3). However, technical violations can be interpreted as effects of the program itself rather than as evidence of criminal activity or recidivism. For one thing, the view of technical violations as a proxy for crime commission is only an assumption. Non-compliant behavior such as disregarding curfews, using alcohol and drugs, and missing treatment sessions may not necessarily signal that the ISP participant is going to commit "new" or "real" crimes.

To test the hypothesis that revoking offenders for technical violations prevents arrests for new crimes, the researchers examined the ISP programs in California and Texas. They computed correlations between number of arrests and number of technical violations and found few statistically significant relationships. In other words, offenders who committed technical violations were no more likely to be arrested for new crimes than those who did not commit them. Moreover, when convictions for arrests during the 1-year followup were examined for all sites, the researchers found no difference in the rates of the ISP offenders and the control group.

ISP's were consistently associated with higher rates of technical violations because of the closer supervision given to those in the programs. If stringent conditions are imposed and people's behavior is monitored, they have more opportunities for violations and for being found out than if there are few conditions and few contacts. For example, the requirement of frequent drug testing alone is virtually guaranteed to generate a large number of technical violations. Few of the sites had many low-risk[17] offenders. The higher the risk, the more likely that offenders are involved with drugs. At most of the sites, drug-related technical violations accounted for a large proportion of all technical violations. Offenders under routine supervision were not subjected to such close scrutiny and would not therefore have had as many opportunities to commit technical violations of the conditions of their probation or parole.

Effect of type of ISP program.   Because only 2 of the 14 sites implemented prison diversion programs and their programs experienced difficulties, the research remains inconclusive regarding the ability of this type of ISP to relieve prison crowding. (See "The Experience of the Prison Diversion Programs.")

The findings for parole and probation enhancement ISP's suggest that commitments to prison and jail may actually increase under the program. The reason is the large number of technical violations, which lead to a higher percentage of ISP offenders than controls being recommitted to jail and prison. At a minimum, ISP programs attempt to increase the credibility of community-based sanctions by making certain that the conditions ordered by the court, including those considered "technical" in nature, are monitored, enforced, and if violated, punished by imprisonment. Depending on how severely ISP staff and their respective courts choose to treat ISP infractions, commitments to prison and jails may rise precipitously.

Exhibit 3. **Offender Recidivism During 1-Year Followup**

	Percentage of Offenders With Any Arrest		Percentage of Offender With Technical Violations		Percentage of Offenders Returned to Prison	
	ISP	Controls	ISP	Controls	ISP	Controls
Contra Costa County, California	29	27	64	41*	2	4
Los Angeles County, California	32	30	61	57	26	22
Seattle, Washington	46	36	73	48*	6	5
Ventura County, California	32	53*	70	73	23	28
Atlanta, Georgia	12	04	65	46	23	4
Macon, Georgia	42	38	100	96	8	21
Waycross, Georgia	12	15	38	31	4	0
Santa Fe, New Mexico	48	28	69	62	14	17
Des Moines, Iowa	24	29	59	55	39	23
Winchester, Virginia	25	12	64	36*	14	8
Dallas, Texas	39	30	20	13	28	17
Houston, Texas	44	40	81	33*	35	20*
Marion County, Oregon	33	50	92	58	50	25
Milwaukee, Wisconsin	58	03*	92	17*	35	3*
AVERAGE	37 [a]	33 [b]	65 [a]	38 [b]	24	15

* Indicates that ISP and control are significantly different, p <.05.

[a] Weighted average of ISP in all sites.
[b] Weighted average of routine probation in Contra Costa, Los Angeles, Seattle; routine probation/parole in Santa Fe, Des Moines, Winchester; routine parole in Dallas and Houston.

The Experience of the Prison Diversion Programs

Prison diversion programs in this study did not provide data on the effect of ISP's on prison crowding. Of the two participating sites that implemented prison diversion programs in the demonstration, one had too few eligible offenders to yield usable results. In the other, the use of randomization was overridden by the jurisdiction, thereby foiling its purpose. The selection process at these two sites therefore makes it impossible to state with certainty the effect of ISP's in reducing prison crowding.

The experience of the two sites (Marion County, Oregon, and Milwaukee, Wisconsin) does reveal a number of insights into the issues jurisdictions face when making decisions about selecting convicted offenders for diversion into the community.

Marion County, Oregon

Marion County set eligibility requirements so stringent that few offenders could qualify for the prison diversion ISP. The study's mandated criterion of excluding offenders currently convicted of violent crimes was extended to exclude offenders with any prior record of violence. Examination of the Marion County data revealed that, in addition, a large percent of potential participants who had current burglary convictions were rejected. Although this offense is considered nonviolent, evidently Marion County did not wish to place burglars into ISP programs.

The three criteria—exclusion of violent offenders, people with any history of violence, and convicted burglars—shrank the pool of eligibles considerably. Furthermore, the local Marion County judge imposed the requirement of informed consent from the offender, producing a sample too small to yield statistically reliable results.

Milwaukee, Wisconsin

In Milwaukee, judges and probation/parole officers overrode the researchers' random assignment of offenders into the experimental and control groups. Milwaukee initially had two pools of eligibles: "front-end" cases consisting of high-risk offenders newly convicted of nonviolent felonies, and "back-end" cases consisting of probation or parole violators who were facing revocation. Regardless of the random designation made by the researchers, most front-end cases were sentenced to prison rather than diversion to an ISP. Of the back-end cases, more than half were sent to routine probation or parole.

That only two sites chose prison diversion suggests the level of concern on the part of the criminal justice system about the risks involved in sending convicted offenders into the community. Further evidence of this concern is the response of these two sites in placing additional restrictions on program implementation.[18]

Data from the Houston site illustrate this point. The Houston ISP was a parole-enhancement program that targeted people under supervision who had a high probability of returning to prison. ISP participants were not arrested for new crimes more often than the controls (who were on routine parole), but were returned to prison more frequently for more technical violations. Fully 81 percent of the ISP offenders had technical violations, compared with 33 percent of offenders in the control group. As a result, five times as many ISP offenders were returned to prison for technical violations as those on routine supervision (21 percent versus 4 percent), and at the end of the 1-year followup, about 30 percent of ISP participants were in prison, compared with only 18 percent of the control group.[19]

Thus, in Houston, putting people on ISP added more offenders to the prison population than did routine parole. This is interpreted as an effect of the ISP program itself—which tends to generate more technical violations—rather than the result of differences between the ISP experimental and control groups. Any other differences were eliminated through random assignment of offenders to both groups.

Cost Benefits

Are ISP's a cost-saving alternative? Like other questions about ISP's, this too has an ambiguous answer—one that depends on what is being compared to what. Compared with routine probation, ISP's are more costly because they are highly labor intensive. Because supervision is intensive, ISP's require lower caseloads—typically 25 offenders per supervisor or team of supervisors. An increase of only 100 offenders in an ISP would call for hiring and training 4 to 8 new employees.

If the cost of ISP's is compared to that of imprisonment, the opposite is true. Virtually no one would question the claim that it is more expensive to keep an offender in prison than on probation. The costs per day for imprisonment are much higher per offender than the costs per day for an ISP. Obviously, ISP's cost less than building new prisons.

Length of time under each sanction also has to be taken into consideration when comparing costs of prison and ISP's. The average cost per year per imprisoned offender is $12,000 and per ISP offender only $4,000. However, if the ISP offender would have otherwise served time in prison (had he or she not been placed in an ISP) for a period of only 3 months, the cost would be $3,000—less than the $4,000 it costs for 1 year of an ISP program. In addition, some of the ISP participants spent part of the followup year incarcerated rather than in the ISP program, thus eliminating part of the cost savings of diversion from prison.

Again, it should be kept in mind in interpreting these findings that the ISP programs resulted in more incarcerations and consequently higher costs than routine probation/parole because of the higher number of technical violations. Across the 12 probation/parole enhancement programs, high violation and incarceration rates for ISP offenders drove up the estimated costs, which averaged $7,200 per offender for the year, compared with about $4,700 for the control group on routine supervision.

Results for Treatment

Treatment and service components in the ISP's included drug and alcohol counseling, employment, community service, and payment of restitution. On many of these measures, ISP offenders participated more than did control group members (see exhibit 4); and participation in such programs was found to be correlated with a reduction in recidivism in at least some sites.

When figures from all sites are examined, they reveal that participation in counseling was not high in either the experimental or control groups, but it was higher for ISP offenders. Forty-five percent of ISP offenders received some counseling during the followup period, compared with 22 percent of the controls.

Overall figures indicate that more than half of the ISP participants were employed compared with 43 percent of the offenders who were on routine supervision. In 4 of the 14 sites (Contra Costa, Los Angeles, Seattle, and Winchester), ISP offenders were significantly more likely than controls to be employed.

Participation in community service varied considerably by site. The highest rate (more than two-thirds of offenders) was reported in the three Georgia sites, where community service has historically played a major role in the ISP design. In seven of the ISP programs, 10 percent or fewer offenders participated in community service, and at no site did ISP offenders participate significantly more often than routine supervision offenders.

Although restitution was paid by only a small minority of offenders, the rate was higher among ISP offenders than those on routine supervision (12 percent and 3 percent, respectively, paid some restitution).

Analysis of the programs in California and Texas revealed a relationship between treatment participation and recidivism. A summary score was created for each offender, with one point

Exhibit 4. **Representative Program Participation**

	Percentage of Offenders in Any Counseling During 1-Year Followup		Percentage of Offenders With Any Paid Employment During 1-Year Followup	
	ISP	Controls	ISP	Controls
Contra Costa County, California	39	14*	41	26*
Los Angeles County, California	16*	02	45	18*
Seattle, Washington	42	14*	31	08*
Ventura County, California	78	76	80	79
Atlanta, Georgia	48	48	54	65
Macon, Georgia	65	50	85	71
Waycross, Georgia	100	88	92	96
Santa Fe, New Mexico	100	59*	86	79
Des Moines, Iowa	59	41*	76	70
Winchester, Virginia	32	12	89	56*
Dallas, Texas	04	02	37	33
Houston, Texas	55	32*	61	61
Marion County, Oregon	50	n/a	33	n/a
Milwaukee, Wisconsin	54	n/a	54	n/a
AVERAGE	45 [a]	22 [b]	56 [a]	43 [b]

* Indicates that ISP and control are significantly different, $p < .05$.

[a] Weighted average of all sites.
[b] Weighted average of routine probation in Contra Costa, Los Angeles, Seattle; routine probation/parole in Santa Fe, Des Moines, Winchester; routine parole in Dallas and Houston.

assigned for participation in any of four treatment or service programs. Analysis revealed that higher levels of program participation were associated with a 10- to 20-percent reduction in recidivism. However, because offenders were not randomly assigned to participate in these activities within the experimental and control groups, it is not possible to determine whether the lower recidivism was the effect of the treatment or of selection bias. In other words, the positive outcomes may be a function not of the treatment but of the type of offender who entered the treatment program. Nevertheless, the results are consistent with literature showing positive outcomes of treatment.

The ISP programs in the demonstration project were by design oriented more toward surveillance than treatment, with funds used largely for staff salaries rather than for treatment service. Sites had to rely on existing treatment programs, which in some communities were quite minimal. This raises the issue of whether participation in treatment would have been higher had more resources been allocated to it.

Policy Implications

Jurisdictions that wish to adopt ISP's might want to revise the model represented in the demonstration to create a better "fit" with their particular needs.

Making controls more stringent. ISP contact levels were greater than with routine supervision, but it might be argued that the programs were not "intensive" enough. It appears that more stringent conditions could be required of ISP's. In the demonstration, ISP contact of any type amounted, on average, to a total of less than 2 hours per month per offender (assuming that 20 minutes, on average, was spent per face-to-face contact). The same is true of drug testing—the average for all sites was just over two tests per month. If the amount of time spent in contacts were greater (that is, if conditions were tougher), the result might be less recidivism. Jurisdictions would have to decide how much more restrictive the conditions should be and would have to weigh possible benefits against the probable higher cost.

Increasing treatment. Jurisdictions might want to strengthen the treatment component of ISP's in hopes of a positive behavioral effect that would lower recidivism. As stated earlier, at the California and Texas sites the recidivism of offenders who received any counseling (for drugs or alcohol), held jobs, paid restitution, and did community service was 10 to 20 percent lower than those who did not.

Overall outcomes might have been even more positive had a greater proportion of the offenders participated in treatment.[20] Participation in drug treatment, in particular, might have had a high payoff. In all the sites, about half the offenders were judged drug dependent by their probation or parole officers. Yet ISP staff often reported difficulties obtaining drug treatment for these people, and at some sites a large percentage of all offenders in need of drug treatment went untreated.[21] It comes as no surprise, therefore, that about one-third of all new arrests were drug-related. A high priority for future research would be evaluation of ISP programs in which treatment plays a major role.[22]

Deemphasizing technical violations.   Jurisdictions might want to reexamine the assumption of technical violations as a proxy for criminal behavior. Offenders who commit this type of violation constitute a considerable proportion of the prison population. On any given day, about 20 percent of new admissions nationwide consist of parole or probation violators, and the resultant crowding means early release for other offenders.

The experience of the State of Washington in rethinking parole and probation revocations is instructive. There, the State legislature, responding to the heavy flow of technical violations attendant on stringent parole and probation conditions, set new rules. The rules require conditions be set according to the specific offense and the particular offender's past criminal behavior; they effectively bar the imposition of conditions affecting all offenders. In addition, the new rules state that prison cannot be used as a sanction for technical violations; the maximum sentence is 60 days in jail.[24]

No empirical studies have been performed yet, but Washington officials believe that as a result of the new rules, revocations for technical violations have decreased while arrest rates for new crimes have remained roughly the same.[25] If Washington is successful, it may mean that jurisdictions will have more prison space for really serious offenders and therefore increase public safety by decreasing the number of people sent to prison for technical violations of parole and probation.

Handling costs.   When considering the issue of affordability, jurisdictions need to keep in mind its relation to program goals. The more constraints a program imposes and/or the more it is service- and treatment-oriented, the higher will be the cost. In Ventura and Houston, for example, stringent conditions and rigorous response to technical violations drove up costs. On the other hand, future evaluations might reveal that the return on investment in programs with these types of emphasis may be lower recidivism.

Judging outcomes. In assessing the success of ISP's (and deciding whether to invest further in them), jurisdictions need to use the same criterion for deciding whether a program is affordable; that is, does it achieve the goals set? One of the study's strongest implications is that jurisdictions need to establish very clearly their intentions for the ISP's they develop and structure the programs accordingly. If jurisdictions are interested primarily in imposing intermediate sanctions, even if the result is not lower recidivism, that goal should be made clear. Otherwise, the public may interpret the recidivism rates as an indication of program failure.

If jurisdictions are primarily interested in reducing recidivism, prison crowding, and system costs, ISP programs as currently structured may not meet all their expectations. These more "practical" objectives were set on the basis of overly ambitious assumptions and on the early results of a few programs that received a great deal of attention and perhaps unwarranted enthusiasm. The findings of this evaluation provide further evidence that surveillance-oriented ISP's will have difficulty in fully achieving these objectives.

If jurisdictions target objectives based more on intermediate sanctions principles, ISP's hold promise. By setting this type of objective, they may be able to impose more stringent controls on offenders than are possible without probation and parole, and they may achieve greater flexibility in sentencing decisions by punishments that more closely fit the crimes committed. Developing an array of sentencing options is an important and necessary first step to creating a more comprehensive and graduated sentencing structure. This goal alone can provide the justification for continued development of ISP and other intermediate sanctions.

Is prison diversion viable?. The evaluation findings indicate that prison diversion and, by extension, reduction of prison crowding, is particularly difficult to implement. This difficulty is reflected in the decision by only 2 of the 14 sites to adopt this type of program. The criteria these two jurisdictions used to assign offenders to the programs also suggest a measure of reluctance. (See "The Experience of the Prison Diversion Programs.") The experience with prison diversion in this study indicates that the criminal justice system and the general public do not at present seem receptive to this type of ISP. A targeted public and judicial education campaign would be required to overcome that reluctance.

Future Research

The major issue for further research is determining whether ISP, a concept that may be sound in theory, might be structured and implemented differently to produce better results. The experience of the California sites suggests, for example, that certain program components could be manipulated. At these sites, a higher level of offender participation in treatment and service programs was associated with lower recidivism. In Ventura, which had the highest levels of surveillance, arrest rates were lower than among the controls. A revised ISP model could answer these and other questions:

- Would ISP's reduce recidivism if resources were sufficient to obtain treatment drug offenders need?
- Would more intensive surveillance lower recidivism?
- Would more selective conditions of parole and probation lower revocation rates?
- What combination of surveillance and treatment would produce the best results?

The study findings indicate a number of additional areas for research:

The potential of ISP as prison diversion.   The limited number of study sites selecting this option and their restrictions on the programs indicate major concerns about ISP for prison diversion. Researchers may want to examine the nature of the potential pool of eligibles, document the most commonly utilized criteria for ISP eligibility, and depending on the criteria, simulate the prison population that would qualify.

Testing of different offender populations.   The ISP model in this study was tested primarily on drug-involved offenders who had committed serious crimes. Studies have shown that the more experienced the offenders, the lower they rate the risk of being caught and confined.[26] For this reason, models using a population of less serious offenders might result in greater deterrence.

The effects of different ISP components.   The random assignment in this study permitted testing the effect of the entire ISP "package," but made it impossible to test the effect of a particular program component. By extension, it was not possible to determine how changing a component might change the effects. Future research could be designed specifically to test the incremental impact of various ISP conditions (such as drug testing and drug and alcohol treatment) on offender behavior.

Effectiveness over time.   Recent research indicates that a 1-year followup, the time period on which the evaluation of outcomes was based, may not be long enough.[27] Future research might focus on whether longer followup might ultimately result in behavioral differences between ISP offenders and controls.

Technical violations and criminal behavior.   The study revealed that technical violations resulted in many recommitments to prison and jail. As noted earlier, the view that such recommitments prevent crime may be only an assumption. The policy significance of technical violations suggests that research is needed in a number of areas:

- Empirical evidence of the relationship of technical violations to criminal behavior.
- The types of technical conditions currently imposed at sentencing.
- How technical conditions are used by community corrections to manage offenders, encourage rehabilitation, and protect the community.
- Trends in the growth of the technical violator population and the effect on jails and prisons.
- Innovative programs, policies, and statutes that have emerged to deal with technical violators.

Appropriate outcome measures.   Recidivism is a key outcome used in evaluating all types of interventions, and because success in rehabilitation has been far from complete, it is almost the only measure used in corrections.

In reaffirming its commitment to ISP and to its focus on rehabilitation, the American Probation and Parole Association issued a position paper that identifies behavioral change, not recidivism, as the appropriate outcome measure. Such change includes negotiation skills, managing emotions, and enhanced values and attitude shifts.

Given the centrality of recidivism to research and practice, it is essential to examine its appropriateness as a measure for certain interventions. For some programs, recidivism may be one of many measures, but perhaps not the primary one.

These are not the only issues for a future criminal justice research agenda, but they are currently the most pressing for research on the future of intensive supervision probation and parole.

Notes

[1] The results of NIJ-sponsored research into four major types of intermediate sanctions are summarized in Gowdy, Voncile B., *Intermediate Sanctions*. Research in Brief. Washington, DC: U.S. Department of Justice, National Institute of Justice, 1993.

[2] Bureau of Justice Statistics, *Probation and Parole 1990*. Bulletin. Washington, DC: U.S. Department of Justice, Bureau of Justice Statistics, November 1991.

[3] The figure for felonies is 48 percent, and for misdemeanors, it is 31 percent, according to Bureau of Justice Statistics, *Correctional Populations in the United States, 1990*. Washington, DC: U.S. Department of Justice, Bureau of Justice Statistics, July 1992.

[4] Langan, Patrick A., and Mark A. Cuniff. *Recidivism of Felons on Probation, 1986–89*. Special Report. Washington, DC: U.S. Department of Justice, Bureau of Justice Statistics, February 1992.

[5] A discussion of recent findings about the rise in the rate of violent crime despite the increase in the number of people incarcerated is presented in the National Research Council's *Understanding and Preventing Violence*, ed. Albert J. Reiss, Jr., and Jeffrey A. Roth, Washington, DC: National Academy Press, 1993: 292–294.

[6] Macguire, Kathleen, and Timothy J. Flanagan, eds. *Sourcebook of Criminal Justice Statistics—1991*. Washington, DC: U.S. Department of Justice, Bureau of Justice Statistics, 1992.

[7] General Accounting Office. *Intermediate Sanctions: Their Impacts on Prison Crowding, Costs, and Recidivism Are Still Unclear*. Gaithersburg, Maryland: General Accounting Office, 1990.

[8] For descriptions of the Georgia program, see Erwin, Billie S. "Turning Up the Heat on Probationers in Georgia." *Federal Probation*, vol. 50 (1986):2. See also: Petersilia, Joan. *Expanding Options for Criminal Sentencing*. Santa Monica, CA: RAND Corporation, 1987. Byrne, James M., Arthur J. Lurigio, and Christopher Baird. "The Effectiveness of the New Intensive Supervision Programs." *Research in Corrections*, vol. 2 (1989). The results of a National Institute of Justice evaluation of the program are presented in Erwin, Billie S., and Lawrence A. Bennett. *New Dimensions in Probation: Georgia's Experience With Intensive Probation Supervision (IPS)*. Research in Brief. Washington, DC: U.S. Department of Justice, National Institute of Justice, January 1987.

[9] Byrne, Lurigio, and Baird, "The Effectiveness of the New Intensive Supervision Programs."

[10] General Accounting Office, *Intermediate Sanctions*. See also Morris, Norval, and Michael Tonry. *Between Prison and Probation: Intermediate Punishments in a Rational Sentencing System*. New York: Oxford University Press, 1990.

[11] For more information on the experiences of the site in implementing the experiments, see Petersilia, Joan. "Implementing Randomized Experiments: Lessons for BJA's Intensive Supervision Project." *Evaluation Review*, vol. 13, 5.

[12] The training component was directed by Rutgers University, the technical assistance by the National Council on Crime and Delinquency.

[13] In the Georgia and Ventura sites, the control programs were another form of intensive supervision. References to all ISP's mean all 14 experimental programs. References to ISP enhancement programs mean all experimental ISP's except Milwaukee and Marion, which adopted prison diversion programs. References to routine supervision probation and parole mean the control programs in eight sites: Contra Costa, Los Angeles, Seattle, Santa Fe, Des Moines, Winchester, Dallas, and Houston.

[14] This meets the definition of effective sentencing proposed by Morris and Tonry. It involves "the curtailment of freedom either behind walls or in the community, large measures of coercion, and enforced diminutions of freedom." (*Between Prison and Probation*)

[15] A violation that does not consist of committing a crime or is not prosecuted as such is usually called a technical violation. It is behavior forbidden by the court order granting probation or parole but not forbidden by legal statute. Examples

are failure to observe curfew, abstain from alcohol, or attend treatment sessions.

[16] General Accounting Office, *Intermediate Sanctions.*

[17] The risk score was constructed from the following variables: drug treatment needs, age at first or current conviction, previous probation terms, previous probation and parole revocations, previous felony convictions, and type of current offense.

[18] NIJ has provided support to RAND to evaluate a prison diversion program in Minnesota that promises to furnish more reliable evidence on the impact of this type of sanction.

[19] Turner, Susan, and Joan Petersilia. "Focusing on High-Risk Parolees: An Experiment to Reduce Commitments to the Texas Department of Corrections." *Journal of Research in Criminology and Delinquency*, vol. 29, 1 (1992):34–61.

[20] Some recent literature gives credibility to this notion. See Anglin, M. Douglas, and Yih-Ing Hser. "Treatment of Drug Abuse." In *Crime and Justice: An Annual Review of Research, Volume 13: Drugs and Crime.* ed. Michael Tonry and James Q. Wilson. Chicago: University of Chicago Press, 1990; and Paul Gendreau and D. A. Andrews. "Tertiary Prevention: What the Meta-Analyses of the Offender Treatment Literature Tell Us About 'What Works.'" *Canadian Journal of Criminology*, vol. 32 (1990):173–184.

[21] For a more complete presentation of this finding, see Petersilia, Joan, Susan Turner, and Elizabeth Piper Deschenes. "Intensive Supervision Programs for Drug Offenders." In J. Byrne, A. Lurigio, and J. Petersilia. *Smart Sentencing: The Emergence of Intermediate Sanctions.* Newbury Park, CA: Sage Publications, 1992.

[22] NIJ is providing RAND with support for a randomized field experiment, currently being conducted in Maricopa County, Arizona, that will test the impact on probationers of different levels of treatment.

[23] Petersilia, Joan, and Susan Turner. "Reducing Prison Admissions: The Potential of Intermediate Sanctions," *The Journal of State Government*, vol. 62 (1989):2.

[24] Washington State Sentencing Guidelines Commission. *Preliminary Evaluation of Washington State's Sentencing Reform Act.* Olympia, WA: Washington State Sentencing Guidelines Commission, 1983.

[25] Greene, Richard. "Who's Punishing Whom?" *Forbes*, vol. 121, 6 (1988):132–133.

[26] Paternoster, R. "The Deterrent Effect of the Perceived Certainty and Severity of Punishment: A Review of the Evidence and Issues." *Justice Quarterly*, 4 (1987).

[27] Anglin, M. D. and W. H. McGlothlin. "Outcomes of Narcotic Addict Treatment in California." In *Drug Abuse Treatment Evaluation: Strategies, Progress, and Prospect*, ed. F. M. Tims and J. P. Ludford. National Institute on Drug Abuse Research Monograph No. 51. Rockville, MD: U.S. Department of Health and Human Services, National Institute on Drug Abuse, 1984.

Section *II*

Correctional Personnel

Correctional personnel form three broad categories—administrators, treatment or supervisory personnel, and correctional officers (guards). In all of these categories males and whites predominate by wide margins, but otherwise there are wide variations both in the characteristics of personnel involved in the three types of positions and in the duties they perform.

Administrators tend to have the longest terms of employment in the corrections field. They may have obtained their present positions by political appointment, civil service examination, or advancement through the ranks. The managerial style of an administrator may be the result of personal experience or philosophy; acquaintance with styles of administration apparently being used successfully elsewhere; or pressures to adopt current emphases or fads in correctional organization and/or treatment in vogue on federal, state, or local levels. As the range of activity covered by corrections has expanded, administrators have been called upon to demonstrate management skills in institutional management, prerelease and work release program planning, residential community-based treatment, juvenile institutional and residential treatment, innovative pretrial diversion programs, probation, parole, juvenile aftercare, and various types of adult and juvenile diversion activity. They also must be prepared to deal with prisoner rights issues, disturbances within institutions, and close monitoring of institutional activity by civil libertarians and other interest groups.

Correctional treatment or supervisory staff occupy the next step in the descending hierarchy of correctional personnel. The majority hold baccalaureate degrees, and many have pursued graduate studies. The vast majority of personnel on this level work outside institutions, in probation, parole, juvenile aftercare, furlough or work release programs, educational program supervision, or residential correctional treatment. Those within institutions serve as psychiatrists or psychologists, social workers, instructors in educational programs, or treatment personnel.

At the lowest level of the correctional personnel ladder, in terms of prestige, education, and salary, are the correctional officers (guards). They make up the vast majority (approximately two-thirds) of prison employees. The chief responsibility of correctional officers is maintaining the security of the institution, although in some instances they are regarded as part of the "treatment team" and asked to participate in rehabilitation efforts. This is most often true in juvenile corrections. Corrections officers have the highest levels of direct interaction with offenders and bear chief responsibility for the orderly operation of the institution. Their operational styles vary, but there is frequently a sense of "accommodation" between successful correctional officers and inmates, which benefits both.

The rapidly expanding field of corrections has suffered severe manpower problems, including shortages of specialized professional personnel, poor working conditions, and underrepresentation of women and members of ethnic minorities in the correctional manpower workforce.

One of the most troublesome problems involved in recruitment of corrections personnel is the low status of corrections work in the public's mind. Those involved in corrections work, particularly correctional officers, have rarely chosen this profession but have entered it by chance after service in the military or because of the need for a secure job. The location of large institutions in rural areas has allowed the entry into correctional work of poorly trained and poorly motivated personnel, chiefly because better qualified individuals were not available. Media exposés of prison corruption and brutality have done little to enhance the public image of correctional work.

Manpower shortages in corrections are related to the emerging roles of private firms and individuals as providers of correctional services. Although involvement from the private sector has been in place for many years, more recently private firms have expanded from providing a few specific services to financing, building and operating correctional institutions. Involvement of the private sector in correctional activity provides another area of correctional employment and presents the possibility of many more corrections-related positions. (Privatization is discussed in more detail in section nine.)

The third article, "Corrections Looks Toward the Twenty-First Century: Needs and Opportunities," by Peter Kratcoski, describes the range of employment opportunities and the higher education preparation regarded as appropriate for corrections positions. A survey of the types of degrees held by administrative and treatment personnel working in corrections today would reveal backgrounds of higher education in such fields as political science, public administration, social work, history, education, psychology, and sociology. Entrants to the field in the past ten years may have more specialized degrees in criminal justice or corrections, but it is typical for personnel working in corrections to have been educated for work in a general "helping" occupation rather than to have specifically prepared for a career in corrections. The selection presents specifics on salary ranges and advancement opportunities and also describes research and teaching opportunities related to corrections.

Selection four, "Reflections on the Education Factor in the Correction Officer Role," by Robert Blair and Peter Kratcoski, is based on information obtained from correction officers and administrators working in state correctional facilities. It was found that it is difficult to differentiate a specific type of education that best prepares a person for correctional work in an institution, and that no form of formal education is comparable to the knowledge obtained through "on-the-job" experience. Most of the correction officers must develop a whole range of skills, including those that pertain to working with a culturally diverse population, if they are to be effective in their work.

The fifth selection, "Burnout: Avoiding the Consequences of On-The-Job Stress," by Richard M. Morris, describes the stressful features of correctional work which also occur in other occupations and those which are specifically tied to the identity of "correctional officer." Stress management strategies for the correctional worker and his or her family are described.

3

Corrections Looks toward the Twenty-First Century
Needs and Opportunities

Peter C. Kratcoski

The field of corrections offers a wide range of career opportunities, including administrative and supervisory positions in institutions or agencies, work as a practitioner, or activity in program development, evaluation, research, and teaching. In *Career Planning in Criminal Justice* (DeLucia and Doyle, 1994), job titles given as career opportunities in corrections include: correctional treatment specialist, corrections counselor, corrections officer, juvenile justice counselor, parole officer, pre-release program correctional counselor, pre-release program employment counselor, recreation counselor, academic teacher, HIV caseworker specialist, education counselor, substance abuse specialist, classification and treatment director, management coordinator, inmate records coordinator, correctional facilities specialist, prisoner classification interviewer, and penologist (73–86).

Current Employment Opportunities in Corrections

In January, 1993, 186,510 supervisory and nonsupervisory correctional uniform staff members were employed in state and federal correctional institutions housing adult offenders. Of these, 9,244 (5%) were employed in federal facilities. Of the total number, 161,363 (86%) served in nonsupervisory, correctional officer

A version of this chapter originally appeared in the *Journal of Applied Sociology* 2 (1975):23–31, and was reprinted in *Correctional Counseling and Treatment*, 2nd edition.

capacities, and 22,830 (12%) had been hired in 1992 and therefore had been working in their current positions one year or less (Camp and Camp, *Adult Corrections*, 1993: 68–69).

The number of correctional agency employees increased by 26% from 1989 to 1993, as shown in Figure 1.

Figure 1

Total Correctional Agency Employees on January 1, 1993

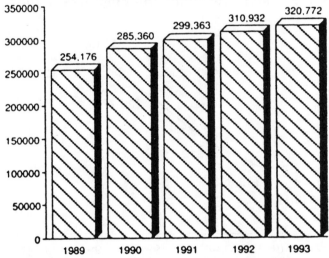

Source: George M. and Camille Graham Camp, *The Corrections Yearbook 1993, Adult Corrections* (South Salem, NY: Criminal Justice Institute 1993: 74).

In January, 1993, there were 8,887 treatment staff employed in adult corrections. These persons served as psychiatrists, psychologists, social workers, case workers, recreation therapists, and counselors. Nationally, the average salary for a corrections officer in 1993 was $20,444 at the completion of a mandatory probation period, with the salary range at the completion of the probationary period extending from a low of $14,100 to a high of $35,760 (Camp and Camp, *Adult Corrections*, 1993: 78, 79, 81). Salaries for treatment staff employed in corrections work are difficult to ascertain, since many of them are contract employees.

In January, 1993, there were 5,522 supervisory staff, 27,575 probation officers, 11,089 administrative and support staff, and 2,744 persons employed in other categories in probation and related services. The average entry level salary for probation officers in 1993 was $22,303, with a range from $15,000 to $32,287 (Camp and Camp, *Probation and Parole*, 1993: 9, 15–16). From 1987 to 1993, as shown in Figure 2, the average entry level salary rose 23%, from $18,113 in 1987 to $22,303 in 1993 (Camp and Camp, *Probation and Parole*, 1993: 17).

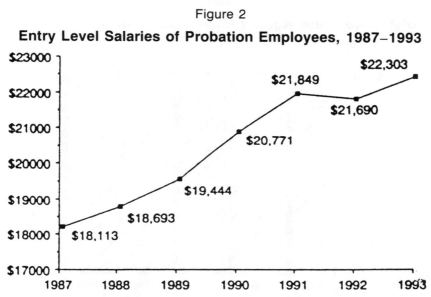

Figure 2

Entry Level Salaries of Probation Employees, 1987–1993

Source: George M. and Camille Graham Camp, *The Corrections Yearbook, 1993, Probation and Parole* (South Salem, NY: Criminal Justice Institute, 1993: 17).

The estimated number of parole employees in January, 1993, was 34,313, an increase of 44% from 1988 (Camp and Camp, *Probation and Parole*, 1993: 37).

In January, 1993, 42,654 employees worked with state juvenile corrections agencies. A large number of these (nearly 40%) served as youth workers in juvenile institutions. In these facilities, there were 9,677 employees who were classified as treatment staff. Their positions included psychologist, psychiatrist, counselor, social worker, caseworker, paraprofessional counselor, academic teacher, and vocational teacher (Camp and Camp, *Juvenile Corrections*, 1993: 47, 51). The percentages of staff working in various capacities in juvenile agencies are shown in Figure 3.

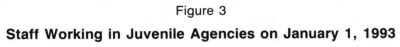

Figure 3

Staff Working in Juvenile Agencies on January 1, 1993

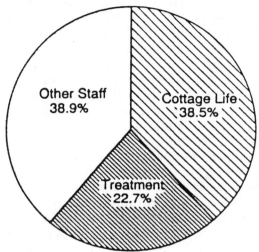

Other Staff
38.9%

Cottage Life
38.5%

Treatment
22.7%

Source: George M. and Camille Graham Camp, *The Corrections Yearbook, 1993, Juvenile Corrections* (South Salem, NY: Criminal Justice Institute, 1993: 52).

The average salary for youth counselors at the completion of a probationary period was $18,998, with a range from $12,856 to $31,632 (Camp and Camp, *Juvenile Corrections*, 1993: 56–57).

Although the figures are not complete for the entire country, there were 33,852 persons employed in some form of correctional work in jails in January, 1993. Of these, 697 were employed as treatment staff (psychologists, psychiatrists, social workers, case workers, recreation therapists, or counselors). The average starting salary for corrections officers or deputies working in the jail system was $21,431, with a low of $13,608 and a high of $36,150 (Camp and Camp, *Jail Systems*, 1993: 15–16, 21). The information on those employed in jails is incomplete, and so the employment figures and salary ranges are approximate. Obviously, the number of jail employees is much greater than reported.

Women and minorities are well represented among corrections workers. A January, 1993 survey found that 51% of the employees hired in 1992 were female, as were 39% of the new employees hired in 1992 (Camp and Camp, *Juvenile Corrections*, 1993: 47–53). In adult agencies, the same survey revealed that 17% of the custodial staff and supervisory and non-supervisory personnel were females, as were 33% of the new employees hired in 1992 (Camp and Camp, *Adult Corrections*, 1993: 68, 71). Forty-nine percent of the probation employees and 49% of the parole employees were female (Camp and Camp, *Probation and Parole*, 1993: 9, 35). Of the employees of jail systems, 27% were female, as were 24% of those hired in 1992 for jailer/officer/deputy positions (Camp and Camp, *Jail Systems*, 1993: 5, 10). In juvenile corrections, 37% of the employees were non-white, as were 34% of those hired in 1992 (Camp and Camp, *Juvenile Corrections*, 1993, 47, 53). In adult corrections agencies, 31% of the custodial staff and supervisory and non-supervisory staff members were non-white, as were 20% of those hired in 1992 (Camp and Camp, *Adult Corrections*, 1993: 68, 71). Fifteen percent of the probation employees and 21% of the parole employees were non-white (Camp and Camp, *Probation and Parole*, 9, 35). Among jail system employees, 34% were minorities, and 31% of those hired in 1992 for jailer/officer/deputy positions were minorities (Camp and Camp, *Jail Systems*, 1993: 5, 10).

The substantial increases in the number of persons employed in corrections in recent years indicate that employment opportunities exist and that they are likely to be available into the twenty-first century. When closely related positions, such as work in group homes, diversion, or substance abuse programs, which are not specifically designed as corrections work but are tangential to the field, are taken into account, the possibilities are even greater.

New job titles are constantly being introduced that require very specialized education and training. For example, those who may be employed to work specifically with offenders who are mentally ill or mentally retarded, or with sex offenders, need a type of education and training that is interdisciplinary. This is particularly true in juvenile and community corrections.

Higher Education Preparation for a Corrections Career

Specific academic programs in corrections were not available until the 1960s. Before that time, students drawn to the general area of correctional work were likely to major in sociology, social work, or psychology. There were few textbooks dealing specifically with corrections, and those available took a non-theoretical, technical approach to the subject.

A major factor in the delay in the emergence of corrections as a field of study was the fact that the image of what constitutes corrections was not well defined. In the eyes of the public, corrections was equated with institutional work in prisons or jails.

It was not until the 1960s, when increased federal funding created many new programs in law enforcement and corrections, that varied career opportunities in criminal justice appeared.

In the turbulent 1960s, inner city disturbances, campus unrest, public fear of crime, revelations of abuses and primitive conditions in institutions, and demands by prisoners for better conditions and recognition of their rights led to legislation which provided funds for expansion of existing programs in criminal justice and the creation of many new programs. The Law Enforcement Assistance Administration, which provided colleges and universities with curriculum development grants for programs in law enforcement and corrections and gave students training grants and tuition loans, supplied a powerful economic incentive for institutions of higher learning to become involved. Many new programs were hastily formulated to take advantage of the available federal funding. In 1960, only 26 colleges and universities in the United States offered full-time programs in any law enforcement related field. However, by 1970, the Law Enforcement Education Directory listed 292 institutions which offered 340 different programs, and many other colleges and universities offered a specialization in some type of law enforcement related field within their sociology or political science departments, making the actual number of existing programs much higher (Tenney, 1971).

Tenney (1971) developed a model to characterize programs in the criminal justice field, labeling them "training," "social science," and "professional." The training oriented programs are primarily designed to teach the mastery and application of rules, the development of mechanical skills to operate equipment, and the mastery of mechanical skills in the performance of maneuvers. The social science programs, in contrast, approach the field from a general theoretical perspective and do not prepare a student for specific work in the subject area. The professionally oriented program is designed to provide both a theoretical foundation and experiences in the field, but goes beyond job training and gives students opportunities to view their experiences in criminal justice and corrections from a wider perspective through internalization of values and setting of goals.

As new higher education programs in criminal justice and corrections developed, the tendency was to create separate departments of criminal justice or law enforcement rather than develop them as specializations within existing departments of sociology or social science. Since the available sociological solutions called for broad changes in the political and economic systems of the community and the country that would require years of effort to implement, there was a movement to create new departments and programs which emphasized training in social control skills. In addition, many of the social science and sociology programs were not designed or prepared to provide the types of field experience and direct training for employment which were now viewed as important. The new departments and programs that were created tended to rely heavily on part-time faculty members who were employed in the field and could offer the students practical advice and the benefit of their expertise.

During the 1980s, many of the hastily designed programs that emphasized training were eliminated. Most of these were located in community colleges or were two-year programs within large colleges or universities that were heavily dependent upon federal subsidies. When funding for the Law Enforcement Assistance Administration was severely reduced and eventually eliminated, these institutions were unable to attract students for the programs or to continue to support them, and they were eventually dropped. Other programs survived and became part of independent departments of criminal justice. By 1980, 816 institutions of higher education were offering crime related programs. This included 1,209 associate level programs, 589 baccalaureate programs, and 222 graduate programs (Myren, 1980: 23). When members of the American Society of Criminology and the Academy of Criminal Justice Sciences were asked to rank graduate programs in criminology and criminal justice in order of prestige, it was found that the majority of programs ranked high in prestige were the older, established programs, which existed before the creation of the Law Enforcement Education Program, administered by the LEAA, in 1968 (DeZee, Joint Commission on Criminology and Criminal Justice Education and Standards, 1980: 18–20). Many of the faculty members teaching in these programs received their degrees in sociology, political science, or psychology.

In 1991, *Anderson's Directory of Criminal Justice Education* (Nemeth, 1991: iii) reported that 1,041 educational institutions offered one or more criminal justice degrees. This was a 10.5% increase in the number offering such degrees since the 1986–87 directory was published.

The current emphasis on criminal justice education is on the types of programs which Tenney characterized as "professional," which stress a strong interdisciplinary curriculum and frequently include courses in professional ethics and in research methods and statistics.

Opportunities for Career Advancement

Most of the individuals who pursue careers in corrections eventually move into administrative and supervisory positions. In the past, those who held such positions were predominantly holders of the Master of Social Work degree, and this degree was considered the highest needed to move into the more responsible and better paying positions. This dominance of the administrative levels of institutions and agencies by social workers has gradually eroded, and those who hold M.A.s or Ph.D.s in criminal justice, corrections, or applied sociology are now being given equal consideration for administrative positions.

Once an individual reaches an administrative or specialized position, the opportunities to advance or to make a parallel move into another agency increase. The management and supervisory skills needed to be effective in administering the juvenile court system, for example, are quite comparable to those needed to administer a county mental health facility. Once a certain level of administrative expertise is developed, it is quite common for persons to transfer from one correctional or social service agency to another.

The job opportunities which require the use of skills of research design, evaluation procedures, and statistics are increasing in the field of corrections. Most of the agencies are required to submit various types of periodic statistical reports and to complete records on their operations. In addition, even the smaller agencies have computerized their records and office procedures. The skills needed to fill these positions do not necessarily have to be obtained in a corrections degree program. Since much of the research and theoretical development in corrections and criminal justice has emanated from sociology, political science, and psychology departments, graduates of a variety of academic programs who have an aptitude for research and some experience with statistics and the use of computers can fit into these positions. However, those with degrees in corrections have an advantage because of their familiarity with the criminal justice process, the terms used in statistical reports, and the legal facets of criminal justice and corrections work. In addition, they are likely to have completed an internship which further familiarizes them with the types of reports involved and the legal and criminal justice terminology used.

Teaching in the corrections area on the college level is another career opportunity. We noted earlier that more than 800 colleges and universities offer programs in criminal justice, law enforcement, or corrections. A large number of these programs are offered out of two year technical schools or community colleges, and part-time teaching opportunities exist for practitioners who wish to pursue them. While full-time teaching positions in colleges and universities are virtually unavailable in many subject areas, they still exist in the criminal justice and corrections areas. A doctorate is the usual entering qualification for those seeking tenured positions. The specific doctorate which the candidate for such a position holds is not as crucial as the emphasis of the coursework and specialization.

New faculty members in criminal justice and corrections programs are drawn predominantly from applicants with doctorates in criminal justice, sociology, political science, psychology, or law. Advertisements for candidates for such positions generally state the minimum requirements as including a doctorate in criminology, criminal justice, or a closely related field.

Summary

The field of corrections is broad enough to allow for a large number of persons with varying educational backgrounds, interests, and skills to carve out satisfying careers. There are opportunities to work in the community and in institutions, and to deal with adults and juveniles through various agencies and widely different types of interaction. While the majority of careers in corrections involve direct contact with offenders in a supervisory or counseling role, there are also positions in administration, training, research, evaluation, and education.

References

Camp, George M. and Camille Graham Camp. 1993. *The Corrections Yearbook, Adult Corrections*. South Salem, NY: Criminal Justice Institute.

_____. 1993. *The Corrections Yearbook, Jail Systems*. South Salem, NY: Criminal Justice Institute.

_____. 1993. The Corrections Yearbook, Juvenile Corrections. South Salem, NY: Criminal Justice Institute.

_____. *The Corrections Yearbook, Probation and Parole*. South Salem, NY: Criminal Justice Institute.

DeLucia, Robert C. and Thomas J. Doyle. 1994. *Career Planning in Criminal Justice*. Cincinnati, OH: Anderson Publishing Company.

DeZee, Matthew R. 1980. "The Productivity of Criminology and Criminal Justice Faculty," Report prepared for the Joint Commission on Criminology and Criminal Justice. Chicago: University of Illinois at Chicago Circle.

Myren, Richard A. 1979, "Criminology and Criminal Justice: Definitions, Trends, and the Future" Pp. 23–38 in *Two Views of Criminology and Criminal Justice: Definitions, Trends and the Future.* Washington, D.C.: U.S. Department of Justice.

Nemeth, Charles P. 1991. *Anderson's 1991 Directory of Criminal Justice Education.* Cincinnati, OH: Anderson Publishing Company.

Tenney Charles W., Jr. 1971. *Higher Education Programs in Law Enforcement and Criminal Justice.* Washington, D.C.: U.S. Government Printing Office.

4

Reflections on the Education Factor in the Correction Officer Role

Robert B. Blair
Peter C. Kratcoski

Introduction

Much of the literature on the educational achievements of correction officers is less than complimentary (Davidson, 1974; Toch, 1978). If one were to take at face value the assertions of some authors, being a dim-witted Neanderthal is a prerequisite for employment as a correction officer. Jacobs' (1978) classic study of officers working in nine correctional facilities in Illinois revealed that most guards were not attracted to correctional work because of a desire to dominate or punish people, but because they were looking for a job with security, and the prison was conveniently located near their place of residence. When the correctional officers were asked why they chose this occupation, 57% stated that they "just needed a job" (187). In fact, 41% reported that they were unemployed at the time they specifically "aspired to become a guard" (187). Crouch and Marquart (1980) point out that in the past, most of the people found working as correction officers did not plan on corrections work as a life career, but rather drifted into it when they reached a "turning point" in their lives. Examples of such turning points included leaving the military, becoming dissatisfied with other employment, being laid off or fired from another job, or relocating to a town near a correctional institution.

In the past, most guards received on-the-job training, which was generally completed under the direction of one or several veteran officers and which involved trial-and-error experiences. A new guard was quickly made aware of what was expected of him or her. The experienced guards let new guards know subtly or directly that loyalty toward other officers was demanded and that prison administrators were not likely to be competent or trustworthy. The only way to learn one's job was from the instruction given by the other guards. A small minority of the personnel employed in correctional facilities were college educated, but these generally worked in administration, personnel, or in the specialized areas of social and psychological services. For example, Jacobs (1978) found that slightly more than half of the guards had a high school diploma or equivalent, while only 11 guards in the entire state of Illinois at the time of the study had a four-year college education (187).

In contrast, many, if not the majority of correction officers recruited in recent years, actually chose this type of employment and prepared for it through formal college-level education. Formal education for those working in the corrections field received a tremendous boost with the Report of the National Advisory Commission on Criminal Justice Standards and Goals, in which it was recommended that "each unified state correctional system should insure that proper incentives are provided for participation in higher education programs" (1973: 490). In the 1970s and 1980s, thousands took advantage of Law Enforcement Assistance Administration grants by attending colleges and universities that developed educational programs in corrections. Perhaps most of these students expected to be employed in supervisory or counseling-type positions within the correctional facilities, but a large number of them began their careers as correction officers. The correction officer occupation ranks among the top growth occupations in the U.S. (Benton, 1988; Silvestri and Lukasiewicz, 1989). The number of students enrolled in criminal justice programs has continued to increase, and one can predict that the correction officer ranks will continue to be filled by college graduates and that they will eventually take over the administrative positions. In the 1990s, Blair and Kratcoski (1992) found a wide variation in the educational levels of correctional officers, with 27% having a bachelor's degree or above, 67% having a high school diploma or its equivalent, and only 6% having completed less than a high school education (8).

It has been suggested that a college educated person who has developed a degree of professionalism is not likely to be very satisfied working as a correction officer, since the expectations of the role tend to demand that the officer be authoritarian, rigid, obedient, and punitive, whereas the concept of professionalism implies having a degree of personal autonomy in decision making, dedication to service, and self-regulation. It has also been suggested that learning about correctional work in a classroom has little relevance to the actual job performance, since there is a wide gap separating the theory pertaining to correctional work and the actual practice of such work.

There are numerous studies that include education as a variable in their research designs, but the findings of the research on the importance of education in correctional work are not definitive. One reason for this may be that education is often one of many variables involved in the analyses rather than being the primary focus of the studies.

Most of the earlier research work on correction officers or guards (Clemmer, 1940; Giallombardo, 1966; Jacobs, 1978) tended to portray the correction officer as having completed a limited amount of formal education. Duffee (1972) noted that the conventional training program for correction officers, which is based on the university classroom lecture model, is not likely to be effective in preparing persons for work in correctional institutions, and Jurik et al. (1987) suggested that the attainment of high levels of education by correction officers led to alienation within the institution, since correction officers did not have an opportunity to perform in the manner in which they were prepared.

No relationship was found between correction officers' levels of education and their attitudes toward punitiveness (Crouch and Alpert, 1982) or between levels of education and the correction officers' beliefs about the rehabilitative potential of prisons (Shamir and Drory, 1981). Likewise, neither Jurik (1985) nor Kassebaum, Ward and Wilner (1964) found a relationship between correction officers' education levels and their attitudes toward inmates. Poole and Regoli (1980) reported that education was inversely related to a custody orientation by correction officers. Blair and Kratcoski (1992) found a weak, but non-significant, correlation between education and the professionalism scores of correction officers.

Qualitative Research Methods

The data for this study were derived from interviews with the corrections officers that included a self-completion questionnaire. Completed responses were received from 274 officers employed in nine state prisons in Pennsylvania. A systematic random sampling design was used to select officers employed in the nine prisons. Care was taken to select subjects from rosters for each eight-hour shift in the nine state facilities. Only one officer refused to complete the interview process and the one-hour questionnaire. The interviews were conducted as part of a participant observation field study that took place over a 12-month time period. The questionnaire included the usual demographic data (age, gender, education, years of experience, and rank) as well as various questions pertaining to their attitudes on the use of authority and punishment, their orientation toward their work, levels of professionalism and alienation, and correctional policy orientations.

Although all of the correction officers included in this study completed questionnaires and were also interviewed, and considerable quantitative information was collected and analyzed, this chapter focuses primarily on the information gleaned from the responses of the officers to the questions posed during the interviews. We interviewed several hundred officers and supervisors over a period of one year. We were attempting to understand how education is interpreted by staff members with different backgrounds and how the context of the work environment shapes attitudes and behavior patterns of staff in state correctional facilities.

One of the most obvious problems of conducting research in prisons concerns the amount of autonomy outside researchers can be granted in prison settings. Access to officers and inmates is often controlled and carefully monitored by shift supervisors; the time allotted for most interviews is, therefore, usually restricted. Moreover, the location and opportunities for observing officer behaviors do not usually permit the recording of data that lead to "thick description." Fortunately this was not the case in this study. The researchers were given a free reign to come and go at their convenience and to spend as much time with the inmates and COs as they wished, as long as it did not interfere with the activities and duties of those being interviewed. We learned in the early stages of fieldwork to pay attention to what officers have to say, but to also observe and record the emotional intensity of their response. The qualitative methodological approach we used included a long interview and intensive structured observations. Many of the facilities were visited several times before interviewing was started. As operationalized in the fieldwork, we gathered information that pertained to cultural factors and personal qualities that come into play when officers supervise and interact with inmates and other staff members. Along with the disciplining, counting, and locking, we also observed and recorded the quality of the exchanges, the humor, the hostility, and the compassion.

Qualitative Research Findings

On one level, we discovered that officers adopt a defensive posture toward formal education; they view education as possibly dysfunctional for many of their duties; appropriate education for the officer role is conceptualized in terms of hands-on training, and the most effective teachers are thought to be experienced officers or supervisors who work side by side with the officers and who serve as their mentors. The interview and observation data are rich with evidence that documents this generalization.

When asked to define the knowledge needed to perform their job, the officers discussed security functions and emphasized the importance of structural or institutional variables for shaping role performance. One officer's comment is typical of the responses we recorded in all nine institutions: "A college diploma carries no guarantee that you'll make it on the inside." In fact, many officers view a college education as a potential liability, a preparation for, what one supervisor referred to as, "trained incapacity." A lieutenant explains how education might work against an officer:

> The inmates resent the newer officers more than they used to. The average inmate has an education level of eighth grade to high school, and the new officer who has an education tries to show it, and to really communicate you have to get down to their level. (Interview by R. Blair with a lieutenant)

An experienced officer was asked to comment on the increasing numbers of entry-level officers with advanced degrees. He concluded his observations with the following comment: "The CO today is better educated test-wise but not street-wise. It takes a long time to become street-wise, and you should always be picking up stuff [on the job]. . . ."

The officer force as a group tends not to make direct connections between formal education and on-the-job functioning. Many officers view the process of learning the CO role as being caught rather than taught. Hence, the representative comments of officers in two separate institutions who addressed the issue of the utility of pre-institutional training for new recruits:

> They require you to spend four weeks at the Academy, but it's hard to prepare an officer for [his local state prison] by going down there [to the Academy]. It was too much like the classroom

thing. There's not much in the way of practice or hands-on type of training.

It's [the CO role] like working around people who speak French. When you have to speak it, you begin to pick it up. . . . (Interview by R. Blair with several correction officers)

Supervisory staff also see more value in on-the-job training than they do in other forms of education. A captain with 28 years of experience commented on the evolving role of the correction officer. His comments reflect the emerging concessions being made to education, but suggest the importance of grounding an education for corrections in the local institution of the CO.

The biggest and most recent change is the overcrowding and added responsibilities. We have had little increase in staff. The actual duties that officers are asked to do have tripled, and if you're going to triple the duties, you should at least double the manpower! Over the past twenty years the COs have come to see their jobs as a career, and now it's evolved into a highly scientific career-type job and the only way to learn it is on the floor. If you could work a guy a half-day, and then send him to school too, then [education] would have a very valuable impact. It's the "in thing" to go the training Academy, but it just doesn't mean that much. (Interview by R. Blair with a captain)

Finally, supervisors of a military-type organization, whose primary function is to lock up offenders against their will, tend almost naturally to expect officers to acquire fundamental skills related to security. Training supervisors tend to see the base information for the role as shaped by technical security skills that are more effectively learned by on-the-job training than through formal education. A number of the supervisors emphasized the need for officers to have good communication skills, but most typical of all responses we recorded are views that reflect the following comment that argues for the primacy of security "training."

It's mostly a matter of socializing [the new officers], and there is not enough information on security techniques. So I worked on training on the job for officers, and designed it for places where the need was maximal, such as in the use of weapons, corridor duty, cell search and packing [of inmate belongings]. (Interviewed by R. Blair with a lieutenant)

These quotations were selected for their value as typical statements of the correctional staff who were asked questions related to the role of education for the CO. The overwhelming weight of the evidence in our data support the generalization that correction officers as a group nurture a skeptical attitude regarding the usefulness of formal education for performing the correction officer role.

What are we to make of these reflections on education? If these are the only results that we could report, we would add little to what we already know about the education factor in the CO role. We decided, therefore, that limiting our study to data gathered through one-shot survey interviews would not do justice to the complexity of the issues. We also reasoned that terminating the study after the first wave of standard interviews would constitute a premature closure of inquiry on an important topic that warrants more intensive investigation. The purpose in adapting the field design followed in the research was to acquire data that capture the subtlety, complexity, and varied aspects of the CO role and, in the same way that quantitative researchers use an elaboration model to check for spuriousness, we attempted to specify the conditions under which our first set of findings might vary. Specifically, we were searching for "counterfactuals" in the data that suggest diversity of views regarding education. Increasingly there is recognition that correction officers are a diverse group and that their roles involve a flexibility that permits qualities to come into play that reflect, among other things, their unique cultures, backgrounds and the type of correctional facility in which they are employed. The discussion that follows focuses on three questions that represent variables that account for a richer and more in-depth understanding of the education facts than those revealed in our initial findings. The second round of interviews was completed for the purpose of answering the following questions:

1. Do unique characteristics of individual correctional institutions influence the way officers and supervisors think about the importance of education?
2. What are the variables that account for differences in opinions on the relevance of formal education for the officer role?
3. What evidence is there that the CO role would benefit from efforts to upgrade education requirements?

Regarding the first question of institutional characteristics, we begin the discussion by challenging what is frequently a common assertion: a prison is a prison. Prisons vary, we discovered, and their unique locales, employment practices, and histories all contribute to diversity in the orientations and performance styles of their COs and supervisors. One institution studied, which we will refer to as Valleyview, is known throughout the state as a prison that is "tight" on security; officers in Valleyview are proud of their roles, and their children might come about as close as any to voicing an unfamiliar aspiration: "I want to be a CO when I grow up." Morale is high among staff and there is a good working relationship between the correction officers' union and management. The prison is perceived by inmates as a "no bullshit operation," and despite the complaints of "redneck" behavior from a few officers, several of the dozen or so inmates we interviewed expressed appreciation for the relative safety they enjoy in an institution that "belongs to the guards." Officers tend to have a "we" versus "they" view in regard to the other prisons in the state, and they often stated that the "system" is "sending us all the bad apples." Of course this feeling was also pervasive among staff in the other state prisons, but the isolation of Valleyview accentuates the distrust of outside change; directives that disrupt traditional authority patterns, regardless of their sources of origin, are usually interpreted as meddling by outsiders.

Part of the success of "running a good shop" like Valleyview, argues one officer, can be explained by the prison's strategic role as a major source of employment in the area. Community attitudes toward the prison are so positive that local leaders petitioned the state to locate and build a second prison in the Valleyview area. A cohesive officer force is one of the consequences of these unique geographical and employment patterns, as suggested in one of our interviews.

> At _____ we help officers. There are lots of relatives working together in here. We have 31 sets of brothers in the institution and aunts and cousins too. The community is so small that everyone knows everyone here, and in some way or another everybody socializes together. Ninety percent hunt and fish and shop and boat together and are closely related through blood or friendship. There are fifteen officers I went to high school with who are working in here. There's a thing here of evaluating officers. Even the poorest officer in here would get some backing [by other officers].

The superintendent of Valleyview had considerable formal education in corrections and had attended college at a time when the treatment and rehabilitation of inmates were given a great deal of emphasis. We were interested in the way a superintendent with a counseling background would articulate the types of skills a correction officer needs to be effective. His statement reaffirmed the statements of the correction officers on this matter. Security concerns at Valleyview take precedence over all other matters, but an officer's knowledge must extend far beyond the mechanical aspects of the job.

> Officers are becoming more professional. The professional carries himself with pride and dignity. He treats his peers as well

as inmates with respect; he respects his superiors. He respects the chain of command, the hierarchy of authority, and there's more of that here than anyplace else in the state. He understands how the institution functions, and he understands his role in relation to the roles of other people in the institution. The guy knows the rules and regulations, and he knows how to deal with inmates without being a hard nose about rules and regulations. He can reason with them and talk them out of situations. He also has basic skills in first aid and CPR; he has basic safety skills; he knows how to conduct a security search—he's good at it, thorough—and knows how to handle security equipment, whether it's handcuffs, shackles, weapons, whatever it might be. That's professionalism. (Interview by R. Blair with an anonymous superintendent)

The superintendent traced the development of large numbers of professional officers in his institution to legitimated authority. The communal ties that cut across ranks, position, and job categories provide the cement that reinforces a security-oriented chain of command.

This institution has been here for a hundred years. It has grown up and the community has grown with it. This is the only [prison] I've ever seen where people aspire to a career in corrections. I mean actually grow up and say they want to work in corrections, and you have grandfathers, fathers, and sons working in this institution. Employees come back to visit the facility after they retire. When you walk through the institution and talk to people in any department here, they treat it and talk about it like it's theirs, and it is. They have a vested interest in it; it's their own. They carry themselves more professionally. Any time we send a couple of our officers for training and officers show up from other institutions in the state, everybody from staff training and development comment; they say, "Look at the officer from _____; they even look better, they carry themselves better." (Interview by R. Blair with anonymous superintendent)

These sets of comments contrast sharply with those offered by another superintendent whose major labor supply includes graduates from a state university criminology program. Reflecting upon the ingredients that make up professionalism in the officer force, he responded as follows:

We are a profession. We have a formal training program . . . you have to have a background [education] and you have to learn a philosophy; you have to learn goals; you have to learn procedures.

You have individuals who are what we would call a "professional officer." He has to make the grade by taking the test, and so you have the whole business of selection. He starts out with formal training and then has on-the-job training. If I had to compare it with a similar profession, I would say the nursing profession. Another comparison would be with law or lawyers, [but at a time when] lawyers did not bother going to law schools and did their clerkships, and then were able to pass the boards. To some extent we're doing the same thing because the training is the equivalent of a clerkship, and passing the bar is in effect too when you move into a particular status after you've been around awhile. . . . (Interview by R. Blair, with an anonymous superintendent)

Of course more information is needed about the superintendents and their institutions, but the results are suggestive of possible ways that personal orientations interact with institutional milieus in shaping understanding and interpretations of the education factor. Returning to the Valleyview example, we also discovered that education was never really a significant factor in hiring or promotion. A strong nepotism in employment practices that favored "who you know" over "what you know" indirectly contributed to a strong communal system that minimized the importance of education. For an institution that has always socialized its officer force through on-the-job training, it is understandable that there would be resistance among officers to Academy training and to other state directives that attempted to implement court-mandated changes. It is understandable, therefore, that officers naturally resisted changes in promotion policies that gave an added edge to officers with formal educational backgrounds. Officers who had accumulated considerable seniority were very negative toward the new state regulation which required the completion of a written test in addition to a specified number of years experience for those seeking promotion to a higher rank. This change was interpreted as unfair and as a violation of local traditions. A block sergeant shared his personal reactions to the indirect effects that education had on the promotion system.

A man with two years [experience] can be academically inclined, and can take tests and beat out the others, yet never be able to run a block; yet they're the guys who are going to get the high score. A older guy, even with the five points extra that they give veterans, may not have a chance. Now they [Bureau promotion policy] are calling for a minimum time of five years before you are eligible for promotion. In the beginning, when they made these changes, maybe I was jealous, but it affected me to see a younger officer with education move ahead. Later I could see

> it, but it took me eight years to make sergeant and yet it only
> took him seven years to make lieutenant. But now he's got both,
> the education and the experience, and now it's OK. He carries
> a great deal of respect and he is a potential captain. (Interview
> by R. Blair with a correction officer)

The sergeant's comment is particularly poignant, because in
addition to its typicality, it illustrates the fact that even the "old
timers" were beginning to accept the importance of education as
a major change in the way their roles are defined. The point is,
different interpretations of education do not just happen in a
vacuum; they reflect combinations of institutional and individual
variables working together.

Another source of diversity in thinking about the role of education
is represented in the court-mandated hiring of minorities and
women as correction officers. As the superintendent of Valleyview
suggested, his prison "lags behind most other institutions" in hiring
minority COs. The few minority officers who work at Valleyview
were interviewed, and they expressed concerns about practices in
Valleyview that reflect their definition of the situation. A minority
officer with two years of experience offered these comments.

> There is a black versus redneck thing in here. In this county
> most of the black people live in _____, and yet they hire their
> people from _____ where there are no blacks. With the black
> [inmate] population growing in here, it's like sending the pope
> to talk to a bunch of Jews. I never see these people [other officers]
> on the outside. They don't get enough race training at the
> Academy, and they don't recruit blacks. There is a lot of
> nepotism here too. There are [racist] jokes all the time. When
> they come at me with them I just play the dozens with them,
> and they can't take that. All they want to do is talk about
> hunting and fishing and their four-wheel drives, and if they kick,
> it's on somebody else. (Interview by R. Blair with a black
> correction officer)

The "good-old-boy network" at Valleyview is viewed by minority
officers as impervious to change. Implied in the following assessment of conditions at Valleyview, as voiced by a minority officer
with 10 years experience, is an argument for changing employment
patterns at Valleyview as well as upgrading education requisites.

> They don't recruit right. You have to deal with them [prospective
> minority employees], you have to go to their community and
> get them. They screen us out. They put in their friends and
> relatives. There is so much nepotism here! When we were on
> A ward we ran it well, and we weren't big guys either; we ran
> it well because we're from the same community as the inmates.
> You need streetwise people in here.

> If you're looking for black officers you got to put it in the paper, take the job information to colleges and to programs where there are blacks. If they really want to get some good officers, why don't they go to the south? Go to the colleges in the south! You get coal region guys here who can't talk to a black man. It's a communication barrier and it takes 5 years to learn their lingo. (Interview by R. Blair with a black correction officer)

The data we collected from interviews with approximately 50 minority officers contain numerous appeals for COs to have specialized educational experiences that would better equip them for working with a growing minority inmate population. Nearly every one of the minority officers cited specific academic subjects, such as "race and ethnic relations," or "what it's like to live in a ghetto" as requisite courses for white correction officers who interact with nonwhite inmates.

Still another source of diversity in thinking about the relevance of education for the CO role comes from the increasing number of female officers in male prisons. Valleyview did not employ female COs at the time of our interviews, but the data drawn from an institution with characteristics similar to Valleyview typify the responses of female officers. If this officer is correct in her assessment of the contributions that women bring to supervising inmates, implications for change in training and education might be significant.

> The presence of male officers in a female institution very often comes across to the female inmate as a physical threat; whereas a female officer in a male institution often becomes an emotional lift for inmates and introduces a more human aspect to the institutional setting of all-male surrounding. Concerning a female doing a "male" job—a female not just in corrections, but in any predominantly male occupation must or is expected to do sometimes two or three times as much [work], both in quantity and quality, than the best male on the job to be given half the credit that is extended to the poorest male performer in that particular institution. In plain English, a man can really "screw up" the particular assignment: eyes will roll toward the heavens, but then it is overlooked. (Note to R. Blair from a female correction officer; emphasis added)

Another variable that is pushing the education factor to the fore of officer training is the growing diversity in the inmate population. Officers in all institutions shared their reservations about the need for communication skills and supervisory techniques that would equip them to more effectively work with special-need inmates. At the time of the interviews, inmates with mental disabilities were becoming more visible. A correction officer offered this view of the situation:

> Six years ago we didn't have as many insane people, and Christ, today, we're polluted with them. When you deal with them, they can't listen like other inmates; they're out in left field; you can't talk with them. Like down here in RHU [Restricted Housing Unit], they're throwing stuff at you all the time. What can you do? About the only option is to move them to B block; once they're there we get them declared insane and from there they are sent to an insane asylum. But it's frustrating because they only keep them at _____ for a few months and we get them right back again. In relation to them you have to change your strategy. They're different from the regular type. You can't use the same talking technique; you have to try cigarettes, humor; some guys just forget it. (Interview by R. Blair with anonymous correction officer; emphasis added)

Some officers, as this one suggested, "just forget it." Others do not, and we frequently were informed that supervisors were careful to assign officers with the requisite communication skills (or natural talents) to supervise inmates with mental disabilities. Other inmate groups are receiving specialized attention as well, including those with AIDS and the elderly. One institutional training coordinator reflected on the relevance of CO education for the growing diversity in the inmate population and on the need for officers to have an enriched repertoire of skills:

> The lower the level of education you have, the less likely you are to do the job, and the less objective you are about the work. I definitely see a need for education of officers. You need education to be a professional in here. Education helps you make a decision quickly and objectively. Also, it helps if you have lived in a lot of different neighborhoods, because you're getting all different kinds of offenders, and you're getting more difficult types of offenders who resist supervision.
>
> The all-male society is at the heart of it. Among the officers, there is competition for promotions; inside the fence there is competition for survival, both physical and psychological. You need the proper tools in your own mind, and if you don't have them, you tend to fall back on basic force. (Interview by R. Blair with an anonymous training coordinator)

Even the older officers are beginning to see the need for upgrading educational requisites for an increasingly complex role. An officer with 25 years of experience shared the following assessment of changes he observed.

> Fifteen years ago there was a line between the officers and inmates, and each knew where he stood. In the '70s, the inmates

got court appointed rights. At the time we were considered guards, and that's what we did; now we have to evaluate a man, and we have to put this evaluation on paper, and the evaluation can be taken to court. If you blow the evaluation in court, the state won't back you up. And when you do this evaluating of inmates, you can't just give orders like in the service.

Things have really changed. Inmates now know their civil liberties; we have younger and younger drug users, and we have middle-class people too. We're not just dealing with the lower classes, and our roles are not clearly defined like they used to be. You have a different inmate now, and the education standards for officers have gone up. In the past, only a few officers had an education, but it wasn't needed then. (Interview by R. Blair with a correction officer)

The increasing diversity in both the inmate population and the officer force is paving the way for a variety of changes, many of which have implications for education that is relevant for the officer role. The final test of the efficacy of education, however, is in the behavior of officers. How does education influence interaction between officers and inmates?

One of the dozen female officers discussed the importance of education for the correction officer role. Education involves more than just being able to identify with the culture and "rap" with inmates. She traces the sources of her professionalism to her college education in the areas of law enforcement and corrections.

I see the job as a profession and a career. I see the need for a sharp uniform, professional conduct, training, a particular way of relating to inmates. I have become more relaxed, use more slang in my speech, talk more, but I still only speak with inmates if it's a necessity, and I am careful not to rap with them. Instead of doing their job, a lot of officers are into rapping and in doing that, they just aren't paying attention all the time; they walk around with a slouch, talk at inappropriate times, and so forth. (Interview by R. Blair with a correction officer)

An officer who had been viciously attacked by an inmate had returned to duty after a prolonged period of recovery. He was a liberal arts college graduate. With some reluctance he agreed to discuss the unfortunate incident. His analysis was not unlike that of an athlete who blew an assignment and lost the big game. He seemed to be blaming himself, not the inmate, for his misfortune.

It was a hard lesson. All the cues were right there, but I didn't read them. Instead of picking them up I misread them, because, for one thing, it was a sunny day and I was feeling good. Another thing, it was Sunday, and I was a little too relaxed. But when I look back on the attack, I can feel the signals: the number of

> guys on the block; there were no people in the divide at the time
> when it's usually crowded. A few guys were milling around
> watching me. I just wasn't paying attention to the environment.
> I pay attention to a lot more things now, and even when I'm
> making my rounds, I listen more and try to look around more.
> My senses have developed. . . . (Interview by R. Blair with a
> correction officer)

There is no suggestion in the quote that a liberal arts education
made any difference at all in the incident that occurred. When we
probed for perceived connections with his background, the officer
repeated a familiar refrain: education helps, but it needs to be
combined with a set of skills that include being able to
"communicate with inmates" and, he added, "the officer has to
know himself." Officers are less reticent to discuss the implications
of training for on-the-job functioning. Those who do not dismiss out-
right their Academy training, tend to cite specific tools and
techniques that they learned at the Academy, or they give a
generally unqualified endorsement to training. The following quote,
however, is reflective of views shared by many officers that suggest
possibly new thinking about the relevance of education:

> For the past years, a new breed of officers has entered this prison.
> They are younger and have lived in the atmosphere of our
> society and know more about criminals. Guys who went through
> the basic training class with me come to the institution with a
> different kind of knowledge than the old timers. We have, as our
> goal, to make things better in here. I don't mean we're soft
> hearted, but trying to encourage decency and respect. Our goal
> is to treat men as humans. The older breed didn't attend training
> school and learn this, and they did not live in the environment
> where there was a mixture of races. (Interview by R. Blair with
> a correction officer)

Perhaps inmates are the best source for documenting the effects
of education on the correction officer role. A routine part of our
fieldwork was to interview inmates. We followed a procedure of
randomly selecting a ward or block and then selecting every other
cell for interviewees. The education factor was not our usual topic
of conversation in the interviews, but a number of inmates cited
the importance of education when we asked them to reflect on the
characteristics of a good or poor officer. The following quote is
typical of comments of inmates in the institutions we studied.

> Usually the more adept guards have more education. But the
> good guards are street-smart too. They have seen the hard times
> and can identify with us. They are consistent in application of

the rules. They have common sense and can tell the difference between types of people. They know the types and take the time to discern the differences between them. They allow privacy and know when to bend. They use good common sense in situations. (Interview by R. Blair with an inmate)

Discussion

Our question on higher education was not specific enough to tap the type of education that may be applicable to being effective as a correction officer. For example, we did not establish whether the correction officer who had completed college had a degree in criminal justice, corrections, sociology, business, or another field. Our findings also suggest that the education factor is very closely intertwined with other factors such as experience, rank, age, the security level of the institution, and even the characteristics of the community in which the facility is housed. Our findings suggest that the college educated correction officer is likely to adhere to a professional standard regardless of the institution in which the person is employed. We expected that those college educated officers working in maximum security facilities would experience more alienation and dissatisfaction than those working in minimum security facilities. This did not turn out to be the fact. Perhaps the knowledge gained from attending college is useful to the correction officer who must be flexible, resourceful, and adaptable to various settings and situations. This may explain the similarity in their responses, even though the college educated officers were working in drastically different settings. On the other hand, many officers working in the minimum security facilities complained of the "hardcore offenders" being sent to the minimum security institutions. In fact, they contended that the only difference between working in a maximum and minimum security facility is the structure of the building, with the inmates and programs being the same for both types of facilities. Correction officers with a college education are often isolated in an institution because many inmates, correction officers, and administrators are not sure what to expect from college educated officers. They are usually coming from the outside and bringing in "foreign notions and ideas." Thus the staff is not always eager to accept those with a college education. Once the college educated officer becomes aware that he or she is not being accepted, alienation can result.

From our qualitative analysis we found that the meanings and interpretations the prison staff placed on the role of education are many and varied, and they reflect attitudes and rationalizations that result from a combination of variables working together: cultural background, individual traits of officers, role situations, and the unique qualities and history of a given institution.

Additional research would have to be completed to determine if a generalized or a more specialized educational program best serves the interests of the correction officer. In addition, the responses of the supervisors who commented on the importance of education to the role of correction officer must be interpreted with some caution, because their comments may in fact be in regard to training, not general education. As noted, many of the supervisors indicated that the college educated correction officer brings to the job a more professional orientation than the typical non-college educated correction officer. While the supervisors may also concede that college educated correction officers tend to be more adept at understanding the behavior of different ethnic and racial groups and overall more skilled in interpersonal communication and human relations, nevertheless, they hold fast to the belief that the job cannot be learned in a classroom. They are the first to admit that even the technical type of training which is received in the correction officer training academy falls short in preparing the officer for the experiences he or she will face in a correctional institution.

We tend to be in complete agreement with this view. Correctional work in the final analysis is no different from that of most other professions. Just as a doctor, nurse, or teacher completes an internship, residency, or student teaching assignment, the correction officer learns the subtleties of the correction officer role while on the job, and no amount of formal education is an adequate substitute. Unfortunately, too often this on-the-job training is completed in a trial-and-error manner without appropriate guidance and instructions.

References

Benton, Ned. 1988. "Personal Management: Strategies for Staff Development," *Corrections Today*, 50(5) (August): 102–106

Blair, Robert and Peter C. Kratcoski. 1992. "Professionalism Among Correctional Officers: A Longitudinal Analysis of Individual and Structural Determinants," in Peter J. Benekos and Alida V. Merlo (eds.) *Corrections: Dilemmas and Directions*. Cincinnati, OH: Anderson Publishing Co.

_____. 1992. "The Education Factor in the State Correction Officer Role," Paper presented at the annual meeting of the American Society of Criminology, New Orleans, LA.

Clemmer, Donald. 1940. *The Prison Community*. New York: Rinehart and Co.

Crouch, Ben M. and Geoffrey P. Alpert. 1980. "Prison Guards' Attitudes Toward Components of the Criminal Justice System," *Criminology* 18(2) (August): 227–236.

Crouch, Ben M. and James W. Marquart. 1980. "On Becoming a Prison Guard," in Ben Crouch (ed.), *The Keepers*, Springfield, IL: Charles Thomas Publishers, 63–106.

Cullen, Francis, Bruce Link, Nancy Wolfe, and James Frank. 1985. "The Social Dimensions of Correctional Officer Stress." *Justice Quarterly* 2(4) (December): 505–533.

Davidson, R. Ted. 1974. *Chicano Prisoners: The Key to San Quentin*. New York: Holt, Rinehart & Winston.

Duffee, David. 1972. *Using Correctional Officers in Planned Change*. Washington, D.C.: National Institute of Law Enforcement, National Technical Information Service.

Giallombardo, Rose. 1966. *Society of Women: A Study of a Women's Prison*. New York: John Wiley & Sons.

Hepburn, John R. and Nancy Jurik. 1986. "Individual Attributes, Occupational Conditions and the Job Satisfaction of Correctional Security Officers," Paper presented at the annual meeting of the American Society of Criminology, Atlanta (October).

Jacobs, J. B. 1978. "What Prison Guards Think: A Profile of the Illinois Force." *Crime and Delinquency*, 25 (April): 185–196.

Jurik, Nancy C. 1985. "Individual and Organizational Determinants of Correctional Officer Attitudes Toward Inmates." *Criminology*, 23: 523–539.

Jurik, Nancy C., Gregory J. Halemba, Michael C. Musheno, and Bernard V. Boyle. 1987. "Educational Attainment, Job Satisfaction, and the Professionalization of Correctional Officers." *Work and Occupations*, 14: 106–125.

Jurik, Nancy C. and Russ Winn. 1986. "Describing Correctional Security Dropouts and Rejects: An Individual or Organizational Profile," Paper presented at the annual meeting of the Academy of Criminal Justice Sciences, Orlando, FL.

Kassebaum, G., D. Ward, and D. Wilner. 1964. "Some Correlates of Staff Ideology in the Prison," *Journal of Research in Crime and Delinquency*, 1: 96–109.

National Advisory Commission on Criminal Justice Standards and Goals: Corrections. 1973. Washington, D.C.: U.S. Government Printing Office.

Philliber, S. 1987. "Thy Brother's Keeper: A Review of the Literature on Correctional Officers." *Justice Quarterly*, 4 (March): 9–37.

Poole, Eric D. and Robert M. Regoli. 1980. "Examining the Impact of Professionalism on Cynicism, Role Conflict, and Work Alienation Among Prison Guards." *Criminal Justice Review*, 5: 57–65.

Rafter, Nicole H. 1992. "Criminal Anthropology in The United States." *Criminology*, 30 (November): 525–545.

Shamir, Boaz and Amos Drory. 1981. "Some Correlates of Prison Guards' Beliefs." *Criminal Justice and Behavior*, 8(2) (June): 233–249.

Silvestri, George and John Lukasiewicz. 1989. "Projections of Occupational Employment, 1988–2000," *Monthly Labor Review*, 112: 42–65.

Toch, Hans. 1978. "Is a 'Correctional Officer' by Any Other Name a 'Screw'?" *Criminal Justice Review* 3(2): 19–35.

5

Burnout
Avoiding the Consequences of On-The-Job Stress

Richard M. Morris

Stress and its presence in the workplace are undergoing close examination. Once looked upon as a factor in productivity and creativity, stress is now viewed as a debilitation factor in a worker's performance. The intention of this article is to outline the causal factors in stress and to suggest that the factors be treated as a group.

A certain amount of stress is needed for one to perform at peak ability. Stress is the agent that causes action and reaction, and certain amounts of stress are necessary for life. The same as a banjo string that if too tightly wound would snap or too loosely wound would produce no sound, the correct amount of tension that gives the desired sound can be compared to the factor of stress in daily life.

Most health care professionals know there is an enormous degree of stress engendered in law enforcement and security work. Repeated confrontations in what is perceived as impossible situations requiring a response (damned-if-you-do, damned-if-you-don't situations) create feelings of inadequacy for those who must make ambiguous decisions during constant ambiguous situations. Shift work, constant fear and anticipation of danger and death, confrontation with injury and violence, negative attitudes that prevail during the course of a workday, prejudice, and hostility and suspicion by the general public add to this, invariably causing anxiety, disillusionment, and disappointment with the job.

Reprinted by permission of the American Correctional Association, Inc. from *Corrections Today* 48(6) (August 1988): 122–126.

Correctional officers and others involved in security work are prime targets for this type of stress. Working in a correctional environment can drain one's senses. Because an officer's senses must be operating continuously when on duty in a correctional facility, the drain on his/her senses is also continuous.

In the private sector, an individual who works 10 or more hours a day and gets the job done quickly is often considered a successful executive. The criterion for success is completing a project in the shortest amount of time. In this atmosphere, the strongest of survivors reaches the top. This type of environment, although successful in the short run, is very costly in its long-term effects. Absenteeism and employee turnover are two of the most immediate symptoms of this work environment. Quite simply, the pressure is too much.

Lately, the analysis of stress has moved into the public sector, with surveys being conducted to determine job burnout. People who work in social programs under government auspices (i.e., programs for the mentally handicapped, physically handicapped, or educationally deficient) often experience what is known as job burnout. Viewed as stress in its most extreme form, job burnout is simply the inability of an employee to continue performing his/her function. Many of the reasons for job stress are reasons for job burnout. Burnout occurs when stress has been so intense for such a long period that it is difficult for an employee to perform even the most basic requirements of his/her job.

Stressors in Correctional Work

There are certain stressors shared by employees in both the private and public sector. Some stressors found in correctional work are also found in other occupations, including administrative policy concerning work assignments, procedures and policy, and lack of administrative backing and support (including the relationship and rapport between correctional officer and supervisor). Stress is also caused by job conflict—a situation in which officers are caught between discrepant situations. Other common stressors in the workplace are inactivity, physical and/or mental work underload and idleness, shift work, working hours other than the normal work schedule, responsibility for the lives and welfare of others, inequities in pay or job status, and being underpaid and under-recognized for one's work.

Correctional officers are also subject to specific stressors including unfavorable attitudes held by the public toward correctional officers, daily crisis situations, daily situations posing a threat or overwhelming officers emotionally, racial situations, confrontations among officers and minority groups, and court rulings that make it seem almost impossible not to violate someone's human or civil rights.

The stressors encountered in security work affect both the organization and individual. Stress can be a prime factor in employee absenteeism, employee turnover, increased costs for overtime, and early retirements. Various studies have indicated excessive stress can lead to alcoholism, drug dependence, heart attacks or other illnesses, divorce, and other family problems.

There are two methods of identifying excessive stress in the workplace. A review of employee sick leave, absentee records, and the job-turnover rate can be used as empirical indicators, but the concerned supervisor will generally recognize that something is wrong. For example, poor or reduced performance, lack of enthusiasm for work, and sudden changes in employee work habits are all common indicators. A review of both the empirical data and the impressions of supervisors is usually the first step in developing a stress management program.

Recommendations for Stress Management

Most stress management programs share three common ingredients. First, the components of stress are defined. Second, warning signals and effects of stress are explained. Third, participants in the program are taught a method of overcoming, reducing and/or dealing with stress. This method can include relaxation techniques, self-hypnosis, and behavior modification. The general principle of stress management is that, although a particular stressful situation cannot be changed, an individual's perception of that situation and his/her subsequent actions can be.

Health maintenance is one further item that is part of most, but not all, stress management programs. Programs focusing on nutritional needs and physical exercise are included in health maintenance. For those individuals who deal in security work, health maintenance is probably an important aspect of a stress management program. An individual in good physical shape may be able to sustain long periods of stressful activity much better than an individual not physically fit.

One factor in stress often overlooked is the physical environment. A stressful environment is generally perceived in terms of an individual's relationship with his/her work and the human contacts in that workplace. The physical environment (i.e., lighting, heating, coolness, dampness, and spacial relationships) can affect individuals in ways that are not readily noticeable. This would seem entirely applicable to those involved in security work. Correctional officers are generally confined to a limited area. A poorly lit area, where the officer is unable to observe the activity of those who are confined, can easily raise the stress level of that officer. Dampness, coldness, or excessive heat can also affect that officer's performance.

Stressful Environments

Ways the organizational structure contributes to employee stress should also be examined. A stress program directed at individuals—and not at the organization—may be effective in the short run, but it will not have any long-term benefits. An employee can be taken out of the stressful environment and recharged, but the stressful environment will once again wear him/her down.

A comprehensive stress management program can also include the family in reducing the level of stress in the individual. Essentially there are two parts to daily life. The first is the relationship between self and family; the second is the relationship between self and the workplace. For the security officer, this is a severe contrast. He/she moves from a comfortable and friendly environment into one that is the complete opposite. This sudden shift undoubtedly affects the amount of stress in an officer's life, and that amount of stress, in turn, affects that officer's family.

One method of reducing stress in a correctional officer's life may be to include the family in the initial training given to that officer. For example, one or two days in the training program of an officer can be set aside so the type of work the officer will be doing can be explained to spouses and other family members. This way the family can have a greater understanding of the stress the individual officer is under. At the least, inclusion of family in the officer's training will establish a bond between the two distinct parts of that officer's daily life.

To summarize, an effective and comprehensive stress management program may include, but certainly not be limited to, the following items:

- A definition of the components of stress.
- An explanation of the warning signals and effects of stress.
- A method for overcoming, reducing, and dealing with stress.
- A health maintenance program, including physical fitness.
- An analysis of the physical environment.
- An analysis of the organizational structure.

- The inclusion of the family in a stress management program.

Individuals in the security field involved in stress management programs strongly suggest that the stress program be conducted by fellow officers. They do so for two reasons: 1) officers generally relate better to fellow officers, and 2) the cost of the stress management program can be effectively reduced by using individuals already included in the personnel budget.

As this article indicates, the study of stress in security work has not fully matured. There are people conducting studies, but the scope of the problem almost defies explanation due to over-crowded institutions, changing work forces, changing inmates, court decisions, the question of custody versus treatment, etc. Also, an important first step in a stress program is diagnosis of the seriousness of stress problems in an organization.

It is clear that stress cannot be treated in short training programs. An individual can be told what is happening to him/her, but unless something can be done about it the stress remains.

There is more to stress management than just learning how to stay calm. Personal health management is important. Breaking away from the only-those-inside-can-know attitude is also important. Peer counseling, not just peer instruction, is important. Nobody has a lock on the best method, if there is one.

Section *III*

Classification for Correctional Treatment

The American Correctional Association defines classification as "the means by which offenders are assigned to different programs in an effort to provide the best available programs to fit the individual offender's needs."[1] Classification of offenders, if properly executed, enables correctional agencies to maximize the use of their personnel and resources to provide treatment that will enable the offender to fulfill his or her specific needs and to assure, as well, that the concerns of other interested parties are met.

The most basic and familiar classifications of offenders are those made according to sex, age (juvenile or adult), severity of offense (misdemeanor or felony), and types of statutes violated (federal, state, or local). The classification of juvenile offenders has been complicated by rulings that require status offenders (those who have committed offenses that are not illegal for adults) to be housed in nonsecure settings and not be mixed with delinquent offenders.[2]

Classification may be made at a diagnostic or reception center, which receives newly sentenced adults and uses various indicators to assess the level of security at which each offender should be held and the type of treatment that may be given. After an offender is sent to a specific institution, an in-house classification may also be made. Juveniles placed in the custody of a state youth authority or youth commission are customarily remanded to a diagnostic and reception center where the type of setting in which the youth will be held is decided. However, in some jurisdictions judges have the power to sentence adults or send juveniles to specific institutions.

Classifications made under the guise of treatment are also developed for more effective management of prisoners. Correctional facilities are frequently typified as being maximum, medium, or minimum security; offenders are placed in terms of their perceived risk to the community and to each other. Maximum security facilities may be surrounded by outside walls or high electrified fences, have internal divisions into cell blocks, and use armed guards. Medium security facilities may be surrounded by walls or fences, but have less intense segregation of prisoners and a lower level of internal surveillance. Minimum security institutions may have no readily visible security measures around the institution and may use cottage living or honors sections for many of the prisoners.

One of the first attempts to develop a prisoner classification system was made by Howard Gill in 1927. His plan included separation of prisoners into distinct groups, either within an institution or by housing them in separate facilities. Gill believed that new prisoners should be isolated from the others for purposes of observing their behavior and determining their potential for rehabilitation. From this point, prisoners would be classified as *tractable*—able to respond to treatment efforts and change their behavior; *intractable*—resistant to change and requiring forcible methods of control; *defective*—mentally ill, retarded, or physically handicapped; and those who could be handled best in some type of work-release or community placement facility.[3]

As classification systems became more refined, it was thought possible, through an elaborate diagnostic process, to match a specific offender with an exact form of treatment that would best suit his needs. Dr. Herbert C. Quay developed a system of classification termed *differential treatment*, which employed such specific matching. First used with delinquents at the National Training School for Boys in Washington, D.C., the program involved testing and then matching each new student with a counselor who had been trained to "treat" the type of problem behavior the youth was believed to manifest.

When rehabilitation became a paramount goal of corrections, it was necessary to develop treatment modalities to enhance the rehabilitative effort. It was also necessary to ascertain which offenders were likely to benefit from specific treatment programs. Article six, "The Functions of Classification Models in Probation and Parole: Control or Treatment-Rehabilitation?" by Peter C. Kratcoski, notes that highly complex methods of classifying probationers, inmates, and parolees have been developed for administrative and management purposes, as well as for treatment and rehabilitation. The

National Advisory Commission on Criminal Justice Standards and Goals, in its *Report on Corrections*, made the point that classification made supposedly for purposes of treatment may in fact be used for control, convenience of the staff, evening out of the number in each treatment program, or cost efficiency.[4]

The range of available correctional treatment is subject to the security level of the institution to which the offender is assigned. For example, total milieu therapy or guided group interaction would not be a likely treatment possibility in a maximum security institution, while behavior modification therapy would be readily available.

On the community level, a probation, parole, or juvenile aftercare officer often divides the caseload into maximum, medium, and minimum supervision levels after calculating the needs of each offender and the risk each presents to the community. Clients under maximum supervision might be seen rather frequently (once or twice a week), while those in minimum supervision may be required to report monthly, or only if some problem arises.

Selection seven, "The Case Management System Experience in Ohio," by Clifford W. Crooks, provides information on the step-by-step development, implementation, and revision of a classification system for offenders utilized by the Ohio Adult Parole Authority. Specific instruments illustrate how offenders are assigned to maximum, medium, or minimum supervision, using risk and need assessment scales. Adaptations of the classification system, based on evaluation findings and officer input, are described, and methods for training officers in risk and needs assessment are reported.

The U.S. Bureau of Prisons developed the functional unit management model in the early 1970s as a means of dividing facilities into smaller units of offenders who are housed together and receive a specific form of treatment. The inmates were supervised by a specially trained team. Functional units were developed to handle offenders with common problems, such as substance abuse or emotional problems. Other units included academic or vocational education emphases.[5]

In article eight, "Functional Unit Management," Hans Toch discusses the origins of the functional unit management model, the premises on which the model rests, the types of units that have been developed in various correctional facilities, and the settings in which functional unit management is likely to be effective.

Selection nine, "An Evaluation of Juvenile Intensive Aftercare Probation: Aftercare Versus System Response Efforts," by Henry Sontheimer and Lynne Goodstein, describes, analyzes, and evaluates an intensive aftercare probation program for serious juvenile offenders. They found that juveniles who were placed under intensive supervision when they were released from an institution committed fewer offenses than a control group of juveniles who were placed on regular supervision upon release from the institution. The constant supervision and quick intervention by the supervising officer when the youths appeared to be moving toward delinquency activity seemed to be important in explaining the effectiveness of the intensive supervision approach.

Notes

[1] Committee on Classification and Casework, American Prison Association, *Handbook on Classification in Correctional Institutions* (Washington, D.C.: American Correctional Association, 1968), 10.

[2] Public Law 93–415 (September 7, 1974), Title II, Part B, Sec. 223 (a), (12).

[3] Howard Gill, "A New Prison Discipline: Implementing the Declaration of Principles of 1870," *Federal Probation* 34 (June 1970): 31–33.

[4] National Advisory Commission on Criminal Justice Standards and Goals, *Report on Corrections* (Washington, D.C.: U.S. Government Printing Office, 1973), 202–203.

[5] Robert B. Levinson and Roy E. Gerard, "Functional Units: A Different Correctional Approach," *Federal Probation Quarterly*, 37 (December 1973), 8–16.

6

The Functions of Classification
Models in Probation and Parole
Control or Treatment-Rehabilitation?*

Peter C. Kratcoski

The use of classification systems in corrections is not a new development. When corrections moved from a punishment model to a rehabilitation or treatment emphasis in the early 20th century, classifications systems, such as that developed by Howard Gill, were used to separate prisoners according to their potential for treatment or training. Gradually, classification systems became more complex and multipurposive, and today they are used not only to classify offenders within institutions but also to assess the amount of supervision needed by offenders placed on probation in lieu of institutionalization or those paroled from prisons.

Classification systems now in use are complex and multipurposive. A distinction can be made between those that are used for administrative and management purposes and those designed to treat and rehabilitate the offender. Those of a management nature are designed to enhance control and to predict the likelihood that an offender will commit new criminal acts after release. The treatment-rehabilitation systems try to differentiate the offenders on the basis of their needs, attitudes, motivations, and attributes and then provide the treatment necessary to bring about the desired changes in values, attitudes, and skills that will inhibit the offenders from recidivating. The treatment-rehabilitation systems of classification are based on the concept of differential treatment,

* The research presented in this article was funded by a grant to the Ohio Department of Rehabilitation and Correction from the National Institute of Corrections, NIC E-P-6.

Source: *Federal Probation*, 49(5) (December 1985): 49–56.

which implies that the needs and problems of inmates and those in community supervision must be defined and treated on an individualized basis. The offender is matched with the specific treatment program which best addresses these problems and needs.

According to Edith Flynn, an effective classification system should meet the following criteria:

(1) There must be an explicit statement regarding the function and purpose of the classification system.

(2) The classification system should be dynamic and theoretically based so that it may serve to increase the system's predictive powers and its success in reducing recidivism.

(3) The assumption on which the classification system is based must be explicit.

(4) The critical variables of the classification typology applied must be specific so that the utility of the system can be empirically tested.

(5) The classification system should be useful and feasible and facilitate efficient management and optimum use of available resources.[1]

Classification of offenders within institutions was closely related to programming, while the use of classification for those placed on probation and parole was initially directed toward predicting recidivism, and levels of supervision were set up according to the assessed risk that the offender would become involved in criminal activity after release.

Since 1980, the Federal Probation System has used a Risk Prediction Scale (RPS 80) which classifies offenders for "high activity" or "low activity" supervision. The items used in this scale include completion of a high school education, the age of the offender, arrest-free status for 5 or more consecutive years before the previous offense, few prior arrests, a history of freedom from opiate usage, and a steady employment period of at least 4 months prior to arraignment for the present offense. Each item is weighted, and a cutoff point on the total score determines whether the offender will initially be assigned to low or high activity supervision.[2] Before initiation of this new system, survey data collected by the Probation Division of the Administrative Office of the U.S. Courts in 1974 and by the Research Division of the Federal Judicial Center in 1977 indicated that a variety of caseload classification methods were used by Federal probation officers. These methods ranged from purely subjective assessments to statistical prediction devices.[3]

When the National Institute of Corrections placed the development of statewide classification systems for probation and parole as a high priority funding project, various states developed systems of classification of those under supervision. These statewide systems considered both control and treatment in their classification procedures. One of the earliest states to receive funding for a new classification program was Wisconsin, and a statewide system was put into effect there in 1977. More than 30 other states have now adopted some form of statewide classification model, and the current emphasis in the field is for county level probation departments to incorporate some features of the state models in their supervision programs. Because of its early start in this area and the wide publicity given to its features, the Wisconsin classification system is often considered the prototype for development of new classification systems.

Classification models tend to have common features. One would be an assessment of the risk (danger to the community) presented by the offender. The risk classification device is designed to assess a client's potential for future criminal behavior. Items related to the offender's criminal history and socioeconomic-personal adjustment background are weighted, and a total score is used to place the offender at a specific level of supervision, with the intensity of supervision designed to reduce the threat of recidivism to a minimum. For example, the instrument used to assess risk in the Wisconsin system included the following:

(1) Number of address changes in the last 12 months;

(2) Percentage of time employed in the last 12 months;

(3) Alcohol usage problems;

(4) Other drug usage problems;

(5) Attitude;

(6) Age at first conviction;

(7) Number of prior periods of probation/parole supervision;

(8) Number of prior probation/parole revocations;

(9) Number of prior felony convictions;

(10) Convictions or juvenile adjudications for burglary, theft, auto theft, or robbery, worthless checks or forgery; and

(11) Conviction or juvenile adjudication for assaultive offense within the last 5 years.[4]

When the various states or local probation and parole departments developed their own risk instruments, there was acceptance of the format used in Wisconsin, but each supervising authority tended to vary somewhat in the number of items included, the specific focus of the items, and the weight given to each item in relation to the total score. For example, those responsible for developing a risk instrument for the Tennessee system reasoned that:

> Since laws vary from one state to another, law enforcement varies from one state to another, and people differ from one state to another, those individuals who find themselves in prison and then on parole will differ from one state to another. This . . . requires that the processes of determining levels of risk and need should be reflective of the clientele in the Tennessee Parole System.[5]

This approach of adjusting the instrument to the local conditions seems appropriate. It also apparently does not detract from the predictive power of the instrument. In classifying offenders supervised under the Federal system, several predictive devices used were found to have comparable predictive power, even though the specific items used in the instrument and the method of scoring and assignment to risk levels varied.[6]

Another feature of classification models is use of a needs instrument, which assesses the offender's needs in such areas as family support, employment, emotional problems, or drug or alcohol abuse treatment. As an offender's score on the needs instrument increases, it is assumed that the amount of time and the number of resources directed toward the case will also increase. The needs assessment instrument is most effective when clients are reassessed on a regular basis and determinations are made as to whether progress is occurring in meeting the offender's needs and working on his or her problems.

Both risk and needs instruments allow officers and supervisors the opportunity to categorize all those supervised in a matrix format: offenders with a high risk and low needs, and those with low risk and low needs. Management and officers get a very clear picture of the distribution of cases which are currently under supervision, and workload distributions can be made according to the intensity of supervision required for the offenders. The models move away from caseloads and incorporate a "work unit" concept, which is set up on the basis of the supervision levels of the offenders, the geographic distribution of the cases, the types of duties required of officers (preparation of presentence investigations or supervision only), and special types of cases handled (transfers or interstate compact cases). Theoretically, this approach should equalize the amount of work expected from each officer. Under past systems, caseloads were defined in terms of the number of cases supervised. Little attention was given to the intensity of supervision required or the amount of time needed for each case.

After assessments have been completed, the classification procedure takes place. Classification in the case management approach involves grounding the specific classification in an evaluation of the interacting forces of the case. The specific classifications of offenders generally include maximum, medium, and minimum supervision levels. They may also provide for cursory levels of supervision, with little or no contact between officer and offender. The specific classification of offenders may vary from jurisdiction to jurisdiction, even though these offenders may have common characteristics. A case perceived as low risk in one jurisdiction may be classified as a medium risk in another because of the small number of serious cases serviced there. The risk score cutoff points may vary significantly, depending on the number of cases supervised and the number of officers available. For example, Ohio and Wisconsin use essentially the same risk and needs instruments, but in Wisconsin the maximum supervision category begins at a score of 15 on the risk instrument, while in Ohio it begins at 26.

In addition to risk factors, other methods are used to classify offenders. Rather than basing classification on criminal activity, other behavioral and personality characteristics of the offender are taken into account. This information is obtained through an interview with the client or from case file information. In Ohio, four Case Supervision Approaches (CSA) are defined, including criminal orientation, multiproblem, socially deficient, and situational offenders. An individual is assigned to one of the CSA's on the basis of a structured interview. After placement at a risk level and a CSA, a case management plan for providing services to the client is developed. The offender is expected to provide input in developing this plan and should agree that the activities required of him or her are appropriate and achievable.

Once the supervision level is defined for a case, the supervision is conducted according to a formula set up for the number and types of contacts required at this level. The specifications of the case plan will direct the officer toward referrals to agencies, the amount of counseling needed, requiring drug presence tests, and setting of special conditions. Case monitoring involves verifying employment, place of residence, participation in required programs, and compliance with probation and parole conditions.

In California, the classification system differentiates both types of offenders and types of parole officers. Offenders are classified as "control," "service," or "minimum-supervision" cases. Those with high risk assessment scores are designated "control" and given intensive supervision by officers who handle only control cases and whose only function is surveillance. "Service" cases, classified by high needs assessment scores, are under the supervision of a service officer, who acts as a broker in obtaining referrals to appropriate community agencies. If a service category offender commits a new offense the service officer cannot arrest him—this function is reserved for control officers. Minimum supervision cases (those with low risk and needs scores) are seen only at a time of release from prison and at the end of the year parole, with monthly mailed-in reports from the offender taking the place of visits to the parole office. Minimum supervision specialists handle these cases, but perform no other functions. In 1981, 84 percent of the parolees were classified as control cases, 8 percent as service cases, and 8 percent as minimum supervision cases. The California parole officers were assigned to control as opposed to service or minimum supervision in a 6 to 1 ratio.[7]

Most classification systems provide for periodic reassessments of the cases. These may take place at specified time intervals (6 months, for example) or if there is a charge in jurisdiction from one unit to another or if the person supervised has committed a new offense. The reassessment instruments shift emphasis from past criminal behavior to overall performance or adjustment during the current probation or parole. The reassessment instrument taps the offender's adherence to the rules and special conditions, use of community services recommended, and overall adjustments in the areas of work, family, and personal functioning. At the time of reassessment the level of supervision may be reduced or increased, although there would be a tendency to reduce rather than increase supervision.

At the time of final evaluation before release a summary of the changes and progress which occurred during supervision is developed. Once the case has been terminated, the information available on all of the classification instruments is stored for future access, if needed.

The Effects of Classification Systems on Clients and Staff

Although the majority of states have developed some form of offender classification which attempts to provide a control and treatment formula within the same model, the evaluation of the effectiveness of these models has generally been rather sketchy. Each state has attempted some internal evaluation, and on occasion detailed evaluation by a neutral agent has taken place. The bases for the determination of effectiveness have varied, but recidivism reduction is the primary factor considered. The purpose of this section of the article is to draw attention to areas in which the departments might be affected regardless of the changes in criminal behavior which may occur after the classification system is put into operation. The manner in which the system affects the staff is generally not even considered in evaluations of its effectiveness. In this article we will look at effects of new systems on both clients and officers, including the degree to which administrators and officers accept and commit themselves to the new system, opinions of the new system's efficiency in comparison to prior systems, and the effects of standardization and the reduction of discretion on the officers' perceptions of their role and their job satisfaction. Does the new system remove autonomy and professional discretion, require upgrading of skill levels, vary or consolidate responsibility areas, increase tedious paperwork, improve communications with other officers and superiors, and reduce or enhance overall job satisfaction? For the clients, what is the expectation in regard to recidivism and community adjustment? The new systems are geared to efficiency and productive use of resources. Recidivism is not expected to decline at all supervision levels. Instead, those offenders who are placed in a maximum supervision category and who also have high needs are given the most intense supervision and concentration of services, and for them the model predicts that criminal behavior will significantly decline and that individual and social adjustment will increase. For offenders placed at lower intensity of supervision levels it is predicted that their present level of performance will not deteriorate and that they will not commit criminal offenses at levels greater than their prior performances.

A study conducted by the National Institute of Corrections involved 474 probation and parole officers who were working in nine states in which some new case management system had recently been introduced. In responding to questions about their new system, more than three of every four respondents viewed it as beneficial. The majority of negative comments about the systems dealt with very specific policy issues indigenous to the particular state system. Some of these comments centered on the inability to adequately perform as expected because of an extremely high caseload, the inclusion of juveniles in the system, problems in rural areas related to finding appropriate settings for conducting interviews, and lack of social-community support systems for referrals once the problems of offenders had been assessed. In this study 32 percent of the respondents rated the system as being "very helpful" in their job, 46 percent considered it "helpful," 14 percent considered it "moderately helpful," and 8 percent regarded it as "not helpful." Seventy-three percent indicated that the system increased their knowledge and understanding of the clients, 53 percent said that it helped improve their case planning, and 54 percent said it helped them improve their ability to anticipate problems on the job.[8]

The degree of satisfaction with new case management systems seems to depend on the commitment to the system by administrators, the preparation for changes, and the ease of the transition from one system to the other. The nature of change is also an important point. In New York City, the Department of Adult Supervision Services had to introduce radical changes in the manner in which it supervised clients because of the influx of more than 13,000 new cases annually and budget reductions. The system introduced, called the Differential Supervision Program (DSP), had three levels of supervision assigned according to risk. However, the minimum supervision level contacts consisted of a monthly telephone call by the offender to a data entry telephone operator. If the call did not occur, a computer-generated letter was sent to remind the probationer to make the call. If the call still was not received, the probation officer was notified and appropriate action taken. Carol Rauh, in evaluating the New York City program, found that two factors were important in determining acceptance or rejection of the model by the rank and file officers. One was whether the automated support services portion of the system performed adequately and actually fulfilled the standardized routine tasks expected of it. The assumption of the program was that the computer would relieve the officers of much of the routine paperwork which was extremely time consuming but contributed to the offenders' welfare. In actual operation, the computer frequently broke down or was in error, and the officers were required to handle a deluge of calls, which led to dissatisfaction and general disillusionment with the system. The second factor mentioned by Ms. Rauh as important in acceptance of the new system was the administration's support and direction. To assess administration and staff commitment, a number of interviews were completed. The higher levels of administrators were very enthusiastic and unanimous in their belief in the importance and effectiveness of the new system. However, satisfaction with the system decreased in the lower levels of administration, and was at its lowest point among the unit supervisors. Only one of the six supervisors interviewed spoke enthusiastically about the new system. This lack of belief in the system was reflected in the attitudes of the probation officers. Half of the officers interviewed reported that while it was a good idea in theory they saw little practical value in the new system. Rather than reducing their workloads, they felt that the new system had added to them. About two-thirds of the officers reported that they did not find the forms used to classify clients helpful, and only two of all the officers interviewed felt that the forms helped them focus on client problems.[9]

An extensive evaluation of the Ohio Case Management System was conducted in selected regions of the state one year after the new system had been in operation. I was the person selected to design and carry out this evaluation. As part of the evaluation, officers in one of the first regions to receive training in the new system were asked to complete an Attitude Assessment Questionnaire before they were trained in the new system. They completed the same questionnaire approximately one year after the training was received and the system had been in operation in that region. The questionnaire explored officers' perceptions of administrators' attitudes toward officers, administrators' effectiveness as perceived by the officers, and officers' positive attitudes toward change. Comparison of the results of the two administrations of the questionnaire revealed that in the post-test there was some change toward more positive attitudes, with the most significant change occurring with regard to officers' perceptions of the administrators' effectiveness.

A second phase of the evaluation of attitudes and opinions of personnel involved a qualitative assessment of the system by supervisors and officers in another region of the state in which the new Case Management System had been implemented. A semistructured interview format was used. The supervisors' responses ranged from total acceptance to a somewhat skeptical "wait and see" attitude. Problems identified included the need for an increase in personnel and adjustment in the number of work units allotted for each supervision level case and for emergency situations for cases which involved revocation procedures. The supervisors also saw a need for additional officer training in the development of case management plans. The officers in general accepted the new system as a useful tool, regarded the standardization in the new system as good, and felt it professionalized the officer's position, promoted efficiency and gave the officers the security of making case management decisions based on objective criteria. Some officers felt that it did involve more paperwork, but the majority felt that the new system was more efficient than the former system because it assisted in developing a case plan earlier and offered direction as to what would be appropriate referrals to social service agencies. Some indicated that it led to an improvement in communications with immediate supervisors. In the past, if there were some confusion or disagreement about how a case should be supervised, the officer would have to accept the supervisors' directions. Now, because of the standardized procedures, it was quite easy to explain to a supervisor how a decision on a case was reached.

In contrast to the New York City probation program, the Ohio case management system was given firm support at all administrative levels. The top administrators supported it through communications and personal appearances to discuss the merits of the system. Regional supervisors and unit supervisors were involved in the Case Management System Development Committee, which designed the instruments in conjunction with the Research Division of the Adult Parole Authority. This support by the administrators was reflected in the comments by the officers, who indicated that in the beginning they thought the new system was just a gimmick or even a way of increasing caseloads and reducing staff, but after its introduction they believed that the administration was committed to it, that the system was here to stay, and that they might as well work with it.[10]

Perhaps the most drastic change in the role of officers occurred in the California system. We noted earlier that the roles of the officers became quite specialized. The acceptance of the case management model in California by administrators, supervisors, and field officers varied. Administrators and supervisors appeared to accept the model because of its emphasis on the protection of the community. Given the current emphasis on "just desserts" for the offenders, and the fact that parole was actually abolished for a period of time in California, a model which emphasizes the control facet of parole work had strong appeal. Some of the field officers also appeared to be quite pleased with the system. They found the concept of the minimum supervision of some cases to be logical and efficient. Some also liked being responsible for only one facet of parole work. Many did not feel competent to handle the dual roles of control and service. On the other hand, some officers lamented the loss of discretion, the ability to use their own judgment in making decisions. This discretionary power was a factor which gave the officer a professional status. Others also felt that the process was more complex and cumbersome than the old system. Their most frequent complaint was that the new system has generated more paperwork, and this detracts from the main job of supervision.[11]

A latent product of extreme specialization by officers only vaguely recognized is a tendency for the department personnel to factionalize on the basis of their assignments. Officers tend to develop a perspective or orientation toward their job which reflects the major goal of their work. The control officers might begin to perceive themselves as law enforcement officers, while the service officers would view themselves as social service workers. The communication gaps and internal dissension between custody and treatment personnel are well recognized in institutional settings on both the juvenile and adult levels. The competition for resources and personnel, in particular when budgets become tight, leads to a general decline in interpersonal relations, morale, and common goal orientation. In most cases, when these conflicts occur the custody factors take priority over treatment.

Recidivism

Although the success or failure of case management systems should not necessarily be dependent on the reduction of recidivism produced, when the basic question, "Does it work?" is asked, reduction in criminal behavior tends to be the criterion which can justify an affirmative response.

The case management models developed by the various states do not suggest that an across the board reduction of criminal behavior will result after the system commences operation. If the model functions according to design, the significant reductions in recidivism should occur in the maximum supervision category. The minimum supervision category should not change, even with the reduction in supervision, and the medium supervision cases might show a reduction in criminal behavior because of the employment of a more individualized case management plan.

Systematic research on the effects on recidivism of new case management plans is trickling in, but the data only give hints regarding the long-term effects. Those who have considerable experience in the corrections field are knowledgeable enough to expect dramatic changes in criminal behavior for the maximum supervision cases. An offender whose deviant behavior dates back to childhood and whose life has followed a pattern of repeated offenses, supervision and/or incarceration is not going to change over night because of more intense supervision or a different approach to supervision.

In Wisconsin, a sample of offenders who were placed in the maximum supervision group were compared with a matched sample of cases who had not yet been included in the case management plan. Those in the control group were matched with those in the experimental group in age, sex, race, probation or parole status, employment, and items on the risk and needs instruments. The maximum supervision group under the new case plan had significantly lower recidivism than those in the control group. Thirty-seven percent of those in the control group had a new offense reported, compared to 18 percent of the experimental group. Twenty percent of the control group members had their probation or parole revoked, compared to 11 percent of the experimental group.[12] For the medium supervision cases a smaller percentage of those supervised under the new system recidivated when they were compared with the control group, but the differences were not large enough to be considered statistically significant. The recidivism in the minimum supervision group was quite low for both the experimental and control groups, confirming the hypothesis that this category of offenders can be given only cursory supervision and still not show an increase in their criminal behavior.

The findings that only 18 percent of the maximum supervision group committed a new offense and only 11 percent had their parole or probation revoked appears incredible when compared to the much higher recidivism rates generally considered to be normal for maximum supervision probationers and parolees. However, it should be noted that the Wisconsin Bureau of Community Corrections is responsible for the supervision of all adult probationers and both juvenile and adult parolees[13] and the overall characteristics of this offender population may not be comparable to what one would find in a more urban-industrialized state.

A study by the Wisconsin Bureau of Community Corrections after 2 years of experience with the case management system revealed that there was a strong correlation between the score the offenders obtained on the risk instrument and revocation rates. The higher the risk score, the higher was the revocation rate. For example, of 4,231 probationers and parolees who were terminated within 2 years after commitment to the program, 1,124 (27 percent) had a risk score between 4 and 7 and had a revocation rate of only 2.49 percent. However, at the other extreme 60 offenders (1.4 percent) had a risk score of 30 and above, and they had a revocation rate of 42.55 percent.[14]

In Wisconsin, both risk scores and needs scores were used to assign cases to supervision categories. The risk scores, however, appear to be more predictive of new criminal activity. In Wisconsin, a risk assessment score of 15 and above would lead to a maximum supervision classification, a score of 8 to 14 would result in medium supervision, and a score of 7 and below in minimum supervision.[15] About 50 percent of new clients were placed in maximum supervision.

The evaluation of the Ohio Case Management System I conducted involved a two-faceted research design. In one facet, an experimental region of the state, the first region where the new system was implemented, was used to develop a comparison of recidivism in the region before and after implementation of the system. Cases for the months of September, October, and November

1981, when the new system had been put into effect, were compared with those in the months of September, October, and November 1980. All cases which originated in parole and probation units selected for the experimental region were included. The 1980 sample had 276 cases, while the 1981 sample had 261 cases. The case files of all offenders in the samples were examined, and all criminal offenses which resulted in convictions, all alleged parole and probation violations which were confirmed, and all probation and parole "violator at large" statuses which occurred during a 12-month period from the date that the offender was placed on parole or probation were considered. The offenders were divided according to supervision level (maximum = risk score of 26 or higher; medium = risk score of 18 through 25; minimum = risk score of 0 through 17) and compared with regard to recidivism, as shown in Table 1.

Table 1

Recidivism of Cases in the Experimental Region by Supervision Level Before and After Implementation of the Case Management System

Supervision Level	Recidivism 1980		Recidivism 1981	
	N	% of Total[1]	N	% of Total[2]
Maximum	40	70%	50	63%
Medium	26	42%	32	47%
Minimum	27	17%	25	22%
TOTALS	93	34%	107	41%

[1] In 1980, there were 57 maximum supervision offenders, 62 medium, and 157 minimum.
[2] In 1981, there were 79 maximum supervision offenders, 68 medium, and 114 minimum.

As shown in Table 1, recidivism was lower for the 1981 maximum supervision group than for the maximum supervision group in 1980, although the decrease was not statistically significant. Although the recidivism increased from 1980 to 1981 in both the medium and minimum supervision levels, the increases were not statistically significant. This comparison, while not conclusive, gives some support for the assumptions underlying the Case Management System model. In the maximum supervision category, where the intensity of supervision was increased, there was a decline in the percentage who recidivated. At the minimum supervision level, where supervision was decreased, no substantial increase in recidivism occurred. The only group which performed contrary to the model's expectations was the medium supervision level. It was expected that recidivism here would remain constant, but it increased.

Of those parolees who committed new offenses, 58 percent of those in the 1980 sample committed felonies, compared to 49 percent of those in the 1981 sample. The percentage of parolees revoked and sent to prison was slightly higher for the 1980 sample (24 percent) than for the 1981 sample (23 percent). Of the probationers committing new offenses, 50 percent of those in the 1980 sample and 47 percent of those in the 1981 sample committed felonies, and 11 percent of the 1980 probationers in the sample were returned to prison, compared to 9 percent of the probationers in the 1981 sample.

The second facet of the research design involved a comparison of the sample of offenders in the experimental region, where the new Case Management System had been implemented (1981), with a sample in a control region of the state, where the system had not been implemented in that year. Since the offenders in the control region were not classified, the researchers classified them according to maximum, medium, or minimum supervision qualifying status, using the same instruments used by Parole Authority staff to classify the offenders in the experimental region. A comparison of the recidivism of the offenders in the experimental and control regions is given in Table 2.

As shown in Table 2, recidivism was almost three times as great at the maximum supervision level as at the minimum level for both the experimental and control group samples, and the recidivism for the medium level was more than twice that of the minimum. These patterns follow the projections made for the Case Management System model. However, it was projected that the recidivism for the maximum level experimental group would be lower than that for the maximum level control group because of the intense amount of supervision given to the maximum offenders in the experimental group, where the new Case Management System had been applied. This did not occur. The higher proportion of offenders in the maximum supervision category in the experimental group sample, when compared with the control group sample, no doubt had some bearing on the lack of recidivism reduction at this level. For the medium and minimum supervision

Table 2

A Comparison of Recidivism by Supervision Level in the Experimental and Control Regions

Supervision level	Experimental[1] Region		Control[2] Region		Significance
	N	%	N	%	
Maximum	50	63%	28	60%	Not significant at .15 level
Medium	32	47%	34	44%	Chi Square Test
Minimum	25	22%	19	17%	

[1] In the Experimental Region, there were 79 maximum supervision offenders, 68 medium, 114 minimum.

[2] In the Control Region, there were 47 maximum supervision offenders, 77 medium, and 114 minimum.

levels, slight increases in recidivism also occurred in the experimental group sample, although it was projected that recidivism at the medium level would be reduced.

When the severity of new offenses by those who recidivated was compared by supervision level, the maximum level offenders in the control group had a greater proportion of felonies (33 percent) than did the maximum level experimental group (27 percent). In the medium level, the percentage committing felonies was the same for the two groups (25 percent). At the minimum level the experimental group (7 percent) and the control group (8 percent) had similar percentages committing felonies. This offense pattern follows the Case Management System model, with the maximum level offenders in the experimental group having a reduced percentage of serious offenses.

Table 3 compares the offenders revoked and sent to prison in the experimental and control regions.

As shown in Table 3, slightly higher percentages of the control region offenders in all supervision levels were revoked and sent to prison. Although these differences are not statistically significant, they support the projection of the Case Management System model that increased supervision of the maximum level cases will have positive results.[16]

Table 3

A Comparison of Supervision Level of Offenders Sent to Prison After a New Offense or Technical Violation in the Experimental and Control Regions

Supervision Level	Experimental[1] Region		Control[2] Region	
	N	%	N	%
Maximum	24	30%	17	36%
Medium	14	21%	18	23%
Minimum	6	5%	11	10%

[1] In the Experimental Region, there were 79 maximum supervision offenders, 68 medium, and 114 minimum.

[2] In the Control Region, there were 47 maximum supervision offenders, 77 medium and 114 minimum.

One should be cautious about generalizing findings from one state program to another, even if a comparable case management system were used. In Ohio, risk and needs classification instruments were adopted which are quite similar to those used in Wisconsin. However, the cutoff points in the risk instruments used to delineate the Ohio supervision levels were considerably higher (26 and above for maximum supervision, 18 to 25 for medium supervision, and 17 and below for minimum supervision) than those used in Wisconsin (15 and above for maximum, 8 to 14 for medium, and 7 and below for minimum). If one compared Wisconsin and Ohio by supervision level without taking into consideration the actual risk scores used to delineate the various levels, it would appear that recidivism was considerably higher for the Ohio offenders than for those in Wisconsin. However, if the cases from the two states were matched by actual risk scores, the proportion committing new offenses would not vary significantly in the two states.

In conclusion, it is apparent that the case management models should be evaluated in relationship to their utility and not necessarily in relationship to a reduction in criminal activity. The systems work if officers make better decisions on cases, make more appropriate referrals to community service agencies, are more efficient in their work, establish better communications with supervisions, and are more confident and satisfied with their own job performance. If the agency administrators can live with the programs, even though recidivism rates do not drop significantly, case management systems will continue to be refined and this should result in a significant improvement in community corrections.

Notes

[1] Edith Elisabeth Flynn, "Classification Systems," in *Handbook of Correctional Classification* (Cincinnati: Anderson Publishing Company, 1978), p. 86.

[2] Administrative Office of the U.S. Courts, *Guide to Judiciary Policies and Procedures: Probation Manual*, Vol. x–0§4004 (February 15, 1979).

[3] James B. Eaglin and Patricia A. Lombard, *A Validation and Comparative Evaluation of Four Predictive Devices for Classifying Federal Probation Caseloads* (Washington, D.C.: Federal Judicial Center, 1982), p. 1.

[4] S. Christopher Baird, Richard C. Heinz, and Brian J. Bemus, *The Wisconsin Case Classification/Staff Deployment Project* (Madison, Wisconsin: Department of Health and Social Services, 1979), p. 7.

[5] James W. Fox, Mitchell Stein, and Gary Ramussen, "Development of the Tennessee Case Management for Delivery of Parole Services." Paper delivered at the 1983 Convention of the Academy of Criminal Justice Sciences, San Antonio, Texas, 1983, p. 7.

[6] James B. Eaglin and Patricia A. Lombard, *A Validation . . . Caseloads*, pp. 99–122.

[7] Stephen Gettinger, "Separating the Cop for the Counselor," *Corrections Magazine*, Vol. 7, No. 2 (April 1981), p. 35.

[8] National Institution of Corrections, *Client Management Classification System Officer Survey* (Washington, D.C.: National Institute of Corrections, 1982).

[9] Carol Rauh, "Important Considerations in Ensuring the Success of a Case Management/Management Information System Model." Paper presented at the annual meeting of the Academy of Criminal Justice Sciences, San Antonio, Texas, 1983.

[10] Peter C. Kratcoski, *An Evaluation of the Case Management System Probation and Parole Sections: Division of Parole and Community Services, Ohio Department of Rehabilitation and Correction*, report submitted September 1983, pp. 171–173.

[11] Stephen Gettinger, "Separating the Cop from the Counselor," pp. 36–37.

[12] Baird, Heinz, and Bemus, *The Wisconsin Case Classification/Staff Development Project: A Two Year Follow-Up Report* (Madison, Wisconsin: Department of Health and Social Services, 1979), p. 26.

[13] *Ibid.*, p. 6.

[14] *Ibid.*, p. 10.

[15] *Ibid.*, p. 20.

[16] Peter C. Kratcoski, *An Evaluation of the Case Management System . . . Ohio Department of Rehabilitation and Correction*, pp. 174–178.

7

The Case Management System Experience in Ohio

Clifford W. Crooks

Introduction: The Wisconsin Contribution

The probation and parole case management systems currently in place at the state and county level in Ohio are by no means unique. They are, in fact, based upon the system developed and implemented in Wisconsin in the previous decade. Needless to say, a great deal has been written about the Wisconsin model and its total systems approach to the classification process. In order to fully understand Ohio's case management systems, it is important to summarize the major achievements in Wisconsin.

Responding to a legislative mandate to improve services for offenders and measure the workload of probation and parole agents, the Wisconsin Division of Corrections, Bureau of Community Corrections secured federal funds and formed the Case Classification/Staff Deployment Project (CC/SD Project) in 1975. During development and implementation, every effort was made to maximize staff input and support. Supervisors and line staff worked together, for example, to define standards. Staff were also encouraged to evaluate new procedures and predictive scales and to make suggestions for improvement.

This article first appeared in *Correctional Counseling and Treatment*, Second Edition. All rights reserved.

When the Wisconsin Classification System was implemented statewide in 1977, it contained the following integrated components which met the objectives of the CC/SD Project:

1. A risk assessment scale developed by multiple regression analysis to identify and weight offender characteristics and criminal history items that best predict further criminal behavior.

2. A risk reassessment scale developed to identify and weight offender items that reflect overall adjustment during the course of supervision.

3. A needs assessment scale and treatment guidelines developed by supervising agents to identify noncrisis, offender problem or need areas, and potential strategies and resources to service them.

4. A Client Management Classification (CMC) system and treatment strategies developed empirically in the form of a semistructured interview and agent impressions to assist in placing offenders in one of five differential treatment groups, and to provide information concerning appropriate treatment strategies for casework planning.

5. A standardized classification and reclassification process was developed for probationers and parolees. At admission to supervision, the risk and need assessment scales are scored and the offender is assigned to one of three supervision levels (specific agent contacts are required at each level). At six month intervals during supervision, the risk reassessment scale and needs scale are scored and an offender is reclassified if appropriate and assigned to the appropriate level.

6. A workload budgeting and deployment system developed as a result of time studies that measured the time required by agents to perform activities and meet supervision standards, and used in the budgetary process and to deploy staff.

7. A management information system generated as a product of the classification and reclassification process and used as a foundation for evaluation, planning, and operations.

In 1979, Wisconsin released a two year follow-up report and analysis of the CC/SD Project. In part, the report concluded that:

• Assignment to different levels of supervision based upon risk and needs assessment had a significant impact on probation and parole outcomes. There were fewer new convictions, rules violations, absconding and revocations with high need/high risk offenders as a result of increased contacts. Decreased contacts with low need/low risk offenders resulted in no adverse effects.

- The risk assessment scale demonstrated effectiveness in predicting success or failure in completing terms of probation or parole supervision.
- The needs assessment scale demonstrated high inter-rater reliability.

Components of the Wisconsin Model were duplicated in a number of probation and parole agencies throughout the country, including Ohio. The Wisconsin Model became, in fact, a National Institute of Corrections (NIC) Model Probation/Parole Classification System.

The Adult Parole Authority
Case Management System (CMS)

The Ohio Department of Rehabilitation and Corrections, Adult Parole Authority staff were first exposed to the Wisconsin Classification System at an NIC funded Case Management Institute in 1979. As a result, federal grant monies were secured and a Case Management Task Force (CMTF), made up of research, management and line staff was formed. It was generally understood that the completed case management product would contain components applicable to both the probation and parole populations serviced by the Adult Parole Authority.

The following is a summary of the integrated CMS components developed by the Task Force:

1. A comprehensive classification process was developed. As in Wisconsin, researchers reviewed a random sample of closed offender cases and used multiple regression analysis to identify strong predictors of future criminal behavior. The resulting risk assessment scale contains ten weighted items. (See Figure 1.)

   A risk reassessment scale, containing eight items, was constructed as well to evaluate an offender's adjustment during supervision. (See Figure 2.)

   Supervisory and line staff developed a needs assessment scale. It contains 13 problem or need areas (two more than the Wisconsin scale), and input for the officer's impressions of the offender's needs. It was designed, like the Wisconsin scale, to be used for classification and case planning. Need treatment guidelines comparable to Wisconsin's, were devised to assist officers in more accurately identifying and treating offender need areas and making appropriate community resource referrals. (See Figure 3.)

Figure 1   Assessment of Client Risk

Processor # _____

Client Name _____ Last First Mi	Client Number _____ Date _____
Officer _____ Last Social Security Number	Unit Location Code_____

Select the appropriate answer and enter the associated weight in score column. Total all scores to arrive at the risk assessment score.

Score

Number of Prior Felony Convictions: (or Juvenile Adjudications)	0 None 2 One 4 Two or more	_____
Arrested Within Five (5) Years Prior to Arrest for Current Offense (exclude traffic)	0 No 4 Yes	_____
Age at Arrest Leading to First Felony Conviction (or Juvenile Adjudications)	0 24 and over 2 20 to 23 4 19 and under	_____
Amount of Time Employed in Last 12 Months (Prior to Incarceration for Parolees)	0 More than 7 months 1 5 to 7 months 2 Less than 5 months 0 Not appplicable	_____

Alcohol Usage Problems (Prior to Incarceration
for Parolees)
	0 No interference
	    with functioning
	2 Occasional abuse; some
	    disruption of functioning
	4 Frequent abuse; serious
	    disruption; needs treatment
		_____

Other Drug Usage Problems (Prior to Incarceration
for Parolees)
	0 No interference with
	    fuctioning
	2 Occasional abuse; some
	    disruption of functioning
	4 Frequent abuse; serious
	    disruption needs treatment
		_____

Number of Prior Adult Incarcerations in a State or Federal Institution	0 0 3 1-2 6 3 or more	_____
Age at Admission to Institution or Probation for Current Offense	0 30 or over 3 18 to 29 6 17 and under	_____
Number of Prior *Adult* Probation/Parole Supervisions	0 None 4 One or more	_____
Number of Prior Probation/Parole Revocations Resulting in Imprisonment (Adult or Juvenile)	0 None 4 One or more	_____

Total _____

Figure 2 Reassessment of Client Risk ☐ During Supervision
☐ At Final Discharge

Processor # _____

Client Name _____	Client Number _____	
Last First Mi	Date _____	
Officer _____	Unit Location Code_____	
Last Social Security Number		

Select the appropriate answer and enter the associated weight in score column. Total all scores to arrive at the risk assessment score.

Score

Number of Prior Felony Convictions
(or Juvenile Adjudications)
- 0 None
- 3 One
- 6 Two
- 7 Three or more _____

Age at Arrest Leading to First Felony Conviction
(or Juvenile Adjudications)
- 0 24 and over
- 2 20-23
- 5 19 and under _____

Age at Admission to Probation/Parole Supervision
for Current Offense
- 0 30 and older
- 4 18-29
- 7 17 and under _____

Rate the following based on period since last (re)assessment:

Type of Arrests (indicate most serious
excluding traffic)
- 0 None
- 2 Technical PV only
- 4 Misdemeanor arrest(s)
- 8 Felony arrest _____

Associations
- 0 Mainly with noncrimnally oriented individuals
- 5 Mainly with negative individuals _____

Alcohol Usage Problems
- 0 No interference with fuctioning
- 2 Occasional abuse; some disruption of functioning
- 3 Frequent abuse; serious disruption needs treatment _____

Other Drug Usage Problems
- 0 No interference with functioning
- 1 Occasional abuse: some disruption of functioning
- 2 Frequent abuse: serious disruption; needs treatment _____

Attitude
- 0 No adverse difficulties/ motivated to change
- 2 Periodic difficulties/ uncooperative/independent
- 5 Frequently hostile/ negative/criminal orientation _____

Total _____

Figure 3 Assessment of Client Needs

Processor # _____

Client Name _____   Client Number _____
                Last   First   Mi
                                                   Date _____

Officer _____   Unit Location Code_____
         Last   Social Security Number

Score

Emotional and Mental Stability

0 No symptoms of emotions and/or mental instability

2 Symptoms limit, but do not prohibit adequate functioning

6 Symptoms prohibit adequate functioning and/or has Court or Board imposed condition

8 Severe symptoms requiring continual attention and/or explosive, threatening and potentially dangerous to others or self   _____

Domestic Relationship

0 Stable/supportive relationships

3 Some disorganization or stress but potential for improvement

7 Major disorganization or stress   _____

Associations

0 No adverse relationships

2 Association with occasional negative results

4 Associations frequently negative

6 Associations completely negative   _____

Drug Abuse

0 No disruption of functioning

2 Occasional substance abuse: some disruption of functioning and/or has Court or Board conditions

7 Frequent abuse; serious disruption; needs treatment   _____

Alcohol Usage

0 No disruption of functioning

2 Occasional abuse; some disruption of functioning and/or has court or Board conditions

7 Frequent abuse; serious disruption; needs treatment   _____

Employment

0 Satisfactory employment, no difficulties reported; or homemaker, student, retired, or disabled

2 Underemployed

4 Unsatisfactory employment; or unemployed but has adequate job skills/motivation

5 Unemployed and virtually unemployable; needs motivation/training   _____

Academic/Vocational Skills/Training

0 Adequate skills, able to handle everyday requirements

2 Low skill level causing minor adjustment problems

6 No identifiable skills and/or minimal skill level causing serious adjustment problems   _____

Financial Management

0 No current difficulties

1 Situational or minor difficulties

5 Chronic/severe difficulties   _____

Attitudes

0 No adverse difficulties/motivated for change

2 Periodic difficulties/uncooperative/dependent

4 Frequently hostile/negative/criminal orientation   _____

Residence

0 Suitable living arrangement

1 Adequate living, i.e., temporary shelter

4 Nomadic and/or unacceptable   _____

Mental Ability (Intelligence)

0 Able to function independently

1 Some need for assistence; potential for adequate adjustment

3 Deficiencies severely limit independent functioning   _____

Health

0 Sound physical health; seldom ill

1 Handicap or illness; interferes with functioning on a recurring basis

2 Serious handicap or chronic illness; needs frequent medical care   _____

Sexual Behavior

0 No apparent dysfunction

2 Real or perceived situational or minor problems

6 Real or perceived chronic or severe problems   _____

Officer's Impressions of Needs

A. Low **0**   B. Medium **3**   C. Maximum **5**

Total _____

After the risk and need assessment and risk reassessment scales were developed, research staff tested the scales against offender case data to determine ranges of risk and need cut-off scores for three supervision levels:

Maximum: High failure potential or great number of problem/need areas requiring services.

Medium: Lower failure potential or problem/need areas, but requiring officer involvement.

Minimum: Least failure potential or few significant problem/need areas.

The CMTF added a fourth supervision level, Extended, to be used at reclassification. To be assigned to Extended, an offender must have been under active supervision for at least a year and at the Minimum level for the previous six months.

Classification is a straightforward process using the risk and need scales. Available information about an offender such as a Presentence or Parole Board Investigation, police reports, interviews or institutional records are reviewed by the officer and the scales are scored. The offender is placed in one of the three supervision levels based upon the higher classification of *either* scale.

The following are current risk and need cut-off scores for the three supervision levels:

Risk Score	Level of Supervision	Need Score
26 and above	Maximum	25 and above
18 to 25	Medium	15 to 24
17 and below	Minimum	14 and below

The following case summary and accompanying scales for Paul S., a 24-year-old male offender on parole supervision for burglary, illustrates the classification process:

> Three years ago, Paul and an accomplice went to the apartment of a female known to the accomplice. They forced open a door, entered and ransacked the rooms (the female was not there at the time). They took money a loaded revolver a butcher knife, and keys. They stole the female's automobile from a nearby lot.
>
> Both were arrested a short time later in the stolen vehicle. The accomplice had the loaded revolver and Paul had the money and knife. When questioned, Paul admitted his involvement, and told police that he and the accomplice had originally gone to the apartment to "punish" the female for

"leaving" the accomplice. Paul was convicted of burglary and sentenced to the Department of Rehabilitation and Corrections. He served three years before he was paroled.

As a juvenile, Paul was adjudicated and convicted at age 14 for the theft of a teacher's purse and placed on indefinite probation. At age 15, Paul threatened a school principal with a hammer was convicted of menacing and continued on probation. Paul was committed to a Department of Youth Services' institution at age 16 as a result of a burglary conviction and a probation violation finding. Following release, Paul served a juvenile parole period which terminated at age 18.

As an adult, Paul was convicted of felony theft at age 19 and placed on probation. Within months Paul was arrested while driving a stolen van. He was convicted for receiving stolen property, his probation was revoked and he was sentenced to the institution. Paul was released on Shock Parole and completed his supervision period without major problems. The current offense of burglary occurred when Paul was 21; it is only the second offense committed with an accomplice.

Paul was raised by his older brother. Paul completed high school and a number of basic auto mechanics courses. As a teen, he had a history of acting out when angered. A recent evaluation described Paul as "argumentative, criminally motivated and lacking in positive direction." Paul has an average intelligence.

Paul has worked primarily as a restaurant cook and dishwasher. In the year prior to his arrest for the current offense, Paul worked only three months. He was fired from his last job for chronic absenteeism.

Paul has been unemployed since his release on parole and has resided with his brother. The brother is employed, owns his own home and has no criminal record. The brother is willing to provide Paul with a residence and spending money until Paul is employed and able to rent an apartment. Paul is actively seeking employment according to his brother. (See Figures 4 and 5.)

As the scales indicate, Paul's risk score is 28 and his need score is 24. Thus, Paul would be classified as a Maximum level offender.

There are two classification exceptions. Sex offenders are not classified by the risk or need scale. In addition, officers can override the scales, with supervisory approval, and assign an offender to a higher or lower level of supervision.

Figure 4 Assessment of Client Risk

Processor # _____

Client Name __*Paul S.*_____   Client Number _____
           Last   First   Mi

                                     Date _____

Officer _____   Unit Location Code_____
         Last   Social Security Number

Select the appropriate answer and enter the associated weight in the score column. Total all scores to arrive at the risk assessment score.

                                                               Score

Number of Prior Felony Convictions: (or Juvenile Adjudications)	0 None 2 One 4 Two or more	**4**
Arrested Within Five (5) Years Prior to Arrest for Current Offense (exclude traffic)	0 No 4 Yes	**4**
Age at Arrest Leading to First Felony Conviction (or Juvenile Adjudications)	0 24 and over 2 20 to 23 4 19 and under	**2**
Amount of Time Employed in Last 12 Months (Prior to Incarceration for Parolees)	0 More than 7 months 1 5 to 7 months 2 Less than 5 months 0 Not appplicable	**0**
Alcohol Usage Problems (Prior to Incarceration for Parolees)	0 No interference with functioning 2 Occasional abuse; some disruption of functioning 4 Frequent abuse; serious disruption; needs treatment	**0**
Other Drug Usage Problems (Prior to Incarceration for Parolees)	0 No interference with fuctioning 2 Occasional abuse; some disruption of functioning 4 Frequent abuse; serious disruption needs treatment	**0**
Number of Prior Adult Incarcerations in a State or Federal Institution	0 0 3 1-2 6 3 or more	**3**
Age at Admission to Institution or Probation for Current Offense	0 30 or over 3 18 to 29 6 17 and under	**3**
Number of Prior *Adult* Probation/Parole Supervisions	0 None 4 One or more	**4**
Number of Prior Probation/Parole Revocations Resulting in Imprisonment (Adult or Juvenile)	0 None 4 One or more	**4**

                                                                 Total   **24**

Figure 5 Assessment of Client Needs

Processor # _____

Client Name _Paul S._ _____ Client Number _____
         Last   First   Mi
                                            Date _____

Officer _____ Unit Location Code_____
      Last   Social Security Number

Score

Emotional and Mental Stability

0 No symptoms of emotions and/or mental instability   **2** Symptoms limit, but do not prohibit adequate functioning   **6** Symptoms prohibit adequate functioning and/or has Court or Board imposed condition   **8** Severe symptoms requiring continual attention and/or explosive, threatening and potentially dangerous to others or self   _8_

Domestic Relationship

0 Stable/supportive relationships   **3** Some disorganization or stress but potential for improvement   **7** Major disorganization or stress   _0_

Associations

0 No adverse relationships   **2** Associations with occasional negative results   **4** Associations frequently negative   **6** Associations completely negative   _2_

Drug Abuse

0 No disruption of functioning   **2** Occasional substance abuse: some disruption of functioning and/or has Court or Board conditions   **7** Frequent abuse; serious disruption; needs treatment   _0_

Alcohol Usage

0 No disruption of functioning   **2** Occasional abuse; some disruption of functioning and/or has court or Board conditions   **7** Frequent abuse; serious disruption; needs treatment   _0_

Employment

0 Satisfactory employment, no difficulties reported; or homemaker, student, retired, or disabled   **2** Underemployed   **4** Unsatisfactory employment; or unemployed but has adequate job skills/motivation   **5** Unemployed and virtually unemployable; needs motivation/training   _4_

Academic/Vocational Skills/Training

0 Adequate skills, able to handle everyday requirements   **2** Low skill level causing minor adjustment problems   **6** No identifiable skills and/or minimal skill level causing serious adjustment problems   _2_

Financial Management

0 No current difficulties   **1** Situational or minor difficulties   **5** Chronic/severe difficulties   _1_

Attitudes

0 No adverse difficulties/motivated for change   **2** Periodic difficulties/uncooperative/dependent   **4** Frequently hostile/negative/criminal orientation   _4_

Residence

0 Suitable living arrangement   **1** Adequate living, i.e., temporary shelter   **4** Nomadic and/or unacceptable   _0_

Mental Ability (Intelligence)

0 Able to function independently   **1** Some need for assistence; potential for adequate adjustment   **3** Deficiencies severely limit independent functioning   _0_

Health

0 Sound physical health; seldom ill   **1** Handicap or illness; interferes with functioning on a recurring basis   **2** Serious handicap or chronic illness; needs frequent medical care   _0_

Sexual Behavior

0 No apparent dysfunction   **2** Real or perceived situational or minor problems   **6** Real or perceived chronic or severe problems   _0_

Officer's Impressions of Needs

A. Low **0**   B. Medium **3**   C. Maximum **5**   _3_

Total _24_

Reclassification occurs at six month intervals, when a significant event alters an offender's status, and at the termination of supervision. The risk reassessment and needs scale is scored based upon the offender's adjustment, and the offender is placed in the appropriate supervision level, as determined again, by the higher classification of either scale. Offenders may be placed in the Extended level at reclassification if they meet established criteria. The scales can be overridden at reclassification, as well.

2. A supervision policy was developed. The CMTF discovered that the Adult Parole Authority lacked a cohesive definition of supervision. The CMTF also discovered that the parole and probation sections of the agency had different policies for common tasks such as arrests, violations and the processing of terminations.

   A supervision mission was defined in terms of a fluid process encompassing information gathering, case assessment, classification, case planning, service delivery, monitoring and evaluation. In addition, nearly every Adult Parole Authority supervision policy was revised to correspond with case management concepts.

3. A process to help officers determine appropriate supervision strategies was selected. A variety of strategies were examined by the CMTF including negotiated contracts, behavioral objectives, force field analysis and Wisconsin's CMC system. The CMTF chose the CMC system and its accompanying treatment strategies. The CMC is administered to an offender within the first 30 days of supervision.

4. Structured levels of supervision were developed, with criteria for placement and movement between levels. The CMS was designed, like Wisconsin's system, to move offenders to lower supervision levels as problems are resolved or reduced and needs met. A negotiated case planning process was devised that focuses both officer and offender on problem identification, case plan behavioral objectives, the action plan necessary to achieve the objectives and the date when objectives are achieved. The case plan is written and completed by the officer at classification and reclassification. (See Figure 6.)

5. Standards for officer functions were defined. Required minimum standards for the four levels of supervision were developed by the CMTF in terms of face-to-face contacts with the offender and officer's verification of the offender's residence, employment, program participation and compliance with

Figure 6 Case Plan

Client Name _____ Client Number _____

(Last)   (First)   (Middle)

Problem/Need (From Instrument)	Objective	Action Plan	Achieved

special conditions imposed by the court or Parole Board. Requirements are minimal for an extended case, but increase proportionally as the supervision level increases.

6. A workload system was developed to accommodate the investigative and supervision functions of the agency. Researchers conducted three work/time studies. In one of the studies, a representative number of officers used self-report forms to track time spent with cases in ten standard activities over a four month period. Study results were used to establish specific work units for supervision cases and for court and Parole Board investigations, and to define monthly workload standards.

7. A data system for management information purposes was devised. Supervision forms were designed to collect a variety of data, including demographics, classification, reclassification and termination information and workload statistics. Since implementation, the data has been collected and collated manually and used primarily for staff deployment and budgeting.

   A computerized, statewide supervision data base with entry and report retrieval capability is scheduled to be on line by 1989. Case management information will be more accessible to staff and can be used for a wider variety of purposes.

In 1980 and 1981, the CMS was implemented throughout the state, one region at a time. As part of the implementation process, staffs were trained in the use of the scales, classification and reclassification, the CMC system and case planning. Ongoing supportive contact was maintained between the CMTF and staff during training and implementation.

An evaluation of the CMS, based upon data generated in the initial implementation region, was conducted in 1984; it yielded mixed findings. The evaluator found, for example, that staff using the system were generally positive about it and that case planning and use of outside community resources by officers had improved. The risk scale was also found to be effective (the needs scale was not evaluated).

However, it was also concluded that officers supervised Minimum and Maximum offenders with the same contact frequency. There were, in fact, too many contacts for Minimum offenders and about half the required contacts for Maximum offenders. Because officer efforts were not concentrated in the appropriate areas, the CMS failed to impact upon the criminal behaviors of Maximum offenders.

Significant steps were taken to strengthen the effectiveness of the system. Follow-up training was provided to staff to reinforce supervision standards, and emphasis was placed on monitoring officer activities.

A follow-up study of the Case Management System, using methodology from the previous evaluation, was released in 1986. Overall, the findings were positive. The risk scale, for example continued to function as a solid predictive instrument. In addition, a marked increase in the referral of offenders to community service agencies was revealed. This suggested that the need scale and case planning process were effective in identifying with no apparent solution.

As in the 1984 evaluation, it was discovered that officers over-supervised Minimum level offenders and under-supervised Maximum level offenders. Despite these findings, the study documented some decrease in the criminal behavior of Maximum and Medium level offenders.

Transfer of CMS Technology

When fully implemented, the CMS applied to all parolees in Ohio, and probationers (primarily felons) under Adult Parole Authority supervision in 51 of Ohio's 88 counties. The majority of other counties had separate probation departments, each with its own individual organizational structure, policies and practices. In 1981, numerous probation departments expressed an interest in learning more about the CMS to NIC and the Adult Parole Authority. Ultimately, NIC agreed to fund a transfer of CMS technology from the state to the counties but stipulated that the counties and the state work together during the process.

Despite a history of inter-governmental conflict and adverse relations, the Adult Parole Authority and 15 urban and rural counties combined their efforts and expertise within a supportive environment of capacity building. Early in the process CMTF members conducted an orientation session for urban county personnel that focused on the concepts and benefits of CMS. During the technological transfer process, CMTF members collaborated with county staff to solve implementation and resistance problems. NIC acted as both a technical consultant and a catalyst during the transfer process.

County and state staff worked closely together in the training design and system development arena. CMTF members, for example, provided county participants with information about the various classification, reclassification and case planning components of the CMS. Adult Parole Authority staff trained urban county CMC trainers. They in turn, trained the rural county line staff in CMC interview techniques.

County and state staff also jointly developed a CMS Entrance Training Program. The four day session is designed to provide new county and state officers with an overview of the purpose and function of the risk reassessment and need scales, and the classification process (officers receive specifics concerning policies and procedures when they return to their county department or state unit). The Program also provides practical training in conducting the CMC interview using the recommended treatment strategies and writing case plans.

In addition to participating in training during the transfer process, the urban and rural counties came together to discuss common issues and problems as they reached the same level of implementation. The county departments also worked with NIC to refine their respective management information and workload systems. County implementation team members first explored creating a professional organization for Chief Probation Officers of Ohio during the transfer process.

By 1984, the 15 urban and rural counties had developed and implemented a CMS for their respective probation departments. Previously tested state classification components such as the risk, risk reassessment and needs scale were duplicated by the county departments (some of the counties later developed their own). A number of counties, however, added an assaultive indicator to their risk and risk reassessment scales. (See Figures 7, 8 and 9.)

The management information and workload technology were transferred from the state to the counties, as well. They too were reshaped to meet the individual needs of the county departments. Wisconsin's CMC system was transferred but not altered.

No formal evaluations of the various county systems have been conducted. However, the transfer of Case Management System technology from the state to county probation departments has undoubtedly resulted in improved inter-governmental relations. More importantly, professional probation practices throughout the State of Ohio have been enhanced significantly.

Figure 7 Assessment of Client Risk

Name: Risk Level: _____

Case Number:

Date: P.O.'s Name: _____

Select the appropriate answer and enter the associated weight in score column. Total all scores
to arrive at the risk assessment score.

Score

1) Number of Prior Felony Convictions: 0 None
   (or Juvenile Adjudications)   2 One
                                               4 Two or more   _____

2) Arrested Within Five (5) Years Prior to Arrest   0 No
   for Current Offense (exclude traffic)   4 Yes   _____

3) Age at Arrest Leading to First Felony Conviction 0 24 and over
   (or Juvenile Adjudications)   2 20 to 23
                                                     4 19 and under   _____

4) Number of Prior Adult Incarcerations in a State 0 0
   or Federal Institution   3 1-2
                                                    6 3 or more   _____

5) Age at Admission to Institution or Probation   0 30 or over
   for Current Offense   3 18 to 29
                                                  6 17 and under   _____

6) Number of Prior *Adult* Probation/Parole   0 None
   Supervisions   4 One or more   _____

7) Number of Prior Probation/Parole Revoked   0 None
   or termination Due to Incarceration   4 One or more
   (Adult or Juvenile)   _____

8) Alcohol Usage Problems   0 No indication of alcohol
                                                    abuse
                                                 2 Occasional abuse
                                                 3 Some disruption of
                                                    functioning
                                                 4 Frequent abuse; serious
                                                    disruption; needs treatment _____

9) Other Drug Usage Problems   0 No indication of drug abuse
                                                 2 Occasional abuse
                                                 3 Some disruption of
                                                    functioning
                                                 4 Frequent abuse; serious
                                                    disruption needs treatment   _____

10) Amount of Full Time Employment in Last   0 More than 7 months
    12 months   1 5 to 7 months
                                                 2 Less than 5 months
                                                 0 Not applicable   _____

                                                                    Total _____

11) Adult Felony Conviction or Juvenile Felony Adjudi-   Yes _____
    cation for Offense Involving Threat of Force, Posses- No   _____
    session of Weapon, Physical Force or Sexual Assault
    within the Last Five Years

If answer to item 11 is yes, then supervision level is
increased to next highest level.

Figure 8 Assessment of Client Risk

Client Name _____ CR_____   Probation
                                           Placement Date _____

Risk: L   M   H   Reassessment Date _____

Assessing P.O. _____   Date _____

Select the appropriate answer and enter the associated weight in the score column. Total all scores to arrive at the risk assessment score.

Score

Number of Prior Felony Convictions:	0	None	
(or Juvenile Adjudications)	2	One	
	4	Two or more	_____
Arrested Within Five (5) Years Prior to Arrest	0	No	
for Current Offense (exclude traffic)	4	Yes	_____
Age at Arrest Leading to First Felony Conviction	0	24 and over	
(or Juvenile Adjudications)	2	20 to 23	
	4	19 and under	_____
Amount of Time Employed in Last 12 Months	0	More than 7 months	
(Prior to Incarceration for Parolees)	1	5 to 7 months	
	2	Less than 5 months	
	0	Not appplicable	_____
Alcohol Usage Problems (Prior to Incarceration	0	No interference	
for Parolees)		with functioning	
	2	Occasional abuse; some	
		disruption of functioning	
	4	Frequent abuse; serious disruption;	
		needs treatment	_____
Other Drug Usage Problems (Prior to Incarceration	0	No interference with fuctioning	
for Parolees)	2	Occasional abuse; some disruption	
		of functioning	
	4	Frequent abuse; serious disruption	
		needs treatment	_____
Number of Prior Adult Incarcerations in a State	0	0	
or Federal Institution	3	1-2	
	6	3 or more	_____
Age at Admission to Institution or Probation	0	30 or over	
for Current Offense	3	18 to 29	
	6	17 and under	_____
Number of Prior *Adult* Probation/Parole Supervisions	0	None	
	4	One or more	_____
Number of Prior Probation/Parole Revocations	0	None	
Resulting in Imprisonment (Adult or Juvenile)	4	One or more	_____

Total _____

Officer Override — Alternate level of supervision felt to be appropriate (see reverse side for explanation).   ☐

Assault Factor — If client has been convicted of 2 assaultive misdemeanors or 1 assaultive felony (including present offense), the level of supervision is moved up one step.   ☐

Figure 9 Reassessment of Client Risk

Client Name _____ CR_____ Probation
Placement Date _____

Risk: L   M   H

Reassessment Date _____

Assessing P.O. _____   Date _____

Select the appropriate answer and enter the associated weight in the score column. Total all scores to arrive at the risk assessment score.

Score

Number of Prior Felony Convictions (or Juvenile Adjudications)	0 None 3 One 6 Two 7 Three or more	_____
Age at Arrest Leading to First Felony Conviction (or Juvenile Adjudications)	0 24 and over 2 20-23 5 19 and under	_____
Age at Admission to Probation/Parole Supervision for Current Offense	0 30 and older 4 18-29 7 17 and under	_____

Rate the following based on period since last (re)assessment:

Type of Arrests (indicate most serious excluding traffic)	0 None 2 Technical PV only 4 Misdemeanor arrest(s) 8 Felony arrest	_____

Associations	0 Mainly with noncriminally
	   oriented individuals
	5 Mainly with negative
	   individuals
		_____

Alcohol Usage Problems	0 No interference with fuctioning
	2 Occasional abuse; some disruption
	   of functioning
	3 Frequent abuse; serious disruption
	   needs treatment
		_____

Other Drug Usage Problems	0 No interference with functioning
	1 Occasional abuse: some disruption
	   of functioning
	2 Frequent abuse: serious disruption;
	   needs treatment
		_____

Attitude	0 No adverse difficulties/
	   motivated to change
	2 Periodic difficulties/
	   uncooperative/dependent
	5 Frequently hostile/
	   negative/criminal orientation
		_____

Total _____

Officer Override — Alternate level of supervision felt to be appropriate (see reverse side for explanation). ☐

Assault Factor — If client has been convicted of 2 assaultive misdemeanors or 1 assaultive felony (including present offense), the level of supervision is moved up one step. ☐

References and Further Readings

Arling, G., B. Bemus and P Quigley (1983) *Workload Measures For Probation and Parole.*

Baird, C., B. Bemus and C. Heinz (1979) *The Wisconsin Case Classification/ Staff Deployment Project: A Two Year Follow-up Report.*

Farmer, G. (1978) *Final Report: National Institute of Corrections Capacity Building Grant FQ 2.*

Kratcoski, P. (1984) *An Evaluation of the Case Management System.*

Natter, G. (1986) *A Follow-Up Study on the Case Management System.*

8

Functional Unit Management
An Unsung Achievement

Hans Toch

A recent issue of this journal contains a list of "BOP First and Mosts."* It is an impressive list, but there is one entry that I miss—there is no mention of the introduction of unit management and of its dissemination through the Federal system in the mid-1970s. This development was unquestionably a "first." And it is an ongoing development: we have just begun to explore what units can achieve, and what we can do with them.

The idea of functional units was simple: take a prison and divide it into smaller groups of inmates and staff members. Each group of inmates (50–100 in 1970) would have its own staff team. The inmates would stay with their units and would be individually programmed. Each unit would become a specialized "mini-prison" within a larger prison and share the institution's facilities with other units.

The arrangement is analogous to neighborhoods in a city. Each neighborhood can be intimate, but is part of and has access to the amenities of the city. Each neighborhood receives municipal services, but has its own cultural flavor, which is different from those of other neighborhoods. Another analogy—which emphasizes programming—is between a prison and General Motors, which has disparate assembly areas for different cars, and "can continue production of Cadillacs even when the Chevy assembly line has run into some snags."[1]

Robert Levinson, a pioneer in conceptualizing unit management, created an imaginary automotive empire as another example:

*See *Federal Prisons Journal*, 1(4) (Summer 1990).

Source: *Federal Prisons Journal*, 2(4) (Winter 1992): 15–19.

So FL [Flivvers Limited] establishes several subsidiaries, one for each model—Bearers, Seattles, and Tallyhoes. In this way some of the expensive effectuation equipment can be shared while workers specialize and develop expertise in producing exemplary automobiles of each type. Moreover, if there is trouble with the brakes on the Bearers, FL can still go on producing acceptable Seattles and Tallyhoes.[2]

The flexibility of Levinson's assembly lines does not spell anarchy: Flivvers Limited decides whether market trends favor small cars (Tallyhoes) or limousines (Bearers). It sets policies that affect what its assembly lines do. Levinson and Roy Gerard write that "one of the dangers in a decentralized facility is that the Functional Units may become totally 'out of step' with one another, so that the institution appears to be headed in all directions at the same time."[3] It follows that there must be ways of coordinating what the units do. As an example, "the Unit Program Plans can become part of a total Master Program Plan for the entire facility."[4]

On the other hand, units need some autonomy so that they can run programs that meet the unique needs of inmates and use the special skills of staff who design and run these programs. Autonomy also lets units develop their own cultures and identities. But the unit still functions as part of the whole prison. A few programs have lost sight of this, and ultimately have been abolished.[5]

What Can Units Do Best?

Levinson and Gerard distinguished between functions of units. One is *correction*, the concern with helpful and constructive experiences that are shaped by staff who are closest to the inmate. The second is *care*, which means efficient use of relevant resources to assist the inmates in doing time. The third use is *control*, which means keeping and monitoring inmates as they remain in the unit, so that staff can work with them.

I have listed three functions, though some would say that only two (care and control) are still alive, and that the third (correction) is dead. A discontinuance of correction, however, is hard to envisage. It would mean that inmate programming could no longer be of concern to staff in units, and that an inmate would receive neither sympathy nor assistance with efforts at self-improvement from staff members who know him. It is true that different functions may be emphasized over time, and from unit to unit. However, care and control and correction are inextricable aspects of functional inmate management, which is the task of unit staff.

One fact is critical for all three functions: the fostering of staff-inmate relationships that benefit from a shared environment and closer acquaintanceship. The foundation for this notion had been laid 15 years before the advent of unit management in a study of the Bureau of Prisons run under Ford Foundation sponsorship. The director of the study, Dan Glaser, had complained that

> . . . by randomizing his caseload through the last number assignment system, the caseworker in a large prison inadvertently reduces his chances of knowing the social environment in which his clients live. By scattering his caseload throughout the prison population, the caseworker minimizes the probability of his also knowing the cellmates or dormitory colleagues, coworkers, recreational partners, or other close inmate friends or associates of any specific client. . . . Also, when the caseload is scattered, it clearly becomes more difficult for the caseworker to see his client's customary behavior in the institution.[6]

In Glaser's reports to the Bureau of Prisons, he suggested attaching caseworkers to tiers or work assignments, in which each caseworker could get to know inmates in their natural environment, observing the pressures to which they were subjected and their capacity to cope with them. Glaser also talked of staff teaming and of "facilitating communication across traditional intra-staff lines."[7]

Among innovations he reviewed, for example, were "treatment teams" at the Federal Correctional Institution, El Reno, Oklahoma, that included custody officers assigned to dormitories to observe inmate behavior. Such experiments of the early 1960s anticipated current concerns about job enrichment for correctional officers.[8] With respect to El Reno, Glaser reported that "before long the line custodial staff seemed unanimous in considering the new system 'the best thing that ever happened' in the prison. They feel it gives them a chance to be heard, and it raises their prestige with the inmates."[9]

Another long-standing question was how to deal with antistaff norms of "inmate subcultures" in custodial prisons. Glaser speculated that "inmate pressure on other inmates to avoid communication with officers varies directly with the extent to which there is an impersonal and authoritarian orientation of staff to inmates."[10] The corollary is that a setting in which inmates and staff can relate to each other would be inhospitable to the advent of an antistaff prisoner culture. Such a setting might do more. Gerard and Levinson have observed that:

> Both staff and residents come to feel a sense of pride in "their" unit and its accomplishments. Rather than offenders finding a common cause to organize against staff, competition develops along more desirable lines, e.g., which Unit has the best record in achieving some positive goal.[11]

Functional units call for participation and involvement. Just as correctional officers, teachers, and clerical staff could be involved in teams, inmates could play an active role:

> Ways must be found to offer opportunities for Unit residents to take intramural roles of increasing responsibility both for their own activities, as well as for the smooth functioning of the Unit. In the area of decision making, as it relates to a particular individual, he should be viewed as a member of the Unit team and have a voice in program decisions affecting him.[12]

Putting the issue of inmate team membership aside, the point is that staff and inmates would have more control over their environment, and new means to enhance their own development. Self-development is enhanced where the personal contributions of team members are prized, and routinization is resisted.

Early Experiments

Like any invention, unit management is a tool. Units have to show that they can earn their keep as they are put to use.

In 1970, the Bureau of Prisons had two obvious needs. One was the need to reduce disruption and violence in prison and to protect weaker inmates from exploitation. Units could help because staff could use them to separate predatory prisoners from those susceptible to predation. Such sorting had occurred in the past, but the separating could now be done on a larger scale, based on observations at intake. Disciplinary incident rates could be measured before and after sorting inmates, to verify the efficacy of the sorting.[13]

The second need was to house substance-abusing offenders who were being committed to the system. The units made it possible to keep these offenders in regular prisons, as opposed to special institutions such as the Public Health Service's "narcotics farms." They also made it possible to experiment with treatment approaches to addiction. Most approaches capitalized on the fact that the offenders lived together as a residential community, which made it easy to use experiences of living and working as grist for treatment, and enabled teams to mobilize constructive peer pressure in resident groups. This combination is a treatment modality, called the therapeutic community.[14] It can be combined with other modalities—such as token economies—or used by itself. This makes definitions difficult, but the Bureau soon had 13 "official" therapeutic communities. Some had "siblings" outside, to which they sent graduates. Others thrived in places such as the

Federal Correctional Institutions at Lexington, Kentucky, and Fort Worth, Texas. One community (Asklepieion) ran for 6 years at the U.S. Penitentiary, Marion, Illinois.

Types of Units

Therapeutic communities are examples of units that provide *treatment*. Inmates are selected for such units because they have problems such as alcohol or drug addiction that can be ameliorated or remedied.

Other units provide *education*, *training*, or *work experiences*, and "an appropriately designed counseling program."[15] The inmates in such units have obvious deficits (marginal literacy, lack of employment skills, and so forth) that can be addressed by the unit. A third type, which covers most units in the Federal system, is *management-related*.

"Management-related" does not mean that the prison gets what it wants and the inmate loses out. For example, inmates can be sorted by personality type to separate "aggression-prone" from "victim-prone" inmates, which reduces rates of predation. Management obviously benefits through fewer incidents, but the real beneficiaries are the inmates who did not become victims. The same rule applies to other sortings in which prisoners are isolated to avoid trouble or conflict.

One can form groups to facilitate service delivery. A unit composed of elderly inmates, for example, can adjoin medical or pharmaceutical services. Young inmates can be assigned to teams that have expertise in adolescence (a side benefit is that older inmates get peace and quiet). Other teams can have expertise in problems of long-teamers, Cuban detainees, persons diagnosed HIV-positive, or other homogeneous groupings.

But classification and sorting—which means specialization of programs and staff—require time and attention and (as far as possible) uncrowded conditions. Where compromise is necessary, a bifurcated situation arises in which classification and specialization are reserved for high-priority programs, and the remaining units receive prisoners on a first-come, first-served basis. Thus, a few units are specialized and serve treatment, training/vocational, or management functions for special populations. Most units receive representative intake subpopulations, and are programmed in more or less standard fashion. Teams can still introduce program variations (if they have autonomy). But they cannot apply Levinson's model and produce Bearers, Seattles, and Tallyhoes under the auspices of specialized experts.

Patterns of Unit Management

Unit management survives crises such as extreme crowding by changing the ratio of special to general units in the system. The challenge for management is to create special units that serve the needs of the system and the inmates, given available resources. Today, resources are scarce, but drug-related offenders need specialized drug-treatment units. Other programs could be inspired by intake disproportions involving long-term offenders, violent offenders, emotionally disturbed persons, non-English-speakers, or other groups that could benefit from special programs. With respect to this issue, managers must ask questions such as:

- How seriously would the inmates be handicapped if they were integrated into the general population?
- What problems would be created for others if these offenders became part of the population?
- Do these offenders require a specialized program, and are staff available who can administer the program?
- Can the program at issue be effective without dealing with the offenders as a group?
- Is there an institution in the system in which the program (say, residential drug treatment) can be set up without playing a wholesale game of musical chairs; i.e., creating serious disturbances in the rest of the system?

Should the answers to these questions favor the creation of a unit, other questions arise having to do with how units are patterned in the system. One model that may appeal involves the creation of institutions that are conglomerates of special units—perhaps different types of units, perhaps of the same kind. Another option places one or two special units in prisons that are otherwise unspecialized. The former model permits the concentration of resources, and the latter allows partial mixing of special and general populations and commonality of custody grading.

Beyond these immediate questions we face long-term questions, involving a future in which special programs can be routinely created, and we can afford to decide whether to move an illiterate drug addict from a therapeutic community to a remedial education unit, or vice versa. When that time comes I shall plan to write a sequel to this essay.

Notes

[1] Robert B. Levinson, "TC or not TC? That is the question," in Hans Toch (ed.), *Therapeutic Communities in Corrections*. New York: Praeger, 1980, p. 51.

[2] Robert B. Levinson, "Try softer," in Robert Johnson and Hans Toch (eds.), *The Pains of Imprisonment*. Beverly Hills, CA: Sage, 1982, p. 244.

[3] Robert B. Levinson and Roy E. Gerard, "Functional units: A different correctional approach," *Federal Probation*, 1973, 37, 8–18, p. 15.

[4] Ibid.

[5] See, for example, Joseph E. Hickey and Peter L. Scharf, *Toward a Just Correctional Community*, San Francisco: Jossey-Bass, 1980; also Elliot E. Studt, Sheldon L. Messinger, and Thomas P. Wilson, *C-Unit: Search for Community in Prison*. New York: Russell Sage Foundation, 1968.

[6] Daniel Glaser, *The Effectiveness of a Prison and Parole System*. Indianapolis: The Bobbs-Merrill Company, 1964, p. 193.

[7] *Op. cit.*, p. 197.

[8] Hans Toch and J. Douglas Grant, *Reforming Human Services*. Beverly Hills, CA: Sage, 1982.

[9] Glaser, p. 205.

[10] *Op. cit.*, p. 128.

[11] Levinson and Gerard, p. 9.

[12] *Op. cit.*, p. 14.

[13] Herbert C. Quay, *Managing Adult Inmates: Classification for Housing and Program Assignments*. College Park, MD: American Correctional Association, 1984. Further reduction of disciplinary incidents can be documented after disaggregating inmates through classification *within* units for programmatic separation. See Diane J. Spieker and Timothy A. Pierson, *Adult Internal Management System (AIMS): Implementation Manual*. Washington, DC: National Institute of Corrections and Human Resources, 1987.

[14] Hans Toch (ed.), *Therapeutic Communities in Corrections*. New York: Praeger, 1980.

[15] Levinson and Gerard, p. 10.

9

An Evaluation of Juvenile Intensive Aftercare Probation
Aftercare Versus System Response Effects

Henry Sontheimer
Lynne Goodstein

In recent years, many jurisdictions have implemented "intensive" supervision regimens for offenders on probation or parole as alternatives to routine probation and/or incarceration. Prior studies often failed to distinguish between two distinct potential effects of intensive supervision. The first effect is a reduction in the propensity to commit any new offenses, and may be viewed as reflecting a rehabilitative or deterrent model. The second possible effect is a reduction in the opportunity to reoffend, caused by the court's response to misbehavior on the part of the probationer or parolee—a risk control or selective incapacitation model. The current study is an experimental evaluation of an intensive aftercare probation program for serious juvenile offenders. The program had a dramatic impact on the frequency, but not the incidence, of recidivism. This finding suggests that the value of intensive supervision lies in its risk control components (a system response effect) rather than in its ability to reduce the propensity to reoffend (an aftercare effect).

The major purpose of the correctional branch of the juvenile justice system is to reduce the likelihood that juvenile offenders, once "treated" by the system, will continue to engage in criminal

*Reprinted with permission of the Academy of Criminal Justice Sciences from *Justice Quarterly* 10(2): 197–227.

behavior. This concern is especially pressing in the case of serious high-risk juvenile offenders, who have a history of committing multiple offenses that would be considered felonies if they were adjudicated in the adult system.

Various types of institutional programs have been developed to reduce serious juvenile criminality, including those which focus on vocational training, education, control of chemical dependency, improvement in self-esteem, and the development of self-reliance through wilderness experiences. The effectiveness of these residential programs has been subject to scrutiny by researchers, who generally have found few differences among them in their abilities to reduce recidivism among juvenile releasees (Goodstein and Sontheimer 1987; Whitehead and Lab 1989). Others, however, interpret the evidence in a more positive light, finding some indications of reductions in recidivism (Andrews et al. 1990; Gendreau and Ross 1987; Greenwood and Zimring 1985).

In recent years, juvenile justice practitioners and researchers have changed their focus from institutional interventions to the social and environmental context of the postrelease period as a potentially important influence on recidivism (Altschuler and Armstrong 1991). This change stands to reason because the effect of the institutional experience on postrelease behavior is likely to be less salient than the effect of the immediate environment. Whether or not a juvenile releasee is enrolled in school, has a job, is relating well to family, is involved with illicit substances—these factors may be most critical in determining whether that individual will be motivated to reengage in criminal activity.

One of the most direct means by which the juvenile justice system can influence juveniles' postrelease environment is aftercare (parole) supervision by local juvenile probation departments. The probation officer is in an excellent position to encourage juveniles to remain in school or to work, to counsel them and their families, to make referrals to other agencies for needed services, and in general to function as monitors of probationers' conduct. Yet because officers in some jurisdictions have caseloads of more than 100 probationers each, little of substance can be expected to occur between the probation officer and his or her released client.

Greater promise exists in the model of intensive probation, in which a probation officer is assigned a small number of cases and is expected to frequently deliver specified services to the releasee and his or her family. If the probation officer has enough time to establish a personal relationship with the releasee, to broker appropriate social services, and to monitor his or her behavior, the juvenile's chances of remaining crime-free may increase. Moreover, if the juvenile does relapse into delinquent behavior, the intensive probation officer may be more able to make an informed and timely recommendation to the court as to whether the youth should be prosecuted as a probation violator and returned to placement, if applicable.

Intensive Probation for Juvenile Offenders

Intensive probation initially was conceptualized as an alternative to institutionalization and was used primarily with adult populations in its early stages (Armstrong 1991). It gained visibility in the mid to late 1980s and has proliferated widely in a relatively brief time, primarily because of several apparently successful, highly visible programs (Erwin 1990; Erwin and Bennett 1987; Pearson 1985; Pearson and Harper 1990). Moreover, it has been extended from a modality intended as an alternative to imprisonment to one which operates in conjunction with institutional placement (Altschuler and Armstrong 1991). Specifically, offenders assigned to intensive aftercare probation are released from institutional placement to probation supervision, which involves intensive prerelease planning, the probation officer's involvement with the offender's family and significant others, and frequent contacts with the offender.

Although the effectiveness of these programs in reducing recidivism is still being debated by researchers (Clear, Flynn, and Shapiro 1987; Gendreau and Ross 1987; Petersilia 1987), the concept recently has made significant inroads into the juvenile justice system, with certain modifications. In light of the traditional commitment of the juvenile justice system to treatment of offenders, intensive probation programs for juvenile offenders generally blend concerns for treatment and service with those of enhanced supervision and surveillance (Armstrong 1991).

The common attribute of virtually all intensive probation programs for juveniles is a small caseload, generally ranging from 12 to 25 juveniles per officer. In addition, most programs specifically target high-risk juveniles who, on the basis of their offense history, the severity of current criminal charges, and/or their personal needs and problems, are predicted as likely to engage in recidivistic behavior. Other common program characteristics are 1) specific goals and activities, 2) objective selection criteria, and 3) a variety of consequences available for violations (Clear 1991). Armstrong notes, however, that "considerable conceptual and definitional confusion continues to persist over exactly what these programs look like, what they share in common, and what they are trying to accomplish" (1991:8).

Effects of Intensive Probation Supervision

Intensive probation programs for juveniles are designed primarily to offer a more accountable type of community-based intervention, which would result in a reduction of recidivism among the serious, chronic juvenile offenders to whom these programs are directed. Less clear, however, is the specific mechanism or model through which recidivistic behavior is likely to be reduced by such programs. Theoretically, various aspects of the programs could work in different ways to effect change in offenders' criminal behavior. In this paper we propose two general models through which intensive probation programs could operate to reduce offenders' recidivism. We call the first the *aftercare effect*, the second the *system response effect*.

The aftercare effect model presumes that intensive probation supervision actually reduces youthful offenders' predilections to crime. It operates through two related, though independent, processes. The first process reflects the effects of specific deterrence. Because of the increase in monitoring and surveillance by the probation officer, youthful offenders may desist from criminal activity, at least temporarily. In this sense, the increased salience of the presence of the probation officer in the juvenile's life may serve as a deterrent to crime. A youth's awareness that a probation officer is monitoring his or her behavior and is willing to take action to thwart illegal acts may serve to reduce the incidence of those acts.

The second process could reflect a genuine set of behavioral changes in the supervised juvenile, caused by lifestyle changes mandated through the intensive probation program. This element of the aftercare effect reflects a genuine impact of the increase in treatment, counseling, and other rehabilitative services provided to the offender by the intensive probation officer. Theoretically, by enforcing juveniles' participation in school and/or work, by counseling or other prosocial group activities, and by fostering more positive relations between the probationer and his or her immediate family, the traditional social casework strategies of an intensive probationary regime could serve to strengthen youths' bonds with the prosocial community. This model, which draws essentially on Hirschi's (1969) control theory, presumes that strengthening bonds with prosocial individuals and institutions leads to changes in offenders' value systems and behaviors which will reduce the likelihood of reinvolvement in criminal behavior.

Theoretically, if the aftercare effect is operating through the process of genuine rehabilitation, the presumed desistance from criminal behavior would be permanent; in the specific deterrence model, one would expect criminality to reappear after the intensive probation surveillance is removed.[1] The important point, however, is that both elements of the aftercare effect would reflect an actual change in the probationer's propensity to criminality, a desistance from crime that would be at least temporary. With respect to actual recidivism, the operation of an aftercare effect would be manifested in lower rates of recidivism: that is, the proportion of offenders not rearrested would be higher than among comparable offenders receiving traditional probation supervision.

The system response effect model does not presume an actual change in youthful offenders' propensity to crime. Rather, it presumes that a reduction in recidivism may occur as an indirect result of the intensive probation officer's improved knowledge of the offender, afforded by a significant increase in contact. The system response effect would be assumed to operate by selective incapacitation through early intervention. The probation officer's increased knowledge of the juvenile offender's behavior patterns would enable him or her to identify early tendencies toward "relapse" and would allow sufficient time to initiate community crime prevention efforts such as house arrest or court review. If these interventions are ineffective, the officer would have the time and the evidence necessary to initiate probation violation proceedings. This quick response would serve to reduce the number of offenses that a given juvenile would have the opportunity to commit.

With respect to actual recidivism rates, this model does not assume a reduction in any given juvenile's propensity to commit criminal offenses if he or she had the opportunity to remain in the community. It assumes, however, that recidivistic offenders would be removed from the community more rapidly, thus reducing the number of offenses they would have the opportunity to commit. Therefore offenders involved in intensive probation supervision would be expected to be arrested at rates similar to those of offenders under traditional supervision, but would commit fewer total offenses than traditionally supervised youths.

Research on the Effectiveness of Intensive Probation for Juveniles

Available evaluations of intensive probation programs do not distinguish between aftercare and system response effects. Indeed, we have only a handful of scientific studies of the effects of intensive probation on juvenile offenders' recidivism; most of these have found no program effects at all.

A test of three different levels of probation supervision on a sample of relatively serious delinquents was conducted in Utah by the National Council on Crime and Delinquency (1987). Probationers subject to intensive supervision (at least one face-to-face contact and one phone contact per week) fared no better as to recidivism than did those subject to routine (two contacts per month) and nonreporting supervision. About 70 percent of the probationers were rearrested within one year; the average number of new arrests was about two per subject.

Barton and Butts (1990) conducted a test of three Michigan in-home programs designed as alternatives to incarceration. Incarceration-bound male juveniles were diverted into these programs, which differed from one another with respect to program philosophy (emphasis on monitoring versus treatment) and auspices (one was court-operated; two were contracted out to private agencies); all three, however, prescribed intensive contact with a probation officer. The experimental youths were compared with a control group of randomly assigned youths who were committed to the state for supervision and placement. After time at risk was controlled, the control group and the three experimental groups manifested levels of reoffending equivalent to a rearrest rate of about 1.8 arrests per year at risk. The authors found no statistically significant differences among the groups on either the incidence or the frequency of reoffending.

Wiebush (1991) evaluated another intensive supervision program designed for incarceration-bound juveniles in Ohio. This program provided the youths with an average of about six face-to-face contacts per month with their probation officers and 10 additional face-to-face and telephone contacts per month with part-time surveillance monitors. Youths under intensive supervision also were referred for services such as substance abuse treatment, counseling, and educational support more often than were their counterparts who were placed on routine probation or committed to the state. Wiebush also found no reduction in the incidence or frequency of criminal recidivism among youths in the program, as compared with a group of felons placed on routine probation and a group committed to the state for placement. After 18 months, about 70 percent of the youths placed on intensive supervision or committed to the state had been reconvicted at least once for a new criminal charge. The only difference among the three treatment groups was that youths on intensive probation were more likely than others to incur probation violations.

An experimental test of the Violent Juvenile Offender (VJO) program (Fagan 1990) reported mixed results. VJO program participants across four program sites initially were committed to secure facilities, then were moved to less restrictive residential programs, and finally were placed under intensive supervision in the community. Control subjects were assigned to "mainstream juvenile corrections programs" and tended to spend more time in secure, rather than community-based, programs. Although a smaller percentage of experimental subjects were rearrested in most comparisons across sites and observation periods, the differences rarely were statistically significant. The results were mixed when the frequency of rearrests was compared: experimentals accounted for significantly fewer arrests at only one of the four sites. Fagan (1990) concludes that the VJO programs were at least as successful as the control treatment and did not jeopardize community safety.

The Current Study

We designed the present study to evaluate an intensive aftercare probation program for juveniles developed by the Juvenile Probation Department of the Family Court of Philadelphia. This program was developed in conjunction with a 1988 proposal by the Juvenile Court Judges' Commission of Pennsylvania for the establishment of intensive aftercare programs in selected counties. Funding for the program gave us the opportunity to devise an experimental research design; thus, simultaneously with the implementation of the intensive aftercare program, we undertook an evaluation study. This paper presents the results of the evaluation as they relate to recidivism in a group of serious, habitual male juvenile offenders in Philadelphia who were committed to a state training school.

The sample subjects were male delinquents committed to the Bensalem Youth Development Center (YDC) by Philadelphia Family Court. Only juveniles committed to this institution were eligible for the intensive aftercare program. To be eligible for admission to the program, juveniles at the YDC must have had at least one prior adjudication for aggravated assault, rape, involuntary deviate sexual intercourse, arson, robbery, or a felony-level narcotics offense, or at least two prior adjudications for burglary.

The Experimental Group
(Intensive Aftercare Probation)

Guidelines for the Intensive Aftercare Probation (IAP) program specify that IAP officers are restricted to a caseload of no more than 12 offenders, in contrast to the "regular" aftercare caseload for

Philadelphia County of 70 to 100 cases. IAP officers are expected to assume supervision of probationers immediately after disposition, at entry to placement. While the juvenile is in placement, the IAP officer is required to make monthly visits to the juvenile, to appropriate program staff members at the YDC, and to the parents or guardians. During this time the IAP officer is expected to work with the juvenile and his family to initiate and implement aftercare planning.

The frequency of the IAP officer's contacts with the juvenile and with significant others increases significantly after the juvenile is released from placement. For the first six weeks, guidelines require that the IAP officer make at least three face-to-face contacts per week with the juvenile. Satisfactory adjustment may result in a reduction to two face-to-face contacts per week after six weeks and to one per week after 12 weeks.

In addition to contacts with the juvenile, the IAP officer must maintain face-to-face or phone contact with the juvenile's parents or guardians at least once a week throughout the course of supervision. One collateral contact with school authorities, employer, or other significant others must be made at least once every other week throughout the course of supervision (phone contacts are permitted). IAP officers must make at least 30 percent of their contacts with their juveniles on postplacement supervision "outside normal probation office hours" (i.e., in evenings and on weekends).

Other than the above standards, probation officers received few guidelines with respect to the philosophy or mission of the program. The program was not defined, for example, as emphasizing a social control or rehabilitative perspective. No effort was made to articulate whether the emphasis of the program would be on enhancing family ties and prosocial relationships, on facilitating educational or vocational growth, on increasing probationers' perceptions of accountability through surveillance, or on some other combination of principles assumed to reduce criminality. Rather, the designers of the IAP guidelines provided probation officers with the specific behavioral objectives listed above, which they were expected to meet in the course of supervising their specified number of probationers. Our interviews with the IAP officers revealed that in fact they provided a number of traditional casework services, which are detailed below.

A strong emphasis was placed on developing educational and/or vocational plans for youths. Most of the juveniles returned to the community with firm plans to attend school (high school, technical school, or college) and with a job (Sontheimer, Goodstein, and Kovacevic 1990:78–79). Officers provided or arranged for counseling services and generally functioned as advocates for their clients. Officers also were urged to develop relationships with their clients' families to facilitate crisis intervention when necessary.

The IAP program did not feature any electronic monitoring or regular drug testing of clients. A few juveniles were screened for drugs on the basis of firm suspicion of use, but regular testing as a condition of probation was rare. On balance, the program may be characterized as having a strong treatment orientation as well as a surveillance function, inherent in the rather stringent reporting (contact) requirements.

The Control Group (Traditional Aftercare Probation)

In Philadelphia Family Court, all juvenile probation services are provided from one central downtown location. Probation services are delivered from one of more than a dozen units, each with its own supervisor. Eight of the units are geographically oriented; clients receiving in-home services such as probation supervision generally are assigned to units according to their place of residence. Other units provide specialized services such as intensive probation supervision and house arrest for pretrial cases. Delinquents committed to residential placement traditionally are supervised from one centralized aftercare unit. During the time of the study, this unit was burdened with very high caseloads (70 to 100 cases per officer). Current and former officers from the unit report that much of their time was devoted to completing necessary paperwork; each juvenile typically appeared in Family Court at least four times during a routine nine- to 12-month commitment, and each appearance required a written report.

According to the guidelines of the aftercare unit at the time of the study, institutionalized clients were to be seen monthly. The unit employed 20 officers, and caseloads were structured so that many officers were responsible for clients at only one or two facilities. Thus they could meet the monthly contact standard for institutionalized clients by making only one or two trips per week. Once clients were returned to the community under aftercare supervision, it was expected that they would be seen twice a month by the aftercare probation officer, the same standard that applied to clients on routine probation. In practice, this guideline was much harder to meet than the monthly contact requirement for committed cases because juveniles in the community were spread out over a wide area.

Services were provided to clients on traditional aftercare

supervision at the discretion of each officer. In view of their large caseloads and paperwork burden, one would not expect them to have much opportunity to provide individualized attention to their clients. In fact, our data show that half of the control group cases had no reported face-to-face contacts with their probation officers during the first six months after institutional release. Nonetheless, control group probation officers reported that about half of their clients returned to the community from the YDC with plans for work and/or school in place.

Research Questions

This study aims to determine whether juveniles on intensive aftercare probation experience fewer subsequent arrests, adjudications, and placements than their counterparts who have not been exposed to these enhanced services. We consider how the social casework and surveillance components of the enhanced probation supervision may affect both the incidence and the prevalence of reoffending. Our analysis considers two issues: 1) Whether the IAP program was implemented successfully and 2) whether it affected recidivism. We measure implementation in terms of compliance with the stated behavioral guidelines discussed above. We measure recidivism in terms of the incidence and prevalence of reoffending. Arrests are the primary indicator of recidivism, although convictions, incarcerations, and probation violations also are reported. We examine rearrests for any criminal offense and for felonies only.

Research Design and Methodology

Sample Selection

The evaluation study used a classic experimental research design: subjects who met the criteria for program eligibility were assigned randomly to either the experimental or the control condition. We set a target goal of 60 experimental and 60 control cases. Because the IAP staff consisted of five probation officers with a maximum caseload of 12 clients each, 60 cases were needed to fill the available IAP program slots and 60 to form the control group.

Service delivery for the IAP began in January 1989; case selection began in October 1988. During October 1988 we reviewed the files of the approximately 150 youths at the Youth Development Center and identified 106 who met the offense criteria for eligibility. Half of these individuals (N = 53) then were assigned randomly to the experimental group (IAP supervision) and half (N = 53) to the control group. The control group cases were supervised by the court's existing aftercare unit, which employs a supervisor, two assistant supervisors, and about 20 line probation officers. Once we had divided the eligible YDC residents randomly into two groups, the two unit supervisors were free to assign a case to any probation officer in their respective unit.

We considered an additional 52 cases for inclusion in the program and the study during the first few months of program operation, both as replacements for cases from the original group who had to be dropped and to increase the size of each group to the 60-person target. Accordingly we screened the records of Philadelphia delinquents committed to the YDC from November 1988 through May 1989. Juveniles who met the IAP offense criteria for eligibility were identified by us as "replacement cases" and then were assigned randomly to the experimental or the control group.

It was necessary to replace 42 of the originally selected 106 subjects for a number of reasons. One major cause of attrition (n = 11) was absconding, either from the institution or as a result of failure to return to the institution after a furlough. We dropped these cases whether they had been assigned to the experimental or the control group. The second major cause (n = 20) was early release; a number of subjects were released from placement before the IAP unit was operational. These juveniles did not receive any prerelease probation services while in placement or any intensive aftercare services in their community for substantial periods after release. Thus, to maintain comparability between experimental and control cases with respect to follow-up periods, we also dropped the youths released early from the control group. The remaining cases lost either were assigned mistakenly to another probation unit instead of IAP (n = 5), were released too late to be tracked for the study (n = 3), or were dropped for other reasons (n = 3; one juvenile was transferred to adult jail on a prior detainer, one was released to live out of state and thus could not be tracked, and one juvenile's court records could not be found).

After allowing for sample attrition for all reasons, this study is based on the results of 44 experimental and 46 control cases. All cases included in the study were released from the YDC between December 1988 and January 1990, and were tracked until May 1990; as a result, follow-up periods ranged from three to 16 months. Although the extent of sample mortality is cause for concern, case attrition was comparable for the two groups, and the randomization process was maintained for the replacement cases.[2] The most serious consequence of the sample attrition is the loss of statistical power. Our design called for 60 subjects per group, the maximum number of clients that could be served by the IAP unit. The final sample, however, provides only about 45 subjects per group.

Data Collection

Complete details of the data collection process and the research instruments are provided in the full report of the study findings (Sontheimer et al. 1990); only the highlights are presented here. We consulted Family Court and institutional case files for each youth in the study to obtain information concerning his criminal, educational, social, and institutional background. We obtained information on the arrest leading to the current placement, on up to 15 additional prior arrests, and on all prior institutional placements. We also obtained additional data on the youth's social history and adjustment to placement, and report them by means of indexes that we constructed. These indexes are described in the full report (Sontheimer et al. 1990).

We tracked subjects' subsequent involvement in both the juvenile and the criminal justice systems. (In this article, the two types of recidivism are aggregated.) We used several sources to detect juvenile and adult recidivism. The first was the Philadelphia Family Court computerized record system, which contains information on all hearings in Family Court involving new arrests or probation violations. Although this source revealed any new arrests, dispositional information often was unavailable because many cases involving arrests in early 1990 were still pending when data collection ceased. A second source for checking juvenile recidivism was the statewide data base of all juvenile court dispositions, maintained by the Pennsylvania Juvenile Court Judges' Commission. Although only the 1989 cases were then available, this source revealed rearrests that occurred outside Philadelphia County.

We also consulted two sources to detect rearrests in the adult (criminal) court system. First, to trace possible rearrests throughout Pennsylvania, we checked names of all subjects against the Pennsylvania State Police Automated Master Name Index data base. This source contains arrest information received from all police jurisdictions statewide. The second source was the Philadelphia Municipal Court computerized record system, which contains information on all disposed and active adult arrests in Philadelphia County. Both sources of adult recidivism, however, often lacked dispositional information. For this and other reasons discussed below, arrests are considered the primary indicator of recidivism in this paper.

Recidivism has been defined variously as rearrest, reconviction, or reincarceration. These distinctions are important from a policy standpoint. Some arrests eventually result in dismissals or acquittals, which may indicate that the subject did not in fact commit a crime. Sometimes, however, dismissals result from administrative decisions (as part of a plea bargain involving other arrests, for example), so that lack of culpability cannot be inferred reliably. One also could argue that reincarcerations are the most valid indicator of program "failure" because in this study the subjects are serious delinquents, all of whom were incarcerated previously; some "relapse" into the delinquent lifestyle (as measured by arrests) is almost inevitable (Murray and Cox 1979). In addition, reincarcerations impose a high financial cost on the juvenile and criminal justice systems.

In our case, only rearrest data give an unbiased picture of recidivism because dispositional information is missing in a large proportion of known rearrests. The preponderance of missing dispositional data is partly a result of the relative shortness of follow-up periods in this study (about 11 months on average).[3] The level of recidivism observed in any group of released offenders is partly a function of the follow-up period during which subjects are tracked. All things being equal, persons observed longer will have more opportunity to reoffend. In this study, the observation period is defined as the time from each subject's release date until the end of the data collection period in May 1990. Because subjects were released between December 1988 and January 1990, this period varies from about three months to about 17 months.

Although the observation period is important in the interpretation of the study results, it is equally important to control for "street time" (Barton and Butts 1990; Sontheimer 1990). Street time is the length of time a subject was actually at large in the community. This period may be less than the overall observation period if the subject was reincarcerated or if he left the state and therefore could not be tracked. We used the following decision rules to calculate each subject's follow-up period, controlling for street time. In the absence of any evidence indicating time "off the street," each subject's follow-up period or time at risk is defined as the time from his institutional release until May 4, 1990 (the end of the data collection period). For subjects who were permitted to relocate out of state after a period of probation supervision, the follow-up period ends on the reported date of relocation. For reincarcerated subjects, the period ends on the reported date of incarceration. In some cases, subjects were reincarcerated but then were released before May 4, 1990. This generally occurred when IAP subjects were sent back to the YDC for a technical violation of probation; such stays averaged about 90 days. For these subjects, time at risk is defined as the length of time from the *original* YDC release until May 4, 1990, minus the length of the subsequent incarceration.

Description of the Sample

Although the eligibility criteria do not explicitly restrict the program to habitual offenders, the great majority of delinquents assigned to IAP had extensive records of arrests for offenses that would have been considered violent felonies if committed by adults. Sample subjects had on average more than five prior arrests for misdemeanors and felonies combined.

Experimental and control groups do not differ significantly from each other on most factors that we considered. Table 1 contains a summary description of the sample, disaggregated into experimental and control groups. We found no differences between the two groups on the following items: race; age at placement; age at first arrest; number of prior arrests, convictions, and incarcerations; most serious prior offense; most serious committing offense; Drug and Alcohol Problem Index; Family Instability Index; Institutional Problem Index; length of institutional stay; and age at release from placement. Differences are observed in school problems and committing offense, but in view of all other comparisons in regard to prior record, social factors, and so on, we believe the two groups are quite comparable.

The majority of sample subjects (81.1%) are black; only 7.8 percent are white; the remaining 11.1 percent are of other races, primarily Hispanic. The average age at placement was 17.1 years. Before their offenses leading to the current YDC placement, sample subjects averaged 5.1 arrests (status offenses excluded), 2.7 convictions, and 1.2 placements. Only two subjects had no prior arrests; 10 had no prior convictions; 25 had no prior placements. The average age at first arrest was 13.8 years. More than 90 percent of the subjects had at least one prior arrest for a felony. Slight differences exist between groups in the distribution of committing offenses: experimental subjects were more likely to be committed for "other" offenses (e.g., escape, simple assault, probation violation), and more control subjects were committed for robbery.

The average scores for the experimental and the control groups on the School Problem Index are 9.2 and 8.6 respectively, a statistically significant difference ($t = 2.29$, df $= 87$, $p < .05$, two-tailed) showing that experimental subjects experience more school problems. A score of 9 (range of 6 to 12) indicates problems in at least three of the six areas (e.g., truancy, suspensions, failure)

Table 1. Profile of Sample (N=90)

	Experimental		Control	
	N	%	N	%
White	2	(4.5)	5	(10.9)
Black	36	(81.8)	37	(80.4)
Other	6	(13.6)	4	(8.7)
Total	44		46	

Most Serious Alleged Prior Offense[a]

	Experimental		Control	
	N	%	N	%
Serious Person[b]	5	(11.4)	8	(18.2)
Robbery	28	(63.6)	27	(61.4)
Burglary	5	(11.4)	7	(15.9)
Other	6	(13.6)	2	(4.5)
Total	44		44	

Most Serious Alleged Offense Leading to Placement

	Experimental		Control	
	N	%	N	%
Serious Person[c]	7	(15.9)	7	(15.2)
Robbery	6	(13.6)	10	(21.7)
Burglary	4	(9.1)	3	(6.5)
Drugs (felony)	9	(20.5)	9	(19.6)
Other	18	(40.9)	17	(37.0)
Total	44		46	

	Experimental		Control	
	mean	sd	mean	sd
Age at placement	17.2	1.0	17.0	1.1
Age at first arrest	13.8	1.4	13.8	1.8
Number of prior arrests	5.0	3.0	5.2	3.6
Number of prior convictions	3.0	2.3	2.5	2.2
Number of prior placements	1.2	1.1	1.1	0.8
School Problem Index[d]	9.2	1.2	8.6	1.4
D&A Problem Index[e]	5.5	2.0	4.9	1.6
Family Instability Index[f]	11.5	2.7	11.5	3.0
Institutional Problem Index[g]	4.5	1.2	4.3	0.9
Number of months at YDC	11.2	3.5	10.4	4.4
Age at release from YDC	18.1	1.1	17.9	1.1

[a] Two control subjects had no prior arrests.
[b] Includes rape, involuntary deviate sexual intercourse, and aggravated assault.
[c] Includes homicide, rape, involuntary deviate sexual intercourse, and aggravated assault.
[d] Range: 6-12. Based on six items: truancy, suspensions, disruptive behavior, lack of achievement, alternative program involvement, and grade failure. Group means different at $p < .03$, based on two-tailed t-test.
[e] Range: 3-9. Based on three items: drug use, alcohol use, and prior substance abuse treatment.
[f] Range: 8-20. Based on eight items: neglect, ineffective parental control, physical and/or sexual abuse, runaway, parental drug and/or alcohol use, and family criminality.
[g] Range: 3-7. Based on three items: rule infractions, escapes, and program participation.

composing the index. The average score on the Drug and Alcohol Problem Index for both groups was about 5 (range of 3 to 9), indicating at least some use of both drugs and alcohol, or significant use of one substance. The two groups had identical averages of 11.5 on the Family Instability Index (range of 8 to 20). Scores in this range indicate moderate problems in at least three or four areas of family functioning (e.g., lack of parental control, parental neglect or abuse, or parental substance abuse), or serious problems in fewer areas. According to the Institutional Problem Index, the majority of subjects did not encounter major problems in adjusting to placement. Scores of 4 or 5 (range of 3 to 7) indicate problems in no more than one of the three areas considered (rule infractions, escapes, and program participation).

Length of stay at the YDC varied widely, from two to 27 months. Stays shorter than six months were rare (six cases). The average length of incarceration was 10.8 months; a few very long periods of incarceration, however, skewed the distribution. The median length of stay (9.8 months) represents more accurately the typical duration of placement. About half of the subjects were age 18 or older at the time of their "YDC release.[4]

Results: Program Implementation

In this section we compare the number of youth and collateral contacts made by IAP and by regular probation officers. The data on contacts were provided by probation officers on questionnaires that we distributed bimonthly. Problems with missing data may have led to underestimates of the actual number of contacts delivered, because missing data were coded as "no contacts" for the months in question. We did attempt, when possible, to obtain the missing data directly from Family Court files of IAP subjects. As will be seen, however, the differences between the number of contacts made by IAP probation officers and by their control group counterparts are so great that they overshadow any problems with incomplete data. Nonetheless, the unexpectedly low level of experimental contacts (in relation to the prescribed level) leaves the implementation issue unresolved to this point.

The results discussed in this section are summarized in Table 2. On average, IAP probation officers made 10.1 face-to-face institutional contacts per youth, compared to 5.1 contacts per youth in the control group, over the youth's entire period of incarceration at the YDC. The level of telephone contacts between probation officers and incarcerated youths was twice as high in the experimental group as in the control group (1.3 and 0.6 contacts

Table 2. Average Number of Reported Contacts during YDC
Placement and First Six Postrelease Months

Type of Contact	Experimental (N=44)	Control (N=46)
During YDC Placement		
Face-to-face with youth	10.1	5.1
Face-to-face with family	2.6	0.7
Postrelease (aftercare)		
Face-to-face with youth		
Month 1	4.8	0.3
Month 2	3.9	0.2
Month 3	3.4	0.3
Month 4	1.9	0.2
Month 5	1.6	0.1
Month 6	0.9	0.2
Months 1 to 6 (total)	16.7	1.3
Months 1 to 6 (weekend)	1.7	0.1
Phone contacts with youth	3.5	0.7
All contacts with family	4.5	0.5
All contacts with others	3.5	0.4

Note: All differences between groups are significant at $p < .01$, based on one-tailed t-test with df=88.

respectively). IAP probation officers also made considerably more face-to-face and telephone contacts with youths' families during this period.

The data show that IAP probation officers made far more aftercare contacts than did control group officers—about 10 times as many. For example, when we totaled all face-to-face contacts with each client during the first six months after release, we found that the experimental group averaged 16.7 face-to-face contacts during this period, compared with only 1.3 contacts in the control group. These data, broken out for each of the first six months after release, are presented in Table 2, along with data on family and collateral contacts.

In the IAP group, face-to-face contacts were highest during the first postrelease month (4.8 contacts) and then declined steadily through Month 6, when probation officers made an average of 0.9 contacts. In the control group, contacts remained fairly stable at about 0.2 contacts per month. The latter figure is not surprising in light of typical control group caseloads of 70 to 100 clients per probation officer.

Telephone contacts between probation officers and their clients followed the same pattern as face-to-face sessions. Table 2 also summarizes information on aftercare contacts with clients' families and with other significant individuals (e.g., school personnel, employers, social service providers). For families and others, face-to-face and phone contacts are combined. Once again, the IAP officers made about 10 times as many contacts as did the regular aftercare probation officers.

The IAP standards direct that 30 percent of all aftercare contacts with juveniles be made during nontraditional hours, defined as weekends and evenings. For each of the first six postrelease months, approximately 10 percent of the contacts by IAP probation officers occurred on weekends. In the control group, the number of weekend contacts was virtually zero. No data are available on services provided during evening hours.

A careful review of the program guidelines concerning contacts and of the actual data on contacts displayed in Table 2 suggests that

IAP probation officers did not attain the mandated minimums for each of the first three postrelease months. The mandated minimum numbers of contacts for Months 1, 2, and 3 respectively were 12, 10, and 8; the actual numbers observed were only 5, 4, and 3. This apparent "dilution" of the experimental treatment raises serious questions about program implementation. Other sources of documentation, however, suggest that the actual number of contacts made or *attempted* was equal to the mandated minimums.[5] Later we show that these observations are consistent with our interpretation of the effects of the program.

In this section we have attempted to show that experimental youths (and their families) received far more attention from their probation officers than did control youths. During the institutional phase, IAP clients and their families saw their probation officers at least twice as often as did control group clients. IAP probation officers maintained regular contact with their clients and others (frequently on weekends) for at least the first three months after release. Control group clients and their families, by contrast, had only sporadic contact with their probation officers. We now examine the primary research question: does the provision of intensive aftercare service to high-risk habitual juvenile offenders reduce their subsequent recidivism?

Results: Recidivism

We report both binary and interval-level recidivism measures. According to the binary criterion, a subject is a success if no rearrests occurred and a failure if one or more rearrests were observed. We counted only arrests for misdemeanors or felonies;

we excluded status offenses and probation violations that did not involve new offenses. The binary criterion is a relatively insensitive measure because it does not distinguish between one-time and multiple offenders; nor does it differentiate between those arrested for minor and for serious offenses (Maltz 1984). This indicator, however, permits straightforward interpretation of the effect of the independent variable, which in this case is the type of probation supervision.

We hypothesized that the superior aftercare planning and the increased level of contact by the IAP probation officers would cause more experimental than control subjects to refrain altogether from reoffending. We call this the aftercare effect without specifying whether the improvement is attributable to specific deterrence or to genuine changes in the juvenile's lifestyle and/or values.

The interval-level criterion that we employ is the number of arrests observed after release from an institution. This criterion differentiates between single and multiple offenders, and therefore may be regarded as a clearer indicator of the propensity to reoffend. The interpretation of this indicator, however, is complicated by what we term "system response effects." For example, if offenders from the experimental group are "taken off the street" quickly in response to an initial rearrest while offenders from the control group are allowed to remain in the community, the most criminalistic experimental subjects will be incapacitated while their criminalistic counterparts in the control group will be free to reoffend again. In fact, we observed this pattern in the current study. Our analyses based on the interval-level measure therefore control for street time.

Percentage of Subjects Rearrested

We begin by examining the percentage of subjects rearrested in each group; this is the simple binary criterion for recidivism. Subjects with no observed rearrests are classified as successes; those with any known rearrests, as failures. The results are presented in Table 3.

When all criminal arrests are considered, the percentage of rearrestees is significantly lower for the experimental group. The types of offenses for which subjects were rearrested were fairly similar between groups, although experimentals were more likely to be arrested for drug charges (primarily misdemeanors) and controls were more likely to be arrested for theft. The pattern is the same when only felony arrests are considered, but the difference between groups is statistically insignificant.

Despite this evidence in favor of the experimental treatment, the

Table 3. **Percentage of Subjects Rearrested over Entire Observation Period**

	Experimental (N=44)	Control (N=46)	X^2 (p)
Misdemeanor or Felony Arrest	50% (22)	74% (34)	4.50 (.04)
Felony Arrest	25% (11)	41% (19)	2.01 (ns)

Note: Significance tests are based on chi-square with df=1, using Yates correction for 2 x 2 table.

interpretation of these results is complicated by the fact that average observation times were not equivalent between the experimental and the control groups. The experimental group averaged 9.9 months of follow-up as compared to 11.7 months for the control group, a significant difference ($t = -2.06$, df = 88, $p < .05$, two-tailed). Because of the unequal follow-up times, the significant difference in favor of the experimental group, apparent in Table 3, cannot be interpreted unambiguously as evidence that the Intensive Aftercare Program is "working."

One way to control for differing follow-up times is to designate a shorter observation period for which data are available on all cases (Maltz 1984). For example, we tracked all 90 cases in the final sample for at least three months. This period therefore provides an unbiased comparison of the percentage of subjects rearrested. When follow-up periods longer than three months are employed, one method of controlling for unequal observation periods is to drop cases not followed for the entire period. Table 4 compares the experimental and the control groups on the recidivism criterion "percentage of subjects rearrested" over three different periods: after three, six, and nine postrelease months. For each comparison, only cases observed for the entire period in question are included.

Experimental subjects manifested less recidivism than control subjects at each point surveyed, although the differences are not statistically significant. The figures based on the first three postrelease months are of particular interest because that is the period during which probation officers are to provide the most contacts to the experimental cases. Because the entire sample was tracked for three months, this comparison maximizes our statistical power by including all cases (as opposed to the comparisons based on six and nine months). Although the intergroup difference is strongest for this period, the results are not statistically significant.

The results for six and nine months should be interpreted with caution for several reasons. Not only are the sample sizes smaller;

Table 4. **Percentage of Subjects Rearrested for Misdemeanor or Felony within Three, Six and Nine Months after Release**

Follow-Up Period	Experimental	Control	X^2 (p)
3 months			
% rearrested	21%	35%	1.64 (ns)
(n) rearrested	(9)	(16)	
[n] at risk	[44]	[46]	
6 months			
% rearrested	42%	51%	0.36 (ns)
(n) rearrested	(15)	(20)	
[n] at risk	[36]	[39]	
9 months			
% rearrested	50%	64%	0.66 (ns)
(n) rearrested	(14)	(21)	
[n] at risk	[28]	[33]	

Note: Percent rearrested is based on percentage of clients at risk during each period. Significance tests are based on chi-square with df=1, using Yates correction for 2 x 2 table.

in addition, the cohorts of youths tracked for longer periods differ qualitatively. That is, juveniles who were reincarcerated soon after release "drop out" of the sample because they were not on the street during the latter months of our observation period. Also, the rather rapid escalation in the percentage arrested from the three-month to the nine-month mark raises the possibility that a substantial majority of each group would have failed if the follow-up period had been longer.

Frequency of Rearrests

Next we consider the average number of rearrests as the criterion for recidivism. The definition of the follow-up period in these analyses is different from that used in the previous section. Previously we referred to the overall "observation period" for each subject; now we refer to each subject's "time at risk" (street time), which takes into account known periods of reincarceration or out-of-state residence.

The decision rules for calculating time at risk were discussed earlier. By definition, average time at risk is less than the average observation period. For this sample the average time at risk is 9.2 months for the experimental group and 10.3 months for the control group, a small and statistically insignificant difference ($t = -1.16$, df = 88, ns). Comparisons based on total time at risk therefore should be unbiased; we begin this stage of the analysis by comparing the groups' frequency or incidence of recidivism based on all known rearrests. For each group, the total number of rearrests observed is divided by the number of subjects in the group. The results are presented in the first row of Table 5. The control group accrued more than twice as many arrests as the experimental group, a statistically significant difference.

One could argue that the results based on the entire follow-up period are not reliable, even though the *aggregate* observation periods for each group are equal. Therefore we calculated each *individual* subject's "annualized rearrest rate" by dividing his total number of new arrests by his time on the street (time at risk), in years. As shown in the second row of Table 5, the experimental group again manifested a significantly lower level of recidivism, based on the mean number of annualized arrests. The results also favor the experimental group when recidivism is defined in terms of felony arrests only.[6]

The results based on the frequency of rearrest are much more robust than those based on the percentage of subjects rearrested. The issues of small sample size and short follow-up period are less problematic here because we control for time at large in both aggregate and case-specific fashion. On the basis of our entire sample of 90 subjects, the differences favor the experimental group by a large margin for all rearrests, felony rearrests, and annualized rearrests.

Probation Officers' Responses to Relapse by Clients

As shown in Table 5, we found a striking difference in the volume of rearrests between the experimental and the control groups. Because the two groups were more similar on the "percentage of subjects rearrested" criterion, we suspected that the larger

Table 5. Frequency of Rearrests over Entire Time at Risk

	Experimental (N=44)	Control (N=46)	t	(p)
Mean Number of Rearrests	1.02	2.07	−2.66	(.01)
Mean Number of Annualized Rearrests	1.65	2.79	−1.92	(.03)
Mean Number of Felony Rearrests	0.41	0.76	−1.65	(.05)
Mean Number of Annualized Felony Rearrests	0.78	0.97	−0.53	(ns)

Note: Significance tests are based on one-tailed t-test with df=88.

difference in the total volume of rearrests was due in part to differential responses to initial signs of relapse. Specifically, this difference was consistent with our hypothesis that IAP clients who committed new crimes or violated probation would face swift and meaningful sanctions, whereas control group recidivists would not. The court actively informed IAP probation officers and their clients that sanctions would be imposed for new convictions and/or probation violations. Several observations show that the system responded differently to undesirable behavior in the experimental and the control groups.

Among those (n = 23) youths who were *rearrested and recommitted*, we note considerable disparities between experimentals and controls in the average "system response time" from first arrest to recommitment. For subjects rearrested and sentenced to incarceration as either juveniles or adults, the average amount of time spent on the street after the first arrest but before recommitment was about two months for experimentals, compared to about six months for controls. When we consider that control youths received minimal levels of probation supervision in the community, these additional four months on the street may have provided control youths with added opportunities to engage in criminal behavior. We also observed that some control group subjects accumulated substantial rearrest records during the period from the first rearrest to eventual reincarceration, including one control case with eight (8) rearrests.

Experimental and control group probation officers also manifested different types of system responses to probation violations. For example, five experimental cases were returned to the YDC as juvenile probation violators, even though no new crimes had been committed; no control cases were recommitted in the absence of a new arrest. This proactive approach by the IAP officers also was evident in their responses to those of their cases who were arrested as adults. IAP officers revoked the juvenile probation of six experimental youths after their arrest as adults, using the probation violation to remove them quickly from the community rather than waiting for possible court sentencing. Control officers apparently preferred to let the criminal courts respond to arrests of older youths on their caseload: probation violation procedures were never initiated after their clients' arrest as adults.

Recidivism Based on Conviction and Incarceration

The quick response of IAP officers to cases that were manifesting difficulties appeared to reduce the comparative frequency of their reoffending. Moreover, such a response ultimately may have been related to the youths' receiving less severe sentences when eventually they were seen before the court: proportionately fewer IAP youths who were prosecuted for either juvenile or adult arrests were convicted or sentenced to confinement. This outcome may be the result of more immediate intervention by the IAP officers, which kept to a minimum the extent and perhaps even the severity of reoffending among IAP youths.

Recidivism criteria based on convictions or incarcerations are related, by definition, to "system response effects." Whether a given arrest results in conviction or in incarceration depends on many discretionary factors, not simply on the offender's culpability. The fact remains, however, that the two groups differed widely on new convictions and incarcerations—differences several times as great as the intergroup differences on new arrests. For example, only 11 percent of the IAP subjects were reconvicted for a new offense, as compared with 37 percent of the control subjects. Moreover, although control subjects accounted for twice as many new arrests as experimentals, they accounted for about six times as many new convictions and sentences to incarceration.[7] In other words, about 14 percent of all new arrests for experimentals led to convictions, whereas more than 40 percent of new arrests for controls resulted in conviction. In terms of the overall benefits of the IAP program, the far lower conviction and incarceration rates of the experimental group are very impressive. In view of the high cost of incarceration, these differences in favor of the experimental group represent considerable savings to the county and the state.

Discussion

The Intensive Aftercare Probation program implemented by the Philadelphia Juvenile Probation Department has been shown to be effective in reducing the frequency, although not the incidence, of criminal behavior in a group of high-risk serious juvenile offenders during the period immediately following institutional release. After release from institutional placement, juveniles who were supervised by an IAP officer committed fewer offenses, on average, than a control group that was supervised under the model of "regular" aftercare probation, involving large caseloads and minimal intervention.

On the other hand, the results of the study prevent us from concluding unequivocally that intensive aftercare reduces the likelihood that supervised youths will engage in their first instance of criminal behavior. Although we found consistent patterns showing proportionately lower rates of recidivism among experimental than among control subjects, these patterns were not statistically significant when the observation periods for each group were held constant. Thus we cannot conclude that intensive aftercare, as operationalized in the Philadelphia programs turns youths away from their propensity to crime. Rather, it appears that the program succeeds in providing IAP officers with the resources, guidelines, attractive backing, and motivation to intervene rapidly, when appropriate, to prevent youths who are failing to make successful adjustments to community life from incurring multiple rearrests. Officers report using a graduated response to clients' adjustment problems, when possible; their options included imposition of consequences such as early curfew or house arrest, in camera or formal hearings in front of the committing judge, and short recommitments to the YDC (Goodstein and Sontheimer 1991).

Findings Concerning the Aftercare and System Response Effects

The Intensive Aftercare Probation program was intended to create both aftercare and system response effects. The aftercare effects theoretically would encompass both rehabilitation and special deterrence. With drastically reduced caseloads, IAP probation officers were expected to have time to work with the juveniles, their families, and representatives of employment, counseling, treatment, and educational organizations to ensure that the youths were participating successfully in prosocial experiences. In interviews, IAP officers told us that their reduced caseloads allowed them to serve as advocates for their youths, much like parents in more affluent families when their children encounter difficulties. Officers expressed pleasure that they had time to "shop" for appropriate agencies for each youth and to follow through with agencies providing services to their youths, finding out how each youth was performing, confirming the appropriateness of the program, or making changes in the services when necessary. In many cases they reported success in establishing a relationship with the juvenile, which enabled them to help him with difficulties.

As stated in our description of the study sample, these youths have histories of severe social dysfunction, including high incidences of drug and alcohol use, family disorganization, and school-related problems. In light of their histories, it was reasonable to expect that IAP juveniles might encounter serious adjustment problems upon reentering the community. The rehabilitative value of the IAP program comes from the additional attention that officers can give to youths when difficulties arise, and from the potential to avert more serious difficulties when first signs of "relapse" occur.

Ideally an Intensive Aftercare Probation program would create measurable, noticeable behavioral change in participating probationers, including reductions in their propensity to return to criminal behavior after a period of incarceration. Although we found consistent patterns reflecting higher rates of recidivism among control cases over time, the differences between experimental and control groups remained relatively small and in some cases were based on less than the full sample. Moreover, it is likely that the differences would have been even smaller if the IAP officers had not stepped in to initiate probation revocation proceedings for several experimental juveniles showing signs of relapse. In this regard, the percentage of youths rearrested perhaps primarily indicates the aftercare effect but reflects system response as well.

One could even argue that the differences in the frequency of rearrests which we observed between groups—what we term a "system response effect"—are the result of a "program effect." That is, IAP officers may have decided to revoke probation or to incarcerate reconvicted clients simply to make the IAP program "look good" rather than basing these decisions on risk control and community protection. Our interpretation is that the two types of effects are essentially indistinguishable here. Removing noncooperative clients from the street was consistent with the mission of the program as defined by the judge in charge of the IAP.

Our results are consistent with other research which found that increased levels of contact alone are not associated with reductions in the propensity to reoffend (Barton and Butts 1990; NCCD 1987; Wiebush 1991). As in previous studies, it appears that the IAP treatment of three contacts per week for 12 to 24 weeks, plus some collateral contacts, is simply not powerful enough to make significant changes in youths' criminal proclivities. The failure to demonstrate significant differences on arrest rates between experimentals and controls is consistent with most studies of other interventions targeted at the habitual or serious delinquent (Fagan 1990).

The findings of our study are important in that they demonstrate the effectiveness of an innovative probation program in significantly reducing the frequency of recidivism in perhaps the most difficult group of juveniles to treat: serious, habitual, violent offenders. The study results show that participants in the Intensive Aftercare Probation program committed about half as many offenses as did comparable youths receiving regular aftercare services. This effect appears to be the result of IAP officers' willingness to be a proactive in dealing with juveniles who demonstrated signs of failure to conform to conditions of probation. The norms of the IAP required that youths manifesting signs of adjustment difficulties be threatened with, and ultimately faced with, return to institutional placement. This policy was evident in the violations of probation by six IAP youths who had not committed new offenses, as well as in the probation violations that soon followed youths' first rearrests, either as juveniles or as adults.

Probation violations effectively removed poorly adjusting youths from the community and prevented them from repeating their patterns of criminality. For the control group, the time during which such repetition might occur was sometimes an extended period between arrest and adjudication. Clearly, this strategy worked; no experimental youth whose probation was revoked during the follow-up period committed more than one offense. In contrast, control youths, who were not subject to probation violation, committed twice as many offenses per capita. This difference is unequivocally a benefit from a public safety perspective. The rapid response of the IAP officers, however, was part of a selective rather than a blanket policy. Not every juvenile rearrest resulted in reincarceration; nor did every adult rearrest result in a juvenile probation violation. Rather, the IAP probation officers' increased awareness of probationers' activities—as indicated by the relatively large number of contacts—apparently enabled them to make informed, individual decisions regarding the juveniles' ability to remain in the community. Moreover, the court knew that IAP officers who recommended continued probation for marginally adjusting clients were able to closely monitor the juveniles' behavior. Control officers could not reasonably make these individual decisions because their large caseloads precluded such close monitoring. In other words, IAP officers were able to practice a form of "risk control" with their probationers (Clear 1991).

These observations provide clues to help us explicate the recidivism results reported earlier. If the court's first response to relapse does not halt the youth's inappropriate behavior, or if the behavior is serious, it appears that IAP officers respond by taking actions which will remove the youths from the community. Apparently such behavior sometimes occurs during the "relapse phase," before the youth actually commits new offenses (or at least is caught), through the process of probation violation. New juvenile or adult arrests, of course, are a clear indication that some relapse has occurred; it appears that IAP officers were proactive in removing these cases from the streets as well. Revoking the juvenile probation of a client arrested as an adult for a serious offense was viewed as a legitimate means of removing him from the community quickly, before any further arrests occurred. This strategy sometimes was used when clients arrested as adults were released on bail and thus were expected to remain at large for several months, awaiting trial.

Implications of the Study

One possible inference from the study's results is that the Philadelphia Juvenile Probation Department should institute a policy of revoking probations of all serious, chronic juvenile offenders immediately after the first arrest following release. After all, if the success of the program appears to be due to the swift response of IAP officers to offenders' recidivism, perhaps the most cost-effective intervention might be to do away with the extensive service delivery component of IAP, to maintain probation officers' caseloads of 70 to 100, and to direct the funds saved on the IAP program to cover increased incarceration costs incurred by higher levels of probation revocations.

We do not support this interpretation. We suspect that the effectiveness of the IAP program in reducing the number of offenses committed by the experimental group reflects two factors specific to this program: 1) the increased knowledge of each case provided to IAP officers and 2) the IAP officers' ability to devote considerable attention to each case, especially the more problematic ones. Our interviews with the IAP officers support this interpretation (Goodstein and Sontheimer 1991). First, the officers believe that the knowledge they gained from their frequent contact with youths and their families enabled them to make sound individual assessments of their clients' situations. Officers were able to recommend that some youths who were experiencing adjustment difficulties (or even rearrest) could remain in the community under IAP supervision. In other cases, IAP officers were in a position to recommend that even without a new arrest, serious signs of probation violation behavior justified removal of youths from the community.

The second factor which contributed to the success of IAP and which would be inconsistent with a generalized mandatory revocation policy is the IAP officers' ability to give considerable attention to each case. When faced with uncooperative clients, IAP officers devoted considerable time to maintaining contact with the youths. Even in cases where youths failed to appear for scheduled contacts, the IAP officers located them and ensured that they could be taken into custody, if necessary, for probation revocation. The process of tracking uncooperative youths, who may believe that they can elude revocation if they simply lie low, is often time- and energy-consuming. The IAP officers' ability to remove some experimental youths from the community depended on their freedom to spend considerable time on tracking each case. Officers with significantly larger caseloads would not be able to prevent some uncooperative youths who deserved to have their probations revoked from "slipping through the cracks."

The success of the IAP probation officers in reducing the number of offenses committed by their clients can be attributed to the officers' ability to decide which youths required removal from the community and to their swiftness and effectiveness in the removal process. Many practices of the IAP officers could not be emulated by officers in conventional aftercare situations with significantly larger caseloads. The results of this study, however, make it clear that public safety is enhanced by quick, selective responses to repeated criminal behavior in this high-risk group of juvenile offenders.

Notes

[1] This distinction has implications for evaluation of this model. If recidivism is measured only during the supervision period, as is frequently the case in evaluation studies, it would not be possible to determine which of the two processes of the aftercare effect was operating.

[2] As a further check on the effect of sample attrition, we tracked all juveniles in the original sample of 108 subjects, including those who were dropped. Our primary findings, as detailed later, held both for the original sample of 108 subjects and for the final sample of 90 subjects, which is the focus of this article.

[3] Although some subjects were tracked for only three months after release, the average period of time at risk (street time) is considered adequate to detect reoffending in this high-risk population. The 9.8-month average time at risk here is comparable to that for the incarceration control group in Barton and Butts's (1990) experimental test of intensive probation (10.7 months at large).

[4] Any new arrests incurred by these subjects would necessarily fall under the jurisdiction of the adult (criminal) court system. Many other subjects who were under 18 at the time of release turned 18 before the end of the study. Therefore it is not surprising that most of the observed recidivism was based on new arrests handled by the criminal, rather than the juvenile, justice system.

[5] In a program compliance audit conducted by the Juvenile Court Judges' Commission during August 1989, aftercare contacts met program guidelines if contacts attempted but not completed (e.g., because probationer was not at home) were also counted. The IAP program supervisor also reported that he carefully monitored the number of contacts made or attempted; his records showed substantial compliance with the mandated minimums for each month when attempted contacts were included. In addition, the number of contacts made with the experimental group, as reported in Table 2, would be higher (by about one contact per month) if a two-month period of very low contact rates were deleted. During this period the six-person IAP unit experienced 100 percent turnover; not surprisingly, many caseloads were left without a probation officer of record for extended periods.

[6] Felony arrests, based on the most serious alleged charge, involve murder, rape, robbery, aggravated assault, burglary, and felony-level drug offenses.

[7] Convictions and incarcerations reported here reflect only dispositions that were known to us when data collection ended. Because many rearrests had not yet reached the disposition stage, the reported number of convictions and incarcerations probably understates the actual levels.

References

Altschuler, D. and T. L. Armstrong (1991) "Intensive Aftercare for the High-Risk Juvenile Parolee: Issues and Approaches in Reintegration and Community Supervision." In T. L. Armstrong (ed.), *Intensive Interventions with High-Risk Youths: Promising Approaches in Juvenile Probation and Parole*, pp. 45–84. Monsey, NY: Criminal Justice Press.

Andrews, D. A., I. Zinger, R. D. Hoge, J. Bonta, P. Gendreau, and F. T. Cullen (1990) "Does Correctional Treatment Work? A Clinically Relevant and Psychologically Informed Meta-Analysis." *Criminology* 28(3):369–104.

Armstrong, T. L., ed. (1991) *Intensive Interventions with High-Risk Youths: Promising Approaches in Juvenile Probation and Parole*. Monsey, NY: Criminal Justice Press.

Barton, W. H. and J. A. Butts (1990) "Viable Options: Intensive Supervision Programs for Juvenile Delinquents." *Crime and Delinquency* 36(2):238–51.

Clear, T. R. (1991) "Juvenile Intensive Probation Supervision: Theory and Rationale." In T. L. Armstrong (ed.), *Intensive Interventions with High-Risk Youths: Promising Approaches in Juvenile Probation and Parole*, pp. 29–44. Monsey, NY: Criminal Justice Press.

Clear, T. R., S. Flynn, and C. Shapiro (1987) "Intensive Supervision in Probation: A Comparison of Three Projects." In B. McCarthy (ed.), *Intermediate Punishments: Intensive Supervision, Home Confinement and Electronic Surveillance*, pp. 31–50. Monsey, NY: Criminal Justice Press.

Erwin, B. (1990) "Old and New Tools for the Modern Probation Officer." *Crime and Delinquency* 36(1):61–74.

Erwin, B. and L. A. Bennett (1987) *New Dimensions in Probation: Georgia's Experience with Intensive Probation Supervision (IPS)*. Washington, DC: U.S. Department of Justice.

Fagan, J. (1990) "Treatment and Reintegration of Violent Juvenile Offenders: Experimental Results." *Justice Quarterly* 7(2):223–63.

Gendreau, P. and R. R. Ross (1987) "Revivification of Rehabilitation: Evidence from the 1980s." *Justice Quarterly* 4(3):349–407.

Goodstein, L. and H. Sontheimer (1987) *A Study of the Impact of Ten Pennsylvania Residential Placements on Juvenile Recidivism*. Harrisburg: Pennsylvania Juvenile Court Judges' Commission.

———— (1991) "The Implementation of an Intensive Aftercare Program for Serious Juvenile Offenders: A Case Study." Paper presented at the annual meetings of the American Society of Criminology, San Francisco.

Greenwood, P. W. and F. E. Zimring (1985) *One More Chance: The Pursuit of Intervention Strategies for Chronic Juvenile Offenders*. Santa Monica: RAND.

Hirschi, T. (1969) *Causes of Delinquency*. Berkeley: University of California Press.

Maltz, M. D. (1984) Recidivism. Orlando: Academic Press.

Murray, C. A. and L. A. Cox Jr. (1979) *Beyond Probation: Juvenile Corrections and the Chronic Delinquent*. Beverly Hills: Sage.

National Council on Crime and Delinquency (NCCD) (1987) *The Impact of Juvenile Court Intervention*. San Francisco: NCCD.

Pearson, F. S. (1985) "New Jersey's Intensive Supervision Program: A Progress Report." *Crime and Delinquency* 31(3):393–410.

Pearson, F. S. and A. G. Harper (1990) "Contingent Intermediate Sentences: New Jersey's Intensive Supervision Program." *Crime and Delinquency* 36(1):75–86.

Petersilia, J. (1987) *Expanding Options for Criminal Sentencing*. Santa Monica: RAND.

Sontheimer, H. G. (1990) "The Suppression of Juvenile Recidivism: A Methodological Inquiry." Doctoral dissertation, The Pennsylvania State University.

Sontheimer, H., L. Goodstein, and M. Kovacevic (1990) *Philadelphia Intensive Aftercare Probation Evaluation Project*. Shippensburg, PA: Center for Juvenile Justice Training and Research.

Whitehead, J. T. and S. P. Lab (1989) "A Meta-Analysis of Juvenile Correctional Treatment." *Journal of Research in Crime and Delinquency* 26:276–96.

Wiebush, R. G. (1991) *Evaluation of the Lucas County Intensive Supervision Unit: Diversionary Impact and Youth Outcomes, Final Report*. Toledo: Lucas County Juvenile Court.

Section IV

Correctional Counseling and Crisis Intervention

Much of the effort of those involved in correctional treatment consists of attempts to discover those factors or occurrences that have some causal relationship to the offender's deviant behavior. Self-introspection helps the law violator uncover his or her motives and motivations and realize the types of reactions, urges, or views of life that have led to problem activity. The offender may also be led to be aware of or develop certain internal strengths, abilities, or qualities that can assist in his or her rehabilitation.

The treatment approach most often used in this form of correctional treatment is termed *casework counseling*. It involves a one-to-one contact between the client and the counselor. The counselor (a therapist, social worker, probation officer, parole officer, or youth worker) seeks to assist the client in becoming better adjusted to his or her current environment and also helps him or her prepare for the future. Hatcher describes correctional counseling as being concerned with the "application of validation techniques designed specifically for bringing about a predictable change in criminal and delinquent behavior."[1]

The specific goals of correctional casework may involve one or more of the following:

1. Increased insight into one's problems and behavior
2. Better delineation of one's self-identity
3. Resolution of handicapping or disabling conflicts

171

4. Changing undesirable habits or reaction patterns
5. Improved interpersonal relationships or other competencies
6. Modification of inaccurate assumptions about oneself and one's world
7. Opening a pathway to a more meaningful and fulfilling existence[2]

Correctional casework does not differ significantly in its goals from casework performed in any of the helping disciplines. The criminal or delinquent has many of the same problems as other individuals who seek counseling. These include facing responsibility, being able to make wise decisions, experiencing self-doubt or anxiety, and developing feelings of self-worth.

There are important differences between casework counseling in corrections and other types of counseling, however. The most profound is that correctional casework counseling *is not voluntarily sought*. The offender is not asked if he or she desires the counselor's advice and services, nor does he or she have a choice of caseworkers. This type of counseling, in which a client is required to accept counseling, is sometimes termed coercive counseling. The amenability of offenders assigned to such counseling may range on a spectrum from total rejection and refusal to cooperate to complete acceptance and cooperation. Also, the fact that the counseling is coercive increases the probability that the client will not be completely honest and open with the counselor but will try to say the kinds of things most likely to speed his or her release from the institution or from supervision. This makes it much more difficult to establish an open, honest relationship in correctional counseling than in other types of casework.

Nevertheless, the caseworker has certain advantages when counseling is coercive. He or she can require a client to enroll in an educational or job training program, submit to psychological testing, or become involved in an alcohol or drug rehabilitation program. Although the client may initially resent such direction, the positive outcomes that may result would not have been attained if the offender had been left to his or her own devices.

Although a correctional caseworker operates under general guidelines set by the courts or the institution (rules of probation or parole, institutional policies), the form of interaction between counselor and client may vary widely, and the counselor's own skills and creativity come into play in the choice of counseling style used with each client. In some instances, the counselor may involve the offender's family in the counseling process as a method of motivating the offender or helping the family change the environment that contributed to the offender's problems. In other cases, the counselor may uncover an area of interest that will open up new employment or educational opportunities for the client and help the client make a new start or turn from criminal associations.

In the tenth selection, "Stages of Counseling" written by Michael E. Cavanagh, it is noted that for counseling to be effective, a developmental process must be followed. The author lists and explains six stages of the helping process: information gathering, evaluation, feedback, the counseling agreement, changing behavior, and termination. These stages are applicable to all forms of counseling including crisis intervention. The veteran probation officer, correctional officer, or social worker who has the responsibility of providing counseling services to offenders may be thinking more in terms of getting the job done than following the developmental stages of the counseling process, but nevertheless to be effective, the various stages mentioned must be adhered to.

In his book *Multicultural Counseling*, John M. Dillard notes that the ethnic and cultural movements of the 1960s to '70s had an important effect on counseling programs because these movements drew attention to the fact that "Since ethnicity plays a valid role in any pluralistic society, skilled counseling professionals also need to be able to communicate effectively with clients of diverse cultural groups."[3] Communication is essential in any counseling situation and good communication between the counselor and the client may never be developed if intercultural barriers exist. Not being cognizant of value differences, engaging in ethnic group or racial group stereotyping, and being insensitive to the beliefs, customs, or styles of living of others can all lead to communication barriers which make any form of counseling impossible.

Selection eleven, "Recognizing and Utilizing Diversity in Counseling Approaches" by Dave Yonas and J. Neal Garland, provides some guidelines for correctional counselors who are working with clients of different ethnic origins. They note that not all individuals identify with their ethnic heritage to the same degree, and it is necessary for the counselor to be aware of the effect the heritage has on their daily lives.

A special form of counseling is that termed *crisis intervention.* Any offender who has been remanded to correctional treatment has already experienced a number of personal crises, including arrest, imprisonment, court hearings and trial, sentencing, and imprisonment or assignment to correctional supervision. However, it is not likely that the offender received crisis intervention counseling during these events, except for the assistance given by a lawyer. The special, intense counseling called "crisis intervention" is directed primarily at the crises that occur within the setting of correctional treatment. Such a need might arise when a prisoner is subjected to homosexual rape, learns that a loved one has died or is terminally ill, experiences anxiety attacks or other emotional problems as a result of imprisonment, becomes aware that his or her family is in dire financial straits or that his or her spouse is filing for divorce, experiences a drug-related episode, or attempts suicide or some other type of self-mutilation. The counseling given in such crises is necessarily more intense and of a different nature than counseling designed for long-term, less stressful interaction.

Zusman defined crisis intervention in the following way:

> Crisis intervention is one term that can be used to describe a whole series of recently introduced, brief treatment techniques employing a wide variety of personnel, service organizations, auspices, and formal labels. Crisis intervention includes, for example, suicide prevention services using telephone and in person interviews, teen-age counseling as offered through "hot line" and "drop-in centers," pastoral counseling, brief psychotherapy offered in emergency "walk-in clinics," family dispute intervention provided by specially trained policemen, window-to-window programs, and a host of similar programs.[4]

The premise that at the time of a crisis a client may be more open to positive suggestions and more strongly motivated to change his or her life than at other times is behind much of the current emphasis on crisis intervention.

Chester E. Sigafoos notes in article twelve, "Conflict Resolution: Primer for Correctional Workers," that conflict situations usually have common characteristics, and correctional workers can follow a general set of guidelines to resolve such situations. It is suggested that the correctional officers faced with a crisis situation should keep the "fight or flight" response in check, listen and assess the situation, summarize his or her initial positions, read between the lines, resolve the situation through compromise and cooperation, and implement the solution.

Notes

[1] Hayes A. Hatcher, *Correctional Casework and Counseling* (Englewood Cliffs, NJ: Prentice-Hall, 1978), 3.

[2] James C. Coleman, *Abnormal Psychology and Modern Life* (Glenview, IL: Scott, Foresman, 1964), 564.

[3] John M. Dillard, *Multicultural Counseling* (Chicago: Nelson-Hall, 1983), 3.

[4] Jack Zusman, "Secondary Prevention," in Alfred M. Freedman, Harold I. Kaplan, and Benjamin J. Sadock, eds., *Comprehensive Textbook of Psychiatry, Volume II* (Baltimore: Williams & Wilkins, 1975), 2335.

10

Stages of Counseling

Michael E. Cavanagh

Like any other developmental process, counseling follows a sequence. It is important for counselors to recognize a sequence so that they will have a framework within which to function and a means to evaluate where in the process they are. As in human development, these stages tend to be somewhat flexible and overlapping, and each stage must be passed through successfully if counseling is to be effective. There is more than one way to view the stages of helping. The format presented here best fits the philosophy of counseling reflected in this text.[1]

The helping process can be divided into six stages: (1) information gathering, (2) evaluation, (3) feedback, (4) the counseling agreement, (5) changing behavior, and (6) termination. Figure 1 reflects this process. It demonstrates an important concept—namely, that both the person seeking help and the counselor have two major choice points with regard to beginning the counseling relationship. The first point occurs when the person seeking help and the counselor initially meet. The person has made an uninformed decision to get help, and the counselor has made an uninformed decision to see the person; that is, the counselor does not know whether or not the person is a reasonable candidate for counseling.

The second choice point occurs after the first three stages, when both the person in counseling and the counselor have gained sufficient knowledge upon which to make an informed decision. The decision is whether to continue counseling or to seek an alternative that would be more appropriate and helpful.

Figure 1

Counseling stages.

Uninformed decision			Informed decision		
Stage 1	*Stage 2*	*Stage 3*	*Stage 4*	*Stage 5*	*Stage 6*
Information gathering	Evaluation	Feedback	Counseling agreement	Changing behavior	Termination

The six stages can be telescoped so that they fit both short-term and long-term counseling, just as basic surgical procedures are the same whether an operation lasts a half-hour or ten hours. Counseling meant to last only five or ten sessions would pass through each of the stages in an abbreviated manner. Long-term counseling could spend 5 sessions on the first three stages and 50 to 150 sessions on the last three. However, it is doubtful that any kind of counseling could be effective without spending at least some time in each stage. If a counselor skipped the information-gathering stage, there would be no foundation for counseling; if the evaluation stage is skipped, the counselor would not know what the person's problems are; if the feedback stage is eliminated, the person could not make an informed decision; if there is no counseling agreement, there would be no course to follow; if behaviors are not changed, there is no counseling; and if the termination stage is ignored, the person will be left with no sense of closure.

This does not imply that counseling does not actually begin until the fourth stage. Counseling begins the moment the counselor and the person in counseling meet. The first three stages can be therapeutic in themselves in that to progress through them, the person and counselor are relating on levels that deal with cognition, emotions, needs, values, and conflicts. As the counselor listens, probes, reflects, understands, and clarifies, the person can be growing in insight, confidence, and hope. The main difference between the first three stages and the last three is that the focus of the first three is on sharing important information, which can be therapeutic in itself. The focus of the last three stages is on helping the person change behavior so that he or she can live more effectively.

Stage 1: Information Gathering

The more information counselors have, the more valid their evaluations, the more accurate their feedback, and the more sound their recommendations. Therefore, it is helpful for counselors to recognize the various areas of information that must be tapped. The information index in Figure 2 represents the main sources of information for the counselor.

Continuum A-B represents the time dimension. Information about the person's past helps the counselor understand how the person got where he or she is. Information about the present indicates how well the person is functioning currently, and information about the future tells the counselor who the person wishes to become. As these pieces of information are brought together, they can give a reasonably good picture of who the person is and why the person is seeking help.

Continuum C-D reflects the importance of getting both intrapsychic and interpersonal information. Intrapsychic information consists of learning about the person's perceptions of reality; his inner conflicts and how they are handled; the relationship between who the person is, thinks he is, and wants others to think he is; as well as the person's beliefs, values, and hopes. Interpersonal information comprises the dynamics involved in how the person relates with others, whether these relationships are satisfying or dissatisfying to the person or to the people with whom he or she relates.

Continuum E-F denotes what the person thinks and feels about herself, others, and relevant events. It is not only important to know the content of the person's thoughts and feelings, but to recognize how they interact and perhaps conflict. For example, when asked how she viewed her father, a woman responds "I have nothing but the utmost respect for him." When she is asked how she *feels* about her father, she replies "I resent him more than words can say."

Figure 2

An information index.

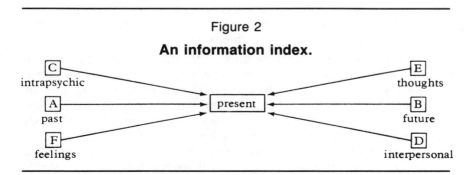

The information index highlights cautions in information gathering. Typically, people seeking help lure counselors into talking about the past, discussing interpersonal relationships, and focusing on ideas. The counselor who is successfully lured will have a fragmented and inaccurate picture upon which to make a clinical evaluation.

Questions

In addition to being aware of the various dimensions of information, it is helpful for counselors to have a clear idea of what specific information they want. The information must be relevant and gathered in a relatively short time. The following format of questions can be helpful in accomplishing this goal. Whether one asks specific questions or gathers the information indirectly depends on the counselor and the situation.

1. "Why do you feel it would be a good idea to talk with me?" This question is meant to ascertain the person's motives for seeking counseling and his or her view of the problem. A person may reply "I didn't think it would be a good idea—my mother did." A person may present the problem as feeling depressed, worried, insecure, confused, or scared. The counselor can then help the person describe the nature of his or her problem more specifically.

2. "How long have you felt this way?" The answer to this question gives the counselor some idea as to whether the problem is long-standing or of short duration. Counselors can be aware that people sometimes describe their problem as short-lived, but further probing indicates that it was present for a long time and only recently became activated.

3. "What do you think is causing these problems?" This question is meant to disclose how much insight the person has and how much responsibility he or she is taking for the problem. A person may answer "I don't have the slightest idea" or "My boss is the cause of the problem" or "I've always been insecure, and this new job is hitting every insecurity I have."

4. "How have you been dealing with the problem up to this point?" The answer to this question will give the counselor some idea of the person's defenses, adaptive responses, and use of environmental supports. The person may answer "I don't think it's a problem; my husband does" or "I've been distracting myself with work and probably eating and drinking too much" or "I have tried several alternatives that I thought a good deal about, and I've discussed it with my family, but I still need a little more help."

5. "How do you expect counseling will help you?" The question is meant to elicit the person's expectations of counseling. One person may answer "I don't have the slightest idea." Another person may respond "I think you can tell me what I should do." A third person may react "I hope you will be able to help me see what I'm doing wrong, so I can stop it."

6. "How much time and effort are you willing to invest in working on your problem?" Answers to this question will tell the counselor how accurately the person assesses the seriousness of the problem and how much personal motivation he or she has to solve it.

7. "Can you tell me some things about your past that you think may be helpful to my understanding of who you are today?" This question is meant to get a psychological snapshot of the person. A detailed case history is rarely necessary as part of the information-gathering stage and may only serve to distract from current issues and affects.

8. "What are some of your strong points?" This question is meant to give the counselor some idea of the person's strengths and also gives the person an opportunity to bolster his or her self-esteem, which may have been diminished in talking about the problem.[2]

Interaction and Reaction

In addition to having the person tell the counselor about himself or herself, the counselor must have an opportunity to see the person in action. The information the person has given is hearsay; that is, its validity depends upon the person's willingness and ability to perceive and communicate accurately. Counselors who restrict themselves to hearsay information are likely to get an inaccurate picture of the person, which will negatively affect the evaluation and feedback. Two ways counselors can become eyewitnesses to the person's dynamics are through interaction and reaction.

Interaction means two things: challenging and relating warmly with the person. *Challenging* means probing the person in a gentle, tentative way. Challenging differs from confronting, which is ordinarily inappropriate at this stage (see Stage 5 for a definition and description of confronting). When a counselor challenges the person's perceptions, motives, insights, defenses, expectations, and values, he or she invites the person to entertain the possibility that his or her way of perceiving reality and reacting to it may not be entirely accurate or helpful.

For example, a counselor may ask "Bill, you say your mom is pretty unreasonable. Is it possible that sometimes she is being

reasonable but you don't want to see it that way?'' The counselor
creates some natural stress to see how the person reacts to it. Does
he handle the stress differently than he says he handles stress? On
being challenged, does he show some behavior that he has
successfully covered up until now? Does he respond by attacking,
withdrawing, or deftly avoiding the challenge? Does he respond
well, seeing the challenge as an opportunity to learn something
about himself or to clarify a situation?

Counselors who are reluctant to challenge a person at this stage
are taking the same risks as a physician who declines to thump a
person's sensitive abdomen. Sometimes the best way to see where
it hurts is to probe, even when it causes some pain.

Warmth is another part of interacting. Relating warmly means
that the counselor naturally and genuinely communicates positive
feelings toward the person by smiling, encouraging, and complimenting the person when it is appropriate. This affords the
counselor a chance to see firsthand how the person responds to
positive feelings, whether he or she accepts them naturally. Does
she freeze and become suspicious? Does he ignore them? Does she
seek them and cling to them? Does he respond well only when
positive feelings are forthcoming? The answers to these questions
will give the counselor some important information as to how the
person handles warmth: whether the person accepts it and grows
from it or rejects it and deprives himself or herself of valuable
psychological fuel.

A second way to elicit firsthand information is by *reacting*. This
means that the counselor is finely attuned to his or her own
reactions to the person. The counselor is like a harp. When a chord
is struck, the counselor knows *somebody* struck it. And, if the
counselor knows he or she did not strike it, then it must have been
the person. The counselor can reasonably assume that the ways
the person ''plays'' him or her are similar to the ways the person
''plays'' other people. Some typical chords that are struck are
feelings of threat, anger, sympathy, tenderness, affection, sexuality,
frustration, confusion, distrust, repulsion, curiosity, and caution.

This information can tell the counselor how the person tends to
''make'' other people feel, at least under certain circumstances. This
material can give the counselor otherwise unobtainable information
as to how the person ''gets'' others to treat him or her.

The information gained from interaction and reaction affords
counselors material that they could not obtain simply by asking
questions and letting the person tell a consciously or unconsciously
edited story.[3]

Stage 2: Evaluation

As information gathering nears an end, the counselor begins to evaluate it. This evaluation evolves around five issues.

Symptoms

Symptoms are signs indicating that a person is overloaded with stress. Academically, there are two kinds of symptoms: those included in the formal diagnostic categories—for example, those presented in the *Diagnostic and Statistical Manual* of the American Psychiatric Association (DSM III)—and those not included in any formal diagnostic classifications. Some examples of symptoms presented as diagnostic categories are depression, anxiety states, phobias, obsessions, compulsions, personality disorders (such as antisocial and passive-aggressive), sexual dysfunctioning (such as impotence and frigidity), and sexual disorders (such as child molesting and rape). Some examples of symptoms that do not fit the traditional diagnostic categories are: inordinate fear, anger, guilt, confusion, frustration, procrastination; feelings of inadequacy, hypersensitivity, fatigue, jealousy, distractibility; interpersonal conflicts; job inefficiency; and religious desolation. Many people who seek counseling refer to their symptoms as their problem. For example, a person may tell a counselor "My problem is that I'm depressed . . . or can't sleep . . . or am tense all the time."

It is important for counselors to assess the nature and severity of the symptoms. Some symptoms need immediate and direct intervention. For example, people who are deeply depressed, severely anxious, have such acute psychosomatic symptoms as severe headaches and insomnia, are currently addicted to alcohol or drugs, or are an imminent danger to themselves or others need immediate symptomatic relief because their symptoms are seriously damaging and preclude the effective use of counseling.

Other symptoms are less damaging and either do not significantly interfere with counseling or actually create sufficient distress in the person that they facilitate it. These symptoms can be monitored and may be used to gauge the progress of counseling. As the person grows in counseling, the symptoms should diminish.

Cause of Symptoms

There is one generic cause of symptoms; namely, something is significantly interfering with, or threatening to interfere with, a basic psychological need. Some of these basic needs are the need to experience a reasonable degree of security, love, esteem, accomplishment, stimulation, freedom, joy, and purpose. When an important need is interfered with, stress results. And when stress is left unmitigated, it will immediately or eventually cause symptoms, depending upon the intensity of the stress and the coping skills of the person. Basic needs can be significantly interfered with in four ways:

1. An objectively psychologically damaging event occurs (loss of a loved one, divorce, termination of a love relationship, imprisonment).

2. The person seeking help is in an important relationship with someone who is behaving in ways that significantly interfere with the person's basic needs (a woman is married to a man who treats her destructively).

3. The person seeking counseling behaves interpersonally in ways that discourage others from meeting his or her needs. For example, a man acts abrasively with women and gets rejected; a woman behaves seductively with men and gets used.

4. The person seeking counseling has intrapersonal dynamics that ultimately interfere with need fulfillment. For example, a man feels inadequate and therefore does not allow others to get close enough to meet his needs; a woman has unrealistically high expectations of herself, which she pursues to the detriment of getting her basic needs met.

These causes may not be mutually exclusive. A man may behave abrasively with women (interpersonal maladaptive behavior) because he perceives himself as inadequate and fears rejection (intrapersonal maladaptive behavior). Hence, he rejects women before they can reject him. There also may be more than one cause underlying a symptom, and two or more causes may interact. The more skilled a counselor becomes, the better he or she can see the interrelating of causes and symptoms and causes with causes. Figure 3 shows the interaction between symptoms, stress, and the causes of stress. It is important that counselors assess the cause(s) of the symptoms accurately because they will dictate the methods of resolution. If the cause is misdiagnosed, the method of resolution will be ineffective.

Relief of Symptoms

What can be done to modify the behavior that is causing the symptoms depends upon the nature of the cause. If the cause is an objectively stressful event, then cognitive restructuring, ventilation, and reassurance may gradually allow the person to feel more secure, loved, or competent. This in turn reduces the stress, which diminishes the symptoms. If the cause is a significant other interfering with the person's need fulfillment, then the person can be helped to perceive and handle the situation more constructively or to withdraw from it. If the person's maladaptive behavior in interpersonal situations is causing the symptoms, then the counselor can help the person develop better social competencies or a better sense of self, depending on the basic problem. If the cause is the person's intrapsychic conflicts, they can be isolated and the person can be taught how to deal with them more creatively. The specific steps taken and the time they require depend upon the nature of the behavior, its duration and severity.

Figure 3

Interaction between symptoms, stress, and causes of stress.

SYMPTOM

↑

OVERLOADING OF STRESS

↑

SIGNIFICANT INTERFERENCE WITH NEEDS

- Psychologically damaging event
- Significant other interferes with needs
- Person relates maladaptively with others
- Person relates maladaptively with self

Readiness for Counseling

Not everyone who seeks counseling is a reasonable candidate; that is, not all people will be able to use counseling to their advantage. The following are some factors counselors may consider when assessing the person's readiness for counseling. Each of these factors is on a long continuum. Obviously, if a person were to be at the positive end of the continuum on all these factors, it is likely that he or she would not need counseling.

1. People who accept responsibility for their problems are likely to be better candidates than those who blame others. People who express some variation of "I need to learn how to handle things better" are likely to be better candidates than those who say "If only my husband . . . wife . . . boss . . . friends . . . treated me better, everything would be all right."

2. People who are willing to work to earn feeling better are likely to be better candidates than those who want to feel better without changing their maladaptive behavior. Perls said "Very few people go in therapy to be cured, but rather to improve their neurosis."[4] Although Perls may be overgeneralizing, there is sufficient truth in his sentiment to evoke caution.

3. People with strong, intrinsic motivation to change are likely to be better candidates than those with weak intrinsic or primarily extrinsic motivation.

4. People who are psychologically minded are more likely to be good candidates than those who are not. Psychologically minded people are insightful and able and willing to appreciate the cause and effect dynamics of their behavior. For example, a person who can recognize that when she gets angry at a person she denies it but later subtly punishes the person who made her angry is likely to be a better candidate than someone who absolutely denies anger and can see no connection between her anger and her passive-aggressive behavior.

5. People who have good environmental supports that reward growth are likely to be better candidates that those who lack such supports.

6. People whose fears cause significant distress will likely be better candidates than those whose symptomatic behavior greatly reduces anxiety or provides pleasure. People who are addicted to alcohol, drugs, or food; those who compulsively gamble, steal, or sexually act out; and those whose symptoms act as effective tools to get much needed attention or as weapons with which to punish others are less promising candidates for counseling.

7. People who are capable of communicating in ways that can be understood and of listening in ways that allow them to assimilate information are likely to be better candidates than those whose symptoms significantly interfere with their ability to communicate. For example, people with severe depression, agitation, withdrawal; those with cognitive disturbances such as hallucinations, delusions, disorientation, or memory impairment; and people with speech disorders such as mutism, verbigeration, or echolalia are not good candidates for counseling.

Great caution must be exercised in deciding who is a reasonable and who is a poor candidate for counseling. Persons who are not good candidates at present can be referred by the counselor to a more appropriate type of intervention (detoxification, chemotherapy, weight-control programs, behavior modification, hospitalization), which may enable them to become reasonable candidates in the future. It is possible for a counselor to accept a poor candidate into counseling. This can be done as long as the counselor does not give the person false hope regarding the effects of counseling.[5]

Person/Counselor Fit

Not all counselors can help all people who seek their help, and it is a destructive expectation for counselors to think otherwise. Counseling relationships are similar to marriages: when serious, ongoing problems arise, it is often a consequence of two people trying to stay together who never should have started together. Counselors who feel that they can help and should agree to help anyone who makes an appointment are deluding themselves. The main medium through which a counselor works is the therapeutic relationship. Ordinary relationships are delicate and tenuous; counseling relationships are much more so.

Counselors are human beings with weaknesses, biases, fears, angers, and values. They can learn to recognize what their delicate areas are and work to strengthen them. However, they can also recognize that once in a while a person in counseling rubs one or all of these delicate areas the wrong way. When this occurs, it is better to refer the person to someone else. One counselor may have a difficult time relating with very hostile, powerful, demanding people. Another counselor may experience inordinate stress relating with very passive, docile, clinging people. A third counselor may have difficulty accepting the person's presenting problem: homosexuality, child molesting, child beating, alcoholism, drug addiction, abortion, sexual promiscuity, rape. The more counselors are in touch with their humanity, the more sensitive they will be to the kinds of people and problems they are more likely to be able to help.

It is both a professional and ethical responsibility to screen people for counseling. Ordinarily, a counselor who agrees to see someone in counseling is communicating that he or she has *good reason* to expect that counseling will be *reasonably successful*, that the *counselor can work effectively* with the person, and that the *time, energy, hardship, and financial investment will be worthwhile.* If any one of the four italicized factors is absent, a serious professional and ethical issue arises.

One factor that greatly contributes to tarnishing the reputation of counseling is the counselor who agrees to work with people who cannot be adequately helped through counseling. This leads to the conclusion that "counseling doesn't work" instead of "counseling doesn't work with certain people," who should have been referred to a more appropriate source of intervention. Counselors who are intelligently selective are providing a positive service to people who are seeking help and to the counseling profession.[6]

It is unlikely that an evaluation will be made with absolute confidence and certainty. Human behavior is usually too complex for that. However, counselors can develop working hypotheses with a reasonable amount of confidence. When they do, they are ready for Stage 3.

Stage 3: Feedback

Feedback consists of the counselor sharing relevant information with the person seeking help. The purpose of the feedback is to provide sufficient information to enable the person to make an informed decision with regard to beginning a counseling program. Four principles can help counselors provide feedback that is meaningful and helpful.

Characteristics of the Information

The information can be given as clearly, succinctly, concretely, and prudently as possible. "Clear" means simple, jargon-free language. "Succinct" means short, without drawn-out descriptions and analogies. Feedback, even with the most psychologically disturbed people, can be given in one session. "Concretely" indicates down-to-earth, easily grasped concepts. Sometimes a simple diagram helps. "Prudently" means that the counselor instills a sense of concern (when it is appropriate) without creating a state of alarm. A helpful attitude is "You've got some problems that do need attention, but there is something you can do about each of them."

Strengths and Weaknesses

The feedback can include both strengths and weaknesses. Usually it is better to begin with strengths and finish with weaknesses. When the procedure is reversed, the person may become so defensive or demoralized that he or she may not hear some important part of the discussion of the problem. Another option is to inter-sperse strengths and weaknesses.

Inviting Questions

The person can be invited to ask questions both during and after the feedback. Questions can be answered in a straightforward yet supportive way. Sometimes people ask a litany of questions in order to forestall the feedback process. When this is the case, the person can be invited to hold his or her questions until the end of the session.

Recommendations

After communicating the feedback to the person, the counselor makes recommendations. The counselor can explain that recommendations are not orders but serious, well-thought-out suggestions. The following are some common recommendations:

Continue counseling on a weekly basis or more or less frequently as the seriousness of the problem dictates.

Continue individual counseling; or begin group, marital, or family counseling; or combine individual counseling with one of the other types.

Continue counseling, but with another counselor. This would occur when the counselor feels that someone else would be significantly more helpful, either because of a personality conflict or because the person's problem requires help outside of the counselor's area of expertise. When this recommendation is made, it should be done prudently and without communicating to the person that he or she is being rejected.

Recommend a more suitable type of intervention—for example, substance abuse counseling, a weight-control program, readings or a course in psychological health, a support group, or religious direction.

Recommend no further intervention because the person's difficulties are quite normal and are simply a part of the person's development and growth.

Recommend no further intervention because, as a result of the sessions up to this point, the person has gained sufficient insight and courage to handle the problems without further professional help.

Recommend no further intervention because, although the person has problems that merit counseling, he or she is not psychologically ready for counseling. The person may not be experiencing sufficient stress or is experiencing stress, but it is controlled by defenses that are currently impenetrable. In either case, the person's motivation and accessibility are less than those necessary for effective counseling. Counselors can exercise care not to convey that the situation is hopeless. The difference between "not being ready" and "hopeless" can be explained, accompanied by an open invitation to return at some time in the future if the person so chooses. On the other hand, these people should not be led to believe that they do not need counseling.

If the sessions preceding the feedback progressed the way they should, neither the feedback nor the recommendations will be a surprise. Counselors need not feel that the feedback should consist of dramatic insights and discoveries. Consciously and unconsciously, the counselor has been preparing the person for the feedback and recommendations as the evaluation progressed.

No matter what the recommendation, it is unhelpful for the person to make a decision on the day of the feedback. The person can be invited to think about the feedback, assimilate and discuss it with others if he or she chooses. The counselor is careful not to convey the attitude that the person would be foolish not to accept the recommendation or that the counselor does not care if the person follows the recommendation. A more helpful attitude is one that conveys "I think the recommendation is a sound one, but what is more important is that it is *your* decision."

At this point, the person in counseling has a second choice point as to whether or not to begin counseling. This time the choice is an informed one. The person understands much more about himself or herself, about the nature of counseling, and about the personality of the counselor. If the person chooses to continue counseling, he or she will be a much stronger candidate and counseling will continue with good momentum. If the person chooses not to continue counseling, this decision may save the person and the counselor a great deal of time, energy, and frustration.

Stage 4: Counseling Agreement

Although counseling has been taking place during the first three stages, both the counselor and the person in counseling possess much more information than they did when they began. Using this information as a frame of reference, the counselor and the person in counseling can come to an agreement on four issues: the practical aspects of counseling, roles, expectations, and the goals of counseling.

Practical Aspects

Practical aspects include how often the person and counselor will meet, the length of the sessions, the policy regarding canceled and failed appointments, and the billing procedures. If there is no need to modify these based on the information gained from the first three stages, it is helpful to restate them in order to underline their importance. However, sometimes the counselor has learned information that causes him or her to adjust some of the practical aspects to fit a particular person and situation. When this is the case, the counselor can explain the modifications and the reasons for them.

Roles

The second part of the agreement deals with role expectations. The specific roles depend on the counselor, the person in counseling, and the situation. For example, the counselor may explain that his or her role will be the same as it was during the first three stages or more passive, reflective, varied, confrontative, direct, ambiguous, questioning, silent, active, or listening. It is helpful for the counselor to offer a brief explanation why he or she feels the nature of the role will facilitate growth.

It is important to remember that *assuming* a role is not the same as *playing* a role. When a man returns from work, he assumes the role of father, which is helpful and appropriate. Hopefully, he does not play the role, which means that he is acting a part that is not he. A counselor may legitimately assume a role in a counseling situation that would be inappropriate to assume in other circumstances, but the role should be a part of him or her and not simply an ill-fitting cloak.

The role of the person in counseling is also discussed. A counselor may feel it is more helpful for the person to bring to each session whatever is on his or her mind or may suggest that the person's past needs more attention and should be the area of focus for a time. Another counselor may wish to concentrate mostly on the present and on feelings, or a counselor may want to focus mostly on what goes on inside the counseling room. One counselor may invite the person to relate personally as well as professionally, asking questions and getting to know the counselor, while another counselor may wish to remain more impersonal.

When both the counselor and person in counseling clearly understand and agree that their roles feel comfortable and will facilitate growth, they are in a better position to work as a synchronized team rather than stumbling over each other at every turn.

Expectations

Expectations can become more explicit than they were during the first three stages because each person has a better grasp of the situation. The counselor shares his or her expectations that involve the responsibilities of the person in counseling. These issues might deal with honesty, making concerted efforts to reach the goals of counseling, placing a high priority on counseling, doing homework assignments, discussing counseling with others, and viewing counseling as a seven-day-a-week experience rather than a 50-minute-a-week visit.

The person in counseling can also share his or her expectations of the counselor. The person can tell the counselor what he or she would find helpful and unhelpful. Often in this early stage of counseling people are not in a position to articulate clearly how the counselor can be of more help. Consequently, the counselor can help the person along these lines and invite the person to keep the counselor apprised of growing and changing expectations as counseling progresses.

Goals

As a result of the first three stages, both the person in counseling and the counselor have a clearer picture of the problems and the possible solutions. Goal setting in counseling is perhaps the most important part because it ties the whole process together. For this reason it requires a certain amount of time and care. The goals of counseling should have certain characteristics.

First, they are specific and measurable. For example, an agreed-upon goal is that a person overcome his or her fear of getting a job. This goal is specific in that it zeros in on a clear target. It is measurable because the steps toward the goal can be readily charted, and it is relatively easy to tell how much progress has been made toward accomplishing the goal.

In contrast, a person may have as a goal to be more happy, less anxious or depressed, to become a better husband or mother, or to get to know him- or herself better. These goals are so general, abstract, and difficult to measure that they are unworkable. This counselor and the person in counseling need to target in on what specifically does "more happy" mean? Why exactly does the person feel tense? Why specifically does the person think he is not a good husband? The more vague and abstract the goals, the less chance counseling has to approximate them.

Second, they are realistic. The goals of counseling are always restricted by the potential of the person in counseling and the limitations in the person's environment. For example, two 38-year-old women wish to enter law school. They seek counseling to help them make the psychological changes necessary to bring this about. For one of these women, this may be a realistic goal and for another it may not be. One woman is divorced, intelligent, and energetic. She worked as a court clerk and feels that she has the motivation, skills, and understanding of what it means to be a lawyer. She seeks counseling because she is not sure if she wants to leave the security of her present job, whether she wants to make the sacrifices that both law school and a career as an attorney demand, and whether it will deprive her two adolescent children of the parenting they still need. She knows what she wants, but she is not sure that pursuing it would be a wise choice.

The second woman is married to a man who does not want her to go to law school. He wants her home with the four school-age children, and he would have to get another job to secure a loan to finance law school. The woman is of modest intelligence and has been depressed. The thought of going to law school has served to raise her from her depression. She has no knowledge of law or law as a career but came upon the idea when she read about another woman whose life was changed when she became a lawyer. She seeks counseling because she wants to learn how she can go to law school and keep her husband happy and children healthy. It is unlikely that the second woman's goal is one that can be attained in counseling, even though it is essentially the same goal as that of the first woman.

A second aspect of realistic goals is that few of them are of an all-or-nothing nature. For example, a man seeks counseling to help him relate more effectively at work. "More effectively" for this particular man may mean increasing his effectiveness by 20, 50, or 70%. It would be unrealistic to expect counseling to allow him to function with complete effectiveness.

Third, the goals are psychologically healthy. Some people's proposed goals are consonant with psychological growth. They want to become more assertive, autonomous, and confident; less angry, fearful, and confused. Other people, however, may seek counseling to maintain equilibrium through means that are not psychologically healthy. For example, a person may want to learn to survive in a work situation that is intractably damaging, to leave a family situation in ways that would be injurious to self and others, or to begin a project for which he is not prepared and that is doomed to fail. While it is the prerogative of those in counseling to choose their own goals, it is the counselor's responsibility not to become a collaborator in destructive behavior.

Fourth, they are often hierarchical. Some people have only one goal in counseling. The previously mentioned woman who wishes to go to law school could be an example of this. Many people, however, have several goals. For example, a man may list the following goals: to be more comfortable sexually, to change jobs, to have a less conflictual relationship with his parents, to recapture religious fervor, to relate more comfortably with women on dates, and to lose 30 pounds.

The items on this list do not automatically lend themselves to a hierarchical arrangement. Once the counselor knows the man better, it may become clear that the goals cannot be arranged in alphabetical order and pursued. It may be that the inordinate pressures at work are causing ongoing damage, and until they are alleviated, the man is in no position to work on any of the other goals. Once that pressure is alleviated, the next step may be to refer the person to a medically supervised weight-control program through which he can lose weight and feel more presentable. While he is losing weight, the next step may be to explore the reasons for feeling sexually confused or uncomfortable about himself. When this issue is on its way to resolution, the next step may be to examine what makes dating an anxiety-producing experience and then to date. When the dating anxiety gets under control, the next step may be to understand and work on his conflict with his parents. When all these are reasonably under control, he may be at peace enough to be able to work on his religious doubts and conflicts.

Sometimes when the first two or three goals in the hierarchy are attained, the rest take care of themselves. For example, in the case above, the man's conflicts with his parents and his religious conflicts may be resolved as side effects of achieving the previous goals.

There are two points of caution with regard to placing counseling goals in a hierarchy. One is that the counselor must walk the middle path between excluding all material in the counseling session except that dealing directly with the current target goal and allowing the person to dabble in one target after another, which results in no consistent movement toward any goal.

The second caution is that agreed upon hierarchical goals must not be set in cement. When the counselor understands more about the person, it may become imperative to rearrange the hierarchy. In the case of the man, the counselor may discover that until his religious conflicts are resolved, there will be no movement toward any of the other goals. A shift in the hierarchy may be necessary when the person and the counselor work hard at attaining a subgoal with no meaningful results. This could indicate that another goal in the hierarchy or a hitherto unrecognized goal must be dealt with first.

Fifth, the goals belong to the person in counseling. Sometimes, especially when people bring general, abstract, or vague goals to counseling, the counselor gets trapped into making them more concrete and manageable. For example, a woman may say she is depressed but doesn't know why because she has a beautiful husband, children, and home—all any woman could ever want. After several unsuccessful attempts to help the woman articulate the cause of her distress, the counselor may decide why she is depressed: she is denying her disappointment with a marriage that has become drab; she resents the fact that her husband won't let her go back to work; she feels guilty about having recently placed her father in a convalescent hospital; and she is repressing sexual feelings because she has no place to get them met.

On the basis of these hypotheses with which the person reluctantly and tentatively agrees ("You're the doctor—I expect you know more about these things that I do"), they launch into trying to reach the counselor's goals. Of course, nothing good is likely to result from this counseling relationship because the goals are the counselor's and not those of the person in counseling. Even if the counselor is correct on all the hypotheses, the woman has never claimed the goals for herself.

It is essential that the counseling goals be clearly owned by the person and that counseling not continue until this occurs. To spend a few sessions trying to clarify goals could be appropriate. But when the goal of counseling is to discuss the goals of counseling, this usually results in unproductive expeditions in which both the counselor and the person continually meet themselves exactly where they began.

Sixth, goals are frequently evaluated. Aiming at goals in counseling is similar to aiming at any kind of target. After attempting to hit the target a few times, it is sensible to examine it to see how successful the efforts have been.

Since goals are specific and measurable, it should not be too difficult to gauge progress toward them. When the counselor and the person agree that they are progressing in the right direction and on schedule, it provides a mutual sense of confidence and accomplishment that can add momentum to their quest. If, after a reasonable time, it becomes clear that the counselor and the person have gradually strayed from the target or that they are on target but progressing too slowly, they can consider questions like the following: Is there a condition that must be met first? For example, the person may need more time to trust the counselor before becoming committed to the goal. Is there some deep ambivalence developing toward the goal as it gets closer to realization? Maybe a man is becoming less confident that divorce is the best thing for him at this point. In any case, it is much better to look at the target early and at short intervals to see the path counseling is taking than to assume counseling is squarely on track, only to discover later that it has been spiraling out of control.

Developing a counseling agreement may take one session or three or four. If the counselor and the person are still struggling and negotiating over an agreement after five sessions, it is likely that the person is not sufficiently motivated to use counseling, there is a problem in the counselor-person relationship, or else the counselor is not sufficiently skilled to develop the agreement.[7]

Stage 5: Changing Behavior

Exactly what occurs during this stage depends upon the person and his or her problem. However, there are some common experiences that occur during this stage with which counselors can be familiar. These issues may arise before this stage, but they arise more obviously and regularly at this time. The following are ten situations with which counselors frequently must deal while helping the person change behavior.

Focusing on Responsibility

This crucial issue often arises, despite the counselor's previous efforts. People in counseling frequently view counselors as psychological architects whose role is to provide a blueprint telling the person who he is, what his problem is, how he should solve his problem, and when he should take each step in the process. Even the most experienced counselor can be insidiously trapped into assuming this role. When this occurs, the counselor is taking responsibility not only for the person's changing behavior but for the person's life.

Counselors can resist the manipulations and temptations to become managers for people in counseling. If persons in counseling need someone to take the reins of their life, they likely need more intensive treatment than traditional outpatient counseling can afford. The counselor's stance toward the person in counseling should always be:

> *You* tell me who you are today.
>
> *You* tell me what your problem is today.
>
> *You* tell me how you wish to solve it.
>
> *You* tell me when you are going to try what strategies.

Obviously, a person could respond "If I could tell you all these things, I wouldn't be in counseling in the first place." And in one sense this retort is valid, but in a deeper sense it is not. The assumption underlying counseling is that the answers to these questions can lie only within the individual. The counselor's role is not to answer these questions, but to provide an environment and a relationship conducive to helping the person grow in the insight and courage necessary to answer the questions and translate the answers into practice. In other words, one of the general goals of counseling is to help a person become his or her own counselor.

Inward Searching

People who are in counseling, like most people, operate almost solely on an external level. Their approach to life is "I've got a problem here, and I have to figure out a way to solve it." The focus is almost entirely on the problem outside of them and not on the person inside. As a result, they are likely to experience the same types of problems continually.

For example, a 30-year-old woman comes to counseling because she is depressed that she cannot find a marriageable man. The more frantic and depressed she becomes, the more she sabotages her relationships with men. After several sessions of internal searching, she makes the following discoveries:

> She has a void within her that is comprised of feeling unimportant, unlovable, and purposeless, and she believes only a man can fill that void.
>
> She looks upon marriage as a psychological and social validation of herself. As long as she is unmarried, she and society look upon her as psychologically lame; as soon as

she gets married, she will be seen as psychologically
healthy. A good deal of the pressure she feels is not to get
married but to feel good about herself.

She thinks the best way to get a man is to be sexually active
and has not realized that this is not going to get her the man
that meets her qualifications. In other words, she is
attracting exactly the kind of man that she dislikes.

She is very ambivalent about marriage. On one hand she wants
to get married, but on the other she resents men because
she needs them to make her happy. She fears her deep need
for a man will enslave her just as her mother became
enslaved to her father. She is fearful that if she does marry,
she may find herself disillusioned, which would rule out her
last hope for happiness on this earth. Her deep ambivalence
is reflected in her behavior with men, causing her
unnecessary conflicts.

As she works through these insights, which until now had been
unconscious, she feels far less pressure to get married. She has
begun to fill her void intrapsychically with a clear appreciation for
her worth and goodness, to which counseling introduces her.
Extrapsychically, she fills the void with new friends, a more fulfilling
job, and hobbies she always enjoyed until she began her
"manhunt."

When she does date, she is more selective, acts in keeping with
her deeper values, and relates more comfortably. Dates are no
longer examinations that she can pass or fail, but evenings to enjoy
in themselves. She still would *like* to marry, but she does not *have*
to marry.

People in counseling often resist inward exploration because they
are fearful of what they will discover. Therefore, it is necessary for
counselors to develop skills that allow them to help people work
through the resistance and a sense of timing that helps them judge
the right time to explore a given insight.[8]

Utilizing Insights

There are two points of view about the insights gleaned from
inward searching. One is that the insights alone may bring about
the psychological equilibrium necessary to reduce symptoms and
create growth. The person's problem may remain, but the person
has outgrown it; so it is less or no longer a nuisance.

A second point of view is that inward searching provides the
blueprint for external behavioral changes and that both are

necessary for maximum personality growth. This view recognizes that not all human problems are solvable, but as long as one is in counseling, one might as well try to solve the ones that are. This view combines the benefits of inward searching and problem solving into a two-part process.

The woman in the previous example did not simply rest with her inner reflections and discoveries, but used them to chart some concrete, observable changes in her daily life. She finished college, changed jobs, broadened her circle of friends and interests, changed her way of relating with men, returned to her religion, and used the psychological dividends of this change to fill her void and strengthen her being. As a result, she has not only solved the problem she brought to counseling, but has grown as a person.

Mirroring

Counselors act as mirrors in which people can see themselves. There are two ways of mirroring: intrapsychically and interpersonally. "Intrapsychically" means that counselors reflect back to people who they are so that they can make appropriate changes in their behavior. Often there is steam on the mirror that people look into daily, and it hides the parts they don't want to see. In mirroring, the counselor says, in effect, "This is the way you look to me now. If you agree that's who you are, what changes, if any, would you like to make? If you don't agree that's who you are, let's figure out why we have different perceptions." This is important because most people in counseling don't have a clear and complete picture of themselves, which leads them to behave in inappropriate and unhelpful ways. It is also important because very few, if any, people in the person's life would have the skills, concern, benevolence, and courage to reflect back to the person how he or she appears. When a person gets a clear, unbiased picture, he or she is in a position to make some meaningful changes.

Equally important is interpersonal mirroring. This means that the counselor reflects back to the person how he or she "comes on" with people and what responses this behavior elicits. The counselor might say "I'm starting to feel angry (manipulated, anxious, confused, distracted, sympathetic, bored, frightened, stupid, guilty, hurt; or warm, relaxed, comfortable, happy, empathetic, interested)." The message that the counselor is conveying is "When you act the way you are, this is the response you are likely to elicit from people. If you want that response, it's okay; but if you don't want it, let's see how and why you elicit it."

As long as counselors are affectively neutral about the issue at hand, they can trust that their reactions to the person are similar to those that other people would have. This is priceless information for people in counseling because they may be oblivious to the effects of their verbal and nonverbal communication on others. People may wonder why others "always" manipulate, reject, seduce, misunderstand, or avoid them when all they ever do is behave in friendly and reasonable ways.

Both intrapsychic and interpersonal reflection must be done as nonthreateningly as possible. It is likely to be threatening to some extent because people generally become anxious when they hear something about themselves that they didn't know, even when the feedback is positive. The only purpose of mirroring is to be helpful; it is never to put a person "in his place."

Confronting

A counselor may point out significant discrepancies in the person's behavior or lifestyle. This is different from mirroring, which simply reflects back to people who they appear to be. It also differs from challenging in that challenging is more gentle and invites people to reexamine the accuracy of their perceptions; confrontation is more assertive and focuses on people's deeper motives and contradictory behavior.

Confronting is one method of interpretation. The message in confrontation is "You say you are this, but is it possible that you are something different?" For example, a counselor may say "Bill, you keep saying you want to save your marriage, but the way you've been acting makes me wonder if there is a part of you that does not want to save it" or "Nancy, you tell me that you want to use counseling, but you consistently forget what we talk about from one session to another and seldom work on anything between sessions."

Some cautions must be exercised regarding confrontation. It is important that the relationship between the person and the counselor is strong enough to support the confrontation. In other words, although people may not enjoy confrontation, they realize it is being done in their best interests. In addition, counselors must have reasonable certitude that any confrontation has a sound basis in reality.

Timing is also important. The confrontation should take place at an appropriate time; that is, not be introduced "out of the blue" or when the person is not sufficiently strong or insightful to learn from it.

Finally, counselors can be sensitive to the nature of their motives.

Is the confrontation actually a personal attack disguised as a helpful strategy, or does it stem from a counselor whose sole interest is helping the person learn something important? If it is an attack, the tone will be "Tim, who do you think you're kidding." If it's a valid response, the tenor will be "Tim, I'd like to share some perceptions with you and see what you think about them."[9]

Giving Support

Counselors offer reassurance and positive reinforcement and reduce people's anxiety by showing them the positive and hopeful aspects of a situation and by rewarding positive behavior with genuine and spontaneous smiles, encouragement, and support. Giving support can be a very effective aid to the counseling process. On the other hand, it can also be an area for caution.

When reassuring the person, it is important that such support is justified by reality and is not a hollow pep talk that will backfire. Statements such as "I'm sure things will turn out fine" or "I have faith in you that you'll do well" are usually ill advised. A better type of reassurance is reflected in "Let's do our best, and, whatever happens, we'll work very hard together to handle it well." This communicates a more reality-based reassurance that focuses on the counseling relationship as a source of support and not on the success or failure of a particular event.

Positive reinforcement also has areas of caution. Counselors can be careful about what they reward. A man may tell a counselor that he was *finally* able to assert himself at work. He proudly relates the incident to the counselor, who congratulates him for his willingness to take a risk and for successfully asserting himself. However, if the counselor had delved more deeply into the matter, he would have seen that the "assertiveness" was a ploy to escape some rightful responsibility at work. In effect, the counselor rewarded the person for being manipulative and shirking responsibility.

It is often difficult for counselors to delve into situations that the person proudly presents as evidence of progress. There is a pressure for the counselor to allow the person to bask in the feelings of accomplishment. For the counselor to examine the situation appears distrustful and rude. However, in keeping with the axiom "All that glitters is not gold," counselors could do well to gently examine situations lest they reward a problematic behavior.

A second caution regarding positive reinforcement is that it can create a situation in which the person in counseling is growing to earn the praise of the counselor. This counseling relationship can never end because, as soon as talk of termination begins, the person regresses as he or she realizes that growth without the praise of the counselor is meaningless. Ideally, growth should be its own reward, and, as people progress in counseling, there should be less need for counselors to reward their efforts. However, in the first phases of counseling, when people's efforts are not yet sufficiently effective to merit rewarding results, it is necessary for counselors to reward their efforts. Under most circumstances, positive reinforcement should be given judiciously and probably more sparingly than it ordinarily is.

Reverse Shaping

The counselor helps shape the behavior of the person in counseling. By a judicious use of reward, expectation, insight, and confrontation, the counselor helps the person modify behavior. Reverse shaping is when the person does the same thing to the counselor. Because conscious and unconscious shaping is almost continually operative in all human beings, the shaping attempts of the person in counseling probably equal those of the counselor. People in counseling can subtly and not so subtly reward and punish counselors. Counselors who behave in ways that please people may be rewarded either by people showing new evidence of growth or by people complimenting them. When a counselor displeases a person in counseling, the person is apt to regress or attack the counselor.

When people's shaping efforts are obvious, they can be dealt with easily. But people who are "cooperative" and whose only wish is "to get strong enough to handle my own problems" can adroitly shape the counselor without the counselor being even slightly aware of it.

Some people bring a script to counseling that has a bad ending. They hire the counselor as an actor who will help them bring about the desired destructive ending in the most "officially approved" way possible. The ending of the story may be suicide, getting fired, getting rejected by loved ones, remaining in a destructive relationship, proving that one is hopeless, getting hospitalized, or making the counselor a failure. Each progressive act is an escalated attempt to shape the counselor's behavior so that he or she will help the person bring about the desired end of the story.

Counselors can react constructively to shaping behavior in two ways. The first is that, every time the person creates a situation in which the counselor feels quite pleased or quite displeased, the counselor can ask: Why is this person telling me this (doing this)?

How does he (or she) expect me to respond? Will my response be feeding into the person's strengths or weaknesses?

Second, it is helpful for counselors to focus on the agreed-upon goals of counseling, despite the person's pressures to ignore them. This will eventually either spotlight the destructive ending of the script and allow the counselor to invite the person to change the ending or cause the person to terminate when he or she sees that the counselor is not willing to be shaped. If the latter happens, it is better to have it occur early than to have the counselor continue as a co-conspirator in the person's destructive behavior.

Transference

This means that a person displaces onto a counselor feelings, attitudes, or impulses that were part of a previous relationship. The counselor who represents an authority figure likely will be reacted to in the same ways the person has reacted to authority in the past—for example, with attitudes that are defensive, hostile, or ingratiating. The person may react to the counselor's personal qualities with positive or negative transference. The way the counselor looks, speaks, sits, thinks, emotes, and values may trigger a transference reaction. A person may say "I hate it (you) when you get that god-almighty expression on your face (because you are my father when you do that)" or "I like coming here (I like you) because I feel comfortable and understood (the way my mother always made me feel)."

Sometimes the transference is direct ("I don't like you"); at other times, it is indirect—that is, directed at the counselor's profession ("I always felt people went into psychology to solve their own problems") or directed at the domain of the counselor ("Why is this room always so cold?").

Counselors can be aware that not all of a person's reactions in counseling stem from transference. People can relate to counselors directly, without transferring any residuals of past relationships. For example, the fact that a person is angry at a counselor does not mean he is manifesting negative transference. The person's anger may be present and appropriate, and to deal with it as transference would be uninsightful of the counselor and demeaning to the person in counseling. Moreover, all conflicts between the counselor and the person in counseling need not be transference. A person with a devout religious faith may not agree with some of the values of a counselor who views religion as neurotic. To label this person's value conflicts with the counselor as transference misses an important reality conflict that needs resolving.

Counselors can also be aware that all transference reactions have a quality of resistance. As long as people are spending time and energy loving or hating the counselor, they are not progressing toward the mutually agreed upon goals.

How much resistance the transference creates determines whether the counselor should interpret it or let it slide. In general, indirect expressions of mildly positive transference should receive the least attention, and direct manifestation of intensely negative transference should receive the most.

Another point of view on transference reactions is that they can be dealt with in a direct, interpersonal manner rather than in an analytical, working-through fashion. For example, a counselor may reply to a woman who challenges him on being sexist: "I agree that a sexist counselor would not be helpful to you. However, why don't we refocus on our goals, and if you see any concrete data to substantiate your concern as we go along, we can deal with it at that time." This type of response respects the woman's concern yet does not allow it to distract her and the counselor from the main purpose of counseling.

Countertransference

Countertransference consists of inappropriate reactions by the counselor to the behavior of the person in counseling. It can be positive; that is, the counselor has caring and affectionate feelings of a kind and degree that are not merited by the reality of who the person is. Countertransference also can be negative; that is, the counselor feels angry or bored with a person who has done nothing to merit these reactions. As with transference, not all pleasant or unpleasant feelings toward a person in counseling are necessarily countertransference. A counselor may have reason to like or to be upset with a person, and these reactions should not be stifled or worked through as countertransference, but dealt with appropriately.

Countertransference can be both an advantage and a hindrance to counselors. It can be an advantage when it teaches counselors something about themselves. For example, a person may have a habit of responding that angers the counselor. The counselor can then scrutinize himself or herself as to what vulnerability was tapped by the person's behavior. Countertransference can be a hindrance to counseling because strong, inappropriate feelings of liking or disliking a person can sufficiently interfere with the counselor's clinical judgment and helpful responses, causing progress in counseling to be seriously impeded. When this occurs, the counselor must assume responsibility for working through the feelings or, if necessary, refer the person to another counselor.

Interpretation

Interpretation introduces to people in counseling previously unknown information about themselves. In other words, the counselor pulls back the blinds and permits the person to see behaviors that were relegated to the subconscious or unconscious layers of personality. The goal of interpretation is increasing self-knowledge. The more self-knowledge people have, the more able they are to change their behavior.

Most interpretation centers on self-deceit. People do not wish to acknowledge parts of themselves and so repress and deny them. However, these hidden behaviors (thoughts, feelings, defenses, motives, conflicts, or values) do not disappear but influence people's actions in ways of which they are unaware. This allows people to vent these less than conscious behaviors without having to accept responsibility for them. For example, a man has unconscious, negative feelings toward his family. He thinks he comes home quite late every night because he is too busy at work. His late arrival allows him to shorten his time in an unpleasant situation and to upset the people who are upsetting him without having to face exactly what he is doing and why. In the meantime, both he and his family are unhappy, and they feel there is nothing that can be done about it.

Interpretation ordinarily poses a threat to the person in counseling because the repressed material being introduced is not pleasant or it would not have been repressed in the first place. Also, the new information that stems from interpretation means that the person will have to let go of old behaviors and adjust current behaviors to the new information. For example, once the man who gets home late discovers what he is doing and why, he will feel more anxious and have to use the anxiety to change the situation in one direction or another. Therefore, it is not unusual for people to resist interpretation.

Because interpretation in counseling is a delicate operation, counselors can be familiar with the important issues involved. Counselors need to know *what* to interpret. Generally, it is more helpful to interpret the person's defenses before the person's conflicts so that the interpretation doesn't get intercepted and defused by the defenses. It is also generally more helpful to interpret process (how and why the person is doing or not doing something in the counseling session) than content (what the person is saying).

Interpretation should be selective in that only behaviors that are significantly affecting the person need to be considered.

Counselors should also know *when* to interpret. Interpretations are more likely to fall on fertile ground when the person in counseling is close to the level of awareness required to grasp the interpretation, when the person is sufficiently relaxed and comfortable with the counselor, and when the counselor has reasonable certainty that the interpretive hypothesis is correct.

The counselor also needs to know *how* to interpret. Counselors can explain the nature of interpretation to the person and begin gradually by offering less threatening interpretations. Interpretations should be phrased tentatively ("Could it be that . . .?") and concisely since unnecessary words serve only to distract.

Interpretation plays less of a role in crisis intervention and short-term counseling than it does in counseling that is of longer duration and addresses deeper problems.[10]

Stage 6: Termination

It is helpful to remember that termination is a *stage* of counseling and not simply the last few sessions. This stage could encompass the last quarter of counseling. During it, the counselor begins preparing the person to leave counseling. The counselor increasingly points out the success the person is achieving. The message is "You seem to be doing more and more on your own and doing it well." This helps the person see that the distance traveled in counseling is a good deal longer than the distance that remains.

The counselor also begins pulling back as a source of support, feedback, and guidance. This does not mean he or she diminishes interest in the person; it only means that the counselor demonstrates the interest in a different way, much as parents show their concern for a child differently as the child matures.

Counseling becomes a place to check in. The sessions consist more of the person saying "I've got a problem that came up last week. Let me tell you what I'm going to do about it, and if you've got any thoughts you can let me know." This level of autonomy is later elevated to the final level: "Let me tell you how I solved a problem this week. I purposely didn't tell you about it because I wanted to handle it on my own. If you've got any thoughts when I'm through, I'd be glad to hear them."

Usually at about this time someone introduces the topic of termination. While it is sometimes said that it is better for people in counseling to initiate the subject of termination, this does not appear to be necessarily true. Sometimes the fact that the counselor brings it up first is supportive because people view it as a validation of their own thoughts and a compliment to their progress. Also, some people assume that bringing up termination is the rightful role of the counselor.

When initiating the topic, the counselor might say "You seem to be doing so well that I'm wondering if you have given any thought to tapering off our sessions?" Of course, the counselor would ask this question only when the person has had good momentum for a reasonable period of time. The person may respond "It's funny you ask that. We must be on the same wavelength because I have been thinking about it, too." Other responses might be "I haven't given it much thought, but I suppose it is something we should start planning for" or "No, I haven't. Why? Do *you* think I'm ready to stop?" The counselor must deal with the dynamics underlying the responses. This final response likely indicates that the person and counselor are viewing things differently or the person is dependent on counseling and resistant to even the thought of terminating.

The person in counseling who initiates the topic of termination might say "You know, I've been thinking that I may not need to come here as often because I'm handling things pretty well." The counselor may respond "Why don't you tell me what you've been thinking about it?" and react appropriately to the person's explanations.

After there is agreement that counseling has progressed to a point where terminating is an issue, the next step is usually to taper off the number of sessions. Generally, the longer the counseling relationship, the longer the tapering-off period. Tapering off usually means reducing the number of sessions from four each month to two. Sometimes that is sufficient but, with some people, it is helpful to continue tapering off to once each month and then to a "come in as the need arises" basis. Tapering off is meant to avoid the shock of autonomy that can cause separation anxiety and regressive behavior.

It is helpful to recall at this stage the nature of a goal; that is, it is something to be aimed at that may not be totally achieved. Hence, counseling does not necessarily continue until the goals are ultimately and irrevocably attained. More often, counseling helps people to approximate more closely their goals and to live more effectively with what distance remains between where they are and where they would like to be.

An adjacent concept is that a person's growth toward goals does not terminate with the end of counseling. By the time people terminate counseling, they should have built up a momentum that will continue to carry them in the direction of their goals.

The clinical judgment regarding termination considers the

relationship between how far a person has progressed in counseling and how much more counseling can or should do for the person. When people have a clear picture of their ultimate goals and good momentum in the right direction, they are ready to finish the job on their own.[11]

Finally, people do not always terminate counseling with profuse feelings of gratitude toward the counselor. Although this can be discouraging or confusing to the counselor, it is understandable. When counseling has been a difficult experience for a person and has cost a great deal of time, energy, tension, hard work, and money, the person may feel like a football player after a grueling victory. He truly enjoys the victory but he feels that he put at least as much into the victory as the coach, and the coach is getting paid. Consequently, he feels no special need to express appreciation. He's happy he's won; he feels it was worth it; he's glad it's over; and he wants to go home.

Some people still have not completely resolved the fact that they needed help or needed to depend on another person. Therefore, to thank the counselor would be admitting that they needed him or her. Obviously, it would be nice for people to resolve these feelings before the termination of counseling, but what is "nice" and what is "real" are sometimes two different things.

Some people have not been good at showing gratitude and saying goodbye for the 20 or 40 years they've been on earth; so counseling may not have changed that. It doesn't mean these people did not receive a great deal from counseling; it simply means they cannot adequately express their gratitude.

On the other hand, the fact that some people show profuse gratitude does not necessarily indicate they received a great deal from counseling. They may just be thankful that counseling is finished or that they escaped from counseling without having to face their deepest, most dreaded problem.

Counselors can take satisfaction from the fact that they helped people and that these people's lives will be better, even though some people's lives will never be more than marginally fulfilling. If a counselor expects to receive greater satisfaction than that, he or she may have to find it outside of the counseling room.

Summary

It is important that counselors recognize the developmental dimension of the counseling relationship. When counselors possess a general theoretical and practical frame of reference, it lends both direction and order to what otherwise could be a chaotic and frustrating experience.

An understanding of the stages of helping is beneficial to both counselors and people in counseling. It is helpful to counselors because the stages act as directional markers that help counselors steer a steady course toward growth. It is also helpful to people in counseling because, once the sequence of stages is explained to them, they can feel a sense of security and purpose.

Thought Questions

1. If you were limited to only *one* question in the information-gathering stage, what would you ask? Why would you ask it?
2. With regard to selecting candidates you would see in counseling, what is one type of person and one type of problem that you think would be best referred to another counselor? Why do you feel this way?
3. After a few sessions, your antagonism toward the person you are seeing reaches such a peak that it is obvious you can no longer be of help to him. When you recommend that he see another counselor, he retorts "You just don't like me. That's why you want to get rid of me." What do you respond?
4. When you experience negative countertransference toward a person in counseling, how are you likely to show it? When you experience positive countertransference toward a person, how are you likely to show it?
5. What specifically would you like to hear from a person in counseling after the successful termination of a counseling relationship? What will it mean to you if you don't hear it?

Notes

[1] Other formats can be found in Brammer (1979), Carkhuff & Anthony (1979), Weiner (1975), and Egan (1982).
[2] For self-evaluation questions that counselors can ask themselves regarding the effectiveness of their information gathering, see Benjamin (1974), pp. 20–24. He discusses questioning by the counselor on pp. 65–90.
[3] Some counselors find that psychological testing gives them an added source of information. For a summary and evaluation of tests that can be used for this purpose, see Osipow et al. (1980). For a discussion of what clients should look for in counselors, see Goldberg (1977), pp. 237–249.
[4] Perls (1969), p. 39.
[5] For further discussion of the selection of candidates for counseling, see Garfield (1980), pp. 41–68.
[6] A different discussion of evaluation can be found in Weiner (1975), pp. 51–72.

[7] A thorough discussion of the importance of counseling agreements can be found in Goldberg (1977), pp. 31–61.
[8] For a fuller discussion of inward searching, see Bugental (1978).
[9] For a thorough discussion of confrontation, see Adler & Myerson (1973).
[10] For further discussion of transference, countertransference, and interpretation, see Singer (1965).
[11] Termination, like any other stage of counseling, can have its unique difficulties.

References

Adler, G., & Myerson, P. F. (Eds.). *Confrontation in psychotherapy.* New York: Science Housse, 1973.

Benjamin, A. *The helping interview* (2nd ed.). Boston: Houghton Mifflin, 1974.

Brammer, L. M. *The helping relationship process and skills* (2nd ed.). Englewood Cliffs, NJ: Prentice-Hall, 1979.

Bugental, J. F. T. *Psychotherapy and process: The fundamentals of existential-humanistic approach.* Menlo Park, CA: Addison-Wesley, 1978.

Carkhuff, R. R., & Anthony, W. A. *The skills of helping.* Amherst, MA: Human Resource Development Press, 1979.

Egan, G. *The skilled helper* (2nd ed.). Monterey, CA: Brooks/Cole, 1982.

Garfield, S. L. *Psychotherapy: An eclectic approach.* New York: Wiley, 1980.

Goldberg, C. *Therapeutic partnership: Ethical concerns in psychotherapy.* New York: Springer, 1977.

Osipow, S. H., Walsh, W. B., & Tosi, D. J. *A survey of counseling methods.* Homewood, IL: Dorsey, 1980.

Perls, F. S. *Gestalt therapy verbatim.* Lafayette, CA: Real People Press, 1969.

Singer, E. *Key concepts in psychotherapy.* New York: Random House, 1965.

Weiner, I. B. *Principles of psychotherapy.* New York: Wiley, 1975.

11

Recognizing and Utilizing Ethnic and Cultural Diversity in Counseling Approaches

David Yonas
T. Neal Garland

Introduction

The concept of *ethnicity* has been defined in numerous ways. To clarify the meaning of the term as it is used in this chapter, it should be pointed out that *ethnic group* refers to a group of people who have common ancestral origins, share certain cultural traits (including values, beliefs, and ways of doing things), have a sense of peoplehood and of belonging, are from a migrant background, and whose membership in their group is involuntary (Isajiw, 1974; Schermerhorn, 1970). *Ethnicity* refers to the extent to which individuals accept, follow, and identify with their ethnic group.

The United States is an ethnically pluralistic society. In other words, Americans can trace their ancestry to a great variety of different nations. The cultures of these ancestral nations cover virtually the entire range of variations in values, beliefs, and customs found throughout the modern world. Indeed, even within a specific ethnic group the range of variations in values and behaviors can be enormous. For example, among Italian American families there are some that are extremely traditional and follow old-world customs as closely as they can. On the other hand, others

This is the first publication of "Recognizing and Utilizing Ethnic and Cultural Diversity in Counseling Approaches." All rights reserved.

identify with their Italian heritage on an emotional level but practice few of the old customs. Still others have forgotten or rejected their Italian heritage to such an extent that it exerts no meaningful influence on their lives. Conflicts within ethnic families may arise when the parental or grandparental generation tries with great determination to maintain "the old ways" while the younger generation tries with equal determination to reject them. For example, an "old world" parent may use extreme corporal punishment in an attempt to force a "wayward" child to accept parental authority. The child, in turn, may use violence against the parents as a way of asserting his/her independence from such traditional authority. At times conflicts can reach a point where violence within the family brings the family members into contact with the criminal justice system.

Alba (1990) wrote that following the Second World War there was a widely held expectation in this country that ethnic Americans would be assimilated into the dominant WASP (White Anglo-Saxon Protestant) culture and that ethnicity would gradually cease to be an issue of concern to the society. An opposing point of view, however, also was quite strong. This view was that third and higher older generations of ethnic Americans were becoming increasingly comfortable with their status in the society and were therefore more likely to retain and even to emphasize their ethnic heritage (Rose, 1981).

Debates about the place of ethnicity in American society have viewed it as waxing and waning at various points in the nation's history. While it was seen as greatly decreasing in importance during the 1950s, the civil unrest of the 1960s and early 1970s is credited with creating a resurgence of interest in "roots" and, therefore, in ethnic backgrounds. Some writers argue that while the influence of ethnicity in today's America is sometimes subtle, it is nevertheless quite powerful (Greeley, 1971).

This history of the United States is essentially the history of immigrant groups, both voluntary and involuntary. The influence of the distinct beliefs, values, and practices of this multitude of ethnic backgrounds upon the identities of individual Americans and upon the society as a whole is potentially very large. When people identify themselves as members of ethnic subcultures, they may develop values and expectations related to this identity which are different from the values and expectations of members of other subcultures and of the mainstream society. This likelihood often has been ignored or minimized in analyses of American social life because of the American tendency to emphasize the individual more than the collective. A consequence of this emphasis is the assumption that all Americans share basically the same values as all other Americans. This would appear to be an unrealistic assumption, given the ethnic, social class, racial, religious, and other sources of diversity which are undeniable facts of American society.

Consistency in values and expectations allows people to assume that they know themselves and others, and it allows for behavior (of one's self and others) to be predictable. When such consistency is lacking, interaction among members of the society can become highly problematic (Gordon, 1978).

It can be said that it is commonly believed that identification with an ethnic background is widespread among Americans and that this identification has important implications for the individual's self-concept, for interactions among individuals from different ethnic backgrounds, and for the cohesiveness of the society in general. At the same time, debates have continued over the past decades—at least since the 1950s—regarding the actual importance of ethnicity in American society. It therefore is important for criminal justice professionals to take into consideration differences among people which are due to ethnic backgrounds and to understand the dynamics of their own backgrounds. Differences in behavior sometimes should be viewed as adaptive means for ethnic group members and must not be confused with individual weaknesses or automatically labeled as deviance.

Individuals learn their basic value systems within the families in which they grew up. If we assume that the United States is composed of a myriad of different ethnic groups, each of which has a value system that is somewhat different in important ways from the value system of the dominant society and from the value systems of other ethnic groups, an important question arises. This question is that of how the individual, as a member of an ethnic group, is able to learn to be a member of the larger society and to form a stable self-identity in the face of such diversity. In order to provide at least a partial answer to this question, the focus of this chapter is on the degree to which the value systems of various ethnic groups in America are similar to or different from each other and from "mainstream" American values, and on the degree to which individual members of various ethnic groups identify with their ethnic subcultures.

Dominant American Values

In order to compare the values of any ethnic group with those of the dominant or "mainstream" society, it is necessary to examine those dominant values. A *value* can be defined as ". . . an enduring belief that a specific mode of conduct or end-state of existence is personally or socially preferable to an opposite or converse mode of conduct or end-state of existence" (Rokeach, 1973, p. 14).

American institutions, including the criminal justice system, have values that are consistent with the dominant American value system. There have been numerous attempts to identify the values which characterize the dominant (White Anglo-Saxon Protestant) segment of American society. Ruesch (1967), for example, has cited the following as the dominant value orientations in American society: individualism, achievement orientation, mastery over nature, and a future orientation.

Robin Williams (1970) also has identified a number of value orientations as characteristic of the dominant culture in the United States. These value orientations include achievement and success, work, humanitarianism, efficiency and practicality, progress, material comfort, equality, freedom, external conformity, science and rationality, nationalism-patriotism, democracy, individualism, and the superiority of certain racial, ethnic, and religious groups. Williams pointed out that some of these values contradict others.

J. Katz (1985) has identified cultural values of the dominant group in the United States that are similar to those discussed by Williams. The list prepared by Katz includes rugged individualism, competition, an action orientation (including mastery and control of nature), hierarchical structure of decision making, direct communication but controlled emotions, adherence to time schedules, a Western orientation in history, the Protestant work ethic, planning for the future, emphasis on the scientific method, status and power based on economic position and material possessions, the nuclear family structure, acceptance of religion, celebration of holidays, and aesthetics based on Western beliefs. She also implied that the dominant white culture can be seen simply as one more subculture existing among a myriad of other subcultures.

Do Different Ethnic Groups Hold Different Values?

There are many popular stereotypes about the supposed characteristics of various ethnic groups. People from Scotland, for example, are said to be "thrifty." The British keep a "stiff upper lip" in the face of adversity, while "mainstream" Americans are "assertive" in nearly every situation. McGoldrick and Rohrbaugh (1987) note that a review of relevant literature reveals the following list of characteristics that are assumed to be associated with particular ethnic groups.

- Jewish American families are claimed to value such things as education, success, encouragement of children, democratic principles, verbal expression, shared suffering, guilt, and eating (Herz and Rosen, 1982; Papajohn and Spiegel, 1971; Zborowski and Herzog, 1952).

- British Americans generally place a high value on control, personal responsibility, independence, individuality, stoicism, keeping up appearances, and moderation in everything (McGill and Pearce, 1982).

- Italian Americans are described as placing a high value on the family rather than on the individual. Food is viewed not only in terms of physical nourishment, but as a major source of emotional nourishment as well. Male and female roles are clearly specified along traditional patriarchal lines. Loyalty in personal relationships is very important (Rotunno and McGoldrick, 1982).

- The stereotypes of Irish American families has included the view that strong mothers and weak or distant fathers are typical. Instead of consumption of food, drinking is the central social activity. Children are taught to behave well and to "not make a scene." They are seldom praised for doing well. Anger is not to be expressed, except against outsiders. Religious rules play a major role in the determination of family values. Suffering is a normal and expected part of life and is to be born in silence or "offered up" in atonement for one's sins (McGoldrick, 1982).

- Black Americans are seen by some as constituting a single homogeneous group, but subgroups within racial categories vary too much to allow for a meaningful single characterization of race in any particular way, although societal forces impose perceived characteristics on certain racial groups. For black families, subcultural differences with the dominant society have been exaggerated by American culture's history of institutionalized racism. The church plays an extremely important role in black culture. Family members' ability to survive under any and all conditions is an important value. Families often must make heroic efforts in order to help their children achieve a better life (Hill, 1972). In part because of the effects of the legacy of racism on males, women disproportionately have become the heads of families. Relationships between men and women exhibit a greater flexibility in roles than is the case in the dominant culture. The extended family is very important (Hines and Boyd-Franklin, 1982; Pinderhughes, 1982).

- Asian subculture in the United States also is represented by a complex mixture of different groups, including Chinese, Japanese, Laotian, Vietnamese, Cambodian, and others. In general, most Asian groups are said to place high value on the family and to emphasize the importance of respect and obligation toward older family members. Sex roles are clearly divided, with men handling the outside world and women maintaining the inner world of the family. Great emphasis is placed on children's education as an avenue to success (Shon and Ja, 1982). Form— that is, the manner in which things are said and done—is very important, as is not "losing face" (McGoldrick and Rohrbaugh, 1987). Despite these commonalities, each Asian subculture has its own differences from the others.

McGoldrick and Rohrbaugh (1987) note that while the ethnic characteristics described in the family therapy literature are basically consistent with popular stereotypes, there was little empirical research to support the existence of these descriptions. They therefore conducted an empirical study to test the extent to which the stereotypes actually described certain ethnic groups. A sample of 220 mental health professionals who identified themselves as having three out of four grandparents belonging to a single ethnic group answered questionnaires that asked about the extent to which certain values and behaviors were characteristic of the homes in which they grew up. The authors concluded that the actual life styles of the ethnic groups tested were basically consistent with popular stereotypes.

Strength of Ethnicity

Criminal justice professionals must not automatically assume that ethnicity makes people different or even assume that when a client identifies himself or herself as a member of an ethnic group that this is an important characteristic for that person. Instead, it is important for professionals to have an effective means by which to explore whether ethnicity is in fact an important part of that person's identity.

The content of an ethnic subculture is the result, among other things, of historical migration patterns, social class factors, religious beliefs, political conditions, and geography. While it is widely held that ethnic subcultures have their own unique features, there has been a tendency for ethnic Americans to move closer to the dominant American value system over time, especially as they improve their socioeconomic status. However, this assimilation process is sometimes limited by various social barriers as well as by the individual members' needs for a sense of belonging and identity (McGoldrick and Preto, 1984).

When a client identifies himself or herself as a member of an ethnic group, the ethnic identity may or may not be a truly important factor in that person's life. An important question for the criminal justice professional to explore is "To what extent does identification with an ethnic background reflect particular experiences in the individual's life?" These experiences are likely to influence the individual's values, beliefs, and actions.

McGoldrick (1982) has identified a number of factors which are likely to be indicators of the strength of an individual's ethnic identity. These factors are:

1. Place of birth of the client;
2. Place of birth of the client's mother;
3. Place of birth of the client's father;
4. Presence of relatives other than the immediate family in the client's household;
5. Most recent time (by generation) that someone in the client's family immigrated to the United States;
6. Population size of the client's area of residence;
7. Whether or not members of the client's extended family live nearby;
8. Upward socioeconomic mobility of the client;
9. Perceived importance which the client places on teaching an ethnic heritage to his or her children;
10. Whether the client's ancestors moved to the United States alone or with other family members;
11. Knowing why the client's family moved to the United States;
12. Whether or not the client wishes to visit the country of origin;
13. Whether a language other than English was spoken in the parental home;
14. Having experienced prejudice and/or discrimination because of ethnic group membership;
15. Whether or not the client lives in an ethnic neighborhood;
16. Degree of the client's participation in ethnic cultural events;
17. Having a desire to raise children with the same values as the client's parents taught him or her;
18. Whether or not the client's political preferences are based on ethnic influences;
19. Degree to which the client participates in ethnic rituals.

Nine of the questions (feeling it is important to teach one's children about their ethnic heritage, knowing why one's family migrated to the United States, wishing to visit one's country of origin, having spoken a language other than English in the parental home, having experienced discrimination because of one's ethnic membership, participating in ethnic cultural events, wanting to teach ethnic values to one's children, basing political preferences on ethnic value, and participating in ethnic rituals) have been found to be strongly related to the strength of ethnic identity (Yonas, 1992). These nine questions would be especially helpful for criminal justice professionals to ask clients, since ethnicity appears to be a "voluntary" identity for many individuals whose families have lived in the United States for many generations.

Conflicting Values of Professionals and Clients

Criminal justice services are embedded in the larger society, and, as a result, they reflect the dominant values, perceptions, and assumptions of the larger society. However, many who rely on these services do not share the dominant perspectives. Covert differences may result in conflict, friction, and misunderstandings.

Professionals, as others, are often not aware of cultural conflicts. Differences in values, goals, knowledge, and resulting expectations are further complicated by other social and economic differences.

When a client's ethnic background differs from that of a service provider, a resulting difference in values may be a significant source of friction. Communication may be impaired, and expectations may go unmet on both sides of the interaction. Conflicting perspectives imposed on members of subordinate groups have caused harm to individuals (Sue and Sue 1990). If a professional is not aware of subcultural differences in values, behavior of the members of some groups may be labeled as a "problem" or found to be lacking in some respect, while in reality such behavior may be entirely appropriate and understandable in terms of the values of those groups. A professional who can maintain an objective stance in terms of values will be better able to detect his or her own assumptions about how the client views his or her problem. Thus, in an accepting fashion, the professional can improve the quality of care and allow for a more cooperative relationship.

Utility of the Study of Ethnicity

The knowledge to be gained from a study of differences in values of different ethnic subcultures can be applied in a wide variety of settings within the criminal justice system. One such setting is that of counseling. In the field of counseling, it is the dominant culture which provides the primary values and norms for counseling theory, research, and application (Katz, 1985). As a result, many clients of counseling tend to view counselors as professionals who attempt to help others adapt or adjust to the dominant society's values (Szasz, 1974). On the other hand, professionals in a heterogeneous society like the United States find it "important to become aware of the world views of the culturally different client and how the client views the definition, roles, and function of the family" (Sue and Sue, 1990, p. 125).

Many potential problems in counseling can be eliminated or reduced in significance by the application of knowledge of ethnic differences and ethnic identities of clients. Such knowledge, for example, can reduce the tendency of some practitioners to impose their own values, standards, and solutions (derived most often from the dominant culture) upon others. A criminal justice system practitioner's sensitivity to the variations in values and beliefs between cultures and subcultures—and even within ethnic subcultures—may decrease this tendency. An "ethnically aware" practitioner will be better able to explore the important ethnic subcultural aspects of a client and the degree to which the ethnic traditions are observed. Problems between generations, intercultural relationships, perceived personal inadequacies, needs, goals, and values can be seen more clearly through an exploration of the place ethnicity and the client's culture occupy for that client. By exploring the ethnic context of the client's presenting problem and including this in the assessment and treatment plan, the practitioner may be able to address more readily the treatment needs of the client.

Sensitizing Against Stereotyping

Some criminal justice professionals (as well as others in society) may have a tendency to stereotype people of various ethnic subgroups because it is easy to see similarities among the members and therefore assume they are all alike. An appreciation of ethnic diversity will affect this tendency to generalize or to stereotype members of these groups. The differences and the related behaviors of members of the groups must be considered, and the strengths and adaptive nature of each value system should be examined in a respectful manner. In addition, each individual must be seen as unique, with characteristics that stem from factors that are stronger than ethnicity.

Future Considerations

The following are ways in which the consideration of ethnic variation may be utilized by criminal justice professionals:

1. To sensitize practitioners to ethnic variations in approaches to problem solving;
2. To provide a greater understanding of the general perspectives, common problems, and specific needs of people from specific ethnic group backgrounds;
3. To clarify the likely sources and probable nature of conflicts between service providers and clients from specific ethnic groups;
4. To suggest ways in which the organization structure and operating procedures of the criminal justice system complement or come into conflict with the value orientations and life styles of people from specific ethnic backgrounds.

Counseling the Offender Who Identifies with an Ethnic Group

Criminal justice professionals need to be aware of the cultural variations which exist within ethnic groups as well as those between ethnic groups. For example, there are variations in what is considered "family," ranging from the isolated nuclear family to the extended family or even to people who are not relatives. Approaches to problem solving vary, also, from an individual orientation to a group orientation. Varying degrees of sharing of feelings also exist. Professionals might do well to consider the following questions:

1. How are "outsiders" perceived by members of this ethnic subculture?
2. What expectations are members likely to have when involved in the criminal justice system?
3. How is authority perceived?
4. Is fate an important factor?
5. If unique values exist for an ethnic subculture, how do these values influence the lives of the members of the group?

This list of questions is not an exhaustive one. One of the best ways to learn about ethnic subcultures is to ask clients to teach service providers about their backgrounds.

References

Alba, Richard. 1990. *Ethnic Identity: The Transformation of White America.* New Haven: Yale University Press.

Gordon, M. 1978. *Human Nature, Class, and Ethnicity.* New York: Oxford University Press.

Greeley, Andrew. 1971. *Why Can't They Be Like Us?* New York: Dutton.

Herz, F., and E. Rosen. 1982. "Jewish Families," in *Ethnicity and Family Therapy,* edited by McGoldrick et al., 364–392. New York: Guilford Press.

Hill, Robert B. 1972. *The Strengths of Black Families.* New York: National Urban League.

Hines, Paulette, and Nancy Boyd-Franklin. 1982. "Black Families," in *Ethnicity and Family Therapy,* edited by McGoldrick et al., 84–107. New York: Guilford Press.

Isajiw, Wssvolod W. 1974. "Definitions of Ethnicity," *Ethnicity,* 1: 111–124.

Katz, Judith. 1985. "The Sociopolitical Nature of Counseling," *The Counseling Psychologist,* 13(October): 615–624.

McGill, D. and J. Pearce. 1982. "British Families," in *Ethnicity and Family Therapy,* edited by McGoldrick et al., 457–482. New York: Guilford Press.

McGoldrick, Monica. 1982. "Irish Families," in *Ethnicity and Family Therapy,* edited by McGoldrick, J. Pearce, and J. Giordano, 310–339. New York: Guilford Press.

McGoldrick, Monica and Nydia Preto. 1984. "Ethnic Intermarriage: Implications for Therapy." *Family Process,* 23: 347–364.

McGoldrick, Monica and M. Rohrbaugh. 1987. "Researching Ethnic Family Stereotypes," *Family Process, 26:* 89–99.

Papjohn, J. C. and J. P. Spiegel. 1971. "The Relationship of Culture, Value Orientation, and Rorschach Indices of Psychological Development," *Journal of Cross-Cultural Psychology,* 2: 257–272.

Pinderhughes, E. 1982. "Afro-American Families and the Victim System," in *Ethnicity and Family Therapy,* edited by McGoldrick et al., 108–122. New York: Guilford Press.

Rokeach, Milton. 1973. *The Nature of Human Values.* New York: The Free Press.

Rose, Peter. 1981. *They and We: Racial and Ethnic Relations in the United States.* New York: Random House.

Rotunno, Marie and Monica McGoldrick. 1982. "Italian Families," in *Ethnicity and Family Therapy,* edited by McGoldrick et al., 340–361. New York: Guilford Press.

Ruesch, Jugen. 1967. "Sociological Techniques, Social Status, and Social Control," in *Personality in Nature, Society, and Culture,* edited by Kluckhohn and Murray, 117–131. New York: Alfred A. Knopf.

Schermerhorn R. 1970. *Comparative Ethnic Relations: A Framework for Theory and Research.* New York: Random House.

Shon, S. and D. Ja. 1982. "Asian Families," in *Ethnicity and Family Therapy,* edited by McGoldrick et al., 208–228. New York: Guilford Press.

Sue, D. W. 1990. "Evaluating Process Variables in Cross-Cultural Counseling and Psychotherapy," in *Cross-Cultural Counseling and*

Psychotherapy: Foundations, Evaluations, Cultural Consideration, edited by A. Marsella and P. Pedersen. Elmsford, NJ: Pedgamon Press.

Sue, David and Derald Sue. 1990. *Counseling the Culturally Different*, 2nd ed. New York: Wiley & Sons.

Szasz, T. 1974. *The Myth of Mental Illness*. New York: Harper and Row.

Williams, Robin. 1970. *American Society*, 3rd ed. New York: Alfred Knopf.

Yonas, David. 1992. *A Study of Variations in Ethnic Value Orientation*. Dissertation, Kent State University.

Zborowski, M. and E. Herzog. 1952. *Life Is With People*. New York: Schocken Books.

12

Conflict Resolution
A Primer for Correctional Workers

Chester E. Sigafoos

Resolution of potentially volatile situations is a primary ingredient in the successful management of inmates. Often, correctional staff are faced with verbally assaultive, intimidating inmates. These inmates may be directing their assaults at each other, or at staff. It is not always necessary for staff to resolve less severe conflicts by writing incident reports, or by physically overpowering the inmate. If such tactics are used, they serve to undermine the relationship staff have with inmates in three ways:

- They establish a pattern of interaction between staff and inmates that heightens tension.
- They provide examples of behavior that other inmates may then decide to use on staff.
- They reinforce the self-fulfilling prophecy some staff may have about inmates—that the only way one can handle them is with force.

Conflict resolution is a method of dealing with anyone whose behavioral and verbal actions indicate he or she is in a state of belligerence. It can be a particularly useful strategy for correctional officers to use in their daily contact with inmates. For example, each day prison staff may encounter inmates whose physical behavior may show them to be agitated, excited, or nervous. Other conflictive inmates may stand firmly, defying staff to come close to them. Their verbal actions may include talking more loudly than normal. They

Source: *Federal Prisons Journal*, 3(2) (Fall 1992): 17–23.

may shout and speak more quickly, running their words together in an unintelligible jumble of syllables.

Imagine this situation: an inmate stands firm, leaning slightly towards you; he points his finger at you while he places his other hand on his hip. He talks louder and faster than normal, slurring his speech at times, possibly even hitting you with saliva as he barks out his thoughts. What would you do in this case? What would you say? There are no textbook answers to how you should respond or what you should say when confronted with this or any other conflict situation. Each situation is different. What upsets one inmate may not upset another. People sometimes "wake up on the wrong side of bed," and are irritated by normal daily routines of life. Even though the contents of the inmate's "message" are different, what is the same about conflict situations is their context.

Most conflict situations share common elements: a heightened state of agitation, a changed facial expression, and a charged mode of speech. By examining these common elements, we can establish some basic guidelines by which conflictive inmates can be handled.

Keep "Fight or Flight" Response in Check

Let's examine the conflict situation more closely. For every action there is a reaction, and nothing could be truer when you're faced with a conflict situation. Before you can even think of what to say, your body will react. Depending on your experience and the level of hostility directed to you, you may find yourself going to the extreme reaction of "fight or flight." In the "fight or flight" response, your body secretes hormones that prepare it to defend itself. This is a natural response when the body feels threatened, but it doesn't help solve the conflict and will probably make it worse. Although it's difficult, we need to try and temper our bodies' immediate reactions to a conflict situation. Put the response in a holding pattern. (Be happy it's there, for you may need it if the inmate goes completely "off" on you.)

Try to maintain a calm, defensive posture. If you assume a hostile, aggressive stance, this may only stimulate the already agitated inmate into a more aggressive mode. Assuming a posture that is calm (but not relaxed) and firm (but not too hard) sets the tone for conflict resolution. Your body language is just as important as your voice for sending a message.

Other inmates may be watching you. They may not be able to hear what you say, but they can see how you look. The image you project will send a message. You need to maintain a defensive posture because the inmate may try to assault you. A mentally disturbed inmate may have difficulty relating to what you say. You may think you're communicating with him when suddenly he swings at you. Standing in a good defensive posture, with your body partially to the side, will give you an edge in countering an attack. If an assault takes place, you'll be in a better position to bring the inmate under control.

So far, you've been confronted with a hostile inmate, your body has reacted, you keep the reaction in check, and you place yourself in a calm, defensive posture. You haven't said a word yet. What should you say? Should you listen or speak? Should you gain the upper hand immediately, or let the inmate "get it off his chest?" Is the inmate angry at you, or at someone or something else? Do you take this personally, or do you need to remind yourself that this particular inmate often acts this way?

Listen and Assess the Situation

In many conflict situations we find that we say something before we think about it. You are already in your calm, defensive posture. So what's your hurry? Instead of talking or yelling back at the inmate, count to five. Give yourself time to hear what he's saying. One of the most frequent complaints you'll hear from inmates is that no one listens to them. They develop a belief that what they say "falls on deaf ears." The inmate may be yelling just because he believes no one will listen. The answer to resolving this conflict, then, is to listen. Some inmates need to "unload" on someone. They vent their frustration and anger in a matter of minutes and then feel better.

Heitler (1990), in her book *From Conflict to Resolution*, presents a useful concept—the "expression of initial positions"; that is, what each side says at the beginning of the conflict resolution process. Listening is a very important component of this phase. A good listener is an active listener. Good listeners focus on what the speaker is saying. This is crucial to assessing the inmate. Is the speaker talking coherently? If not, the inmate may be under the influence of drugs or alcohol, or suffering from a serious mental disturbance. The only way you would know this is by listening. You would handle this inmate differently from one who is coherent but also agitated. If you started arguing immediately with the inmate, he might shut up, and thus deprive you of information necessary to your assessment.

Even though you may not agree with the conflictive inmate, now is not the time to argue with him. Listen to his story; don't criticize or try to demonstrate your superior knowledge. Listening doesn't mean you agree with him, it just means you've heard him.

An active listener also provides feedback to the speaker. This feedback can be both verbal and nonverbal. Nonverbal feedback includes nodding the head at appropriate times, maintaining eye contact with the speaker (not necessarily staring at him or looking through him), and, if appropriate, leaning toward the speaker (but maintaining your defensive posture).

Verbal feedback tells the speaker he's being heard and can be simple utterances like "uh huh," "yes," "I see." If the inmate says something you don't understand, perhaps because he's speaking so fast, ask him to clarify what he means. Some people are afraid to interrupt an agitated person for fear they'll "set them off." Asking the speaker for clarification shows that you are listening. Convey the message that what the speaker is saying is important, and you want to be sure you clearly understand.

In addition, when you ask someone to clarify what he's said, his reaction will usually be to talk slower and more distinctly. Have you ever heard yourself give directions to a foreign visitor? You talk much slower, make your sentences simpler, and enunciate more clearly. This is what happens when you ask a conflictive inmate to clarify what he's said. This sets a different pace of speech and tone of delivery. Instead of rambling and screaming, the inmate needs to slow down and temper his words. Many times this tactic will be sufficient to reduce the hostility level.

A second element of the assessment phase is the role of *equal time sharing*. This aspect needs to be examined more closely because of the different dynamics operating in the correctional setting. When you're dealing with a hostile inmate, he'll want to dominate the interaction by talking louder and longer. The normal staff-inmate "distribution of power"—who has control of the situation—favors the staff member. Staff become used to being in control and comfortable with a distribution of power in which the inmate is subordinate.

This "normal" asymmetry of power becomes disrupted in a conflict situation. The normally subordinate inmate acts as though he has become dominant and the staff subordinate. Staff need to be aware that power relationships frequently vary. Generally, staff dominate interactions with inmates, but that domination may be 51 percent on one occasion and 80 percent on another. The important thing to remember is that even if the inmate acquires 51 percent of the power in an interaction, eventually the power will shift back to normal levels.

Thus, if the staff member perceives that the inmate is shifting the power dimension, he or she needs to be reassured that this may only be an illusion. Just because the inmate is talking louder, faster, or longer doesn't necessarily mean the staff member has lost power in the relationship. The staff member needs to stand firm and self-confident. By doing this, the staff member holds on to the power base, which will return to its normal, asymmetrical nature once the conflict has been resolved.

In society, daily interactions between people are also characterized by fluctuations in the power dimension. Asymmetrical relations (boss and subordinate, for example), if accepted by the participants, are usually satisfactory. Healthy relationships among friends and family, however, are characterized by symmetrical power dimensions. In these, friends maintain a balance of power, thereby allowing give and take in the relationship and the mutual satisfaction of each friend's needs.

When power relationships in corrections become symmetrical, a different problem arises. Allowing a relationship between staff member and inmate to become balanced may scare some staff members. They may fear that they will not be able to regain control of the situation once the inmate dominates the interaction.

We need to recognize that by giving an inmate time to yell and scream, we are not losing power. In fact, what we are doing is maintaining control over the situation, since it is "we" who are allowing the inmate to speak. All inmates do not thoroughly think through what has caused their conflicts. Letting them talk may give them the first opportunity to actually hear what they've been thinking. Sometimes, after they've heard themselves, they recognize the flaws in their thinking, and resolve the conflict themselves.

But in other instances, the inmate's logic may not be flawed. Allowing symmetry in the relationship opens the way for the exchange of information. Symmetrical relationships mean that each person has equal time to present a point of view. Some inmates don't want to allow staff equal time. The egotistical nature of the antisocial personality wants only to hear itself. These types of inmates have always had difficulties in social interactions. They don't have the ability to "decenter," or see things from another person's point of view.

Identification of the antisocial inmate can be accomplished with experience during the assessment phase of conflict resolution. If you find that the inmate yelling and screaming at you is not receptive to an even exchange of information, consider another course of action. In some situations, walking away—while saying something like "I'll come back when you're calmer"—is a possible alternative. The presence of the staff member creates a "target" or stimulus for the inmate. If that stimulus is not there, the inmate may not respond anymore. This is not to suggest that the inmate will not be dealt with. The staff member can always return to the inmate at a later time, hopefully after he has calmed down.

In most conflict situations needing resolution, however, the staff member will not have the option of walking away.

Summarize Your Initial Positions

So what do you say to the agitated inmate? Ask him if you can say something. Asking permission to speak when confronted with a hostile inmate is like throwing a curve ball when the batter expects a fast ball. Inmates are seldom asked their permission, they are usually told what do to. Some staff may balk at the idea of asking an inmate's permission to speak. But remember, this technique allows you to maintain control of the situation.

You will accomplish several things by asking permission to speak. You'll find out if he's finished talking. If he's not, he will probably tell you so. In this way you're letting him know you want to speak, but will allow him time to finish. This will set the stage for a symmetrical interaction—I'll let you speak, then you let me speak. More importantly, you will be showing respect. You'll be giving him the message that what he says is important, and you don't want to interrupt.

When the inmate indicates he is finished speaking, you're on. The delivery of your message is as important as the content. If you've just listened to a hostile, screaming inmate, you've had an excellent example of how not to talk. Speak in a clear, direct manner—loud enough to be heard, but soft enough that the inmate has to work a little to hear you. This will force him to redirect his attention from shouting and screaming to push his message out, to processing incoming information instead.

Deliver your message at a slower than normal pace. Talking rapidly to a conflictive inmate will only exacerbate his anxiety. In fact, he's liable to model your behavior and increase his talking speed. Talking slower will hopefully set a precedent.

Do not criticize, ridicule, or make fun of what the inmate said. Some staff may think the inmate's actions are a "put on." But making a joke out of what he's said will only add fuel to the fire. It's important to speak in a professional, business-like manner. Some staff successfully use humor when dealing with a conflictive inmate. This can be risky. It is wiser to use a technique you're safe with than one that could backfire.

It is important to convey that you recognize the need to listen to different points of view. You are taking the time because it is important for you to offer your thoughts in an effort to help resolve the conflict.

Feedback is a way to offer verbal information to the conflictive inmate. For example, if you respond to the inmate, saying "yes, but . . .", this does not show cooperation. The "but" is an indication that the inmate is wrong and you are right. Changing the word to "and", as in "yes, and . . .", creates a different atmosphere: "Now we can cooperate in resolving this conflict."

If we put this all together, we should end up with an atmosphere in which both participants have an equal opportunity to express their points of view. The conflictive inmate may have started out in a hostile, agitated manner, but through the use of controlled speech patterns, the staff member is able to set a tone that will promote the sharing of information.

By summarizing the initial positions, you tell the inmate you've heard what he's said. In return, and in a symmetrical fashion, the inmate has heard your point of view. This does not say that either point of view is right, just that we know where each stands. From this, a working relationship can be developed to find solutions to the conflict. Studies of interactions between people have shown how working toward a common goal enhances the relationship between enemies. This does not suggest that a staff member be "buddy-buddy" with an inmate. But it is important for staff to have positive relationships with inmates.

The goal of conflict resolution is to obtain a "win-win" situation. If one side is not allowed to present its position, we end up with "win-lose." The inmate loses by being locked up after not being allowed to talk, or the staff loses by fueling inmate animosity.

During the presentation of initial positions, each participant states what he wants. It is difficult to develop a path to a goal if neither side knows what goal is being sought. Some goals can never be attained—for example, if the inmate says his goal is to get out of prison "right now!" Other goals may be more logical.

Take the example of the inmate who is furious, upset, and "not going to take it any longer." He's been held in the reception unit, living with two other inmates, for the past 3 weeks, waiting for bedspace in the housing unit. We know what his goal is, but what about your goal? Is ensuring a safe environment for the inmates all there is to it?

Read between the Lines

The next phase involves an examination of the initial positions, and the "true" underlying reasons for those positions. One of the most difficult jobs a staff member has is being able to decipher what some inmates mean. Inmates can be experts at concealing the truth. They've been rewarded for it in the past. But one of the drawbacks of being good at deception is that sometimes you don't know what the truth is anymore. When this happens, inmates may not know why they are so upset. This makes the job of resolving the conflict more difficult.

Another source of false information could be staff members if, instead of being active listeners, they just listened to their own thoughts, focused on what they thought they heard was wrong, or began to overinterpret the inmate's position.

Exploring underlying concerns requires the participants to shift their focus. At this time, the staff member could move the discussion to other surroundings. Inmates will "front" a staff member, given the opportunity—that is, they will attempt to embarrass or upset a staff member in front of other inmates. Resolving conflict situations in front of other inmates creates additional problems. First, the inmate wants to continue to be seen as dominant. If the staff member can convince the inmate to move to another location, he or she also removes the inmate from his source of support.

Second, the onset of the conflict may have occurred in the inmate's room, or some other familiar surrounding. Removing the inmate from this surrounding creates an advantage for staff. The staff member also wants to be in familiar surroundings, thereby gaining a nonverbal edge over the inmate. Further, the initial surroundings have been linked to the onset of the conflict. Staying there may only keep the memory of the initial confrontation fresh.

Third, the staff member has reached a point with the inmate in which a mutual relationship exists. They are now in a state of cooperation rather than confrontation. It becomes easier for both to cooperate if they work in a more private setting. Some inmates may object to a staff member's suggestion of going to "their" office. This could be seen as a sign of weakness or defeat in the inmate. If that's the case, agree upon a neutral spot. When choosing the location, privacy needs to be weighed against security. You are not out of the woods yet. The inmate may have calmed down, but could be doing so in an effort to assault you when you least expect it. Sometimes walking around the compound provides all the privacy you need.

In this stage a mutual effort is undertaken with the goal of resolving the conflict. Prior to this, the atmosphere was oppositional, the perspectives were narrow, and the focus was on "I." Now the focus should be on looking at the broader picture. Change the pronoun in your sentences from "I" to "We." This establishes a new mindset in which the staff member is no longer the enemy, and the inmate is no longer the subordinate. Now you are working together to resolve the issue.

Examining underlying concerns begins with a restatement of the initial positions. Time has now passed, and the inmate may be in a clearer frame of mind. Ask the inmate to restate his position. Follow with a restatement of your position. In the example of the inmate demanding a housing unit change, the inmate now states, "I don't feel comfortable living in there." This is not the same initial position. The initial position was a demand to be moved. Now, he doesn't "feel comfortable." Why the change?

A change from the initial position may take place for several reasons. The inmate or staff member may have gained some insight into the problem, making the true reason for the conflict easier to understand. Conversely, the passage of time may create second thoughts, and the true reason may have moved farther away.

Some inmates are able to be honest with themselves and with others. For these inmates, conflict resolution will probably end up in win-win situations. For others, the ability to be honest with themselves has long been distorted and flawed. As a staff member, you may not be interested whether an inmate is being honest with himself. But at this phase of conflict resolution, your ability to accept the inmate, and show a nonjudgemental interest in his conflict, is important. Guard against the introduction of any personal bias into the relationship.

Inmates are very sensitive to being questioned. In fact, they are probably experts in the "art" of interrogation and its tactics and techniques. Just a short time ago, this inmate was yelling and screaming. The one thing we didn't want to do was antagonize him, or appear hostile or offensive. Now we are at a point at which it's necessary to obtain information. We don't want to appear offensive, because if the inmate feels he's being interrogated we're liable to end up where we started.

Here a little role playing may help. Jack Webb, in the television series "Dragnet," was famous for one expression, "just the facts." That's what we're looking for, "just the facts." And we are doing so for the purpose of achieving "our" goal, resolving the conflict.

Information is contained in the mind at various levels. Often, the surface levels do not provide the facts needed to understand underlying concerns. As you delve deeper into the reasons for the conflict, you will need both awareness and a sense of history. You'll need to be aware of how specific things affect this inmate. Why does he "feel uncomfortable"? Is it because the beds are terrible, or does he have back problems? The more you talk, the more history will be uncovered. We all have a personal history, which influences what we think about, how we think, and how we react to things.

Earlier, the role of listening was discussed. It is important in this phase too. But the listening you do now will be different. When you listen to deeper concerns, it helps if you "soften" your stance. By this, you seem more compassionate and understanding.

Here's how our hypothetical example might resolve: as you listen to the inmate talking about his problems with his housing situation, you realize something else is bothering him—family problems, perhaps. Or one of his cellmates might be trying to extort something from him. Or perhaps the other inmates in his cell are having a sexual relationship and he is upset by it. You might ask if he's ever had this problem before. There's no need to pry, and he may not want to explain fully, but the more you can talk to him on this level, the likelier you are to discover the true reason for his conflict.

During the dialogue, you have your side to present too. You'll probably want to explain the procedures for housing and the rationale behind the system. Emphasizing the aspect of fairness in placement for all inmates is important. The system isn't designed to benefit one person only. While the inmate focuses on his specific needs, the narrow perspective, the staff focuses on the needs of the institution, the broader perspective. But now you see how one inmate's problem comes in conflict with the system you represent. At this point, you would again summarize each position.

Resolve the Situation through Compromise and Cooperation

The needs of both parties have been identified. Now we must provide options that serve those needs. The generation of alternatives is a group process. Both inmate and staff member need to offer ideas. Brainstorming is most effective when it is unrestricted, free-flowing, and involves more than one person. The goal is to generate as many options as possible.

Once the possible alternatives are listed, a mutually satisfying choice can be made. Of course, the solution may not always be totally satisfactory to each person. In corrections, resolution of the conflict may not mean the inmate gets what he wants. Some needs cannot be satisfied because of policies against the proposed solution, circumstances beyond staff's control, or the irrational nature of the demands. Does this mean that conflict resolution failed? No. Just calming the inmate down, and reducing the volatility of the initial situation, is conflict resolution in itself. The goal of conflict resolution need not be the totally successful resolution of every problem.

A realistic resolution will involve compromise and cooperation. Part of picking the solution involves compromise, the give and take of negotiation. As each person presents alternatives, the pros and cons can be discussed.

Some inmates, no matter how many alternatives you look at, no matter how hard you've tried, will just not be satisfied. These rigid-thinking inmates will continue to have difficulty adjusting to prison life. With these inmates, the staff member can at least say, "I've done the best I can." Most inmates learn to adjust, but there will always be a few who seem to thrive on being miserable—that's their choice.

Implement the Solution

The final step is to review what you've both done and ensure that no unfinished business remains. In the example of the inmate seeking different housing, the staff member was able to move the inmate to a new cell within the reception unit. The inmate wasn't able to move to a housing unit like he wanted. But after the underlying reasons for his distress were revealed, the solution was easier to find.

After a conflict is successfully resolved, the relationship between inmate and staff changes. The asymmetrical nature of the relationship returns, but the quality of the relationship is now different. Inmates and staff who work together learn that with a little patience, listening, and understanding, results can be obtained—maybe not the results the inmate originally wanted, but positive results nonetheless.

Inmates come away from the experience with a different attitude. They have learned that other alternatives exist by which they can change their environment. If resolving the conflict through communication works once, perhaps it will work again. If one inmate finds it works for him, he'll probably tell others. For staff working with inmates, the little bit of time you take today may pay off tomorrow.

Section V

Reality Therapy and Responsibility Training

Reality therapy is based on the principle that an individual must accept responsibility for his or her behavior and the goal of the reality therapist is to lead the person being treated to act "responsibly."

According to William Glasser, pioneer of the reality therapy concept, those in need of treatment have been unable to meet their own needs because they deny the reality of the world about them.[1] Reality therapy seeks to help the one being treated to perceive the world as it really is and to behave in a reasonable, responsible manner in the light of this perception. Glasser defines two basic human needs as the key to human behavior—the need to love and be loved and the need to feel that we are worthwhile to ourselves and to others.[2] He regards all irresponsible (socially unacceptable) behavior as caused by the client's inability to fulfill one or both of these needs. Glasser views a close involvement with other humans as essential to the achievement of responsible behavior and the reality therapist is called upon to become personally involved with clients.

Reality therapy differs from other types of therapy in a number of ways. It does not examine the client's past or recognize the existence of mental illness. It views all behavior as conforming to or deviating from the concept of responsible behavior. The concept of morality plays an important role in the therapy, and all acts are defined as being right or wrong. Against this background, the therapist actively instructs the client in ways to become responsible and better fulfill his or her needs.

The use of reality therapy in corrections has a strong appeal for a number of reasons. Since the therapist does not require extensive training and the therapy does not involve complicated terminology, categorizations, or treatment procedures, reality therapy can be implemented by correctional workers who operate on a paraprofessional or volunteer level, as well as by professionals in the field. It follows the basic tenets of common sense and the "golden rule" and does not involve the preparation of detailed case histories, psychological test results, or progress reports.

Critics of reality therapy maintain that it is unrealistic to deny the existence of mental illness and to maintain that any type of individual, no matter how severe his or her problem behavior has become, can be treated in this manner. As the sole judge of the responsibility or acceptability of the client's behavior, the reality therapist is in a position to guide the behavior of the client without feedback from other professional staff, who might be critical of the manner in which the case is being handled. Finally, the therapist is seen as a strong authority figure who may alienate those whose criminal behavior is a reaction to or rebellion against authority or those who are unable to meet the expectations of authority figures.

The two selections in this section are designed to introduce the reader to the principles of reality therapy and then provide a discussion of the issues and concerns related to its use. In selection thirteen, "Reality Therapy: Helping People Help Themselves," Richard L. Rachin describes the step-by-step procedures used by an effective reality therapist to gain the client's trust and lead him or her toward responsible behavior.

In selection fourteen, "Reality Therapy: Issues and a Review of Research," Carl A. Bersani reviews the success of the application of reality therapy in such settings as schools, corrections, private practice, state mental hospitals, substance abuse centers, and similar programs. Of particular interest is his finding that reality therapy is utilized in 80% of juvenile institutions contacted in a national survey. He also describes the issues and concerns related to the application of reality therapy, including the definition of responsible behavior and the influence of the moral convictions or preconceived notions and prejudices of the counselor in shaping the client's behavior. Acceptance of the counselor's values and judgments uncritically can lead to a client's overdependence on the counselor and inhibit the client's ability to make independent decisions.

Notes

1 William Glasser. *Reality Therapy* (New York; Harper & Row 1965), 7.
2 Ibid., 9.

13

Reality Therapy
Helping People Help Themselves

Richard L. Rachin

"The realities of mental-health operations," said Anthony Graziano two years ago, "seldom match the idealism with which they are described in the rhetoric."

> Our professional rhetoric is powerfully reinforcing when it enables us to obscure our own doubts and to disguise our own shortcomings. We seldom actually do what we say we are really doing. Sustained by their own deception, individual clinicians believe they are performing noble functions in essentially bureaucratic, unsympathetic, and doubtfully effective agencies.[1]

Graziano was not saying anything new. This same message has been delivered, with increasing volume, since the early fifties. Only recently, however, have the efficacy and ethical underpinning of classical treatment procedures been openly attacked.[2] Today it seems almost fashionable to expose, if not castigate, psychoanalysts for defects of character and purpose—faults which they have always shared with the rest of us.[3]

While psychotherapy, particularly of the psychoanalytic type, has never proven to be more effective or dependable than less pretentious kinds of help, orthodox practitioners tend to be as defensive as shamans in examining this incongruity. With certain notable exceptions, there is a remarkable absence of discussion among psychotherapists concerning the efficacy of their treatment techniques in spite of the paucity of evidence mustered to support the

From *Crime and Delinquency*, January 1974. Reprinted by permission of Sage Publications, Inc.

belief that psychotherapy is more effective than other treatment procedures.

The influence of mental health practitioners is largely responsible for acceptance of the view that socially disapproved behavior is evidence of emotional illness. Too often the label becomes a self-fulfilling prophecy building impenetrable barriers between *them* (those labeled) and the rest of us.

People in trouble, whether they are patients in mental institutions, drug dependents, or kids who play truant, often are not in a position where they can choose to be treated or not be treated. Public agencies armed with clinical evaluations make the choice for them. The recipient of such public largesse and his family have had little to say about rejecting or terminating treatment, even when the service seems to endanger his health and well-being.[4] Explanations designed to justify these practices are patronizing and lack the evidence that would support continuing them.

Ponder Graziano's theme that American mental health practitioners seem more concerned about improving their status and enhancing their power base than they are about treating. Clinical services have not been freely available to persons needing such care—especially in correction, where both the quality and the quantity of clinical personnel have left something to be desired. Considering juvenile correction alone, the President's Crime Commission reported that, of the 21,000 persons employed during 1965 in 220 state-operated juvenile facilities, only 1,154 were treatment staff. While the accepted national standard required one psychiatrist for every 150 juvenile inmates, the actual ratio in American institutions for children was 1:910. Forty-six psychiatrists (over half of them concentrated in five states) were then listed as the treatment backbone of juvenile correction.[5] As Donald Cressey observed, "The trap is this: We subscribe to a theory of rehabilitation that can be implemented only by highly educated, 'professionally trained' persons, and then scream that there are not enough of these persons to man our correctional agencies and institutions."[6]

Dissatisfaction with the Medical Model

The following are some of the reasons for the accelerating development of alternatives to traditional, medically based approaches to helping troubled people:

1. "The recidivism rate for offenders," writes Seymour Halleck, "remains depressingly high and the number of psychiatrists interested in treating the delinquent remains shamefully low."[7]

Publicity given to crime and the problems of our criminal justice system has not led to any significant increase in the number of clinicians devoting themselves to correction.

2. Even if there were enough conventionally prepared clinicians available, it is doubtful that government would be able or willing to assume the cost of their employment. Psychiatric attention is expensive and psychiatry's patients in the correctional system have never been high on the list of public priorities.

3. Important class, cultural, and racial barriers between those treating and those being treated have hindered the development of rapport and effective treatment programs. This problem has been magnified by our dependence on institutional care and the location of most of the institutions in rural areas, where staff recruitment beyond the surrounding communities (when attempted) is usually unsuccessful. Generally, in a state with a relatively large urban population, few of the staff—but, conversely, a disproportionately large part of the inmate population—are members of city-dwelling minority groups.

4. Research has not demonstrated that people receiving conventional treatment are any better off than those not receiving treatment. While this may be disturbing to advocates of the status quo, it is well to recall Jerome Frank's words: "Comparison of the effects of psychotherapy and placebos on a group of psychiatric outpatients suggests certain symptoms may be relieved equally well by both forms of treatment and raises the possibility that one of the features accounting for some of the success of all forms of psychotherapy is their ability to arouse the patient's expectation of help."[8] We are witnessing an accelerating growth of more humane, socially accountable therapies in which people with problems depend on other people with similar problems for help. The influence that human beings have on one another has long been noted, but has not been applied in practice.[9]

Although middle-class values and standards provide no valid measure for assessing mental health or mental illness, this yardstick has been customarily employed to measure deviation and the need for correctional care, especially in juvenile courts. Fortunately, simple economics has forced a re-examination of the traditional treatment orthodoxy. We have finally come to question the concept of mental illness as behavior that deviates from an established norm and its concept of cure as intervention by professionally trained mental health practitioners.

There should be little argument about the pervasive long-term ineffectiveness of most "treatment" programs. Although poorly trained staff, crumbling and inadequate physical plants, skimpy budgets, and overcrowding contribute to their futility, it is doubtful that unlimited resources alone would make it possible to rehabilitate significantly more offenders. Many private child-care agencies with budgets and per capita costs several times those of their public counterparts have discovered this when they become involved with court-referred children—even though they have been highly selective when deciding which court-committed children they will accept. A major reason for the poor results may be that many of the ways in which most well-adjusted adults once behaved are now viewed as symptomatic of underlying pathology. Two important circumstances are usually overlooked: (1) usually behavior brought to the attention of the courts and other official agencies is disproportionately that of poor and minority group children; (2) as George Vold observed, "in a delinquency area, delinquency is the normal response of the normal individual. . . . The nondelinquent is really the 'problem case,' the nonconformist whose behavior needs to be accounted for."[10]

The imprimatur of the court clinician is usually sufficient to dispose of children whose true feelings and needs are probably better known to their peers than to anyone coming into contact with the child for the first time. As Martin Silver found, "The detection of a 'proclivity to bad behavior' is facilitated by the court's 'treatment' process." Silver goes on to quote Dick Gregory: "Being black is not needing a psychiatrist to tell you what's bugging you."[11]

Offenders who have proved to be poor candidates for traditional treatment approaches in many cases seem responsive to peer group "here and now" therapies. As Carl Rogers expressed it, "It makes me realize what incredible potential for helping resides in the ordinary untrained person, if only he feels the freedom to use it."[12] The medical model for understanding and treating essentially psychosocial, ethical, or legal deviations makes it, as Szasz suggests, "logically absurd to expect that it will help solve problems whose very existence has been defined and established on nonmedical grounds."[13]

Nevertheless, when available in correction and more than just in name, diagnostic and treatment services essentially remain cast from the same orthodox mold. Vested interests and ignorance combine to apply a method of treatment that even Freud himself was to disavow in later life.[14] Ironically, proposals made to improve treatment services are usually accompanied by pleas for more psychiatrists, clinical psychologists, and psychiatric social workers. The influence which mental health practitioners have had on the design and delivery of treatment services seems accounted for not by any greater success in helping people but by seemingly convincing arguments disparaging alternative approaches. Put to the test, conventional treatment practices based upon the mental health/mental illness model have been as unsuccessful with offender groups as they often have been unavailable. Operating in the penumbra of the clinician and frequently in awe of him, legislators and correctional administrators have clung tenaciously to procedures about which they understand little and feel the need to understand less. And this problem has not been restricted to correction.

The development of less costly, more effective, and readily attainable treatment alternatives can be traced to three conditions: first, a quest for involvement, understanding, and clear communication by significant numbers of people—a need which could hardly be met by the small coterie of conventional mental health practitioners; second, voluntary patients' dissatisfaction with the time and expense required for treatment; and third, a crescendo of criticism directed by practitioners and researchers at a treatment methodology that has never been validated.[15]

William Glasser shared this concern. Near the completion of his psychiatric training he began to doubt much of what he had been taught. "Only a very few questioned the basic tenets of conventional psychiatry. One of these few was my last teacher, Dr. G. L. Harrington. When I hesitatingly expressed my own concern, he reached across the desk, shook my hand and said 'join the club.' "[16]

Reality Therapy

Glasser's theories departed radically from classical procedures. He postulated that, regardless of the symptom—be it drug use, fear of heights, suspicion that others may be plotting against one, or whatever—the problem could be traced in all instances to an inability to fulfill two basic needs:

> Psychiatry must be concerned with two basic psychological needs: *the need to love and be loved and the need to feel that we are worthwhile to ourselves and to others.*[17]

Glasser believed that the severity of the symptom reflected the degree to which the person was failing to meet these needs. No matter how bizarre or irrational the behavior seems to be, it always has meaning to the person: a rather ineffective but nevertheless necessary attempt to satisfy these basic needs.

Regardless of behavior, people who are not meeting their needs refuse to acknowledge the reality of the world in which they live. This becomes more apparent with each successive failure to gain relatedness and respect. Reality therapy mobilizes its efforts toward helping a person accept reality and aims to help him meet his needs within its confines.

We fulfill our needs by being involved with other people. Involvement, of course, means a great deal more than simply being with other people. It is a reciprocal relationship of care and concern. Most people usually experience this relationship with parents, spouses, close friends, or others. When there is no involvement with at least one other human being, reality begins to be denied and the ability to meet one's needs suffers accordingly.

Glasser points out that advice given to a person who needs help is of little value. People who deny the reality of the world around them cannot be expected to respond to exhortations to do better or to behave. Involvement means having a relationship with another person who can both model and mirror reality. The reality therapist presumes that people who are experiencing difficulty in living are having difficulty meeting their needs within the confines of the "real world." To help someone adopt a more successful lifestyle, the reality therapist must first become involved with him. Involvement is the reality therapist's expression of genuine care and concern. It is the key to his success in influencing behavior. Involvement does not come easily. The therapist must be patient and determined not to reject the person because of aberrance or misbehavior.

Reality and Traditional Therapy Compared

Reality therapy rejects the classical system whereby problem-ridden people are viewed as mentally ill and their behavior is labeled according to a complex and extensive classification scheme. Instead of the terms "mental health" and "mental illness," reality therapy refers to behavior as "responsible" or "irresponsible." The extensive, ambiguous, and unreliable diagnostic scheme on which conventional practitioners depend is discarded. As diagnostician the reality therapist simply determines whether the person is meeting his needs in a manner that does not interfere with others meeting theirs. If he is, he is acting responsibly; if he isn't, he is acting irresponsibly.

Conventional procedures lead the patient back through a maze of old experiences in search of the origin of his problem, because, the analyst assumes, the patient will be unable to deal with the present until he understands how the problem began in the elusive link in the past. Reality therapy concentrates on the present, on the "here and now" rather than the "there and then." Nothing can change the past, no matter how sad or unfortunate it may have been. The past does not influence present behavior any more than the person permits it to. The focus of the reality therapist, therefore, is on present behavior, about which something can be done.

Conventional therapy emphasizes the process during which the patient relives significant occurrences in his past and projects his past wishes, thoughts, and feelings onto the therapist; through interpretation of these past events the therapist helps the patient understand his present inadequate behavior. In contrast, reality therapy rejects the need for insight into one's past; the reality therapist relates to the person as he is and does not relive the past. The conventional practitioner seeks to uncover unconscious conflicts and motivations and to help the patient gain insight into these mental processes; he deemphasizes conscious problems while helping the patient understand his unconscious through dreams, free associations, and analysis of the transference. The reality therapist insists that the person examine his conscious self and behavior; conceding that efforts to understand motivation or other complex mental processes may be interesting, he doubts that the results merit the time spent to obtain them: it has yet to be demonstrated, he argues, that these pursuits have anything to do with helping the person.

Conventional practice makes no ethical judgments and frees the patient of moral responsibility for his actions; it views the patient as being under the influence of a psychic illness which makes him incapable of controlling his behavior. In reality therapy the patient is forced to face the consequences of his behavior: Was it right or wrong? What were the results for him?

Finally, the conventionally schooled practitioner insists that his role remain inexplicit, almost ambiguous, to the patient; he does not take an active part in helping him find a more productive way to live. Although the reality therapist does not take over for the person, he helps him—even teaches him when necessary—to learn better ways to meet his needs.

Fourteen Steps

The reality therapist follows certain steps in attaining involvement and influencing responsible, realistic behavior. Responsibility, the basic concept of reality therapy, is defined simply as the ability to meet one's needs without depriving others of the ability to meet theirs. Realistic behavior occurs when one considers and compares the immediate and remote consequences of his actions.

Step 1: *Personalizes.* The reality therapist becomes emotionally involved. He carefully models responsibility and does not practice something other than he preaches. He is a warm, tough, interested, and sensitive human being who genuinely gives a damn—and demonstrates it.

Step 2: *Reveals Self.* He has frailties as well as strengths and does not need to project an image of omniscience or omnipotence. If he is asked personal questions he sees nothing wrong with responding.

Step 3: *Concentrates on the "Here and Now."* He is concerned only with behavior that can be tested by reality. The only problems or issues that can be confronted are those occurring in the present. Permitting the person to dwell on the past is a waste of time. He does not allow the person to use the unfavorable past as a justification of irresponsible action in the present.

Step 4: *Emphasizes Behavior.* Unlike attitudes or motives, behavior can be observed. The reality therapist is not interested in uncovering underlying motivations or drives; rather, he concentrates on helping the person act in a manner that will help him meet his needs responsibly. Although the person may be convinced that new behavior will not attain responsible ends, the reality therapist insists that he try.

Step 5: *Rarely Asks Why.* He is concerned with helping the person understand what he is doing, what he has accomplished, what he is learning from his behavior, and whether he could do better than he is doing now. Asking the person the reasons for his actions implies that they make a difference. The reality therapist takes a posture that irresponsible behavior is just that, regardless of the reasons. He is not interested in time-consuming and often counter-productive explanations for self-defeating behavior. Rather, he conveys to the person that more responsible behavior will be expected.

Step 6: *Helps the Person Evaluate His Behavior.* He is persistent in guiding the person to explore his actions for signs of irresponsible, unrealistic behavior. He does not permit the person to deny the importance of difficult things he would like to do. He repeatedly asks the person what his current behavior is accomplishing and whether it is meeting his needs.

Step 7: *Helps Him Develop a Better Plan for Future Behavior.* By questioning *what* the person is doing now and *what* he can do differently, he conveys his belief in the person's ability to behave responsibly. If the person cannot develop his own plan for future action, the reality therapist will help him develop one. Once the plan is worked out, a contract is drawn up and signed by the person and the reality therapist. It is a minimum plan for behaving differently in matters in which the person admits he has acted irresponsibly. If the contract is broken, a new one is designed and agreed upon. If a contract is honored, a new one with tasks more closely attuned to the person's ability is designed. Plans are made for the contract to be reviewed periodically.

Step 8: *Rejects Excuses.* He does not encourage searching for reasons to justify irresponsible behavior: to do so would support a belief that the person has acceptable reasons for not doing what he had agreed was within his capabilities. Excuses do not improve a situation; they do not help a person to see the need for an honest, scrutinizing examination of his behavior. Excuses only delay improvement.

Step 9: *Offers No Tears of Sympathy.* Sympathy does little more than convey the therapist's lack of confidence in the person's ability to act more responsibly. The reality therapist does not become inveigled into listening to long sad stories about a person's past. The past cannot justify present irresponsible behavior. The therapist has a relationship with the person which is based upon genuine care and concern; sympathizing with a person's misery or inability to act in a more productive and need-fulfilling manner will do nothing to improve his ability to lead a responsible life. The therapist must convey to the person that he cares enough about him that, if need be, he will try to force him to act more responsibly.

Step 10: *Praises and Approves Responsible Behavior.* People need recognition and esteem for their positive accomplishments. However, the reality therapist should not become unduly excited about a person's success in grappling with problems that he previously avoided or handled poorly. But just as a person's irresponsible behavior is recognized when he is asked what he plans to do about it, so should his responsible behavior be recognized.

Step 11: *Believes People Are Capable of Changing Their Behavior.* Positive expectations do much to enhance the chances of a person's adopting a more productive lifestyle regardless of how many times he may have failed in the past. Negative expectations, on the other hand, serve to undermine progress. It is easier to do things well when others are encouraging and optimistic.

Step 12: *Tries to Work in Groups.* People are most responsive to the influence and pressure of their peers. It is much easier to express oneself with a group of peers than it is to relate to a therapist alone. People are also more likely to be open and honest with a peer group. Problems one often imagines are unique are quickly discovered by group members to be similar to the difficulties others also are encountering. Group involvement itself is immediate and helpful grist for observation and discussion. Learning experiences derived from interaction in treatment groups carry over to personal group encounters.

Step 13: *Does Not Give Up.* The reality therapist rejects the idea that anyone is unable to learn how to live a more productive and responsible life. There are instances when a person may be unwilling to do anything about his life, but this does not mean that, given another opportunity, he will not work to change it. Failure need not be documented in a detailed case record. Case records too often become little more than repetitive and largely subjective harbingers of failure. Sometimes professionals seem more involved with records than with the people the records pretend to describe. The reality therapist does not let historical material interfere with his becoming involved with people or prevent him from beginning afresh.

Step 14: *Does Not Label People.* He does not believe that elaborate diagnostic rituals aid involvement or help the person. Behavior is simply described as responsible or irresponsible. The therapist does not classify people as sick, disturbed, or emotionally disabled.

The principles of reality therapy are common sense interwoven with a firm belief in the dignity of man and his ability to improve his lot. Its value is twofold: it is a means by which people can help one another, and it is a treatment technique, applicable regardless of symptomatology. It is simple to learn albeit somewhat difficult for the novice to practice. Experience, not extensive theoretical grooming, is the key to accomplishment.

Correctional clients who have proven least amendable to conventional treatment methods respond well to reality therapy. That its employment involves only a fraction of the time as well as the cost required by traditional (and not more effective) psychoanalytically oriented treatment modalities only further underscores its value. Until research can demonstrate its relative effectiveness and permanence, these reasons alone make its utilization well worth a try.

Notes

[1] Anthony M. Graziano, "Stimulus/Response: In the Mental-Health Industry, Illness Is Our Most Important Product," *Psychology Today*, January 1972, p. 17.

[2] *Los Angeles Times*, June 26, 1972, p. 3.

[3] Phyllis Chester, "The Sensuous Psychiatrists," *New York*, June 19, 1972, pp.52–61.

[4] Frontal lobotomy, electric shock, and insulin therapy to relieve anxiety were far from being the most humane procedures. See Percival Bailey, "The Great

Psychiatric Revolution," *American Journal of Psychiatry*, Vol. 113, 1956, pp. 387–406. Those who have complete confidence in the new wonder drugs should see Richard Elman's "All the Thorazine You Can Drink at Bellevue," *New York*, Nov. 22, 1971, pp. 40–46; also, *New York Times*, July 15, 1972, p. 7.

[5] President's Commission on Law Enforcement and Administration of Justice, *Task Force Report: Corrections* (Washington, D.C.: Government Printing Office, 1967), p. 145.

[6] Donald R. Cressey, remarks on "The Division of Correctional Labor," *Manpower and Training for Corrections*, Proceedings of an Arden House Conference, June 24–26, 1964, p. 56.

[7] Seymour L. Halleck, "The Criminal's Problem with Psychiatry," *Morality and Mental Health*, O. Hobart Mowrer et al., eds. (Chicago: Rand McNally, 1967), p. 86.

[8] Jerome D. Frank, *Persuasion and Healing* (New York: Schocken Books, 1964), p. 74. See also R. G. Appel et al., "Prognosis in Psychiatry," A.M.A. *Arch. Neurol. Psychiat.*, Vol. 70, 1953, pp. 459–68; O.H. Mowrer, *The Crisis in Psychiatry and Religion* (Princeton, NJ: Van Nostrand, 1961), p. 121; Hans D. Eysenck, *The Effects of Psychotherapy* (New York: International Science Press, 1966), p. 121.

[9] J. Dejerine and E. Gauckler, *The Psychoneuroses and Their Treatment* (Philadelphia: Lippincott, 1913), p. 17.

[10] E. Lovell Bixby and Lloyd W. McCorkle, "Discussion of Guided Group Interaction and Correctional Work," *American Sociological Review*, August 1951, p.460.

[11] Martin T. Silver, "The New York City Family Court: A Law Guardian's Overview," *Crime and Delinquency*, January 1972, p. 95.

[12] Carl Rogers, *Carl Rogers on Encounter Groups* (New York: Harper & Row, 1970), p. 58.

[13] Thomas S. Szasz, "The Myth of Mental Illness," *American Psychologist*, Vol. 15, 1960.

[14] J. Wortis, *Fragments of an Analysis with Freud* (New York: Simon and Schuster, 1954), p. 57.

[15] Eysenck, *op. cit. supra* note 8, p. 94, quotes D. H. Malan, the Senior Hospital Medical Officer at London's Tavistock Clinic, the locus of orthodox psychoanalysis in England: "There is not the slightest indication from the published figures that psychotherapy has any value at all."

[16] William M. Glasser, *Reality Therapy: A New Approach to Psychiatry* (New York: Harper & Row, 1965), p. xxiii.

[17] *Id.*, p. 9.

14

Reality Therapy
Issues and a Review of Research

Carl A. Bersani

Introduction

This introductory section identifies several important characteristics of reality therapy. Reality therapy in action will be discussed in the following section. The primary foci in this section are correctional settings and school settings. A subsequent section identifies a variety of issues and concerns in the application of reality therapy. The concluding section briefly reviews Glasser's recent publications.

For those who work with people with a diverse range of problems, reality therapy has increasingly become the treatment of choice. Its popularity is evident in school settings, in rehabilitation settings, among the clergy, with offenders, and in private practice. Reality therapy offers us a rather simple but clear approach for growth and behavioral change.

Although trained in psychology and psychiatry, William Glasser's disillusionment led him to devise a practical method in the treatment of clients which he labeled reality therapy. The catalysis leading to the creation of this innovative intervention strategy initially took place during his experiences with confined female delinquents. This led to the first paper dealing with reality therapy

This article first appeared in *Correctional Counseling and Treatment*, Second Edition. All rights reserved.

(1964), followed by his exceptionally well received book titled
Reality Therapy (1965). Reality therapy is distinct from other
therapies in a number of ways. We will identify several important
distinctions.

Conventional therapy goals do not include client responsibility
or personal actions as primary. Rather, the primary thrust of much
of our therapeutic strategies is to probe into a client's past thereby
gaining insight. Glasser would argue that in the process of
continually examining the past in order to understand current
behaviors, rationalizations for current behaviors are,
unintentionally, given recognition. One of the many distinctions of
reality therapy from many other therapies is the treatment focus
on the here-and-now. A basic belief of reality therapy, therefore, is
that clients refuse to accept responsibility for their current
behaviors. Accordingly, reality therapy is designed to enable clients
to develop a sense of personal responsibility for their actions and
to acquire conscious control over their subsequent behaviors. This
process occurs as the reality of their behaviors, their environments,
and the consequences of their behavioral choices become known
to them. In this therapy, dwelling on unconscious thought
processes, feelings, attitudes, and the past are considered self-
defeating. Attention is directed instead to the present and into the
future. The client-counselor efforts are to explore which current
behaviors are self-defeating and what behavioral substitutes better
serve the client's needs.

All therapies encounter clients who are depressed, drug addicts,
delinquents, spouse abusers and many other categories too
numerous to list. However, Glasser is not concerned with the actual
symptoms employed by individuals (Ososkie and Turpin, 1985). In
describing the central premises of reality therapy Glasser (1965)
identifies another basic belief which underlies and begins to unfold
a distinction of his therapy from other therapies. He considers that
all the symptomatologies expressed by clients signify they are
failures because they have not grasped reality and, therefore, their
need satisfactions cannot be achieved. Furthermore, they invite
failure for they tend to select ineffective behaviors in their striving
to meet their needs. In Glasser's (1965) own words:

> . . . all patients have a common characteristic: *they all deny the*
> *reality of the world around them.* Some break the law, denying
> the rules of society; some claim their neighbors are plotting
> against them, denying the improbability of such behavior. . . .
> Millions drink to blot out the inadequacy they feel but that need
> not exist if they could learn to be different; and far too many
> people choose suicide rather than face the reality that they could
> solve their problems by more responsible behavior. . . . therapy

will be successful when they are able to give up denying the world and recognize that reality not only exists but that they must fulfill their needs within its framework.

What are these needs? For Glasser, the single, most basic psychological need required by all is the establishment of an identity (Glasser, 1975). The identity is characterized by success and self-esteem. Central in achieving a successful identity are the major psychological routes of loving, being loved and in feeling worthwhile to oneself and to other people. Most important, the shift from a failure identity to a successful identity (and eventual changes in attitudes and beliefs by clients and others) is contingent on changes in the client's behaviors within meaningful interpersonal relationships. In effect, behavioral changes by the client induces behavioral changes in those with whom the client interacts.

Throughout his writings, Glasser continuously reminds us of another major difference between reality therapy and conventional therapies. This difference is the type of client-counselor involvement desired in reality therapy. To varying degrees, conventional therapists remain impersonal and objective. Other therapies view involvement—the therapist becoming a separate and important person in the client's life—as undesirable (Glasser, 1976).

For Glasser, the eventual achievement of involvement (which reduces isolation and facilitates increased need satisfaction) begins with a distinctive type of client-counselor relationship that goes beyond understanding and empathizing with the client. It requires counselors to share openly their own personal struggles with clients, to allow their own values to be challenged by clients, and to confront and challenge clients only when involvement evolves into a special kind of relationship (Glasser, 1965). One earns trust and the privilege of confronting and challenging. It is achieved through a process of involvement where both the counselor and client convey respect, genuineness, and acceptance of each other as unique persons. Without this type of involvement, the underpinnings have not been achieved for a helping process.

Reality Therapy in Action

For over 20 years the helping professions as well as society in general were witness to the intensification of people problems. During this period, the limitations of traditional therapeutic approaches to treatment became apparent. The 1960s to the present can be characterized as a persistent search for demonstrably effective and practical models for intervention (Cohen and Sordo, 1984). Glasser's model of reality therapy and its use in a variety of settings throughout this period is evidence of this search for a practical model of intervention which could be utilized by a wide range of contemporary practitioners.

In the years since the publication of *Reality Therapy* (1965), Glasser's counseling and therapy model has received enthusiastic support and use by highly skilled professionals as well as less skilled workers in service agencies. This popularity is in keeping with Glasser's (1984) statement that the therapy is appropriate to a wide range of behaviors and emotional problems—from mild emotional situations and maladjustments to severe anxieties, perversions and psychoses. Numerous accounts of the successful application of reality therapy with a variety of clientele in diverse settings is evident in the literature (Banmen, 1982a).

Its popularity and application have been reported in settings such as schools, corrections, private practice, state mental hospitals, substance-abuse centers, etc. Two major works convey the successful application of reality therapy by counselors working with a variety of clientele in diverse settings. *The Reality Therapy Reader* (Bassin, Bratter, and Rachin, 1976) brings together accounts of the application of reality therapy in private practice, in education, and in corrections. An edited work by Naomi Glasser (1980) includes two dozen accounts of how reality therapists have worked with a variety of clients. The range of clients helped with reality therapy include: divorced parents, self-destructive adolescents, depressed clients, psychotics who learn to acquire more responsible behavior, clients with severe handicaps, alcoholics, principals helping teachers, and teachers and school counselors helping children (Glasser, N., 1980).

Despite the numerous illustrations mentioned above of the successful application of reality therapy, Banmen (1982b) states that very little formal research evaluating the effectiveness of reality therapy exists. He further states that Glasser and many other reality therapists are increasingly concerned by this lack of formal research. Although reality therapy has not been formally researched in all possible settings and with the full range of potential clients, an examination of the existing limited research could increase our insight regarding the circumstances under which reality therapy appears successful, thereby suggesting promising endeavors and avenues for future research.

In practice, the use of reality therapy is evident in numerous and diverse types of settings. Additionally, general descriptions and testimonies of success by those practitioners utilizing reality therapy are quite apparent in the literature and in conversations with practitioners.

The limited efforts to measure the effects of reality therapy have primarily focused on the correctional and school settings. However, one can offer examples of scattered pieces of research in other settings. Browne and Ritter (1972) selected reality therapy for 16 of the most regressed patients at a V.A. hospital containing 190 psychiatric, medically infirm patients in geriatric wards as a pilot effort. Patients in these wards were diagnosed as long-term, chronic schizophrenics. With the exception of one patient, all achieved personal pride and improved sufficiently in self-care, social abilities, and personal relations making them eligible to be placed in facilities outside the hospital. One study (Zaph, 1974) researched the effects of the use of reality therapy in the community to enhance the personal growth of retarded adult women. Indications of personal growth were measured by improvements in minimum behavioral standards and in goal achievements. Success was achieved on some of these measures.

Another study used reality therapy in efforts to free 65 addicts who were in a methadone dependence program (Raubolt and Bratter, 1976). After one year, significant results in detoxification (remaining drug free, being employed, and no arrests) were achieved.

Correctional Settings

Reality therapy has many supporters among counselors. Its greatest impact appears to be in correctional settings. Vinter (1976) indicates that reality therapy is utilized in 80 percent of the juvenile institutions which were studied in a national survey. It is not known whether the use of this therapy is widespread because it fits the reality as staff understand it or because of the assumption that highly trained professionals are unnecessary in the use of this therapy. Despite its popularity and extensive use in corrections, only a small amount of formal research has been done on reality therapy.

Practitioners have frequently stated that offenders who are alienated by conventional treatment methods respond positively to reality therapy. Using reality therapy in a prison with a group of 43 inmates for 15 weeks, Williams (1976) supports this general impression. All participants found reality therapy to be at least somewhat helpful with 80 percent rating the program as very helpful to them. Many of these inmates felt that reality therapy helped them to take a more realistic and responsible outlook on life in general and prison in particular. Furthermore, none of these inmates received a disciplinary report during the 15 weeks of the program. Williams concludes that reality therapy works because its strengths coincide with many of the weaknesses of incarcerated offenders. One such connection identified by Williams is: "Where many inmates tend to live in a fantasy world of—'if onlys,' reality therapy focuses on the way life is."

One serious problem facing staff is the unrealistic vocational goals of inmates. Prior to release, many inmates avoid facing reality or pursuing a responsible course of action. A main ingredient of the Maryland Comprehensive Offender Model Program was testing and assessing in order to evaluate training or employment possibilities. Since one goal of this program was to get inmates to face reality and assume responsibility in being available for work possibilities, individual and group counseling were based on the reality therapy model. Within a one-year period 2,795 inmates were in the program; 2,170 of them were released from institutions and available for work. At the time of this report, half of those placed in jobs were self-placements. Bennight (1975) concludes that overall placement of these males exceeded normal placement by applicants who did not have the multiple barriers to employment characteristic of these males.

The research by Falker (1982), German (1975) and Molstad (1981) studied behavioral change. The Magdala Halfway House in St. Louis changed to reality therapy as its primary treatment modality. This facility handles 70 young, adult male offenders per year. Falker (1982) states that previous attempts by staff to control and change the behaviors of residents through positive and negative reinforcements were futile. The reality therapy approach was used to allow both staff and residents an opportunity to examine and evaluate their behaviors.

Among the principles of reality therapy stressed was teaching residents to plan better behaviors when their current behaviors were not fulfilling. Unable to control residents by use of punishment, staff opened new lines of communication leading to cooperative behaviors that fulfilled needs of both workers and residents. For example, "can do—let's try" atmosphere of conciliation along with rules generated by the common group to benefit both staff and clients almost eliminated negativism and various forms of hostile behaviors. Such problems at one time were the norm. Falker found that within a three-year period dramatic reductions by residents in absconding and in terminations occurred, and a significant increase occurred in residents who were successfully released. Successful release meant release to the community with a job, in training, or in school.

Glasser (1965) initially established reality therapy principles within the Ventura School for Girls in California. Considering their prior juvenile history, the Ventura School was the last stop prior to being committed to an adult prison. Of the 370 girls released on parole, only 43 violated parole. German (1975) investigated the effects of group reality therapy on juvenile inmates and staff leaders of the therapy groups. As a consequence of systematic exposure to the principles of reality therapy during group therapy sessions, it was expected that changes in certain behaviors, self-esteem, etc. would occur. German found that the experimental group viewed themselves and were viewed by their teachers as more responsible, more mature, and more acceptable persons. However, self-esteem did not increase. They did exhibit significantly fewer behaviors in the dormitory which required disciplinary action compared to the control group. It was also hypothesized that since staff leaders of the group therapy sessions were exposed to the inmates within a transactional environment, they would change their perceptions of people in general. German's findings indicated that staff leaders changed by viewing people as more positive, complex, and changeable.

Molstad (1981) assumed a position with a residential treatment facility for emotionally disturbed adolescents which had experienced close to total staff turnover. Runaways occurred almost daily; vandalism, theft, fist fights, and other aggressive behaviors were common. Treatment intervention had been based on the Transactional Analysis model. Molstad indicates the new staff felt that TA was too cognitive for these adolescents to understand.

Social workers were given intensive training in reality therapy, and the entire staff (cooks, janitors, etc.) was given a working knowledge of the approach (Molstad, 1981). For the inmates, individual, group, and family therapy were also based on the principles of reality therapy. As long as they remained in keeping with reality therapy principles, policies for each treatment unit were formulated with input from residents. Such involvement (i.e., deciding on rules, tasks, and consequences) increased the likelihood of adhering to the rules. The weekly individual sessions centered on the present, evaluating behavior, developing problem-solving techniques, developing relationships, formalizing resident plans, and developing increased resident responsibility. Daily group reality therapy sessions dealt with school problems, peer problems, family difficulties, problems in the facility, future planning, etc. Each family also experienced group reality therapy sessions. Changes in family relationships, activities, and types of interaction were common areas for discussion. Actual discharge was based on increased level of responsibility in the institution, within the family, within the school setting, and the local community.

Molstad found that behavior in the facility improved greatly when discharge responsibility was turned over to the residents. These adolescents viewed the program more seriously and worked harder toward the goal of discharge. Since accountability was stressed at both the individual and group levels, disruptive behavior and vandalism decreased quickly and drastically.

For the effects of reality therapy on the self-concept of alienated, unmotivated, drug abusing adolescents, see Brown and Kingley (1973). See Thatcher (1983) for a before and after design and a within-group comparison of the effects (for group home delinquents trained in the concepts and practices of reality therapy) on self-concept and locus of control.

There does exist a literature on the use of restitution which we will not review here. Although restitution is clearly grounded on the ideas of reality therapy, the research is not formally structured to examine reality therapy. For a discussion of how reality therapy ideas can be operationalized in traditional restitution programs, see Matthews (1979). Therapists may be especially interested in Lackman's (1986) proposal and operationalization of the behavior equivalent (undoing) to traditional restitution using the steps of reality therapy.

School Settings

The ideas of reality therapy have direct implications in school settings. Glasser first became concerned not only about behavior but also learning, since virtually all the girls at the Ventura School for Girls experienced a history of school failure (Corey, 1977). In his book *Schools Without Failure* (Glasser, 1969), he proposed a program to eliminate failure and other school related problems.

A major problem expressed by teachers in achieving an atmosphere for learning is the issue of serious behavioral problems in the classroom. Several studies have examined the application of reality therapy to classroom discipline problems. Gang (1976) selected two 4th and 5th grade teachers for training in the principles and methods of reality therapy. Each teacher selected three male students whom they considered to be serious behavior problems. Each teacher was trained in reality therapy by the researcher and through participation in a system-wide training program conducted by an associate from Glasser's Educator Training Center. Each teacher met with the researcher at least two times a week and the researcher observed each teacher at least three times a week and provided feedback. Also, trained observers monitored each student in the classroom environment, three times a week, with observations recorded in ten-second intervals.

Gang's study was divided into four phases:

Baseline: In this phase, teachers continued their natural teaching practices in the classroom. This determined where each of the six target students were in relation to the rated behaviors before the beginning of the intervention strategy.

Initial Involvement Intervention: In this phase, teachers were instructed to give each student 15 to 20 seconds of special, personal attention. This was to occur at least three times during each class period. The purpose of this was to develop an ongoing, personal relationship between teacher and student.

Varied Intervention: The teacher continued to give personal attention during this phase, but three modified reality therapy conditions were also used. In the first condition, the teacher responded only to the student's undesirable behavior by following those steps of reality therapy which ask four questions. During the second condition, the teacher responded only to desirable behavior and would follow the steps of reality therapy. In the third condition, the teacher responded to both desirable and undesirable behaviors and followed the steps of reality therapy.

Follow-up: At the conclusion of the intervention phase, trained observers continued recording classroom behavior to determine the durability of any student behavior changes that had occurred as a result of the intervention treatments.

Gang reports that the results clearly supported reality therapy as a solution for those identified as serious behavior problems. For all the target students, a highly significant decrease in the frequency of undesirable behavior occurred; a highly significant increase in the frequency of desirable behavior occurred over baseline conditions during the treatment and follow-up phases of the study. Both teachers felt the establishment of an ongoing, genuine relationship—an outcome of the plan—accounted for the successful outcomes.

The Thompson and Cates (1976) study is similar in goal and method to the Gang (1976) study. Six female elementary teachers each selected the student representing the most difficult discipline problem—a student they would most like to have absent from the school setting. Each teacher received training in a ten-step plan developed by Glasser for teaching discipline to students. The ten-step plan can be divided into three categories. First is the involvement stage. Among other things, it required teachers to stop using unhelpful behaviors and to reinforce helpful behaviors. The counseling stage required teachers to counsel students using the reality therapy process including a written contract with students that outlines a plan for changing behavior. The time-out stage includes logical consequences for misbehavior as well as written plans for correcting misbehaviors. The phases of this study and the method of monitoring/analysis were very similar to the Gang (1976) study. As in the previous study, all six students achieved significant increases in appropriate behavior and decreases in inappropriate behavior during the treatment stage compared to the baseline stage. The two studies taken together appear to support reality therapy as a tool for behavior change. Large gains in appropriate student behavior were achieved through a modest amount of positive behavioral changes on the part of teachers. For the effectiveness of reality therapy on discipline and behavior problems using an experimental and control design, see Matthews (1973).

The primary purpose of the study by Dakoske (1977) was to explore not only the short-term but also the long-term effects of reality therapy on both discipline and self-concept. Thirty selected fifth graders were randomly assigned to either a reality therapy session group or a group which received the Open Language Arts Program. Self-concept and problem behaviors were measured before and after the reality therapy sessions.

Dakoske (1977) indicates reality therapy sessions were led by a classroom teacher with assistance by the elementary school counselor. On a weekly basis, fifteen sessions were held for one hour each week. Classroom topics as recommended by Glasser (1965, 1969) were discussed by the students. The teacher provided encouragement to students to explore their ideas, feelings, and values. The principles of Glasser's approach were followed in the classroom discussions and included efforts to build interpersonal relationships and provide mutual support.

Dakoske found significant differences in favor of the group exposed to reality therapy sessions on post-test versus pre-test measures of problem behaviors and self-concept. However, post-test one year later which included no treatment for either group revealed no significant difference between the groups on self-concept. For additional studies using experimental/control groups with a pre- and post-testing design reporting favorable effects of the reality therapy process on self-concept, see Omizo and Cubberly's (1983) study of learning disabled children and Slowick, Omizo and Hammet's (1984) study of Mexican-American adolescents. Other studies which have measured the effects of the reality therapy process on school achievement, locus of control, and self-concept are: Hawes (1971), Thatcher (1983), Matthews (1973), and Shearn and Randolph (1978).

Banmen (1982b) has commented on the issue of the practitioners' skills in using reality therapy. He offers this as a possible explanation for some of the inconsistencies in some of the findings on reality therapy. In reviewing reality therapy studies, Banmen (1982b) found that positive results were more likely for behavioral changes. This review also finds increasing positive results for changes in self-concept but mixed results on locus of control. Thus, we can identify areas where reality therapy appears promising. We should also recall that in many settings and populations reality therapy is the primary treatment mode despite the lack of research validation. Thus, more research is needed in those settings and populations virtually ignored by formal research.

Issues and Concerns in the Application of Reality Therapy

When one views edited works (Bassin, et al., 1976; Glasser N., 1980), volumes by William Glasser, and diverse monographs, the numerous virtues of reality therapy appear to be common knowledge. Yet, like other therapies, reality therapy in practice is only as good as the individual counselor using it (Trojanowicz and Morash, 1983). Considering the particular mode of intervention used in reality therapy, it is one of the methods especially subject to misuse and misunderstanding, despite the fact other therapies may encounter similar problems (Ivery, 1980).

In the application of reality therapy, therefore, issues and concerns have been expressed. A number of writers raise a variety of concerns. For example, what constitutes responsible behavior? If behavior does not harm others, who decides? What is moral and correct? In practice, who really decides? Is the counselor expected to function as a value catalyst and as a model for responsible behavior? Do the principles of reality therapy contain ingredients both for involvement and for rejection? In his more recent works (see references), Glasser increases the emphasis on a nonjudgmental, noncritical, and supportive therapeutic relationship (Corey, 1986). Nevertheless in the applying of principles of reality therapy, a number of writers continue to express the concerns just mentioned. (For example, see Corey, 1986; Peterson, 1976; May, 1967; Ivery, 1980; and Arbuckle, 1975.) Ivery (1980) also cautions that reality therapy must achieve a balance in working with clients which includes environmental circumstances. What follows are some of the major problem areas with reality therapy and its application.

All counselors adhere to moral standards particular to them. Clients are confronted with the disparity between a variety of behaviors which the counselor deems conventional and acceptable versus the specific behavior of the client. Distinct from some therapies, Glasser's (1965, 1972) position is that people are failures not because their standards are too high, but because their performances (irresponsibilities) are too low. Accordingly, there is the need to enhance greater maturity to reduce irresponsible behavior. (As an aside, reality therapy is appropriate for over-socialized clients, but the statement above does not appear appropriate to this category of client.)

We should be concerned with moral standards because therapy counselors are free to incorporate their own values into the interaction process. At times counselors unconsciously incorporate their values because they assume these are the preferred ones. Clients can be especially victimized when they do not have firm convictions with regard to the allocation of responsibilities within their family, aspirations for their children, or attitudes toward homosexuality. The client may be victimized for being involved in a lifestyle not consistent with the counselor's preferred values. Reality therapy counselors continually evaluate the current behaviors of clients and may unduly assist in suggesting options for future behavior—based more on personal value sets than on those which could emerge from clients. To the extent this occurs, it is the preconceived notions and prejudices of these counselors which shape future planning. Thus far, Glasser's writings do not provide a systematic methodology for clearly separating the moral standards of the counselor from that of the client. Those who should be best able to cope with this dilemma are reality therapists who are experienced and certified.

This apparent lack of reasonable amount of uniformity by diverse counselors in the application of reality therapy creates other concerns troublesome to many adherents of reality therapy. Attention will be given to a selected number of those concerns which are central when one attempts to implement reality therapy. Beyond moral standards, another concern deals with the issue of involvement. Essentially, the problem involves the importance of the uncritical acceptance of the client as the central feature in establishing involvement. Sometimes, a subsequent shift occurs toward critically evaluating a client's future behavior. Because of this shift, the possibility does exist that the underpinnings for the relationship and for changing behavior may have changed. The mandate to accept or at least to give recognition to much of what the client has to say initially offers a solid foundation for establishing a firm emotional and cognitive relationship. After the counselor determines that the special type of involvement desirable in reality therapy has been achieved, the counselor revises the relationship in the eyes of the client by also becoming a person whose acceptance of the client appears, now, to be highly conditional on successfully achieving agreed upon behavioral changes. The counselor becomes a judge, and, perhaps, unconsciously conveys that love comes as a result of good behavior.

Thus, the concern here is the potential for the client to perceive the counselor's behavior and statements as rejection. For a client with a history of failures in relationships, this relationship is then like all others. Worse, because it may not be as apparent, in order to sustain acceptance from the counselor, the client makes behavioral changes to please the counselor. But this occurs at the expense of enhancing the client's self-determination which is the reason for the therapy and the relationship. These scenarios also bring into question whether the client is developing involvements with others beyond the therapist. The whole purpose of planning responsible behavioral changes is to become involved with others, not to expend one's energies on rescuing the involvement with the therapist.

The question of dependency as well as the termination of therapy are issues for many therapies. For reality therapy, these are serious concerns when we consider its ideas and that it is short-term therapy. Central to reality therapy is that self-worth can only be achieved by becoming involved with others in the client's real world. Despite the successes of the therapy in helping clients become more behaviorally responsible, (as the earlier research review suggests) not all clients achieve independence. Some practicing reality therapists were aware early on that some clients concluded that the counselor's evaluation and guides for behavioral changes had greater validity than their own judgments. Yochelson and Samenow (1977) state that a shortcoming of reality therapy is the lack of specifics in teaching processes of decision making that would apply beyond the immediate situation. We need to acknowledge the problem of dependency and include as part of reality therapy a strategy for learning that enables what is learned to transfer beyond the immediate behavioral change. If the counselor is perceived as the expert and concrete behavior changes are not generalized to other aspects of life, then clients are likely to sustain a dependency relationship. They are also likely to experience a crumbling of the degree of self-confidence they have attained when therapy does end.

Szasz, like Glasser, feels strongly that mental illness is not an illness. Immediately upon publication of *Reality Therapy* (1965), Szasz (1966) expressed concern that Glasser had merely relabeled everything called mental illness as irresponsibility. It is clear even in Glasser's recent writings that he continues to view all behaviors as the sole creation of the inner workings of the individual. Further, if the behavior is disruptive to elements of conventional society, one is behaving irresponsibly.

It is not difficult to concur with Glasser's major thrust. However, behavioral expressions stem from greater complexities than choosing to be irresponsible. We will identify only a few issues here. At times what others are doing is vastly more important than the irresponsible behavior of the client. The labeling processes directed toward an individual may be so pervasive that the irresponsible behavior of the client is but a symptom of a larger problem. This issue is not adequately dealt with by the principles of reality therapy.

Also, given insufficient recognition are subcultures. Indeed, some people do behave irresponsibly toward others. Yet, they may believe they possess successful identities, not failure identities. Some persons are simply happy not conforming. Some pimps may illustrate this point. Drug trafficking provides another example. Can we really assume that they consider themselves to be failures or concur with our standards of responsible behavior? Glasser does not adequately deal with this issue except to say that if the client does not critically assess existing behavior, therapy can be of no help.

Another principle of reality therapy is: "Accept no excuses." Many practitioners have difficulty following this in practice. The principle is critical since many clients have histories of using excuses as rationalizations so as not to conform. In effect, excuses are used to sanction irresponsible behavior. Yet, who does not need self-esteem defenses to preserve credibility—to smooth over interactional encounters? Those who don't are few in number. Eliminate the use of excuses for a month from the thousands of interactions experienced during that period. Now what is the status of your informal and formal relations? How are you perceived? It is apparent that valid and even invalid excuses are vehicles for orderly social interaction and relationships. In fact—at least in our society—a major feature among members is to use excuses when expectations are not fulfilled. Therefore, literally permitting no excuses can affect relationships. No excuses permitted in the "problem" area is absolutely crucial. On the other hand, permitting *normal* usage of excuses in marginal areas around the core problem is realistic and is in keeping with how people normally behave.

There is the question of whether reality therapy should explicitly include a principle dealing with the client's social relations. It would be helpful if a principle existed which emphasized and provided guidelines for the counselor to monitor what others, in addition to the client, are doing in the relationship. Explication here is critical if the counselor is to be effective in helping the client plan strategy.

One walks a precarious path when the plan for action is based mainly on what ability the client possesses in grasping and in conveying what others are like in the relationship. For this reason, some counselors have contacts with others in the relationship.

The negative influences of environmental circumstances is not directly dealt with in the steps of reality therapy. This is a major concern to therapists who incorporate this therapy in their actual practice. Reality therapy does attempt to help the client to accept and to meet the circumstances which actually surround the client. For emotional stability and to establish a successful identity, one must learn to cope with certain environmental circumstances which cannot easily be changed. Nevertheless, for many ex-cons the actual adjustments to the neighborhood can be overwhelming. Despite the plan for behavioral change, there are basic questions about the availability of appropriate associates, available employment, and the holistic exposure to an environment kindly described as negative.

The above suggests that reality therapy lacks a guide for addressing the all-embracing roles and positions within which clients are physically and mentally entrapped. What should be done after one grasps the client's relationships? At the very least we should attempt revisions, after client consensus evolves, in the fabric of the client's social web. However, once the counselor does grasp the reality of our multiple worlds, realistically achieving a successful identity should not be equated to living a conventional lifestyle.

What constitutes some of the elements of a comprehensive approach? There are some elements which are immediately apparent. But these hardly exhaust all possible elements. First, reality therapy at the individual level is primary. All other elements are supportive players for achieving the goals of the therapy. Environmental "manipulation" is a necessary tool for therapists. After client consensus evolves, the client is assisted in gradually securing appropriate relationships through groups/associates, work, and residential placement. There comes a time when group counseling serves well clients with similar problems, and those to whom the client must relate. In our society many may be striving for identity first, then goals as Glasser (1975) states. Eventually, the core of who we can be is supported and reinforced by job satisfaction. Therefore, it is the responsibility of the therapist that the maximum vocational and educational potential of the client is understood and acted upon. Lastly, any good therapist would grasp the disabilities (including social skills) and potentials of clients and routinely take advantage of the extensive network of social services actually available. Far too many therapists are not really aware of all the types of services which are available to their clients. On this point, Bratter (1976) similarly argues that the counselor's role should be one of advocate to help the client obtain needed services. Glasser (1972) has proposed a Community Involvement Center to serve failing people. Although the CIC is restricted in vision, many of the elements proposed in this comprehensive approach can easily be included in an expanded version of Glasser's center.

Recent Works

Recent works by Glasser are consistent with his discussions in his earliest writings about the principles of reality therapy. Thus, the basic beliefs conveyed in earlier writings such as *Reality Therapy* (1965); *Schools Without Failure* (1969); and *Identity Society* (1975) have not been subject to profound revisions. It does appear that Glasser's recent writings give more emphasis on particular points. For example, Corey (1986) concludes that these writings encourage the counselor to be less critical, less judgmental, and to be more accepting, less confrontational in the therapeutic milieu. This shift addresses a few concerns mentioned previously. But these concerns are not fully resolved by Glasser's recent statements. Certainly, they are unresolved in the actual practice of reality therapy.

Some of Glasser's recent writings are consistent with his earliest writings, others complement or expand reality therapy. In *Positive Addiction* (1976), Glasser appears to enrich reality therapy by recognizing the difficulties of developing one's potential including the entrapment of self-involvement which leads to *negative* addiction (drugs, overeating, etc.). Glasser's solution is addiction. The addiction to which he refers is *positive* addiction. Glasser recognizes the needs of clients to cultivate strength if reality therapy plans for behavioral change are to be successful. Positive addictions to Glasser are unlimited and very regular: running, studying, meditating, volunteering, and so on. Glasser states this lets the client's "brain spin free" (the brain becomes free from the undesirable consequences of negative addiction). Heavy involvement with positive addiction is fruitful because this mental achievement generalizes to the individual's overall pleasure and competence in other areas of life. Accordingly, Glasser would encourage the counselor to use this approach as a means for the client to acquire the needed strength to accomplish the goals of reality therapy.

Other recent works by Glasser which extend beyond reality therapy but are useful as a resource for reality therapists are

Stations of the Mind (1981), and *Control Theory* (1984). Control theory and elements of brain functioning are combined to involve theory of perception. Stated very briefly, the heart of the theory is the relation between our inner world perceptions which are internally motivated and external happenings which have no meaning until we internally interpret external happenings. It is not external forces which cause us to behave in a certain way. Instead, it's what our inner behavior makes of external behavior. In effect, we choose our emotions. For example, others are reacting to us. Others may view us as short or ugly. We may have been deceived. Reactions of being depressed or being hostile are not the only outcome. Why? Because we ought to satisfy our inner needs and therefore it is we who should control how we desire to perceive the external. It is we who choose how we perceive and that determines our view of external reality. In short, Glasser feels we cannot let the external world shape the personal world within us. We take control, interpret and interact with the external; we thereby, in turn, influence external elements in the course of satisfying our inner needs.

For reality therapists these two recent works appear to be far more practical and useful than is traditional behavioral psychology. These writings complement Glasser's reality therapy and are worth the attention of those counselors committed to this therapy.

References

Arbuckle, D. S. 1975. *Counseling and psychotherapy—an existential-humanistic view*, 3rd ed. Boston: Allyn and Bacon.

Banmen, J. 1982a. *Reality therapy bibliography*. Los Angeles: Institute for Reality Therapy.

_____. 1982b. "Reality therapy research view." *Journal of Reality Therapy*, 2(1): 28–33.

Bassin, A., Bratter, T. E., and Rachin, R. L., eds. 1976. *The Reality Therapy Reader*. New York: Harper and Row.

Bennight, K. C. 1975. "A model program for counseling and placement of offenders." *Journal of Employment Counseling*, 12(4): 168–173.

Bratter, T. E. and Raubolt, R. R., 1976. "Treating the methadone addict." In *The Reality Therapy Reader*, Bassin, A., Bratter T. E., and Rachin, R. L. (eds.). New York: Harper and Row.

Brown, L. J. and Ritter, J. I. 1972. "Reality therapy for the geriatric psychiatric patient." *Perspective in Psychiatric Care*, 10(3): 135–139.

Brown, W. and Kingley 1973. "Treating alienated, unmotivated, drug abusing adolescents." *American Journal of Psychotherapy*, 27(4): 585–598.

Cohen, B. Z. and Sordo, I. 1984. "Using reality therapy with adult offenders." *Journal of Counseling Services and Rehabilitation*, 8(3): 25–39.

Corey, G. 1986. *Theory and practice of counseling and psychotherapy*, 3rd ed. Monterey, CA: Brooks/Cole Publishing Company.

Dakoske, T. J. 1977. "Short- and long-term effects of reality therapy on self-concept and discipline of selected fifth grade students." Ph.D. diss., University of Cincinnati. *Dissertation Abstracts International*, 1977, 2338.

Falker F. (1982). "Reality therapy: a systems level approach to treatment in a halfway house." *Journal of Reality Therapy* 1(2): 3–7.

Gang, M. J. 1976. "Enhancing student-teacher relationships." *Elementary School Guidance and Counseling*, 11(2): 131–137.

German, M. L. 1975. "The effects of group reality therapy on institutionalized adolescents and group leaders." Ph.D. diss., George Peabody College for Teachers, 1975. *Dissertation Abstracts International*, 1975, 1916b.

Glasser N., ed. 1980. *What are you doing? How people are helped through reality therapy*. New York: Harper & Row.

Glasser, W., 1964. "Reality therapy: A realistic approach to the young offender." *Crime and Delinquency* 10, 135–144.

_____.1965. *Reality therapy: A new approach to psychiatry*. New York: Harper & Row.

_____. 1969. *Schools without failure*. New York: Harper & Row.

_____. 1975. *The identity society*. Rev. ed. New York: Harper & Row.

_____.1976a. "Notes on reality therapy." In *The reality therapy reader*. Bassin, A., Bratter, T. E., Rachin, R. L., (eds.) New York: Harper & Row.

_____. 1976b. *Positive addiction*. New York: Harper & Row.

_____. 1981. *Stations of the mind*. New York: Harper & Row.

_____. 1984a. *Control theory*. New York: Harper & Row.

_____. 1984b. "Reality therapy." In *Current psychotherapies*. Corsini, R. (ed.). Itasca, IL: Peacock.

Hawes, R. M. 1971. "Reality therapy in the classroom." Ph.D. diss., University of the Pacific, 1971. *Dissertation Abstracts International*, 1971, 2483.

Ivery, A. E. 1980. *Counseling and psychotherapy: Skills, theories and practice*. Englewood Cliffs, NJ: Prentice-Hall.

Lachman, S. J. 1986. "Restitution: A behavioral analog for undoing." *Journal of Reality Therapy*, 5(2): 3–10.

Matthews, D. B. 1972. "The Effects of reality therapy on reported self-concept, social adjustment, reading achievement, and discipline of fourth and fifth graders in two elementary schools." Ph.D. diss., University of South Carolina,1972, *Dissertation Abstracts International*, 1973, 4342–4843.

Matthews, W. G. 1979. "Restitution programming: Reality therapy operationalized." *Offender Rehabilitation*, 3: 319–324.

May, R. 1967. *Psychology and the human dilemma*. Princeton, NJ: D. Van Nostrand Company.

Molstad, L. P. 1981. "Reality therapy in residential treatment" In *Journal of Reality Therapy* 1(1): 8–13.

Omizo, M. M. and Cubberly, W. F. 1983. "The effects of reality therapy meetings on self-concept and locus of control among learning disabled children." *Exceptional Child* 30(3): 201–209.

Ososkie, J. N. and Turpin, J. O. 1985. "Reality therapy in rehabilitation counseling." *Journal of Applied Rehabilitation Counseling*, 16(3): 34–37.

Peterson, J. A. 1976. *Counseling and Values—A Philosophical Examination*. Cranston, RI: Carroll Press Publishers.

Raubolt, R. R. and Bratter, T. E. 1976. "Treating the methadone addict." In *The Reality Therapy Reader*, Bassin, A., Bratter, T. E. and Rachin, R. L. (eds.), New York: Harper & Row.

Shearn, D. F. and Randolph, D. L. 1978. "Effects of reality therapy methods applied in the classroom." *Psychology in the Schools*, 15(1): 79–83.

Slowick, C. A., Omizo, M. M., and Hammett, V. L. 1984. "The effects of reality therapy process on locus of control and self-concepts among Mexican-American adolescents." *Journal of Reality Therapy* 3(2): 1–9.

Szasz, T. S. 1966. "Equation of opposites." *The New York Book Review* Feb. 6:6.

Thatcher, J. A. 1983. "The effects of reality therapy upon self-concept and locus of control for juvenile delinquents." *Journal of Reality Therapy* 3(1): 31.

Thompson, C. L. and Cates, J. T. 1976. "Teaching discipline to students." *Elementary School Guidance and Counseling*, 11(2): 131–137.

Trojanowicz, R. C. and Morash, M. 1983. *Juvenile delinquency*, 3rd ed. Englewood Cliffs, NJ: Prentice-Hall.

Vinter, R. D., ed. 1976. *Time out: A national study of juvenile correction programs*. Ann Arbor: National Assessment of Juvenile Corrections.

Williams, E. W. 1976. "Reality therapy in a correctional institution." *Corrective and Social Psychiatry and Journal of Behavior, Methods and Therapy*, 22(1): 6–11.

Yochelson, S. and Samenow, S. E. 1977. *The criminal personality—The change process*, Volume II. New York: Janson Aronson.

Zapf, R. F. 1974. Group therapy with retarded adults: A reality therapy approach. Ph.D. diss., Fordham University 1973. *Dissertation Abstracts International* 1974, 4889–4890.

Section *VI*

Behavior Modification

Of all the treatment techniques described in this book, behavior modification holds the distinction of being the most debated. Proponents of this technique applaud its ease of implementation; clearly observable results; and applicability to a wide range of populations, ranging from autistic or hyperactive preschoolers through nursing-home residents troubled by problems of senility. Those who oppose or would severely restrict its use argue that it borders on "thought or mind control," reduces the production of acceptable human behavior to the level of training an animal, or has such a strong potential for abuse that it must be carefully monitored.

The truth about behavior modification's benefits and hazards certainly lies somewhere between these two extremes. Much of the criticism of behavior modification has arisen from public confusion about what it is and references to the use of electric shocks and drug therapy in some types of behavior modification. Selection fifteen, "Behavior Modification: Perspective on a Current Issue," clearly defines just what behavior modification is and is not, gives examples of the types of positive reinforcement and aversion stimuli that are common to behavior modification programs, and discusses the special considerations attendant upon the use of behavior modification programs in a correctional institution.

The use of behavior modification in an institution poses special problems. A therapist must walk the line between working to modify the inmates' behavior in a manner that will make them more law-abiding citizens *after* they leave the institution and changing their behavior to accommodate living *within* the walls—that is, making them more docile, easier to handle, or respectful of authority. The correctional setting provides opportunities for abuse of behavior modification techniques that would not be likely to occur elsewhere. For example, the "time out" method of aversion stimulus, which amounts to removing the offender to a room, alone, for a short period of time, could easily be expanded to punitive periods of solitary confinement. Denial of privileges could be misused in the same manner.

On the positive side, the institution offers the most controlled environment for behavior modification, since inmates are less open to outside influences and a wide range of privileges or desirable items can be offered as positive reinforcements or rewards to encourage or sustain good behavior.

Students and evaluators of behavior modification therapy generally conclude that the individual doing the reinforcing or applying aversion stimuli is the key factor in the program's success. A number of studies of behavior modification involving delinquents discovered that positive reinforcement is most important at the beginning of a program;[1] that the personalities of the therapists providing the reinforcement or aversion were important factors in behavioral changes;[2] and that the more clearly defined the expected behaviors were, the greater the chance of achieving them.[3] After reviewing and summarizing fourteen studies of behavior modification programs involving almost 2000 delinquents in the United States, Romig concludes that "Behavior modification is certainly no panacea for juvenile delinquency. Behavior modification did work to change certain behaviors, such as school attendance, test scores, promptness, and classroom behavior. However, it did not affect something as global as delinquency or arrest rate."[4]

Selection sixteen, "Establishing Behavioral Contracts with Delinquent Adolescents," explores the strategies that have proven most successful in this type of contracting. Input from the adolescent into the design and setting of rewards and regulations was found to be very important. Examples of behavioral contracts that utilize positive influences already available in the adolescent's life and are designed to fit various types of delinquent activity are given in this article.

Notes

[1] R. L. Bednar; P. F. Zelhart; L. Greathouse; and W. Weinberg, "Operant Conditioning Principles in the Treatment of Learning and Behavior Problems with Delinquent

Boys," *Journal of Counseling Psychology* 17 (1970):492–497.

[2] V. Tyler and G. Brown, "Token Reinforcement of Academic Performance with Institutionalized Delinquent Boys," *Journal of Educational Psychology* 59 (1968):164–168.

[3] S. B. McPherson and R. S. Cyrille, "Teaching Behavioral Methods to Parents," *Social Casework* 52 (1971):148–153.

[4] Dennis A. Romig, *Justice for Our Children* (Lexington, MA: Lexington Books, 1978), 20.

15

Behavior Modification
Perspective on a Current Issue

Bertram S. Brown
Louis A. Wienckowski
Stephanie B. Stolz

Introduction

In the history of civilization, people have continuously tried to control their environment and to find ways of teaching themselves and their children better means of acquiring new skills and capabilities. Common-sense notions of the ways that reward and punishment can change behavior have existed since time immemorial. Thus, elements of what is now referred to as behavior modification were used long before psychologists and other behavioral scientists developed systematic principles of learning.

As behavior modification procedures are used ever more widely, many different concerns have been expressed. On the one hand, the public and mental health professionals are concerned about whether behavior modification procedures are sufficiently well demonstrated through research for these procedures to be generally recommended and widely disseminated. On the other hand, behavior modification has acted as a conceptual "lightning rod" in the midst of stormy controversies over ethical problems associated with attempts at social influence, drawing to it such

Source: U.S. Department of Health, Education and Welfare, National Institute of Mental Health. Washington, D.C.: U.S. Government Printing Office (1976).

highly charged issues as fear of "mind control" or concerns about the treatment of persons institutionalized against their will. Apparent or actual infringements of rights, as well as some abuses of behavioral procedures, have led to litigation and calls for curbs on the use of behavior modification.

Everyone tries continually to influence his own and others' behavior, so that the individual using behavior modification procedures is distinctive only in that he is attempting to influence behavior more systematically. Commenting on this issue, one attorney has said that to be opposed to behavior modification is to be opposed to the law of gravity. Rather, the key issue is what sort of care, caution, and control should be exercised when behavioral principles are applied precisely and systematically.

This report is intended to provide an objective overview of the history and current methods of behavior modification and to review some critical issues, in an effort to aid the reader in differentiating between warranted and unwarranted concerns. We will also make some suggestions regarding ethical standards and practices.

What Is Behavior Modification?

To understand behavior modification, it is helpful first to clarify its relationship to a broader concept, behavior influence.

Behavior influence occurs whenever one person exerts some degree of control over another. This occurs constantly in such diverse situations as formal school education, advertising, child rearing, political campaigning, and other normal interpersonal interactions.

Behavior modification is a special form of behavior influence that involves primarily the application of principles derived from research in experimental psychology to alleviate human suffering and enhance human functioning. Behavior modification emphasizes systematic monitoring and evaluation of the effectiveness of these applications. The techniques of behavior modification are generally intended to facilitate improved self-control by expanding individuals' skills, abilities, and independence.

Most behavior modification procedures are based on the general principle that people are influenced by the consequences of their behavior. The current environment is believed to be more relevant in affecting the individual's behavior than most early life experiences or than enduring intrapsychic conflicts or personality structure. Insofar as possible, the behaviorally oriented mental health worker limits the conceptualization of the problem to observable behavior and its environmental context, rather than including references to hypothesized internal processes such as traits or feelings.

In professional use of behavior modification, a contractual agreement may be negotiated, specifying mutually agreeable goals and procedures. When the client is an adult who has sought therapy, the contract would be between him and the mental health worker. When the behavior modification program is to benefit a mentally disadvantaged group, such as the retarded, senile, or psychotic, the contract is often between the individuals' guardians or other responsible persons and the mental health worker. Parents, who usually make decisions affecting their young children, generally are consulted by the mental health worker regarding treatment for their children. Who the appropriate person is to make the contractual agreement for a prisoner is a complex and unsettled issue, taken up later in this report in connection with the discussion of the use of behavior modification procedures with prisoners.

Behavior therapy is a term that is sometimes used synonymously with behavior modification. In general, behavior modification is considered to be the broader term, while behavior therapy refers mainly to clinical interventions, usually applied in a one-to-one therapist-patient relationship. That is, behavior therapy is a special form of behavior modification.

Behavior modification typically tries to influence behavior by changing the environment and the way people interact, rather than by intervening directly through medical procedures (such as drugs) or surgical procedures (such as psychosurgery). Thus, behavior modification methods can be used in a broad range of situations, including the child-rearing efforts of parents and the instructional activities of teachers, as well as the therapeutic efforts of mental health workers in treating more serious psychological and behavioral problems. The effects of behavior modification, unlike the results of most surgical procedures, are relatively changeable and impermanent.

Behavior modification procedures require that the problem behavior be clearly specified. That is, the mental health worker must be able to define objectively the response that the service recipient wants to learn or to have reduced. Thus, certain kinds of problems treated by dynamic psychotherapy are simply not appropriate candidates for behavior modification. In particular, the patient who seeks therapy because of an existential crisis—"Who am I? Where am I going?"—is not an appropriate candidate for behavior modification. This quasi-philosophical problem does not lend itself to an approach that deals with specific identifiable behavior in particular environmental contexts. It is possible that a patient who describes his problem in this way actually has some specific behavioral deficits that may underlie his existential difficulties or occur alongside them. Whether a careful behavioral analysis of the patient's difficulties would reveal such deficits is not now known, however.

While it has been alleged that secret, powerful psychotechnological tools are being or would be used to control the masses, researchers in behavior modification point out that they have encouraged the dissemination of information about behavior processes. In fact, workers in this area believe that increased knowledge will help people to understand social influence processes in general and actually would enable them to counteract many attempts at control, if such attempts occurred. Many persons using behavior modification methods not only evaluate the effectiveness of their procedures, but also measure the consumers' satisfaction with the behavior modification program used.

Is Behavior Modification Merely Common Sense?

Many persons who learn about the general procedures of behavior modification say that they seem to be nothing more than common sense. To some considerable extent, this is true. For example, parents are using these techniques whenever they praise their children for good report cards in the hope of encouraging continued interest and application. On the job, promotions and incentive awards are universally accepted as ways of encouraging job performance. The very structure of our laws, with specified fines, penalties, and the like, is intended to modify behavior through aversive control.

Behavior modification, however, like other scientific approaches, imposes an organization on its subject matter. While common sense often includes contradictory advice (both "out of sight, out of mind," and "absence makes the heart grow fonder"), the principles of behavior modification codify and organize common sense, showing under what conditions, and in what circumstances, which aspect of "common sense" should be applied. The mothers and grandmothers who use what could be described as behavior modification procedures may often do so inconsistently, and then not understand why they have failed.

What Behavior Modification Is Not

As more publicity has been given to this approach, the term "behavior modification" has come to be used loosely and imprecisely in the public media, often with a negative connotation. Thus, behavior modification has sometimes been said to include psychosurgery, electroconvulsive therapy (ECT), and the noncontingent administration of drugs, that is, the administration of drugs independent of any specific behavior of the person receiving the medication. However, even though procedures such as these do modify behavior, that does not make them "behavior modification techniques," in the sense in which most professionals in the field use the term. In this report, the use of the term "behavior modification" will be consistent with its professional use; that is, behavior modification will be used to refer to procedures that are based on the explicit and systematic application of principles and technology derived from research in experimental psychology, procedures that involve some change in the social or environmental context of a person's behavior. This use of the term specifically excludes psychosurgery, electroconvulsive therapy, and the administration of drugs independent of any specific behavior of the person receiving the medication.

History of Behavior Modification

Even though behavior modification is new within the behavioral sciences, the basic experimental work designed to obtain a precise understanding of the principles of learning dates back at least 75 years. Pavlov's first book, *Work on the Digestive Glands*, was published in Russian in 1897. Since then, those initial studies have been followed up with extensive laboratory experiments on learning in both animals and humans. It is on this broad foundation of experimental research that behavior modification principles are based.

The clinical use of behavior modification has a somewhat shorter history, since reports in the scientific literature of such applications have occurred mainly within the past 15 years, although some work was done as early as the 1920s and 1930s (e.g., Jones 1924; Mowrer and Mowrer 1938). Building on animal research by Skinner and his students, the pioneering work of Lindsley (Lindsley and Skinner 1954) and Ferster and DeMyer (1961) demonstrated that the behavior of even such severely disturbed individuals as adult psychotics and autistic children actually followed the same psychological laws as that of normal persons. Wolpe (see, e.g., 1958), working from a more neurophysiologically based theory, developed the method of systematic desensitization, a technique for treating neurotic behavior patterns. Psychologists and psychiatrists in England (Shapiro 1961; Eysenck 1952) also contributed to the early growth of behavior modification.

Once these and other researchers had shown that the principles of learning applied to severely disturbed persons, the development of the field of behavior modification began to accelerate. On the whole, applied researchers have found that the principles developed in laboratory research can be applied effectively to many behavior problems in the real world.

Behavioral treatment interventions were first used with regressed psychotics and neurotic adults (Ayllon and Michael 1959; Ayllon and Azrin 1965; Wolpe and Lazarus 1966). Extensive clinical work has shown that behavior therapy techniques can be effective in eliminating many incapacitating neurotic fears, such as fear of flying in planes. Behavior therapists working with regressed psychotics have been able to develop a variety of adaptive behaviors in these patients so that the patients' lives were enriched by the availability of many new choices (e.g., Ayllon and Azrin 1968).

From these beginnings, the field of behavior modification has expanded to new clinical populations and new settings, including delinquents in halfway houses, the retarded, preschool and deaf children and drug abusers. Some autistic children, who might otherwise be continuously restrained in straightjackets because of their attempts at severe self-mutilation, have been helped by properly designed programs to control their own behavior effectively (e.g., Lovaas et al. 1973). Severely retarded children previously considered incapable of any learning other than the most basic, have, in some instances, been shown capable of acquiring some intellectual skills (e.g., Baer and Guess 1971). Delinquents who would otherwise have been incarcerated at great cost to themselves and to society have often been successfully helped in behaviorally oriented community settings, their own homes, and schools (e.g., Phillips et al. 1971). Some of the drug abusers who have chosen abstinence as a goal have been helped to attain this objective and carry on a normal life without opiates (e.g., Thomson and Rathod 1968).

A large amount of behavior modification research has been done with normal children, including research on improving classroom management, teaching methods, and parent-child relations. Children whose behavior is only mildly maladaptive can be treated by their parents or teachers, because behavior modification lends itself to use by persons not professionally trained in therapy. Most recently, behavior modification has been extended to social problems such as the facilitation of cooperative living in a public housing project, decreasing littering, encouraging the use of public transportation, and enabling unemployed persons to find jobs.

Behavior modification procedures are now used by psychologists, psychiatrists, educators, social workers, speech therapists, and members of other helping professions.

Current Practice of Behavior Modification

Behavior modification is a family of techniques. The diverse methods included under the general label have in common the goal of enhancing persons' lives by altering specific aspects of their behavior. Ideally, the mental health worker and the service recipient decide together on a mutually agreeable set of treatment goals and on the means for attaining these goals. The service recipient or his representative should be kept fully informed of the results of the treatment as it progresses, and also participate in any modification of goals or techniques.

The initial analysis of the problem typically should begin with a detailed description of the behavior that is causing distress or interfering with optimal functioning of the individual in familial, social, vocational, or other important spheres of activity. The behavioral goals are to be viewed in the context of everything the person is able to do, and also in terms of what kinds of support his usual environment is capable of providing over the long term.

This description, whenever possible, should be based on observations of the individual in the setting in which he reports that he is distressed. These observations may be careful quantitative records, or they may be statements about the relative frequency of various behaviors. The person making the observations may be the therapist or his agent, a peer of the individual receiving the service, or the individual himself. For example, a parent might be trained to tally the frequency with which a child stutters, a teacher or hospital aide might keep a record of a child's aggressive outbursts, and a well-motivated individual can count the frequency of occurrence of an unacceptable habit such as nail-biting.

In addition to obtaining this description of what the individual does and does not do, the behavioral mental health worker should try to find how the individual's behavior relates to various events and places in his current and past experiences. Relevant for behavior modification are the events that immediately precede and that immediately follow the behavior. The goal should be to determine the circumstances under which the behavior seems to occur and the environmental consequences that might be maintaining it.

Behavior modification, then, involves the systematic variation of behavioral and environmental factors thought to be associated with an individual's difficulties, with the primary goal of modifying his behavior in the direction that, ideally, he himself (or his agent) has chosen.

Transition to the Nontreatment Setting

The goal of all treatment is the maintenance of improvement after the termination of therapy. The ideal behavior modification program would include a specification of the environment in which the individual normally would be living, and a provision for establishing and strengthening behavior desired or useful in that environment. Generalization to the natural environment is helped if the behavior modification program includes a planned transition between the therapeutic program and the natural environment. The following example illustrates this principle:

> *O. Ivar Lovaas (UCLA) has been studying autistic children for a number of years.[1] He has found that when parents have been trained to carry on with a behavior modification program, children continue to improve after they have left his special treatment ward. On the other hand, the children regress if they are returned to institutions after leaving the ward, and no longer participate in a special training program.*

Examples of Behavior Modification Methods

This section briefly describes some of the most common behavior modification methods. This is a young field, and other techniques are continually being developed and evaluated by clinical researchers. Thus, the methods included here should not be considered an exhaustive list.

Methods Using Positive Reinforcement. Positive reinforcement is a technical term that is roughly synonymous with reward. A positive reinforcer is defined as any event following a given response that increases the chances of that response recurring. Typical positive reinforcers include tangible items, such as money or food; social events such as praise or attention; and activities, such as the opportunity to engage in recreation or to watch television. However, what is reinforcing or motivating for some people—what they will work for—is not necessarily reinforcing for others. As a result, when using behavior modification procedures with any individual, the mental health worker needs to determine what particular items and activities will reinforce that person's behavior at that time.

Methods that use positive reinforcement form the major class of methods among behavior modification techniques. In general, positive reinforcement is used to develop and maintain new behavior, and the removal of positive reinforcement is used to decrease the frequency of undesired behavior. Positive reinforcement has been used in teaching social behavior, in improving classroom management, in motivating better and faster learning of academic materials, in maintaining necessary weight loss, and in teaching new skills of all sorts.

> *Positive reinforcement is being used to help disruptive underachieving children, in one research project.*[1] *Among a variety of procedures being used, teachers praise the children for appropriate behavior and send home daily reports. The children's parents reward them for good daily reports. The researcher, K. Daniel O'Leary (State University of New York, Stony Brook), reports that the children's disruptive behavior has been reduced as a result of this program.*

Although some positive reinforcers are much more effective if a person has been deprived of them for a while, others continue to be reinforcing virtually regardless of how often an individual is exposed to them. Thus, by carefully selecting reinforcers, it should not be necessary to deprive an individual beyond the natural deprivations that occur in daily life in order to be able to reinforce him positively.

One increasingly common use of positive reinforcement is in the group management procedure called a *token economy* (Ayllon and Azrin 1968). In a successful token economy program, the participants receive tokens when they engage in appropriate behavior, and, at some later time, exchange the tokens for any of a variety of positively reinforcing items and activities, just as money is used in society at large. Thus, the token economy is basically a work-payment incentive system. As such, it can be used with institutionalized persons to strengthen behavior that is compatible with that needed in the society at large, such as regular performance on a job, self-care, maintenance of one's living quarters, and exchange of currency for desired items.

One advantage of the token economy, given the limitation in professional manpower, is that nonprofessional personnel are typically the actual agents of therapeutic change. If therapeutic procedures are going to be extended to the many persons who require help, professional personnel must make increased use of those who are in direct contact with the persons requiring service. Those persons who can administer a token economy without special advanced training include nurses, aides, correctional officers, and friends and family members of the individual receiving the service. Such persons should, of course, receive appropriate professional supervision.

The early development of the token economy system took place almost exclusively in closed psychiatric wards. Token economies were found quite useful in preventing or overcoming the deterioration of normal social behavior, or what Gruenberg (1967) has called the "social breakdown syndrome," that accompanies prolonged custodial hospitalization, whatever the initial diagnosis. The token economy method is now being extended to acute psychiatric programs, to public school classrooms, and to classrooms for disadvantaged, hyperactive, retarded, and emotionally disturbed children (Anderson 1967; O'Leary and Drabman 1971). Such programs have also been used with delinquents and persons with character disorders to enhance educational achievement and to improve adjustment to military or civilian environments (Cohen and Filipczak 1971; Colman 1971). Tokens have been used to increase children's attention span and to improve self-help skills in retardates (e.g., Minge and Ball 1967).

In the behavior modification technique of *shaping*, a desired behavior is broken down into successive steps that are taught one by one. Each of the steps is reinforced until it is mastered, and then the individual is moved to the next one. In this way, the new behavior is gradually learned as what the individual does becomes a closer and closer approximation of the behavioral goal.

New behavior can also be taught by means of *modeling*. In this method, a person who already knows how to engage in some desired behavior demonstrates it for the individual who is learning. For example, if a client were learning socially appropriate ways to greet members of the opposite sex, another person might demonstrate them for the client.

> *The model demonstrating the appropriate behavior can be an actual one or an imaginary one. Alan E. Kazdin (Pennsylvania State University) is conducting a study of some facets of imaginary or covert modeling.*[1] *Subjects in his study are college students who have problems in assertiveness. They are taught to imagine one or several other persons engaging in the sort of assertive behavior that the subjects hope to learn, and then are tested to see how much their own assertiveness has increased.*

In *contingency contracting*, the mental health worker and the client decide together on the behavioral goals and on the reinforcement that the client will receive when the goals are achieved. For example, a parent and child might agree that it would be desirable if the home were neater, specifically, if the child's playthings were appropriately stored after a certain time in the evening. The child might request that the parent agree to take him to a favorite activity after the child had put away his playthings for a specified number of days. A contract often involves an exchange, that is, each person entering into the contract agrees both to change his own behavior and to provide reinforcement for the changes that the other person makes. Such a mutual contract is frequently used in marriage counseling.

> The methods of contingency contracting are being studied by Henry M. Boudin (University of Florida) to see how they can be made effective for dealing with the special behavior problems characteristic of drug abusers.[2] The goal of this project is to reduce drug dependence in addicts who are being treated in an outpatient setting. The contracts made between the drug abusers and the therapists cover a large number of aspects of the addicts' lives. For example, an addict might agree to set up a joint bank account with his therapist, to which the addict deposits his own money. If a urine test indicates that he has broken his promise not to use illegal drugs, funds are taken from that account by the therapist and sent to some organization that the addict strongly dislikes. Contracts work both ways: If the therapist is late for an appointment with the addict or misses a therapy session, he can be required to deposit money to the addict's account. A contract involving positive reinforcement might specify that if the addict completes some amount of time on a job, he would receive a few movie passes or discounts on some number of phonograph records.

Aversive Control.   Some types of inappropriate behavior, such as addictions and certain sexual behaviors, appear to be maintained because their immediate consequences are naturally reinforcing for the individual. In such cases, aversive control techniques are sometimes used to combat long-term consequences that may be much more detrimental to the individual than the aversive methods themselves. Aversive methods are also used for behaviors that are life-threatening, such as severe self-mutilation.

In general, an aversive stimulus, that is, something that is unpleasant to the person, is used to help the person reduce his desire to carry out the inappropriate behavior (Rachman and Teasdale 1969). After aversive therapy, for example, a man who formerly became excited sexually only when thinking of women's shoes, might report that he had lost interest in the shoes. With aversive techniques, the aversive stimulus will not occur, that is, the individual is able to avoid it, as long as he does not perform the behavior that he and the mental health worker have agreed is undesirable. When aversive therapy is appropriately conducted, it is accompanied by positive reinforcement of normal behavior.

Perhaps the most commonly used aversive stimulus in behavior modification is a brief, low-level electric shock. This type of aversive stimulus has been highly effective in ameliorating severe behavioral problems such as self-injurious behavior (see, e.g., Bucher 1969). When properly used, the shocks are very brief. Shock used this way causes no lingering pain or tissue damage and can be administered with precise control (Baer 1970). The use of shock as an aversive control procedure is entirely different from its use in electroconvulsive therapy, a procedure completely outside the scope of behavior modification.

A different type of aversive control method is the removal of positive reinforcement, such as a loss of privileges following a given behavior. This is a technique commonly used by American parents (Sears, Maccoby, and Levin 1957). One example of a technique involving the removal of positive reinforcement is the *time-out* procedure, in which an inappropriate behavior is followed by a period of brief social isolation.

The time-out procedure is one of a number of behavior modification techniques being used in a study of preschool children with poor social, language, and cognitive skills.[1] The goal of the investigator, Donald M. Baer (University of Kansas), is to reduce these children's hyperactive and rebellious behavior. When a child engages in disruptive behavior, he is placed for a brief period in a small room adjoining the classroom. This aversive control for disruptive behavior is combined with a wide variety of positive reinforcing procedures for appropriate behavior. Positive reinforcers used in this study include attention, praise, access to preferred activities, and snacks.

Fines are another example of aversive control; fines require the individual to give up some positive reinforcement following an instance of inappropriate behavior.

One common use of aversive stimuli is in attempts to reduce excessive drinking by associating the drinking experience with an aversive stimulus. For example, recent research on alcoholism has employed electric shock as an aversive stimulus to teach the alcoholic patient to avoid continued drinking beyond a criterion blood alcohol level. This has reportedly been successful in helping problem drinkers learn to limit their intake to moderate levels typical of social drinking (Lovibond 1970).

In research by Roger E. Vogler (Patton State Hospital and Pacific State Hospital, California), alcoholic persons being treated either in the hospital or as outpatients receive electric shock if they drink too much alcohol in a bar-like setting in

*the hospital.[3] Shock is also used to train the patients to
discriminate when their blood alcohol concentration exceeds
a specific level, and to teach them to drink slowly.*

Drugs such as Anectine and Antabuse have also been used as
aversive treatment for alcoholic persons (see section on Methods
Using Drugs, below).

The other relatively common use of aversive stimuli is to control
self-injurious and self-destructive behavior such as head-banging
or tongue-biting. Such behavior can apparently be eliminated with
a brief application of a strong aversive stimulus immediately after
the response (Risley 1968; Bucher and Lovaas 1968).

*Occasionally, infants, young children, and some mentally
retarded persons "ruminate," that is, they apparently
voluntarily reject food from their stomachs into their mouths
where it may be reswallowed or further ejected from their
mouths. When this problem is severe, it can be life-threatening
and may have serious detrimental effects on the physical,
emotional, and social development of the child. Thomas
Sajwaj (University of Mississippi) has developed a procedure
using lemon juice as a mild aversive stimulus to control the
ruminative behavior: when the infant or child regurgitates, a
small amount of lemon juice is immediately squirted into his
mouth by an attendant.[1] Preliminary results with a few
children suggest that this aversive therapy eliminates the
rumination, and that no other maladaptive behavior appears.*

A consistent finding from research on aversive control is that the
effects of the therapeutic use of aversive stimuli seem to be
restricted to the particular behavior that is associated with the
aversive stimulus, in that particular situation, with that particular
therapist. That is, the effects of aversive stimuli do not seem to
generalize very much (Risley 1968; Bucher and Lovaas 1968).

In contrast to the somewhat limited effects of aversive stimuli in
controlling undesirable behavior, the positive side effects of this
treatment seem to be rather widespread. For example, it is
commonly reported that once the use of aversive stimuli has
eliminated a patient's self-injurious behavior, he avoids people less
and is more responsive to other therapy aimed at teaching him
adaptive responses.

While the effects of aversive stimuli may, in many cases, be only
temporary, the individual will not make the undesirable response
for at least some period of time. During that time, he is more
amenable to learning new, appropriate responses. On the whole,
research suggests that the most effective way of eliminating
inappropriate behavior is to follow it with aversive stimuli, while

at the same time positively reinforcing desired behavior. If the environment then continues to support the new, desired responses, the inappropriate behavior will soon cease to occur. Since the aversive stimuli are used only following inappropriate behavior, they will no longer be administered. The effects of the initial aversive control will, however, be lasting, because the individual will now have learned to make appropriate responses.

It is important to note, however, that in the absence of rewarded alternatives, the response that had been suppressed by an aversive technique is likely to recur. To ensure that it does not, the individual being treated should learn behavior that will be maintained by rewards that occur naturally in his environment. In some instances, simply stopping the undesirable behavior enables the individual to get natural rewards. For the "ruminating" child, for example, stopping the ejection of food in itself allows proper digestion of food, greater comfort, and normal eating, growing, and developing. In addition, the infant is now more receptive to normal learning experiences.

Overcorrection. Overcorrection is a behavior modification method combining positive reinforcement and aversive control that is used to discourage inappropriate or disruptive behavior. In this procedure, the person who has engaged in the inappropriate behavior not only remedies the situation he has caused, but also "overcorrects" it. That is, the person is required to restore the disruptive situation to a better state than existed before the disruption. For example, a violent patient in a mental institution who overturns a bed in a dormitory might be required not only to right that bed and make it up again, but also to straighten the bedclothes on all the other beds in that dormitory. Making up the bed that was overturned corrects the situation that the violent behavior disrupted; making up all the other beds is, then, an "overcorrection."

Often an inappropriate or disruptive behavior has been receiving some sort of reinforcement. For example, stealing results in the thief acquiring goods he desires; turning over a bed might get a patient attention and concern from an otherwise busy ward staff. Thus, one function of the overcorrection procedure is to terminate any such reinforcement associated with the inappropriate behavior: the thief must return the stolen goods, for example.

Moreover, overcorrection is an aversive stimulus, because it requires effort to complete the overcorrection, and because the person cannot be engaging in other behavior while he is completing the overcorrection task. In addition, the overcorrection procedure itself may often be educative, in that the process of restoring the original situation generally requires the individual to engage in appropriate behavior.

Overcorrection has been a particularly effective technique in eliminating aggressive and disruptive behavior in institutionalized patients (Foxx and Azrin 1972; Webster and Azrin 1973). One of the advantages of overcorrection over other methods for dealing with these problems is that severe aversive stimuli may not be involved in overcorrection.

Systematic Desensitization.   Gradual, progressive exposure to feared situations has long been advocated as a means of eliminating or reducing maladaptive anxiety or avoidance behavior. In systematic desensitization, the exposure is preplanned in graduated steps. In general, this procedure involves teaching the patient to relax, and then having him imagine or actually encounter increasingly disturbing situations. The patient usually does not move on to a more disturbing item until he can remain deeply relaxed with a less disturbing one. Recent research, however, has suggested that some degree of forced exposure can also be effective in reducing fears.

If a patient is afraid of heights, for example, the therapist works together with the patient to develop a list of increasingly fearful situations. For example, the patient might say he is very afraid of looking out from the top of the Empire State Building, but hardly afraid at all of climbing a small ladder. He then is trained to relax, and the therapist asks him to imagine each of the series of situations, starting with the one he is least afraid of, the one arousing little or no tension or fear. Over a series of therapy sessions, the patient will be exposed systematically to the whole list of fearful situations, and, at the end of treatment, will be able to maintain his relaxed state even while imagining scenes that were initially extremely fearful. Patients are usually encouraged to try out their newly learned ability to relax in the face of the formerly fearful situation outside of the therapy setting. Generalization of the effects of systematic desensitization from the treatment setting to real life is typically found, especially when the patient has done the "homework" of gradually facing what used to be fearful.

Systematic desensitization has been used clinically by behavior therapists to treat unreasonable fears, frigidity, insomnia, interpersonal anxiety, and other clinical problems in which anxiety is a core problem.

> *Systematic desensitization is being used with a variety of problems. For example, Thomas L. Creer (Children's Asthma Research Institute and Hospital, Denver) has demonstrated the effectiveness of systematic desensitization in the treatment of*

children's asthma.[1] As a result of the treatment, the children learned to be less afraid of having asthma attacks and used significantly less medication. Desensitization is also being used as a treatment for insomnia (Richard R. Bootzin, Northwestern University)[1] and as a component of treatment for marital sexual dysfunction (Joseph LoPiccolo, State University of New York, Stony Brook).[1]

Assertive Training. When a person fails to stand up for his rights in an appropriately firm manner, he may not have acquired appropriate assertive behavior, or he may not be engaging in behavior that he actually knows how to do. Similarly, persons who do not express positive feelings in appropriate situations also may lack appropriate assertive skills or an appreciation of the situations in which those skills should normally be used.

Assertive training is taught by a combination of methods, including modeling of appropriate behavior by the therapist or some other person, and reinforced practice by the patient. The overall goal of this type of behavior therapy is the alteration of the patient's interpersonal interactions.

Methods Using Drugs. On the whole, behavior modification procedures emphasize environmental manipulation. However, drugs have occasionally been used as an integral part of a behavioral treatment, either following a particular behavior, or as an adjunct to a behavioral program.

A few case studies in the literature report the use of drugs as aversive stimuli, when the therapist was attempting to reduce some inappropriate behavior. For example, succinylcholine chloride (Anectine) was given to one individual who had a severe dependency on sniffing various substances such as airplane glue. In the treatment, the patient sniffed one of these substances and was immediately injected with Anectine, which produces an extremely unpleasant sensation of drowning and suffocating. The treatment was conducted under the supervision of an anesthesiologist. After this treatment, the patient refrained from sniffing the substance that had been associated with the Anectine (Blanchard, Libet, and Young 1973).

Anectine, and emetic drugs such as Antabuse, have also been used as aversive treatment for alcoholic persons, although the evidence suggests that they are not strongly effective treatments.

When drugs are used as part of an aversive control program in behavior modification, they must take effect immediately after the occurrence of a specific inappropriate behavior. This temporal relationship between the behavior and the aversive action of the drug is considered to be an essential aspect of the therapy. As noted later in this paper, giving aversive drugs independently of a person's behavior is not behavior modification, in the sense in which we are using that term.

Drugs are also sometimes used to facilitate the progress of a behavioral program. Brevital is a drug that enhances relaxation. Some practitioners who do systematic desensitization give their patients small doses of Brevital, if the patients are otherwise having trouble learning to relax in the therapy session (Brady 1966). Usually the dosage level of the drug is gradually adjusted so that the patient soon relaxes without the assistance of the drug.

Evaluation of Behavior Modification

Collecting evidence that would show whether behavior modification is effective is not as easy as it would seem. Several conceptual issues first need to be resolved. In order to evaluate behavior modification, the types of problems for which it is appropriate must be delimited, suitable outcome measures must be selected, and appropriate comparison conditions must be chosen.

While therapists who use behavior modification feel that it is appropriate for a wide range of problems, other persons have questioned the appropriateness of a behavioral approach to many mental health problems because of their belief that the therapy for a particular problem must direct itself to the root cause of the problem. In that view, disorders of biological origin should be treated with biologically based principles, while those of psychological origin should be treated psychotherapeutically.

A substantial body of opinion insists that there need not be a relationship between the etiology of a problem and the nature of the treatment that is effective in ameliorating it (Birk et al. 1973; London 1972). A disorder with an organic or neurophysiological etiology may be responsive to a biological therapy, but it may also be markedly improved by one of the procedures based on behavior modification. Similarly, difficulties that have an environmental origin may be responsive to biological intervention, such as psychopharmacologic treatment, as well as to a behavioral treatment. Behavior modification is based on learning principles, and so is particularly suitable for those problems, whatever their etiology, where the appropriate treatment involves retraining or learning new skills.

Therapists who use behavior modification methods would choose an objective, preferably quantifiable, measure of behavior as the outcome measure for evaluating the efficacy of treatment procedures. This selection contrasts with the outcome measures preferred by classical psychodynamically oriented therapists, who feel that personality tests reflect the changes that they seek to achieve in therapy. These psychotherapists may, in fact, regard as "mere symptoms" what the behaviorally oriented therapists regard as the focus of treatment. One of the consequences of this difference in viewpoints is that it is extremely difficult to obtain general agreement on a set of outcome measures for a comparison of the effects of behavior modification and psychotherapy.

The ideal evaluation of the effectiveness of behavior modification would tell us whether behavioral procedures bring about improvement more often, more quickly, to a greater degree, longer, or at less cost than do alternative procedures, such as psychotherapy. Unfortunately, at least in part because of the difficulty in obtaining agreement among professionals on what constitutes "improvement," this sort of direct comparison has been made systematically in only a few studies.

Despite the conceptual problems in making comparisons of different kinds of treatments, however, researchers have recently begun to conduct comparative evaluations in which one group of individuals receives a standard, well-accepted treatment, conscientiously applied, while another receives some kind of behavior modification, again conscientiously applied. This kind of research is aimed at answering the important questions of relative therapeutic efficacy and cost-effectiveness. By comparing results obtained on a variety of outcome measures with existing, standard procedures and with behavior modification, researchers will begin to provide the evidence necessary for deciding whether the costs of introducing new procedures, training staff in those procedures, and making changes in supervision and recordkeeping, will be adequately repaid with a significant improvement in the functioning of the persons treated.

Although few comparisons have been made of behavior modification with other forms of treatment, large numbers of case studies and systematic evaluations of behavior modification have been reported in which the researchers have shown experimentally that the behavior modification methods were responsible for the improvements obtained. To summarize these many reports briefly, behavior therapy has been shown to be effective with some persons suffering from unjustified fears, anxiety reactions, and stuttering. Problems that have shown some improvement when individuals have been treated by behavior therapy procedures include compulsive behavior, hysteria, psychological impotence, frigidity, exhibitionism, and insomnia.

Behavior modification procedures have been used to analyze and produce significant changes in the language of institutionalized retardates who were initially deficient in language skills. Control of self-destructive and self-mutilating behavior has been achieved in a number of cases through behavior modification, as has the elimination or great reduction of milder forms of disruptive behavior, such as tantrums, whining, screaming, fighting, and destruction of property. Positive behaviors developed in institutionalized persons with behavior modification procedures include proper eating techniques and the complete range of self-care skills frequently absent in such persons. In otherwise normal preschool children, behavior modification has been used to facilitate the development of those motor, social and cognitive skills thought especially appropriate to the preschool environment, yet not appearing in the normal course of events in that setting. For example, social isolates have acquired social skills, and silent children, a readiness to speak. Hyperactive children have been taught to attend to tasks, and predelinquents have been taught friendly speech and have learned to perform skills necessary for school achievement, to take appropriate care of their living quarters, to interact cooperatively with their families, and to stop stealing and aggressive behavior (Baer 1973).

Token reinforcement systems have been shown to be effective in many classrooms for modifying behavior problems such as classroom disruption, failure to study, and low academic achievement. Chronic mental patients on wards throughout the country have learned a wide variety of appropriate social behaviors after the introduction of a token economy. The token economy has recently been introduced in a few nursing homes and wards for senile patients, and the early results appear promising. When the behavioral program is in effect, the patients come to interact more with each other and engage in more activities. Studies have shown that careful implementation of behavioral techniques can often produce improvements in the verbal and nonverbal behavior of psychotic and schizophrenic children.

Behavioral treatments have been quite successful with toilet training and most nervous habits, but somewhat less successful with alcoholism, smoking, and tics other than in a few special cases. To the extent that the symptoms of asthma are maintained by environmental consequences, the number and severity of asthmatic attacks can be reduced by behavioral programs designed to rearrange those consequences. Systematic desensitization has also been effective with some asthmatics (Price 1974).

Overall, then, much more evaluative research needs to be done with the behavioral treatments, although they do show considerable promise. With many clinical problems, behavioral procedures have been used only on a few individual cases, so that experimental evidence is lacking for the efficacy of the specific methods used. Thus, while a great range of problems appears to be responsive to behavioral treatment, for many types of problems, validating data are yet to be obtained. The existing evidence is strong enough, however, that an expert task force of the American Psychiatric Association recently concluded that behavior therapy and behavior principles employed in the analysis and treatment of clinical phenomena "have reached a stage of development where they now unquestionably have much to offer informed clinicians in the service of modern clinical and social psychiatry" (Birk et al. 1973).

Current Behavior Modification Programs: ADAMHA

The Alcohol, Drug Abuse, and Mental Health Administration (ADAMHA) is supporting behavior modification research in a wide variety of areas; the amount of that support exceeds $3 million a year, out of a total of over $121 million spent on research. Behavior modification research being conducted with ADAMHA support covers a wide range of problems and populations. Research is being done on the behavioral problems of children and adults, on persons with mild behavior problems and quite severe ones. Researchers are attempting to develop better behavioral techniques for dealing with asthma, insomnia, and hypertension, as well as evaluating new child-rearing techniques and classroom management methods. Behavioral treatments for problems of alcoholism, drug addiction, and juvenile delinquency are also being studied.

Many current projects have been described above as examples of specific behavior modification procedures. A few other projects will be described here, as further indication of the range and scope of support currently being provided.

Montrose M. Wolf, Elery L. Phillips, Dean Fixsen, and others (University of Kansas)[1] have developed a halfway house for predelinquent adolescents that uses procedures of behavior modification. This halfway house, called Achievement Place, is a community-controlled, community-based, family-style residential home for six to eight adolescents who have typically been adjudicated there by the juvenile courts. The program is designed to provide a maximum amount of motivation and instruction to the youths when they first enter, and then, as they develop skills and self-control, to reduce the amount of structure, replacing it with more natural reinforcement conditions. Behavior modification procedures include a token economy; positive reinforcement to shape appropriate social, academic, prevocational, and self-care behavior; and fines for inappropriate behavior. In addition, the adolescents' parents are trained in child management procedures so that the parents can be more successful in guiding their children toward productive lives.

Preliminary findings indicate that Achievement Place youths progress far better than do comparable youths placed on probation or sent to a State training school. This model has been copied widely, and there are now more than 30 such homes in operation in eight States, supported by State and local funds.

Nathan H. Azrin (Anna State Hospital, Illinois) has developed an extensive life-intervention scheme for alcoholic persons, based on behavior modification principles.[3] In this treatment program, vocational, family, and other social reinforcers are rearranged so that the alcoholic person learns new behavior patterns incompatible with drinking. The clients are given marital and job counseling and are introduced to alcohol-free social situations especially established for them. The effectiveness of this treatment package is being compared with that of existing hospital procedures.

A. J. Turner is receiving support for a project in which behavior modification procedures are being used in all possible service areas of the Huntsville-Madison County (Alabama) Mental Health Center.[1] The results obtained on a wide variety of measures administered to the patients in this center are being compared with results on the same measures obtained from patients in a comparable community mental health center that uses standard procedures. Thus far, the experimental community mental health center has reported a much greater decline in State hospitalizations from their catchment area than that shown by comparable counties, as well as decreases in other measures, such as average number of days in the hospital.

Critical Issues in Behavior Modification

Recently, concerns have been widely expressed over the ethical and legal aspects of behavior modification techniques.

The Fear of Control

Some people fear behavior modification and control because of prevalent contemporary attitudes of distrust and skepticism of authority in general, and "mind control" in particular; others have more specific concerns that are related to the practice of behavior modification or, often, to myths and misconceptions about the practice of behavior modification.

General Concerns About Control.   Behavior modification is most often criticized when it is used to alter the behavior of persons who are involuntary participants in therapy. Involuntary patients or subjects include those who are disadvantaged, vulnerable, or powerless because of institutionalization, age, social position, or discrimination.

Perhaps the most frequent complaints are in connection with the treatment of hospitalized mental patients and institutionalized delinquents and criminals. There has been a growing sensitivity to the ambiguity that can underlie diagnosis and choice of treatment goals for these populations. According to this view, a thin line separates social deviance from a mental illness that requires hospitalization. Society can often find it more convenient to institutionalize the deviant individual than to deal with the problem he represents. The hospitalization or incarceration thus may be more in the interest of social control than in the interest of the person's welfare.

The growing distrust of the exercise of control over the helpless and the disadvantaged even challenges the legitimacy of the authority of those who attempt to treat these persons. The authority to treat the institutionalized mentally disordered, for example, has been eroded by the growing dissemination of the notion that mental "illness" is a myth. According to this view, people should accept responsibility for their own behavior, including behavior that might otherwise be termed "mentally ill." Further, an emerging sociological model views the mentally disordered patient as a victim of stresses and strains that reside primarily within the social structure, rather than within the individual.

Credence has been increasingly given to the picture of the mental patient as a victim who is hospitalized for the convenience of society. In that view, treatment is seen as either a form of punishment or a procedure designed to make the patient conform to the requirements of an oppressive society. The mental health worker who proposes to modify the patient's behavior thus can be seen as serving the interests of the oppressor, rather than favoring the right of the person to express his individuality.

The news media, popular books, and movies have given voice to these general concerns. Also, several organizations have, in the last few years, called conferences to explore these issues. For example, the Institute of Society, Ethics, and the Life Sciences, of the Hastings Center (Hastings-on-Hudson, New York), held a series of meetings between 1971 and 1973 in which leaders in mental health research, practice, and public policy explored the problems of behavior control by drugs, the media, and physical manipulation of the brain, and discussed issues relating to the use of behavior control in education and in total institutions such as prisons and mental hospitals. The Institute has released reports summarizing these discussions.

Specific Fears of Behavior Modification.   The general concerns mentioned above are relevant to all types of psychotherapy, as well as to behavior modification. In addition, people have expressed other concerns that are more specific to behavior modification procedures.

Behavior modification has been criticized with respect to its theoretical foundation, its goals, and its methods. Some mental health professionals have attacked behavior modification on the grounds that its underlying assumptions are at variance with their basic values and tend to dehumanize man (see, e.g., Carrera and Adams 1970). Contingency contracting, for example, has been said to foster a manipulative, exchange orientation to social interaction, and token economies, an emphasis on materialistic evaluation of human efforts. Mental health professionals, including persons with a behavioral orientation, have also questioned the appropriateness of accepting a patient's definition of his own problem, on the grounds that the patient's self-attribution of deviance can, like his behavior, be seen as learned behavior that is a function of consequences provided by society (Davison 1974; Begelman, 1977).

Another type of concern about the goals of behavior modification was expressed in a detailed law review critique which argued that behavior modification could be used to impose "an orthodoxy of 'appropriate conduct'" on the community (Heldman 1973), and thus to silence social and political dissent. Extremist activist organizations have described the procedures of behavior modification as "crimes against humanity."

The media and literature have incorrectly linked behavior modification with techniques such as psychosurgery, chemotherapy, electroshock, and brainwashing. The fantasied potency of imaginary or untested mind-controlling techniques, popularized in such works as *Brave New World, 1984, The Manchurian Candidate*, and *A Clockwork Orange*, has been extended to encompass standard, carefully evaluated behavior modification techniques.

Further, procedures that are encompassed within behavior modification can be misused. When this happens, critics decry behavior modification, even though the misuse is such that the procedure can no longer accurately be called "behavior modification." For example, Anectine, a drug that produces the sensation of drowning or dying, and Antabuse and other emetic drugs, have occasionally been used as components of behavior modification procedures. In aversive therapy for problems such as glue-sniffing and alcoholism, such drugs may be used as the aversive stimulus. However, these drugs have also been seriously misused, especially in prison settings, where they are given to persons in retribution for real or imagined lack of "cooperation" on their part, or as a way of keeping recalcitrant persons "in line." The noncontingent use of drugs lies outside the purview of behavior modification.

A Perspective On the Issue of Control.   Like any technology, behavior modification can be used ineptly, or for ends that could be considered immoral. The technology of behavior modification, says Skinner (1971), "is ethically neutral. It can be used by villain or saint. There is nothing in a methodology which determines the values governing its use" (p. 150). When psychoanalytic therapy was first introduced, it too raised the spectre of unethical authoritarian control. It is likely that any approach to the alteration of human behavior raises these same questions.

In the view of persons working in the field of behavior modification, it is the nature of social interaction for people to influence each other. In other words, behavior is continually being influenced, and it is inevitably controlled. Therapy without manipulation is a mirage that disappears on close scrutiny (Shapiro and Birk 1967). That is, in all kinds of therapy, the therapist hopes to change the patient in some way. Bandura (1969) formulates the issue in this way: "The basic moral question is not whether man's behavior will be controlled, but rather by whom, by what means, and for what ends." Behavior modification, then, involves altering the nature of the controlling conditions, rather than imposing control where none existed before.

Behavior modification is not a one-way method that can be successfully imposed on an unwilling individual. By its very nature, behavior modification will succeed only when the individual who is receiving the consequences is responsive to them and cooperates with the program. If the environmental events following an individual's behavior are not reinforcing to him or are less reinforcing than some alternative, his behavior will not change. Similarly, if the aversive consequence that follows his behavior is less unpleasant to him than some alternative, his behavior will not change. For many persons, it is highly reinforcing to be resistant to attempts to alter their behavior and highly aversive to succumb to external control. Even though such an individual may be participating in a behavior modification program, the person conducting the program may not be able to find any consequence strong enough to compete with the individual's desire to remain unchanged. Thus, in the long run, each of us retains control over his own behavior.

This characterization is equally true, whether the persons in the behavior modification programs are voluntary, adult, clinic patients, or institutionalized individuals with senile psychotic syndrome. Even for the latter group of persons, environmental consequences will succeed in altering their behavior only if the new consequences are more reinforcing than some alternative. Because mentally disadvantaged groups, such as the senile, often are in settings lacking an array of alternative reinforcers, special care needs to be exercised in developing programs for them. Later in this paper, some procedures are suggested that might help protect disadvantaged groups from inappropriately designed programs.

Although aversive therapy procedures seem more coercive than those using positive reinforcement, the individual still must cooperate fully with the procedures in order for them to be effective. While aversive procedures may reduce the individual's motivation to engage in the undesirable behavior, the motivation probably will not be reduced to zero. Rather, the goal of the therapy generally is to reduce the motivation to the point where the individual is able to exercise self-control and avoid engaging in the undesirable behavior.

Recent fiction has dramatically portrayed individuals supposedly unable to overcome the effects of aversive therapy. This, however, is not realistic. If coercion is used in therapy—whether positive or aversive—that may indeed force the individual's cooperation for a time. But, in real life, once this coercion is removed, the individual will be able to return to his former ways if he is motivated to do so.

It is important to remember that in addition to its emphasis on environmental control, the behavioral approach also assumes that persons are able to learn behavioral principles and understand how environmental events can control their own behavior (Ulrich 1967). As behavioral principles are more widely disseminated, an increasing number of persons will have access to them. Hopefully, through the knowledge that people gain from discussions of behavioral principles in courses, workshops, articles in the public press, television "talk shows," and other such sources, they will have a better understanding of their own behavior.

As public awareness increases, the likelihood of behavior being manipulated by more knowledgeable individuals lessens. Just as a professional in behavior modification may use his understanding of behavioral principles in an attempt to alter other persons' behavior, so those other persons can make use of their own understanding and control of themselves and their environment to resist, or indeed to counterinfluence the behavior of the professional.

The behavior influence process is always a reciprocal one: The behavior manager attempts to shape the behavior of some other person through changing the consequences of that person's behavior, but, at the same time, the manager's behavior is in turn shaped by the other's response. Control always results in countercontrol.

In the ideal situation, the mental health worker using behavioral procedures would plan the goals and methods of the therapy together with the client. Persons using behavioral approaches would follow the same generally accepted ethical principles guiding other therapists, and so would strive to maintain a suitable balance between the rights of individuals and of society.

Thus, when there is controversy over the application of behavior modification, it often seems to be in instances in which these ideal conditions have not, for some reason, been met. One important benefit of the public attention to and criticism of behavior modification has been increasing sensitivity on the part of all mental health workers to issues that were formerly often neglected. For example, many therapists are only recently becoming aware of the need to involve the client or his representative more realistically in the planning of the treatment program, including the selection of both goals and methods. In the past, the mental health worker often used simply his own clinical judgment and experience as the basis for determining treatment goals and methods.

Also, the significance of the imbalance in power that is usually found between the therapist and the client is only now coming to be understood by mental health workers. Typically, the therapist comes from the more powerful classes or has a higher status within an institution, while the client is from a less powerful class or is of a lower status. In all mental health fields, including behavior modification, therapists have tended to view problems from their own perspective, so that treatment goals chosen were those that they would want for themselves or that would benefit those to whom the therapist had allegiance. In many instances, the inclusion of the client or his representative in the decision-making process is beginning to redress this imbalance. The power imbalance is a particularly serious problem, however, when the clients are involuntarily confined in an institution. Later in this report, the issues surrounding the use of behavior modification in prisons are discussed in detail.

On the whole, the goal of behavior modification, as generally practiced, is not to force people to conform or to behave in some mindless, automation-like way. Rather, the goals generally include providing new skills and individualized options and developing creativity and spontaneity.

Persons working in behavior modification have tried to be sensitive to the issue of control and to face the issue directly. Task forces on ethical issues in behavior modification have been established by each of the major professional societies whose members work in this field—the American Psychiatric Association, the American Psychological Association, and the Association for Advancement of Behavior Therapy. The first of these has published an extensive report (Birk et al. 1973).

In summary, people do fear control of their behavior, and they fear any method that seems to be effective in changing behavior. However, people need an understanding of what controls behavior and how behavior can be changed. Skinner (1971) has a thoughtful statement on this issue: "Good government is as much a matter of the control of human behavior as bad, good incentive conditions as much as exploitation, good teaching as much as punitive drill. . . . To refuse to exercise available control because in some sense all control is wrong is to withhold possibly important forms of counter-control" (pp. 180–181). Dissemination of information about behavior modification methods will make techniques of resisting oppressive control generally available, so that new methods of control can be met by new methods of countercontrol (Platt 1972).

The Use of Aversive Control

Aversive procedures can be and have been seriously misused so that they become means by which a person in power can exercise control or retribution over those in his charge. The abusive treatment may then be justified by calling it therapeutic and labeling it "behavior modification."

A Perspective on Aversive Control.   While many behavior modification aversive techniques, such as shock and time-out, are effective, it is unfortunately true that they are also cheap and easy to apply, requiring little if any specialized knowledge on the part of the person using—or misusing—them. Further, aversive techniques are widely known to be included in the family of behavior modification methods. Thus legitimized, these simple aversive methods are subject to indiscriminate use and other abuses, without regard for individual rights. For example, time-out, which appropriately used should be for only short periods of time, has, in some settings, involved extraordinarily long periods of isolation in small quarters.

Aversive techniques have been used successfully to eliminate life-threatening self-destructive behavior in clinical populations.

Although the techniques themselves are unpleasant to consider, the gain from their use can be potentially great, especially when compared to the alternative, which may be long-term confinement in an institution or prolonged periods in total restraint. Thus, aversive techniques are appropriately used when the risk to the patient of continuing the self-injurious behavior is serious, alternative treatments appear to be ineffective, and potential benefits to the patient from the treatment are great. On the other hand, aversive methods should not be used to enforce compliance with institutional rules.

Suggested Procedures. When aversive methods are used, appropriate safeguards should be included for the protection of the rights and dignity of those involved. Severe aversive methods, involving pain or discomfort, should be used only as a last resort, when the person's behavior presents immediate danger to himself or others, and when nonpainful interventions have been found to be ineffective. Aversive therapies should be conducted only under the surveillance of an appropriate review panel, preferably one including representatives of the group to which the person receiving the treatment belongs; and they should be used only with the continuing consent of the person receiving them, or of his representative. The person supervising the use of aversive methods should continually monitor the results, which should also be available to the review panel. Any method not providing significant help should be abandoned. The technique used should not violate generally accepted cultural standards and values, as determined by the review panel.

Behavior Modification in Prisons

Behavior modification has become an increasingly controversial yet important law enforcement tool. Many persons feel that the use of behavior modification in prisons conflicts with the values of individual privacy and dignity.

Persons using behavior modification procedures have been particularly criticized for their attempts to deal with rebellious and nonconformist behavior of inmates in penal institutions. Because the behavioral professional is often in the position of assisting in the management of prisoners whose antagonism to authority and rebelliousness have been the catalyst for conflict within the institution, the distinctions among his multiple functions of therapy, management, and rehabilitation can become blurred, and his allegiance confused. While the professional may quite accurately perceive his role as benefiting the individual, he may at the same time appear to have the institution, rather than the prisoner, as his primary client.

Frequently, the goal of effective modification in penal institutions has been the preservation of the institution's authoritarian control. While some prison behavior modification programs have been designed to educate the prisoners and benefit them in other ways, other programs have been directed toward making the prisoners less troublesome and easier to handle, adjusting the inmates to the needs of the institution.

A related problem is that in prisons as elsewhere, the term "behavior modification" has been misused as a label for any procedure that aims to alter behavior, including excessive isolation, sensory deprivation, and severe physical punishment. Behavior modification then becomes simply a new name for old and offensive techniques.

The question of voluntary consent is an especially difficult problem when the persons participating in a program are prison inmates (Shapiro 1974). It is not clear whether there can ever be a "real volunteer" in a prison, because inmates generally believe that they will improve their chances for early parole if they cooperate with prison officials' requests to participate in a special program. There are other pressures as well; for example, participation in a novel program may be a welcome relief from the monotony of prison life.

The use of behavior modification in the prisons came to national attention recently when the Law Enforcement Assistance Administration (LEAA) withdrew its support from some behavior modification programs. According to a spokesman for LEAA, this was done because the agency staff did not have the technical and professional skills to screen, evaluate, or monitor such programs. The termination of the programs was criticized by the American Psychological Association (APA) as an injustice to the public and to prison inmates. The APA's news release (Feb. 15, 1974) said that the LEAA decision would tend "to stifle the development of humane forms of treatment that provide the offender the opportunity to fully realize his or her potential as a contributing member of society."

A similar point of view has been expressed by Norman A. Carlson, Director of the Federal Bureau of Prisons, in discussing the difficulty of determining which programs should be described as behavior modification: "In its broadest sense, virtually every program in the Bureau of Prisons is designed to change or modify behavior. Presumably, the Federal courts commit offenders to custody because their serious criminal behavior is unacceptable to society. The assumption is that during the period of incarceration, individuals will change their patterns of behavior so that after release, they will not become involved in further criminal activity." In general, when behavior modification programs are introduced in Federal prisons, it is important that they be consistent with this philosophy.

A Perspective on the Use of Behavior Modification in Prisons.   A major problem in using behavior modification in prisons is that positive programs begun with the best of intentions may become subverted to punitive ones by the oppressive prison atmosphere. Generally, behavior modification programs are intended to give prisoners the opportunity to learn behavior that will give them a chance to lead more successful lives in the world to which they will return, to enjoy some sense of achievement, and to understand and control their own behavior better. Unfortunately, in actual practice, the programs sometimes teach submission to authority instead.

Thus, critical questions in the use of behavior modification in prisons are how goals are chosen for the program and how continued adherence to those goals is monitored. Behavior modification should not be used in an attempt to facilitate institutionalization of the inmate or to make him adjust to inhumane living conditions. Further, no therapist should accept requests for treatment that take the form "make him 'behave,'" when the intent of the request is to make the person conform to oppressive conditions.

Currently, a common position is to recommend the elimination of behavior modification programs in prisons, on the grounds that such therapy must be coercive, since consent cannot be truly voluntary. However, before this drastic step is taken, careful consideration should be given to the consequences. If constructive programs were eliminated, it would deny the opportunity of improvement for those inmates who genuinely want to participate and who might benefit from the programs. It would seem far better to build in safeguards than to discard all attempts at rehabilitation of prison inmates, whether behavior modification or any other rehabilitative method is involved.

Suggested Procedures.   The appropriate way to conduct treatment programs in prisons, and, in fact, whether such programs should even be offered, are matters by no means settled. Because of the custodial and potentially coercive nature of the prison setting and the pervasive problem of power imbalance, special procedures are needed to protect the rights and dignity of inmates when they engage in any program, not only behavior modification. Some procedures are suggested here, in an attempt to add to the dialogue about ways to give prisoners the option of participating in programs and yet not coerce them into doing so.

A review committee should be constituted to pass on both the methods and goals of proposed treatment programs, and to monitor the programs when they are put into effect. The committee should be kept continually informed of the results of the programs, including short- and long-term evaluations, and of any changes in goals or procedures. A meaningful proportion of the members of this committee should be prisoner representatives, and the committee should also include persons with appropriate legal backgrounds. The person conducting the behavior modification program should be accountable to this committee, and ultimately, to all the individuals participating in the program.

As is always the case with such review panels, conflicting philosophies and differing loyalties may make it difficult for the panel members to agree unanimously on decisions. Such a panel does, however, provide a regularized opportunity for conflicting points of view to be expressed, an opportunity generally not otherwise available. Thus, the group's discussions can, at a minimum, sensitize program administrators and prison officials to the critical issues.

When this committee, including both prisoners and staff members, has chosen the goals and methods of the program, each potential participant should have a realistic right to decline participation. If a prisoner does refuse to cooperate, he should neither lose privileges he already has, nor receive additional punishment, for so declining. The presentation of the program given to him should include a description of the benefits of participation, both in the institution and after the prisoner has left there. Ideally, the prisoner should be offered a choice among several different kinds of programs, rather than the single alternative of a behavior modification program or nothing.

Implications for Behavior Modification of Emerging Legal Rulings

In the last few years, the courts have begun to make rulings on the rights of institutionalized persons, including the mentally ill. The emerging law may have a major impact on behavior modification programs, in particular, because the recent rulings extend rights that are considered basic and that must presumably be available to all persons. While even the major decisions apply legally only in the jurisdiction where they are announced (unless they are ratified by the U.S. Supreme Court), often other areas will adopt rules or pass legislation that is consistent with the decisions, so that they often have impact far beyond a circumscribed geographic area.

The recent decisions are an important step forward in defining the rights of patients more clearly. In particular, the identification of specific items and activities to which the patients are entitled under all circumstances seems to be a major advance. Even though these legal rulings have the effect of requiring the behavioral worker to be far more ingenious in selecting reinforcers for use in institutions (as explained below), this professional inconvenience is far outweighed by the gain in human rights for the patients. No therapeutic program should have to depend for its existence on the continuation of a dehumanizing environment.

Judicial rulings are not necessary to emphasize that aversive techniques are neither legally nor ethically acceptable when they are used solely for oppressive purposes or without the consent of the person on whom they are used, or his guardian. The recent legal reinterpretations relating to human welfare have been concerned mainly with limiting possible abuses of positive reinforcement.

For example, one of the most common ways for mental hospital patients to earn money or tokens for token programs is by working in on- and off-ward jobs. Such employment is justified by mental health professionals on the grounds that it has an educational purpose: It teaches the patients skills needed in the outside world. The decision in *Wyatt v. Stickney*[4] seems to have restricted the use of hospital work as a means of earning money or tokens. In that decision, the court barred all involuntary work by mentally handicapped patients on hospital operations and maintenance, and specifically said that privileges should not be contingent on the patients' work on such jobs. A similar ruling was made in *Jobson v. Henne*.[5]

Usually when patients work on hospital jobs, they are compensated at a level far below the prevailing wage, or even below the minimum legal wage. This practice of employing institutionalized persons without normal compensation to perform productive labor associated with the maintenance of the institution has been called "institutional peonage" (Bartlett 1964). The *Wyatt* decision specified jobs that may be done by mentally handicapped patients and held that the patients must be compensated for that work at the prevailing minimum wage. Another recent case, *Souder v. Brennan*,[6] extended the principle of minimum wage compensation to all institutionalized persons in non-Federal facilities for the mentally ill and mentally retarded. While the minimum wage requirement may seem reasonable on the face of it, it may be a problem for many mental institutions and institutions for the retarded that cannot afford even the minimum wage. Under

Wyatt, apparently the only types of work exempt from minimum wage coverage are therapeutic work unrelated to hospital functioning, and tasks of a personal housekeeping nature (Wexler 1973).

Among the reinforcers used in some token economies are such basic aspects of life as food, mattresses, grounds privileges, and privacy. That is, in these programs, the patients have been able to have these items or engage in these activities only if they were able to purchase the item or activity with their tokens. According to recent legal developments, such as the *Wyatt v. Stickney* case, patients have a constitutional right to a residence unit with screens or curtains to insure privacy, a comfortable bed, a closet or locker for personal belongings, a chair, a bedside table, nutritionally adequate meals, visitors, attendance at religious services, their own clothes or a selection of suitable clothing, regular physical exercise including access to the outdoors, interaction with members of the opposite sex, and a television set in the day room. In other cases (*Inmates of Boys' Training School v. Affleck*[7] and *Morales v. Turman*[8]), similar kinds of activities and amenities were ordered to be available to juveniles in residential facilities. Thus, these legal rulings appear to have defined as basic rights many of the items and activities that have till now been employed as reinforcers in token economies.

The *Wyatt* decision was upheld on appeal by the U.S. Court of Appeals for the Fifth Circuit.[9] Even before that action, the ruling was already influential. However, because of inconsistencies among rulings, it is not clear at the moment just how much these rulings entitle the members of various institutionalized populations to have, and what sorts of items and activities can be restricted to those persons with sufficient tokens to purchase them (Wexler 1973).

Further, the new rulings do not totally prevent the inclusion in a token economy of the various items and activities named in the rulings. Rather, the result of the rulings is to permit the restriction in availability of these items and activities only with the consent of the patients or representatives of the patients. That is, these constitutional rights, like other constitutional rights, can be waived in suitable circumstances by the individuals involved. For example, a patient may consent to having his access to television restricted so that television programs might be available to him only following changes in his behavior that he desires to make.

Mental health workers who want to use the token economy procedure are now beginning to search for new types of reinforcers or new methods of reinforcement delivery that will not require special waivers of the constitutional rights of the patients. Suitable reinforcers would be those beyond which any patient would ordinarily be entitled, or to which he would normally have access. Many professionals believe that such new types of reinforcers will be developed, that behavior change can be produced without depriving patients of the basic necessities or asking them to waive their constitutional rights, and that this entire legal development is a significant step forward. The rulings, however, are recent ones, and extensive changes in practice have yet to occur.

Recent legal rulings have implications for behavior modification procedures other than the token economy. For example, *Wyatt* specified in detail the conditions under which electric shock devices could be used with mentally retarded residents. That ruling, and *New York State Association for Retarded Children v. Rockefeller*[10] also, set limits on the use of seclusion with mentally retarded and mentally ill patients.

Other legal rulings (e.g., *Rouse v. Cameron*[11] and *Donaldson v. O'Connor*[12] have held that patients have a right to treatment. Possible implications of this might be an extension of patients' rights with concomitant restrictions on the use of some behavior modification techniques. At the same time, a right to effective treatment might result in a requirement that all therapies include the sort of continual monitoring of effectiveness that is generally standard practice in behavior modification. Judicial rulings in this area have been inconsistent, however, some supporting a right to treatment (e.g., *Rouse v. Cameron* and *Wyatt v. Stickney*), and some holding that there is no legal obligation to provide treatment (e.g., *Burnham v. Department of Public Health of the State of Georgia*[13] and *New York State Association for Retarded Children v. Rockefeller*). In the 1974 appellate court decision upholding *Wyatt*, the court also overruled the lower court decision in the *Burnham* case. Thus, the Fifth Circuit Court has ruled that, for that jurisdiction, mental patients as a class have a Federal constitutional right to adequate treatment when they are committed against their will to State institutions. Inconsistencies remain, however, especially in decisions regarding voluntary hospitalization (Budd and Baer, in press). It is still too early, also, to draw clear implications for behavior modification from the appellate court decisions on right to adequate treatment.

Ethics in Behavior Modification

Recently, many persons have expressed increasing concern that those who conduct behavior modification programs should take special care that their methods are ethical and that the individuals undergoing behavior change are protected. While, on the whole, researchers and therapists using behavior modification methods have exercised normal caution, some aspects of the problem have not always received the attention that they deserve.

One difficulty in establishing ethical standards for behavior modification is that the issues and problems are different for different populations in different settings. Informed consent, for example, is clearly meaningful when a normal adult voluntarily goes to an outpatient clinic to obtain guidance in altering a specific behavior that he wants to change. However, when prisoners are offered the opportunity of participating in behavior modification, it is by no means clear that they can give truly voluntary consent.

A further difficulty in this area is that the appropriate person to determine the means and goals of treatment is different for different populations in different settings. The mental health professional must decide in each instance who his client is, that is, who the person or group is with whom he should negotiate regarding the choice of means and goals for a behavior modification program. It is often both obvious and correct that the ostensible client is the actual one. For example, a neurotic patient comes to a clinic to be relieved of his fear of flying in planes: The patient, determining for himself the goal of therapy, is the true client. Or, when a husband and wife are referred to a mental health worker to learn contingency contracting as a method of improving their marriage, it is generally clear that both partners have chosen the goal of improvement of their interpersonal relations. The mental health worker's responsibility is to assist them in achieving this goal.

On the other hand, when a behavioral consultant is asked to help a teacher keep her pupils in their seats, working quietly at all times, the ethical situation is less clear. Are these the optimum classroom conditions for learning, and are the children's best interests served by teaching them to be still, quiet, and docile (Winett and Winkler 1972; O'Leary 1972)? The mental health professional may want to suggest alternative goals, or work together with the class and the teacher in developing appropriate goals.

Similarly, when an administrator of an institution for the retarded asks a behavioral professional to establish a token economy so that the inmates will be motivated to work on jobs for the hospital, the professional may want to work together with an advisory committee to determine the relative value of that work activity for the hospital and for the retardates. While he is being asked to have the hospital as his client, he needs also to consider the rights of the patients, the potential benefits to them of the activity, and any risks that may be involved. The professional may decide, for example, that such hospital jobs have minimal benefit for the patients, and thus may feel that the institution's goal is an inappropriate one. Identifying the true client is also a critical problem when behavior modification programs are used in prisons.

Suggested Procedures. Ethical safeguards for behavior modification programs need to take a number of factors into account: client involvement, a balance of risk and benefit, appropriate review by outside persons, the efficacy of the proposed procedures, and the plans for accountability of the program.

In discussing these complex issues, we are aware that the procedures we suggest have relevance for all types of mental health programs, not just for behavior modification. In this paper, we do not attempt to address these complex issues in that broader context. However, we recognize that the full range of concerns mentioned here applies in all mental health settings.

Ethical responsibility demands that members of the client population or their representatives be seriously consulted about both the means and the goals of programs, before the programs are introduced to change behavior. The persons planning the program need to evaluate the extent to which the members of the target population can give truly informed consent to the program. This involves (1) preparation of a description of the program and its goals so that the persons will know what is to be involved, (2) an assessment of the extent to which they are competent to understand the proposal and make an appropriate judgment about it, and (3) an evaluation of the degree to which their consent can be truly voluntary.

The client himself, or the advisory committee, together with the mental health worker, should weigh the potential benefits to the client of the change that is expected to result from the proposed behavior modification program, against an evaluation of possible risks from using the procedure. This balance can be a difficult one to reach, because the various persons involved may well each see the situation from his own point of view. Thus, the mental health worker might find a proposed technique acceptable because it produces rapid improvement in seriously maladaptive behavior, while client representatives might object to the same technique because it violates the client's rights or restricts his freedom, however briefly, and regardless of ensuing benefits. The client may disagree entirely with the goal of the program that has been chosen by the institution in which he is confined, on the grounds that he is not interested in the supposed benefits offered.

The definitions of risk and benefit will be different in different settings and will also change over time, as customs, knowledge, and values change. Thus, while all the members of an advisory committee may share the goal of helping the client, reaching consensus on how to achieve that goal may involve considerable compromise by persons representing differing points of view.

In many cases, the individual whose behavior is to be changed will be able to negotiate the proposed means and goals directly with the professional personnel. In that way, mental health worker and client can arrive at a mutual agreement or contract that would specify the rights and responsibilities of each of them. However, when the program concerns individuals who have been shown to be incapable of making their own decisions, it will be necessary for the mental health worker to deal with a representative or surrogate for the specific persons who would participate in the proposed program.

The less directly the persons are involved in the initial determination of means and goals, the more protections of those persons should be built into the system. Thus, when the mental health worker is not directly accountable to his client, an advisory committee should be established that would cooperate with the mental health professional in choosing the methods and goals of the behavior modification program. This committee should include either representatives of the persons whose behavior is to be modified, their guardians, or advocates.

The establishment of a suitably constituted review committee does not automatically guarantee that approved programs will include appropriate protections. The official guardians of the persons in the program may, for example, have a vested interest in controlling those persons in a way more convenient for the guardians than beneficial for the persons in the program. The mental health professional, too, cannot be viewed as an entirely disinterested party, especially when he is employed by the institution charged with the care of the persons in the program. In general, members of review committees need to be aware of the conflicting interests involved, and sensitive to the factors influencing their own and each other's behavior, so that subtle coercions are not used to manipulate the decision.

Effectiveness and accountability are other key elements of ethical responsibility in behavior modification. The results of the behavior modification program must be carefully monitored to ensure that the goals agreed on by the advisory committee, or by client and therapist, are being achieved. If they are not, sound practice requires a reevaluation and revision of the methods being used. In addition, the persons conducting behavior modification programs must be accountable to those whose behavior is being changed, or to their representatives. Information on the effectiveness of the program should be made available to the consumers on a regular basis.

Behavior modification programs have an additional special ethical problem because the procedures are generally simple enough to be used by persons lacking the training to evaluate them appropriately. Thus, a further safeguard that should be built into behavior modification programs is a limitation on the decision-making responsibilities of program staff to those matters in which they have expertise. Persons with appropriate professional qualifications, such as a suitable level of training and supervised clinical practice, are able to design and organize treatment programs, develop measurement systems, and evaluate the outcome of behavior modification programs. Such persons should be familiar with the ethical guidelines of their particular profession. Technicians, paraprofessionals, and other workers with only minimal training in behavior modification generally can function in the setting in which behavior is being modified, but should not initiate decisions affecting the welfare of other individuals, unless those decisions are reviewed by the professional staff (Sulzer-Azaroff, Thaw, and Thomas 1975). Given such a delegation of responsibility, review of behavior modification programs should be concerned both with the individuals who make the critical treatment decisions and with the adequacy of supervision of nonprofessional staff.

Ethical Safeguards: The Professions.   The need to adhere to sound ethical practices is accepted by all trained mental health practitioners. Practitioners using behavior modification methods are expected to adhere to existing codes of ethics formulated by their professions. In addition, the Association for Advancement of Behavior Therapy (AABT) is currently formulating a set of standards for practice. The Behavior Therapy and Research Society publishes a list of behavior therapists whose qualifications have undergone peer evaluation.

The AABT also has a system of consultative committees that are coordinated by the president of the Association. Persons who are associated with institutions or programs and who are concerned about present or proposed behavior therapy procedures can ask the AABT president to appoint a committee of persons to go to the site, investigate, and make an advisory report. These reports are compiled into a casebook of standards of practice.

Ethical Safeguards: DHEW Policy and Protections.   Much of the biological, medical, and behavioral research conducted in this country is supported by funds from the Department of Health, Education, and Welfare (DHEW). According to the current DHEW policy, which was established by the May 30, 1974, regulations (Chapter 45, Code of Federal Regulations, Subtitle A, Part 46), in activities involving human subjects, the rights and welfare of the subjects should be adequately protected; the risks to an individual from participation should be outweighed by the potential benefits to him and by the importance of the knowledge to be gained; and informed consent should be obtained by methods that are adequate and appropriate.

According to DHEW policy, risks are defined to include not only potential physical harm, but also adverse psychological reactions or social injury. The policy gives as the basic elements of informed consent: a fair explanation of the procedures to be followed and their purposes, including an identification of those that are experimental; a description of any expected discomforts and risks; a description of the benefits to be expected; a disclosure of appropriate alternative procedures that would be advantageous for the subject; an offer to answer any inquiries concerning the procedures; and an instruction that the subject is free to withdraw his consent and to discontinue participation in the project or activity at any time without prejudice to himself.

As applied to research on behavior modification, this policy means that the person receiving the service or his representative should be told that the person will be receiving behavior modification treatment, and what the treatment program will involve. He should be told what problems might arise, if any, and what the goal of the treatment is. It should be made clear to him that he should feel free to drop out of the study at any time. Not mentioned in the official regulations, but part of recommended practice in this area, is that the client or his representative should cooperate with the mental health worker in specifying the goals of the behavior modification treatment.

The DHEW regulations place primary responsibility for safeguarding the rights and welfare of subjects on the organization conducting the activities. The responsibility, however, is shared by the organization's review committee and the DHEW staff and advisory committees, each of whom determines independently the adequacy of proposed procedures for the protection of human subjects. According to the regulations, any institution conducting DHEW-funded research, development, or related activities involving human subjects must establish a committee with responsibility for reviewing any application for support of such activities, to insure that the protocol adequately fulfills the policy for the protection of the subjects.

The National Institutes of Health established a study group that is charged with reviewing various aspects of the DHEW policy on human subjects. The group drafted proposed rules dealing with protection of subjects in prisons and mental institutions, and with protection of subjects in research involving pregnant women, abortion, fetuses, and products of *in vitro* fertilization. Public comment on these proposals has been received.

Many hospitals and research institutions have used the DHEW regulations as a model for structuring their own policy for the protection of human subjects. Others have gone beyond the regulations to require, for example, the presence of the subject's personal physician, personal lawyer, and immediate kin, with specific periods of time being allocated for discussion before consent is given. This is an area that is receiving increasing attention.

The National Research Act (PL 93–348) provided for a National Commission for the Protection of Human Subjects of Biomedical and Behavioral Research, which will be in existence for 2 years, beginning in 1974. This Commission is charged with investigating a number of issues, including the problems of obtaining informed consent from children, prisoners, and the institutionalized mentally infirm when they are asked to participate in experiments. The Commission has also been asked to determine the need for a mechanism that will extend the DHEW regulations beyond DHEW-funded research activities to all activities with human subjects, including research and health services.

Summary and Conclusions

Behavior modification currently is the center of stormy controversy and debate. We have attempted to put these problems in perspective, through a discussion of what behavior modification is and what it is not, and a review of the major issues.

Many years of laboratory research provide the basis and rationale for the development of behavior modification techniques and behavioral treatments. The behavior modification methods currently being used include procedures suitable for use in the clinic, such as desensitization, and in the mental institution, such as the token economy. The procedures can be used with normal adults and children and with the mentally disadvantaged, including the retarded, the senile, and the psychotic. Behavior modification methods have been used to ameliorate a wide range of problems, including mutism, self-destructive behavior, inappropriate fears, and nervous habits. Also, behavior modification methods have been used to teach a great variety of appropriate, normal behaviors, including normal speech, appropriate social behavior, and suitable classroom skills.

The Federal Government continues to support and encourage research and demonstrations that test new behavior modification techniques, that seek to refine existing ones and apply them to new clinical populations and new settings, and that promote the dissemination of techniques that have been positively evaluated. A particularly strong need is for additional research comparing the efficacy of behavior modification methods with that of alternative treatment approaches. Research is also needed on ways to deliver behavior modification techniques to larger numbers of persons in less restrictive settings than the institutions where much of the research, until now, has been done.

Concern has been expressed that behavior modification methods may be used by those in power to control and manipulate others. Some critics have charged that the use of behavior modification methods is inconsistent with humanistic values. However, all kinds of therapies involve attempts to change the patient in some way. Behavior modification, like other therapeutic methods, requires a cooperative individual in order for it to be effective. Countercontrol, especially countercontrol based on knowledge of behavioral principles, is a major way that individuals can respond to any attempted manipulation.

The concerns that have been expressed about behavior modification have stimulated a reexamination of the assumptions and ethics of all psychosocial therapies. Ethical problems are particularly serious when therapies are used within institutions such as mental hospitals and prisons, or with the institutionalized mentally retarded and senile. In these settings, mental health workers have to be sensitive to the implications of the imbalance in power between them and their clients.

Aversive procedures, easy to abuse, have also raised serious concerns. These methods can, however, be used to benefit patients greatly, as when aversive techniques are used to eliminate life-threatening self-destructive behavior. Appropriate safeguards need to be provided, whenever aversive control techniques are proposed. Greater involvement of clients or their representatives in decisions about the means and goals of treatment programs will help protect persons participating in the programs.

Perhaps the most controversy has arisen in connection with the use of behavior modification in prisons. Behavior modification programs have, in some places, been designed to preserve authoritarian control and discipline, rather than to teach skills that would benefit the prisoners, once they are released. It is not clear whether prisoners are ever able to be true volunteers in any experimental program held in a prison. Here, too, safeguards must be built into the structure of any behavioral program.

Recent legal rulings have provided significant gains in human rights, especially for involuntarily committed patients. The rulings have called attention to possible abuses of the use of positive reinforcement and have extended the limits of institutionalized persons' basic rights.

In addition to discussing these issues, we have suggested some ways that safeguards might be designed for behavior modification programs. The issues are relevant to all types of mental health programs, and many of our proposed solutions would be applicable more generally as well. They are discussed here, however, only as they apply specifically in behavior modification.

Ethical responsibility demands that members of the client population or their representatives be consulted about both the means and goals of programs, and that these persons have an opportunity to weigh the balance of risk and benefit in any proposed program. Programs should be monitored to ensure that they are effective, and those persons conducting the programs should be accountable to those whose behavior is being changed, as long as the program is continued.

The Department of Health, Education, and Welfare is currently developing new regulations for the protection of human subjects, and the National Commission for the Protection of Human Subjects of Biochemical and Behavioral Research is also investigating related topics.

Public debate will surely continue concerning the issues that surround the use of behavior modification techniques. Professional evaluation of these techniques and public discussion of them can help prevent abuses in the use of behavior modification procedures, as well as foster public understanding and acceptance of beneficial procedures. London (1974) contends that " . . . a decent society regulates all technology that is powerful enough to affect the general welfare, at once restricting the technicians as little as possible and as much as necessary." In that context, both continued monitoring of behavior modification by the public and further research on this important technology are needed to serve society and the individuals who make it up.

Notes

[1] This project is being supported by the National Institute of Mental Health.
[2] This project is being supported by the National Institute on Drug Abuse.
[3] This project is being supported by the National Institute on Alcohol Abuse and Alcoholism.
[4] 325 F. Supp. 781 (M.D. Ala. 1971), 334 F. Supp. 1341 (M.D. Ala. 1971), 344 F. Supp. 373 (M.D. Ala. 1972), and 344 F. Supp. 387 (M.D. Ala. 1972). This case was known as *Wyatt v. Aderholt* on appeal.
[5] 335 F. 2d 129 (2d Cir., 1966).
[6] 367 F. Supp. 808 (D.D.C. 1973).
[7] 346 F. Supp. 1354 (D.R.I. 1972).

312   Section VI: Behavior Modification

[8] 364 F. Supp. 166 (E.D. Tex. 1973).
[9] *Wyatt v. Aderholt*, No. 72–2634(5 Cir., Nov. 8, 1974).
[10] 357 F. Supp. 752 (E.D. N.Y. 1973).
[11] 373 F. 2d 451 (D.C. Cir., 1966).
[12] 493 F. 2d 507(5 Cir., 1974).
[13] 349 F. Supp. 1335 (N.D. Ga. 1972), appeal docketed, No. 72–3110, 5 Cir., Oct. 4, 1972. This case was consolidated for argument on appeal with *Wyatt*.

References

Anderson, R. C. Education psychology. *Annual Review of Psychology*, 18, 129–164, 1967.

Ayllon, T., and Azrin, N. H. The measurement and reinforcement of behavior of psychotics. *Journal of the Experimental Analysis of Behavior, 8*, 357–383, 1965.

Ayllon, T., and Azrin, N. H. *The Token Economy*. New York: Appleton-Century-Crofts, 1968.

Ayllon, T., and Michael, J. The psychiatric nurse as a behavioral engineer. *Journal of the Experimental Analysis of Behavior*, 2, 323–334, 1959.

Baer, D. M. A case for the selective reinforcement of punishment. In Neuringer, C., and Michael, J. L., eds. *Behavior Modification in Clinical Psychology*. New York: Appleton-Century-Crofts, 1970.

Baer, D. M. The control of developmental process: Why wait? In Nesselroade, J. R., and Reese, H. W., eds. *Life-span Developmental Psychology: Methodological Issues*. New York: Academic Press, 1973.

Baer, D. M., and Guess, D. Receptive training of adjectival inflections in mental retardates. *Journal of Applied Behavior Analysis*, 4, 129–139, 1971.

Bandura, A. *Principles of Behavior Modification*. New York: Holt, Rinehart and Winston, 1969.

Bartlett, F. L. Institutional peonage: Our exploitation of mental patients. *Atlantic*, 214(1), 116–119, 1964.

Begelman, D. A. Ethical and legal issues of behavior modification. In: Hersen, M.; Eisler, R.; and Miller, P., eds. *Progress in Behavior Modification*, Vol. 1. New York: Academic Press, 1977.

Birk, L. et al. *Behavior Therapy in Psychiatry*. Washington, D.C.: American Psychiatric Association, 1973.

Blanchard, E. B.; Libet, J. M.; and Young, L. D. Apneic aversion and covert sensitization in the treatment of a hydrocarbon inhalation addiction: A case study. *Journal of Behavior Therapy and Experimental Psychiatry*, 4, 383–87, 1973.

Brady, J. P. Brevital-relaxation treatment of frigidity. *Behaviour Research and Therapy*, 4, 71–77, 1966.

Bucher, B. Some ethical issues in the therapeutic use of punishment. In Rubin, R. D., and Franks, G. M., eds. *Advances in Behavior Therapy, 1968*. New York: Academic Press, 1969.

Bucher, B., and Lovaas, O. I. Use of aversive stimulation in behavior modification. In Jones, M. R., ed. *Miami Symposium on the Prediction of Behavior, 1967*. Coral Gables: University of Miami Press, 1968.

Budd, K., and Baer, D. M. Behavior modification and the law: Implications of recent judicial decisions. *Journal of Applied Behavior Analysis*, in press.

Carrera, F., III, and Adams, P. L. An ethical perspective on operant conditioning. *Journal of the American Academy of Child Psychiatry*, 9, 607–623, 1970.

Cohen, H. L., and Filipczak, J. *A New Learning Environment*. San Francisco: Jossey-Bass, 1971.

Colman, A. D. *Planned Environment in Psychiatric Treatment*. Springfield, IL: Thomas, 1971.

Davison, G. C. Homosexuality: The ethical challenge. Paper presented at the meeting of the Association for Advancement of Behavior Therapy, Chicago, November 1974.

Eysenck, N. J. Discussion on the role of the psychologist in psychoanalytic practice: The psychologist as technician. *Proceedings of the Royal Society of Medicine*, 45, 447–449, 1952.

Ferster, C. B., and DeMyer, M. K. The development of performances in autistic children in an automatically controlled environment. *Journal of Chronic Diseases*, 13, 312–345, 1961.

Foxx, R. M., and Azrin, N. H. Restitution: A method of eliminating aggressive-disruptive behavior of retarded and brain damaged patients. *Behaviour Research and Therapy*, 10, 15–27, 1972.

Gruenberg, E. M. The social breakdown syndrome—some origins. *American Journal of Psychiatry*, 123, 12–20, 1967.

Heldman, A. W. Social psychology versus the first amendment freedoms, due process liberty, and limited government. *Cumberland-Samford Law Review*, 4, 1–40, 1973.

Jones, M. C. The elimination of children's fears. *Journal of Experimental Psychology*, 7, 382–390, 1924.

Lindsley, O. R., and Skinner, B. F. A method for the experimental analysis of behavior of psychotic patients. *American Psychologist*, 9, 419–420, 1954.

London, P. The end of ideology in behavior modification. *American Psychologist*, 27, 913–920, 1972.

London, P. Behavior technology and social control—turning the tables. *APA Monitor*, April 1974, p. 2.

Lovaas, et al. Some generalization and follow-up measures on autistic children in behavior therapy. *Journal of Applied Behavior Analysis*, 6, 131–165, 1973.

Lovibond, S. H. Aversive control of behavior. *Behavior Therapy*, 1, 80–91, 1970.

Minge, M. R., and Ball, T. S. Teaching of self-help skills to profoundly retarded patients. *American Journal of Mental Deficiency*, 71, 864–868, 1967.

Mowrer, O. H., and Mowrer, W. M. Enuresis—a method for its study and treatment. *American Journal of Orthopsychiatry*, 8, 436–459, 1938.

O'Leary, K. D. Behavior modification in the classroom: A rejoinder to Winett and Winkler. *Journal of Applied Behavior Analysis*, 5, 505–511, 1972.

O'Leary, K. D., and Drabman, R. Token reinforcement programs in the classroom: A review. *Psychological Bulletin*, 75, 379–398, 1971.

Phillips, E. L., et al. Achievement Place: Modification of the behaviors of predelinquent boys within a token economy. *Journal of Applied Behavior Analysis*, 4, 45–59, 1971.

Platt, J. Beyond Freedom and Dignity: "A revolutionary manifesto." *The Center Magazine*, 5(2), 34–52, 1972.

Price, K. P. The application of behavior therapy to the treatment of psychosomatic disorders: Retrospect and prospect. *Psychotherapy: Theory, Research and Practice*, 11, 138–155, 1974.

Rachman, S., and Teasdale, J. *Aversion Therapy and Behaviour Disorders*. Coral Gables: University of Miami Press, 1969.

Risley, T. R. The effects and side effects of punishing the autistic behaviors of a deviant child. *Journal of Applied Behavior Analysis*, 1, 21–34, 1968.

Sears, R. R.; Maccoby, E.; and Levin, H. *Patterns of Child-Rearing*. Evanston, IL: Row, Peterson, 1957.

Shapiro, D., and Birk, L. Group therapy in experimental perspective. *International Journal of Group Psychotherapy*, 17, 211–224, 1967.

Shapiro, M. B. The single case in fundamental clinical psychological research. *British Journal of Medical Psychology*, 34, 255–262, 1961.

Shapiro, M. H. Legislating the control of behavior control: Autonomy and the coercive use of organic therapies. *Southern California Law Review*, 47, 237–356, 1974.

Skinner, B. F. *Beyond Freedom and Dignity*. New York: Knopf, 1971.

Sulzer-Azaroff, B.; Thaw, J.; and Thomas, C. Behavioral competencies for the evaluation of behavior modifiers. In Wood, W.S., ed. *Issues in Evaluating Behavior Modification*. Champaign, Ill.: Research Press, 1975.

Thomson, I. G., and Rathod, N. H. Aversion therapy for heroin dependence. *Lancet*, ii, 382–384, 1968.

Ulrich, R. Behavior control and public concern. *Psychological Record*, 17, 229–234, 1967.

Webster, D. R., and Azrin, N. H. Required relaxation: A method of inhibiting agitative-disruptive behavior of retardates. *Behaviour Research and Therapy*, 11, 67–78, 1973.

Wexler, D. B. Token and taboo: Behavior modification, token economies, and the law. *California Law Review*, 61, 81–109, 1973.

Winett, R. A., and Winkler, R. C. Current behavior modification in the classroom: Be still, be quiet, be docile. *Journal of Applied Behavior Analysis*, 5, 499–504, 1972.

Wolpe, J. *Psychotherapy by Reciprocal Inhibition*. Stanford, CA: Stanford University Press, 1958.

Wolpe, J., and Lazarus, A. A. *Behavior Therapy Techniques*. Oxford: Pergamon Press, 1966.

16

Establishing Behavior Contracts with Delinquent Adolescents

Robert Bruce Rutherford, Jr.

The effectiveness of behavior modification (applied behavioral analysis) principles and techniques has been demonstrated repeatedly with children and adults in a variety of learning environments. Some behavioral techniques are more effective than others depending upon the environment where intervention is to take place. The custodial or institutional setting has the potential for controlling the widest range of variables competing with the intervention strategy. Intervention strategies which originate in the home, school, or community, on the other hand, may be limited in their behavioral influence because the individual will have access to many other sources of reinforcement. Older subjects such as delinquents may be more adept at developing alternate strategies for obtaining reinforcers and avoiding manager or mediator-imposed interventions. It appears, especially with the more sophisticated adolescent, that in order to maximize the effectiveness of the behavioral intervention, and to bridge the gap between the institutional setting and real life, the adolescent must be given the power to negotiate various aspects of the tasks and reinforcers included in the intervention strategy. The strategy which lends itself most appropriately to the adolescent's involvement is behavioral contracting.

Behavioral Contracting

Behavioral contracting involves the systematic negotiation between mediator (parent, teacher, probation officer, social worker,

Source: *Federal Probation*, 39(1)(March 1975): 28–32.

unit counselor, or supervisor) and a target (delinquent adolescent) of the behaviors to be performed within a given environment, and the specific reinforcing consequences or "payoffs" to be provided when performance requirements are met.

Behavioral contracting is based upon an applied behavior analysis model whereby the environmental dynamics which maintain behavior are assessed. In behavioral contracting, a behavioral analysis involves specifying: (A) the antecedents which will cue the contract behavior, (B) the contract behavior to be developed, (C) the consequences which will maintain the contract behavior (see figure 1).

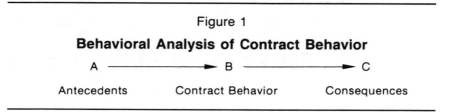

Figure 1
Behavioral Analysis of Contract Behavior

A ⟶ B ⟶ C

Antecedents   Contract Behavior   Consequences

The "antecedents" are events which are present in the environment to cue behaviors. They include those stimuli, cues, directions, or prompts that set the occasion for a given behavior and a specific, predictable consequence. The antecedent cues for doing 20 arithmetic word problems at home may be a math book, a sharp pencil, 3 sheets of paper, directions at the top of the page, and a quiet, well lighted room. These cues may signal that the "consequences" of completing the "contract behavior," e.g., math problems done correctly by 9:00 A.M. the following morning, will be positive. The positive consequences may be a higher letter grade, praise from teacher and parents, and/or a specifically contracted item or event such as a coke or 20 minutes of free time at midday. Behavioral analysis makes the assumption that consequences which are positive will result in an increase in the frequency of the desired behavior.

In summary, behavioral analysis involves planning before the fact and behavioral programming after the fact of a given behavior. Sound behavioral contracts specify systematically each of the three steps of the behavioral analysis model.

Rules for Establishing Behavioral Contracts

The following are steps which appear to be most crucial for the development of sound behavioral contracts:

1. A behavioral analysis must be made of the behavior to be contracted. As mentioned earlier, analysis must be made of the antecedents and consequences of the contracted behavior, as well as of the behavior itself.

2. The behavioral contract must be precise and systematic. Each condition of the contract must be specified. Dates, times, criterion behaviors, amounts and/or range of consequences, names of contractor and contractee, and names of others involved in the contract should all be included. The terms of the contract must be adhered to strictly and systematically at all times.

3. The behavioral contract must be fair to both the contractor and the contractee. A contract implies the power of both parties to negotiate terms. If the terms are unfair, the contract will fail. The contracted behaviors and the consequences must be balanced to the satisfaction of both parties.

4. The terms of the behavioral contract must stress the positive. A behavioral contract which implies positive reinforcement for appropriate behavior rather than punishment for inappropriate behavior will be more readily adhered to by the contractee. Positive reinforcement strengthens the behavior which it follows; punishment only temporarily suppresses behavior.

5. The concept of "shaping" may be used when establishing behavioral contracts. If a behavior initially does not exist or exists at only a minimal level, the contract must reinforce approximations of a final specified behavior. Opportunities for easy initial success must be enhanced. It should be emphasized that behaviors that are already in the contractee's behavioral repertoire *must* be built into the contract.

6. A consultant or arbitrator may be helpful at first in the negotiation of behavioral contracts between the contractor and the contractee. In many contracts, both the contractor and the contractee must change their behaviors; under these circumstances a consultant or arbitrator permits the terms of the contract to be fair to both parties.

7. The behavioral contract should be a formal written document which specifies all privileges and responsibilities of the parties involved. It should be signed by both parties. The behavioral contract is a negotiated agreement between two people which allows the contractor and the contractee to predict the consequences of the contracted behaviors. Signatures enhance the formality and commitment of the contract.

8. Both the consequences which follow the completion of the contracted behavior (*the A clause*), and the consequences which follow the noncompletion of the contracted behavior (*the B clause*), must be specified. By specifying the consequences for completing and not completing the contract, the possibilities for misinterpretation of the contract are reduced. Inclusion of both the A and B clauses reduces the chances of error.

9. Reinforcing consequences must always follow the completion of the contracted behavior and must be delivered immediately. In establishing a behavioral contract, the opportunity should be available to receive some portion of the reinforcing consequence immediately upon completion of the contracted behavior. Contracts are often negotiated which allow for small but continuous payoffs for daily behaviors, while at the same time making a large payoff contingent upon completion of a whole series of daily behaviors.

10. Behavioral contracts should progress from contractor-initiated to contractee-initiated as rapidly as possible. While behavioral contracts are negotiated documents, it is generally true that the terms of the initial contracts are designated and controlled by the contractor (parent, teacher, probation officer, unit supervisor, etc.). Behavioral contracting will have more generalized results when the contractee (adolescent) proposes the privileges and responsibilities to be included in the contract.

Case Studies and Sample Behavioral Contracts in Four Settings

In order to demonstrate the diversity of the environmental settings where behavioral contracts may be negotiated with delinquent adolescents, four cases are presented along with sample behavioral contracts. The contracts described include a family contract (between mother and son); a school contract (between teacher, counselor, and student); a community contract (between probation officer and probationer); and an institutional contract (between unit supervisor and inmate).

Family Contract

John is a 15-year-old boy. His parents have been separated for several years and he lives with his mother and younger brother and sister. John's mother is concerned that John has been suspended from school because of his poor attendance record. His mother has been trying to reason with him because the school counselor has told her that unless he attends for the rest of the semester and turns in all work assignments, John will not be readmitted to that school. His work assignments consist of two take-home assignments per week. Only 4 weeks remain until the end of the semester. As a last resort, John's mother has threatened to withhold enrollment in a driver's education course unless he can stay in school. John has expressed a strong interest in the driver's education course and in getting his driver's permit in August.

Several other problems exist in the home. John has been going out on weekends without permission and staying out past curfew, a situation which worries his mother because he has been picked up twice by the police and brought home. In order to try to gain John's confidence, his mother has started buying him cigarettes by the carton. She has discovered John is selling unused cigarettes to his friends.

When John is not at home, he frequently visits his mother's friend, Rick Blackley, who lives a few houses away. Rick has a garage full of tools and an old car on which John has worked since his suspension from school. However, the work that John was doing on the car was completed several weeks ago.

CONTRACT

Date _____

1A For each day that John attends all classes, he will earn the privilege of ten (10) cigarettes per day or one (1) package of cigarettes every other day.

1B For each day that John does not attend all classes, ten (10) cigarettes per day will not be earned.

2A If John attends 90 percent of the full school days between Monday, May 21, 1973, and Friday, June 14, 1973 (20 days), he will earn one (1) driver's education course. The driver's education course will begin on June 18, 1973.

2B If John does not attend school for 90 percent of all classes between May 21, 1973, and June 15, 1973 (20 days), the privilege of the driver's education course will be withdrawn.

3A For each take-home assignment that John turns in to his teachers between Monday, May 21, 1973, and Friday, June 15, 1973, John will earn one evening out on the weekend, provided his mother knows his whereabouts and the time that he will return home.

3B For each take-home assignment that John does not turn in to his teachers between Monday, May 21, 1973, and Friday, June 15, 1973,

John will stay in one evening during the weekend.

As negotiator and overseer of this contract, Mr. Rick Blackley will see that all sections of this contract are followed and that said consequences will be paid.

As representative of the Central High School, Mr. Tom Anderson, counselor, will act as the monitor of the behaviors in the school (i.e., attending classes and turning in assignments).

Mr. John Wright, Student	Mrs. Judy Wright, Mother

Mr. Rick Blackley,
   Negotiator
	Mr. Tom Anderson,
	   Counselor

School Contract

Ron is a 16-year-old boy of above average intelligence who is quite disruptive in all of his 10th grade classes except math. His grades, in all but the math class, have been D's and F's for the last two 6-week periods. He is currently maintaining an A in math. He enjoys being with his math teacher, Mr. Leigh, as demonstrated by his appearances in Mr. Leigh's classroom before and after school to discuss math problems and backpacking (a hobby both he and Mr. Leigh have in common). When Ron is not actively disrupting his other classes, he is usually doing math problems rather than the assigned task.

Ron was arrested twice in the last 4 months for selling pills after school near the high school. In addition, he was accused of beating a 14-year-old boy for allegedly failing to make good a debt related to his drug sales. The charges were eventually dropped. However, Ron is still on probation for the drug arrests and his probation officer has stated that if he does not pass all of his courses at the end of the school year, Ron will remain on probation.

Ron's disruptive classroom behavior includes being verbally abusive to his teachers and his peers, making loud noises when others are speaking, walking around the classroom and poking constantly at his classmates. Presently he is excluded from English and machine shop classes due to his behavior. His counselor, Mr. Quinlin, and his math teacher, Mr. Leigh, have discussed establishing a contract with Ron to facilitate his getting back into English and machine shop classes and raising all of his grades to passing level.

CONTRACT

1A If Ron returns to both his English and machine shop classes and attends at least 4 days out of 5 days each week, he will be allowed to spend his last period (formerly a study hall) in Mr. Leigh's intermediate math class as a math assistant and tutor.

1B If Ron either fails to return to his English and machine shop classes or fails to attend at least 4 out of 5 days, he will not be allowed to be Mr. Leigh's math assistant and tutor.

2A If Ron's behavior in both his English class and his machine shop class is judged appropriate by the teachers (criteria of appropriateness to be determined before this contract is to be initiated), he will earn one chit per class per day to be turned in to Mr. Quinlin, the school counselor. Thus a maximum of 10 chits per week can be earned for attendance.

Ron will earn one chit per letter grade on the math, the social studies, the English and the machine shop tests each Friday. An F = 0 chits, a D = 1 chit, a C = 2 chits, a B = 3 chits, and an A = 4 chits. These chits will also be turned in to Mr. Quinlin. Thus a maximum of 16 chits per week can be earned for grades.

For each week that Ron earns at least 18 chits, Mr. Quinlin will issue Ron a pass to spend one half hour a day for three days of the following week with Mr. Leigh, after school. These three 1/2-hour periods will be spent discussing any topic Ron wishes.

2B If Ron does not earn a total of 18 chits per week, he cannot spend the 1/2-hour periods after school with Mr. Leigh.

All terms of this contract have been negotiated freely between me, *Ron Chan*, and Mr. Leigh, my math teacher, and Mr. Quinlin, my counselor. I also understand that Mr. Mock, my machine shop teacher, and Mrs. McGlothlin, my English teacher, will assist in this contract.

_____ Ron Chan	_____ Mrs. McGlothlin
_____ Mr. Leigh	_____ Mr. Mock
_____ Mr. Quinlin	_____ Date

Community Contract

Pamela is 14 years old. She has a record of being a runaway for periods of up to 1 year. When she leaves it is usually to be with older men. When she was 9 years old she had her first sexual experience with a 19 year old. She now has a 4-month-old baby, fathered by her 21-year-old ex-boyfriend. She has also been treated a number of times for venereal disease.

Pamela's mother is mainly concerned with two of Pamela's problems. The first of these problems is her constant running away from home. Pamela says that the argument that usually precedes her running away deals with the mother's placing too much responsibility for household chores on Pamela. She has three sisters in the home, but she is expected to do the major portion of the work. The second problem area that the mother identifies deals with the $96.00 which Pamela receives every 2 weeks from the County for her baby. Pamela thinks that she should have control of it. Currently the County is making the check payable to the mother.

Pamela enjoys parties with her friends, watching television, and listening to music. She has shown a great deal of interest in going to Disneyland and going out to a nice dinner. She also greatly enjoys the peer group activities that are periodically provided by the County Probation Department, i.e., trips to the mountains, beaches, sports events, museums, and movies.

CONTRACT

Date: _____

1A Pamela receives $96.00 every 2 weeks. Of that $96.00 she will pay her mother, every 2 weeks:

Food $30.00
Board   20.83
Utilities   3.00

Total $53.83   Every 2 weeks

2A For following the chore chart each week (which divides the household chores evenly between Pamela and her sisters), Pamela will be able to attend any and all group activities provided by the Probation Department that week.

2B For not following the chore chart each week, Pamela will not be able to attend group activities provided by the Probation Department that week.

3A For each Friday or Saturday night that Pamela goes out and is home by 1:00 A.M. her mother will provide free baby sitting for the baby that evening.

3B For each Friday or Saturday night that Pamela goes out and is not home by 1:00 A.M., she will pay her mother fifty cents (50¢) per hour for the time that she is gone past 1:00 A.M.

4A Pamela will receive free baby sitting from 9:00 A.M. to 1:00 P.M. from her mother on weekdays when Pamela is attending summer school.

4B Pamela will pay fifty cents (50) per hour to her mother for baby sitting if she does not attend summer school.

As negotiator and overseer of this contract, Mr. Glen Hamilton, County Probation Officer, will see that all sections of this contract are followed and that said consequences will be paid. Mr. Hamilton will see that both Pamela and her mother are treated fairly by the contract.

Ms. Pamela Brooke, Student

Ms. Sue Brooke, Mother   Mr. Glen Hamilton,
            Probation Officer

Institution Contract

Unit III of the County Detention Facility contains 20 girls whose ages range from 13 to 17 years. The average length of confinement is 13 months. The major reasons for confinement include drug use, incorrigibility, theft, assault, and prostitution.

Problem behaviors on the Unit include fighting, refusal to obey staff orders, attempts to run away, refusal to go to school, refusal to work on Unit projects such as group behavioral counseling sessions and Unit cleaning and decorating activities, destroying property in the dayroom and in the dormitory, and stealing from the staff and the other girls.

Possible positive reinforcers available include shortened sentences, having one's own room, weekend passes home, staying up late, special materials to decorate rooms, radios and televisions in one's room, and items from the token economy store.

A token economy system has been established in order to reinforce the girls systematically for performance of appropriate behavior. All of the girls earn tokens for specific behaviors: 5 points for being at breakfast at 7:30 A.M., 3 points for each 20 minutes on-task in the school classroom, 5 points for brushing teeth and hair in the evening, etc. Each girl can also negotiate individual contracts to deal with behaviors unique to herself.

Barbara is a 13-year-old who was placed in the County Detention Facility for being an accomplice to an armed robbery committed by her 19-year-old boyfriend. Barbara, who has lived in nine foster homes since she was 18 months old, was at the County Detention Facility 5 weeks when the first contract was negotiated with her. She participated in the basic token economy of Unit III, but she refused to take part in either the school program or the daily group counseling sessions on the Unit. When she was forced by the staff to attend these activities, she did not speak or in any way acknowledge the other participants.

Barbara has expressed a great deal of interest in visiting her current foster parents. She has been with them over a year and they seem to be as attached to Barbara as she is to them. Also, Barbara has beautiful long black hair which she spends a great deal of time brushing and combing. Barbara's hair is very important to her as she has received many compliments on it both before she entered the Detention Facility and in the Facility itself.

BEHAVIORAL CONTRACT

Date: _____

1A I, _____, agree to attend the school from 9:00 A.M. to 12:00 noon for at least 4 out of the 5 days of the week contingent upon receiving 25 *bonus* points per day and being allowed to stay up until 9:30 to watch TV or play cards with staff.

1B I, _____ , agree that if I do not attend school from 9:00 A.M. to 12:00 noon for at least 4 out of 5 days of the week, I will not receive 25 *bonus* points per day and I will have to go to bed at 8:30.

2A When I, _____ , am in school, I will complete, 80 percent correctly, 5 of 6 lessons per day contingent upon 5 *bonus* points per lesson and the use of the hairdryer for 30 minutes each evening.

2B When I, _____, am not in school or do not complete, 80 percent correctly, 5 of 6 lessons per day, I will not receive 5 *bonus* points per lesson nor will I be allowed to use the hairdryer that evening.

3A When I, _____, attend each behavioral counseling session, I will receive 5 *bonus* points and the use of all of the hair conditioner, shampoo, curlers, hairnets, bobby pins, and scotchtape I need to do my hair that evening.

3B When I, _____, do not attend a behavioral counseling session, I will not receive 5 *bonus* points and I will not get to use the hairsetting materials.

4A If I, _____, contribute to the behavioral counseling session (as judged by Mr. Denison, the behavioral counselor, and the other girls on a scale of 1 to 15) with an average score of 10 or above, I will receive 10 *bonus* points.

4B If I, _____, receive a score below 10 on my contribution to the behavioral counseling session, I will not receive 10 *bonus* points.

 5. When I, _____, receive 3150 *bonus* points, I can visit my foster

parents at home from 4:00 P.M. Friday until 4:00 P.M. Sunday of the weekend following my earning the 3150 *bonus* points.

_____   _____
Ms. Barbara Russell   Teacher

_____   _____
Unit Supervisor   Behavioral Counselor

Conclusion

Applied behavioral analysis, in the form of written behavioral contracts, can be an effective intervention strategy with delinquent adolescents. The contract provides the adolescent with: (1) maximum negotiation power, (2) directly observable contractor responsibilities, and (3) a system for predicting the behavior of the contractor. The contract provides the contractor or mediator with: (1) the power to negotiate change in the adolescent's behavior, (2) observable contractee behaviors and contingencies, and (3) a system for predicting contractee behavior.

Section *VII*

Group Counseling in Corrections

Group counseling, which involves group activity under the direction of a therapist or group leader, differs from individual, one-to-one interaction between counselor and client in a number of ways. Hatcher defines it in the following manner.

> Group counseling is a planned activity in which three or more people are present for the purpose of solving personal and social problems by applying the theories and methods of counseling in a group. It can be either structured or relatively unstructured in regard to purpose or leadership. It can be an intensive emotional experience or a superficial "bull session." Its primary focus, ideally, is upon the presentation of personal and interpersonal reality in such a way that one has an opportunity to learn about self and others.[1]

Group counseling and group treatment techniques evolved during World War II and in the postwar years. A type of group therapy termed "guided group interaction" was developed by McCorkle and Wolf as a method of treating offenders who were members of the armed forces. Following World War II, the technique was modified and adopted by civilian institutions. The most notable experiment using the guided group interaction technique was undertaken by McCorkle and Bixby in the early 1950s as part of a delinquency treatment program known as the Highfields Experiment. In this project, as in earlier group work of this type, the group members were called upon to help each other set and work toward specific goals; to lend strong peer support to efforts at positive change; and to exert sanctioning power over negative behavior. The key element of guided group interaction is the problem-solving activity that takes place in the group meetings.[2]

Group counseling was introduced into the correctional system in the 1940s and 1950s for reasons of increased efficiency in handling prisoners rather than because treatment personnel had strong convictions that it would be more effective than individual counseling. Initially, group counseling had a strong educational or training emphasis and only dealt incidentally with efforts to assist offenders in solving their emotional problems. Two new types of group therapy emerged in the 1950s. Although not specifically developed for correctional treatment, they proved to be readily adaptable to correctional settings. Moreno originated "psychodrama," a type of group counseling in which the subject acts out his or her problems while other group members serve as the various "characters" for the "drama."[3] Psychodrama episodes might include simulations of dialogues with spouses, parents, or acquaintances, with other group members acting the parts of these significant others in the subject's life. Role playing, a similar technique used by Slavson, calls upon various group members to assume certain roles and simulate situations, under the guidance of a therapist or counselor.[4]

The 1960s provided two additional forms of treatment that can be applied in a group setting, reality therapy and transactional analysis. Reality therapy involves having the correctional client gain an idea of what his or her immediate needs and behavior requirements are and accept responsibility for them. A group may be the ideal setting for a client to learn just how his or her behavior is perceived by others, realize that others care what happens to him or her, and develop a plan for better behavior in the future. Transactional analysis was originated by Berne and modified by Harris. Berne believes that behavior is directed by one of three "ego states": the "Adult" ego state, characterized by rational, mature, responsible behavior; the "Parent" ego state, which is judgmental of the behavior of others; or the "Child" ego state, which involves emotional, self-centered responses.[5] In transactional analysis, the dialogues taking place in the group situation are constantly analyzed and categorized by the group and group leader as representative of one of these ego states. The goal of TA is to help group members learn to interact at the "Adult" ego level.

The 1970s witnessed another development in group counseling. Harry H. Vorrath, who was involved in the earlier Highfields Experiment in guided group interaction, modified and redeveloped this technique into what he called "positive peer culture." This approach, used with juveniles, involves interaction of small groups of youths (approximately nine) under the guidance of a group leader. The influence of peers is brought to bear in identifying problems, deciding how to solve them, developing interest in and concern for all members of the group, and feeling a stake in the success of others. Those involved in positive peer culture groups define their difficulties and seek to solve them with the aid of a list of general and specific problems, which are defined when they exist and when they are solved. The list is given below.

Positive Peer Culture Problem-Solving List

1. *Low self-image:* Has a poor opinion of self; often feels put down or of little worth.
   When solved: Is self-confident and cannot easily be made to feel small or inferior. Is able to solve his problems and make positive contributions to others. Doesn't feel sorry for himself even though he may have shortcomings. Believes he is good enough to be accepted by anybody.

2. *Inconsiderate of others:* Does things that are damaging to others.
   When solved: Shows concern for others even if he does not like them or know them well. Tries to help people with problems rather than hurt them or put them down.

3. *Inconsiderate of self:* Does things that are damaging to self.
   When solved: Shows concern for self, tries to correct mistakes and improve self. Understands limitations and is willing to discuss problems. Doesn't hurt or put down self.

4. *Authority problem:* Does not want to be managed by anyone.
   When solved: Shows ability to get along with those in authority. Is able to accept advice and direction from others. Does not try to take advantage of authority figures even if they can be manipulated.

5. *Misleads others:* Draws others into negative behavior.
   When solved: Shows responsibility for the effect of his behavior on others who follow him. Does not lead others into negative behavior. Shows concern and helps rather than taking advantage of others.

6. *Easily misled:* Is drawn into negative behavior by others.
   When solved: Seeks out friends who care enough about him not to hurt him. Doesn't blindly follow others to buy friendship. Is strong enough to stand up for himself and makes own decisions. Doesn't let anyone misuse him.

7. *Aggravates others:* Treats people in negative, hostile ways.
   When solved: Gets along well with others. Does not need to get attention by irritating or annoying others. Gets no enjoyment from hurting or harassing people. Respects others enough not to embarrass, provoke, or bully them.

8. *Easily angered:* Is often irritated or provoked or has tantrums.
   When solved: Is not easily frustrated. Knows how to control and channel anger, not letting it control him. Understands the put-down process and has no need to respond to challenges. Can tolerate criticism or even negative behavior from others.

9. *Stealing:* Takes things that belong to others.
   When solved: Sees stealing as hurting another person. Has no need to be sneaky or to prove himself by stealing. Knows appropriate ways of getting things he wants. Would not stoop to stealing even if he could get away with it.

10. *Alcohol or drug problem:* Misuses substances that could hurt self.
    When solved: Feels good about self and wouldn't hurt self. Does not need to be high to have friends or enjoy life. Can face problems without a crutch. Shows concern for others who are hurting themselves by abusing alcohol or drugs.

11. *Lying:* Cannot be trusted to tell the truth.
    When solved: Is concerned that others trust him. Has strength to face mistakes and failures without trying to cover up. Does not need to lie or twist the truth to impress others. Tells it like it is.

12. *Fronting:* Puts on an act rather than being real.
    When solved: Is comfortable with people and does not have to keep trying to prove himself. Has no need to act superior, con people, or play the show-off role. Is not afraid of showing his true feelings to others.[6]

In addition to the obvious cost-efficiency factor of treating more than one offender at the same time, group counseling has been rated as having a number of other advantages in the correctional setting. Chief among these is the fact that it can be used to counter the influence of the inmate subculture, which makes strong demands for the prisoner's loyalty and attention. The types of openness and amenability to change that can be developed in group treatment can work to counter the strong pull of the inmate code. In addition, the brain-storming or problem-solving experience of the group as a whole may provide solutions that offenders may not have thought of or may be reluctant to accept from staff members but will try because peers who have "been there" suggest them. Another advantage of group counseling is that many members of the staff may become involved and have a stake in the treatment outcome. Although trained therapists are needed for certain types of group work, other groups can be ably directed by regular staff, student interns, or even offenders who have received training in the treatment techniques.

There are certain disadvantages to group counseling as well. These include the fact that, unless guided skillfully, sessions may become little more than occasions to air grievances. Offenders, who have the one constant goal of "getting out," may see the group setting as an appropriate spot for "conning" staff members and may display little sincerity. Deep-seated fears of revealing information that may delay release or result in physical reprisals or ostracism by other inmates can prevent candor in a group setting. Finally, personality characteristics of some offenders make it very difficult for them to feel comfortable or to participate in group sessions.

The choice of the specific treatment technique to be used in a group setting is dependent upon the leader's training, preference, assessment of the group's needs, and the goals set for the group activity. Treatment possibilities for groups designed to be primarily instructive or to attack a specific problem (alcohol or drug addiction, for example) are necessarily more limited than for groups structured for the more general purpose of improving offenders' adjustment within the correctional setting. Problem-solving group work, such as reality therapy, guided group interaction, or positive peer culture, may involve role playing or psychodrama; while group counseling geared to improving the offender's general adjustment to life would be more likely to use such techniques as transactional analysis.

In selection seventeen, "The Process of Group Counseling," Trotzer notes that an effective group process must involve five stages, if the knowledge gained in the group is to be transferred to activity outside it. These stages are: (1) the security stage, in which the group member is made to feel comfortable and not threatened in the group setting; (2) the acceptance stage, in which the group member comes to know that he or she is an important part of the group, that others care about him or her, and that he or she has certain problems; (3) the responsibility stage, in which the group member takes responsibility for his or her own actions and for finding solutions to problems; (4) the work stage, during which things found to be unsatisfactory in one's life must be changed; and (5) the closing stage, when the group member accepts the support and encouragement of the group as he or she gradually detaches from it.[7] Romig's findings about the ineffectiveness of the majority of group counseling programs seems to indicate that many of the groups failed to get beyond the "acceptance stage" and did not plan specific procedures for the "work stage," when the problems defined by the group should be attacked.

In article eighteen, "The Use of Groups," by Richard A. Stordeur and Richard Stille, the provision of treatment for violent males is considered. Spouse-to-spouse violence has become an important concern, and innovative treatment approaches are desperately needed. The authors, who had considerable experience in counseling violent males, developed some guidelines for counseling assaultive offenders in a group setting. They note that group counseling for batterers has many advantages over individual counseling, including the reduction of the batterer's isolation from others, the opportunity to develop interpersonal skills (so that means other than violence can be used to deal with frustrations), and chances to elicit aid and support from peers. The article also focuses on the dynamics of the group, the size, structure, number and length of sessions, leadership styles, and the mix of economic and social backgrounds that appear to create the best chance for controlling or constructively channeling anger in those being treated.

Notes

[1] Hayes A. Hatcher, *Correctional Casework and Counseling* (Englewood Cliffs, NJ: Prentice-Hall, 1978), 152.
[2] Lloyd McCorkle, *The Highfields Story* (New York: Holt, Rinehart and Winston, 1958).
[3] J. L. Moreno, *The First Book on Group Psychotherapy* (New York: Beacon House, 1957).
[4] S. R. Slavson, *An Introduction to Group Therapy* (New York: Commonwealth Fund, 1950).
[5] Eric Berne, *Transactional Analysis in Psychotherapy* (New York: Grove Press, 1961), 19.
[6] Harry H. Vorrath and Larry K. Brendtro, *Positive Peer Culture* (Chicago: Aldine, 1974), 37–38.
[7] James P. Trotzer, *The Counselor and the Group* (Monterey, CA: Brooks/Cole Publishing, 1977), 53–63.

17

The Process of Group Counseling

James P. Trotzer

Background

The process of group counseling presented in this chapter has emerged from experience in a variety of settings and with a wide range of clients and age groups. Contributing to this model have been my involvement and leadership experience in schools with upper elementary, junior high, and senior high students, at the Minnesota State Prison working with inmates and staff, at the university level working with undergraduate and graduate students, in numerous human-relations workshops with a variety of educators, in church-related youth retreat groups, in interracial groups, and in other diverse settings as a consultant. This process model was developed first (Trotzer, 1972), and the rationale supplied later. In this sense the model is experience-based rather than theory-based and is rooted in observation of actual group interaction rather than in empirical assessment of hypothetical constructs.

Nature of the Process

The model described presents a developmental perspective of group counseling, which is intended for use as an aid in under-

From *The Counselor and the Group: Integrating Theory, Training, and Practice*, by J. P. Trotzer, Copyright © 1977 by Wadsworth, Inc. Reprinted by permission of the publisher, Brooks/Cole Publishing Company, Monterey, CA.

standing and directing the group process and as a framework for many different theoretical approaches and techniques. The group process itself is divided into five stages. However, the stages are not autonomous or independent of each other. Each stage has certain characteristics that distinguish it, but their meaning and impact are obtained only within the context of the total group process. The duration of each stage is dependent on the nature of the leader and group members. In some cases, the stages turn over very rapidly; in some, the stages are almost concurrent; and in others, a particular stage may continue for a long period of time and can lead to stagnation in the group process, especially if this occurs early.

Rogers' (1967) description of the group process correlates well with this idea of stages emerging and submerging in group interaction.

> The interaction is best thought of, I believe, as a varied tapestry, differing from group to group, yet with certain kinds of trends evident in most of these intensive encounters and certain patterns tending to precede and others to follow. (p. 263)

Each stage of the group is like a wave that has momentary identity as it crests but whose beginning and demise are swallowed up in the constant movement of the sea.

The Group Process and Problem-Solving

The stage cycle of the group process reflects characteristics of our basic human needs and depicts the essential qualities of good interpersonal relationships. The model also mirrors a basic pattern for successful problem-solving. The integration of the stages into a conceptualization of a method for resolving problems is readily evident. The stages of security, acceptance, responsibility, work, and closing are easily translated into a step-by-step procedure for resolving personal concerns. First of all, as we experience problems we can't solve, there is a natural tendency to hide or deny them because we don't want negative repercussions in our self-image or in reactions of others around us. Problems threaten our security as persons and our relationships with others. Therefore problems are only shared with others if an atmosphere of safety is part of our relationship with them. Feelings of trust and confidence reduce risk and facilitate our sharing of personal concerns with others. The amount of trust necessary for disclosing our problems is a product of the combined emotional seriousness of the problem and the quality of our relationships. Some problems we experience force us to use disclosure as a means of developing a trusting climate. For example, a client who has recently undergone a traumatic experience—say a close friend was injured while riding in a car the client was driving—may be motivated by intense emotional feelings to share the problem without first determining if the atmosphere is safe. Such risks are sometimes taken without a foreknowledge of trust in the relationship. However, other problems may have emotional or social overtones that demand an atmosphere of confidentiality before any self-revelations occur. In these cases the relationship must develop first and self-disclosure follows. Examples of these kinds of problems include sex problems, drug problems, and difficulties in relationships with significant others such as parents, teachers, or marriage partner. In any event, step one in resolving our problems is to find a safe place in which we can talk about them.

The second step is associated with acceptance. Although the term *acceptance* encompasses a broad range of concepts, such as acceptance of self, acceptance of others, and acceptance by others, a key point in solving a problem is to accept that problem as a part of ourselves. Until we recognize that the problems we experience are part of us, we cannot act constructively to resolve them. Denial and unwillingness to face our problems are the biggest deterrents to their resolution. In order to accept our problems, we need to know that recognition of them as our own will not be devastating to ourselves or to our relationships with others. In other words, our own acceptance of our problems is contingent to a large degree on the reactions or the perceived reactions of others. If we are accepted by others in total, if we feel we can show them all of ourselves including our problems and be received with an empathic ear, we are more willing to identify, share, and acknowledge our problems.

Taking responsibility is the third step in the problem-solving process. After we acknowledge our problems, we must also admit to our part in their cause and shoulder the responsibility to act positively to resolve them. Responsibility brings into focus the action phase of problem-solving. The realization that problem-solving is an active process and that the individual with the problem is primarily responsible for that action is a difficult but necessary step toward resolution. Clients often hope that once they have admitted to, identified, or accepted their problems something almost magical will occur and the problem will be resolved. They sometimes feel that because they have made the courageous effort to reveal themselves, their reward should be instant resolution, or at least that the counselor should take over. Therefore the process of getting clients to take responsibility for themselves is another key step in successful resolution.

The fourth step is to work out the means whereby the problem can be solved. This involves understanding the problem, identifying alternative solutions, evaluating them, planning and practicing new attitudes or behaviors, and trying them out in the real world. The helping relationship at this point is a working relationship in which all parties exert energy and intelligence toward helping the individual find and implement a successful solution.

The final step is to terminate the relationship when clients begin to experience success more than failure in their attempts to integrate changes into their lives. Terminating counseling clients should not only realize their problems are resolved but should have learned the problem-solving process and increased their confidence to use it. The following discussion will describe the life cycle of a group in which the problem-solving characteristics just detailed will be related to the group-counseling process. Each stage will be discussed separately, considering factors such as major identifying characteristics, focus, leader role, and resulting impact.

The Security Stage

The initial stage of the counseling group is characterized by tentativeness, ambiguity, anxiety, suspicion, resistance, discomfort, and other such emotional reactions on the part of both the members and the leader. The members experience these reactions because they are entering a new situation in which they cannot predict what will occur, and they are not confident of their ability to control themselves or relate well to the group. Even though orientation procedures are used, once the group comes together and interaction begins, the cognitive preparation gives way to the normal emotional reactions experienced in new social situations. Uncomfortable feelings also arise because each member is aware that he or she is in counseling and has personal concerns that are not easily shared under any circumstances.

An example of the inner turmoil a group member experiences was demonstrated by a young woman who requested admittance to a therapy group at a university counseling center. During the first session she paced and stood outside the room, struggling with the decision of whether to enter or not. The group leader, aware of her fears and misgivings about the group, left the door open and indicated to her that she could come in when she was ready. Toward the end of the session she entered the room and stood against the wall but did not join the group until the second session. So extensive was her discomfort that she did not participate until the fourth session and did not risk disclosing anything about herself until much later. Although most group members do not experience reactions to that extent, feelings of discomfort in the early sessions are always prevalent.

The security stage is a period of testing for the group members, and much of this testing takes the form of resistance, withdrawal, or hostility. Bonney (1969) points out that "resistance and hostility toward the leader and conflict among group members are . . . expected outgrowths of the basic insecurity of procedural direction and uncertainty concerning the capacity of the group to achieve its proposed aims" (p. 165). The testing takes many forms and is aimed in many directions but the most common challenges are leveled at leader competency, ground rules, and other members' actions. Rogers (1967) feels that negative expressions are a way of testing the trustworthiness and freedom of the group. All persons in the group experience some form of nervousness that generates defending types of behaviors rather than the authentic sharing of feelings.

The focus during this initial period must take into account these insecure feelings of the members. Underlying concerns that brought the members to the group should be set aside for the moment, and the here-and-now discomfort facing the group should be worked with. Some leaders like to use group warm-ups to help members express and work through these initial feelings and to establish a comfortable rapport within the group. The individual problems of the members, though they may be categorically similar, are most likely quite dissimilar in the perception of each member at this point. Thus it is important to establish a common ground so that members can make contact with each other and open lines of communication.

Since each member is preoccupied with dissatisfactions in his or her own life, an immediate focus on any one problem would lead to a rather disjointed process, which would run a high risk of losing the involvement and cooperation of all the members. This type of emphasis might also allow some members to go too deeply too quickly and scare off others. Cohn (1973) warned leaders to avoid this possibility and stressed that one essential feature of the group process is that members must be moved to deeper levels of interaction together. By initially focusing on the discomfort that all are experiencing, a common ground is established, which moves the group toward more cohesiveness. This identification with one another helps members overcome feelings of isolation and lays the foundation for the development of trust (Trotzer, 1972).

A significant aspect of the security stage is the leader's part in sharing the discomfort. Seldom will a leader enter a group without some feelings of uneasiness and hesitancy. These feelings do not reflect the skill and experience of the counselor but rather are indicative of the effort involved in working toward closeness between people and helping people with problems. If leaders do not enter groups with some of these feelings, they are probably not prepared to become involved in the very personal worlds of the members.

The leader's role in the security stage is to perform what Lifton (1966) calls "security-giving operations." Leaders must be able to gain the confidence of the members, display warmth and understanding, provide for the various needs of the members, and create and maintain a friendly and safe atmosphere in the group. Sensitivity, awareness, and an ability to communicate feelings and observations to the group without dominating it are important qualities of group leadership at this stage of the group's development.

As the group resolves the discomfort of the artificial situation, members can begin delving into the problems in their lives, and as members share their common feelings and perceptions, trust develops. Cohn (1964) emphasizes this concept of trust, suggesting that once group members trust and are trusted the groundwork is laid for making the effort needed to improve their real-life situations. Rogers (1967) states that the "individual will gradually feel safe enough to drop some of his defenses and facades" (p. 8). The members will become more willing to show their inner selves rather than just their outer selves. They will begin to direct energy toward expression—communication that allows oneself to be known to others authentically and transparently—rather than impression—communication that involves putting on a face in order to attract others (Schmuck & Schmuck, 1971).

Ohlsen (1970) also described the impact of the security stage:

> *When clients come to feel reasonably secure within their counseling group, they can be themselves, discuss the problems that bother them, accept others' frank reactions to them and express their own genuine feelings toward others. (p. 91)*

In other words, the development of trust provides the basis for getting down to the business of working on one's problems. Vorrath (n.d.) adds that the most dynamic experience members "gain from the group is that they learn to trust people" (p. 9). So trust has a process dimension and an outcome dimension, which give it a two-fold impact in the group process. During the security stage the development of a trusting, nonthreatening atmosphere is the primary objective. This objective is in accord with each member's basic human need for security. As trust increases, the willingness for personal involvement and commitment increases. Members are more likely to risk letting themselves and their problems, frustrations, joys, and successes be known. Because of the atmosphere created by the movement toward trust, the individual members feel freer to be themselves. When this occurs the transition into the second stage of the group-counseling process takes place.

The Acceptance Stage

The acceptance stage is directly related to our need for love and belonging and therefore has many derivatives that influence the direction of the group process. Generally this stage is characterized by a movement away from resistance and toward cooperation on the part of group members. As members begin to overcome the discomfort and threat of the group, the grounds for their fears dissipate and they become more accepting of the group situation. As they become more familiar with the group's atmosphere, procedures, leader, and members, they become more comfortable and secure in the group setting. They accept the group structure and the leader's role. This acceptance does not mean the purpose of the group is clear to members, but it does mean they are accepting the method. The meaning and purpose of the counseling group must be derived from the group members not from the group structure.

Inherent in the group members' acceptance of the group as a vehicle for their interaction is their need to belong and the need for relatedness. The members' desire to be a part of the group emerges as an important motivating factor. This desire is inwardly evident to the individual from the outset of the group. But at first it's stifled for fear of acting in a manner that might ultimately jeopardize that belonging. However, with the foundation of trust established, the members are more willing to be their real selves and risk being known for the sake of being accepted. A journal entry of a 24-year-old Vietnam veteran who chose an alcohol treatment center rather than jail effectively depicts the acceptance stage of the group process:

> At first there was no way I was going to admit to being an alcoholic or even that I had a drinking problem. But as I listened to the other guys talk about booze in their lives I began to realize they were all talking about many of the same experiences I had. The first thought that came to me was "Hey, you can't fool these cats because they've been there." I felt lots of pressure to 'fess up' but still held back because I wasn't sure

*how they (the group) would take me nor was I sure I could
stomach myself if I did. I finally decided to share my drinking
problems when I saw the group treat another Nam vet in the
group in a sensitive way, giving him support and help with
a problem I thought was even worse than mine. When I did
admit I had a drinking problem the group seemed to open up
to me and let me in, and I also liked myself better.*

As acceptance is experienced, relationships grow, and cohesiveness develops. Cohesiveness is important to the group process
because it makes group members more susceptible to the influence
of each other and the group. It also provides the impetus for group
productivity. It is a key factor in the helping process in groups
because "those who are to be changed and those who influence
change must sense a strong feeling of belonging in the same group"
(Ohlsen, 1970, p. 88). Thus group cohesiveness meets the members'
needs to belong, provides them with a temporary protective shield
from the outside world, and is a potent therapeutic factor in the
change process.

The therapeutic influence of cohesiveness makes use of peer-
group dynamics as its key resource in the group. As members
experience genuine acceptance by fellow members, self-esteem is
enhanced, ego is strengthened, self-confidence is bolstered, and they
develop more courage in facing up to their problems. The impact
of feeling accepted by a group of one's peers is stated succinctly
by Gawrys and Brown (1963):

> *To be accepted and understood by the counselor is a satisfying
> experience: to be accepted and understood by a number of
> individuals is profound. (p. 106)*

Within this context, then, the potential of peer-group influence can
be used in a positive manner by the counselor. The group leader's
role in this stage is no small factor in generating an accepting
atmosphere in the group and contributing directly to the individual
members' experience of feeling accepted. Leaders must be models
of acceptance from the onset of the total group process. They must
demonstrate a genuine caring for each of the group members. Their
leadership must be characterized by acceptance of each person
regardless of the behaviors he or she has exhibited outside the
group. The process of acceptance is initiated by leaders who practice
Rogers' (1962) concept of unconditional positive regard. As the
members experience acceptance from the leader, they feel more
accepting of themselves and follow the leader's model in their
actions toward one another. As members feel more accepting of
themselves and other members, a total atmosphere of acceptance
is created.

This brings us to the primary objective of the acceptance stage from a problem-solving perspective—developing acceptance of self. For members' problems to surface in the group they must feel free to be truly themselves without fear of rejection or reprisal. As already stated, members cannot deal effectively with their problems without recognition that the problems are a part of them. Further, they must know that even though they have problems they are still persons of worth and importance. All people have the desire to like and accept themselves and to be liked and accepted by others. It is this desire that the group utilizes in helping members deal with their problems. When each member can accept feelings, thoughts, and behaviors, whether good or bad, as part of themselves and still feel accepted and respected as a person of worth, a big step has been taken in the helping process of the group.

The focus during the acceptance stage should be on the whole person and not just on isolated problem areas. In order to attain self-acceptance and acceptance of others, members must work with the total picture of themselves and others. Getting to know oneself and each other, engaging in "who am I?" and "who are you?" activities, serve to promote self-disclosure. As individuals share themselves and describe their problems, accepting problems as part of themselves occurs more naturally and is less threatening. Many leaders like to incorporate the first two stages of security and acceptance, using structured personal-sharing activities and techniques to do so. In this way sharing promotes trust, and trust encourages sharing. And members find that many of their concerns are similar to those of other members. This similarity among members leads to identification with each other and the group and facilitates openness. As members can speak more freely about their problems, they find they can embrace them without losing self-esteem or position in the group; and this experience paves the way for the more individualistic stage of responsibility.

The results of the second stage of the group-counseling process include acceptance of the group structure and the leader's role, meeting individual needs for love and belonging, acceptance of self, acceptance of others, and acceptance of problems as part of oneself. This may sound like a big order to fill, and it is. But acceptance is also a powerful force in facilitating the problem-solving process. When established, it removes many of the roadblocks in the counseling process. It enables the group to begin constructive individual help. The development of acceptance accomplishes three main objectives (Trotzer, 1972).

1. *It aids the group in becoming cohesive and close thus
   meeting Gendlin and Beebe's (1968) guideline that*

"closeness must precede unmasking."

2. *It helps each individual feel accepted as a person of worth even though life is not satisfactory at the moment. This meets Gendlin and Beebe's (1968) guideline of putting "people before purpose."*

3. *It releases the potential of peer-group influence to be used in a positive rather than negative manner.*

The Responsibility Stage

The third stage of the group-counseling process is characterized by a movement on the part of group members from acceptance of self and others to responsibility for self. There is a subtle but distinct difference between acceptance of and responsibility for self. Acceptance helps members realize and admit that problems are a part of their selves. However, acceptance alone leaves members with an avenue of retreat away from working on their problems. Members can say "yes, that's the way I am" or "that's my problem" but can disclaim any part in its cause or rectification. Acceptance allows members to claim no fault and negates any responsibility for doing anything about changing. The inclusion of responsibility, however, moves members toward resolution. The combination of acceptance and responsibility encourages members to state "yes, that's my problem, and I have to do something about it." The ground is thus made fertile for constructive change to take place.

A single mother with two children who shared her problems and frustrations in a women's counseling group at a mental-health center exemplifies the difference between acceptance and responsibility. During the fourth group meeting, she talked extensively about the pain of her divorce and the subsequent difficulties of trying to raise her children alone. She became very emotional at times, and the group facilitated catharsis in a very sensitive manner. At the end of the session the group leader helped the woman put herself back together emotionally and solicited feedback from the group couched in terms of support. During the following session she was again the focus of attention, but this time members began to suggest alternatives that could possibly help her improve her life. To each alternative she responded by saying, "I already tried that" or "I don't think that would work." After several attempts to get her to consider alternatives failed, one member observed that maybe she really didn't want to do anything different in her life to overcome the problems. The woman denied that but soon afterward asked that the focus of group attention be directed elsewhere. During the following sessions this woman's problem was brought up several times by herself, other group members, or the leader, but the discussion always stalemated at the point of her taking any responsibility for the problems or for initiating changes. Eventually she told the group that she felt her problems were the result of others being unfair and insensitive to her and that she was a victim and not a cause in her situation. Soon afterward she left the group. She was willing to share her problems in the group but was not able to see herself as a contributor or take the initiative to work toward resolving them.

The issue of responsibility in the group emanates from both our needs as human beings and the nature of the problem-solving process. Members can only meet their need for esteem and respect through actions and achievements that require the person to take responsibility. If members feel causes are external they will also feel the cures must come from sources external to themselves and not from within.

Our needs are reflected in the pressure of the counseling group to move on. The social aspect of cohesiveness developed in the acceptance stage wears thin after a while, and there is a natural tendency toward getting down to the business of problems. This tendency, according to Bonney (1969), is a mark of group maturity in that group members begin to accept responsibility for the management of the group and exert their energies to the task of problem-solving. As members take increased responsibility for themselves and the therapeutic process, their chances for growth within the counseling group improve. In fact, Lindt (1958) found that only those who accepted responsibility in the helping process of the group benefited from their experience.

During the early stages of the group process the task is to develop trust and acceptance by focusing on similarities among members. This process universalizes. It helps members recognize that their problems are experienced by others (universalization), even though individual differences are apparent (Dinkmeyer and Muro, 1971). During the responsibility stage the focus changes to individualization and differentiation based on each person's uniqueness and responsibility. The atmosphere of the group provides for considerable personal freedom with the implication that members have permission to explore their weaknesses, strengths, and potentialities, to determine a way of working on problems, and to express feelings. The here-and-now emphasis is a key component in the responsibility stage, but it takes on a broader, problem-oriented perspective. During the early stages of the group the here-and-now is restricted to present feelings about the group and one's part in it and to help members focus on their here-and-now problems outside the group as well. This can be done in a step-by-step process in which expression of feelings is the starting point. The expression of personal feelings and perceptions about self and others is one basis for learning responsibility in the group. To emphasize taking responsibility for what one feels, leaders can ask members to state their own perceptions and to tack on the statement "and I take responsibility for that feeling." In this manner members learn to take responsibility for expressing hostility and caring without the threat and risk usually associated with the expression of such feelings.

As the members learn to accept responsibility for their personal feelings it becomes easier to accept responsibility for their actions and eventually their problems. These steps must be taken if the counselor and the group are to have any significant impact on the individual member's life. Mahler (1969) emphasizes the importance of responsibility for oneself:

> Counselees must realize the importance of being responsible for their own lives, behavior, and actions, making their own decisions and learning to stand on their own perceptions. (p. 140)

He adds that:

> People need opportunities to learn that only by taking actions, making decisions, and accepting responsibility for their own lives can they become adults in the full sense of the word. (p. 141)

Group counseling gives them that opportunity.

The leader's role during this stage centers around helping members realize self-responsibility. Lakin (1969) and Glasser (1965) stress the modeling nature of the leader role in which the counselor's actions must depict the proper attitude toward responsibility. Glasser feels that responsibility can only be learned through involvement with responsible people. Therefore the member's primary example to follow in the group is the leader. The leader must help members maintain a focus on themselves and their problems at this point, rather than on events, people, or situations external to the group and beyond its influence. The counseling group can only affect people and situations through its effect on the person in the immediate presence of the group. The counselor must stress an internal frame of reference rather than an external one. The question that ultimately must be faced is not "what can others do?" but "what can I do?"

The leader faces a crucial issue during the responsibility stage, and a word of caution is apropos. In our concern for our clients to "make it on their own," we often see opportunities in the group process that could be used to "teach" members responsibility. This situation must be avoided. For group members to become responsible they must experience responsibility, not be told about it. It is appropriate at times to bring up the issue of responsibility or even to confront members with it, but the choice to be responsible should be left to the members. Mahler (1969) feels that "counselors who teach in group counseling violate the concept that basic responsibility for management of one's own life is up to the individual" (p. 103). Therefore leadership should be directed toward helping members feel accepted and responsible without domination. When successful, members will feel more personal, individual responsibility and will exhibit less dependency.

The responsibility stage sets the tone for the remainder of the group-counseling process. Once members realize their responsibility for themselves and understand that neither the leader nor the group will infringe upon it, the members can direct their entire attention to problem-solving. The responsibility stage affirms the inherent worth of the members, assures them of respect as human beings, and points out the qualities necessary to enhance self-worth and resolve problems. Those qualities are self-assessment, congruence, honesty, responsibility, and commitment. When the members willingly engage in the introspective process, self-disclose, demonstrate their acceptance of others and willingness to help others, and—with very little or no help from the leader—take responsibility, the work stage of the counseling process is imminent.

The Work Stage

The character of the work stage organizes itself around the individual problems and concerns of the group members. As trust, acceptance, and responsibility are experienced and learned, it becomes increasingly evident that there are some areas in each members' life that are not satisfactory and could benefit from change. When these areas are pinpointed and discussed specifically, the work stage goes into full operation. Vorrath (n.d.) feels that the core of the group process is reached at this point, because the goal of this type of group is to work on problems and get them solved.

The work stage of group counseling is exemplified by the interaction of a human-relations group designed to improve communication and relationships between racial groups in a large urban high school. The members decided that the basic problem was not knowing how to approach students who were racially different from themselves. They tended to be hesitant, fearing overtones of prejudice might be communicated. To work on this problem, the leader first had racially similar members discuss their perceptions of racially different groups and then make suggestions that they felt would facilitate better relationships. After each subgroup had discussed their perceptions and made their suggestions, a comprehensive list of suggestions was developed in terms of skills. The leader than formed racially mixed dyads to try out the suggestions. During their work stage, partners were rotated periodically to give members the experience of trying out alternatives and building their skills and confidence with all racial groups represented.

The basic purposes of the work stage are to give group members the opportunity to (1) examine personal problems closely in an environment free of threat, (2) explore alternatives and suggestions for resolving the problems, and (3) try out new behaviors or attitudes in a safe setting prior to risking changes outside the group (Trotzer, 1972). The energy of the group is concentrated on accomplishing these three purposes through the use of feedback, clarification, and information-giving. Once in motion the productivity of the group is quite amazing and at times needs to be held in check because of the tendency to begin to solve problems before they are fully understood.

The leader role in the work stage is extremely vital from two perspectives. Leaders must be both facilitator and expert. They must be able to facilitate the discussion of problems, bringing out as many facets as possible, and create an atmosphere where alternatives can be suggested. These two processes entail mustering the total perceptual and experiential resources of the group. After a particular problem has been discussed and alternative solutions suggested, leaders must use their expertise to provide vehicles for examining the consequences of the suggestions as a means of aiding the decision-making process. These activities can take the form of role-playing, sociodramas, communication exercises, or discussion. In this way alternatives can be assessed and evaluated, thus avoiding shot-in-the-dark failures. This type of reality testing in the group provides the group member with an idea of both the feasibility of a specific alternative and the effort involved in using it to resolve the problem. It also provides the member with an opportunity to develop self-confidence before attempting to make any specific changes in the more threatening world outside the group.

Another important facet of the group process that surfaces during the work stage is the dual role of the group member as both the helper and the helped. When any one member of the group is working on a particular problem, the other members provide help through their feedback, sharing, suggestions, discussion, and participation in group activities. The experience of being in the helper role increases the members' feelings of self-worth because now they are in the position of giving rather than receiving. The giving of assistance to others also produces a more congenial attitude toward receiving assistance from others. The two-way process of helping and being helped is thus established. This process makes good use of members' altruistic tendencies, as well as allowing them to engage in "spectator therapy" where they benefit from watching others work out their problems.

During this stage the group also represents "society in microcosm" (Gazda, 1968c); that is, group members represent, as best they can, the forces, attitudes, reactions, and ideas of the world outside the group. Through the process of feedback the group helps each member develop realistic alternatives to problems that can reasonably be applied in their lives outside the group. This minisociety function is important because of its transitional value in preparing members for the task of implementing changes.

In the work stage the "healing capacity" (Rogers, 1967) of the group emerges, and the specific goals and objectives of the counseling group are dealt with. Each group has different objectives based on the diversity of the group membership and the setting in which the group is formed. However, since most counseling groups are usually organized to deal with specific problems, it is at this point in the group process where efforts are focused on resolving them. The work stage prepares members for reentry into the world where they are experiencing their problems. They are armed with a well-conceived and evaluated plan, and self-confidence has been shored up through practice and personal encouragement. However, individuals do not have to make the changes and implement their plans without some support, which brings us to the final stage of the group process, closing.

The Closing Stage

The final stage of the group-counseling process is mainly supportive in nature and is characterized by feedback, encouragement, and perseverance. Although group members may successfully work through their problems within the group, they still face the difficult task of modifying their behavior and attitudes outside the group. The expectations of significant others outside the group are still based on past experience with the group member, thus making it difficult to give encouragement or reinforcement to the member for acting in new or different ways. The group is a place where members can share their frustrations, successes, and failures and also reassess their actions for possible changes that will increase their effectiveness. Without a source of support, the chance of regression to old ways is greater.

The group also serves as a motivator. Part of this function entails rejecting excuses and confronting members with their own lack of commitment and effort if need be. Sometimes members need to be pushed out into the real world when they cannot venture forth on their own. The group has uncanny competence in assessing whether members are authentic in their efforts and whether they have performed up to their capability. During this stage the group can be both a sounding board and a control board.

Group support facilitates the integration of change into the client's life. Efforts to change and the change process itself are supported until reinforcement occurs in members' lives outside the group. As the changes become more natural parts of their life-styles, the difficulty of adapting new behaviors, feelings, and attitudes decreases. The support of the group is only necessary until the balance between ease and difficulty in implementing change swings to the ease side of the scale.

The focus of the group thus turns to members' behavior and experience outside the group and deals with progress they are making. The leader helps members discuss their experiences and feelings, offering support, understanding, and encouragement. The leader also helps members begin to take credit for their own changes instead of giving credit to the group or the counselor. In this way the individual members can integrate their new behaviors and attitudes into their everyday lives and can feel reinforcement from within themselves rather than from the group.

The closing stage for individuals may take many different forms. For example, a student who had been a member of a therapy group at a college counseling center for three years began to miss group meetings, showing up periodically but with longer time lapses between attendance. As she entered the final semester of her senior year, she relied less and less on the group for feedback and support taking more and more responsibility for herself. Her need for the group and her involvement in the group lessened, with termination coinciding with graduation.

Another example of the closing stage is the standard procedure used at an alcohol treatment center when individual patients are preparing to leave treatment. The patient's group holds a graduation ceremony for the departing member during which that person makes a commencement address reviewing and summarizing the treatment and describing goals and objectives for the future. The group then engages in a serenity prayer during which group members give support, feedback, and encouragement to the graduating member. The person is then presented with a coin that has a missing piece symbolizing the unending process involved in rehabilitation and growth. The ceremony thus serves to summarize and reinforce changes that have occurred but also prepares the person for the rigors of adjusting to life outside of the treatment center.

The point at which a group or individual member should terminate is sometimes difficult to determine. For this reason groups are often terminated on the basis of a preset time schedule, for example, after ten sessions or at the end of a quarter or semester. However, ending a group is also appropriate when group members experience more success than failure in solving their problems and feel intrinsic rather than extrinsic reinforcement for their actions in doing so. As members become more dependent on themselves, they lose their dependence on the group. As they resolve their problems and learn how to solve problems, they no longer need the group. When any of these situations occur the group has run its course and should be disbanded.

A Precautionary Note

Viewing group counseling as a developmental sequence of a set number of stages raises the possibility of unnecessary and undesirable rigidity in conceptualizing the group process. To circumvent this and maintain flexibility in this group model, it is necessary to remember that within each stage there can be many levels. Different degrees of trust, acceptance, and responsibility are reached by the group and its members at different times. Some problems discussed in the group require less trust than others. At other times it may be necessary for the process to recycle, developing deeper levels of trust, acceptance, or responsibility in order to deal with a particular problem. Bonney (1969) refers to this occurrence as the retransition stage in which the group goes back through the early phases of group development before proceeding to a deeper level. At any one time and with any one problem or person the group may have to retreat to a previous stage before it can move on to the next one. In fact, all stages may recur several times before the group has run its course.

Another consideration is that components of two or more stages may be prominent in the group at the same time. The group may be learning trust, acceptance, and responsibility while working on a particular problem. The group does not develop in a lock-step manner even though general trends can be noted and specific characteristics consistently appear at certain points in the group's development. Neither can the group process be forced to conform to an external standard or model. Rather it is a responsive and flexible process that is influenced by the leader's personality, by differences between people and their problems, and by variations in the rate at which different people develop relationships and work out individual change.

Concluding Comments

Group counseling brings into perspective the relationship between psychological needs and the socialization process, whereby human learning and problem-solving occurs through interaction. It accentuates the social learning process by focusing on the dynamics of the group itself rather than on some environmental context. Group members are given the opportunity to learn how they function individually and interpersonally. They can do this because the leader and other members have created a climate or atmosphere characterized by psychological safety and acceptance where they can take responsibility for their own lives. In such a situation members can experience the healthy attributes of individuality or uniqueness and relatedness or conformity. They learn both independence and interdependence.

Members can express themselves freely and engage in open and honest interaction with other members without the fear of rejection or reprisal that so often tempers interaction in one's environment. Within the group members can experience and learn responsibility. They can confront problems openly, knowing they will obtain support and assistance as needed. Members experience the interchanging role of being the helper and the helped as they work on their own problems and assist others with theirs. The member can discover and evaluate alternative solutions to personal concerns while at the same time building self-confidence and personal security, which serve as enabling factors in implementing change outside the group. Thus group counseling provides both a setting and a process whereby the basic objectives of a counseling program can be attained.

Learning Activities

The exercises presented here are organized in sequence to relate to the stages of group development discussed in this chapter. Although the primary characteristic and use of each activity is stage-related, there are also many other purposes for which they can be used. These activities are versatile and adaptable, depending on the leader's approach and the nature of the group.

Trust Ring[1]

Option I. This exercise is useful in demonstrating the characteristics of trust and confidentiality that are necessary for a group to work effectively. Have all group members stand in a circle in an area that is free of material objects such as chairs or tables. Members should have a strong grip on each of their partners hands or wrists. Then have the group extend out as far as possible forming a taut circle. Instruct all members to lean back exerting pressure on the circle and slowly move their feet toward the center of the circle creating a centrifugal pressure on the group. Have the group move in a clockwise direction maintaining this centrifugal pressure. After a few moments reverse the direction. Follow the exercise with a discussion of each person's reaction in terms of the amount of pressure they were personally willing to place on the group and their feelings regarding their partners and the total group. Stress the importance of the whole group going to the aid of individuals who were slipping in order to protect them and maintain solidarity in the group. Discussion can also focus on the amount of pressure the group as a whole exerted relating it to risk-taking in self-disclosure and feedback.

Option II. A variation of this exercise is to have members stand in a circle shoulder to shoulder. Instruct the members to interlock their arms around the back or waist of the persons beside them. Then have the group members lean inward and slowly move their feet away from the center of the group creating a centripetal force on the group. Have the group move alternately in a clockwise and counterclockwise manner. At the conclusion of the exercise have the group members retain their interlocking positions in the circle and discuss the reactions in the same manner as described above. An added feature of this discussion can be the impact of closeness created by the "arms around each other" dimension, relating it to the effect of warmth and closeness in developing cohesiveness and trust in the group.

Option III. This exercise is useful in working with individual members who are having difficulty developing, feeling, or understanding trust in the group. It is particularly effective in working with individuals who wish to trust the group but are having difficulty doing so. Stand one member in the center of the group and have the other members form a standing circle around him.

The initial distance between the person in the center and the circle members should be relatively small but large enough to allow freedom of movement. Instruct the member in the center to close his eyes and place his feet together. Then instruct him to fall toward the circle without moving his feet and allow the group to move him back and forth and around. The outside circle should vary the distance they allow the person to fall and the roughness they use in handling him but always be responsible for the member's safety. Follow-up discussion should center on the individual's feelings and reactions. The main thrust is to help the individual come to grips with feelings about trust and to point out the important group dynamics associated with individuals sharing problems or disclosing themselves in a group situation.

Closed Fist[2]

This activity lends itself to a consideration of the strategies used by people in negotiating trust in human relationships. It is particularly applicable to group counseling because of the risk intrinsic to the process of sharing. Break the group down into dyads. Ask the partners to exchange some material object that they value (such as a ring, a picture, or a wallet). Have each partner put the object away out of sight for the time being. Then instruct the members to think of something that is extremely valuable to them, something they would not wish to give up under any circumstances. Give the group a few minutes to choose something. Then ask one of the partners to figuratively place the thing of value in a closed fist without telling the partner what it is. Instruct the other partner to try to get it. Allow this process to proceed for a time without any intervention. Then ask for an account of what happened, noting the different strategies that were used to obtain the object and pointing out their relevance to the group process. After this discussion ask the members to try to get back the actual objects they exchanged initially.

Important factors to consider in this exercise are the type of exchange strategies that produce competitiveness, cooperation, ill will, and positive interpersonal feelings. Strategies that are conducive to positive relationships should be used in the group. Also, the value of the objects exchanged reflects the amount of commitment and trust in the relationship. Members will share more willingly and at a deeper level if there is reciprocal sharing by other members.

Life Story

Vorrath (n.d.) uses this technique to introduce new members into the group. It is especially appropriate for ongoing counseling groups that experience member turnover. New members after a brief period of time in the group are asked to tell their life stories as completely and as accurately as they possibly can. The life stories should include a description of the problems that brought the new people into the group. The other group members have the responsibility of facilitating the new member's efforts. Under no circumstances should the views of the person be challenged at this point. After the story is completed the group can begin to work with discrepancies or other factors that might relate to solving the member's problems. The main impact of this technique is that members realize their side of the story is going to be heard first. They receive guarantees that their frame of reference is important and will be considered by the group. They experience acceptance and find the group is a safe place to air their problems.

Poem of Self

This exercise helps establish a minimum level of self-acceptance for each group member and helps the group become involved in introspection and self-disclosure essential to the group process. Use the following directions in carrying out the exercise.

1. List four words (adjectives) that describe what you look like.
2. List four words (adjectives) that describe what you act like (personality).
3. List five words ending in "ing" that describe things you like to do (if you like to read, put reading).
4. List six things (nouns) that would remind people of you (for example, possessions, such as a guitar, or roles you play, such as a student).
5. List four places you would like to be.
6. On a sheet of paper draw the following diagram (you may want to hand out a mimeo form).

```
                ____
            ____    ____
        ____    ____    ____
    ____    ____    ____    ____
        ____    ____    ____
            ____    ____
                ____
```

7. On the first line of the diagram write your full name.
8. Choose one word from list 1 (what you look like) and one word from list 2 (what you act like) and place them in the blanks in line 2.
9. Choose three words from list 3 (things you like to do) and insert them in the blanks in line 3.
10. Choose four words from list 4 (things that remind people of you) and write them in the blanks in line 4.
11. Choose two words from list 5 (places) and write them in the blanks in line 5.
12. On the bottom line write a nickname or any name by which you are called other than your given name. (This may be a derivative of your given name, such as "Toni" for Antoinette.)

On completion of the poem have each member read his or her poem to the group twice, the first time quickly with rhythm and the second time slowly so that they can catch all the words. After everyone has read and explained the meaning of the words in their poems discuss how the exercise contributed to getting to know one another.

Coat of Arms

The coat of arms has more depth to it than the poem of self and can be used in conjunction with it. This activity gets at more varied aspects of each person's life and provides a good beginning for the actual counseling process. It also combines the medium of illustration with verbal description, which makes sharing an easier process. Give each person a sheet of paper with the illustrated diagram on it or have the people draw it. Then have them fill in the numbered sections of the shield according to the following instructions.

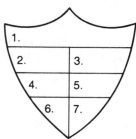

1. In the section numbered 1, write a motto or phrase that describes how you feel about life or that is a guide to your life-style. (Some people create their own; others use quotations, poems, or Bible verses.)
2. In section 2, draw a picture that represents your greatest achievement or accomplishment (no words).
3. Draw a picture that represents something other people could do to make you happy (no words).
4. Draw a picture that represents a failure or disappointment (no words).
5. Draw a picture that represents the biggest goal in your life right now (no words).
6. Draw a picture that represents a problem you would like to work on in this group (no words).
7. Write down three things you would like people to say about you if you died today.

After all the members have completed the shield, have each member describe his or hers to the group, explaining the meaning of each section. This exercise has the positive impact of acceptance since it deals with each person's strengths, weaknesses, goals, relationships with others, and problems. The instructions for the various parts can be changed to meet the demands of the situation and the needs of the members, thus making this exercise a flexible and effective tool in the hands of the group leader.

Strength Bombardment

One means of helping group members accept responsibility for themselves is to approach it from a perspective of strengths, assets, and accomplishments the member is already aware of. This exercise uses the process of self-disclosure and feedback to help members take responsibility for their behavior. First, have each group member develop a list of all positive accomplishments or achievements. Encourage the members to feel completely free about the list and not to think about the reactions of others or about the ego-related emotional connotations such a request usually conjures up. On completion of the list, have the members write a paragraph, starting with "I am," that describes their positive qualities. Assure them that no one else will see the paragraph, but indicate that they should include only positive qualities and not put in any negative ones. When the paragraph is completed have members put it away, stating that they can do what they want with it. Now have the members share their initial list of accomplishments with the group. Then place two chairs facing each other in the center of the circle. Ask one member to volunteer to take one of the chairs in order to receive positive feedback from the other members. When one person has taken a chair, each other person in turn gets up, sits in the opposite chair and gives the first person only positive feedback. There should be no "I would like you if" or "I like you but" comments, and the person receiving the feedback can only respond with expressions of appreciation, not with denials or counter remarks. This process continues until each person has received positive feedback from every other person in the group. On completion of the activity, relate the experience to the issue of responsibility and discuss how one's positive qualities can be used to help overcome one's negative qualities and problems.

Awareness and Responsibility

This technique has developed out of the Gestalt approach to group therapy and combines the concepts of personal awareness and individual responsibility. It has relevance to group counseling because it clarifies where members are personally and helps them take responsibility for their own thoughts, feelings and behavior in the group. Each group member is asked to share with the group present thoughts, feelings, and perceptions or observations using the format: "Right now I am aware . . . [members complete the statement describing what they are aware of], and I take responsibility for that." The last part of the statement is added to get individuals to affirm their own part in feeling, acting, or thinking the way they do and to prevent them from putting responsibility on others. A leader can effectively use the last part of the statement by simply asking members to add it to any statement involving a personal emotion, accusation, interpretation, or perception. In this way, the impact of the statement becomes just one person's frame of reference and allows other members the freedom to respond as they see fit without feeling threatened by the imposition of another person's point of view on them.

Gestalt Interventions

One of the ways we avoid being responsible for ourselves and in control of our own lives is through the words we use in communication (Stevens, 1971). The following intervention techniques drawn from the Gestalt approach to group therapy can be used to help group members take responsibility for their own thoughts, feelings, and behaviors and ultimately for their problems.

1. *Questions or Statements.* Many questions that group members ask are really camouflaged statements. Before responding with an answer ask the questioner to change the question into a statement that expresses personal perceptions, observations, or feelings.

2. *I Can't/I Won't Statements.* Members often use the words "I can't" in discussing problem situations, which give the impression that control is really outside of themselves. When you hear an "I can't" statement ask the member to repeat the statement using "I won't," which conveys the message that the person has a choice in the matter. "I just can't talk to my father" changes to "I just won't talk to my father."

3. *I Have to/I Choose to Statements.* Have group members make a list of "I have to" statements describing all the things in their lives that they feel they have to do. Have them share their lists in the group. Then have them change "I have to" to "I choose to" and discuss the differences between the two lists. Discussion usually pinpoints quite clearly the issue of personal responsibility and choice. As a group leader you can also ask members to substitute "I choose to" for "I have to" during group discussions. In doing this the members realize that they are responsible and that they do have a choice.

4. *I Need/I Want Statements.* Group members often express desires as needs, creating the impression that severe personal consequences will result if needs are not met. They say "I need," which depicts whatever it is as essential to their well-being. To define more accurately what really is needed and what can be done without, have members change "I need" statements to "I want" statements and discuss which is more appropriate, incorporating feedback from other members as to the accuracy of the statement.

Problem Identification and Rating

The work stage is the point in the group process at which problems should be dealt with directly. This exercise pinpoints problems that are pertinent to individual members and are relevant to other members' lives as well. Have the members anonymously write down a description of a problem they would be willing to discuss with the group. Stress the "willing to discuss" aspect. When the descriptions are finished, read them one by one to the group. After each problem is read ask members to individually rate it on a scale (5 is high and 1 is low), showing their interest in discussing the problem and their identification with it. Record each individual rating and after reading and rating all the problems, add up the totals. A hierarchy of problems develops based on the scores. Reread the highest rated problem and ask the person who wrote it to describe it in detail. The group can then work with that specific person and problem.

This procedure results in a hierarchical agenda, but if the group is particularly effective in helping the first person, other members may decide to reveal deeper problems they want help with. The problem agenda and hierarchy should be adhered to only if it is in the best interests of the group. Rigid structuring of the group focus could deter progress.

Go-Round

One of the simplest and yet most versatile and effective exercises that can be used in group counseling is the "go-round." As the name implies this technique involves going around the group person by person, giving each a specific opportunity to respond. This technique has many variations and purposes and fits at any stage of group development. For instance, a "go-round" is a good way to begin with a group to find out what everyone is thinking or feeling and to get some cues about how to proceed. A "go-round" when a group ends gives members the opportunity to say what they have not had a chance to say and is a good way to tie up loose ends. During the group sessions, go-rounds immediately following critical incidents are useful to air feelings and release tension, as well as to move the group on to the next phase of the process.

Notes

[1] The Trust Ring exercises of Options I and II were developed by Jim Ross and demonstrated in my group-counseling class at the University of Wisconsin-River Falls.

[2] This exercise was demonstrated by Dr. Dan Ficek in a Human Relations Workshop he and I led at Red Wing, Minnesota in the spring of 1974.

References

Bonney, W. C. Group counseling and developmental processes. In G. M. Gazda (Ed.), *Theories and methods of group counseling in the schools.* Springfield, IL: Charles C Thomas, 1969.

Cohn, B. Group counseling with adolescents. In B. Cohn (Ed.), *Collected articles: The adolescent and group counseling* (unpublished). Board of Cooperative Educational Services, Yorktown Heights, NY 10598, 1964.

Cohn, B. *Group counseling presentation.* Spring Group Guidance Conference, University of Wisconsin-Oshkosh, 1973.

Dinkmeyer, D. D. and Muro, J. J. *Group counseling: Theory and practice.* Itasca, IL: F. E. Peacock, 1971.

Gawrys, J., Jr., and Brown, B. O. Group counseling: More than a catalyst. *The School Counselor* 1963, 12, 206–213.

Gazda, G. M., and Larson, M. J. A comprehensive appraisal of group and multiple counseling research. *Journal of Research and Development in Education*, 1968, 1(2), 57–132.

Glasser, W. *Reality therapy.* New York: Harper & Row, 1965.

Lakin, M. Some ethical issues in sensitivity training. *American Psychologist*, 1969, 24, 923–928.

Lifton, W. *Working with groups* (2nd ed.). New York: Wiley, 1966.

Lindt, H. The nature of therapeutic interaction of patients in groups. *International Journal of Group Psychotherapy*, 1958, 8, 55–69.

Mahler, C. A. *Group counseling in the schools.* Boston: Houghton Mifflin, 1969.

Ohlsen, M. M. *Group counseling.* New York: Holt, Rinehart & Winston, 1970.

Rogers, C. R. The interpersonal relationship: The core of guidance. *Harvard Educational Review*, 1962, 32, 416-429.

Rogers, C. R. The process of the basic encounter group. In J. F. T. Bugental (Ed.), *Challenges of humanistic psychology.* New York: McGraw-Hill, 1967.

Schmuck, R. A., and Schmuck, P. A. *Group processes in the classroom.* Dubuque, IA: Brown, 1971.

Stevens, J. O. *Awareness: Exploring, experimenting, experiencing.* Moab, UT: Real People Press, 1971.

Trotzer, J. P. Group counseling: Process and perspective. *Guidelines for Pupil Services.* Madison: Wisconsin Department of Public Instruction, 1972, 10, 105–110.

Vorrath, H. H. *Positive peer culture: Content, structure and process.* Red Wing, MN: Red Wing State Training School.

18

The Use of Groups

Richard A. Stordeur
Richard Stille

Counselors have intervened in wife assault with a variety of approaches: separate individual counseling for men and women, couple counseling, couple groups, family counseling, and gender-specific groups have all been utilized in the attempt to terminate the cycle of violence. For reasons discussed in this chapter, we strongly prefer to counsel abusers in groups. Although other modes may be helpful at later stages, we believe the immediate and primary goal of stopping the violence seems best attained when a man is in a group of his peers.

Groups for assaultive men differ in several important ways from most other problem-oriented groups, general therapy groups, and personal growth groups. Counselors who have been unaware of the differences in structure, objectives, goals, counselors' roles, and facilitator styles have had difficulty when beginning these groups. Failure to tailor an approach in the planning stage to suit the characteristics and the needs of abusers and the aims of an assaultive men's counseling program can produce regrettable results; dropouts, group rebellion, therapist frustration, and marked deviation from the goal of the group can occur. In addressing many of these issues, we aim in this chapter to help counselors prepare for productive, efficiently operated groups.

From *Ending Men's Violence Agtainst Their Partners* by Richard A. Stordeur and Richard Stille, Copyright 1989 by Sage Publications, Inc. Reprinted by permission of Sage Publications, Inc.

Groups for Assaultive Men

Individual Counseling Versus Group

We have counseled batterers both individually and in groups. These contrasting experiences have led us to choose a group setting for this work whenever possible. In part, the reasons emerge from the inadequacies of individual counseling. This mode of helping an abuser is slow and arduous. The requirement to address minimization, externalization, and other problem behaviors overtly is not only difficult, it has the potential to create an adversarial atmosphere in which two roles can be highlighted—persecutor and victim. If a man regards us as persecutors we become his enemies, and it is then only natural that he strengthen his defenses. Where social and emotional isolation are problems for the man, individual meetings with a therapist are a poor remedy. Because an individual counseling relationship occurs behind closed doors, violence remains a secret and the shame associated with it remains. Furthermore, the one-to-one relationship risks reinforcing notions of psychopathology rather than the sociocultural, learned aspects of violence against women.

While the individual approach presents obstacles to change, the use of groups is based on what we believe to be the overwhelming advantages of this mode. Distinct and separate from content or counselor skill level, the group environment itself facilitates change. We can think of at least nine reasons to counsel abusers in groups:

(1) A group helps decrease a batterer's isolation. The group counseling environment requires taking risks, self-disclosure, and being vulnerable in the presence of others. It promotes trust while eroding the harmful facade of pseudoindependence demanded by the traditional male sex role. Social and emotional isolation from others is a mental health deficit, particularly when a man must deal with mounting stress levels. A group provides opportunities both to learn to rely on others and to help others.

(2) A group promotes improved interpersonal skills. A man in a group engages in discussion and role play, learns to give and receive feedback, and must do these respectfully.

(3) A group offers mutual aid among peers. The mutual aid process created by ten men multiplies the potential number of creative responses to any one man's struggle. This maximizes the self-help element while reducing the counselor's responsibility always to have an answer to a problem.

(4) As men learn to be helpful to each other, each individual's

status as a batterer makes him a special kind of expert. His credibility stems from "having been there." Additionally, because help comes from a number of individuals, men's authority issues with the counselor are deemphasized.

(5) The effect of confrontation is maximized in a group. When a therapist confronts one man on an issue, other men who struggle with the same issue are indirectly confronted. When the group observes one man struggle with an issue, each member identifies with that struggle as if he were looking in a mirror. However, because only one man is being confronted directly, defensiveness on the part of others in the group may be diluted.

(6) As a group works for change, a norm is established for attaining group objectives within a certain time. This sense of group time functions as a reference point for members who lag behind, encouraging them to keep up with the group.

(7) A group maximizes rewards for change. As each man reports a success, he is reinforced by the entire group instead of by the therapist alone.

(8) The secrecy surrounding male violence against women and children often leads both perpetrators and victims to believe they are exceptional or sick. A group helps to dispel this notion. When a batterer enters a group, he meets ordinary men who have the same problem. This event begins the consciousness-raising process whereby men learn about the prevalence of abuse and the sociocultural factors influencing ordinary people to be violent. Beyond the educational value of this revelation, we believe shame is reduced.

(9) In view of incessant funding difficulties in social services, the group approach is cost-effective.

A Psychoeducational Approach

The term *psychoeducational* has been used to describe groups for assaultive men (Ganley, 1981b). Although the implications of the term might vary according to who is using it, it seems to be one of the best available for describing a recommended overall approach in batterers' groups. When violence is viewed as learned behavior, it follows that it can be replaced by new learning. Therefore these groups are partially oriented to educating batterers. Counselors teach skills, lead discussion on various issues, facilitate role plays, and assign homework. Interestingly, the learning aspect of abuser groups is reflected by many men's tendencies to refer to the group as a "class."

Education in these groups differs from that found in most classroom situations. Classroom education is most often concerned with subject material that is external to the learner, such as facts, figures, and concepts. Although this does occur in a batterers' group, we select most material for its personal relevance to assaultive men. Members are really learning about themselves. For instance, when we teach a man that certain ways of thinking about a situation profoundly affect the way a person feels about it, he must apply this information to his struggle to be nonviolent through his participation in group exercises and self-disclosure. Therefore, there is a marked personal slant to all material.

The psychoeducational approach that we present also allows for each man to present personal issues and receive help from the counselors and other members. Although this occurs at special, predetermined points in each session, portions of these groups bear strong resemblance to ordinary therapy groups.

Counseling Duration

The duration of a man's counseling varies from one program to another. One New York program provides only 6 sessions in an "educational workshop" format (Frank & Houghton, 1982). A Minneapolis program offers 32 group sessions of assaultive men's group counseling as well as a variety of other services (Stordeur, 1983). Programs differ not only in length, but in philosophical assumptions, subjects covered, and techniques used. Hence comparing programs is complex if not unrealistic.

Our emphasis on violence as learned behavior leads us to believe that eradicating violence and replacing it with alternatives is a long process. Twenty or more years of learning cannot be altered overnight. Herein lies a problem; few agencies or communities have the resources to provide one or more years of counseling to each man. Seen in this light, most programs fall short of an ideal and simply provide what they can. Knowing that there is an ever-present discrepancy between men's needs and service availability, we chose to offer group counseling, specifically aimed at stopping the violence, that has ranged from 24 to 32 sessions. When possible, we now choose the higher figure.

Group Structure

Although we feel most comfortable with eight to ten clients in a group, we typically attempt to begin a group with ten to twelve clients. This is to account for men who drop out at some point along the way. Assuming that the majority of men are not mandated to attend, it is usually necessary to perform assessments on twenty or more men to produce the desired ten to twelve clients. Of the number of men assessed, some will not be appropriate for the group and are refused, some will openly decline an offer to enter, and some who are accepted will not show up. From our experience, we think it is advisable to have approximately fifteen men assessed and appearing to be committed to enter a group. Normally, ten to twelve will follow through and attend the first session.

Although it is possible to operate a group with more than twelve men, it makes it difficult to develop a trusting atmosphere, to give each man the attention he needs, and to finish on time. When beginning with fewer than ten men, the group may stabilize (after dropouts) at a number that decreases the program's efficiency. Sometimes it is advantageous to postpone the beginning of a group until a sufficient number of men are available.

We operate closed groups, meaning that we will not accept new members into the group after the second session. Excepting dropouts, men who begin this group finish with the same group of men 32 sessions later. Although many programs choose to operate open groups and admit new members at any point, we favor the closed group option for two reasons. The first is that it is difficult to integrate new members when considerable amounts of material have been taught prior to their entry. It would involve prohibitive amounts of group time to help new members catch up to the group. Alternatively, it could consume hours of a counselor's time in individual sessions to do the same thing. Attempting to do this would be analogous to admitting students to a course that was half finished. A second reason for running closed groups is that admitting new members after a certain point of group development destabilizes the group. The men will be familiar with each other and a bond of trust will be growing. The addition of new faces can interfere with this process by temporarily reducing spontaneity, comfort, and self-disclosure.

While closed groups have definite advantages over open ones, not all agencies are able to accomplish this. In locales where only one closed group is offered, men who miss an entry deadline could wait several months for the next group. This is no small consideration. In light of the dangerousness of battering, a shorter waiting period may better protect the battered woman. Closed groups may also be unrealistic for programs in small, rural communities, for there may never be enough men at one time to start a closed group of sufficient size. Such communities frequently use open groups and gradually build up their membership.

Our groups meet for approximately two and one-half hours each session.[1] The first two-thirds of the session consists of structured activity, such as teaching a skill, facilitating discussion, or involving the men in an exercise. After a coffee break, the last one-third of the session is Sharing Time—a period in which any man can present an issue or seek help for a problem.

While it is possible to reverse the order by beginning with Sharing Time and then proceeding to structured activity, there are two reasons not to. It can be difficult to terminate Sharing Time in favor of other tasks if many men have problems to present or if there is a man in crisis. Additionally, a man may want to discuss material from the structured portion as it relates to himself during the Sharing Time that follows.

We have also experimented with the frequency of meetings. In one of the best arrangements, the group meets twice a week for the first 16 sessions and once a week for the remainder. One reason for this is that a 32-session group that meets only once a week takes a long time to complete. A more important reason is that the portion most concerned with imparting the skills to avoid abuse needs to be completed without delay.

Confidentiality and the Group

Most counseling relationships are private affairs; the flow of information from that relationship to outsiders is strictly regulated according to "right to know" rules. Almost always it is the client who determines who has a right to know this information. The flow of information in the reverse direction is not so stringently governed. Although it is normally necessary to secure a client's permission to seek information about him (e.g., contacting previous therapists), a therapist sometimes receives information volunteered by others. In everyday therapeutic relationships, therapists often feel uncomfortable receiving unsolicited information about their clients. The ethics and the consequences of using these data in counseling can be perturbing.

Counseling offenders requires the ability to enforce accountability. To aid in this, we have made some changes in the normal flow of information. Programs in which we have worked often have men's partners attending battered women's groups, either in the same agency or in another community service. In this situation we are sometimes informed by the woman's counselor, or the woman herself, of abusive behavior between group sessions. If the woman feels safe enough to allow us to use this information in the men's group, we will confront the man if he chooses not to

report it. There are other information channels we keep open. We
provide probation workers of court-mandated men with general
progress reports and specific reports on abuse or threats of abuse.
Child protection agencies are sometimes involved in a case and may
delay final disposition pending the outcome of treatment. We
sometimes provide them with progress reports. The end result of
this regular flow of information is that our groups are much less
confidential than other counseling endeavors.

Counselors should consider the effect of these practices on the
group's members prior to beginning a group. In every group we
have conducted, the first time we confront a man with accounts
of his abuse that he has chosen to conceal, the entire group seems
shocked. The man under scrutiny may feel angry and betrayed.
Similarly, a member may have strong reactions when he discovers
that his probation worker knows something that he discussed only
in group. For this reason, we strongly recommend that therapists
discuss the confidentiality policy with each man carefully during
the intake process and that each man sign a form indicating he
understands the policy. Therapists should address this issue again
in the first group session. If these policies are explicitly outlined and
explained as nonnegotiable conditions for participation in the
program, clients are more likely to accept them and less likely to
feel betrayed later.

Readers may wonder if these alterations of normal confidentiality
practices interfere with trust and openness in counseling. Some
men become guarded and suspicious, but, in our experience, they
soon regard these practices as normal. We do not see a harmful
effect. Men still disclose very sensitive information under these
conditions. Some men even seem motivated to disclose abuse
precisely because they do not know if the therapists have knowledge
of these events in advance of a group session. They prefer to take
the initiative in disclosing rather than be caught trying to conceal
abusive behavior. The effect is negative only when policy is
explained after the fact.

The Group Counselor

Leadership Style

Assaultive men are generally not self-reflective, self-disclosing,
or self-motivated. They are often highly anxious about relating to
others on the level called for in a counseling group (Ganley, 1981b).
They also employ defenses that are incompatible with addressing

the issue of battering. If the therapist waits for anxiety to disappear and for desirable behaviors to emerge, the group will likely flounder and men will drop out. For these reasons, a nondirective counseling style is inappropriate in these groups.

We agree with Ganley's (1981 b) recommendation that counselors adopt a directive leadership style that implies certain counselor behaviors. The directive counselor is actively involved in the group process. The counselor teaches not only through words but also by modeling or demonstrating skills. Interaction among members is facilitated through structured activities. Member participation is elicited by asking questions. The counselor assigns homework, follows up on assignments, and confronts individual men and the group on their resistance to changing thoughts and behavior. When appropriate, the counselor tells members what to do and what not to do. Furthermore, the counselor sets clear limits on behavior and enforces consequences for violation of those limits.

These examples describe someone who is a very central figure in the group. The term *authoritarian* may come to mind for some readers. This pejorative term suggests a leadership style emerging from a need to wield power over others, a rigid respect for hierarchical structures, and an inability to tolerate dissent. In recommending a directive style, we are not promoting authoritarianism. While the therapist definitely assumes the position of authority in the group, the directive style is not that of a martinet. Power for its own sake is not an issue here. The therapist is always respectful of group members' feelings and rights. While also being a caregiver, the therapist maintains control over the group so that it may do its work.

We believe the directive style is most needed in the earliest stage of the group. As time passes, the therapist can relax this stance as the group gradually develops some measure of constructive autonomy. Group norms emerge, a mutual aid process is born, and members slowly learn to do with each other what the therapist modeled in the earlier sessions.

Guarding the Time

These groups use a highly structured format because the psychoeducational approach necessitates covering much material in a relatively short time. If the group is planned as having a maximum number of sessions, we guarantee that a counselor will feel pressured to keep to the schedule. Many situations will seem to conspire against accomplishing what was planned.

The reader should not underestimate the difficulty of keeping to a schedule. In any single session, a number of factors can wreak havoc. Members may arrive late. Men who have difficulty understanding material may necessitate longer periods of discussion than planned. One or more men may be in crisis while several men may be required to report abuse; a sense of urgency often develops around competing demands. It is common for novice therapists to have difficulty covering the agenda. Consequently, we advise meticulous planning of time in each session. As the therapist becomes more familiar with the material, he or she will develop the sense of timing needed to cover it all

Two and a half hours of group time can easily be consumed by attending to men's individual problems. Therapists trying to keep to a schedule are often deeply affected by the men's needfulness. There can be a temptation to postpone the educational portion of the group for that session so that men can be cared for. This is a common dilemma. Because we recognize that counselors often have to make judgment calls, we are not inflexible on this issue. However, we must caution the reader that the postponing of educational material in a batterers' group might be tempting fate. In particular, the first half of the program contains anger control skills that must be learned rapidly. A particular skill scheduled for a certain night may help prevent an assault.

Group Cofacilitation

A result of adopting a directive style in these groups is that the therapist assumes much responsibility. Attending to the resistance to change, maintaining awareness of group process, and the demands of teaching are a huge load for one person. Those who facilitate these groups alone often perceive the competing demands as an impediment to doing their best work. For this reason, having a cofacilitator, though not absolutely essential, is of tremendous value.

Cofacilitation allows one person to be engaged with the group while the other observes specific interactions and the group's process. It fends off therapist exhaustion by allowing for periodic switching of roles. Additionally, dealing with difficult clients may be easier because the differing characteristics of each therapist offer a greater variety of constructive responses. Often the best qualities in each therapist are complementary and result in effective teamwork. Furthermore, for between-session problem solving, two therapists are better than one.

Counselor's Gender

The subject of the gender of group counselors for batterers raises some interesting issues. Although there seems to be little in the professional literature concerning the gender of therapists in this specific field, most programs face this question sooner or later. The basic question is, Does it matter whether it is men or women who conduct groups for batterers? In some quarters, this is a controversial question.

In conversations with some counselors who believe men alone should do this work, we have heard a number of reasons used to support their position. There is the politically based argument according to which men have an obligation to assume the responsibility of working with other men in stopping violence against women. This frees women to work with victims. Other reasons stem from beliefs about the positive impact of male facilitators in a batterers' group. Some believe it is advantageous when two male therapists model cooperation rather than traditional male competitive behavior. Some believe that the presence of men alone will facilitate disclosures of violence in general and sexual violence in particular, while the presence of a woman would inhibit these. Also stated is the belief that an all-male group forces batterers to learn to accept nurturing from other men and thereby decreases their dependency on women.

While these are intriguing notions, we know women who have successfully conducted these groups with other women. In conversations with those who use mixed-gender teams and seem less concerned with the gender of therapists, we have been told that many North American programs seem no less successful with this approach to abuser counseling. They believe that abusers who practice traditional sex-role stereotyping may benefit from observing women demonstrating strength and equality in relationships with male co-workers. Finally, from a pragmatic perspective, many communities with scarce resources are lucky to find knowledgeable staff to run such programs. Whether these are men or women may seem a luxurious worry in many locales.

While the issue of counselor gender is certainly important in services to female victims of male abuse, we do not believe gender is a key issue in counseling male abusers. Consequently, we do not support exclusionary policies or practices based on gender as some service providers do. A therapist's personal suitability, skillfulness, and general awareness of issues surrounding violence against women seem much more relevant to working well in this area.

Women Counselors in a Batterers' Group

While it is difficult to justify claims that either gender has an advantage in counseling batterers, the presence of women counselors will affect the group in some manner. The effect is neither good nor bad; it will simply be different from groups operated solely by men. A woman entering a group should consider in advance how she will respond to a variety of special issues.

A first issue arises from batterers' curiosities and fears. The group may want to know if the woman has been battered. Beneath this question may be the hidden concern that she will be angry, harsh, and rejecting of abusers if she has been battered. We believe honesty is probably the best policy in this situation. Although she can reassure men that she is there to help, not to punish, the group will ultimately be reassured by how she behaves rather than by a statement of intent.

If she has been battered and this is revealed to the men, the group may attempt to treat her as an expert victim. They may routinely turn to her for the "battered woman's point of view." While this is not necessarily negative, it can become so if the members become preoccupied with victims and lose the focus on themselves. If she feels constrained because her role is too narrowly defined by the group, the cotherapist team should find a way to broaden her role.

A second issue stems from male sex-role conditioning. We believe this conditioning predisposes men to seek nurturing from women. Consequently, the group may attempt to relate to a woman cotherapist exclusively as the nurturer (mother). If she feels pulled in this direction, some planning with the cofacilitator may be necessary to ensure that her role is not narrowly defined for her by the group. For example, in establishing a balance that is not based on sex-role stereotypes, cofacilitators may determine that the man should consciously adopt more than his share of nurturing tasks while the woman assumes more of the directive or confrontive tasks.

Finally, and most important, a man and a woman should be conscious of how they share power between themselves in the group. Assaultive men should witness a working relationship characterized by mutual respect and equality instead of male domination. In a situation where a female trainee works with an experienced male counselor, the difference in experience and the educational aspect of the relationship should be announced to the men. This will provide an accurate interpretation for whatever degree of uncertainty and dependency she may exhibit.

Keeping Records

While there are more interesting aspects to our work, our roles also involve keeping reasonably accurate client files. Although most agencies have specific policies in this regard, we find that many counselors are irregular in making entries to client files. In extreme cases, a therapist may work with a client for months and not make entries until closing the case. We have good reasons for emphasizing this mundane activity. The first stems from our experiences in court. In our work with court-mandated abusers, we sometimes have to terminate their involvement with the program. When termination carries the threat of other penalties, some men will ask for a hearing. Whenever this has happened, we have felt relieved to have reliable, detailed records when called to testify. Second, all of our clients are more susceptible to court involvement because of assaultive behavior. Counselors may be called to court in the event of an assault, a homicide, or a suicide. Finally, detailed records are absolutely precious if the program is ever accused of negligence or malpractice.

Detailed record keeping should extend beyond assessment and individual sessions. We make file entries after every group session for every man. We record his presence or absence, his contributions to the group, and the substance of any personal issues he raises. We are particularly diligent in recording exact details of his abuse accounts or threats of violence. We also note the specifics of any intervention we make.

Communication with Men's Partners

Disclosing Information

Seeking collateral information during assessment involves interviewing the man's partner whenever possible for general information and, in particular, violence data. We believe that, once communication channels between abuser counselors and victims have been established, they should be kept open. One reason for this is that men's partners should have access to reliable information about abuser counseling. Abusers too often lie or distort information about their participation in counseling during disputes with their partners. In misrepresenting the program as supporting them in their behavior, they perpetrate a form of psychological abuse. To help reduce the impact of this tactic, the program should develop a method of imparting the following information to victims:

(1) The program views the man as entirely responsible for his behavior. His partner and children are never responsible for his actions.

(2) The man's partner is in no way responsible for his success or lack thereof in abuser counseling. He is entirely responsible for utilizing information from counseling. Additionally, the program will never attempt to intervene in her life through him. For instance, he cannot correctly claim that she must cooperate with him in some manner when he uses a particular anger control method.

(3) The abuser counseling program content is outlined for her.

(4) Counselors will never take the man's side if he describes a domestic dispute in the group (although other men often do).

(5) Abuser counseling is not a "cure" for a man's abuse. Indeed, he is not diseased. It is no more than an opportunity for him to learn how to handle himself nonabusively in relationships. Whether he learns the material and uses it in his relationships is entirely up to him. This also means the fact of finishing a group program is no guarantee that he will be nonabusive.

(6) The program unequivocally supports her and her children's rights to be free from all kinds of abuse. We will provide as much information as we can on alternatives to enduring abuse or will facilitate a referral for this purpose to an appropriate service.

(7) If the agency offers battered women's counseling, the woman is informed of this and given the opportunity to attend counseling.

This information can be given to women in two ways, each of which will depend on how the agency's abuse services are organized. The first option is that each female partner can be invited to attend an individual session with a counselor. A second, more efficient option is possible when the agency operates battered women's group counseling and a significant number of women have partners attending abuser counseling. A counselor from one of the abuser groups can be invited to a women's group session to give this information and answer questions.

Receiving Information

A second reason to maintain communication with men's partners is that counselors can periodically receive valuable information from partners. Because some men will continue to conceal their abusive behavior while enrolled in a group, we believe it advantageous to invite women to inform men's counselors of abuse. If a man decides not to report an incident of abuse to the group, counselors can confront the man with the incident and with his decision to conceal it. Counselors should never disclose a woman's report without her permission and without being confident that she has made reasonable efforts to protect herself from retaliatory abuse. To facilitate safety when women report abuse, those agencies offering group counseling for battered women should ensure that there are reliable communication channels between men's and women's counselors.

We cannot overstate the counselor's and the agency's obligation to be cautious and vigilant in attempting to ensure the safety of anyone who is a potential victim of violence. We believe this goal should always have the highest priority. As the counseling of abusers becomes more routine within an agency, and as the program proceeds, therapists may slip into complacency. We urge therapists to avoid complacency by beginning service to each abuser with the assumption that he constitutes a lethal danger to others and to himself.

Issues Related to the Use of Groups

Group Heterogeneity

Most of our groups include a broad spectrum of men. They come from a variety of socioeconomic groups, racial and cultural backgrounds, and educational levels. We have had white, upper-middle-class businessmen, teachers, and bank officials blending with the poor, the working class, new immigrants, the physically disabled, and the learning disabled. We have had educational levels ranging from fourth grade to the master's degree in a single group. In groups with a high number of court-mandated men, we have had a higher than usual number of disadvantaged clients; these groups seem to attract more frequent attention from the criminal justice system than groups made up of the more privileged elements of society. In groups containing larger numbers of voluntary clients, the privileged sectors of society have greater representation. Although each group is unique, all groups are heterogeneous.

The heterogeneity of these groups is a challenge for therapists. The program's educational facet, with its emphasis on skill development and attitude change, must be planned and conducted with foresight and care. Members differ in their abilities to read, to abstract, and to follow through with homework assignments. Written material must be selected not only for its content but also for its coherence to a range of members. Unlike a university course, in which written materials are primary learning tools, most written materials in batterers' groups should be supplementary rather than essential to the program score requirements. Because we never assume that an abuser will gain essential knowledge from handouts, we always cover core material through lecture or discussion during group. Counselors following this strategy will minimize a class bias in their approach and be more certain that all members are learning the core material.

When we discover a man having difficulty with the material, we take remedial action. For example, one of us conducted a group in which a blind man attended. His lack of sight sometimes interfered with his remembering lecture material. We remedied this in two ways. Whenever possible, we avoided overreliance on visual aids. When a chart was presented, we took pains to explain the content and assure he understood. Second, we recorded lecture and discussion portions of each group so he could review them between sessions. Programs serving the blind might consider translating written material into braille. In other instances, when we have had semiliterate men in group, we have scheduled occasional individual sessions to be certain they are learning the material. When we present material, we watch the group and look for signs of losing some men's attention. Glazed looks or staring at the walls or out the windows might suggest that therapists should change their language or strive to be more concrete.

Group Members Perpetrating Violence

Clients in batterers' counseling will experience failure from time to time. Particularly in the early portions of a group, it is common for a member to come to a session and report that he was violent. While this behavior contravenes a group rule, we expect this to happen. While a prohibition against violence is obviously necessary, it is unrealistic to expect total compliance. The learning of nonviolent alternatives is a gradual process. Initially there will be awkwardness with new skills and mistakes will abound.

Two of our colleagues began their first group by making any violent behavior automatic grounds for expulsion from the group. Very early in the group, a man was expelled. Thereafter, not a single man spoke about current violence. Instead, the group pretended everything was fine while undercurrents of hostility and suspicion made for a truly miserable experience. Although the counselors abandoned this policy, the group in question remained suspicious of the program.

Although some degree of failure is normal, readers should not infer that we indulge violence. Backsliding in a batterers' group is cause for grave concern. The counselor should feel compelled to reserve time in the group session for any man who has been violent between sessions. At the beginning of each session, we determine if this is an issue by asking the group if any man has been violent or abusive since the last meeting. If anyone has, he is directed to share this with the group and be the first to speak during Sharing Time.

We have several objectives in mind when dealing with a violence report in the group:

(1) The man should relate his version of the events.

(2) When details are lacking (as they often are), the counselor should seek more information.

(3) The therapist should respond to apparent inconsistencies, distortions, blaming of the victim, and other defenses that are obstacles to the man's accepting responsibility for his behavior and understanding his mistakes.

(4) The counselor should help the man understand as precisely as possible the points where he made mistakes.

(5) The man should be helped to see specific alternatives to abuse in that situation.

(6) Input from group members should he encouraged.

(7) If possible, those alternatives should he role-played.

Failures provide opportunities. Each man will learn some of his best lessons from a detailed analysis in group of how he and other group members went wrong. Additionally, each man will be in a better position to avoid abuse in similar future situations if mistakes and nonabusive alternatives are highlighted.

There will be situations where a member has difficulty choosing nonviolence, but counselors are reluctant to expel him from the group because he seems motivated and cooperative. Before expelling the man, counselors can try a less drastic course. For instance, they can offer the man the option of separating from his partner for the duration of the program as a condition of remaining in the group.

Toleration of mistakes, however, does have a limit. When a man is repeatedly violent and this is not remedied by counselor or group input, his continuation in the group becomes an issue. Whether it is an unwillingness to stop his abuse, inability to learn, or habitual defiance of authority, a batterer should not remain in counseling if he is not changing. Counseling may not be the appropriate response to his violence.

Contact Among Clients Outside of Counseling

To address batterers' isolation and to structure support for non-violence between sessions, group members should be encouraged to rely on each other outside the group. Usually, counselors feel reassured about the developing mutual-aid function of the group when relationships between men grow. While this is generally a positive development, it is occasionally destructive. Subgroups of men may form and coalesce around viewpoints that erode the purpose of the group. These subgroups may meet informally over coffee either before or after a group. Favorite activities include criticism of the counselors and program content, and group support for sexist and violent behavior. This may be signaled by a subgroup spokesperson seeming to speak for a number of men by using the pronoun *we*. For instance, "Last week after group we were talking about what you said and we disagreed with . . ." might be a sign that bonding is a problem instead of an asset.

We have encountered very rare, but horrific instances of subgrouping in which the subgroup's behavior was intolerable. In one case, two men formed a subgroup in which they sexually abused the partner of one of the men. While therapists might be tempted to censure the behavior and continue working with the perpetrators, this crosses all reasonable boundaries for toleration of backsliding. When a member uses the group as a recruiting ground from which he can form abusive teams, it is insufferable. As a remedy, we favor ejection of this subgroup. To keep these members in the group is more than a mockery of the program—it communicates an ambiguous message to other members about behavioral limits. We terminate members for other, less harmful transgressions than this.

Requests for Advocacy

Occasionally a member will ask a counselor to intercede on his behalf in difficulties he has with other people and systems. Most often it is a request that the therapist be his advocate. Some common requests are listed below:

(1) With an imminent court appearance on assault charges, he asks the counselor to write a positive personal reference that will help his defense.

(2) He asks the counselor to provide a positive personal reference to help in his child custody dispute.

(3) Fearing the loss of his children, he asks the counselor to intervene in a child protection investigation.

(4) Anxious about losing his partner, he asks the therapist to convince her to remain in the relationship.

Counselors would be justified in feeling discomfort about any of these requests. All of them represent a man's attempts to escape the consequences of his abuse. Counselors complying with these requests may be in an untenable position. While working in a program that ought to support protection of victims and the ability for appropriate social systems to censure abuse, they adopt a stance that undermines these goals. They compromise their own integrity and that of the program. Each of these requests also puts counselors in the position of seeming to support the promise that the batterer will not be abusive in the future. This prediction is impossible to make with any accuracy.

One way to curtail these requests is to formulate a policy outlining what kind of support can be offered to abusers. This policy can be announced to men at intake or at the first group meeting. One kind of representation we believe is appropriate is a written or verbal statement indicating that the man has enrolled in the program, and what portion of the program he has completed thus far. Additionally, an explicit, carefully worded statement concerning outcome separates the fact of completion from an assumption that the man has achieved nonviolence. For example, we commonly qualify letters confirming program participation with this statement: "Completion of this program does not guarantee that the man will not be abusive. Completion indicates that he is equipped with the skills to stop his abuse. The decision to use these skills is entirely his."

We do not mean to dismiss all forms of advocacy. There is another kind of advocacy that is both appropriate and helpful. Since many abusers come to counseling facing criminal charges, separation and divorce, the need to find new living quarters, and other serious stressors, they can benefit from help in negotiating strange systems and from receiving accurate information. This kind of assistance can reduce stress levels and indirectly help prevent abuse triggered by these stressors. Ideally, this as an adjunct service that is not part of the therapist's role. Specialized advocates operating out of a separate program within the agency or from a different social service may be helpful with these matters.

Use of Anger in the Group

The subject material in a batterers' group, the use of confrontation, and the stress associated with struggle periodically elicit powerful reactions from the men. If the arousal were labeled appropriately, it might more often be recognized and expressed as feelings of vulnerability, sadness, helplessness, or confusion. More often these are transformed into anger and there is the danger, however slight, that an angry member will be violent in the group.

Interestingly, this occurrence in the group replicates his problem in his home. The same escalation mechanism is played out except that, in the group, it is less likely to result in him choosing violence.

Although violence in these groups is exceedingly rare, extreme anger can be frightening to therapists and clients. While an angry outburst can be a means of personal tension reduction, it can also have an external function; anger can be used as a conscious or unconscious attempt to control the behavior of others. People the man perceives as threatening will likely alter their behavior if they feel intimidated by his anger. A group in which one or more men frighten others will lack the safe atmosphere necessary for effective counseling. It is the counselor's job to halt such a development.

When a man becomes excessively angry in group, he should be reminded that he is capable of temporarily leaving the room to "cool down." Leaving is not an offense and it is not a sign that he is a coward fleeing confrontation. Instead, it is a sign of self-control. It demonstrates that he is able to make a choice between staying in the situation and being abusive and leaving to avoid abuse.

Concluding Remarks

In this chapter we have made a case for considering batterers' groups as a special phenomenon. While all counseling groups are similar in some ways, groups differ in other ways as a result of the focal problem, any special characteristics of clients having this problem, and the choice of interventions. We have described issues or concerns that may be peculiar to abuser groups, and in so doing, have sought to prepare readers to plan their own group programs.

For therapists beginning this work, we want to stress the need for careful, thorough preparation. Of course, clinical readiness, in terms of counseling skills and group content, is necessary, but clinical preparation is not enough. Though detailed coverage is beyond our scope, we remind the reader of another realm in which it is important to prepare for assaultive men's group counseling. That is the level of program readiness in its relationships with other community services. The professional education and networking aspect of beginning this service should not be neglected. It is important that links among services be established, that respective responsibilities be negotiated, and that other services have a general understanding of the program's approach to men who batter.

Note

[1] The group structure and many of the group rules were adapted from those employed by the Domestic Abuse Project, Minneapolis.

Section *VIII*

Special Areas of Correctional Treatment

In section three, we noted that classification models have been introduced, tested, and refined to assist probation and parole officers and treatment personnel in supervising the client population more effectively. These models are based on the risk presented to the community by the offender, but they also contain components which examine the needs of the offender with regard to job opportunities, medical treatment, substance abuse counseling, mental health assessment, and other factors. The risk element is always the overriding consideration in determining classification as to the need for maximum, medium, or minimum intervention of the officer and counselor in the offender's life. The needs of the offenders, although apparent and identified, become a secondary consideration.

In this section, we will consider counseling for various types of offenders whose needs are so paramount that they must be included in any treatment plan. These include substance abusers, sex offenders, the mentally ill, retarded offenders, and older inmates.

The largest single category of offenders is made up of those involved in substance abuse. For example, in January, 1993, it was found that there were 200,980 inmates in state and federal correctional facilities who were receiving some type of drug treatment.[1] If the number of substance abusers being treated in non-institutional settings is also considered, the total is substantially higher. The manner in which these offenders were involved with drugs determines to a large extent whether any form of treatment is needed. Obviously, those who were distributors of drugs, particularly the top-level dealers, may not have been abusers themselves, while many of the lower level distributors are likely to have been abusers.

A typology of drug-involved offenders was developed by Marcia R. Chaiken and Bruce D. Johnson. They described the characteristics and problems presented by occasional users, persons who sell small amounts of drugs, and those who frequently sell drugs or sell them in large amounts, as shown in Table 1.

The same authors also summarized the types of drug dealers, their level of drug use, and the types of offenses they commit, as shown in Table 2.

The treatment strategies for substance abusers involve four major modalities, according to George DeLeon. These include detoxification, methadone maintenance, drug-free outpatient settings, and residential therapeutic communities (116). According to DeLeon, detoxification is usually conducted in an inpatient hospital setting for a period of one to three weeks, while methadone maintenance is generally pursued on an outpatient basis, after an initial detoxification period. Those involved in treatment in drug-free outpatient settings are targets for individual and group counseling, while those treated in therapeutic communities are counseled in residential settings.[2] The success level with a particular modality is obviously dependent upon a number of factors, including the length and level of substance abuse and the motivation of the offender to change his or her behavior.

Selection nineteen, "The Effects of Intensive Treatment on Reducing the Criminal Recidivism of Addicted Offenders," by G. Field, describes intensive treatment in an institutional setting and presents an evaluation of the programs provided for male and female inmates in the New York State correctional system. Selection twenty, "Reviewing the 'TASC' (Treatment Alternatives to Street Crime) Experience," by James A. Inciardi and Duane C. McBride, illustrates how the "TASC" program can provide a bridge between the drug treatment community and the criminal justice system. The underlying premise of "TASC" is that drug use offenders can be treated more effectively and less expensively in the community than in an institutional setting. It is also noted that the key to the program's success is maintaining open communications and referral possibilities between criminal justice agencies and community social service agencies. Selection twenty-one, "Counseling Alcoholic Clients," was developed as a treatment handbook for those who are involved in such counseling. It provides step-by-step guidelines and instructions on how best to conduct such interventions.

Table 1 Types of drug-involved offenders

Type of offender	Typical drug use	Typical problems	Contact with justice system
Occasional users			
Adolescents	Light to moderate or single-substance, such as alcohol, marijuana, or combination use.	Driving under influence; truancy, early sexual activity; smoking.	None to little.
Adults	Light to moderate use of single substances such as hallucinogens, tranquilizers, alcohol, marijuana, cocaine, or combination use.	Driving under influence; lowered work productivity.	None to little.
Persons who sell small amounts of drugs			
Adolescents	Moderate use of alcohol and multiple types of drugs.	Same as adolescent occasional user; also, some poor school performance; some other minor illegal activity.	Minimal juvenile justice contact.
Adults	Moderate use of alcohol and multiple types of drugs including cocaine.	Same as adult occasional user.	None to little.
Persons who sell drugs frequently or in large amounts			
Adolescents	Moderate to heavy use of multiple drugs including cocaine.	Many involved in range of illegal activities including violent crimes; depends on subtype (see Table 2).	Dependent on subtype (see Table 2).
Adults	Moderate to heavy use of multiple drugs including heroin and cocaine.	Depends on subtype (see Table 2).	Dependent on subtype (see Table 2).

Source: Marcia R. Chaiken and Bruce D. Johnson, "Characteristics of Different Types of Drug-Involved Offenders," Washington, D.C.: U.S. Department of Justice: 4–5.

Table 2 Types of dealers who sell drugs frequently or in large amounts

Type of dealer	Typical drug use	Typical problems	Contact with justice system
Top-level dealers			
Adults (only)	None to heavy use of multiple types of drugs.	Major distribution of drugs; some other white-collar crime such as money laundering.	Low to minimal.
Lesser predatory			
Adolescents	Moderate to heavy drug use; some addiction; heroin and cocaine use.	Assaults; range of property crimes; poor school performance.	Low to moderate contact with juvenile or adult justice system.
Adult men	Moderate to heavy drug use; some addiction; heroin and cocaine use.	Burglary and other property crimes; many drug sales; irregular employment; moderate to high social instability.	Low to high contact with criminal justice system.
Adult women	Moderate to heavy drug use; some addiction; heroin and cocaine use.	Prostitution; theft; many drug sales; addicted babies; AIDS babies; high-risk children.	Low to moderate contact with criminal justice system.
Drug-involved violent predatory offenders: The "losers"			
Adolescents	Heavy use of multiple drugs; often addiction to heroin or cocaine.	Commit many crimes in periods of heaviest drug use including robberies; high rates of school dropout; problems likely to continue as adults.	High contact with both juvenile and adult criminal justice system.
Adults	Heavy use of multiple drugs; often addiction to heroin or cocaine.	Commit many crimes in periods of heaviest drug use including robberies; major source of income from criminal activity; low-status roles in drug hierarchy.	High contact with criminal justice system; high incarceration.

(continued)

(Table 2 continued)

Types of dealers who sell drugs frequently or in large amounts

Type of dealer	Typical drug use	Typical problems	Contact with justice system
The "winners"			
Adolescents	Frequent use of multiple drugs; less frequent addiction to heroin and cocaine	Commit many crimes; major source of income from criminal activity; take midlevel role in drug distribution to both adolescents and adults.	Minimal; low incarceration record.
Adults	Frequent use of multiple drugs; less frequent addiction to heroin and cocaine.	Commit many crimes; major source of income from criminal activity; take midlevel role in drug distribution to both adolescents and adults.	Minimal; low incarceration record.
Smugglers	None to high.	Provide pipelines of small to large quantities of drugs and money.	Variable contact.

Source: Marcia R. Chaiken and Bruce D. Johnson, "Characteristics of Different Types of Drug-Involved Offenders," Washington, D.C.: U.S. Department of Justice: 6–8.

Sex offenders also present unique difficulties for correctional counseling and treatment. Many of the disorders and dysfunctions experienced by such offenders are too complex to be treated adequately by counselors who are not specifically trained to work with them. When the offender's family is closely involved, as is frequently the case, the need for family therapy may be readily apparent, but not easily accomplished. Although treatment for severe disorders, such as sexual psychopathy, is now mandated in many states, sex offenders involved in less dramatic behavior may not be offered the treatment quality or intensity needed to prevent recurrence of their offenses.

Selections twenty-two and twenty-three describe the varieties and types of treatment currently available and the roles offenders' family members can play in the treatment process.

"In Treatment of the Sex Offender," DeZolt and Kratcoski note that many activities formerly defined as improper sexual behavior subject to criminal penalties are no longer liable for criminal prosecution. State codes have been revised to define specifically sexual offenses, and most of these can be categorized as sexual assaults and displays. In this article, particular attention is given to the characteristics of sexual psychopaths, rapist typologies, and typologies of sex abusers of children. The legality of treatment such as psychosurgery-castration or drug therapy is reviewed, and counseling therapies of various types are described. Institutional and community group treatment of sex offenders is discussed and evaluated, and characteristics of therapies which have been effective with sex offenders are described. Group therapy which follows the technique known as rational-emotive therapy is discussed.

In "Northwest Treatment Associates, Seattle, Washington, A Comprehensive, Community-Based Evaluation and Treatment Program for Adult Sex Offenders," Knopp describes specific techniques used to retrain adult sex offenders to deal with and overcome their tendencies toward unacceptable sexual behavior and to develop appropriate sexuality. Guided group work is utilized, and behavioral treatment, geared to the specific needs of individual offenders, is included. Impulse control techniques which can be applied by the offenders themselves and stronger intrusive types of controls which may need to be applied are described. The roles that offenders' spouses and victim counselors can play in changing the behavior of adult sex offenders are given detailed consideration.

Another important area of correctional treatment involves mentally ill or retarded offenders. Public Law 94-142, the Education of All Handicapped Act of 1975, has important implications for both juvenile and adult correctional treatment, because it mandates free and appropriate education for all handicapped persons 21 years of age or younger. Handicapped individuals are defined in the law as mentally retarded, hard of hearing, deaf, orthopedically impaired, visually handicapped, seriously emotionally disturbed, or learning disabled requiring special education and related services.[3] Because of the age range covered in the law's mandate, many offenders incarcerated in adult institutions, as well as those held in juvenile facilities, are required to receive services.

Handling mentally ill and mentally retarded offenders in institutional settings is difficult for many reasons. They must be protected from victimization by the general inmate population, and they require additional attention to help them understand the significance of what is happening to them and reduce the traumatic effects of the incarceration experience. Community treatment, whenever possible, would seem to be the most appropriate setting for retarded or mentally ill offenders who do not pose a threat to the community.

Selection twenty-four, "A Helping Hand: Reaching Out to the Mentally Ill," by Burkhead, Carter, and Smith, describes a program at Central Prison in Raleigh, North Carolina, that is designed for inmates who have been diagnosed as having serious mental disorders and are also considered dangerous and difficult to manage. The authors note that nationwide, the estimates of the number of inmates who have serious mental problems range from 10 to 25%. Generally, such inmates who are incarcerated can function quite well, provided that they take their prescribed medication. After release, however, these same individuals are often quickly reinstitutionalized, because prison out-patient services are non-existent or inadequate to meet their needs. The program described in this selection is designed to prepare mentally ill incarcerated offenders for re-entry into the community. Strong emphasis is placed on the importance of taking prescribed medication and developing the educational, social, and life skills needed for them to function in the community.

Selection twenty-five, "Habilitation of the Retarded Offender in Cuyahoga County," by Bowker and Schweid, describes a program for mentally retarded offenders who were under the supervision of a county probation department. These offenders were supervised at different levels, based on scores obtained from a standardized risk and needs instrument used by the department. The probation officers assigned to the mentally retarded offender unit were specifically trained to recognize the needs of these offenders and provide appropriate support as well as individual and group counseling.

In the final selection of this section, "Older Inmates: Special

Programming Concerns," the author describes the needs of incarcerated older offenders and explores the question of whether older inmates should be housed with the general prison population or placed in separate units. It is noted that health problems are an overriding concern. In addition, special recreational or social activities may need to be developed, if the older inmates are to make satisfactory adjustments.

Notes

[1] George M. Camp and Camille Graham Camp, *The Corrections Yearbook 1993.* (South Salem, New York: Criminal Justice Institute, 1993): 65.

[2] George DeLeon, "Treatment Strategies," in James A. Inciardi, ed., *Handbook of Drug Control in the United States.* (New York: Greenwood Press, 1990): 115–138.

[3] C. Michael Nelson, Robert B. Rutherford, Jr., and Bruce I. Wolford, "Handicapped Offenders Meeting Education Needs," *Corrections Today*, 47 (5) (August 1985): 32.

TABLE 1

Source: Marcia R. Chaiken and Bruce D. Johnson, "Characteristics of Different Types of Drug-Involved Offenders," Washington, D.C.: U.S. Department of Justice: 4–5.

TABLE 2

Source: Marcia R. Chaiken and Bruce D. Johnson, "Characteristics of Different Types of Drug-Involved Offenders," Washington, D.C.: U.S. Department of Justice: 6–8.

19

The Effects of Intensive Treatment on Reducing the Criminal Recidivism of Addicted Offenders

Gary Field

The impact of substance abuse on crime is profound. A 1974 Census Bureau study of 10,400 state prison inmates found that 39 percent of robberies, 47 percent of burglaries, 53 percent of homicides, and 61 percent of assaults were reported to be committed under the influence of alcohol (Roizen and Schneberk, 1977). A survey of 13,700 state prison inmates in 1986 found that 35 percent of inmates admitted using drugs at the time of their crime and that 43 percent reported using drugs on a daily or nearly daily basis within the month prior to committing the crime that led to their incarceration (Innes, 1988). According to a recent National Institute of Justice report on its Drug Use Forecasting System, 73 percent of male arrestees in 11 U.S. cities who voluntarily submitted urine samples tested positive for drugs (Wish, 1988). Individuals with established patterns of both drug abuse and criminality have been shown in studies in Baltimore and Los Angeles to have increases or reductions in criminality with corresponding increases or reductions in drug abuse (Gropper, 1984).

Effective treatment for addicted offenders can be part of the solution to the problems of reducing crime and turning offenders into productive citizens. The most effective treatment programs reported to date with addicted offenders have been intensive treatment programs of considerable duration that are designed as

Source: *Federal Probation*, 53(4) (December 1989): 51–56.

modified therapeutic communities. The Stay N' Out Program in New York (Wexler, Falkin, and Lipton, 1988) and the Cornerstone Program in Oregon (Field, 1985) have both reported substantial reductions in criminality by successfully treated inmates.

This article presents a followup study on reduction of criminal recidivism by inmates treated in the Cornerstone Program. It also presents methods for measuring changes in criminal activity over time that may be helpful to other researchers.

Program Description

The Cornerstone Program has been described extensively elsewhere (Field, 1985). The program is a 32-bed modified therapeutic community located on the grounds of Oregon State Hospital in Salem. Successful residents typically spend the last 10 to 12 months of their sentence in the program, are paroled directly from the program, and are provided with 6 months of aftercare/transitional services while they are on parole. Cornerstone is coeducational, but most of the program participants (95 percent) are male. The following treatment principles summarize the program's characteristics and style:

1. *Separating inmates from the general population.* State prison inmate cultures are antithetical to the environment that is needed for successful treatment. Inmate cultures value lying to authority, glamorizing drugs and crime, and an atmosphere of negativeness and nihilism. Hope for personal change has a difficult time surviving in this kind of context. The cultures of successful treatment programs center around peer support and pressure for personal change, rather than around an obsession with "fighting the system." The social environment of treatment is as important as the information presented.

2. *Clearly understood rules and consequences.* Inmates need to clearly understand what is not acceptable and what the consequences are for breaking rules. Inmates do better at managing themselves and learning new information or behaviors when clear limits are established and held to.

3. *A clear system for earning freedom a little at a time.* It is important for addicted inmates to earn privileges for behavior that supports their recovery and to lose privileges when they begin to relapse into criminal thinking or the early stages of addictive behavior. By this process, systematically managed, the inmates can best learn that they have control over their own lives.

4. *Formal participation by inmates in running the program.* Inmates need to feel "ownership" in the program to fully invest themselves in it. Responsibility for self is a key treatment goal, and inmates need to be given as much responsibility as they can manage.

5. *Intensive treatment.* Addicted inmates need a wide variety of treatment interventions as well as a full weekly schedule. Aside from these people needing habilitation or rehabilitation to a number of life skills, they do best when their days are fully structured and the demand level of what is expected of them is kept high.

6. *Treating addiction and criminality.* Both of these problems exist in the drug dependent inmate. If both are not simultaneously addressed, the untreated one will consistently undermine the other. That is, a criminal lifestyle tends to yield alcohol/drug abuse, and alcohol/drug abuse tends to yield a resurgence of criminal activity.

7. *Transition and aftercare.* Successful treatment needs to focus on helping the inmate prepare to return to the community. Community involvement should continuously expand during the course of treatment. Once paroled and released from residential treatment, parolees need continuing interventions to assure they are following their recovery plan.

Program Population

Table 1 lists some of the critical demographic characteristics of the Cornerstone population during this study. The data in table 1 are taken from the January 1984 population and are typical. The average number of adult felony convictions, average total time incarcerated as an adult, and the average age of first substance abuse document the extreme chronicity of criminality and substance abuse on this group.

Evaluation Design and Method

This is a criminal recidivism study done retrospectively using the Law Enforcement Data System (LEDS), a computerized telecommunications and information system for Oregon law enforcement agencies that lists criminal activity for Oregon and accesses the Federal criminal justice data system.

The 220 unduplicated program discharges from January 1, 1983, through December 31, 1985, were sorted into four experimental

---

Table 1

Characteristics of the Cornerstone Treatment
Population Given in Group Means

Age	31.0
Age first arrest	13.6
No. of adult arrests	13.7
No. of adult felony convictions	6.9
Total time incarcerated as an adult	7 yrs., 7 mo.
Age of first substance abuse	12.5

---

groups: Program graduates (Grads) (N = 43); non-graduates who spent more than 6 months in the program (NG > 6 mo.) (N = 43); non-graduates who spent more than 2, but less than 6 months in the program (NG 2–6 mo.) (N = 58); and non-graduates who spent between 1 day and 2 months in the program (NG 0–2 mo.) (N = 65). Six of the potential NG 2–6 mo. group had to be eliminated from the study because four were deceased and two had failed to be released from prison since leaving the program. Five potential NG 0–2 mo. group members had to be eliminated because they were in the program so short a time (less than 1 day) that adequate identifying information had not been collected by program staff. The remaining 209 subjects were distributed throughout the four experimental groups as noted above.

The dependent variables in this study were arrests, convictions, and prison incarcerations. Arrests were tabulated as "arrest events" as reported in LEDS. These "arrest events" may have included multiple arrest "counts" at the time of arrest. Similarly, convictions were tabulated on the basis of each "arrest event" and did not consider convictions on multiple "counts." Therefore, only one tabulated conviction was possible for each "arrest event." Arrests and convictions included all recorded arrests and convictions: misdemeanors as well as felonies. County jail time actually spent (as opposed to suspended sentences) exceeding 6 months (more than 179 days) on a conviction was counted as equivalent to a state prison incarceration. County jail time of less than 6 months actual duration, alone with fines and probation, were considered as convictions without prison incarceration.

In the first part of the study, absence of any arrests, convictions, and prison time for 3 years after the beginning of parole was compared across all four experimental groups.

In the second part of the study, rates of arrest, conviction, and prison incarceration were compared across the groups for a "3-year" interval after parole and for two "3-year" intervals before incarceration for the offense that led them to the Cornerstone Program. The "3-year" intervals are actually "36-month at-risk intervals," because each of these time periods included a complete 36 months without incarceration time. So if, for example, after 12 months into an interval an individual was incarcerated for 4 months, the actual interval would be extended for 4 months (from 36 to 40). This method creates a full 36-month "at-risk" time interval of study and is a more accurate measure of frequency of criminal activity.

Two problems were encountered with the rate study. Some subjects had not spent sufficient time out of prison since entering treatment (at least 1 year) to have achieved measurable rates of arrest, conviction, and incarceration and had to be dropped from the second part of the study. Other subjects were too young to have had at least three complete years of non-incarcerated time since their 18th birthday. These people were also dropped from the second part of the study. Final numbers for the second part of the study were as follows:

Grads: 43 of 43—100 percent
NG > 6 mo.:   37 of 43—86 percent (1 subject too young, 5 had not been out of prison one full year post treatment)
NG 2–6 mo.:   41 of 58—71 percent (5 too young, 12 not out of prison one full year post treatment)
NG 0–2 mo.:   37 of 65—57 percent (9 too young, 16 not out of prison one full year post treatment, 3 still on escape status)

In each of the experimental groups, about 75 percent of the subjects were old enough to have at least 6 years of "at risk" community time. These are the subjects that were used to gather the data for the 3- to 6-year pre-treatment interval.

Results and Discussion

Table 2 presents absence of arrests, convictions, and prison incarcerations for 3 years after parole for Cornerstone graduates (average stay of 11 months), non-graduates who stayed in the program for more than 6 months (180 days), non-graduates who stayed 2–6 months (60–179 days), and non-graduates who stayed less than 60 days.

Table 2

Rates of Avoiding any Arrest, Conviction, or Prison Time for 3 Years After Parole for Cornerstone Participants From 1983 through 1985

	No Arrests	No Convictions	No Prison Time
Program Graduates (Grads) (N = 43)	37%	51%	74%
Non-Grads who completed at least 6 months (NG > 6 mo.) (N = 43)	21%	28%	37%
Non-Grads who completed 2 through 5 months (NG 2–6 mo.) (N = 58)	12%	24%	33%
Non-Grads who left before 60 days (NG 0–2 mo.) (N = 65)	8%	11%	15%

The order of success as measured by no arrests, convictions, or prison incarcerations in table 2 consistently favors time in treatment. Program graduates consistently do much better than the nongraduate groups, even though many graduates continue to have some contact with the criminal justice system. The two "partial treatment" groups (2 to 6 months and more than 6 months groups) show results that are similar to one another, but again consistently favor time in treatment. The less than 60 day group comes close to being a no-treatment comparison group. The poor results shown by this group without significant treatment are noteworthy.

The consistent ordering of success rates and the constancy of relative success between the groups across arrest, conviction, and prison incarceration data suggest that any of these three dependent variables are an equally usable outcome measure.

Because simple presence or absence of arrests, convictions, or prison incarceration over a lengthy time period hides much of the criminal activity that is occurring, it was decided to measure rates of each of these outcome variables. By comparing post treatment rates with pre-treatment rates, it was hoped that a clearer picture of the effects of intensive treatment would be gained.

Figure 1 presents arrest rates for the four experimental groups

Figure 1

Group Mean Arrest Rates Over Pre and Post
Treatment 3-year "At Risk" Intervals

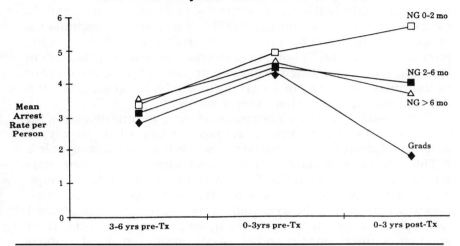

Figure 2

Group Mean Conviction Rates Over Pre and Post
Treatment 3-year "At Risk" Intervals

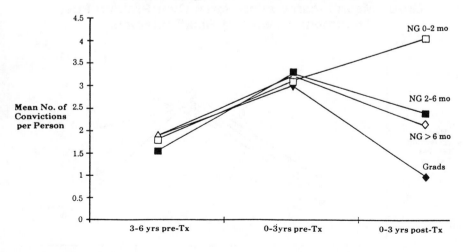

over pre and post treatment 3-year at risk intervals. Figures 2 and 3 present the same data for convictions and prison incarcerations.

The data presented in all three figures are remarkably similar. In each case the four experimental groups are virtually identical at the pre-treatment intervals. In each case all four groups show accelerating criminal activity across the pretreatment intervals. In each case the relatively untreated (NG 0–2 mo.) show a continuation of accelerating criminal activity following their brief exposure to intensive treatment. Finally, in each case the treated groups show a decrease in criminal activity that correlates positively with time in treatment. As in the first part of the study, program graduates do significantly better than nongraduates.

These results present a more thorough and graphic display of the effects of intensive treatment on reducing criminal recidivism among addicted offenders than was possible from the data in table 2.

This study has two obvious limitations. First, subject motivation for change is not controlled for across the experimental groups. Some of the positive effects may have occurred because those inmates who stayed in treatment were simply more motivated, rather than the results being due to specific treatment effects. There are two counterbalances to this study limitation. First, subject motivation at some point is always a part of successful treatment, and second, no motivational differences between the groups are apparent in the pre-treatment data in figures 1, 2, or 3.

Figure 3

Group Mean Incarceration Rates Over Pre and Post Treatment 3-year "At Risk" Intervals

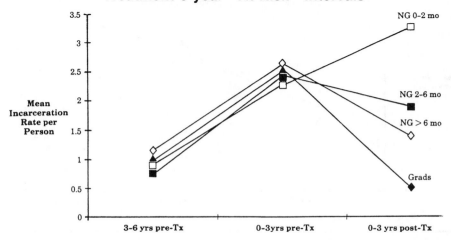

The second limitation in this study occurred because the complexity and requirements of measuring pre and post treatment arrest, conviction, and prison incarceration rates necessitated that significant numbers of subjects in some of the groups be dropped from part of the study. The question is what biasing factor occurred by dropping those subjects from the second part of the study? That question cannot be answered with any certainty at this time. However, the subjects who were dropped from the non-graduate groups were dropped largely because they had recidivated at such a rate that they had not yet achieved 12 full months of community time in the 3 to 5 years since their parole. These individuals, therefore, probably represent the "worst cases" in the non-graduate groups and would likely push the arrest, conviction, and incarceration rates at post treatment even further apart, creating even more separation between the experimental groups.

Conclusions

The following conclusions are drawn from the results of this study.

1. The Cornerstone Program continues to demonstrate a positive effect on decreasing the criminal activity of program participants.
2. Addicted offenders who receive little or no treatment show an accelerating pattern of criminal activity over time.
3. Time in treatment in an intensive treatment program for addicted offenders correlates positively with measured decreases in criminal activity.
4. Many successfully treated addicted recidivist offenders continue to show at least some involvement with the criminal justice system after treatment, even though their involvement is reduced.
5. Arrests, convictions, or prison incarcerations all seem to be approximately equally accurate measures of criminal activity.

References

Innes, C. *Drug Use and Crime*, Bureau of Justice Statistics Bulletin, Washington, DC: Superintendent of Documents, U.S. Government Printing Office, 1986.

Field, G. "The Cornerstone Program: A Client Outcome Study." *Federal Probation, 49*, 1985, 50–55.

Gropper, B. *Probing the Links Between Drugs and Crime*, National Institute of Justice Reports. Washington, DC: Superintendent of Documents, U.S. Government Printing Office, 1984.

Roizen, J. and Schneberk, D. "Alcohol and Crime." In M. Aarens, T. Cameron, J. Roizen, R. Roizen, R. Room, D. Schneberk, and D. Wingard (eds.), *Alcohol, Casualties and Crime*. Berkeley: Social Research Group, 1977.

Wexler, H., Falkin, A., and Lipton, D. *A Model Prison Rehabilitation Program: An Evaluation of the Stay N' Out Therapeutic Community*, a final report to the National Institute of Drug Abuse by Narcotic and Drug Research, Inc., 1988.

Wish, E. *Drug Use Forecasting (DUF): April-June 1988 Data*, National Institute of Justice report, 1988.

20

Reviewing the 'TASC' (Treatment Alternatives to Street Crime) Experience

James A. Inciardi
Duane C. McBride

Introduction

Epidemiological data on the prevalence and incidence of drug use in the United States suggest two alternative and somewhat distinct patterns of involvement with cocaine, heroin, and other illegal substances. For the general population of the U.S., that is, the more stable "at home" residents who do not live on the streets or in jails, prisons, or other institutions, existing data indicate that illegal drug use peaked around 1980, with noticeable declines in subsequent years (Johnston et al., 1989, p. 62). Data from the National Household Survey, sponsored by the National Institute on Drug Abuse, indicate similar trends among adolescents and young adults (Clayton et al., 1988, p. 23).

During the same period, however, research focusing on criminal offenders has documented *increased* drug use. Data from the Drug Use Forecasting (DUF) project indicate that in most of the 20 monitored metropolitan areas, at least 40 percent of sampled felony arrestees tested positive for cocaine. Results in some urban areas— New York, Miami, Philadelphia, Washington, D.C., and Los

From *Journal of Crime and Justice*, 15(1) (1992): 45–61. Reprinted by permission of Anderson Publishing Co., Cincinnati.

Angeles—suggest that the arrestee population is virtually saturated with cocaine. In these cities, more than 60% of sampled felony arrestees test positive for cocaine and at least 75% test positive for at least one illegal drug (Drug Use Forecasting, 1990). As such, it would appear that street criminals have dramatically increased their drug use, and most of this increase involves cocaine—a drug clearly associated with violent aggressive behavior (Inciardi, 1989; Inciardi & McBride, 1989; McBride & Swartz, 1990). These trends have created interest in new treatment initiatives for drug-abusing criminal offenders, especially since they have occurred simultaneously with three other factors bolstering interest in the wider use of drug abuse treatment.

First, prison populations grew dramatically during the 1980s. Second, HIV and AIDS among drug users, and particularly among intravenous drug users, is a large and growing problem. Third, the one helpful development is that recent research has convincingly documented the success of compulsory and coerced treatment for drug-involved offenders (DeLeon, 1988; Hubbard et al., 1989; Leukefeld & Tims, 1988; Platt et al., 1988). These evaluation studies demonstrate that the key variable most related to success in treatment is *length of stay*, and that those coerced into treatment remain longer than voluntary commitments.

These assorted trends suggest a strong need to reexamine the existing linkages between drug abuse treatment services and the criminal justice system, to expand those linkages that have demonstrated effectiveness, and to establish additional connections. The most obvious starting place for such a consideration is the Treatment Alternatives to Street Crime (TASC) program. This national initiative has had as its objectives for some two decades the identification, treatment referral, and monitoring of drug involved offenders.

The Roots of TASC

The earliest roots of TASC can be traced to the recognition that incarceration was not the solution to addiction. Although drug abuse researchers and clinicians had been arguing this for decades (see Lindesmith, 1965; Musto, 1973; Nyswander, 1956), the point had never been addressed in terms of "due process of law." This came in the aftermath of *Robinson v. California* (370 U.S. 660) decided by the United States Supreme Court in 1962. Although *Robinson* dealt primarily with the Eighth Amendment ban against cruel and unusual punishment, its lesser known holding was that a state could establish a program of compulsory treatment for narcotic addiction. Further, the High Court ruled that such treatment could involve periods of involuntary confinement, with penal sanctions for failure to comply with compulsory treatment procedures.

At the same time, government officials as well as the public at large had come to view much of the criminal involvement of narcotics users as driven by economics—the necessity to obtain money to buy drugs. It was believed that if drug dependency could be treated, then drug-related crime could be reduced, or even eliminated. As a result, in 1966 Congress passed the Narcotic Addict Rehabilitation Act (28 U.S.C. §§2901–2903), which permitted federal judges and prison officials to refer narcotic-addicted probationers and inmates to the Lexington, Kentucky and Fort Worth, Texas treatment facilities as an alternative to traditional incarceration. Release from these facilities was followed by mandatory aftercare supervision. This program also permitted voluntary self-commitments by motivated addicts (Weissman, 1978, p. 122). As such, the Narcotic Addict Rehabilitation Act established statutory authority for involuntary inpatient and out-patient treatment and for treatment in lieu of prosecution.

The Nixon administration's "war on drugs" built on these earlier trends with the passage of the Comprehensive Drug Abuse Prevention and Control Act of 1970 (see Uelman & Haddox, 1989, Sec. 3.2). More commonly known as the Controlled Substances Act, the legislation authorized, among other things, the diversion of drug-involved offenders from the criminal justice system into drug abuse treatment programs. Similar legislation was being passed in a number of state jurisdictions. At both the federal and state levels, the focus of diversion was on non-violent first offenders, particularly those whose crimes were associated with heroin addiction.

By 1972, then, several statutory linkages between the criminal justice and drug abuse treatment systems had been created. It was at this point that the Treatment Alternatives to Street Crime (TASC) program was created by President Nixon's Special Action Office for Drug Abuse Prevention. A national program designed to divert drug-involved offenders into appropriate community-based treatment programs, TASC was funded by the Law Enforcement Assistance Administration (LEAA) and the National Institute of Mental Health (NIMH). The first programs became operational in Wilmington, Delaware and Philadelphia, Pennsylvania by the close of 1972 (Perlman & Jaszi, 1976, p. 2).

The Empirical and Theoretical Foundations of TASC

TASC evolved within the context of the prevailing theoretical, clinical, and empirical understandings of the relationship between drug use and crime. TASC attempted to develop an effective alternative to the incarceration of drug-using criminal offenders. At a practical level, the implementation of TASC in 1972 was based on three fundamental assumptions:

1. that in various parts of the United States, and particularly in major metropolitan areas, there are serious problems of drug abuse and addiction that both directly and indirectly affect significant portions of the population.
2. that coupled with drug addiction is a cycle of crime, arrest, incarceration, release and more often than not, continued drug dependence that inhibits efforts to "rehabilitate" the addict and safeguard the community.
3. that the frequency of this contact between the addict and the criminal justice system provides viable opportunities for the introduction of treatment alternatives to street crime (*TASC Guidelines*, 1973, p. 1).

In addition, there were the costs of incarceration. During the years immediately prior to the implementation of TASC, court diversion was seen as one possible cost-effective alternative. The reasons were several:

1. unarguably, diversion would be far cheaper than incarceration;
2. if diversion occurred at the *pretrial* stage, it could reduce court workload and related staff and processing costs;
3. diversion to supervised *treatment* served the dual purposes of avoiding the criminalization process while at the same time addressing the problems of drug use that led to crime; and,
4. because the programs to which individuals would be diverted were usually of shorter duration than prison sentences, societal reintegration would occur at a more rapid pace.

Diversion in general, and TASC in particular, was an outgrowth of these considerations (American Bar Association, 1975).

The Current Structure of TASC

To a very great extent, the roots of TASC can be traced not only to the Law Enforcement Assistance Administration (LEAA), but also to the President's Commission on Law Enforcement and Administration of Justice and the "war on crime" of the late 1960s and early 1970s. TASC was but one among the many initiatives. Well before the 1980s had begun, however, it was all too clear that the national war on crime had failed. The great LEAA experiment had not uncovered the secret to solving the crime problem. What it did show, though, was what *didn't* work to prevent crime: saturation patrolling, quicker police response times, advanced technology, and college education for law enforcement personnel. LEAA studies also served to deflate the optimistic notions about the rehabilitation of offenders, preventive detention, parole, and the death penalty as a deterrent (see Cronin et al., 1981). From its inception in 1969 through 1980, LEAA appropriations totaled almost $8 billion.

On April 15, 1982, LEAA was terminated, and the reasons were numerous. During its formative years, LEAA had struggled to reduce crime and to respond to changing congressional priorities while managing a rapidly expanding budget. But by the mid-1970s, as the crime rate kept accelerating and the criticisms of LEAA continued unabated, inflation-conscious presidents began submitting reduced budget requests for the agency. The major criticisms included mismanagement in grant programs, inefficiency and ineffectiveness, inconsistent objectives, and lack of standards and criteria for evaluating program effectiveness. With inflation reaching new heights at the beginning of the 1980s, LEAA was given only minimal funding for 1981. And finally, there was the "new federalism"—that emergent political consensus that reduced federal involvement in direct services to local communities. With the demise of LEAA in 1982, federal funding was completely withdrawn from TASC. At the time, TASC were operating at 130 sites in 39 different states and Puerto Rico (Bureau of Justice Assistance, 1988, p. 5).

Despite the demise of LEAA, TASC has not only endured, but has done so rather well. Immediately after the withdrawal of federal funding, some 100 programs in 18 jurisdictions were able to secure local support. The Justice Assistance Act of 1984 revived federal endorsement and some fiscal support for TASC. This legislation authorized a criminal justice block grant program to encourage local and state government support of programs deemed highly likely to improve the efficiency and effectiveness of the criminal justice system and to address the problems of drug-related crime and the drug-involved offender. TASC was one of 11 programs certified by the Bureau of Justice Assistance (BJA) for immediate eligibility in this initiative (Bureau of Justice Assistance, 1988, p. 7).

An immediate outgrowth of BJA involvement was the development of TASC parameters, elements, and standards of performance. The product of this endeavor was the TASC "Ten Critical Elements"—the specific steps necessary for a successful

TASC program effort. As such, the critical elements are guidelines—benchmarks as to what is necessary for an appropriately functioning TASC program. Moreover, these elements provided a generic framework for assessing both organizational and operational performance standards, afforded the TASC field the benefit of standardization across sites, and provided a common language upon which to bring a very complex program concept into an operational program framework. The "critical elements" include the following:

Organizational Elements

The first five elements are those administrative systems and services that must be in place before client services can be effective.

1. A broad base of support within the justice system with a protocol for continued and effective communication.
2. A broad base of support within the treatment system with a protocol for continued and effective communication.
3. An independent TASC unit with a designated administrator.
4. Policies and procedures for required staff training.
5. A data collection system to be used in program management and evaluation.

Operational Elements

The last five elements circumscribe client service and supervision.

6. A number of agreed-upon offender basic eligibility criteria.
7. Procedures for the identification of eligible offenders that stress early justice and treatment intervention.
8. Documented procedures for assessment and referral.
9. Documented policies and procedures for random urinalysis and other physical tests.
10. Procedures for offender monitoring that include criteria for success/failure, required frequency of contact, schedule of reporting and notification of termination to the justice system.

TASC Evaluations

The TASC experience has been a positive one. Evaluations since 1976 have repeatedly suggested TASC to be highly productive in 1) identifying populations of drug-involved offenders in great need of treatment, 2) assessing the nature and extent of their drug use patterns and specific treatment needs, 3) effectively referring drug-involved offenders to treatment, 4) serving as a linkage between the criminal justice and treatment systems, and 5) providing constructive client identification and monitoring services for the courts, probation, and other segments of the criminal justice system. Perhaps most importantly, evaluation data indicate that TASC-referred clients remain longer in treatment than non-TASC clients, and as a result, have better post-treatment success (see Collins et al., 1982a, 1982b; Collins & Allison, 1983; Hubbard et al., 1988; System Sciences, 1979; Toborg et al., 1976; Tyon, 1988). Finally, it would appear that through the development and application of its "ten critical elements," TASC has been strengthened both conceptually and operationally. Specifically, a study conducted by the National Association of State Alcohol and Drug Abuse Directors during 1988 and 1989 found that programs with all of the critical elements in place were more likely to be functioning smoothly, with limited fallout in program linkages and TASC assessment and monitoring activities (NASADAD, 1989). As such, it would appear that TASC is poised for expansion in the 1990s.

The Future of TASC

TASC will likely expand in the 1990s, primarily because it has been recognized by the National Institute on Drug Abuse (Brown, 1991; Inciardi & McBride, 1991), the Office of Treatment Improvement (Scheckel, 1991), and the Office of National Drug Control Policy (Lewis, 1991) as a viable program for reducing drug use and related crime. Furthermore, a national evaluation of TASC was funded by the National Institute on Drug Abuse in late 1991, and federal block grant funds have been earmarked for TASC.

In any future expansion of TASC, a basic design issue must be addressed. The "critical elements" require that a TASC program be an independent entity—structurally autonomous and self-governing so that it can objectively serve the needs of the client, the treatment system, and the criminal justice system. Both the Tyon (1988) and NASADAD (1989) studies, however, found that TASC exists in a variety of structural modes, many of which depart significantly from the critical element model. Some TASC programs, for example, in addition to case management, also provide treatment services. Others are located in probation departments. Such arrangements have evolved as the result of the lack of a stable funding source for TASC, and the consequent survival structures that have evolved. This would suggest that

TASC is in need of more secure and consistent funding sources if it is to maintain its role as an independent bridge between the criminal justice and treatment systems.

Going further, there are some very good reasons for expanding TASC. First, there is the changing relationship between drug use and crime. Whereas the drug-involved offender in the early days of TASC was a primary heroin user with a long history of property offenses, the drug-related crime of the 1990s has become more violent (McBride & Swartz, 1990). Moreover, Drug Use Forecasting data document that instead of there being a statistical relationship between drugs and crime, it would appear that there is a saturation of drugs in offender populations (Drug Use Forecasting, 1990).

Research during the 1980s on the specific effects of drug use on patterns of criminal behavior suggests that TASC can play a significant role in reducing drug-related street crime. In a series of excellent research analyses by John C. Ball of the Addiction Research Center and David N. Nurco of the University of Maryland, it was demonstrated that during drug-*free* days, members of drug subcultures are far less likely to commit crimes than during their drug-*using* days (Ball et al., 1983; Nurco et al., 1985). TASC has been effective in identifying, assessing, referring, and monitoring members of such populations.

Second, the 1980s war on drugs and the citizen demands for more drug arrests and convictions have tended to exacerbate the already crowded conditions in court settings throughout the country. The wider use of TASC as a mechanism of pretrial diversion or in conjunction with probation could serve to alleviate portions of this crowding.

Third, there is the link between drug use and HIV/AIDS. In 1987, the United States Public Health Service estimated that there were some 900,000 regular (at least weekly) IV drug users across the nation, 25% of whom were already infected with HIV-1 (CDC, 1987). At the same time, the Centers for Disease Control was reporting that IV drug users represented 24% of all reported AIDS cases in the United States. By late 1991, they had come to represent 28% of known cases in the U.S. (CDC, 1991).

The ready acquisition and transmission of HIV-1 and AIDS among IV drug users is the result of needle-sharing practices, combined with the presence of "cofactors." These cofactors include any behavioral practices or microbiological agents that facilitate the transmission of HIV. For intravenous heroin, cocaine, and amphetamine users, the blood transmission of HIV-1 may occur as a result of using or sharing contaminated drug injection paraphernalia. Prior to injection, for the purpose of making the user's drug of choice go into solution, it is dissolved in tap water that is heated in a "cooker"—typically a bottle cap or spoon. "Cookers," which are often shared by IV drug users and are rarely cleaned properly, represent potential reservoirs for HIV-1.

The injection process poses even greater contamination risks. "Booting" is a risk/cofactor of considerable significance, since the practice increases the amount of residual blood left in drug paraphernalia. Booting involves the aspiration of venous blood back into a syringe for the purpose of mixing the drug with blood, while the needle remains inserted in the vein. The mixed blood/drug solution is then injected back into the vein. Most IV drug users believe that this "premixing" enhances a drug's effects. Since IV users often share needles and syringes, particularly if they are administering the drugs in "shooting galleries"—places where users gather to take drugs—booting increases the probability that traces of HIV from an infected user will remain in a syringe to be passed on to the next user. And finally, genital sores and infections from other viruses have also been found to be cofactors (Quinn et al., 1988), and because of their lifestyles, IV drug users are rather well-known as a population that hosts a wide spectrum of micro-organisms (Des Jarlais et al., 1987; Geelhoed, 1984; Pace et al., 1974; Young, 1973).

An additional risk factor in the AIDS/IV drug connection is prostitution. There is an extensive body of literature offering a strong empirical basis for the notion that prostitution is a major means of economic support for IV-drug-using women (James, 1976; Rosenbaum, 1981). Moreover, it is well established that there is a high incidence of prostitution among women IV-drug users (Goldstein, 1979; Inciardi, 1986). As such, the IV-drug-using prostitute is not only at high risk for contracting HIV-1, but for transmitting it as well (Castro et al., 1988; Chaisson et al., 1987; Newmeyer, 1987). And furthermore, the transmission of HIV-1 infection has likely been increased through the recent phenomenon of trading sex for crack (Inciardi, 1989b).

Drug users, in addition to being the second highest risk group for HIV-1 and AIDS, also represent a population that appears difficult to impact with routine AIDS prevention messages. The potential for HIV-1 acquisition and transmission from infected paraphernalia and "unsafe" sex is likely known to most drug users. Yet most are accustomed to risking death (through overdose or the violence-prone nature of the illegal drug marketplace) and disease (hepatitis and other infections) on a daily basis, and these generally fail to eliminate their drug-taking behaviors. Thus, for a drug user who risks disease and death on a daily basis, warnings that needle sharing or unsafe sex may facilitate an infection that could cause death perhaps five or more years down the road have little meaning.

As such, the more appropriate risk reduction strategy would be drug abuse treatment, as facilitated through TASC programming.

There is also considerable evidence that the criminal justice system is more likely to come into contact with injecting drug users that are at higher risk for HIV infection than the general drug-using population. Analysis of data from over 60 cities demonstrated that intravenous drug users who had spent the most time incarcerated injected drugs with greater frequency, were more likely to rent needles, and were less likely to clean their needles than those with little or no incarceration time (Inciardi et al., 1992).

Fourth, given the demands in recent years for *more* prison sentences and *longer* prison sentences for convicted felons, the American penitentiary system is faced with a situation of massive crowding. And considering that perhaps half or more of all prison inmates are incarcerated as a result of drug use, an ideal area for TASC expansion is the parole setting.

The ideal parole/TASC venture would be a joint effort between a jurisdiction's department of correction, parole authority, and the single state agency that oversees the provision of drug abuse treatment services. Although one might consider such a venture as fraught with overlap and the problems of dual supervision, TASC can be structured to both enhance and complement parole supervision in a number of ways.

1. In the area of *pre-parole screening*, TASC assists the institutional correctional system in its role as a specialist in the identification and assessment of drug-involved offenders.
2. In the area of *service delivery*, TASC offers advantages for both corrections and parole. TASC case managers specialize in developing and implementing aftercare plans for drug-involved offenders. In addition to drug abuse treatment, TASC provides urine monitoring, employment advocacy, client referral to other segments of the local human service delivery network, and follow-up. As such, treatment and support services can be offered within a "clinical" rather than a "correctional" setting.
3. In the area of *clinical efficacy*, the literature suggests that TASC would represent an effective adjunct to parole. In this regard, a variety of research efforts have documented that: a) the key variable most related to successful outcome in drug treatment is *length of stay in treatment*; and, b) clients coerced into treatment tend to stay longer than those admitted voluntarily (Hubbard et al., 1989; Leukefeld & Tims, 1988). The TASC model is a variety of coerced treatment, and as noted earlier, has been proven effective in retaining clients in treatment.

4. In the area of *alleviating prison crowding*, TASC can assist in two ways. First, by relying on a TASC recommendation for treatment, scarce treatment slots will be allocated to those drug users most in need of, and responsive to, treatment. An accurate assessment of client need will increase the chances of success in treatment while reducing the chances of relapse and future criminal behavior, arrest, and incarceration. Second, TASC aids the parolee in successfully completing his/her term of supervision. Periodic urine tests, site visits, and case conferences tend to become a useful deterrent fostering program compliance.

Fifth, and finally, there is the matter of TASC programming within the context of work release. Temporary release from prison as well as partial incarceration in transitional facilities and halfway houses have a notable history in American corrections. Their justification draws upon a variety of theoretical and empirical traditions that emphasize the importance of maintaining significant, nondeviant roles outside the prison community (McBride, 1990, p. 706). Participating in a temporary release or halfway house program is considered to facilitate reintegration into the social and economic structures of the free community, thereby reducing the probability of recidivism. In addition, when the release also involves *work*, the offender is afforded opportunities to make restitution, pay fines, support dependents, obtain job training and experience, and perhaps make contacts for permanent employment upon eventual release from custody.

It would appear that TASC programming as an aspect of a structured work release program would be an ideal approach for prevention/intervention efforts for drug involved offenders. In addition to the benefits of TASC discussed earlier in this report, an even greater potential exists within the context of *TASC as a condition of work release*. The clinical efficacy of compulsory or coerced treatment has been noted. Compulsory treatment for drug abuse has been legally possible in the United States for almost three decades, and for almost as long a time researchers have been examining its relative effectiveness.

Although the benefits of coerced/compulsory treatment accrue within the context of any TASC arrangement, they would be intensified in a structured work release setting because of the closer supervision associated with halfway houses and temporary release centers.

Postscript

There is reasonable evidence that TASC is accomplishing most, if not all, of its objectives. Prior research suggests that it has been successful in identifying drug users in the criminal justice system, assessing their service needs, referring them to treatment services, and monitoring their progress. Further, a variety of follow-up efforts indicate that TASC clients stay in treatment longer and report less drug use than non-TASC clients. However, there have never been systematic, large-scale outcome or process evaluations of TASC. Previous studies tended to focus on but a few programs or included TASC clients as part of other evaluation studies. As such, further appraisal and assessment of the TASC experience appears warranted.

References

American Bar Association Commission on Correctional Facilities Services (1975). *Pre-trial Criminal Justice Intervention Technique and Action Programs*. Chicago: author.

Ball, J. C., J. W. Shaffer and D. N. Nurco (1983). "The Day-to-Day Criminality of Heroin Addicts in Baltimore—A Study in the Continuity of Offense Rates." *Drug and Alcohol Dependence* 12:119–142.

Bureau of Justice Assistance (1988). *Treatment Alternatives to Street Crime (Program Brief)*. Washington, DC: U.S. Department of Justice, Office of Justice Programs.

Brown, B. S. (1991). "Thoughts on TASC." Presentation at the TASC Executive Forum, Key West, FL.

Castro, K. G., S. Lieb, H. W. Jaffe, J. P. Narkunas, C. Calisher, T. Bush and J. J. Witte (1988). "Transmission of HIV in Belle Glade, Florida: Lessons for Other Communities in the United States." *Science* 239:193–197.

Centers for Disease Control (1987). "Human Immunodeficiency Virus Infection in the United States: A Review of Current Knowledge." *Morbidity and Mortality Weekly Report* 36(Supplement).

_____ (1991). *HIV/AIDS Surveillance*. Atlanta: author.

Chaisson, R. E., A. R. Moss, R. Onishi, D. Osmond and J. R. Carlson (1987). "Human Immunodeficiency Virus Infection in Heterosexual Intravenous Drug Users in San Francisco." *American Journal of Public Health* 77:169–172.

Clayton, R. R., H. L. Voss, L. LoSciuto, S. S. Martin, W. F. Skinner, C. Robbins and R. L. Santos (1988). *National Household Survey on Drug Abuse: Main Findings 1985*. National Institute on Drug Abuse. Washington, DC: U.S. Government Printing Office.

Collins, J. J. and M. Allison (1983). "Legal Coercion and Retention in Drug Abuse Treatment." *Hospital and Community Psychiatry* 34:1145–1149.

Collins, J. J., R. L. Hubbard, J. V. Rachal, E. R. Cavanaugh and S. G. Craddock (1982a). *Criminal Justice Clients in Drug Treatment.* Research Triangle Park, NC: Research Triangle Institute.

_____ (1982b). *Client Characteristics, Behaviors and In-treatment Outcomes: 1980 TOPS Admission Cohort.* Research Triangle Park, NC: Research Triangle Institute.

Cronin, T. E., T. Z. Cronin and M. E. Milakovich (1981). *U.S. v. Crime in the Streets.* Bloomington, IN: Indiana University Press.

DeLeon, G. (1988). "Legal Pressure in Therapeutic Communities." *Journal of Drug Issues* 18:625–640.

Des Jarlais, D. C., E. Wish, S. R. Friedman, R. Stoneburner, S. R. Yancovitz, D. Milsvan, W. El-Sadr, E. Brady and M. Cudrado (1987). "Intravenous Drug Use and the Heterosexual Transmission of the Human Immunodeficiency Virus: Current Trends in New York City." *New York State Journal of Medicine* 87:283–286.

Drug Use Forecasting (1990). *1988 Forecasting Report.* Washington, DC: National Institute of Justice.

Geelhoed, G. W. (1984). "The Addict's Angioaccess: Complications of Exotic Vascular Injection Sites." *New York State Journal of Medicine* 84:585–586.

Goldstein, P. J. (1981). *Prostitution and Drugs.* Lexington, MA: Lexington Books.

Hubbard, R. L., J. J. Collins, J. V. Rachal and E. R. Cavanaugh (1988). "The Criminal Justice Client in Drug Abuse Treatment." In C. G. Leukefeld and F. M. Tims (eds.), *Compulsory Treatment of Drug Abuse: Research and Clinical Practice.* Rockville, MD: National Institute on Drug Abuse.

Hubbard, R. L., M. E. Marsden, J. V. Rachel, H. J. Harwood, E. R. Cavanaugh and H. M. Ginzburg (1989). *Drug Abuse Treatment: A National Study of Effectiveness.* Chapel Hill, NC: University of North Carolina Press.

Inciardi, J. A. (1986). *The War on Drugs: Heroin, Cocaine, Crime, and Public Policy.* Palo Alto, CA: Mayfield Publishing Co.

_____ (1989a). "The Crack/Violence Connection Within a Population of Hard-Core Adolescent Offenders." *Technical Review on Drugs and Violence.* Rockville, MD: National Institute on Drug Abuse.

_____ (1989b). "Trading Sex for Crack Among Juvenile Drug Users." *Contemporary Drug Problems* 16:689–700.

_____ (1991). *Treatment Alternatives to Street Crime: History, Experiences, and Issues.* Rockville, MD: National Institute on Drug Abuse.

Inciardi, J. A. and D. C. McBride (1989). "Legalization: A High-Risk Alternative to the War on Drugs." *American Behavioral Scientist* 32:259–289.

Inciardi, J. A., J. J. Platt, D. C. McBride and S. Baxter (1992). "Injecting Drug Users, Incarceration, and HIV." In B. B. Brown (ed.), *The National AIDS Demonstration Research Program*. Westport, CT: Greenwood Press.

James, J. (1976). "Prostitution and Addiction." *Addictive Diseases: An International Journal* 2:601–618.

Johnston, L. D., P. M. O'Malley and J. G. Bachman (1989). *Drug Use, Drinking and Smoking: National Survey Results from High School, College, and Young Adult Populations 1975–1988*. National Institute on Drug Abuse. (DHHS Publication No. ADM 89–1638). Washington, DC: U.S. Government Printing Office.

Leukefeld, C. G. and F. M. Tims (eds.) (1988). *Compulsory Treatment of Drug Abuse: Research and Clinical Practice*. Rockville, MD: National Institute on Drug Abuse.

Lewis, L. (1991). "Thoughts on TASC." Presentation at the TASC Executive Forum, Key West, FL.

Lindesmith, A. R. (1965). *The Addict and the Law*. New York: Vintage Books.

McBride, D. C. (1990). "Temporary Release From Prison: Theory and Practice." In J. A. Inciardi (ed.), *Criminal Justice*. San Diego: Harcourt Brace Jovanovich.

McBride, D. C. and J. Swartz (1990). "Drugs and Violence." In R. Weisheit (ed.), *Drugs, Crime and the Criminal Justice System*. Cincinnati: Anderson Publishing Co.

Musto, D. F. (1973). *The American Disease: Origins of Narcotic Control*. New Haven, CT: Yale University Press.

National Association of State Alcohol and Drug Abuse Directors (1989). *Measuring TASC Program Compliance With Established TASC Critical Elements and Performance Standards* (unpublished). Washington, DC: author.

Newmeyer, J. A. (1987). "Role of the IV Drug User and the Secondary Spread of AIDS." *Street Pharmacologist* 11:1–2.

Nurco, D. N., J. C. Ball, J. W. Shaffer and T. F. Hanlon (1985). "The Criminality of Narcotic Addicts." *Journal of Nervous and Mental Disease* 173:94–102.

Nyswander, M. (1956). *The Drug Addict as a Patient*. New York: Grune and Stratton.

Pace, B. W., W. Dosher and I. B. Margolis (1984). "The Femoral Triangle: The Potential Death Trap for the Drug User." *New York State Journal of Medicine* 84:596–598.

Perlman, H. and P. Jaszi (1976). *Legal Issues in Addict Diversion*. Lexington, MA: Lexington Books.

Quinn, T. C., D. Glasser, R. Cannon, D. I. Matuszak, R. W. Dunning, R. L. Klein, C. Campbell, E. Israel, A. Fauci and E. W. Hook (1988). "Human Immunodeficiency Virus Infection Among Patients Attending Clinics for Sexually Transmitted Diseases." *New England Journal of Medicine* 318:197–203.

Rosenbaum, M. (1981). *Women on Heroin*. Brunswick, NJ: Rutgers University Press.

Scheckel, L. (1991). "Thoughts on TASC." Presentation at the TASC Executive Forum, Key West, FL.

System Sciences (1979). *Evaluation of Treatment Alternatives to Street Crime: National Evaluation Program, Phase II Report*. Washington, DC: National Institute of Law Enforcement and Criminal Justice.

TASC Guidelines (1973) Washington, DC: Law Enforcement Assistance Administration.

Toborg, M. A., D. R. Levin, R. H. Milkman and L. J. Center (1976). *Treatment Alternatives to Street Crime (TASC) Projects: National Evaluation Program, Phase 1 Summary Report*. Washington, DC: National Institute of Law Enforcement and Criminal Justice.

Tyon, L. P. (1988). *Final Report: Baseline Management and Assessment Data Project* (unpublished). Portland, OR: National Consortium of TASC Programs and the Bureau of Justice Assistance.

Uelman, G. F. and V. G. Haddox (1989). *Drug Abuse and the Law Sourcebook*. New York: Clark Boardman.

Weissman, J. C. (1978). *Drug Abuse: The Law and Treatment Alternatives*. Cincinnati: Anderson Publishing Co.

Young, A. W. (1973). "Skin Complications of Heroin Addiction: Bullous Impetigo." *New York State Journal of Medicine* 73:1681–1684.

21

Counseling Alcoholic Clients
A Microcounseling Approach to Basic Communication Skills

National Center for Alcohol Education

Overview of the Training Program

Counseling Alcoholic Clients: A Microcounseling Approach to Basic Communication Skills is designed to help practicing alcoholism counselors upgrade their abilities to use eight basic communication skills—attending paraphrasing, reflection of feeling, summarizing, probing, counselor self-disclosure, interpreting, and confrontation—in one-to-one interaction with a client. On completion of the program, participants will be able to:

- define each skill;
- recognize when each skill is being practiced effectively; and
- demonstrate the ability to use each skill and to integrate all skills appropriately and effectively in a simulated counseling situation.

The eight skills as defined in this program are:

Attending. Demonstration of the counselor's concern for and interest in the client by eye contact, body posture, and accurate verbal following.

Paraphrasing. A counselor statement that mirrors the client's statement in exact or similar wording.

Source: *Counseling Alcoholic Clients.* Washington, DC: U.S. Government Printing Office (1978).

Reflection of Feeling. The essence of the client's feelings, either stated or implied, as expressed by the counselor.

Summarizing. A brief review of the main points discussed in the session to insure continuity in a focused direction.

Probing. A counselor's response that directs the client's attention inward to help both parties examine the client's situation in greater depth.

Counselor Self-Disclosure. The counselor's sharing of his/her personal feelings, attitudes, opinions, and experiences for the benefit of the client.

Interpreting. Presenting the client with alternative ways of looking at his/her situation.

Confrontation. A counselor's statement or question intended to point out contradictions in the client's behavior and statements or to induce the client to face an issue the counselor feels the client is avoiding.

These skills can be classified under the broader headings of listening, processing, and feedback, three elements that comprise communication between two individuals. This program addresses communication from the counselor's perspective.

Listening is defined as receiving messages from a client by focusing attention on what the client is expressing, both verbally and nonverbally.

Processing is the complex series of events that take place within the counselor between his or her listening and responding to the client. Processing may include mentally cataloging data, categorizing, comparing, hypothesizing on significance, exploring implications, and selecting a response on the basis of the counselor's life experience, beliefs, knowledge, attitudes, feelings, self-acceptance, and other factors that influence judgment and performance.

Feedback is the verbal or nonverbal response that the counselor makes as a result of processing the information received from listening to a client.

Attending can be classified as a listening skill; the remaining seven can be classified as feedback, and as such, provide evidence of the quality of the listening and processing that precede the feedback. Processing skills are not covered explicitly in this course.

Paraphrasing, reflection of feeling, and summarizing are primarily the feedback skills that demonstrate to the client that the counselor is paying attention to what the client is expressing verbally and nonverbally. The counselor can also use these skills to help the client recognize and clarify his/her own understanding of what he/she says and the feelings related to these messages. The counselor applies the other four skills—probing, counselor self-disclosure, interpreting, and confrontation—to promote a mutual identification and understanding of the client's problems and ways to deal with those problems.

These eight skills constitute only a partial listing of skills that can be subsumed under the heading of listening, processing, and feedback. Other dimensions of processing include the counselor's knowledge about alcohol and alcoholism; specific treatment techniques (behavior shaping, modeling, goal setting, assertiveness training, relaxation training); various theories of psychological development and human behavior (Maslow, Glasser); self-awareness of feelings, values, and attitudes; and past personal and professional experiences. Other feedback skills include advising, information giving, directing, supporting, and structuring.

Mastery of all the listening, processing, and feedback skills and others such as maintaining confidentiality, record keeping, crisis intervention, and referral are necessary for effective counseling. Mastery of all these skills depends on both training and experience and requires the same focused attention that is being given to the eight basic communication skills in this program.

The eight skills covered in this training program were selected not only because of their fundamental nature but also because they represent the core of communication skills necessary for the largest number of counselor activities in one-to-one interaction. The major activities in one-to-one client interaction can be expressed in a variety of ways. In one such listing, the counselor:

1. Establishes and maintains a climate for counseling.
2. Interviews the client to gather case history information.
3. Provides safeguards for maintaining confidentiality and ethical standards.
4. Prepares and uses necessary client reports and records.
5. Seeks consultation on the client's case when needed.
6. Negotiates an individual treatment plan that is tailored to and acceptable to the client.
7. Plans strategies for intervening in the client's crisis situations outside the counseling setting.
8. Increases client understanding of the severity of the abuse by explaining the nature of alcoholism as an illness.
9. Informs and assists the client in establishing necessary contacts with community services.

10. Coordinates involvement of other resource persons in accordance with a mutually acceptable individual treatment plan for the client.
11. Increases the client's ability to recognize the possible need for counseling assistance in the future.
12. Prepares for and conducts after-care activities with the client.
13. Evaluates client progress and assists the client in doing the same so that individualized treatment plan goals can be redefined if necessary.
14. Given the client's expressed desire to discontinue participation in the treatment process, the counselor leads the client in a review of the accumulated gains of the treatment process.

By matching the eight skills and this list of activities, it is apparent that, regardless of what other skills may be required, attending, paraphrasing, reflection of feeling, and summarizing are essential to "establishing and maintaining a climate for counseling," which is fundamental to and part of all the other activities. In addition, probing, counselor self-disclosure, interpreting, and confrontation are critical to Activities 2, 6, 11, 12, 13, and 14 and are called for in certain phases of Activities 5, 7, 8, 9, and 10.

Other important aspects of the counselor/client interaction include the qualities of genuineness, warmth, empathy, immediacy, congruence, concreteness, and respect. These are not skills, but rather are conditions which the counselor can create partially through the use of the basic communication skills. These conditions are not addressed directly in the training program but will be discussed where appropriate.

In summary, this training program focuses on the presentation and practice of eight basic communication skills. These are not the only skills a counselor uses in the counseling situation; however, they are essential in establishing a foundation of client self-awareness and mutual understanding between client and counselor. Their use in a counseling session or in communicating with colleagues, family, and others will help the counselor to:

- listen effectively to find out what the other person's situation or problem is;
- let the other person know that the counselor is really hearing and understanding him/her;
- check out with the other person that the counselor's perception of the situation or problem is accurate; and
- assist the other person in his or her perception and understanding of self, situation, and possibilities for change.

The eight skills are presented one at a time. The idea is to break down the task of communicating into smaller units or skills. Participants learn and practice the individual skills separately and then practice integrating them.

The skills are presented in ten sessions, one for each of the eight skills and two integrating sessions. The first integrating session comes after the sessions presenting the first four skills and provides an opportunity to practice the integration of those four skills. The second integrating session comes after practicing the other four skills and provides the opportunity to practice the integration of all eight skills. The eight skill building sessions will follow the same basic pattern:

- an exercise illustrating one or more aspects of the skill;
- a description of the skill as it is used in this training program;
- a demonstration of each skill poorly and competently applied;
- skill practice in small groups; and
- a discussion of this skill in counseling clients with alcohol-related problems.

Feedback and Assumptions

Feedback

Feedback was described in the Overview as the verbal or nonverbal response that the counselor makes as a result of processing the information received from listening to the client. With the exception of attending, the communication skills covered in this program are classified as feedback.

Feedback used in another sense is an important aspect of this training program. During skill practice sessions, participants will take turns as counselor, client, and observer. Client and observer will give the counselor feedback dealing with his or her performance of the skill in question.

The definition of feedback as used in the context of the practice sessions is: telling the counselor what you (as observer) heard and saw as he or she practiced a particular skill, or what you (as client) felt in response to his or her practice of the skill.

The extent to which you give each other feedback and the quality of the feedback may be the critical factor in determining whether or not this workshop will be productive for you. For example, if in practice sessions neither the observers nor the clients give you significant feedback about your performance as a counselor, you might complete your training, having gone through all the prescribed activities, and have gained nothing. You may perhaps even take away a more distorted rather than a clearer picture of your capabilities. In addition being a recipient of feedback can help sharpen your perception of what constitutes useful feedback.

When giving feedback, whether positive or negative, keep these guidelines in mind. They apply to both counseling and skill practice situations.

- The purpose of feedback is to be helpful to other people by giving them useful information about what they are doing or the effect they are having on you.
- *Timing* is important. If feedback is given so long after a happening that the recipient can't remember the happening clearly, it is not likely to be helpful. Feedback is most helpful when given as soon as possible.
- *Be specific rather than general.* Generalities often raise people's defenses so that they don't get the message you are trying to give. It's much easier to hear and acknowledge "I felt annoyed when you were late for our appointment today," than it is to hear and acknowledge "You're always late and I'm sick and tired of it." (Even if the other person *is* always late and you are sick and tired of it, it's more constructive to deal with specific situations as soon as possible, rather than not give feedback and sit on your feelings until you finally explode.)
- *Being descriptive rather than judgmental* is also less likely to raise people's defenses and is more helpful."You just went through a stop light and you're driving at 40 MPH in a 20 MPH school zone, and I feel nervous," is more constructive than "You're really a lousy driver."
- The last point to remember about *feedback* is that it *Should be directed toward behavior, which is something the receiver can do something about.* While you may find you simply have to tell someone the effect that his/her height, or age, or color of eyes has on you, this is not feedback. In effect, you're not telling that person anything about himself/herself but something about yourself. Even if it's positive, such as "Darling, I just love your green eyes," you're talking about your own likes or dislikes rather than something someone else has control over and could change if he/she wanted to.

Assumptions

Despite earnest intentions to give accurate and meaningful feedback, we may sometimes unconsciously erect barriers to doing so. These barriers may derive from our own needs, beliefs, prejudices, preferences, values, or fears, and they may frequently take the form of assumptions about others. Sometimes our assumptions are on target; quite often they are far from reality. However, they are accurate often enough to encourage us to keep making assumptions.

Making assumptions often takes the form of taking observable facts about another person, developing a theory to explain those facts, and then treating the other person as if your theory is proven. In alcoholism counseling, this process might mean observing that a client's eyes are bloodshot, assuming that he/she has been drinking, and reacting to the client with anger and disappointment on the basis of your assumptions. The client, however, may actually have hay fever or may not have been able to sleep. This kind of assuming is sometimes called *pigeon-holing* or *stereotyping*.

Making assumptions can also take the form of making another person responsible for our feelings. For example, I may feel frightened; if I assume that some other person is threatening to me, then this assumption justifies or rationalizes my fear. This process could easily take place with a client who may, in reality, be dangerous only to himself/herself or not dangerous at all.

Three things to remember about assumptions are:

- Recognize that you probably have some.
- Don't take them too seriously. You can't know another person's experience, only your own perceptions of that experience. Any conclusions or theories that you may have about another may be accurate or they may be *only* your assumptions.
- Check them out. Using nonjudgmental words and tentative phrases, share your assumptions with the recipient and see whether they are accurate or not—for example, "It seems like you have been drinking today." Remember, the object in counseling another is not for the counselor to be right (and the client wrong) but rather to establish communication, build a relationship, and help the client develop the capacity to deal more effectively with his/her life.

Attending

Definition of Attending

Attending is fundamental to the use of all other counseling skills. As used here, attending implies a concern by the counselor with all aspects of the client's communication. It includes listening to the verbal content, hearing and observing the verbal and nonverbal cues to the feelings that accompany the communication, and then communicating back to the client the fact that the counselor is paying attention.

Purposes of Attending

1. It encourages the client to continue expressing his/her ideas and feelings freely.
2. It allows the client to explore ideas and feelings in his/her own way and thus provides the client with an opportunity to direct the session.
3. It can give the client a sense of responsibility for what happens in the session by enabling him/her to direct the session.
4. It helps the client relax and be comfortable in the counseling session.
5. It contributes to the client's trust of the counselor and sense of security.
6. It enables the counselor to draw more accurate inferences about the client.

Components of Attending

Effective attending has two components: (1) listening and observing and (2) communicating to the client that listening and observing is going on.

The first component of attending behavior is *listening effectively and observing* carefully. For many people, listening is a difficult task to learn. Although society does place great emphasis on spoken exchanges, many people have not learned how to listen effectively. Often, people may think they are listening when they are actually thinking about something else or are debating a subject in their head while waiting for the other person to pause so they can present some comment of their own. A client can usually sense when the counselor is listening with "half an ear."

Effective listening by itself, however, is not enough. Counseling occurs in a face-to-face situation where both participants watch, as well as listen to, each other. The difference in information gathered from seeing and hearing as opposed to hearing alone is illustrated vividly by contrasting television with radio.

The counselor learns much about the feelings of the client through observation. Frequently, nonverbal behavior that expresses feelings may appear to alter or even negate verbal messages. It is common for people to communicate much more than they intend by their body language. As a matter of fact, the nonverbal message is more likely than the spoken words to transmit the real message— for example, a facial expression showing disgust may contradict the statement, "I'm not bothered by the thought of a drunken woman."

Conversely, many of the skills, attitudes, and feelings of the counselor are conveyed to the client through nonverbal behavior such as facial expressions, posture, eye contact, and gestures. The first component of attending occurs when the counselor stays attuned to what the client is expressing verbally and nonverbally. He/she listens closely and observes carefully.

The second component of attending behavior is *letting the client know that he/she is really being heard.* The counselor communicates through his/her attentiveness to the client generally through three methods.

a. *Eye contact*—The counselor should initiate and maintain eye contact with the client. Strong impressions—favorable and unfavorable—are formed depending on the kind and amount of eye contact. In ordinary social interaction, it is considered courteous to look at the person with whom one is speaking. In counseling, this behavior is almost imperative. However, in some cases continuous eye contact might cause the client to feel uncomfortable, as could a fixed stare or an intense gaze. Varied use of eye contact is the most effective and natural behavior for the counselor and the most likely to put the client at ease.

It is important to note that these comments on eye contact are not applicable to all cultures. For instance, maintaining direct eye contact is a hostile act to some Native Americans and may be taken as a lack of respect by some Orientals.

b. *Posture*—Body language reveals a great deal about people; posture and gestures convey distinct messages. Impressions of others are formed even from the way they sit. The counselor wants to communicate to the client by his/her body posture that he/she is interested. An upright seated position with the upper body leaning slightly forward is generally considered to convey attentiveness, but the counselor should adopt a posture in which he/she will feel relaxed and comfortable. The first position the counselor assumes won't necessarily be the only one. The counselor will undoubtedly shift positions during the counseling session, for comfort and as a reflection of his/her feelings.

Again, a word of caution if offered regarding cultural differences in acceptable attending. In some cultures, sitting too close to a client might be considered offensive or threatening; sitting too far away might convey detachment or withdrawal, and individuals vary in the amount of distance or closeness they heed. By watching how the client uses space in relation to the counselor, the counselor will probably have an indication of what is comfortable for the client.

c. *Accurate verbal following*—The counselor communicates to the client by verbal responses that listening and observing are occurring. The most important characteristic of accurate verbal responses is that they relate directly to what the client is expressing. This means the counselor doesn't jump to new topics or interrupt the client but follows the client in what he/she is saying. The counselor takes his/her cues from the client and indicates involvement by simply nodding, using encouraging phrases such as "um-hum" or "I see," repeating key words, or posing one-word questions, such as "Oh?" or "Yes?"

Later in this training program, the counselor will practice more specific types of responses (for example, paraphrasing, reflection of feeling, and summarizing) that convey to the client that the counselor has listened and observed. At this point in the program, the counselor can demonstrate accurate verbal following by offering minimal verbal responses, making head movements, and staying with the topic.

Summary of Attending

In attending, the counselor's goal is to listen effectively, to observe the client, and to communicate his/her interest and attentiveness through direct eye contact, relaxed body posture, and accurate verbal following. The skill of attending is the foundation on which all the other skills in this program are built.

Paraphrasing

Definition of Paraphrasing

Paraphrasing is a counselor response that restates the content of the client's previous statement. Paraphrasing concentrates primarily on cognitive verbal content, that is, content which refers to events, people and things. In paraphrasing, the counselor reflects to the client the verbal essence of his/her last comment or last few comments. Sometimes, paraphrasing may involve simply repeating the client's own words, perhaps emphasizing one word in particular.

More often, paraphrasing is using words that are similar to the client's, but fewer in number.

Paraphrasing and reflection of feeling are very similar and therefore are easy to confuse. In both skills, the counselor must identify the client's basic message, either cognitive or affective (pertaining to feeling or emotion), and give that message back to the client using his/her (the counselor's) own words.

The distinguishing feature between paraphrasing and reflection of feeling is the focus of the counselor's response. A paraphrase focuses on the words the client is speaking. Reflection of feeling focuses on the associated feeling or emotion as expressed in the client's tone of voice, rate and volume of speech, posture, and other nonverbal behavior as well as verbal content.

In actual counseling it is neither realistic nor therapeutic to perform only one skill at a time. However, for the purpose of refining the individual skills in this workshop, it is helpful to concentrate on each skill separately. Reflection of feeling will be discussed and practiced in a separate session.

Purposes of Paraphrasing

1. It communicates to the client that the counselor understands or is trying to understand what he/she is saying. Paraphrasing can thus be a good indicator of accurate verbal following.
2. It sharpens a client's meaning to have his/her words rephrased more concisely and often leads the client to expand his/her discussion of the same subject.
3. It often clarifies confusing content for both the counselor and the client. Even when paraphrasing is not accurate, it is useful because it encourages the client to clarify his/her remarks.
4. It can spotlight an issue by stating it more succinctly, thus offering a direction for the client's subsequent remarks.
5. It enables the counselor to verify his/her perceptions of the verbal content of client's statements.

Components of Paraphrasing

Paraphrasing has two components: determining the basic message and rephrasing.

The counselor uses his/her judgment to *determine the basic message* that is being expressed in the client's verbal content. Much of the time clients tend to speak in short paragraphs. They seldom state a single thought and wait for a reply. So the counselor must attend to all of the client's verbal content, but decide on the basic message being expressed in the "paragraphs."

After the counselor determines the basic message to be responded to, he/she attempts to give this content back to the client in a more precise way by *rephrasing* it. The counselor may want to combine several of the client's related comments into one response to the client.

To paraphrase effectively, then, the counselor determines the basic message from the content and rephrases it, usually in similar, but fewer words.

Checking Out

To minimize the possibility of the counselor's letting his/her assumptions distort what the client is saying, the counselor should get in the habit of checking out his/her paraphrasing. This can be done by adding phrases such as, "Is that right?" "Am I correct?" or "Have I heard you correctly?" to the paraphrase. This procedure will usually evoke a response from the client, and the counselor can then judge whether he/she is making assumptions or is accurately attending to the client. Checking out may not be necessary, however, if the client is clearly indicating agreement either verbally or nonverbally.

Assessing the Outcome of Paraphrasing

How effectively a counselor has used paraphrasing can best be judged by the client's next response after a paraphrase. If the paraphrase is effective, the client may indicate agreement by a word or gesture and may continue to talk further on the same subject.

Sometimes the counselor will not succeed in accurately distilling the client's comments, and the client may reply, "No, that's not what I meant." When this occurs, the counselor's attempt at paraphrasing has still been useful because it allows the counselor to see immediately that he/she has erred either in determining the basic message or in rephrasing the content.

In other instances the client may confirm the accuracy of the counselor's paraphrase, but, having heard his/her meaning expressed in different words, decide to modify or even reverse the meaning entirely to reflect a changed point of view.

Each of these outcomes can be regarded as evidence that the counselor's paraphrase has been effective.

Examples of Paraphrasing

Three examples of client statements and possible paraphrasing responses follow. After reading the examples, (a) indicate below each response whether it is appropriate or poor paraphrasing and why, and (b) formulate another appropriate paraphrasing response for at least one of the examples.

Client: I think I'm going to move out this weekend. All she ever does is complain about my drinking. Never does any housework, just nags me.

Counselor: Nagging and drinking don't mix.

_____

Counselor: Sounds like things are bad at home and you're trying to decide whether to leave.

_____

Counselor: It seems you've made the decision that you can't take it any more.

_____

Counselor: _____

* *

Client: I got stopped again for DWI and may lose my license.

Counselor: So your right to drive could be in jeopardy.

_____

Counselor: Sounds like this new DWI offense could mean trouble.

_____

Counselor: You just can't stop hot rodding around.

_____

Counselor: _____

* *

Client: My boss doesn't understand me at all. He doesn't realize I'm always shaky in the morning.

Counselor: I hear you saying that your boss can't see your situation the way you see it.

_____

Counselor: Your boss is firm about work starting at 9:00.

_____

Counselor: Mornings are a tough time for you.

_____

Counselor: _____

Summary of Paraphrasing

To paraphrase is to determine the basic message in the client's cognitive statements and concisely rephrase it. The rewording should capture the essence of the cognitive verbal content. Occasionally, an exact repetition of the client's remarks may be an appropriate paraphrase. More commonly, the counselor determines and rephrases the basic message of the verbal content using similar, but fewer, words.

Reflection of Feeling

Introduction

Dealing with feelings and emotions—one's own or others'—is probably the most difficult part of human relations. One cause of this difficulty is that the dominant American culture does not value open and free expression of feelings and emotions.

At an early age, we learn to control, mask, or deny our feelings. Unfortunately, with most of us, this process is learned well and reinforced continuously in our schooling. Through primary emphasis on intellectual achievement, we are conditioned to restrain, and even deny, our emotions. However, denied or suppressed feelings do not just disappear. Depending on the intensity of the feelings and how long they have been suppressed, they manifest their presence both psychologically and physically in such ways as difficulty in communicating with others, depression, fatigue, tension headaches, and psychosomatic illness. A more constructive approach is to recognize that feelings and emotions exist, accept them as part of ourselves, and learn to express them in ways that promote individual growth and mutually satisfying relationships.

In counseling, we must communicate with the client not only on the factual, or cognitive, level (meaning events, people, things), but also on the affective level (meaning feelings about events, people, and things). Frequently, we may have as clients people who have controlled, inhibited, or denied their feelings and emotions for years. One of our tasks is to help them understand that it is acceptable, even necessary, to be aware of and express their feelings in the counseling relationship. The ability of the counselor to transmit that message is based on the assumption that the counselor can get in touch with, identify, and express his/her own feelings. Our primary focus here is on helping the client to become aware of, identify, and express his/her feelings.

An important concept to understand with regard to reflection of feeling is *empathy*, which has been identified as one of the essential conditions in counseling. Empathy, in everyday language, means putting oneself in the other person's shoes. More formally, it might be defined as the counselor's attempting to perceive the world through the client's frame of reference. Thus the counselor manifests empathy through his/her ability to perceive what is happening in regard to the client's feelings and to communicate this perception to the client. Reflection of feeling is one of the ways empathy can be communicated.

Definition of Reflection of Feeling

Reflection of feeling is the counselor's expressing the essence of the client's feelings, either stated or implied. In contrast to paraphrasing, reflection of feeling focuses primarily on the emotional element of the client's communication, whether it is verbal or nonverbal. The counselor tries to perceive the emotional state or condition of the client and feed back a response that demonstrates his/her understanding of this state. Reflection of feeling, then, is an empathic response to the client's emotional state or condition.

Purposes of Reflection of Feeling

1. It conveys to the client that the counselor understands or is trying to understand what the client is experiencing and feeling. This empathy for the client usually reinforces the client's willingness to express feelings to the counselor.
2. It clarifies the client's feelings and attitudes by mirroring them in a nonjudgmental way.

3. It brings to the surface feelings of the client that may have been expressed only vaguely.

4. It gives the client the opportunity to recognize and accept his/her feelings as part of himself/herself. Sometimes the client may refer to "it" or "them" as the source of a problem, when he/she really means "I was feeling angry."

5. It verifies the counselor's perceptions of what the client is feeling. That is, it allows the counselor to check out with the client whether or not he/she is accurately reflecting what the client is experiencing.

6. It can bring out problem areas without the client feeling pushed.

7. It helps the client infer that feelings are causes of behavior.

Components of Reflection of Feeling

The reflection-of-feeling skill consists of two components: identification and formulation.

The counselor must first *identify* the basic feeling(s) being expressed verbally or nonverbally by the client. To be able to identify feelings in clients, a counselor must be able to recognize feelings in himself/herself. Although the counselor can't feel the client's feelings, he/she can infer what they might be by processing the verbal and nonverbal information the client is communicating. The counselor matches the information he/she gains with his/her experiences in order to label the feelings the client seems to be experiencing. Since the counselor has experienced feelings such as joy, anger, pain, fear, and boredom, he/she can remember how they felt.

To recognize or be aware of feelings in the client, the counselor attends to both verbal and nonverbal cues. When he/she is listening effectively to the client's statements, the counselor may perceive feelings that are either directly expressed or implied. Sometimes the verbal indications of feelings may not be as straightforward as they seem. Often "I think" and "I feel" are used interchangeably, although they have different meanings, particularly in counseling. For example, if a client says, "I felt overjoyed at the news," the counselor can infer that the client was happy. However, if the client says, "I feel he is too strict," the counselor cannot reliably infer what the client feels, but only what he/she thinks.

Distinct messages of emotional content also will come from nonverbal cues. Nonverbal indicators of feeling include such things as head and facial movements, posture, gestures, and voice tone and quality. Some examples of specific nonverbal cues are lowered head, folded arms, restlessness, crying, and slowness of speech.

Think back for a moment. When you're depressed, how does your voice sound? When you're angry, what happens to your face, mouth, eyes, jaw, and voice? When you're afraid, what happens to your eyes, your body posture, your gestures? Of course, different people will display different degrees and amounts of emotional intensity in different ways. Only after observing and interacting with a person over time can anyone begin to decide what that individual's nonverbal behavior might really be saying about how he/she is feeling.

In general, though, the counselor can be alert to such facial and body expressions as smiles, eyes widening or narrowing, worry wrinkles, drooping shoulders, or tightly clenched hands. Voice quality is an important area to attend to for signs of emotion. Loudness or softness, changes in tone or inflection, and emphasis on one word are indications of feelings. Sometimes the client may convey conflicting messages with his/her verbal and nonverbal behavior. He/she may say "I'm not upset," when his/her hands are shaking and his/her face is red.

Thus, in identifying feelings, the counselor attempts to enter the client's frame of reference by drawing on his/her own experiences with feelings. The counselor must identify the feelings the client is communicating before he/she can reflect them accurately to the client.

The second component of an effective reflection-of-feeling response is to *formulate a response* that captures the essence of the feeling expressed by the client. Although the counselor tries to understand and identify the client's feelings as well as he/she can, it is not possible to *be* the client, so any conclusions drawn should be considered tentative and presented as tentative reflections. By remaining tentative and openminded in formulating verbal responses, the counselor avoids dogmatic-sounding responses that might alienate the client if they are inaccurate.

Examples of appropriate phrases with which a counselor might begin a reflection-of-feeling response are:

It seems that you feel. . . .
Are you saying that you feel. . . .
You seem to feel. . . .
Is it possible that you feel. . . .
I'm picking up that you feel. . . .
You appear to be feeling. . . .
Perhaps you're feeling. . . .
I sense that you feel. . . .

Often, counselors find reflection of feeling one of the harder skills to master. Some common errors counselors tend to make in using this skill follow in the next section. These errors may also occur in using some of the other skills in the program.

Common Errors in Formulating Reflection-of-Feeling Responses

1. *Stereotypical language*—The counselor can fall into a pattern of always beginning reflections in the same way with a phrase such as "You feel. . . ." Some of these phrases were listed above as appropriate, but the counselor should avoid using any one of them too often. The counselor should vary his/her style of reflecting.

2. *Timing*—Sometimes the inexperienced counselor attempts to reflect feelings after every statement the client makes. This can give an impression of insincerity and may dilute the effect of the technique. At the other extreme, the counselor waits until the client has finished a long series of comments and tries to reflect many feelings in one response. Another error in timing involves pauses. Counselors often don't wait out pauses. Long pauses can mean that the client is trying to say things that are difficult for him/her to say, but the uncomfortable counselor may jump in and respond immediately, in effect interrupting and breaking off the client's struggle to express a complex or painful thought or feeling.

3. *Too-shallow or too-deep responses*—The counselor should strive to feed back to the client the essence of what he/she is expressing. The counselor should avoid either reflecting a feeling or taking away from the client's meaning by merely labeling the feeling. The goal is to communicate to the client that he/she is understood on the level where he/she is. For example, a client may say, "I feel bad. I had some drinks at the office party last night after I promised myself I wouldn't." A too-shallow response from the counselor might be, "You mean you're sorry." A too-deep response might be, "You feel *really* guilty about your drinking."

Checking Out

Checking out perceptions is as important in reflection of feeling as it is in paraphrasing, even though the reflection of feeling is phrased tentatively. The addition of a questioning phrase, usually at the end of the reflection-of-feeling statement, will insure that the counselor is not making unfounded assumptions about the client.

For example, "I sense that you feel discouraged today. Is that right?"

Assessing the Outcome of Reflection of Feeling

In reflection of feeling, as in paraphrasing, the effectiveness of the activity can be determined by the client's response. The client may confirm or disclaim the reflection. If the reflection is accurate, the client is more likely to continue discussing the feeling reflected. An inaccurate reflection will often bring a correcting response from the client, which results in clarification. In either case, the net result of reflection-of-feeling responses made by the counselor should be an increased focus on feelings by the client as he perceives that discussing feelings is acceptable in counseling.

Examples of Reflection of Feeling

Three examples of client statements and possible reflection-of-feeling responses follow. After reading the examples, (a) indicate next to each response whether it is appropriate or poor reflection of feeling and why, and (b) formulate another appropriate reflection-of-feeling response for at least one of the examples.

Client: I'm afraid that I have some influence on his drinking. Like I may be one of the reasons he drinks so much.

Counselor: You appear to be feeling guilty that you may be a part of his drinking.

_____

Counselor: You worry that you may contribute to his drinking.

_____

Counselor: You feel he drinks too much.

_____

Counselor: _____

* *

Client: I didn't want to come here. There is nothing wrong with me. I only came to see you because my wife insisted.

Counselor: You seem resentful about coming here.

_____

Counselor: You feel that you're a perfectly normal person.

_____

Counselor: I get the impression that you're annoyed.

_____

Counselor: _____

* *

Client: God, I hate my ma. She tries to run my life for me. I
             feel almost as strongly about my dad. He just sits back
             and lets her run everything. As long as he's got his
             booze, he's ok.

Counselor: You feel guilty because you can't accept the idea that
             you hate your parents.

_____

Counselor: Sounds like you resent your mother for being too strong
             and your father for being too weak.

_____

Counselor: I'm hearing you express two different feelings—
             irritation at your mother and impatience at your dad's
             behavior,

_____

Counselor: _____

Summary of Reflection of Feeling

Reflection of feeling involves _identifying_ the essence of the
feelings the client is expressing and _formulating_ a response that
indicates that the counselor understands. Usually the counselor
offers fresh words that capture the basic verbal or nonverbal feeling
message of the client.

Summarizing

Definition of Summarizing

Summarizing is the tying together by the counselor of the main points discussed in a counseling session. Summarizing can focus on both feelings and content and is appropriate after a discussion of a particular topic within the session or as a review at the end of the session of the principal issues discussed. In either case, a summary should be brief, to the point, and without new or added meanings.

In many respects, summarizing is similar to, or an extension of, paraphrasing and reflection of feeling in that the counselor seeks to determine the basic meanings being expressed in content or feelings and give these meanings back to the client in fresh words. Summarizing differs primarily in the span of time it is concerned with. In paraphrasing, a statement or brief paragraph occurring over a short period of time is rephrased. In summarizing verbal content, several of the client's statements, the entire session, or even several sessions are pulled together.

In reflection of feeling, the counselor responds to the last feeling or feelings expressed or displayed. In summarizing feelings, the counselor reviews numerous feelings expressed or displayed over a longer period of time.

Purposes of Summarizing

1. It can insure continuity in the direction of the session by providing a focus.
2. It can clarify a client's meaning by having his/her scattered thoughts and feelings pulled together.
3. It often encourages the client to explore an issue further once a central theme has been identified.
4. It communicates to the client that the counselor understands or is trying to understand what the client is saying and feeling.
5. It enables the counselor to verify his/her perceptions of the content and feelings discussed or displayed by the client during the session. The counselor can check out whether he/she accurately attended and responded without changing the meanings expressed.
6. It can close discussion on a given topic, thus clearing the way for a new topic.

7. It provides a sense of movement and progress to the client by drawing several of his/her thoughts and feelings into a common theme.
8. It can terminate a session in a logical way through review of the major issues discussed in the entire session.

Components of Summarizing

Accurate summarizing has two components: selection and tying together.

The counselor uses his/her judgment to *select the key points* discussed. As the counselor picks out the highlights of content and feelings, general themes usually begin to emerge. When deciding what material to summarize, the counselor should note consistent and inconsistent patterns that have evolved in the session. For example, the client may keep coming back to one particular issue, implicitly emphasizing its importance, or the client may seem to contradict himself/herself by making conflicting statements at different times during the session.

After selecting the principal points discussed or displayed, the counselor attempts to *tie together* these points and to feed them back to the client in a more concise way. In drawing together the content and feelings, the counselor should avoid adding his/her own ideas, which could well be assumptions. The idea is to give back to the client essentially what he/she has said concisely, using fresh words.

Assessing Outcomes of Summarizing

The outcome of a summarization depends to a large extent on where in the counseling session it occurs. If the summarizing of a particular topic occurs during the session, it is likely to encourage the client to talk further. If summarizing occurs at the close of the session, it is more likely to terminate further discussion.

How effectively a counselor has summarized the essence of the verbal content and feelings the client has expressed can best be determined by the client's response to the summary. The client may affirm that the counselor has tied together points already discusses and, depending on where in the session the summary is made, continue to explore the topic, begin a related or new topic, or accept the counselor's remarks as a wrap-up of the session.

Sometimes the counselor may not have accurately pulled together the essential content and feelings of the client, or may have added assumptions of his/her own to the exchange. In that case, the client may say, "That isn't quite what I said," or "I agree with that except for. . . ." The counselor and client can then resolve areas in question before proceeding or ending the session.

As with paraphrasing and reflection of feeling, the counselor should make a practice of checking out the accuracy of a summary with the client to minimize the chances of making unwarranted assumptions.

Examples of Summarizing

To a divorced woman exploring problems that she is having with a teen-age son, who is drinking heavily:

> As I understand what you've been saying during the past few minutes, you seem to be struggling with three possible ways to handle the situation: you might continue trying to reason with your son yourself; you might ask his father to help you deal with the boy; or you might stop discussing the problem with your son and punish him by taking away his privileges.

At the end of a session with a male client:

> Let's take a look at what we've covered in today's session. It sounds like you've felt inadequate in dealing with several areas of your life—your family, your job, and now your drinking.

Summary of Summarizing

To summarize is to *select* the key points or basic meanings from the client's verbal content and feelings and succinctly *tie them together*. The summarization should accurately reflect the essence of the client's statements and feelings and should not include assumptions of the counselor. Summarizing, then, is a review of the main points already discussed in the session to insure continuity in a focused direction.

Probing

Definition of Probing

Probing is a counselor's use of a question or statement to direct the client's attention inward to explore his/her situation in more depth. A probing question, sometimes called an "open-ended question," requires more than a one-word (yes or no) answer from the client.

When phrased as a statement, the probe contains a strong

element of direction by the counselor; for example, "Tell me more about your relationship with your parents," or "Suppose we explore a little more your ideas about what an alcoholic is."

Purposes of Probing

1. It can help focus the client's attention on a feeling or content area.
2. It may help the counselor better understand what the client is describing by giving him her more information about the client's situation.
3. It may encourage the client to elaborate, clarify, or illustrate what he/she has been saying.
4. It sometimes enhances the client's awareness and understanding of his/her situation or feelings.
5. It directs the client's attention to areas the counselor thinks need attention.

Components of Probing

The two components of probing are identification and open-ended phrasing.

The counselor uses his/her judgment to *identify* a subject or feelings area touched on by the client that needs further exploration. As with the other skills practiced in this training program, it is important that the counselor use probing only after attending to the client. By listening to and observing the client, the counselor may identify matters that either seem unresolved or seem to need further development.

In probing, the counselor decides what areas might need further attention, whereas in paraphrasing, reflection of feeling, and summarizing, the counselor attempts to feed back to the client in a more concise way the same material or feelings the client presented or displayed.

After identifying the area that needs to be explored further, the counselor attempts to *phrase an open-ended question or statement* to help include such words as what, where, when, or how. For example, "When do you feel that way?" "Where does that occur for you?" It is generally best to avoid asking questions beginning with the words are, is, do, or why. The first three words tend to elicit one-word answers. "Why" frequently poses a question that the client cannot answer. As a result, the client may feel defensive and resist further exploration of the topic, or may indulge in vague speculation unrelated to the topic under discussion.

Assessing the Outcomes of Probing

As with other skills studies, how effectively a counselor has probed can best be determined by the client's response. If the probe encourages the client to talk in greater depth about his/her feelings or the content identified by the counselor, then the technique has probably been helpful. Similarly, if the probe seems to make the client more aware of a situation he/she has tended to avoid or ignore, and more apt to discuss it specifically, then the probe has been effective. In general the probe may be seen as effective when the client responds by talking further about the subject or feeling on what seems like a deeper level (as opposed to a superficial, intellectualizing level).

Sometimes, the counselor may probe an area that the client is not yet ready to discuss or deal with. In that case, the counselor might encounter extended silence or some other form of resistance on the part of the client. Or the client may simply say "I'd rather not talk about that." The probe might still be considered effective in this case, because the counselor may have succeeded in directing the client's attention to the problem area which either the client or the counselor might come back to later.

Examples of Probing

Two examples of client statements and possible probing responses follow. After reading the examples, indicate next to each response whether it is appropriate or poor probing and why.

Client: Mother and Dad were fighting and he was pounding on her and knocking her down, so I beat him up and went out and had a steak.

Counselor: How were you feeling at the point where you decided to beat your father?

_____

Counselor: Tell me more about what you were going through as that happened.

_____

Counselor: Do you often have fights with your father?

_____

* *

Client: I've been doing this job for years now and nobody ever
            complained before and now they're saying my job
            performance hasn't been as good.

Counselor: In what ways specifically do they say your work hasn't
            been good?

_____

Counselor: You're not going to blow this job, are you?

_____

Counselor: I'm wondering what your reaction was to criticism of
            your job performance.

_____

Summary of Probing

Probing is the use of a counselor question or statement to direct
the client's attention inward to explore his/her situation in depth.
The counselor identifies an area which seems to need exploration
and then openly phrases a response. Used effectively, probing
should help both the client and counselor to better understand the
client's situation.

Counselor Self-Disclosure

Introduction

The importance of identifying and responding to feelings has been
stressed throughout this program. Although our focus has been on
the feelings of the client, the feelings of the counselor are just as
important. The counselor should be aware of his/her feelings during
the counseling session, and this awareness should lead to congruency between the counselor's verbal and nonverbal behavior.

If the counselor becomes impatient with the client's evasive
statements, this impatience will probably show in his/her own

nonverbal behavior. Therefore, it should be constructively expressed. Showing honest and open involvement with the client by being congruent is one way the counselor can be genuine. When the counselor provides a model of genuineness, the client is more likely to perceive that being genuine is acceptable and necessary in counseling. It may also establish a pattern that the client may apply to his other social interactions.

For the counsellor to be genuine and congruent in counseling, he/she must be aware not only of feelings, but also aspects of himself/herself that others may· see. In an attempt to clarify the kinds of information available about all people, Joe Luft and Harry Ingham contributed their names and ideas to the concept of Johari Window.* The Window is a visual way of describing information available about any person. The four "panes" of the Window are:

1. Information known by all about a person (open area).
2. Information known by the person, but not by others (hidden area).
3. Information known by others, but not by the person (blind area).
4. Information not known by the person or by others (unknown area).

Individual awareness, which contributes to genuineness and congruency, depends on any person's increasing the information in his/her open area while reducing the blind and hidden areas.

Definition of Self-Disclosure

Self-disclosure is a sharing by the counselor of his/her own feelings, attitudes, opinions, and experiences with a client *for the benefit of the client*. Self-disclosure should include significant content and be relevant to the client's situation. Self-disclosure *in the present* (the here and now of the counseling session) occurs when the counselor communicates his/her feelings about the client or the session, such as by saying, "I'm pleased that you can talk about these things." Self-disclosure may also include revealing experiences the counselor has had *in the past* that seem relevant to the client's current situation.

---

* For a diagram of the Johari Window and a discussion of the related concept, see:
   Hanson, P. G. "The Johari Window: A Model for Soliciting and Giving Feedback,"
   J. William Pfeiffer and John E. Jones, Editors. *The Annual Handbook for Group Facilitators.* LaJolla, CA: University Associates, 1973, pp. 114–119.
   Johnson, Vernon, E. *I'll Quit Tomorrow.* New York: Harper & Row, 1973, p. 120.

Purposes of Self-Disclosure

1. It tends to build a sense of trust and rapport between the counselor and the client.
2. It helps reduce the client's feelings that he/she is unique and alone in the situation he/she is experiencing.
3. It often enables the counseling relationship to move to deeper levels.
4. It fosters a feeling of empathy in the counseling relationship when the client perceives that the counselor may indeed be able to see things from the client's point of view.
5. It tends to promote the expression of feelings by the client in the counseling relationship.
6. It may create an atmosphere in which the client feels free to express content that he/she had previously avoided.
7. It may encourage the client to explore further a particular subject or feeling by sharing the counselor's experience with a similar situation.

Guidelines for Self-Disclosure

Self-disclosure requires knowledge of *principles* to guide the appropriate timing and content of the self-disclosure.

1. *The counselor's disclosure should relate directly to the client's situation.* This principle pertains primarily to disclosures about the counselor's past experiences. To help decide whether an experience is relevant to the client's situation, the counselor may first use paraphrasing, reflection of feeling, summarizing, and probing responses to insure that he/she does understand the client's situation.

2. *The counselor should disclose only experiences that have actually happened to him/her.* Using a personal pronoun such as I, me, my, or myself in a self-disclosure can give a clear message to the client that the counselor is telling about an experience that happened to him/her and is not merely relating the hearsay experience of a third party. This principle is most appropriate to the "past" type of self-disclosure.

3. *The counselor has the option of revealing information about himself/herself on various levels of intimacy.* The counselor could reveal information that is in the open area of the Johari Window and probably known to many. Or, if the counseling relationship has

produced a deep level of mutual trust, empathy, and genuineness, the counselor might reveal to the client an aspect of himself/herself that few others know. The guiding principle as to what level of information to reveal lies in the answers to two questions: Will it benefit the client and will the counselor feel comfortable in revealing that information?

Problems of Self-Disclosure

There are also some problems associated with self-disclosure of which the counselor should be aware.

1. *Self-disclosure in the present (the here and now of the session) can have an immediate and sometimes extreme effect on the client.* When the counselor reveals a current feeling about the client (for example, that the counselor feels bored), the client may feel rejected or belittled. In deciding whether to disclose what might be perceived by the client as a negative feeling, the counselor must ask himself/herself whether he/she is disclosing for the sake of the client or out of a personal need. Positive feelings (pleasure, happiness, pride) revealed by the counselor usually do not result in as obvious reactions in the client as do negative feelings. The counselor should recall that he/she is attempting to be a genuine, honest person in the counseling relationship and therefore must consider revealing positive and negative feelings if such disclosures would benefit the client.

2. *The use of counselor self-disclosure shifts the focus of the session away from the client to the counselor.* The counselor must guard against allowing subsequent responses to leave the focus on the counselor and thus tend to deny or downgrade the experiences of the client. The counselor should keep in mind that the self-disclosure is for the benefit of the client. The client is not likely to be helped if the counselor proceeds to work through a need of his/her own.

3. *The premature use of an intimate past experience or a threatening present feeling could make the client anxious and could damage the counseling relationship.* If the counselor is quite sure that he/she understands the client's situation and that the conditions of trust, empathy, and genuineness are present in the relationship, the self-disclosure will probably be appropriate.

4. *There is a certain amount of risk to the counseling relationship any time the counselor uses self-disclosure.* The counselor reveals something personal about himself/herself that the client

may ignore, deny, or ridicule. In exposing himself/herself, the counselor stands to gain by being perceived as an honest, genuine person but runs the risk that the client's perception of him/her may change and thus change the dynamics of the counseling relationship. If the client's perception of the counselor has changed negatively because of an inappropriate self-disclosure, the counseling relationship may be disrupted.

Not all counselors may feel comfortable sharing personal experiences, but all counselors should recognize the value of the "here and now" self-disclosures that foster a climate of trust and openness. Each counselor makes his/her own decision about whether to use self-disclosure in counseling. When self-disclosure is used appropriately, the benefits, in the form of a deeper counseling relationship, can be great. The counselor will probably be using self-disclosure appropriately if he/she continually asks the question "is this disclosure for the sake of the client?"

Examples of Self-Disclosure

Below are three client statements, the first two followed by possible self-disclosure responses. After reading the examples, (a) indicate below each response whether it is appropriate or poor self-disclosure and why, and (b) formulate an appropriate self-disclosure for the third client statement. (Assume that the appropriate conditions in the relationship have been established.)

Past:

Client: You know, I feel so ashamed. All my friends are going to find out that I have a drinking problem and I don't know how I can face them.

Counselor: I think I'm aware of how you might be feeling because I can remember how ashamed I felt, at first, when I had to admit to my friends that I am an alcoholic.

———————————————————————————

Counselor: I think I know how you might feel. I'm not an alcoholic, but my father is and I can remember my shame and embarrassment about the secret getting out.

———————————————————————————

Counselor: I know how you feel. I felt really embarrassed when my father came to my graduation in jeans.

———————————————————————————

* *

Present:

Client: Well, I did have a few drinks before coming here tonight, but it doesn't matter because I'm sticking to my treatment plan.

Counselor: I have to admit I'm feeling disappointed right now. I thought you were doing so well in staying away from alcohol.

_____

Counselor: If you think you've got problems, let me tell you how hard it is for me to go to a cocktail party and not to drink.

_____

Counselor: I'm trying very hard to control my feelings of anger toward you. I think you know that we decided you shouldn't come here if you had been drinking.

_____

* *

Client: Sometimes I feel so discouraged. It seems like nothing will ever change, no matter what I do.

Counselor: _____

Summary of Self-Disclosure

Self-disclosure involves the counselor sharing his/her own feelings, attitudes, opinions, and experiences with a client for the benefit of the client. The self-disclosure of the counselor might be revealing a present feeling or relating a relevant past experience. Both timing and appropriateness of content are central to effective self-disclosure. Used appropriately, counselor self-disclosure should increase the level of trust, genuineness, and empathy in the counseling relationship and reduce the client's feeling of being unique in his/her problems or difficulties.

Interpreting

Introduction

Most people place limits on how they will look at problems or situations. As a result of this restricted outlook, people make comments like "I could never do that." When asked why they couldn't they often don't know. They just know that they have never considered doing such a thing. This kind of thinking produces narrow vision, which hinders people from arriving at other ways of looking at problems or situations. People thus become further entrenched in the one position rather than trying to open up their vision or perspective.

The counselor, as well as the client, is subject to falling into the trap of restricted thinking. After learning the skill of interpreting, the counselor will be able to help clients broaden their perspectives. To do so, the counselor has to broaden his/her own way of viewing problems and situations.

Definition of Interpreting

Interpreting is a technique used by the counselor to present the client with alternative ways of looking at his/her situation. For example, the counselor might use a different perspective to explain events to a client so that he/she might be able to see the problem in a new light and perhaps generate his/her own fresh ways of looking at it.

Interpreting differs from reflection of feeling, paraphrasing, and summarizing in that it usually involves the addition of the counselor's ideas to the basic messages being expressed or manifested by the client. In other words, in reflection of feelings, paraphrasing, and summarizing, the counselor attempts to understand and maintain the client's frame of reference. In interpreting, the counselor offers a new frame of reference to the client. Interpreting, as defined here, is not the "in-depth" type of interpretation that psychoanalysts might do. In this training program, the emphasis in interpretation is not on digging into the client's psyche but on offering alternative points of view in regard to his/her immediate problem or situation.

Purposes of Interpreting

1. It helps the client realize that there is more than one way to look at most situations, problems, and solutions.

2. It offers the client a role model of the counselor seeking alternative ways of viewing events in life.
3. It can teach the client how to use self-interpretation to explore new points of view.
4. It can help the client understand his/her problems more clearly.
5. It often generates new and distinctive solutions to problems.
6. It may prompt the client to act more effectively when he/she sees other solutions to problems.
7. It often enables the client to gain a better understanding of his/her underlying feelings and how these might relate to verbal messages he/she has expressed.

Components of Interpreting

Effective interpreting has three components: determining and restating basic messages; adding counselor ideas for a new frame of reference; and "checking out" these ideas with the client.

The basic framework on which all of the counseling skills presented thus far have been built is the ability to listen effectively and observe carefully. It is especially important that the counselor employ the skills of attending, paraphrasing, reflection of feeling, and summarizing prior to and in conjunction with interpreting. The first step in interpreting *is to determine the basic messages* the client has expressed or displayed and restate them. The counselor seeks to determine the essence of what the client is saying or doing (the client's frame of reference) and then restates this in a paraphrase, reflection of feeling, or summary.

As the counselor is determining the basic messages and restating them, he/she probably will have some ideas or hunches about alternative ways of viewing the client's situation, or may begin to see connections, relationships, or patterns in the events the client describes. When these ideas are included in the material being restated to the client, the counselor is *adding his/her ideas* to offer the client a new frame of reference from which to view his/her situation.

Because the counselor is departing from the client's frame of reference and offering alternative viewpoints, it becomes very important to phrase any interpretation tentatively or *to check out directly* with the client his/her reaction to any new points of view. Tentative phrases such as "The way I see it . . ." or "I wonder if . . ." are appropriate ways to begin an interpretation. Sometimes the counselor might want to phrase the interpretation as a question— for example, "Do you think, then, that you might be uncomfortable with older men because of your poor relationship with your father?" This form of interpretation is more tentative than a statement and thus there is a greater possibility that the client will see the offered interpretation as a possibility rather than as a fact. Whether the counselor is on target or completely off, the client is more likely to react to an interpretation openly if it is offered tentatively.

Another way of checking out how the interpretation is received by the client is to add a question onto the end of the new point of view such as, "How does that hit you?" or "Am I really far off?" However the counselor relays the tentativeness of his interpretation, it is imperative that the counselor let the client know it is merely an alternative way of looking at the situation and not necessarily the only or right way.

Guidelines for Effective Interpreting

Interpreting is a more complex and subtle skill than others included in this program. Because it can be a potent promoter of behavior change, however, it is worth the effort required to learn interpreting and use it effectively. Some general guidelines follow:

1. In formulating interpretations, the counselor should use simple language, close to the level at which the client is operating. He/she should avoid jumping too far ahead of the client, indulging in speculation, or stating the interpretation in such a way as to seem to be showing off psychological expertise. An example of not staying at the same level as the client's is one in which the counselor replies to the client's remark that he wishes his dad would lose some weight, with, "You're suffering from typical castration anxiety complicated by Oedipal conflicts."

2. Added ideas or explanations that the counselor offers to the client are often expressed to the client in terms of a particular theory of behavior and personality, such as Gestalt, behavioristic, rational emotive, or psychoanalytic. Such a theory will probably provide some of the labels the counselor will tend to put on feelings and events in the client's life. The counselor should, of course, be aware of what theoretical position he/she operates from. However, in this training program, no discussion of various theoretical positions is given.

3. The counselor should encourage the client to get in the habit of considering a range of alternative ways to view his/her situation. The counselor may serve as a model for this kind of unfettered thinking by presenting an alternative and then

asking the client to suggest others. For example, to a client who has said that feelings of loneliness have caused him to drink in the past, the counselor might say, "Let's look at some things you might do to deal with that lonely feeling, other than drink. One thing you could do is call your A.A. sponsor and talk to him for a while. What are some other things you might do?"

Outcomes Expected from Interpreting

The effectiveness of interpretation can be determined by the client's reaction to any frame of reference offered. If the alternative point of view is close to what the client has expressed, the client might immediately accept the interpretation as a useful way to rethink the problem. In fact, the client might seem to get a sudden recognition of what the problem is. A response such as "I just realized that's it," could be a typical reply.

If the interpretation varies somewhat from what the client has expressed, several reactions are possible. The client might accept a new frame of reference tentatively—"I'll have to think about that one." On the other hand, he/she might reject the interpretation completely or say "Yes, but . . ." Or the client might accept it too uncritically. The counselor should be cautious in proceeding in the direction of an interpretation that the client accepts without any hesitation, because it could mean that the client does not feel free to challenge anything the counselor says. However, if the counselor keeps in mind the procedure of checking out perceptions with the client, the counselor's interpreting and subsequent responses will be made tentatively or cautiously.

If the interpretation is too extreme, the client might become anxious or threatened and the session could be disrupted. Or the client, again, might accept the interpretation at a cautious or tentative level.

Although the client will usually make some sort of response immediately after an interpretation (as opposed to saying nothing), the actual effect of the attempt to offer an alternative point of view may not be realized by either client or counselor until later. The client may come back to the next session, after having given the new point of view some thought, and report that he/she wishes to explore that or other alternatives to the way he/she had been thinking.

Examples of Interpreting

Following are two brief client/counselor dialogues demonstrating the use of interpreting. After reading the examples, formulate an appropriate interpreting response for one of the examples.

Client: I couldn't let my son help me now that I'm down and out. I've got that shred of pride left—because, you see, I remember when he was a kid and I didn't turn my hand to help him. I traipsed around the country—his mother dies when the kid was born—and I let the relatives push him around and stick him in foster homes—and now . . .

Counselor: Your behavior in the past makes you feel embarrassed about the help your son wants to give you now, is that what you mean? (Reflection of Feeling)

Client: Yeah, yeah, I'm no good to him and then he wants to help me. I mean it felt like a knife stuck in me when we met the other day and he said, "We can make a go of it together, Dad—I've got a little money saved up." No, no, I won't let him do it. I will clear out of here. It'll be hard, but—I haven't done one thing for him, or anyone else for that matter.

Counselor: Sounds like your struggling with whether to leave or accept help from him. (Paraphrase)

Client: Yeah, I guess maybe I have always had this thing about not owing nothing to nobody and them not owing me nothing. But now I don't know—my son really seems to want to help me. I just don't know what to do.

Counselor: At this point you feel you don't deserve any help from your son, yet he seems to want to give it. Have you considered the possibility that maybe he doesn't hold the past against you and really loves you? (Interpreting)

Counselor: _____

              _____

* *

Client: I keep remembering how I walked out on her and the kids. Five years ago—the law never did catch up with me—I thought I was pretty smart—but now—God, I was such a heel. I don't see how I could have done it.

Counselor: As you see it, your past behavior was pretty dreadful. (Paraphrase)

Client: Yeah, that's right. I'm so ashamed I can't look people in the eye. Now I can't find her—not a trace. Her relatives won't tell me where she is. I don't blame them—but how could I have hone it? Just because it was tough going. I tell you, I'll never have any self-respect.

Counselor: Sounds like you're feeling kind of hopeless and down now, but it also seems like you're feeling really guilty about your past. Have you thought that maybe she and the kids wouldn't want to see you after all these years and that your trying to find them is something you are doing to make you feel less guilty and not for their benefit? (Interpreting)

Counselor: _____

            _____

Summary of Interpreting

Interpreting is presenting the client with alternative ways of looking at his/her situation. It involves determining and restating the basic messages of the client, adding counselor ideas to this material for a new frame of reference, and checking out with the client the acceptability of the new point of view. Used effectively, interpreting should assist the client to realize that there is more than one way of viewing most situations and to help him/her apply this kind of unrestricted thinking to all aspects of his/her life.

Confrontation

Definition of Confrontation

Confrontation is the deliberate use of a question or statement by the counselor to induce the client to face what the counselor thinks the client is avoiding. The client's avoidance is usually revealed by a discrepancy or contradiction in his/her statements and behavior. Thus, confrontive responses point out discrepancies either within the client or in the client's interaction with the environment. In confrontation, the counselor frequently identifies contradictions that are outside the client's frame of reference, whereas paraphrasing, reflection of feeling, and summarizing involve responding within the client's frame of reference. In using confrontation, the counselor gives honest feedback about what he/she perceives is actually happening with the client. Confrontation should not include accusations, evaluations, or solutions to problems.

Purposes of Confrontation

1. It helps the client become more congruent (what he/she says corresponds with how he/she behaves) when the client sees how he/she is being perceived by the counselor.
2. It establishes the counselor as a role model in using direct, honest, and open communication.
3. It tends to focus on problems about which the client might take action or change his/her behavior.
4. It often breaks down the defenses of the client which he/she has consciously or unconsciously put up.
5. It tends to enrich the condition of empathy in the counseling relationship when the client perceives the confrontation as being done by a concerned counselor.
6. It encourages the client to acknowledge his/her feelings and behavior by bringing to the surface those he/she has denied. Once the client has accepted ownership of these feelings and behavior, he/she is more likely to accept responsibility for them.

Types of Discrepancies

A discrepancy or contradiction in the client is often a clue to the counselor that confrontation is indicated. A discrepancy or contradiction might be one of the following general types:

1. A discrepancy between how the client sees himself/herself and how others see him/her—for example, the client may describe himself as an outgoing, talkative person, but the counselor perceives the client as extremely quiet and reserved.
2. A contradiction between what the client say and how he/she behaves—for example, the client says she is not depressed, but she is talking slowly, sitting in a slumped posture, looking as if she is ready to cry.
3. A discrepancy between two statements by the client—for example, a client may say he wants to be treated for his drinking problem, but later says the only important thing to him is saving his driver's license.
4. A discrepancy between what the client says he/she is feeling and the way most people would react in a similar situation—

for example, a client may say that if his wife leaves he doesn't care if he ever gets to see his children again.

5. A contradiction between what the client is now saying he/she believes and how he/she has acted in the past—for example, a client may say she has no trouble staying away from the bottle, but she has had three slips in a month.

Using Confrontation Effectively

There are a few guidelines that the counselor should keep in mind when formulating a confrontive response. First, and perhaps more important, mutual trust and empathy must already be firmly established as part of the counseling relationship. Confrontation should come across as a positive and constructive act by a caring counselor, not as a negative and punitive act of a judgmental counselor. This attitude of empathy and caring can be transmitted not only by what the counselor says but also by his/her tone of voice and facial expression when the confrontive response is introduced into the session.

The counselor should also keep in mind that the most effective confrontive responses are those that address specific, concrete attributes of the client's behavior that the client can do something to change. It isn't very helpful to confront general behavior, for example, "You're always talking about changing your behavior, so why don't you do it?" An example of a specific confrontation would be, "You say you want to quit drinking, but what I see you doing is figuring out how to get a pint to get through the day."

Confrontation may be directed toward the client's assets (strengths) or his/her limitations (weaknesses). The counselor should be wary of always identifying contradictions that point up weaknesses in the client. Confrontive responses can be used constructively by focusing on strengths of the client. For example, to the client who expresses lack of confidence in his ability to handle stressful situations without drinking, the counselor might say, "Last time this happened you called me and did most of the work of sorting things out and deciding what to do."

In practical application, the confrontive response often takes the form of a compound statement that sets up a "you say . . ., but you do . . ." format. The second part of the statement points out the discrepancy or contradiction in the client's behavior or message. For example, "You say you don't want to see him again, but you go to places where you know he'll be." In using confrontation, then, the counselor listens to the client's feeling and content messages, observes the client's behavior, and presents evidence of a contradiction or discrepancy to the client.

Risks Involved in Confrontation

Because confrontation is an extremely powerful tool for the counselor to use, there are certain risks involved. Whenever the counselor becomes aware of a discrepancy or contradiction in the client's behavior or messages, the benefits of using confrontation must be weighed against the risks.

Risks to the Client—If trust and empathy have not been firmly established in the counseling relationship, the premature use of a confrontive response could harm the relationship. The client could become distrustful of the counselor or decide that the counselor cannot be of any help to him/her. The use of confrontation can be very threatening and anxiety-producing for the client, and if the proper conditions aren't there to begin with, it can damage or end the counseling relationship.

The use of confrontation may precipitate a crisis in the client's life. Especially if a client seems emotionally unstable about certain areas of his/her life, it might not be wise to confront him/her on those particular areas. For example, if a client has just been fired from his job and is very upset about it, the counselor should probably not confront him at that moment with his job performance.

Risks to the Counselor—Sometimes the counselor does not confront the client because the counselor is protecting himself/herself from risk. The counselor may be hesitant to point out a discrepancy for fear he/she might be wrong and would not be able to substantiate the contradiction to the client. Or the counselor might not like to deal with the extreme emotional reactions that could follow a confrontation. The counselor may not be comfortable with anger, anxiety, or tears. The counselor may pass over an appropriate confrontation situation because he/she would be uncomfortable if the usual defenses were dropped and thus wants to prevent the relationship from getting too close or intense.

In deciding whether to confront or not, the counselor must weigh the possible benefits to the client against the possible harm. In addition, if the counselor is hesitating to confront, he/she should ask himself/herself whether this reluctance is out of concern for the client or out of self-concern. If the counselor recognizes that the reluctance to confront is out of concern for himself/herself, the counselor should search himself/herself to see whether the cause of the apprehension is a legitimate concern, such as fear or physical harm from an intoxicated client, or whether it is a fear the counselor should try to resolve within himself/herself.

The Outcomes of Confrontation

If the counselor's confrontation has been effective, it could lead to exploration of previously blocked or denied feelings or behavior. In addition, an effective confrontation can often bring about a kind of breakthrough in the client's recognition that a behavior change is needed.

In practice, the counselor often may not know whether the confrontation has been effective or helpful until after several more exchanges in the session or until a later session. The client's immediate response to the confrontation sometimes does not indicate its effectiveness.

Frequently, the beginning counselor does not know what to do after he/she attempts a confrontive response. The following general guides might help:

1. If the client accepts the confrontation and agrees with the discrepancy pointed out, the counselor can use the opportunity to reinforce positive behavior. The counselor might say, "It's really a step in the right direction that you can recognize and accept this contradictory behavior so easily."
2. If the client denies the confrontation, the counselor is probably wisest to return to an empathic response, such as, "My even suggesting that seems to bother you a lot." The client may not be ready to deal with the discrepancy at that time and it would not be helpful to persist in the confrontation.
3. The client may simply act confused or ambivalent after a confrontive statement. In that case, the counselor could focus on the current feeling by saying, "You seem to feel confused by my saying that."

Examples of Confrontation

Two examples of client statements and possible confrontive responses follow. After reading the examples (a) indicate next to each response whether it is appropriate or poor confrontation and why, and (b) formulate another appropriate response for at least one example. In addition, indicate the type of discrepancy each example illustrates.

Client   (sitting with hands clenched, face muscles tight): I'm not really angry at my father for being a drunk. I mean he's been embarrassing me in front of my friends all of my life and I've gotten used to it.

Counselor: You say you're not angry, but right here as you talk about it I see you tensing up and looking upset.

_____

Counselor: You say you've gotten used to being embarrassed in front of your friends, but I don't think you really mean that.

_____

Counselor: You still seem angry about this to me and I think what you should do is go tell your father how you feel.

_____

Counselor: _____

_____

Discrepancy is between _____

and _____

* *

Client   (who has admitted past inability to abstain when "out with the boys"): I know I'm getting better. Yes sir, I'm going to be out there with the boys and it's not going to bother me at all when they're stopping for a beer.

Counselor: It's good to hear that you don't think that situation will bother you, but how does that statement fit in with the fact that you told me that you broke down and drank with them when they stopped last week?

_____

Counselor: You're not getting better at all; your past behavior shows you're a drunk and I guess you always will be.

_____

Counselor: You say that won't bother you, but from other things you've said I'm not sure you're convinced of that yourself.

_____

Counselor: _____

_____

Discrepancy is between _____

and _____

Summary of Confrontation

In confrontation, the counselor uses a question or statement to induce the client to face what the counselor thinks the client is avoiding. The counselor may, for example, point out discrepancies between the client's verbal and nonverbal behaviors, between two of the client's statements, or between the client's past behavior and his/her position or behavior in the counseling session. Used effectively, confrontation should help the client become more congruent and accept responsibility for his behavior. It can also reinforce the climate of trust, empathy, and genuineness in the counseling relationship. Because it is one of the most potent techniques the counselor can use, there are also some risks involved in using it. In deciding whether to use it or not, the counselor must determine whether the benefits of confrontation outweigh the possible harm to the client.

Bibliography

Brammer, L. *The Helping Relationship*. Englewood Cliffs, NJ: Prentice-Hall, 1973.

Crawford, J., Stancavage, F., and Jiminez, C. *Individual Counseling for Alcoholism Counselors, Participant's Manual*. Rockville, MD: National Institute on Alcoholism and Alcohol Abuse, 1975.

Gazda, G. *Human Relations Development: A Manual for Educators*. Boston: Allyn & Bacon, 1973.

Hackney, H., and Nye, S. *Counseling Strategies and Objectives*. Englewood Cliffs, NJ: Prentice-Hall, 1973.

Ivey, A., and Gluckstern, N. *Basic Attending Skills, Participant Manual*. Amherst, MA: Microtraining Associates, 1974.

_____. *Basic Attending Skills, Leader Manual*. Amherst, MA: Microtraining Associates, 1974.

_____. *Basic Influencing Skills, Participant Manual*. Amherst, MA: Microtraining Associates, 1976.

_____. *Basic Influencing Skills, Leader Manual*. Amherst, MA: Microtraining Associates, 1976.

Okun, B. *Effective Helping: Interviewing & Counseling Techniques*. N. Scituate, MA: Duxbury Press, 1987.

Shertzer, B., and Stone, S. *Fundamentals of Counseling*. Boston: Houghton-Mifflin, 1968.

Small, J. *Becoming Naturally Therapeutic: A Handbook on the Art of Counseling, with Special Application to Alcoholism Counselors*. Austin, TX: Texas Commission on Alcoholism, 1974.

22

Treatment of the Sex Offender

Ernest M. DeZolt
Peter C. Kratcoski

The concept of "sex offender" creates some difficulty in definition, because of the wide diversity of opinion and moral conviction as to what constitutes normal or acceptable sexual behavior. Researchers at the Kinsey Institute defined a sex offense as "an overt act committed by a person for his own immediate gratification which is contrary to the prevailing sexual mores of the society in which he lives, and/or is legally punishable; and results in his being legally convicted" (Gebhard, et al., 1965:8). In the past two decades, many activities which were defined as improper sexual behavior and subjected to criminal penalties became commonplace occurrences. Although premarital sexual activity, homosexual contacts, and dissemination of birth control information and devices to unmarried persons remained forbidden by statute in many jurisdictions, they were practiced with little fear of prosecution. However in a recent decision the U.S. Supreme Court upheld a Georgia law which prohibits oral or anal sexual contacts between persons (*Bowers v. Hardwick*, 1986).

In the past ten years, notable increases have occurred in the number of reported and prosecuted cases of rape and of sexual abuse of children. These increases have forced mental health professionals to reevaluate the skills and techniques applied when dealing with offenders involved in these and other sex related offenses. State criminal codes have been revised to specifically define sexual offenses and tie penalties attendant to their commis-

This article first appeared in *Correctional Counseling and Treatment*, Second Edition. All rights reserved.

sion. For example, the Ohio Revised Code (1983) classifies sexual offenses as sexual assaults and displays, prostitution offenses, and offenses related to the dissemination of obscenity and matter harmful to juveniles (§2907.02–2907.37). Prostitution and offenses related to the dissemination of obscenity and matter harmful to juveniles are generally penalized through the imposition of fines or short jail terms, and treatment is not a factor in the disposition of such cases. In contrast, the dispositions of cases involving sexual assaults and displays frequently include treatment. Such treatment may be mandated by the courts or offered as an option for the offender.

Offenses defined as sexual assaults and displays include:

Rape, broadly defined as sexual intercourse with females by force, including anal intercourse, cunnilingus, and fellatio. Included are homosexual and lesbian assaults, rape by drugging the victim, and rape as sexual conduct with a pre-puberty victim.

Sexual battery, defined as including sexual conduct by coercion, impaired judgment, or incestuous conduct between parent and child, stepparent and stepchild, a guardian and a ward, or a custodian or person "in loco parentis" with his or her charge. This category includes sexual conduct with a prisoner or hospital patient within an institution by a person with supervisory authority.

Corruption of a minor, defined as sexual conduct by an offender who is age eighteen or over who knows his or her partner is between the ages of 13 through 15.

Gross sexual imposition is analogous to rape, but involves less serious "sexual contact," including any touching of the erogenous zone of another for the purpose of sexually arousing or gratifying either person.

Sexual imposition includes sexual touching when the offender knows or has reasonable cause to believe the touching is offensive. This section of the code further forbids sexual contact when the victim is in early adolescence and the offender is age eighteen or over and four or more years older than the victim.

Importuning prohibits the soliciting of a person under thirteen years of age to engage in sexual activity, or when the solicitor is age eighteen or over and four or more years older than the person solicited.

Voyeurism prohibitions make it illegal to be involved in trespassing, invasion of privacy, and spying for the purpose of obtaining vicarious sexual thrill.

Felonious sexual penetration is the insertion of any instrument, apparatus or other object into the vaginal or anal cavity of another through compelling force, threat of force, or after impairing the other person's judgment through intoxicant, force or deception. (Ohio Criminal Code, as amended through June 30,1983 § 2907.2 through 2907.12).

While this list is not exhaustive, it represents the types of behavior which fall within the range of sexual assault and display offenses.

We noted earlier that the less serious types of sexual offenses may be ignored or punished with fines or short jail terms. However, when serious felonies of a sexual nature occur, several states have formulated laws which specifically designate the type and nature (determinate or indeterminate) of sentence which should be imposed, and even the type of facility where the offender should be housed.

While the vast majority of sexual offenders, if prosecuted and convicted, would be subject to the same types of sanctions and afforded the same treatment options as other offenders, in approximately half of the states statutes have been enacted that focus on the psychopathic sexual offender. Generally these statutes are based on the assumption that such an offender lacks the willpower to control his actions or impulses, is dangerous, and is likely to commit the same offense again if the opportunity arises. The laws are applied to offenders who are considered a serious threat to the community, notably rapists and child molesters. Although they vary in specifics, these statutes allow for commitment of the offender to a mental hospital or an institution for the criminally insane if a psychiatrist has ruled that the individual has the characteristics of a sexual psychopath. Once hospitalized or institutionalized, treatment is mandated for such an offender. The commitment can be for life, if the offender does not respond to treatment.

Washington's Sexual Psychopath Act (1975) provides for treatment in a state mental hospital for sex offenders who have been defined as sexual psychopaths. In such cases, the prosecutor files a petition alleging that the offender is a sexual psychopath who is predisposed to commit sexual offenses in a degree which constitutes a menace to the health and safety of others. After the offender is convicted, sentence is suspended while the offender undergoes a 90-day period of observation in a state mental hospital. If the diagnosis of sexual psychopathy is confirmed, the offender is committed to the hospital until the treatment staff decides that he or she should be released and the court accepts this judgment. The offender may be unconditionally discharged or placed under probation supervision for up to five years.

Sexual psychopath statutes and habitual offender statutes (which frequently are applied to sexual offenders) are grounded in the assumption that there are viable treatment programs which can change the behavior of these persons. In *Allen v. Illinois* (1986), the U.S. Supreme Court upheld an Illinois law providing for commitment to prison psychiatric wards of persons who had demonstrated propensities toward acts of sexual assault, and declared that the state is serving its purpose of treating rather than punishing such persons by committing them to institutions designed to provide psychiatric care and treatment. The fact that the prison psychiatric wards house convicted criminals as well as persons who have not been convicted of sexual offenses does not alter the fact that the state is sending them there with the intention to treat them, not to punish them (*Allen v. Illinois*, 1986).

Treatment is frequently mandated for rapists and offenders who have sexually abused children. Because such offenders present unique problems, their treatment will be the focus of this chapter. The characteristics and motivations of these offenders will be examined and programs which have been developed to treat them will be described.

Rapists—Typologies

Various typologies have been developed to examine the motivations and emotional processes of rapists. One classification, set by Groth, Burgess and Holmstrom, describes rapists in terms of four basic types:

> *The power assertive rapist* regards rape as an expression of his virility and mastery and dominance. He feels entitled to "take it" or sees sexual domination as a way of keeping women in line. The rape is a reflection of the inadequacy he experiences in terms of his sense of identity and effectiveness. . . .

> *The power reassurance rapist* commits the offense in an effort to resolve disturbing doubts about his sexual adequacy and masculinity. He wants to place a woman in a helpless, controlled position in which she cannot refuse or reject him, thereby shoring up his failing sense of worth and adequacy. . . .

> *The anger-retaliation rapist* commits rape as an expression of his hostility and rage toward women. His motive is revenge and his aim is degradation and humiliation. . . .

> *The anger-excitation rapist* finds pleasure, thrills, and excitation in the suffering of his victim. He is sadistic and his aim is to punish, hurt, and torture his victim. His aggression is eroticized. (Groth, Burgess, and Holmstrom: 1977:1242)

In their study of 146 rape victims, these researchers concluded that approximately two-thirds of the offenses were power rape situations, and the remaining third were anger rape situations (1242).

Although a good deal of theory and research related to rapists has been developed, there is considerable confusion about the personality characteristics of the individuals who commit rapes. Some psychologists and sociologists view rape as essentially an act of violence. As a form of violent behavior, rape may be instrumental, that is, used as a means of gaining the rewards of prestige with peers, control over others, and mastery of situations. Many researchers' typologies of rapists support the notion that rape is widely used to make victims helpless, fearful, and totally under the rapists' control (Menachem, 1971; Macdonald, 1971). Such rapists may feel that their behavior will go unreported or unpunished, and this supposition is given some weight by research. In *The Crime and the Consequences of Rape* (1982), Dean and deBruyn-Kops report, on the basis of governmental and research sources, that many incidents of rape continue to be unreported and, of those reported to police, only 25% lead to arrest, while many charges are dropped or reduced to misdemeanors. They reported that only 20% of the offenders who go to trial for rape receive actual prison sentences.

Rape may also be interpreted as pathological behavior which reflects a morally defective personality. There may not be any meaning attributed to the act beyond attempting to satisfy the rapist's sexual needs. The degree of psychological abnormality attributed to the offender would determine whether treatment or punishment is in order.

For example, the *Diagnostic and Statistical Manual of Mental Disorders* (3rd ed.) lists compulsive rape under the sexual deviation category of paraphilia, and notes that sex offenses can be classified under various psychiatric conditions such as schizophrenia and manic depressive psychosis (1978:1–33). Treatment for a compulsive rapist, then, should be grounded in the assumption that this person is mentally ill.

Sex Abusers of Children—Typologies

Sexual abuse of children is regarded as a greatly underreported offense, and actual incidence may be as much as ten times the official reports (Elwell, 1979:227). Children may be abused through rape, sexual battery, gross sexual imposition, sexual imposition, or felonious sexual penetration, The female-to-male ratio of victims of sexual abuse is estimated to be 10 to 12 abused females for every male child abused, but there are indications that sexual abuse of male children is greatly underreported (Roth, 1978:3). Sexual offenses which involve family members (incest) are the least likely to be reported or fully prosecuted. There is evidence that a notable percentage of those involved in this activity were sexually abused themselves as children. Such persons tend to have been part of a disorganized lifestyle which also involved other forms of deviance and drug and/or alcohol abuse (Elwell, 1979:227–235).

The profile of an adult who sexually abuses a child is that of a young, heterosexual male, who is concerned with controlling, not injuring the young child. According to Krasner, et al., (1977:108) no force is used in 54% of all such incidents. Rosenfeld (1979) characterized the adult abuser as an individual who has experienced feelings of rejection or inadequacy and is emotionally estranged from his wife. The mother is often a key figure in the sexual abuse of female children. She may be aware that the child has assumed her sexual role and either does not protest this or even feels relieved about it. An American Humane Association study (1977:6–8) found that more than 10% of the mothers of sexually abused children had themselves been sexually abused as children. The assumption of the abused child of her mother's role may extend to taking over a good deal of the housework and care of the other children, as well as sexual contact with her father.

Gebhard and his associates at the Kinsey Institute, in a study of sexual offenders against children (1965) classified them as pedophiles (offenders who preferred sexual contact with children), sociosexually underdeveloped males (those who suffered from feelings of shyness and inferiority toward women), amoral delinquents (offenders who, when aroused, were apt to employ any convenient human or animal for gratification), mental defectives (who seek petting with children as much for attention and affection as for sexual gratification), psychotics, drunks, and senile deteriorates (characterized by deprivation, loneliness, and impotence) (216).

Issues in Treatment of Sex Offenders

Treatment modalities for rapists and other serious sexual offenders may involve three broad categories: psychosurgery-castration, drug therapy which produces "chemical castration," and counseling therapies. The use of psychosurgery-castration or drug therapy cannot be mandated without the offender's consent. An offender might agree to an operation or to use of a drug such as Depo-Provera, which reduces sexual drive and helps the offender control his sexual impulses, if a guaranteed reduction in sentence were offered as a trade-off. If an offender is diagnosed as suffering from a mental disorder, and if the offender is sentenced under a special section of the criminal code which mandates treatment, it is most likely that counseling therapies will be applied. However, even these cannot be undertaken without the offender'scooperation and consent.

Regardless of whether an offender's behavior is defined in a legal manner (by the type of act committed) or through psychological definition (emphasis placed on learned sexual deviation), once committed to an institution or hospital, the offender has the right to voluntary consent to treatment. Bohmer (1983) notes that: "Without consent from a subject, training professionals—and in some cases institutions, are technically liable for the charge of battery. At a minimum, the person to be treated should be given information about the basic nature of the treatment and the 'material risks' involved" (6). Material risks are defined by Schwitzgebel (1979) as information regarding a patient's position which a reasonable person would view as critical. He believes that information consists of six key elements: the diagnosis or purpose of the treatment, the nature and duration of the treatment, the risks involved, the prospects for success or benefits, possible disadvantages if the treatment is not undertaken, and alternative methods of treatment (6).

Mentally competent persons who have been involuntarily committed to hospitals or institutions have a right to refuse treatment. Their consent, or approval from the court, must be gained prior to beginning treatment. Although such patients have a right to treatment, they are not obliged to accept it. In contrast, mentally competent persons convicted of offenses generally do not have a legal right to refuse standard forms of treatment. However, there has been a trend toward establishing set procedures for obtaining consent from inmates prior to beginning treatment which might be termed "hazardous or exceptionally intrusive." Court decisions which have upheld a prisoner's right to refuse treatment have involved treatment which was considered "unreasonable or experimental" rather than treatment which met professionally recognized standards (Schwitzgebel, 1979:83).

Under Illinois state law, individuals may be committed to the psychiatric ward of a prison if they are proved to have a mental disorder for more than one year and had demonstrated propensities toward acts of sexual assault. Persons accused of being sexually dangerous must under law talk with state psychiatrists, who would evaluate their condition and make a determination whether these persons are mentally ill. If the determination is positive, they are housed in the psychiatric ward. In upholding the constitutionality of this law the Supreme Court noted: "The state serves its purpose of treating rather than punishing sexually dangerous persons by committing them to an institution expressly designed to provide psychiatric care and treatment." (*Allen v. Illinois*, 54 U.S. Law Week: 4966).

Another issue in the treatment of sex offenders is the return of the offender to the community. Although treatment is initiated in a hospital or institutional setting, decisions are made in many instances to gradually return sex offenders who show evidence of responding positively to treatment to the community through placement in group homes of furlough from the hospital or institution while treatment continues. Public concern about the effectiveness of treatment is sometimes coupled with a perception that offenders who have been hospitalized rather than institutionalized have escaped punishment for their misdeeds.

Avery-Clark described the trend for mental health practitioners to lobby for the placement of offenders who are suffering from psychiatric disorders directly related to their crimes in hospitals rather than in institutions. She noted that offenders who served time in hospitals usually had shorter stays than those with comparable offenses who had been institutionalized (1983:69). The concern of the local citizenry that serious sexual offenders who may still be "dangerous" are being released back into the community after a short stay in a mental hospital has resulted in movements to have legislatures establish new regulations which would require that the committing judge approve each release from a psychiatric facility. The judge's decision would be based on an evaluation of the sex offender by a psychiatrist appointed by the court.

Group Therapy for Sex Offenders
in the Institutional Setting

Group therapy has been utilized as a treatment modality for rapists and sex offenders against children who have been committed to institutions. Theorists (Groth, et al., 1982; Alford, et al., 1985) have suggested that these offenders commit their offenses because of personality adjustment problems. Their sexual offenses are manifestations of hostilities and anger resulting from unsolved life issues. The group therapy approach stresses the personal involvement of each offender in improving his or her interpersonal and social skills.

An institution based program which used group therapy was applied at the United States Disciplinary Barracks in Fort Leavenworth, Kansas. Twenty male inmates were divided into two groups: those who had committed sexual offenses against children, and those who had raped adults. The "sexual offenses against children" group met for one hour, once a week, for a year. The entrance guidelines for this group were based on the offender acknowledging his responsibility for the offense, understanding the inappropriate nature of the offense, having concern for the victim's response, and feeling distressed over his behavior (Groth, 1982:94).

The overall objectives of this group were reintegration of the offender's personality through the fostering of self-worth and development of interpersonal and social skills and impulse management. The actual treatment goals consisted of: keeping a written log of the issues and responses discussed in the group setting, writing an autobiography after three months in the program, developing better interpersonal skills in relating to women and forming expectation regarding women, dealing with the possibility that the offender had been a victim of sexual abuse as a child, and detecting impulses toward approaching a child with the need for sexual contact (Alford, et al., 1985).

The entrance guidelines for the rapist group were the same as those for the group of child sexual abusers. The rapist group was serviced by a male/female treatment team who "role modeled competency and self-confidence without putting each other down" (Alford, et al., 1985:84). The purpose of using the male/female team was to help break down the stereotypes of women internalized by the offenders. Therapy goals were developed through personal drawings with disclosure. Offenders were asked to draw pictures of themselves, parents, women, wives, and girlfriends, if applicable. Discussions followed in which the concepts of preference, self-image, expectations, power, control, and competition were evaluated. The offenders were asked to draw a picture of the woman they raped and compare her to the "ideal woman, wife, or mother" (Alford, 1985:84).

Both the child sex abusers and the rapists were pre- and post-tested on the Tennessee Self-Concept Scale (TSCS), which measured identity, self-satisfaction, behavior, physical self, moral-ethical self, personal self, family self, and social self (Alford: 1985). It was found that the rapists had shallow relationships with women, were possessive, lacked commitment, and had a fear of being rejected. The child molesters had a lower self-esteem of and a worse opinion of the act they committed than did the rapists. However, these opinions changed after the group therapy. Molesters were also more prone to become dependent on the therapist. Both groups relied heavily on sexual stereotypes in their relationships (Alford: 1985).

Group therapy has also been used successfully with mentally disordered sex offenders, who had been found guilty of felony sexual offenses. Not all types of mentally disordered offenders are candidates for such treatment. Excluded from participation are "psychotics, mentally retarded, legally insane, and otherwise incompetent offenders, such as those judged to stand trial by reason of insanity" (Annis, et al., 1984:428).

A program for treatment of mentally disordered sex offenders was operated at Florida State Hospital. It involved the treatment of twenty-five offenders ranging in age from 25 to 46. The group treatment involved offenders, therapists, and "victim workers," who had themselves been victims of sexual aggression. Each therapy session lasted 90 minutes, and the offenders were divided into groups of five to eight. Each "victim worker," along with one or two therapists, met with each group one to five times. The sessions involved exchange of information, culminating with the offenders detailing their sexual aggression against the victim. The group process often evolved into highly personal, often very intense, interactions with considerable disclosure by offenders and the "victim workers." (Annis, et al., 1984:430).

Approximately half of the offenders involved in this program were returned to court or prison for failure to gain from therapy, while the remaining half returned to the court or prison with a good report. The successful offenders usually received probation, reduced sentences, or assignment to a less restrictive correctional setting (Annis, et al.:428).

Evaluation of this program was accomplished through self-reports of offenders, therapists, and the "victim workers." These self-reports were administered before, during, and after the sessions, and by follow-up questionnaires. The offenders reported after completing the program that they believed they had helped educate the "victim workers" as to their human quality. They also reported that the program made them better able to share their feelings with women, improved their communication skills, gave them new perceptions of women as more than "objects," personalized their victims, and gave them a more accurate perception of society's perception of them (Annis, et al.:430–31).

The use of the "victim workers" in therapy for offenders was fairly unique. It was found that among forty-four rehabilitation programs serving incarcerated rapists, only four employed rape victims or those who work with survivors of sexual victimization in treatment roles (Annis, et al.:434). The use of victims in counseling other victims is widely applied through rape crisis centers and sexual abuse hotlines, and the possibility of their wider use in treating sexual offenders should be explored.

Behavior modification through group therapy was applied in the Missouri Sexual Offender Program. The philosophical foundation of this program was the belief that sexual offending is a learned behavior and therefore can be modified through a conscious awareness of personal behavior. The theoretical basis of the program is the supposition that when an offender assumes responsibility for his behavior and is given alternate social skills as reinforcement, socially acceptable behavior will result (Clark, 1986: 89).

The Missouri Sexual Offender Program involves two phases. During Phase I, the orientation, weekly two-hour classes were conducted to discuss the concept and the treatment with the offenders. The major possible consequence of failure to participate would be a delay in obtaining parole. After interviews, the offenders were classified as manipulative or aggressive, socially inadequate, or more average individuals who had exercised poor judgment and committed offenses as a result. A wide variety of testing instruments was also used, including the Minnesota Multiphasic Personality Inventory, the Norwicki-Strickland Personal Opinion Survey, the Rathus Assertiveness Scale, and the Anger Self-report Scale. Cognitive, affective, and behavioral disturbances specifically related to sexual concerns were evaluated with the Derogatis Sexual Functioning Inventory and the Thorne Sex Inventory (Avery-Clark, 1983). During Phase II, group therapy based on confrontative techniques, was used to heighten offender awareness regarding learned behavior. Phase II lasted 9 to 12 months with meetings held four hours each week. Evaluation of the program indicated statistically successful results.

Community Group Treatment for Sex Offenders

Community treatment of sex offenders raises the question of whether punishment or treatment should be the major purpose in dealing with sex offenders. One often overlooked benefit of community treatment of sex offenders is the possibility of educating the public regarding the existence of inappropriate sexual activity, its motivations, and the availability of treatment. State legislation in the late 1970s mandated community treatment for sex offenders. Atascadero State Hospital in California and Western State Hospital in Washington are the sites of innovative community treatment programs for sex offenders. At Atascadero State Hospital, the program begins with an orientation to educate offenders in the areas of sexual anatomy and physiology. Small group sessions are then employed to raise the offenders' level of awareness of the needs of others. Role playing is used, and college student volunteers, both heterosexual and homosexual, are brought in to assist offenders in learning to model behavior and gain assertiveness skills.

The therapy at Western State Hospital, in Washington, centers on group processing. MacDonald and Williams (1971) state the group treatment goals as awareness of problem behavior, understanding of treatment goals and expectations, acceptance of responsibility to change problem behavior, and the development of social skills to adopt new behavior patterns. In the first phase of the program, offenders' progress is measured in group living, work assignments, psychotherapy family and sexual relationships, social and recreational activities, and leadership ability. Once offenders successfully complete Phase I, they are granted work furloughs, but return to the hospital at night.

Unlike the community programs described above, which are housed in state hospitals, the Child Sexual Abuse Treatment Program (CSATP) operates in the community, funded by Santa Clara County, California. County probation officers intervene, in crisis situations involving child sexual abuse, and provide individual and family counseling. The therapy process emphasizes treatment of the involved family members separately, then as a family unit with a child, and, if necessary, marital therapy.

A group known as Parents United and a related group, Daughters United, share the counseling responsibilities with the probation officers by attending weekly meetings with the offenders similar to those held by Alcoholics Anonymous. Parents are forced to take responsibility for mistakes or oversights that led to incestuous patterns. Fathers must confront other mothers and fathers at the meetings regarding the abuse of their children. Offenders are not placed into the program until they admit and understand the seriousness of their actions. Those allowed to enter are given suspended sentences and then ordered by the judge to participate in this therapy as a condition of release to the community (Kiersh, 1980:33).

Characteristics of Effective Therapy for Sex Offenders

The counseling programs developed to treat sexual offenders, whether used in an institution, psychiatric hospital, or the community all seem to have a common theme. There is an assumption that the cause of the offense cannot totally be defined as a personality abnormality of the offender. If the offender is to change his behavior, the treatment must call for open, uninhibited communication with others who are affected by this person's behavior, including parents, spouse, other family members, or the victim. Group treatment seems to yield more positive results than individual counseling. If the group consists of offenders and counselors, the interaction may be initially characterized by dislike, distrust, aggressive behavior, insults, refusal to participate, or failure to identify with the other group members, but during the group process insights are gained. The topics and discussions during the meetings may vary tremendously, depending on the members andtheir needs.

VanNess, who supervised group therapy with violent sexual offenders over a number of years, lists the following matters as frequent topics of group discussions:

1. Being honest with yourself about the offense
2. Taking personal responsibility for your actions without blaming others
3. Understanding the laws and why you were sent to the institution
4. Understanding what happened to your victim
5. Dealing with your reputation in your community
6. Being honest with your family
7. Learning what makes you angry
8. Learning how to handle your anger
9. Learning to solve problems without using force
10. Chemical abuse and your offense
11. Building good relationships with people. (VanNess, 1983:14)

During the sessions, various techniques were used to illustrate situations which might arise with family members or institution staff. Role playing, discussions of films, and various exercises and games provided offenders opportunities for communication and learning.

VanNess identified certain patterns of behavior in the rapists' lives which have also been noted by other researchers. These included a lack of close personal relationships with other persons, particularly women, distrust of other males, a view of the world as a hostile and "dog eat dog" place, and conceptions of parents as givers or withholders rather than emotionally bonded persons. In their dealings with others, the rapists viewed power or force as the important element in relating to other persons, and had great difficulty in recognizing that men and women could treat each other as equals. In describing events which immediately preceded the rapes they committed, they invariably described some type of highly emotional incident which aroused their anger (VanNess: 1983:16).

Robinson A. Williams, who served as Assistant Director of the Treatment Center for Sexual Offenders at Western State Hospital, regarded abnormal sexual behavior as a learned method of relieving emotional stress. He maintained that sexual attacks or contacts become habitual ways of finding emotional release for offenders who feel inadequate and insecure in their relationships with women. He noted that sex offenders frequently have experienced troubled childhoods and may themselves have been victims of sexual abuse as children (Denenberg, 1974:58).

Group therapy is beneficial for sex offenders because it provides a setting in which they can relate to fellow sex offenders and feel that they will understand their problems. As the group encourages the offender to reveal his inner conflicts and fears, he becomes aware of the motivations for his offenses and begins to recognize that he must change his behavior. The group provides constant support during this awareness experience. Various steps are established, which give the offender opportunities to take more responsibility for his actions. The steps usually involve increasing degrees of physical freedom to move about the institution or the grounds and acceptance of responsibility for the activities of the group.

Most of the group therapy programs which have some demonstrated success with sex offenders appear to follow the general outlines of the technique known as rational-emotive therapy. This therapy, developed by Ellis in the 1950s, identifies irrational thinking and erroneous belief systems as the roots of problems, and involves a process of reeducation by which the person being treated acquires a more rational and tolerant view of life. The therapist functions as a teacher who leads the offender to understand how his outlook has contributed to his self-defeating behavior and how to begin to behave rationally. The group plays a key role in leading the offender to critically examine his beliefs and behavior and work to change them. The eclectic approach involved may include probing, confrontation, challenging, behavior contracts, role playing, hypnotherapy, assertiveness training, and many other techniques. Encounter groups, marriage and family therapy, and sex therapy may be used. Rational-emotive therapy is most effective with persons who are not seriously emotionally disturbed, and, because of its emphasis on the thinking process, it is unlikely to be successful for persons of limited intelligence (Corey, 1982:96–97).

References

Alford, Jane M., Gary E. Brown and James C. Kasper, 1985. "Group Treatment for Sex Offenders," *Corrective and Social Psychiatry and Journal of Behavioral Technology Methods and Treatment*, 31(3): 83–86.

Allen V. Illinois, 1986. *U.S. Law Week*: 4966

Annis, Lawrence V., Leigh G. Mathers and Christy A. Baker, 1984. "Victim Workers As Therapists for Incarcerated Sex Offenders," *Victimology: An International Journal*, 9(3–4): 426–435.

Avery-Clark, Constance A., 1983. "Sexual Offenders: Special Programatic Needs," *Corrections Today*, 45(5): 68–70.

Bohmer, Carol, 1983. "Legal and Ethical Issues in Mandatory Treatment: The Patient's Rights versus Society's Rights," In *The Sexual Aggressor*, Joanne Green and Irving R. Stuart (Eds.). New York: Van Nostrand Reinhold Company.

Bowers v. Hardwick, 1986. 54 *U.S. Law Week*: 4919.

Clark, Marie, 1986. "Missouri's Sexual Offender Program," *Corrections Today*, 48(3): 84–86.

Corey, Gerald, 1982. *Manual for Theory and Practice of Counseling and Psychotherapy*, 2nd ed., Monterey, CA: Brooks/Cole Publishing Company, 1982.

Dean, Charles and Mary deBruyn-Kops, 1982. *The Crime and the Consequences of Rape*. Springfield, IL: Charles C. Thomas.

DeFrancis, Vincent, 1977. "American Humane Association Publishes Highlights of National Study of Child Neglect and Abuse Reporting for 1975," Washington, D.C.: U.S. Department of Health, Education and Welfare, National Center on Child Abuse and Neglect, Publication OHD 77–20086:6–8.

Denenberg, R. V., 1974. "Profile/Washington State, Sex Offenders Treat Themselves," *Corrections Magazine*, 1(2): 53–64.

Diagnostic and Statistical Manual of Mental Disorders, 3rd ed., 1978. Washington, D.C.: Task Force on Nomenclature and Statistics of the American Psychiatric Association: L1–L33.

Elwell, M. E., 1979. "Sexually Assaulted Children and Their Families," *Social Casework*, 60(4): 227–235.

Gebhard, Paul H., John H. Garnon, Wardell B. Pomeroy and Cornelia V. Christenson, 1965. *Sex Offenders: An Analysis of Types*. New York: Harper & Row.

Groth, A. N., A. W. Burgess and L. L. Holmstrom, 1977. "Rape: Power, Anger, and Sexuality," *American Journal of Psychiatry*, 134: 1239–43.

Groth, A. N., W. F. Hobson and T. Gary, 1982. "The Child Molester: Clinical Observations," In *Social Work and Child Sexual Abuse*. New York: Haworth Press.

Kiersh, Edward, 1980. "Can Families Survive Incest?" *Corrections Magazine*, 6(2): 31–38.

Krasner W., Linda C. Meyer and Nancy E. Carroll, 1977. *Victims of Rape.* Washington, D.C.: U.S. Government Printing Office, 1977.

MacDonald, G. J. and R. T. Williams, 1971. "A Guided Self-help Approach to Treatment of the Habitual Sex Offender," Fort Steilacoom, Washington: Western State Hospital.

Macdonald, John M., 1971. *Rape Offenders and Their Victims.* Springfield, IL: Charles C. Thomas.

Menachem, Amir 1971. *Patterns in Forcible Rape.* Chicago: University of Chicago Press.

Ohio Criminal Law Handbook, 3rd ed., 1983. Cincinnati: Anderson Publishing Company.

Rosenfeld, Alvin A., 1979. "Endogamic Incest and the Victim-Perpetrator Model," *American Journal of Diseases of Children*, 133:406–410.

Roth, R. A., 1978. *Child Sexual Abuse—Incest Assault and Sexual Exploitation*, A Special Report from the National Center on Child Abuse and Neglect. Washington, D.C.: U.S. Department of Health and Human Services.

Schwitzgebel, R. Kirkland, 1979. *Legal Aspects of the Enforced Treatment of Offenders.* Washington: U.S. Department of Health, Education and Welfare.

Smith, Alexander B. and Louis Berlin, 1981. *Treating the Criminal Offender*, 2nd ed. Englewood Cliffs, NJ: Prentice-Hall.

VanNess, Shela R., 1983. "Rape as Instrumental Violence: A Perspective for Theory, Research and Corrections," paper presented at the annual meeting of the Academy of Criminal Justice Sciences, San Antonio, Texas.

Vetter, Harold J. and Ira J. Silverman, 1986. *Criminology and Crime.* New York: Harper & Row.

Washington Sexual Psychopath Act, 1975. Wash. Rev. Code Ann. 71.06.010 Seq. (1975).

23

Northwest Treatment Associates
A Comprehensive, Community-Based Evaluation and Treatment Program for Adult Sex Offenders

Fay Honey Knopp

Northwest Treatment Associates (NWTA) is a partnership of five practitioners[1] who collectively have 50 years of full-time experience in the treatment of sex offenders. Since 1977, in their attractive, three-story converted house, Steven Silver, Timothy A. Smith, Steven C. Wolf, Roger W. Wolfe, and Florence A. Wolfe have provided what is believed to be one of the largest and most comprehensive outpatient sex-offender evaluation and treatment programs in the United States. At any given time, approximately 200 men (and a few women) are involved actively in weekly or twice-weekly treatment in two locations.[2] Nonoffending spouses and other family members also participate in the treatment program.

More than 85 percent of NWTA's clients are attached to the criminal justice system through either court-ordered evaluations or sentences of probation with conditions of treatment.[3] Since probation provides very few treatment subsidies, NWTA's clients are mainly white and middle class.[4] "Probation views treatment as a privilege," says Roger Wolfe (1981b). "If they want community treatment, they have to work for it." The average period of time spent in treatment is 18 months, though a few stay longer. Most felony offenders are on five years' probation.

Fee schedules are on a sliding scale. They range from $40 to $70

Reprinted by permission of Safer Society Press from: *Retraining Adult Sex Offenders: Methods and Models* by Fay Honey Knopp (Orwell, VT: Safer Society Press, 1989), pp. 85–101.

for individual treatment and $13 to $23 for two-hour sessions. On each therapist's caseload, NWTA usually subsidizes at least three particularly hard-working and well-motivated clients who do not have adequate funds to purchase treatment.

Evaluation and Assessment

The majority of the people accepted into the program "graduate" or complete treatment. The reason for this comparatively low dropout rate is the selection of clients prior to treatment. Like most community-based programs, NWTA excludes individuals from treatment if they show patterns of overt physical violence, if they show an extensive history of nonsexual crimes, if they are assessed as being psychotic or suffering from severe mental illness, if they have serious substance abuse problems, if they are identified as "grossly inadequate," or if they have poor motivational levels and counterproductive attitudes that prevail despite modeling, education, and confrontation during the assessment process (R. Wolfe, 1981a, 1984).

Roger Wolfe and his colleagues, like other experienced sex-offender treatment specialists, are justifiably skeptical and often distrustful of their clients' historical perceptions of the sexually aggressive behavior that led them to their present situation. To test a client's perceptions of the behavior for which he was convicted, staff use a polygraphist with an extensive history of working with sex offenders. Staff recount, not without humor, some standard staff responses to the traditional amnesia and shadowy memories of their clients during evaluation and assessment, particularly when the polygraph has indicated that the client was involved in defensive lying:

> I have this kind of standard approach I take and it is usually effective. When a sex offender comes in and I question him about the allegations against him and his perception of them, he may say: "Well, I really don't remember if I did—but it really happened all at once and I've never thought about it before, it never entered my mind before—it was just totally spontaneous" —etcetera. I then go into my old philosopher stance, lean back in my chair, and kind of squint my eyes and say, "Y'know—I guess I believe you. If you really are the way you are representing yourself—a person who just spontaneously with no forethought raped this kid—it says to me that you are so incredibly danger-ous, you should not be on the street even this afternoon. In fact, I'm going to call the cops right now . . ." Then there's a quick

turn around. "Well . . . I suddenly remember very clearly . . ."
(S. Wolf, 1981)

Another client said he remembered his offense but "just had these brief flashes. I'm there with this kid—she's a nameless, faceless figure, and I remember trying to insert my penis, but she is only a five year old . . ." We worked on that for three or four sessions, to no avail, and then I told him we could not continue to treat him. The primary criterion for working with anybody in the community is you have to have honesty. A good client—a really honest client—is going to give us, at most, *maybe* 75 percent honesty. (R. Wolfe, 1981b)

Evaluation and assessment include psychological testing,[5] physiological monitoring via the plethysmograph (also used for monitoring treatment progress), and a period spent in one of the ongoing, guided sex-offender groups. A person under evaluation must obtain unanimous group and treatment-team sanction on four basic issues: (1) that he believes he is a sexual offender; (2) that he strongly desires specialized intervention; (3) that he will be helpful to others in their process of accomplishing similar goals; and (4) that he has demonstrated change in and outside the treatment setting.

Treatment Modalities

The NWTA treatment program consists of two major components: a confrontive, guided-group model modified for community use, and a range of behavioral treatment approaches.[6] Roger Wolfe is a strong advocate for treatment eclecticity:

Behavioral treatment is very important, but not sufficient by itself. We need both group and individual counseling to deal with the offender's characterological problems. I think a great many treatment programs exaggerate the importance of one or the other approach. I am firmly convinced you have to have both. Above all, you need individual assessment and careful, individual treatment planning for each person. It is a great deal of work. (R. Wolfe, 1981b)

Staff at NWTA are aware that one of their most important tasks is to help their clients to develop appropriate sexuality. Sexual reorientation is provided for those men who have no appropriate sexual arousal system or history. Marital counseling, sexual enhancement, and treatment for sexual dysfunction also are provided where appropriate. Says Florence Wolfe (1981), "Many of our clients have poor social skills[7] and no orientation to appropriate sexuality. We help them go through all the steps to establish their own relationships."

Guided Sex-Offender Group

The guided sex-offender group at NWTA is a modified version of the one developed in Western State Hospital's Sex Offender Program.[8] Honesty is a program requirement, so the model is extremely confrontive. The men are expected to challenge directly any rationalization and character traits that make offending easier. The group also provides an arena for education, support for prosocial behavior, and positive role modeling.

Steven Silver, who facilitates the majority of the groups at NWTA, perceives his role as both teacher and therapist. He structures specific written and experiential situations for the men to explore. Silver, a nontraditional group therapist, is a powerful, conscious model of a nondeviant male. Though a highly skilled veteran of group process and therapy with traditional mental health patients, none of these experiences prepared him adequately for running a sex-offender group. He developed his expertise by working with offenders for 12 years and through studying the relevant literature. In describing his NWTA stance, he says,

> It is confrontive and challenging. It is insisting that behavior be totally honest and responsible. I tell our clients, "I may act like a teacher, but this is not a class. It is group therapy and every one of you has a very serious disorder." It is emphasized that the behavior has been seriously abusive and that there is certainly the potential for subsequent dangerous behavior.
>
> If you tolerate one guy minimizing what he did, four weeks later he will come back and he will have minimized it, accepted it, and be sliding backward. It is important, however, to allow the offender room to blame, rationalize, and in other ways misrepresent people and circumstances; otherwise a therapist will obtain lip service compliance without behavioral or characterological change. The offender needs to believe that his side has at least been heard.
>
> This is the hardest group therapy that has ever been structured, because the sex-offenders' therapist has to take the responsibility for ensuring that, when these men walk out of the door, they are not going to reoffend. (Silver, 1981)

In group therapy at NWTA, the offender's character pathology that facilitates sexual offending and other destructive behaviors is brought into awareness, challenged, and gradually replaced with prosocial attitudes, traits, and behaviors. Traits such as impulsivity, manipulation, dishonesty, sexual preoccupation, low frustration tolerance, denial, and deviousness are among those focused upon. The offender must take full responsibility for the harmfulness and severity of the offense. He learns preoffense warning signs (emotional, cognitive, physical, and environmental antecedents) and internal and external controls over impulses and behaviors, and he structures his life to minimize the possibility of reoffense. Learning in group occurs through confrontation, modeling of appropriate behavior, discussion, assignments, experiential exercises and lectures given by people in the field, for example, a counselor for sexually abused children. The client must complete a long series of assignments including assigned texts and pass a comprehensive written examination and a polygraph test prior to any consideration for program completion. All assignments and exercises are offender focused; the client must understand thoroughly his offending cycle and demonstrate by living a positive, prosocial lifestyle that he is willing and able to make the necessary changes (Wolfe & Wolfe, 1984).

If a person reoffends while in the group (almost always these reoffenses are misdemeanors such as exhibitionism and voyeurism), he may be taken back on a provisional basis, depending on the combined decision of probation and NWTA staff. If he does come back, Silver explains,

> I think reaccepting him depends on the level of the offense, how it came to light, and the client's attitude about it and treatment. If an exhibitionist reoffends against an adult, you are going to be considerably more tolerant than if a child molester reoffends. It also depends on how long a person has been in the program. If he has been in the group a significant length of time and reoffends, it means there is a great deal of information regarding offense-related patterns and controls that he is keeping a secret. And there must be lots of things he has not been doing, a lot of cons and scams he has been running and getting away with. It speaks to a continued pattern of deviance and to trying to "beat" treatment. (Silver, 1981)

The average length of stay in treatment groups is 18 months, during which certain tasks must be accomplished. Individuals are evaluated periodically by both their fellow group members and the treatment team. The therapist is present at all group sessions to guide, monitor, and assist the offenders in their process.

Following graduation, a client is encouraged to return to the group at any time, for any reason at no charge. If a client begins to feel himself returning to his deviant pattern or if his family notices some slipping, there is no excuse for not returning and seeking further help.

Behavioral Treatment

Sex-offender clients are given an introductory explanation of the basic principles of behavioral treatment and assigned readings to familiarize them further with the approaches. The men go to their local library, find the readings, do the prescribed work, and bring it back to NWTA.

The behavioral treatment is geared toward reducing and/or eliminating the deviant sexual arousal, which staff believe provides a major motivation for the offender's behavioral pattern. The initial step in treatment is bringing the overt behavior under control:

> Sex-offender behavior is conditioned on a very basic level—sexual arousal. The individual has a long history of carrying out that particular behavior, paired with immediate gratification. A large chunk of that is sexual gratification, but a great many other things go along with that, too. Adrenalin rush, getting away with something, escaping from discomfort or boredom—these often are overlooked. The sex offense gives the offender something to focus on as an escape from tedium, problems, anxiety, and frustration. We are talking about the immediate application of a strong, powerful package of rewards. Our theory is, if you are going to deal with the compulsive nature of that behavior, you are going to have to do some counterconditioning. (R. Wolfe, 1981b)

This procedure involves pairing the deviant behavior and its antecedents with ungratifying, negative results. It also means encouraging nondeviant behavior and pairing it with positive reinforcers.

In the case involving an incest offender, for example, Roger Wolfe might use the following scenario to pair negative imagery with the offender's deviant behavior:

> Imagine you are walking into your daughter's room. You are pulling back the covers, feeling very excited, very aroused. You are reaching down, picking up her nightie. You've touched her, your hand is covered with pus, you can smell the overwhelming stench, you brush your hand against your clothes, the pus is smeared against your clothes, the stench is really making you nauseous, you feel like you have to throw up, you taste the sweet, sickly bile in the back of your throat. . . . (and so forth).

There are many other procedures commonly used by NWTA staff. First we will describe briefly six approaches to teaching impulse control. Next we describe, in greater detail, behavioral methods aimed at reducing deviant arousal and/or increasing appropriate arousal. These include covert sensitization, covert positive reinforcement, masturbatory reconditioning, boredom aversion, and the modified aversive behavioral rehearsal technique. Last, we examine a variety of techniques used in teaching victim empathy.

Simple Impulse-Control Techniques. The methods described here are among the simplest, most concise, and least intrusive interventions taught to the offender to assist him in controlling ongoing impulses. They are considered "bandaids" in that they are short-term pragmatic attempts to preclude reoffense until more long-term modalities can have an impact.

1. *Thought-stopping*[9] is used to disrupt a deviant thinking pattern. An example is given of a heterosexual pedophile walking down the street and noticing a little girl. His eyes may wander to her buttocks. He begins to think how beautiful and little they are. "We want him to stop those thoughts, to block them out," explains Roger Wolfe. "Thought-stopping, simply stated, is to have the offender scream at the top of his lungs—'STOP'—*inside* his head. It disrupts that thought" (R. Wolfe, 1981b).

2. *Thought-shifting* to aversive imagery is equally simple. The pedophile, for example, sees a little girl and finds himself starting to dwell on her. Immediately he must try to think of something aversive. For instance, he imagines a police officer walking up behind him, tapping him on the shoulder, and saying, "I know what you are up to," then kneeing him in the groin and calling in the neighbors to deal with "the local pervert." Realistic aversive imagery disrupts arousal and deviant thought processes and applies a punishment to those behaviors. The probability of reoffense is diminished.

3. *Impulse-charting* is a method used to help the offender to focus on what is going on in his thinking and acting patterns. NWTA gives the client little cards that list the days of the week. After the offender controls an impulse, he records a number from one to 10 that indicates the intensity of that impulse and the difficulty he had in controlling it.[10] "It gives them something to do that takes them one step further away from offending," says Roger Wolfe. "It also gives us an ongoing measure that we can quantify in terms of the strength and frequency of his impulses. We get some idea of how well the person is doing, how good our techniques are, and how well they are working. If his impulses are not decreasing, we had better go back to the drawing board and come up with a new approach" (R. Wolfe, 1981b).

For people having greater difficulty controlling their impulses, or for someone who raises suspicion that he might be on the brink of reoffending, the program utilizes stronger, more intrusive types of controls. These are most appropriate for chronic child molesters or exhibitionists, the clients who usually are the most out of control.

1. *Scheduled overmasturbation* simply places the client on an escalating masturbation schedule, timed by the clock. The frequency of masturbation is increased steadily to reduce sexual drive and thus make it easier to control. "This exercise also gives him a measure of control over his sexuality," says Roger Wolfe (1981b), "since he is used to masturbating willy-nilly. Care is taken that he is utilizing appropriate imagery."

2. *Spouse monitoring* involves asking the spouse or significant other to give the program feedback in terms of how the offender is doing,[11] by signing the checklist of tasks and homework to be completed by the client and by monitoring his behavior. Spouse monitoring is used with nearly all clients.

3. *Environmental manipulation* helps to get the offender out of situations that are high risk for him and his potential victims. For instance, with an incest or pedophile offender, one of the standard procedures is to have him move himself right out of the house, as opposed to taking the victim out of the house and doubly victimizing him/her. Other examples provided by Roger Wolfe (1981b) are practical and creative:

> These are all basic, common-sense approaches that work. Here are some examples we have used with exposers. One person had a great many impulses to expose while he was aimlessly cruising around town. We told him he can no longer cruise, but he must have a specific destination, he must call his friend and tell him to meet him at a designated place at a specific time. In group we changed the time a guy jogged, where he jogged, the way he drove to work, the way he drove home from work, and what he does on Sunday afternoons in football season. These were all situations where he had flashed. One of the most creative kinds of things we do with flashers who exhibit in their cars is to have them put their names on the front, back, and sides of the car. Also, we had one fellow who was a jogger and who flashed while he was jogging. We had him get a T-shirt with his name on it.

If these impulse-control measures are not effective, Depo-Provera may be prescribed.

Covert Sensitization.[12] Approximately 10 weeks of treatment are devoted to covert sensitization. Conditioning sessions are audiotaped, and the 40-minute tape is sent home with the client, who is instructed to listen to it daily. Monitoring by spouses or significant others and quizzing for content make compliance more likely.

Tapes also typically include covert positive reinforcement of alternatives to deviant behaviors (such as not responding to deviant stimulus situations, assertiveness, appropriate sexual behavior, and so forth). In the early sessions, the therapist constructs the tape; later, the client takes over this task, with the therapist serving as a consultant. After 10 weeks, additional elements are included in conditioning tapes.

Staff describe graphically how covert sensitization is used. First, the therapist induces a relaxed phase for about five to fifteen minutes, depending on how well trained and adept the client is in being able to drift down into a relaxed state where he can get good imagery.[13] Next he is given instructions that he is going to focus on the upcoming scenes and they are going to seem very real. The therapist then begins a description of a scene, tailor-made for the client, constructed from a fear inventory of about 175 items, from which the client has chosen those that are most fearful to him.

> We first start with a written checklist and then explore other things they are very afraid of—a bad experience where they nearly drowned, an automobile accident, a particular horror movie that really scared them—all their most relevant and immediate fears. Usually these men are fresh from their court experience, so we do all sorts of marvelous scenes about being taken down to the police station and what the judge said to them. The more impact the better, is the general rule. What you are after is finding the images that produce a strong reaction. (R. Wolfe, 1981b)

Roger Wolfe describes how one person's fear of snakes was paired with a scene reflective of his deviant pattern:

> You are restless. It is about three o'clock in the morning and you cannot sleep. You tell yourself you are going to go to the bathroom. You get up, you go to the bathroom, you urinate, and you continue to stand there. You are thinking, "Little Sally is sleeping in the room next door." You tell yourself, "Maybe I'd better check on her just to see if she kicked her covers off or something." As you are thinking that, you kind of put your hand down on your penis and you feel your excitement. You tell yourself, "She is sound asleep—she won't know if I was in there or not." You go up to her door, telling yourself she is sound asleep and you are just going to check on her, feeling sexual excitement, thinking about touching her, thinking you will just slip up her nightgown a little bit and maybe just look at her, and getting more excited. You are thinking about doing that, with your hand on the doorknob, getting really excited now, really turned on, and you gently, carefully, being really quiet, open that door, you open that door thinking about touching

> her . . . and you suddenly realize there is something on the floor.
> There is something moving on the floor in the bedroom. My God,
> my God, you say—it is a snake! There is more than one. There
> are creepy crawly snakes all over and you can see their little
> forked tongues, see their beady eyes. They are moving toward
> you. You are just terrified standing there, you want to run, but
> you are just scared. A cold chill runs up and down your body.
> Your body gets tight. They are moving toward you. God, these
> cold slimy snakes are moving toward you. One of them is on
> your toe now . . . (R. Wolfe, 1981b)

The client, in an induced state, hears the scene for the first time
at NWTA. Then he writes the scene down in his own words,
monitored by his spouse or friend. A week later the client returns
and guides the therapist through the scene. The therapist will check
the client's memory at various points and ask for a self-report on
what the impact of the tape has been.

"For instance," says Roger Wolfe, "I may ask him, at the place
where his hand is on the doorknob, to tell me what he is feeling
when he is home listening to the tape. Can he feel the coldness and
hardness of the knob? Can he see the shadows of his own hallway?
I'm trying to pick up how clear the imagery is" (R. Wolfe, 1981b).
Wolfe also asks for bodily reactions to the scene. "When he says,
'That snake really scares me,' I say, 'What is your body doing?' I
should hear things like 'My throat is dry, I am swallowing, my
stomach flutters, and I have increased heart beat.'"

Some other measures of treatment impact are self-report of
deviant impulses, plethysmograph assessment, and polygraph
examination.

Covert Positive Reinforcement. The last two scenes on the tape
will pair appropriate behavior with cognitive and material rewards.
There are many approaches that can be used. One scene involves
the offender just leaving a situation that is typical of his deviant
pattern, where he would have had high impulses and temptations
and could have reoffended. The scene would place him safely away
from such temptations, and he would realize, "I didn't even think
about it. By God, that feels really good. Hey, I'm more normal; all
that work I am putting in—it is paying off." The tape would provide
a material reward by having him drive home and find a letter telling
him he had just been granted a job promotion.

A second approach involves an element of cognitive
restructuring.[14] In this scenario, the sex offender starts repeating
some of the excuses he typically has used himself. For instance,
he might say, "Well it won't hurt, she's asleep, she likes it anyway,
this is a good way for her to learn about sex." Then, instead of
continuing this pattern, suddenly he thinks, "That's a bunch of

bullshit! In fact, the reality is, it is harmful, it does hurt people, it is not okay. I don't care if she is asleep or not asleep—that is invading her privacy and that's being damaging and harmful."

Another approach, Roger Wolfe explains, is to take a range of the client's most positive behaviors and reinforce them by loading the end with rewards.

> For instance, you can walk a client through a scene where he is behaving assertively and pair that up with having him sit down in a restaurant where the waiter brings him some marvelous beefsteak. You can smell the aroma, you can see the juices kind of flowing from the steak, and there are mushrooms on top, and french fries, and so forth. The rationale for loading the end with rewards is that we want him to take the whole tape and come out of the experience feeling pretty good about himself. If he comes out of the tape feeling pretty good, it is that much easier for him to go back and do the tape again. If you do just total punishment, the client gets phobic about doing the tape. Scenes are changed with each tape to minimize adaptation and maximize generalization. (R. Wolfe, 1981b)

As mentioned earlier, the therapist makes the first few conditioning tapes and then encourages the client to construct his own. This process of gradually shifting responsibility is an integral part of NWTA's therapeutic plan:

> I think this kind of self-help approach is reflective of our total treatment philosophy. We want to train the individual to change his own behavior. We want him to become his own behavioral therapist. By the time he leaves here he should be as good as we are, if not better, in terms of dealing with his own specific problem. We learn a great deal from the types of tapes he makes. He gets into much more when he is sitting on his own with that tape recorder. The clients do an amazingly good job. We could work with them for years and years, but they know more about their patterns than we do, they know more about what turns them off than we do, and they know more about what turns them on than we do. (R. Wolfe, 1981b)

Masturbatory Reconditioning[15] *and Boredom Aversion.*[16] Staff have combined and adapted the technique of masturbatory reconditioning and boredom aversion to function within outpatient, part-time treatment. The positive masturbatory reconditioning involves having the client masturbate to an appropriate fantasy, until he has an ejaculation. Roger Wolfe points out the need for therapist monitoring:

> Their perceptions of what is an appropriate fantasy are incredible. We have had clients come in with their initial tapes

and say "I had a wonderful appropriate fantasy," and it turns out to be a tape describing what is essentially a rape! Many men in our male culture wouldn't graduate from our groups.

We have the clients focus on the antithesis of offending, that is, on warmth, caring, affectional, close, intimate human aspects of sexuality. We stress the sensual and erotic as well. When they are making their tapes, we want them to throw in lots of adjectives about warm and close, and a lot of respect for the female, what she is wanting, doing, and feeling. They focus on her feelings and responses and on their own feelings and responses. The woman should come across as a person and not a blow-up rubber doll. (R. Wolfe, 1981b)

Staff help the men develop appropriate fantasies. Their assignment at home is to verbalize the fantasy into a tape recorder while masturbating to ejaculation four to seven times a week. "The point is we want to reinforce—through the powerful mechanism of masturbatory conditioning—appropriate sexuality, and not only appropriate sexuality, but the antithesis of sexual offending where you have to make your victim a piece of meat," says Roger Wolfe (1981b).

The boredom-aversion technique is used by the offender after ejaculating to appropriate fantasies. Then he turns the tape cassette over and verbalizes 45 continual minutes of a series of his deviant sexual fantasies.[17] He must continue his fantasies for 45 minutes and cannot turn off the tape recorder until he fills up the whole side with no pauses and no blanks.

We try to have the individual repeat the full fantasy including antecedent conditions (emotional, environmental, physiological, and mental precursors). The actual sexual behavior and the immediate consequences, such as transitory feelings and his methods of resolving them (the false promise), are included. When he completes one fantasy, he begins another. (R. Wolfe, 1981b)

The Modified Aversive Behavioral Rehearsal Technique (MABRT). The MABRT, using mannequins and videotape, is a technique developed for systematically controlling deviant sexual expression in pedophiles and exhibitionists. It was adopted by NWTA's Timothy Smith and borrows many of the components of Aversive Behavioral Rehearsal (Wickramasekera, 1980). Mannequins have been used previously for assessment of sex offenders, where it was found that interacting with a "humanlike" figure elicited behavior not previously reported by the offender (Forgione, 1974).

This technique involves a client in re-enacting his sexual assault on a mannequin that is representative of the age and sex of his victims. This scene is videotaped[18] and viewed by the client, his significant other, and his treatment group. This very close simulation, including even the actual motor behaviors, is paired with powerful negative emotions that the client experiences in this situation. On a cognitive level, the client is confronted with the harmfulness, outrageousness, and absurdity of his rationalizations, feelings, and behaviors. "Sharing with others the impactful, visual depiction of his deviance is a greatly magnified mode of self-disclosure," says Roger Wolfe (Wolfe & Wolfe, 1984). "It forcefully breaks through most remnants of rationalization, justification, and minimization residual in the client."

Negative side-effects reported in the literature are almost precluded by utilizing this technique only after the client has been in treatment a minimum of six months. One unexpected side-effect of this procedure is that the emotional responses of a significant percentage of clients seem focused on the trauma they created for their victims; thus this procedure, in addition to its conditioning and cognitive impact, serves as an influential empathy training procedure (Wolfe & Wolfe, 1984).

Empathy Training. Staff use several techniques, including behavioral ones, to help the offender to come to grips with the reality of his offense and its effects on the victim. Efforts to correct the cognitive distortions in the offender's perception of the victim's feelings about sexual assault include making contact with victim counselors or advocates, as well as the techniques of cognitive restructuring, role playing, and bibliotherapy.

1. *Victim counselors* are invited to attend the group meeting, or the offender is sent to a victim advocate center, where, at his own expense, he must ask a victim counselor to tell him about victims' feelings. Wherever possible, NWTA staff try to arrange to have the counselor of his actual victim be the person to tell him of the victim's perception of the hurt and damage s/he experienced. With many clients, this process seems to have the desired level of emotional and intellectual impact.

2. *Cognitive restructuring.* The offender constructs scenes, casting himself or significant others in the role of the victim. Research such as reading and consultation with victim specialists or their spouses is assigned, to assure a thorough and accurate job. Cognitive restructuring is utilized at this point. The client focuses on his typical rationalizations; for example, an exhibitionist will say, "This will really turn her on." Scenes are constructed where he utilizes and buys the rationalizations. These scenes then are paired with aversive

imagery. Finally, alternate scenes are constructed where he catches himself in the distortion and counters with the reality message; for example, the exhibitionist will say, "That is nonsense! I have done this hundreds of times and the only responses I have ever gotten are derision, disgust, and fear." The scene continues with the client performing some operant behavior to terminate the possibility of deviant behavior. Then the client shifts to a positively reinforcing scene, a "warm pink fuzzy" (Maletsky, 1980; R. Wolfe, 1981a).

3. *Roleplaying.* The group therapist tells the client, "Okay we talked about your view of the sexual assault scene, we talked about your thoughts about what was going on in the victim's head—that she really liked what you were doing. Now we are going to give you the opportunity to do the scene and be your victim." This approach might occur on a variety of levels with the same client. He may begin with a 500-word essay on the effects of the abuse on the victim. The next step might be for him to become that victim in a role play. The offender may protest and start out by saying, "Well, I couldn't do that, because it creates all sorts of psychological trauma for me." Nevertheless, he is asked to become the victim, lying on the floor and simulating getting molested in front of 14 other group members.

Tapes also are used. A scene is reconstructed from his victim's perspective, telling the offender, "You are 11 years old. You lie in your bed at night. You hear your dad get up. You stiffen up. You are just hoping and praying he won't come in your room tonight like he did last night." The therapist then will describe what that particular offender actually did to the victim, while the offender is imagining he is that victim. Roger Wolfe explains, "Part of the offender's rationalization in his self-defense is that the victim never resisted, so we put that into focus. One of the ways we do that is to say to the offender, 'Your victim was three feet tall and weighed about 100 pounds. You are six feet tall and weigh 200 pounds. Imagine a man who was 12 feet tall and weighed 600 pounds coming into your bedroom and saying, 'Hi, you and I are going to do it' " (R. Wolfe, 1981b).

4. *Bibliotherapy.* Clients are asked to read books written by sexual assault victims (e.g., Brady, 1981; Morris, 1982). A report form developed by staff therapist Nancy Nissen asks clients to record arousal points, victim traits, and offender traits as they are reading. With most clients, this enhances perceptions of their victim's pain.

Reoffense Rate

The reoffense rate by graduates of NWTA's sex-offender treatment program is approximately 10 percent, according to Roger Wolfe (1981b). "Since most of the men are on probation for five years, we usually hear of any reoffense through that division. When the offender commits a new offense, it is usually the same or a lesser type for which we treated him." Rarely, the person will progress to a more serious offense.

NWTA also reports a high rate of success where the Modified Aversive Behavior Rehearsal Technique was used as a treatment component. These data show an overall success rate of 95 percent with 92 sex offenders who had engaged in a variety of, and often multiple, paraphilias. Length of follow-up ranged from one to 28 months, with a mean follow-up of 13.5 months.[19]

Northwest Treatment Associates'
Success Rates Where the MABRT is a Treatment Component

Offense Type	Number*	Reoffend	% Success	Type Reoffense
Molests female children	64	2	97	Expose, Child Molest, F. Rape
Exhibitionism	27	4	85	Expose, F. Child Molest
Voyeurism	6	1	83	Expose
Molests male children	17	0	100	_____
Rapes female children	3	1	66	Child Rape
Rapes female adults	3	0	100	_____
Grabs breasts	2	1	50	Expose
Molests boys & girls	8	0	100	_____
Cross-dresses/steals clothing	1	0	100	_____
Total Offenders & Reoffenses:				
Mean Success Rate	92	5	95%	

* Many of the sex offenders had multiple deviancies, so total offenses are greater then number of offenders. Sources NWTA

Wolfe reiterates the importance of continual evaluation and assessment while the offender is in treatment. He recounts the case of a person who came in as an exhibitionist and was in treatment for three or four weeks and doing very poorly. He suddenly disappeared from treatment because he was caught in a vicious rape.

Whatever your relationship to a sex offender, you should keep foremost in mind, he is an *addict*. The individual verbalization, promises, assurances, and contentions should be regarded in the same light as those of alcoholics regarding alcohol or heroin addicts regarding their drug. An approach of healthy skepticism is advised, and behavior should speak to you much louder than words. (R. Wolfe, 1981b)

Notes

[1] Six additional people have an associate status, and a secretary serves as a support staff person.

[2] In 1982 a branch treatment program was established in Bellingham, Washington.

[3] NWTA prefers not to handle paroled sex offenders. They consider perhaps one in 20 is treatable.

[4] NWTA's clientele include a small percentage of ethnic groups. Such groups are underrepresented in almost all community-based adult sex-offender treatment programs.

[5] Psychological tests include the MMPI, the Abel Card-Sort of Sexual Preferences, the Clarke Sexual History Questionnaire, and a general substance abuse overview checklist.

[6] As a last resort, Depo-Provera may be used to reduce sexual arousal and sexual drive.

[7] See Appendix C for description of social skills training used by NWTA.

[8] For a description of this program, see Chapter 9 of this book.

[8] See Cautela (1969).

[10] Staff report that it is not an uncommon experience for clients to falsify these records and advise programs to be cautious and to look for a plausible learning curve. Additional confusion may be caused by the fact that some clients experience a lengthy period of suppression due to the trauma of discovery.

[11] See Appendix D for a sample "Partner Alert List."

[12] See Cautela (1967, 1970).

[13] To train the client in stress-reducing and imagery-enhancing muscle relaxation methods, Roger Wolfe spends about 20 minutes with each client explaining NWTA's systematic format for inducing deep-muscle relaxation, followed by one hour in a taped session guiding the offender through the system. The client then can play the tape at home and do the exercises on his own for one or two weeks. Hypnosis also may be used when an offender is not successful with traditional methods.

[14] See Meichenbaum (1977).

[15] See Abel & Blanchard (1974); Marquis (1970).

[16] See Laws & O'Neil (1979); Marshall & Lippens (1977).

[17] See Appendix E for sample of "Protocol for Boredom Tapes." On occasion, when boredom tapes are being reviewed in the NWTA office, the therapist will ask the client to punish any deviant arousal while listening, by inhaling the noxious odor of placenta culture.

[18] See Appendix F for two release forms for clients involved in MABRT, one is for client consent and the other provides permission for NWTA to use the tapes for the purpose of training professionals in the technique.

[19] Wickramasekera (1980, p. 123) reports a high MABRT success rate also, especially with 23 exhibitionists (95 percent success) followed for 22 months to nine years.

References

Abel, G., & Blanchard, E. B. "The Role of Fantasy in the Treatment of Sexual Deviancy." *Archives of General Psychiatry, 30*:4, 1974, 467–475.

Brady, K. *Father's Days.* New York: Dell, 1981.

Cautela, J. R. "Covert Sensitization."' *Psychological Record, 20,* 1967, 459–468.

Cautela, J. R. "Behavioral Therapy and Self-Control Techniques and Implications." In C. M. Franks (ed.), *Behavioral Therapy: Appraisal and Status.* New York: McGraw-Hill, 1969.

Cautela, J. R. "Covert Reinforcement." *Behavior Therapy, 1,* 1970, 35–50.

Forgione, A. G. "The Use of Mannequins in the Behavioral Assessment of Child Molesters: Two Case Reports." *Behavior Therapy, 7,* 1974, 678–685.

Laws, D. R., & O'Neil, J. A. "Variations on Masturbatory Reconditioning." Paper presented at the Second National Conference on the Evaluation and Treatment of Sexual Aggressives, New York City, May 12, 1979.

Maletsky, B. M. "Assisted Covert Sensitization." In D. J. Cox & R. J. Daitzman (eds.), *Exhibitionism: Description, Assessment & Treatment.* New York: Garland Press, 1980.

Merquis, J. "Orgasmic Reconditioning: Changing Sexual Object Choice through Controlling Masturbation Fantasies." *Journal of Behavior Therapy and Experimental Psychiatry 1,* 1970, 263–271.

Marshall, W. L., & Lippens, K. "Clinical Value of Boredom, A Procedure for Reducing Inappropriate Sexual Interest." *Journal of Nervous & Mental Disease, 165,* 1977, 283–287.

Meichenbaum, D. *Cognitive-Behavioral Modification.* New York: Plenum Press, 1977.

Morris, M. *If I Should Die Before I Wake,* Los Angeles: Tarcher, 1982.

Silver, S. Taped site-interview by F. H. Knopp, September 30, 1981.

Wickramasekera, I. "Aversive Behavioral Rehearsal." In D. J. Cox & R. J. Daitzman (eds.), *Exhibitionism: Description, Assessment & Treatment.* New York: Garland Press, 1980.

Wolf, S. Taped site-interview by F. H. Knopp, September 30, 1981.

Wolfe, F. Taped site-interview by F H. Knopp, September 30, 1981.

Wolfe, F., & Wolfe, R. Letter and notes to F. H. Knopp, May 17, 1984.

Wolfe R. "Northwest Treatment Associates: An Outpatient Approach to the Treatment of Sex Offenders." *TSA News,* August 19, 1981.(a)

Wolfe R. Taped site-interview by F. H. Knopp, September 30, 1981(b).

24

A Helping Hand
Reaching Out to the Mentally Ill

Michael Burkhead
James H. Carter
James A. Smith III

People with psychiatric disorders, especially schizophrenia, are more likely today than ever to wind up in prisons. Several things have led to a rapid increase in the number of chronic mentally ill inmates, including the closing of state mental institutions, which led to the release of these patients without proper discharge planning; the trend away from using abnormal offender statutes; and the growing number of mentally ill young adult alcoholics and drug abusers.

National estimates of the number of inmates suffering from significant mental illness vary widely, from 10 percent, as reported by the U.S. Department of Justice in 1985, to 25 percent, as cited by the U.S. Department of Health and Human Services in 1986.

Mentally ill inmates find everyday living difficult—often because they lack basic coping skills. Adjustment to prison is particularly hard for them, and because of their emotional problems, they are exploited by more aggressive inmates (Carpenter 1986).

Handling the deviant behaviors of other prisoners is also hard for mentally ill inmates. It is also difficult for them to conform to the many rules and restrictions of prison life, and so they have a high incidence of rule violations. With medication and counseling, some offenders can live in the general prison population, but more often they need special housing and mental health services.

Reprinted from the June 1990 issue of *Corrections Today*, vol. 52, no. 3: 88, 90, 92, with the permission of American Correctional Association, Laurel, MO.

Across the country, prison outpatient services are either nonexistent or too crowded, and most cannot give the treatment necessary for successful community living. Unprepared for life in the community and fearful of the outside world, the chronic mentally ill are frequently rehospitalized or reimprisoned.

A specialized treatment program for chronic mentally ill male inmates at Central Prison in Raleigh, N.C., shows how states can help this special prison population. Initially financed in 1984 by a small grant from the National Institute of Justice, the Life Skills Transitional Program is designed for inmates who are within six months to a year of release (Anthony and Liberman 1986).

Many of these patients are simply shuttled from state mental hospitals back to communities. Discharge planning is extremely important to stop this endless cycle. Most of these inmates have histories of mental health treatment, including hospitalization; however, some developed mental disorders after incarceration.

Patients diagnosed with schizophrenic disorders or major affective disorders and a history of hospitalization are eligible for the program, as are those who are found to be grossly mentally ill, dangerous, and difficult to manage in the prison mental health system.

The program is voluntary. Eligible patients are interviewed and the Life Skills Transitional Program is described to them. From March 1, 1985, to Oct. 1, 1988, 132 patients were interviewed. Sixteen decided not to attend, and 32, after initially agreeing to attend, dropped out.

Once in the program, patients are transferred to a self-contained, 24-bed ward in the mental health facility at Central Prison. They stay on that ward until their release date.

The average stay in the program is 5.2 months, although some patients have stayed in the program for as long as 12 months. Monday through Friday, patients attend class for three hours and supervised recreation for one hour each day. The patients also meet regularly with treatment staff for evaluation, goal setting and aftercare planning.

A community meeting is held each week for all patients and treatment staff. Conferences with counselors from the Division of Vocational Rehabilitation and the Social Security Administration are scheduled on an individual basis. Patients who reach appropriate custody levels and demonstrate stability over a period of several months can attend a supervised workshop at the nearby state mental hospital. Patients in this phase of the program receive complete vocational evaluations and are given paying jobs. These jobs help them save money, which is theirs upon release.

A number of services are supplied during the course of the

program. First, patients learn more about chemotherapy and medication. Under the direction of the team psychiatrist, their concerns about medication are informally discussed. The team nurse conducts a more formal class on medication, explaining why medications are prescribed and discussing their side effects, doses and ways they are taken.

Patients also participate in individual and group psychotherapy. The team psychologist schedules and conducts these sessions, depending on each patient's needs and requests.

Adult basic education is also an important part of the Life Skills program. A teacher and an assistant conduct individualized instruction for each patient. Those who have finished high school take college correspondence courses and tutor other patients. The patients also have four microcomputers, and educational software is available.

Classes on social skills are also held, teaching patients basic living skills including budgeting and managing money, shopping, cooking, cleaning and personal hygiene.

Relaxation therapy and biofeedback training are also taught. Patients practice progressive relaxation techniques with biofeedback machines.

Each patient is also interviewed by a counselor from the North Carolina Division of Vocational Rehabilitation, who tells them about post-release resources. If the patient lives outside of Raleigh, the vocational rehabilitation counselor will refer counselors near the patient's home. The counselor also gives vocational testing and counseling for eligible patients and selects some to attend a coeducational program with non-inmates at a state mental hospital.

A social security case worker interviews each patient to determine his social security disability status.

And finally, the Life Skills program helps patients find living arrangements before their release. If the patient does not have an appropriate residence through his family, the program social worker finds a suitable home in a designated community. In some cases, patients are placed in a halfway house or independent living situation.

Aftercare planning begins near the patient's release date. Continuing outpatient treatment is scheduled through community mental health centers, and clinical information is sent to the community-based facility. If possible, a conference is held with the patient and the receiving community program. If the patient plans to live with family members, the family is contacted and the patient's needs are discussed.

While they are in the program, patients must follow the prison rules and attend class daily. Penalties for rule violations include loss of time off from their sentences and segregation; however, violations are relatively rare, especially when compared to previous rates.

The average Life Skills program patient is a 32-year-old black male with a fifth grade education. He is likely to have been convicted of a violent crime or a property crime, have a history of substance abuse, and be diagnosed as a paranoid or undifferentiated schizophrenic. At least 84 percent of the patients were hospitalized for a psychiatric problem before incarceration. The following are general characteristics of the Life Skills program group as of Oct. 1, 1988.

Of the patients admitted, 49 percent were diagnosed as suffering chronic, undifferentiated schizophrenia and 26 percent were diagnosed with chronic, paranoid schizophrenia. Only 1 percent suffered from major depression. The great majority, 77 percent, qualified for a dual diagnosis; they also had histories of alcoholism and/or substance abuse before being incarcerated.

The majority also had an average educational level of about fifth grade, based on Wide Range Achievement Test scores. Their complete range was from a 2.2 grade level to an 11.4 grade level. Thirty-one percent had a high school diploma or the equivalent, and 69 percent never attended high school.

Most patients had multiple convictions: 39 percent for assaults, 44 percent for property crimes, 5 percent for sexual crimes, 7 percent for alcohol and substance abuse, and 5 percent for arson/unlawful burnings.

Of those who dropped out of the program, their ages, diagnoses, achievement levels, race, and custody levels failed to yield any consistent information. More subjective measures, such as the severity of illness and the amount or duration of medication, also did not help predict who would drop out of the program.

Of the patients who finished the program, 15 percent returned to prison within three years, 13 percent were committed to state mental hospitals, 4 percent were paroled to federal sentences, and 9 percent could not be tracked. The number of patients who successfully adjusted after release is 58 percent. This suggests a significant positive effect on the lives of these offenders.

Recidivism is a complex issue and depends on selected criteria. This is a typically transient, homeless population that is very difficult to track. Medical records are notoriously unreliable. The recidivism rate is estimated to be 28 percent, although the length of time for the follow-up is still too short to make definitive conclusions. Only a small fraction of the patients have been out of prison for more than a year. And contact with some of the released patients has already been lost because of their transient life styles.

The fact that a program such as this is permitted in a maximum security state institution shows progress and speaks to our growing concern for the mentally ill prison population.

References

Anthony, W. A., and R. P. Liberman. 1986. The practice of psychiatric rehabilitation: historical, conceptual, and research base. *Schizophrenia Bulletin* 12: 542–559.

Carpenter, W. T. 1986. Thoughts on the treatment of schizophrenia. *Schizophrenia Bulletin* 12: 527–539.

Carter, J. H. 1987. Discharge planning for chronically mentally ill prisoners. *Discharge Planning and Psychiatry* 1: 2–3.

Halleck, S. 1986. *The Mentally Disordered Offender*. Washington, D.C.: U.S. Department of Health and Human Services.

U.S. Department of Justice. 1985. *Sourcebook on the Mentally Disordered Prisoner*. Washington, D.C.: U.S. Department of Justice.

25

Habilitation of the Retarded Offender in Cuyahoga County

Arthur L. Bowker
Robert E. Schweid

Background

In the late 1970s, the Common Pleas Court of Cuyahoga County Ohio,[1] became concerned over the increasing numbers of retarded offenders. Through the concerted efforts of numerous individuals and agencies an attempt was made to identify these offenders and develop appropriate alternatives to imprisonment.

One of the first steps was to develop a profile of the mentally retarded offender (MRO) under adult probation supervision in Cuyahoga County The adult probation department identified 144 cases as retarded from active caseloads during the period November 1977 to November 1978. Only 37 of these cases met the criteria of having a documented intelligence quotient (IQ) of 70 or below or a history of institutionalization in mental retardation facilities. These 37 cases revealed the typical retarded offender was a young black male with a 9th grade education who had committed a nonviolent offense.

Several limitations of this first study were evident. First, probation officers untrained in retardation identified the retarded offenders selected for the study. Second, history of institutionalization was not proof of retardation since some individuals were warehoused

Source: *Federal Probation*, 56(4) (December 1992): 48–52.

in retardation facilities without adequate testing.

Nevertheless, with these limitations in mind, the department concluded the study appeared accurate based on other studies. The study made the following recommendations: 1) train the entire staff on retardation; 2) develop a means of identifying retarded offenders; and 3) develop a special probation caseload to supervise retarded offenders (Federation for Community Planning, 1979).

The following developments resulted from this study: the creation of a Mentally Retarded Offender Unit (MRO Unit) within the probation department; the creation of a clinical director of the MRO Unit within the court psychiatric clinic (clinic); and the separation of MRO's from the general jail population into 10 inmate pods in the Cuyahoga County Correction Center. All three of these components work together to habilitate the retarded offender.

MRO Unit

The MRO Unit, which began supervising retarded offenders in October 1980, had supervised over 300 offenders by 1992. The monthly caseload size is between 55 to 65 compared to a regular caseload of over 200. The reduced caseload is designed to provide high intensity supervision.

The unit's admission criteria have changed several times since the unit's inception. At the beginning the admission criteria were merely evidence of a low IQ based upon "observations," school records, and/or actual psychological testing. It soon became apparent a more objective standard was needed because some offenders placed on the unit based upon "observations" were not retarded.

A measured IQ of 80 or lower was then imposed as an admission criterion. However, this did not eliminate the inappropriate placement of offenders; the unit soon became too large to be adequately handled by one probation officer. To create a manageable size and to ensure appropriate placement, the unit criterion was again changed to 75 or lower IQ[2] on the Weschler Adult Intelligence Scale (Revised) (WAIS-R). The WAIS-R also had to be administered by a licensed psychologist from the clinic, usually the clinical director of the MRO Unit.

Prior to 1988, offenders placed on the unit were supervised in one of four different supervision levels. The decision about level of supervision was based on a standard "risk/needs" instrument used by the probation department. The instrument objectively measures the risk a probationer has of recidivating. Examples of specific areas factored into the instrument are: prior criminal record, substance abuse, mental health, mental ability, and employment record.

The four supervision levels are: 1) High, requires office contacts twice a month; 2) Medium, requires office contacts once a month; 3) low requires office contacts once every 3 months, with mail contacts on the months with no office contacts; and 4) Extended, requires only monthly mail contacts. As a probationer completes his probation he is reevaluated to determine the appropriate level.

In 1988 an additional supervision level, Super High, was added for use on the MRO Unit. The Super High level was created to increase MRO Unit contacts for those cases demanding the most time. Specifically, new probationers and probationers who were in some crisis are placed on the Super High level. Probationers on Super High level are required to report to the probation officer once a week for at least 4 weeks. Probationers may remain on Super High level longer depending on their situation as determined by the probation officer and the officer's supervisor. After the probationer leaves the Super High level he is reassigned to the High level and to subsequent levels based upon the risk/needs instrument.

Interaction takes place between the three MRO components in several important ways. First, the probation officer in charge of the MRO Unit is provided with the names of potential MRO's from both the clinical director of the MRO Unit and the MRO Pod in the Correctional Center. The probation officer then "tracks" these potential MRO's through the criminal justice process. Second, if the offender has an IQ of 75 or lower on the WAIS-R, the sentencing judge is advised by the MRO Unit that the offender is appropriate for supervision in the unit. Third, the MRO Unit acts as a source of information about MRO's to both the clinical director of the MRO Unit and the MRO Pod.

The clinical director of the MRO Unit may receive a request from a probation officer of a general caseload for IQ testing on one of the officer's probationers to determine eligibility for the unit. These requests are coordinated by the MRO Unit to ensure that all collateral information such as medical and school records are obtained for a complete evaluation; that the supervising probation officer is informed if a probationer misses his or her appointment for testing; and that probationers determined by the clinical director of the MRO Unit to be appropriate for the unit are transferred expediently. Fourth, the MRO Unit contacts the MRO Pod when a retarded offender is arrested on a probation violation or new case to ensure that the offender is separated from the general inmate population. The MRO Unit also contacts the pod to keep the retarded offenders advised of their status with regard to such things as probation violation hearings, sentencing, or placement in a substance abuse program.

The MRO Unit operates on a case management model. Each probationer's needs are evaluated by the probation officer, the clinical director of the MRO Unit, and others. The probationer is then referred to an appropriate agency to receive services.

Probationers on the unit may receive "informal counseling," depending upon the skills, expertise, and time constraints of the probation officer. Unfortunately, "high quality counseling," such as psychotherapy or group counseling, is not available from the unit itself. Such services are obtained by referral to the appropriate agencies in the community. It is highly unlikely that the unit will ever be able to provide all the counseling needs of the retarded offender population because of the diversity of these offenders' needs.

In 1988, an interdisciplinary team was formed to coordinate services with MRO. The team consists of representatives from: the Association of Retarded Citizens of Cuyahoga County (ARC); the Cuyahoga County Correction Center; Case Western Reserve University Mental Development Center; the Cuyahoga County Board of Mental Retardation and Developmental Disabilities; the Ohio Bureau of Vocational Rehabilitation; the Cuyahoga County Public Defender's Office; and the clinical director of the MRO Unit. The team is chaired by the probation officer supervising the MRO Unit. The members meet monthly and discuss new assignments to the unit and problem cases. If a community agency is already involved with a probationer, a representative of that agency is asked by the probation officer to attend the meeting.

During these meetings, habilitation plans are designed to address the following areas: substance abuse; psychological needs; vocational/education needs; and any other serious problems that are identified. The plans then are implemented by the probation officer with the assistance of different team representatives. The plan's success or failure is discussed at each meeting, and the plans are modified as needed. Early intervention is designed to prevent further criminal behavior.

The MRO Unit also has special rules designed to assist the probation officer in ensuring the offender comprehends his or her rules of probation. These rules were designed by the probation department, the clinical director of the MRO Unit, the Ohio Department of Mental Retardation and Developmental Disabilities, and ARC.

The rules are the same as the general rules of probation for a nonretarded offender but are written in a manner that retarded offenders find easier to comprehend. These rules are read and explained in detail by the probation officer to all retarded offenders placed on the MRO Unit. In addition to the rules, the unit has probation violation and probable cause hearing rights which also are written in a manner that a retarded offender would find easier to comprehend. These rights are also read and explained to those probationers on the unit who are facing violation hearings.

Finally, the probation officer of the unit sets up a special appointment with probationers whose terms of probation are about to expire. During this appointment, a "closure interview" is held with the probationer to discuss the probationer's successes while on probation and any areas the probationer still may need to work on. During the closure interview, the probation officer discusses 10 specific behaviors the probationer needs to avoid in the future to stay out of trouble. Finally, the probationer is given a list of telephone numbers to obtain assistance if needed after probation in the following areas: residence; substance abuse; health care; psychological needs; and vocational training.

Clinical Evaluation of MRO's

Individuals whom the court or probation department suspect are mentally retarded are referred to the clinic. Judicial referrals of retarded offenders include: Competence to Stand Trial, Sanity at the Time of the Act, Mitigation of the Penalty, or Drug Dependency Evaluations. It was determined at the outset that coordination of these evaluations required a clinical director who is trained in mental retardation, developmental disabilities, and forensic psychology. Specific evaluations may include: gathering developmental, school, and social history/information about the individual; intelligence testing; adaptive behavior evaluations; psychological and psychiatric evaluations; and neuropsychological evaluations. Some evaluations are performed by the clinical director.

Other evaluations are reviewed by the clinical director to aid evaluators in making specific habitation recommendations for the MRO. The clinical director then communicates with the other team members so that the individual is tracked while going through the court system to see that appropriate assistance is given from the public defender's office, the correction center, and the probation department.

MRO Pod

The MRO Pod in the Cuyahoga County Corrections Center was started to prevent more intelligent inmates from victimizing retarded offenders during their incarceration. The pod held 10 inmates in an area separate from the general population.

While retarded offenders are held in the MRO Pod, a counselor from the Case Western Reserve University Mental Development Center provides group counseling to them once a week to facilitate their adjustment in the new environment of the jail. (For an indepth look at the counseling sessions, see "Group Counseling with Retarded Offenders" by Joseph Steiner in *Social Work*, March–April 1984.)

The MRO Pod counselor maintains contact with the MRO Unit on new retarded inmates and is a member of the interdisciplinary team. As a member of the interdisciplinary team, the counselor provides valuable insight into the retarded offender's adjustment to jail.

Unfortunately, in 1989 the separation of the retarded inmates from the regular population was curtailed because of overcrowding. Retarded inmates are now housed with inmates in the medical/ psychological units of the Cuyahoga County Correction Center. More jail space is now being built, and it is hoped the special pod for retarded inmates will return.

Study of the Retarded Offender

A 1989 study reviewed the case files of 67 probationers under active supervision in the MRO Unit through March 31, 1988. A structured data collection instrument was used to obtain information in the following areas: social background; psychological/physiological traits; criminal history; present offense history; and present probation supervision. Most of the information was obtained from presentence/postsentence investigation reports and probationer monthly report forms. These reports were available on all 67 cases because the reports are legally mandated. Court psychiatric clinic reports were the next major source of information. Ninety-nine percent of the cases had clinic evaluations.

Nineteen percent of the cases had both Sanity at the Time of Act and Competence to Stand Trial evaluations done by the clinic. Eight percent of the cases had only Competence to Stand Trial evaluations. The other cases had one or more of the other types of clinic evaluations.

From the study, a profile of the retarded probationer in Cuyahoga County emerged. Ninety-one percent were male; 57 percent were black. Forty-eight percent fell in the 20- to 24-year-old age group. Seventy-three percent were single, and 66 percent had no children.

Fifty-two percent resided in their parents' homes, and 48 percent of the caseload resided in high crime rate areas of Cleveland, Ohio.

In 24 percent of the cases there was a problem at the residence which could have lead to a probation violation hearing (e.g., substance-abusing probationer placed in a residence where ongoing substance abuse is prevalent).

The average highest completed grade was 10th. Only 13 percent had completed high school. Forty-eight percent had no employment for an 18-month period prior to the study. Sixty-six percent had incomes below $300 a month.

The mean full scale IQ was 68. Fifty-one percent were diagnosed as Borderline Intellectual Functioning. Forty-nine percent were mentally retarded. Seventy-one percent were dual diagnosed with mental retardation and substance abuse, mental illness, and character disorder. Thirty-nine percent had special physical difficulties, such as seizures. Twenty-four percent of the cases had been abused as children.

Sixty-seven percent had prior criminal records; 43 percent were for nonviolent offenses. Thirty-six percent had juvenile records. Twenty-one percent of the cases had previously been on adult probation. Only 7 percent had served time in prison.

Twenty-four percent of the defendants were in jail during the pretrial phase; 60 percent were on bail and 12 percent in the Court Supervised Release Program of the probation department. Ninety-seven percent of the offenders had pled guilty, with 83 percent pleading guilty to a "lesser included offense."

Seventy-eight percent were on probation for only one class of crime. The top three crimes were: 1) auto theft offenses; 2) other theft offenses; and 3) burglary/breaking and entering offenses. These three types of crimes accounted for 45 percent of the probation offenses. Sex offenses had the highest percentage (9 percent) in the violent offense category.

Seventy-three percent were given probation sentences of 1 to 3 years. Thirty-four percent had a probation violation hearing for a new conviction and/or violation of probation rules. Ninety-one percent of the hearings resulted in a finding of guilt. In 32 percent of these cases, the probationer received only a verbal warning.

Problems

One problem which has become evident recently relates to diagnosing MRO's and obtaining school records. School districts are allowed to destroy records 5 years after a student has left the system or within 5 years after notification and permission from the parent or guardian. Cleveland public schools, where 75 percent of the cases last attended school, have been destroying these records, making it impossible to substantiate any special programs or needs as well as documentation of disabilities. This has not only been problematic for diagnosis, but agencies such as the Cuyahoga County Board of Mental Retardation and Developmental Disabilities and the Ohio Bureau of Vocational Rehabilitation require these records prior to providing services and financial assistance. This policy will make the difficult task of getting services for the MRO much harder in the future.

A second problem that has quite often plagued the MRO Unit has been a hesitation by some community agencies to service the MRO. Some community agencies specializing in servicing the mentally retarded have been reluctant to serve MRO's because of their probation status. Other agencies that service nonretarded offenders hesitate to serve MRO's because of their retardation. The MRO Unit has found the best way to overcome these hesitations is to educate the respective agencies regarding probation and retardation.

Specifically, those agencies which specialize in servicing the retarded are advised that the MRO's for the most part are nonviolent. It is pointed out that MRO's may be more motivated than their other clients because of their probation status and their concern over going before a judge for not following through on treatment conditions. Finally, retardation service agencies are advised that the MRO Unit is an active agent for change and will assist them if any problem does arise. The MRO Unit frequently proves this statement by providing quick action when a service agency does encounter some difficulty with a MRO.

Agencies that do not normally service retarded offenders are advised that MRO's may take longer to service, but they are more motivated than many nonretarded offenders. Retarded offenders have a strong desire to be accepted, which in many cases translates into a strong motivation to please those who are trying to help them.

An example of MRO Unit assistance to an outpatient substance abuse program that did not normally service retarded individuals concerned the Twelve Steps of Recovery. The program director expressed concern over providing services to a MRO because the director thought the offender may have difficulty understanding the written Twelve Steps of Recovery. The MRO Unit was able to direct the program director to materials developed at Kent State University that explain the steps in a pictorial manner designed for mentally retarded individuals. The substance abuse program obtained the materials and began expanding its services to retarded substance abusers.

Another problem noted earlier is the loss of the MRO Pod in the Cuyahoga County Corrections Center due to overcrowding. MRO's in correctional institutions are frequently the victims of assaults and psychological and emotional abuses and are made "scape-goats" by the more intelligent inmates. These problems are aggravated by the present overcrowding situation. The short-term solution to this problem has been to house MRO's with inmates who are mentally ill and/or have medical problems, i.e., pregnant or HIV-positive. Obviously, this is not much of a solution. Some solutions might be return of the MRO Pod and increased pretrial release opportunities for nonviolent retarded offenders.

Identification of MRO's has been a problem. Individuals who have not been spotted as "unusual" in court or have not been observed by staff in the jail, the psychiatric clinic, or through the probation department may not be recognized as retarded.

Estimates of the retarded in correctional populations have ranged from 5 percent to 10 percent. (McDaniel, 1987; Santamour, 1988). A study completed in 1984 of the Ohio Correctional System found a retardation prevalence rate of 1.3 percent among the inmate population (Denkowski, 1985). The MRO Unit supervises between 55 to 65 MRO's. The probation department as a whole supervises over 8,000 offenders. Based upon these estimates the MRO Unit should be supervising from about 80 to 800 offenders.

A possible explanation for the difference between the estimated level and the actual number of retarded offenders on the MRO Unit is the reluctance of some supervising probation officers to transfer a nonproblematic, frequently "eager to please" retarded offender when there is a strong probability that after the transfer the probation officer will get a "hard-core" offender to take the place of the MRO.

The only solution to the identification problem is the continued training of the entire probation department, the correctional center staff, and the court. They need to understand that the MRO Unit is best suited to serve the needs of both the problematic and non-problematic retarded offender. To allow any mentally retarded offender to remain on a caseload of over 200 probationers is a disservice to that offender.

The Future

The future of the MRO Unit is a bright one. Since the MRO Unit was created in 1980, it has developed contacts in the community for servicing the retarded offender. There is now a concerted effort by numerous community agencies, through the interdisciplinary team, to evaluate and serve the needs of the MRO. With the interdisciplinary team in place, the MRO Unit can find solutions to the problems of servicing the retarded offender and be an effective correctional agent.

Notes

[1] Cuyahoga County has the largest population of the 88 counties in Ohio and includes the City of Cleveland.

[2] The upper limit IQ of 75 was chosen to be consistent with guidelines recommended by the *Classification in Mental Retardation*, 1983 revision published by the American Association on Mental Deficiency (p. 23), and by the *Diagnostic Statistical Manual III-R* published by the American Psychiatric Association (1987).

References

American Psychiatric Association. (1987). *Diagnostic and statistical manual III-R*. Washington, DC: Author.

Day, E., Goodman, M., Griffin, B. W., & Kennedy, M. (1982). *Mentally retarded offenders: A handbook for criminal justice personnel*. Cleveland: Federation of Community Planning.

Denkowski, G., & Denkowski, K. M. (1985). The mentally retarded offender in the state prison system: Identification, prevalence, adjustment, and rehabilitation. *Criminal Justice and Behavior, 12*(1), 55–70.

Federation for Community Planning. (1979). *A study of the mentally retarded probationer in Cuyahoga County Adult Probation Department: A Report of the Probation Task Force of the Committee on the Mentally Retarded Offender*.

Grossman, H. J. (Ed.). (1983). *Classification in mental retardation*. Washington, DC: The American Association on Mental Deficiency.

McDaniel, C. O. (1987, April). Is normalization the answer for MROs? *Corrections Today*, 184–188.

Santamour, M. (1986). The offender with mental retardation. *The Prison Journal, 66*, 3–18.

26

Older Inmates
Special Programming Concerns

Peter C. Kratcoski

Introduction

Those developing programming for state and federal institutions in the 1990s are faced with such concerns as overcrowding, an increasingly violent prison population, care for AIDS infected inmates and the need to prevent its spread, and pressures to direct funding toward highly visible uses. In this climate, the increasing number of older inmates in these institutions and their special problems may not receive a great deal of consideration by correction administrators. It is necessary to draw attention to the older inmates and their needs.

A report completed by the U.S. Bureau of Prisons Office of Research and Evaluation (1989) revealed that almost 12% of the U.S. Bureau of Prisons inmate population was age 50 or above at the time of the report, and it was estimated that in the year 2005 more than 16% will be age 50 or above. A survey of federal prisons and state prison systems found that there were more than 24,000 inmates age 50 and above housed in long-term institutions on January 1, 1989 (Camp and Camp, 1989).

The presence of ever increasing numbers of older inmates in federal and state institutions presents dilemmas for administrators and planners. The declining physical health of persons age 50 and older may create a need for changes in the physical plants, since a number of the prisoners may be unable to climb stairs, and ramps or wheelchair accessibility may be required. Expanded medical and mental health services and recreational, educational, and social programs for the older inmates will also be needed.

Research on the adjustment of older inmates to prison life is rather scarce. One study of imprisoned persons age 50 and above discovered that older inmates who were incarcerated for the first time were more positive in their sentiments about prison life and conditions than were older inmates who had been incarcerated on other occasions. Feelings of fear of being victimized by younger inmates were frequently expressed by older inmates housed in the geriatric unit of one correctional facility. The older inmates also complained more frequently than younger ones about lack of privacy and constant noise. In addition, most reported that they had not developed friendships within the institution (Vito and Wilson 1985).

Older inmates' adjustment is affected by the degree to which they are isolated from families and friends. Sabath and Cowles (1988) found that family contacts, education, and health had effects on the positive institutional adjustment of the inmates. The older offenders who were able to maintain contacts with their families were found to be better adjusted than those who could not do so. Those who had attained enough education to read and take part in institutional activities that required the ability to read were more likely to make a positive adjustment. Poor health contributed to the emotional isolation of the older inmates, since it limited their ability to participate in institutional activities.

A survey (Fultz, 1989) of all of the older inmates aged 60 and above incarcerated in the Maryland correctional system revealed that of the 89 inmates in the system, 20% were housed in maximum security, 72% in medium and 8% in minimum. The largest concentration was at the Maryland House of Corrections in Jessup, where the "old man's unit" consisted of 46 single cells. Fultz found that the older inmates tended to adapt to prison life by not becoming involved. More than 90% of the older inmates wanted to be housed with their own age group.

Correctional administrators and policy makers have generally responded to the older inmate situation in one of the following ways:

1. They have ignored the problem, stating that, since 85 to 90% of the inmate population is in the younger age brackets, the limited resources available for programming should be allocated to them.

2. Some states have constructed new correctional facilities or converted existing facilities for the older inmates. However, this

type of facility is still quite rare and will generally serve the dual function of providing the specific type of housing needed by older inmates and serving the needs of the physically handicapped or those with debilitating illnesses. Often, the older inmates are also those who are handicapped or seriously ill.

3. Older inmates are mixed with the general population, without any special concern for their housing needs. In these instances, provision is made for their recreational needs, work assignments, or special medical problems.

4. A special unit is established for older inmates within the larger institution. Here, the older inmates are housed separately from the others, but may have contact with them in work, recreation, or educational programs, or in the dining halls.

The fourth approach is the least commonly utilized, and is generally considered necessary only when a large proportion of the older inmates have rather severe health problems.

Research Design

To elicit responses from older inmates in regard to their institutional adjustment in the areas of educational, recreational, and security needs, physical and mental health, and social relations, a questionnaire with multiple choice items and a few open-ended questions was prepared. Permission was given to administer this questionnaire to inmates in eight U.S. Bureau of Prison facilities, three state institutions in Florida, and three state institutions in Ohio. Three of the institutions housed female offenders. One of the state facilities in which males were housed was specifically established for older inmates, and one of the federal institutions housing males was developed as a medical/geriatric facility. None of the facilities housing women had established separate units for the older inmates. The older inmates in the other correctional facilities involved in the study were dispersed randomly throughout the facility. At these institutions, age was not a factor considered by the administration when the unit assignments were made.

An interview schedule with questions related to perceived problems of older offenders, institutional responses to these problems, and plans for the future was developed for use with selected administrators, correction officers, and support staff. Several members from each category were interviewed at each of the correctional facilities included in the study.

The research was completed in the following manner. All of the older inmates were asked to report to a specific area in the institution. After an introduction, the purpose of the research was briefly explained. Inmates were told participation was voluntary and they could leave at any time. The questions were read and scored by the research team for those who could not read. It did not appear that there was any significant resistance to the research. Many of the inmates did not participate because they were on work details. Others had just finished work assignments and were sleeping; some were attending school; others just didn't want to be bothered. In several cases, the questionnaires were distributed by the support staff. A total of 482 usable inmate questionnaires and 62 interviews with correction officers, support staff, and administrators were included in the study. The older inmates' adjustment to the institutional setting was measured by a set of questions pertaining to their lives in regard to visitors, institutional activities, health problems, relations with other inmates and staff, feelings of fear, and victimization by other inmates.

Findings and Analysis

The larger portion of the older inmates included in this study were housed in correctional facilities in which an inmate's age was not given special consideration when the specific facility assignment or unit assignment within the institution was made. Most older inmates were classified on the basis of security considerations, which were determined by the nature of their offenses. For example, in the course of our study we had contact with inmates beyond the age of seventy who were living in a maximum security penitentiary.

Comparisons were made between the responses of the inmates housed in the facilities specifically developed for the older inmate and those held in institutions where the older inmates were dispersed throughout the prison population. Special attention was given to the responses of the older female inmates, since the needs of persons in this category tend to be overlooked when correctional policies and programs are designed.

One section of the questionnaire pertained to visitors. Almost half of the older inmates in both types of settings had visitors regularly, while the other half stated that they "rarely" or "never" had visitors. The most frequent types of visitors were spouses, children, and other relatives, with visits from friends, lawyers, social agency representatives, and volunteers being much less frequent.

The inmates in the older inmate institution were less likely to have definite release plans. One-third of this group stated that they would live in a shelter home or didn't know where they would live on release. Most of the older inmates in both categories participated regularly in several forms of recreational activities. There was a tendency for both groups to pick the quiet games and non-physical activities. More than half of the respondents in the older inmate institution were dissatisfied with the number and range of activities, compared to less than one-third in the other facilities who were dissatisfied. More than half of those in the older inmate institutions were involved in some type of educational program, compared to 38% of the older inmate respondents housed in the other institutions. The same held true for involvement in self-help groups such as Alcoholics Anonymous and drug abuse programs (51 to 30%). A significantly larger proportion of those housed in the older inmate institution participated in activities and programs sponsored by external groups, and the respondents housed in the older inmate correctional facility attended religious services more frequently than did the inmates housed in the other facilities included in the study. As would be expected, few of the older inmates in either type of institution were satisfied with their living quarters. Most of the inmates had common complaints such as insufficient space, lack of proper ventilation and stuffy, damp, or cold quarters. However, those living in the institution which housed all age groups were more likely to mention such things as noise, inconsiderate inmates, stale air from smokers, aggressive inmates, being placed on the top bunk, and the location of the dining rooms and toilets as major housing problems.

Approximately one-third of the older inmates in both types of settings stated that the other inmates in the institution were friendly and helpful and there was no difference in the proportion of inmates who stated that they avoided interacting with other inmates. However, a larger number of older inmates in the non-specialized institution found the other inmates, particularly the younger ones, to be aggressive and violent.

The large majority of the older inmates in both types of institutional settings claimed they were never threatened by other inmates, and only a few of the older inmates in either type of institution stated that they were ever beaten by other inmates. Several of the older inmates in both types of institutional settings stated that they were fearful for their life in the institution and afraid of the other inmates. However, they constituted a very small proportion of the respondents. Thus, the findings do not support one of the major arguments for having separate units or institutions for older inmates, that older inmates will be intimidated, exploited and abused by the younger ones if they are not housed in separate units or facilities away from the younger inmates.

It appears that the overall health of those housed in the older inmate institution was significantly worse than that of those housed in the other institutions. Sixty percent of those in the older inmate institution stated that their present health was excellent or good, compared to 92% of the older inmates housed in the other institutions. Forty percent of those in the older inmate institution stated that their health condition was below average or poor.

A large percentage of the older inmates housed in the specialized facilities claimed that their health had declined since coming to the institution. The most persistent health problems mentioned by those in the older inmate institution pertained to mental factors such as worry, depression, and anxiety. Forty-seven percent of the respondents housed in the older inmate institution were given treatment at a prison hospital, compared to 20% of the older inmates at the other facilities.

A significantly larger proportion of the older inmates in the specialized institution was incarcerated for the first time. This may help explain their greater anxiety and concern about their situation.

Older Women in Prison

As previously mentioned, three of the correctional facilities included in the study housed women. Twenty percent of the respondents in the study were female. In general, the older female inmates appeared to have more difficulty adjusting to institutional life than did the older male inmates. Female inmates were less likely to have visitors or to participate in recreational and social activities than were male inmates. Only 19% of the older women stated that they participated in some kind of structured activity on a daily basis, compared to 50% of the older men. When compared with the older male inmates, females were less likely to become friendly with other inmates. In addition, a larger proportion of the older female inmates than of the males stated that they were either occasionally, frequently, or always afraid, and a larger proportion of the older female inmates than of the males claimed that their health was "poor" or "terrible."

The older women were generally dissatisfied with their living quarters. Insufficient space, poor ventilation, noise, lack of privacy, and the hostility of other inmates were very common complaints. The larger majority of the older women would have preferred to live with other inmates who were about their own age. One study by Kratcoski and Babb (1990) revealed that one factor affecting adjustment problems of the older women inmates is the fact that most state correctional facilities for women accommodate all types of offenders, and the security level for women prisons is generally geared toward the most dangerous inmates. Thus, the programs, visiting privileges, and activities are developed in line with the need for greater security required for serious offenders.

The work opportunities available for women in prison are generally not on a par with those available for men, and it was acknowledged that the opportunities to engage in meaningful employment tended to be quite limited. In addition, the older female inmates' lack of skills, poor physical health, and the attitude expressed by many of the women that they were too old to learn new skills or to do anything useful were important factors affecting the adjustment of older women in the area of work.

One administrator noted that new institutional responsibilities have resulted from increases in the number of older female inmates, observing, "I feel that the responsibilities have increased since the influx of older inmates, due to the special problems that have occurred. For example, many are wheelchair bound, overweight, and lack initiative to be a part of the correctional system in terms of productivity."

Programs for Older Inmates in a Special Institution

One of the facilities included in this study was specifically designed to house older inmates. A three-story building originally used as a hospital was converted to a correctional institution. It is classified as medium security and has dormitory style living areas. In the yard there are benches, a miniature golf course, a walking path, volleyball and a horseshoe game. Inmates wear a variety of clothing and have identification badges instead of numbers. Rules tend to be flexible. While everyone who is capable of working is assigned a job, many of the jobs are make-shift. Inmates with physical problems are allowed to ride the elevator. Attending school is considered as full-time employment. A work release program is available to some of the inmates. The mean age of the inmates at this facility was 55 and the range was 38 to 87.

The correctional officers, social service staff, and administrators interviewed at this correctional facility were almost unanimously in agreement that it is better for older inmates to be in such an institution than to be randomly dispersed throughout the various correctional institutions in the state.

While many of the older inmates had committed serious offenses, including murder and rape, this often was their first time in an institution, and they were experiencing considerable adjustment problems. Since the older inmate facility was not specifically designed as a geriatric institution, the inmates were supposed to follow a program similar to that in other correctional facilities of a comparable level of security. All of the inmates were supposed to work. The most difficult task of the administration was to find ways to keep the inmates busy. Many, if not the majority, were incapable of completing strenuous work, and the administration had to be imaginative in its work programming.

For example, they employed elevator operators even though the elevator was self-service. The administration contracted with nearby state and county agencies to provide a letter and flyer stuffing service, a job which could be performed sitting down, allowing inmates who were lame and even in wheelchairs to participate. Attending school was defined as a form of employment, and many of the older inmates took advantage of this opportunity. It was not unusual to see 60- or 70-year-old men learning to read and write.

The staff insisted that the correctional officers and administration needed specialized training if they were to be effective. The correctional staff must be cognizant of the effects of the aging process and the needs of the older inmates. It was pointed out that institutional rules must often be relaxed. Many inmates who violate rules or appear to be disobeying orders may not have heard the orders, or may not have understood the rules. The inmates may be forgetful, misinterpret instructions, or not even be aware of the meaning of the slang terms often used by the staff and correctional officers.

Older inmates need more attention and assistance than the younger inmates, since they do not tend to become involved in the inmate subculture and are less likely to be assisted by family and friends while incarcerated. They are more fearful of being released and having to return to the community, and they are more likely to have serious physical and mental health problems than their younger counterparts. The correctional officers and other staff must be trained to deal with this. For example, some older inmates may be bed wetters, others need to make constant trips to the bathroom or take medicine at regular intervals, and the staff must be willing and trained to help accommodate them.

If given the opportunity, many of the older inmates would be satisfied to vegetate rather than become involved in recreational, social, and educational activities. Thus, it is very important to get every inmate involved in these types of programs to the extent possible. Generally, the educational programs available to the older inmates are not designed to prepare them for jobs, but rather to help raise their self-esteem. If the inmates are functional illiterates, they must participate in the Adult Basic Education Program. Others who have graduated from high school are encouraged to enroll in the college courses which were offered by a near-by college. One of the unit managers had developed a Life Skills Education program, and those inmates who had a reasonable chance of being released before they died were encouraged to complete the program. The program consists of locating housing after release, adjusting to having a criminal record, obtaining financial resources such as food stamps, medicaid, or employment, writing resumes, developing social skills, taking care of personal hygiene and becoming involved in community activities.

As mentioned, a number of the older inmates had committed types of offenses that are extremely upsetting to the community. For example, many were child molesters. This type of offender is generally disliked by both the staff and other inmates, and normally they have an extreme amount of guilt to deal with. Special group counseling sessions were available at the institutions for these offenders. The staff encouraged volunteers of various types to come into the institution. The staff was in agreement that more effort must be made to encourage volunteers to come into the prison. Some of the older inmates were able to maintain some contact with the community through town visits.

The older inmates were encouraged to participate in recreational activities to the extent of their ability. A gym, a weight room, a machine exercise room, and a small outdoor softball field were available. Games were organized to be competitive, but not extremely physical. For example, basketball tournaments were scheduled in which the players shot foul shots instead of scrimmaged. Softball was played with a soft rubber ball. Many of the inmates used the body building equipment and were in excellent physical condition. Thus, the staff in general was quite convinced that older inmates benefitted from being housed in an institution which was programmed for the needs of the older inmates. Rather than vegetate, as many believe happens in such an institution, they tend to have more opportunity to participate in the various social, recreational, work and educational activities available than they would have if they were interspersed in regular facilities. For the staff, a job in an institution for older offenders may actually be much more demanding than one in a regular correctional facility, and correction officers working in these types of facilities need special training if they are to be effective.

The Fort Worth Comprehensive Health Unit

The Comprehensive Health Unit located at the Federal Correctional Institution at Fort Worth is designed to hold 147 offenders who
must meet the following criteria:

1. Are appropriate for a level one, coed facility
2. Have some on-going medical/health problem which precluded
   conventional housing
3. Require 24-hour medical coverage
4. Have ambulatory problems
5. Have limited work ability
6. Require close proximity to both in- and outpatient services
7. Are able to attend to their own personal hygiene such as
   bathing, eating, dressing, and cleaning their own room, not a
   hospital-type inmate (Federal Bureau of Prisons, 1987, p. 6)

Administrators and support staff at Fort Worth were asked it
special programs were needed for the older inmates. Some of the
respondents stated that the existing programs were adequate.
Others cited a "need for additional structured recreational and
cultural programs," "allowances for personal TVs and radios in
their rooms," and "better educational programs that directly benefit
older inmates, since most of them are not interested in traditional
educational programs." Many of the comments centered on the
importance of obtaining the training and experience to assist those
inmates with serious health problems. Comments on this matter
included, "There is a need for special training in medical areas to
learn to deal with severe health problems," and, "Inmates who are
medical cases cannot work and need more attention." It was also
mentioned that older inmates need to receive special counseling
when they are near to their release dates, since "many are retired
or unable to work" and these must learn how to become active in
the community in ways that do not center on work.

The manager of the Comprehensive Health Unit mentioned that
even inmates with rather severe health problems are not excluded
from institutional activities. If able to do so, these inmates are
required to do light jobs for the prisons industry, perform small
janitorial services, or assist at the school.

In an interview, Ron Hixson, the unit manager of the
Comprehensive Health Unit of Fort Worth, mentioned that
cleanliness and access are two major concerns of the staff members
who work with chronically ill or handicapped inmates in a geriatric
facility such as Fort Worth. The environmental design of the facility
must allow for maximum mobility, and a clean living unit is one

way to prevent the spread of disease within the unit. Special health oriented programs for the inmates at Fort Worth include stress management, health wise, drug facts and positive mental attitude. A nurse/counselor is assigned to the regular unit staff for the purpose of medical monitoring and to give information in self-health care and preventative medicine (Kratcoski and Pownall, 1989: 22).

Although the older inmates had more health problems, many of the staff members at Fort Worth were convinced that the older inmates were better adjusted to prison life. It was stated that, "older inmates take advantage of every program made available to them," and "do not require the strong authority figures that the young ones do." One administrator believed that the correction officers could become more effective if they were given specialized training on how to supervise older inmates. He stated, "Custodial [workers] normally don't tune in to the understanding phase of aging. They have to do a better job of simplifying rules and go the extra mile in discussing rules and why we're applying them to aged inmates."

Programs for Older Inmates in the Non-Specialized Institutions

Even if it is shown that special facilities or units are more desirable for older offenders, there is no guarantee that they will be housed in that manner. To date, few of the states have developed specialized facilities for older inmates. The larger majority of the state correctional systems and the U.S. Bureau of Prisons distribute the inmate population on the basis of security needs and regional consideration, rather than on the basis of age.

Most of the staff and administrators of the non-specialized facilities included in this study mentioned the positive effects of having older inmates intermixed with the younger inmates. It was stated that the older inmates tend to have a calming effect on the younger inmates with whom they are housed. Usually they adjust quite well. Even though they are not physically able to protect themselves from younger more aggressive inmates, they will develop a group of friends who will look after them.

It was pointed out by one unit manager working in a federal facility that "black older men have a positive influence on the younger black males. They are seen as father figures and are generally respected and protected. On the other hand, the same relationship does not exist for the white older inmates, who tend to stay by themselves and are ignored by the young white men." However, it was conceded that when mixed in with the younger inmates, there was more resistance by older inmates to participation in educational and physical activities. Even if they were required to attend school in cases in which they tested below the 8th grade level, they would tend to be passive and "just put in the time" (personal interview with unit manager).

The administrators and staff agreed that if predictions are true and a larger proportion of the future inmate population are older offenders, there will be a need for more staff, and it will put a drain on the resources of the facilities. In addition, the staff will need specialized training to work with this segment of the population. For example, a dentist working in a federal facility which houses approximately 150 inmates could affect the quality and the variety of dental work competed, since the older inmate will tend to have more dental needs and complex problems than the typical younger offender.

The administrators and staff at these facilities conceded that the health problems for the older inmates are generally more complex than those of the general population. They will show up at sick call more often, and it is hard to find meaningful work assignments for some of them who are in poor health. In order to prevent or retard health problems, the U.S. Bureau of Prisons has developed a commitment to facilitating health consciousness throughout the system. Most of the Bureau of Prisons administrators emphasize a holistic approach to positive health. Everything that happens in the institutions, including provision of appropriate living quarters, balanced nutritious meals, and anti-smoking campaigns, is designed to promote good health. The older inmates are encouraged, along with all others, to participate in recreational activities and become health conscious. If 10 to 15% of the population of a correctional facility is composed of older inmates, it is possible to develop special recreational, social and educational programs for the older inmates even though they are housed within the general population.

It was stated by several staff members employed in U.S. Bureau of Prisons institutions that inmates' health sometimes improves after they are institutionalized, because they receive proper diet and regular exercise. While this generalization appears to hold true for the older male inmates, it does not seem to be true for the older females. Since increased involvement in institutional activities may improve or at least maintain inmates' health, older inmates, both men and women, should be encouraged to participate in activities to the extent of their ability and should be rewarded for participating.

At one federal penitentiary an "Over 40" league was organized. Several softball teams were formed, and weight lifting competitions and handball and tennis matches were organized. The competitive nature of the events, along with being able to compete at one's own age level, resulted in a much larger participation than would normally be the case before the activities were restricted to a specified age group. The staff at this facility was also able to organize a pre-release program geared specifically to the needs of the older persons who will reenter the community.

The staff in one of the women's facilities indicated that it is difficult to get older women involved in educational, recreational, or health-oriented exercise programs. This may at least partially result from cultural conditioning which emphasizes passivity in women. Moreover, many of the women in these facilities had never been employed outside the home and were not planning on employment after release. One innovative recreation director addressed the older women's reluctance to become involved in activities by starting an experiential drama program. The woman were given hypothetical problems related to aging, family, and other common concerns to which they responded through drama and dance. This program had been successful in increasing the older women's involvement.

Summary

The research presented lends support to some of the arguments for creation of special institutions for older inmates, since they tend to have more needs than those housed in the other facilities. However, most correctional administrations believe that older inmates make the best adjustments when they are housed in the general population.

As long as older inmates continue to be housed in institutions with inmates of all ages, special programs must be developed to serve their needs. Most administrators believe it is best to keep the older inmates mixed in with the other younger inmates, since it is easier to administer the prison when such a policy is followed, but other administrators suggest that it may be best to house them in separate units or even separate facilities because of the great demands they put on the staff and resources. Thus, the positive effect of control enhancement is offset by the negative effect of drawing too much on the staff and resources. Regardless of whether administrators choose to build new facilities, assign special units of prisons for older offenders, or continue to keep them in the general population, health care for older offenders will continue to be a major concern, and the administrators of prisons will have to include provisions for more extensive health care services in their long-range planning.

Since providing adequate health care as mandated by law will become more and more expensive, it would appear that this is an area in which the contracting of services with the private sector could provide a partial solution to the problem.

References

Camp, G. M., and C. Graham Camp. 1989. *The Corrections Yearbook.* South Salem, NY: Criminal Justice Institute, pp. 30–31.

Federal Bureau of Prisons. 1987. "Unit Plan for Comprehensive Health Unit, Fort Worth, Texas." Washington, DC: U.S. Government Printing Office, September.

Fultz, L. 1989. "Older inmates in Maryland." Unpublished doctoral dissertation University of Maryland, College Park, MD.

Kratcoski, Peter C. 1990. "A Study of Older Inmates In Federal Correctional Facilities." Unpublished paper presented at the Annual Meeting of the American Society of Criminology, Baltimore.

Kratcoski, Peter C. and Susan Babb. 1990. "Adjustment of Older Inmates: An Analysis by Institutional Structure and Gender," *Contemporary Criminal Justice* 6(4) (December): 264–281.

Kratcoski, Peter C. and George Pownall. 1989." "Federal Bureau of Prison Programming for Older Inmates," *Federal Probation* 53(2) (June): 28–35.

Sabath, Michael J. and Ernest L. Cowles. 1988. "Factors Affecting the Adjustment of Elderly Inmates in Prison." In Belinda McCarthy and Robert Langworth (eds.), *Older Offenders.* New York: Praeger. pp. 178–196.

Vito, Gennaro F. and Deborah G. Wilson. 1985. "Forgotten People: Elderly Inmates," *Federal Probation* 49(1) (March): 18.

Section IX

Correctional Treatment
Past, Present and Future

Does correctional treatment have a future? The corrections field does not operate in a vacuum, and the various social, economic and political factors that are of importance for the entire country eventually will be manifested in the correctional sphere. Thus the increasing crime rates of the 1970s, which may have resulted from a wide variety of factors, were interpreted by many to be a direct outcome of the failure of correctional treatment, coddling of offenders, and too little emphasis on punishment. Politicians and correctional administrators were quick to realize that they were on safe ground with the general public if they took a "hard line" approach. They could back up their position with studies which seemed to prove that rehabilitative programs, in particular those operated in institutional settings, had not achieved the expected results. Consequently, the 1980s witnessed a greatly reduced commitment to rehabilitation and correctional treatment and an increased emphasis on punishment as a deterrent, which has continued into the 1990s.

A careful examination of correctional treatment programs geared toward rehabilitation reveals that it is not possible to definitively state whether most of the programs were failures, successes, or neutral aspects of the correctional process. Most of the earlier treatment programs did not have a research or evaluation component built into them. Programs of an experimental nature were initiated, completed, and discontinued without any evidence being gathered as to their effectiveness. As the various federal and state agencies funding these programs began to require evaluation reports, the evaluation was generally conducted by the agency directing the program or contracted with a research consulting firm. The findings were frequently open to question.

Inter-agency research on the effectiveness of programs seemed at first glance to be appropriate, since staff members had access to records and information that might be difficult for outside researchers to obtain. However, those given the responsibility of evaluating programs within agencies were usually not well versed in research methodology or program design techniques and not well qualified to make recommendations for further development or program changes. Administrators who had committed themselves to a certain treatment philosophy could successfully ignore findings contrary to their expectations about the success of the programs being conducted under their direction. Evaluations conducted by outside consulting firms also had their limitations. Consulting agency staff usually did not have direct experience or expertise in correctional treatment and were oversensitive to the direction given to them. The incentive to make the programs "look good" to please the agencies and therefore receive more contracts also came to bear in this evaluation approach.

Even considering the questionable nature of some of the evaluative research and although a few programs have been demonstrated to reduce recidivism after release from institutional correctional treatment, there is overwhelming evidence that institutional treatment *does not* make those treated more law abiding after their release. The goal of rehabilitation through institutional treatment has proven to be an unattainable one in spite of the efforts of administrators to develop programs to attack every facet of offenders' problems and the dedicated efforts of workers from many helping areas.

Bartollas and Miller advanced several explanations for the failure of the "rehabilitation model," including disillusionment and rapid turnover of the treatment staff, the fact that the size of the prison population made it impossible to put treatment ahead of security, the gap between the motivations and values of the middle-class treatment staff and the predominantly lower-class prison populations, insincerity and lack of desire for rehabilitation on the part of the inmates, and the inappropriateness of a dehumanizing institutional setting for the application of any type of effective treatment.[1]

In the 1970s, correctional planners and administrators began to turn to community-based treatment as an alternative to institutionalization. Economic considerations played an important part in this emerging trend. Prison overcrowding, lack of funds, and lack of public enthusiasm for the building of new facilities made placement of many offenders in the community a practical necessity. The halfway house movement, which began in the 1860s under the sponsorship of religious or public service groups and initially involved providing for the basic physical needs of homeless or alcoholic individuals, enjoyed a renaissance in the 1950s. Courts began to place offenders in halfway houses as a last resort before incarceration (halfway in); parole authorities allowed certain offenders to live in such settings before they were returned to the community and independent living (halfway out). As government agencies and private foundations offered grants for the development of such facilities to local communities, residential treatment began to emerge as the new hope for correctional treatment. The small-group setting characteristic of most residential treatment centers seemed to be ideally suited to using group treatment techniques being developed during the 1960s, and new hope emerged for rehabilitative treatment in community settings. The lower cost of placing offenders in community treatment also had an appeal, and the possibilities for job placement or educational opportunities for offenders provided an added dimension. By the early 1970s, populations of adult and juvenile correctional institutions were at all-time lows.[2]

Also in the early 1970s, the concept of "normalization" of the correctional experience for juveniles and adults gained wide acceptance. This idea involves providing those who have been placed under the supervision of the justice system with experiences that approximate as nearly as possible the experiences of normal community life.[3] For those who are not hardcore, dangerous, or severely emotionally disturbed and thus do not require institutionalization, the situation most closely approximating "normal" would obviously be supervision in their own homes or in small groups in community residential treatment. Massachusetts pioneered normalization and deinstitutionalization by closing its juvenile correctional institutions in 1972 and developing a completely community-centered program. This program, developed by Dr. Jerome Miller, included an admission, diagnostic, and classification procedure; detention placement for most juveniles in group homes or with foster parents; group homes used for treatment, with placement of youths according to age, sex, and behavioral characteristics; institutional treatment for dangerous or disturbed juveniles; use of counselors to work with juveniles in aftercare who had been placed in foster homes; and special placements for retarded youths or those with other special problems.[4]

In the mid-1970s, it seemed that those who favored rehabilitation as the goal of correction finally had found the way to bring it about—community-based treatment for juveniles and adults and use of individual and small-group treatment techniques in a "normalized" atmosphere. Then, unexpectedly, there were sharp increases in violent crimes and crimes against persons, which gave rise to public outrage and demands or "get tough" policies applied to both juveniles and adults. Prisons that had fallen into disuse were reopened, and the downward trend in institutional placements quickly reversed itself.

Those directly involved in corrections, from the institutional administrators to the correctional officers, realize that the prison experience must include elements beyond punishment. Inactivity and boredom contribute strongly to prison disruptions. Thus, involvement of the inmates in some type of productive activity, such as prison industries or educational programs, has benefits for both the system and the inmates. Within the prison setting, rehabilitation activities emphasized today often are work or education related.

Article twenty-seven, "Federal Prison Industries" by Richard P. Seiter, describes the role of federal prison industries in providing work opportunities for inmates and the benefits derived from inmate participation in these programs. Article twenty-eight, "The Post-Release Employment Project" by Saylor and Gaes, demonstrates that, if inmates are provided with work opportunities while they are incarcerated, the desired effects of decreasing idleness of the inmates, increasing orderliness in the institution, and preparing the inmates for productive activity after release occur. The twenty-ninth article, "We Must Educate Prisoners," by Raymond Bell, stresses the same themes, but with an emphasis on education as the best hope for reducing offender recidivism, particularly among juveniles.

Although the inmate population in the United States is at an all-time high, and there is every reason to believe that it will continue to increase, there has also been a significant rise in the use of community treatment as an alternative to overcrowded jails and prisons. Supervision of those placed in community treatment includes traditional styles of probation or parole supervision as well as some innovative methods. Electronic monitoring is one example. In January, 1993, it was reported that over 5,000 probationers were supervised in this manner, as were more than 3,000 parolees in 1992.[5]

The type of offender being monitored has some bearing on the outcome if a violation occurs. In an article summarizing a 1989 National Institute of Justice survey of offender monitoring in the United States, Renzema and Skelton noted that, although the threat of quick jailing is considered a deterrent for all types of offenders being monitored, the jail overcrowding situation frequently prevents this from occurring. They reported that parolees were more likely than probationers to be incarcerated when violations occurred, and that other responses to monitoring rule violations included intensified reporting requirements, stricter curfews, increases in required community services, or temporary detention (332). Renzema and Skelton also stated that more than two-thirds of the offenders being monitored were required to pay monthly monitoring fees, which were typically between $100 and $300 (334). With regard to length of monitoring, they reported an average term of 79 days, and stated that the rates of successful outcomes were not significantly different for probationers, parolees, or those in community corrections. All of these groups had successful termination rates between 74.3 and 76% (337).[6].

For offenders who are allowed to remain in the community under supervision, it is likely that the use of electronic monitoring devices will expand dramatically. These monitors have been promoted as a means for reducing the cost of supervising non-violent probationers or parolees and providing accurate information on their daily activities. Although use of the monitors has been criticized because their use places the emphasis of correctional activity on controlling the behavior of the offender rather than changing his or her attitudes and values or developing educational or job skills which would produce long-range solutions to the offender's problems, their continued and expanded use is likely. "Electronic Monitors," by Annesley K. Schmidt, examines the acceptability, legality, and cost of monitoring programs.

Another innovative approach to corrections involves the placement of offenders in programs that resemble military "boot camp" operations. These programs have received a great deal of attention as a treatment tool. Some critics of this approach argue that the programs fall into the panacea or "quick fix" category, and that the changes that occur in the behavior and attitudes of those involved are short term, at best. Those who endorse the approach argue that the "boot camp" experience meets the needs of offenders for order and discipline, and that they help develop life skills and self-esteem.

As shown in Table 1, thirty states and the Bureau of Prisons were operating programs in 1992 and 1993. More than 6,000 participants were involved in these programs, the average length of stay being 121 days.[7]

Selection thirty-one, "Shock Incarceration: Rehabilitation or Retribution?" by MacKenzie et al., describes a "boot camp" type of program that operated in Louisiana. The dynamics of the program are discussed, and the rehabilitative components of the program are enumerated.

Table 1   **Growth of Shock Incarceration Programs for Adults**

Date Began	State	Number of Programs in 1992 and 1993	Number of Participants/ Capacity in 1992 and 1993	Average length of stay[a]
1983	Georgia	5	800/800	90
	Oklahoma	4	415/438	90[b]
1984				
1985	Mississippi	1	223/263	120
1986				
1987	Florida	1	93/100	90
	Louisiana	1	64/136	120
	New York	5	1500/1500	180
	South Carolina	2	198/216	90
1988	Alabama	1	140/180	90
	Arizona	1	92/150	120
	Michigan	3	160/600	90
1989	Idaho	1	236/250	120
	North Carolina	1	82/90	92
	Tennessee	1	103/150	91
	Texas	2	329/400	80
1990	Illinois	1	215/230	120
	Maryland	1	332/448	168
	New Hampshire	1	32/65	120
	Wyoming	1	23/24	95
1991	Arkansas	1	150/150	105
	BOP-male	1	192/192	190
	Colorado	1	114/100	90
	Kansas	1	66/104	180
	Nevada	1	60/60	150
	Ohio	1	76/94	90
	Virginia	1	79/100	90
	Wisconsin	1	40/40	180
1992	BOP-female	1	119/120	180
	Massachusetts	1	95/256	120
	Minnesota	1	12/36	180
	Pennsylvania	1	45/50	180
1993	California	1	48/176	180[c]
Total		46	6133/7518	121

1993   Considering beginning programs: Indiana, Missouri, and Rhode Island.

[a] Based upon graduates of the program
[b] Four programs, two 90-day programs and two 45-day programs
[c] The first phase is 120 days with a capacity of 176 and the second phase is 60 days with a capacity of 64.

Source: Doris Layton Mackenzie, "Boot Camp Prisons in 1993," *National Institute of Justice Journal*, 227 (November, 1993): 22.

Given the current and likely to continue emphasis on incarceration and its deterrent effects, the prison population will continue to increase, and correctional services will also grow. Privatization of correctional services has been advanced as one way of dealing with this reality.

Privatization in corrections involves the use of the private sector to perform functions and services which formerly were handled by the correctional agencies themselves. Saxton noted four ways in which privatization has occurred in recent years. These include operation or management of prison industries by private firms, private financing of correctional construction, including lease-purchase arrangements, total private sector operation of correctional facilities, or contracting for services such as medical treatment, food preparation or specialized treatment for offenders.[8]

Philip A. Ethridge and James P. Marquart, who examined the involvement of the private sector in the Texas correctional system, noted that correctional facilities administered by the private sector have smaller inmate populations than those administered by state correctional agencies and that the privately administered facilities are in a better position to prepare the inmates for reentry into the community upon release.[9] While privatization of institutional operations may increase in the future, it is not likely to lead to a solution to the problems of overcrowding and lack of funds. However, privatization through community-based service offerings and residential center management is likely to grow in significance.

In selection thirty-two, "Privatization in Corrections," Donald Walker traces the development of privatization in the United States. He notes that contracting for medical services and psychological counseling has generally been an integral part of correctional management and that the major controversies and issues regarding privatization center on the private ownership and operation of correctional facilities. In selection thirty-three, "Privatization in Juvenile Services: Competition Promotes Quality," Loughran shows how the State of Massachusetts, through privatization, was able to decrease its juvenile institution population drastically while increasing the counseling and services offered to juveniles who were brought into the system.

Current Emphases in Correctional Treatment

We noted in the introduction to this text that the pendulum of correctional thinking has swung back to reemphasis on punishment. Treatment is coming to be viewed as a privilege, which an offender may receive, but to which he or she is not entitled.

Because of this trend, less attention is given to the emotional adjustment of offenders and more emphasis is placed on making the offender into a productive member of society. Career planning and guidance counseling—which could include achievement, interest, and aptitude testing; vocational rehabilitation; and enrollment in educational or job-preparation programs—assume top priority in the counseling hierarchy. Types of counseling or treatment aimed at resolving specific problems, such as substance abuse, are also given priority over treatment geared toward improving the offender's emotional well-being. Certain other "practical" types of therapy, such as peer counseling or assertiveness training, which are seen as more direct approaches toward making the offender into a functioning member of society, are also emphasized.

Role of the Correctional Counselor

Although correctional treatment personnel continue to serve many of their functions in institutional and community treatment settings, they have been called upon to assume new roles. One role is that of "client advocate," not in terms of taking an offender's part in struggles against those in authority, but in terms of helping the client locate needed services and finding the means to obtain such services. As Shulman stated:

> . . . the very institutions set up to solve problems became so complex themselves that new problems were generated. Social, medical, and educational systems are difficult to negotiate, even for individuals who are well equipped to deal with them, never mind those with limited education and resources. The services established for people are often so complex that it is difficult for individuals to make use of them.[10]

The treatment counselor, in addition to having training in various treatment techniques, is called upon to act as a "service broker," that is, the person who discovers and links those in need of specific services with the exact agency in the community that can provide those services most efficiently and effectively. Such activity presupposes a great deal of knowledge and well-developed contacts on the treatment counselor's part. The types of services in which the "service broker" must have connections would include psychological testing and treatment, social welfare, vocational rehabilitation, and educational testing and placement. Telling offenders *where* to seek help at the exact time when they are ready or willing to accept it may be the key activity a correctional treatment counselor performs. In all this coordination, the offender's contribution and efforts toward self-help and self-motivated change cannot be overlooked. Now that the emphasis appears to be on "justice," an offender who has received and accepted a just punishment for his or her misdeeds would also be able to expect a just and compassionate response to his efforts to secure treatment or assistance which, although no longer *required* or even regarded as a *right* of an adult offender, is available when sought in a sincere manner.

Notes

[1] Clemens Bartollas and Stuart J. Miller, *Correctional Administration* (New York: McGraw-Hill, 1978): 2.

[2] John P. Conrad, "We Should Never Have Promised a Hospital," *Federal Probation* 39(1974): 4.

[3] Daniel Katkin, Drew Hyman, and John Kramer, *Juvenile Delinquency and the Juvenile Justice System* (North Scituate, MA: Duxbury Press, 1976): 458.

[4] E. Eugene Miller and M. Robert Montilla, *Corrections in the Community* (Reston, VA: Reston Publishing, 1977): 117.

[5] George M. Camp and Camille Graham Camp, *The Corrections yearbook 1993: Probation and Parole* (South Salem, NY: Criminal Justice Institute, 1993): 28, 56.

[6] Marc Renzema and David T. Skelton, "Use of Electronic Monitoring in the United States: 1989 Update," in Thomas Ellsworth, *Contemporary Community Corrections* (Prospect Heights, IL: Waveland Press, 1992): 330–339.

[7] Doris MacKenzie, "Boot Camp Prisons in 1993," *National Institute of Justice Journal*, 227 (November 93): 22.

[8] Samuel F. Saxton, "Contracting for Services: Different Facilities, Different Needs," *Corrections Today*, 40 (6) (Oct. 1988): 16–17.

[9] Philip A. Ethridge and James P. Marquart, "Private Prisons in Texas: The New Penology for Profit," *Justice Quarterly* 10 (1) (March 1993): 29–48.

[10] Lawrence Shulman, *The Skills of Helping* (Itasca, IL: F. E. Peacock, 1979): 296.

27

Federal Prison Industries
Meeting the Challenge of Growth

Richard P. Seiter

Much of the Federal Bureau of Prisons' ability to manage complex and often overcrowded institutions has been due to its ability to maintain productive work programs for inmates, thereby reducing idleness. As the Bureau responds to an influx of a large number of new inmates, it is essential that the availability of programs expands at the same pace. Federal Prison Industries (FPI) provides the greatest opportunity to involve inmates in this kind of endeavor.

FPI is a wholly owned, non-appropriated Government corporation, created by Congress in 1934 to sell solely to the Government. Its goods are marketed under the trade name UNICOR. A prison program managed by correctional professionals, it was created to provide work for inmates, instill a work ethic for individuals with little past work experience or training, and teach inmates skills so that they will be better prepared to return to the community.

Currently, more than 14,000 inmates are employed by FPI; fiscal year 1989 sales were approximately $360 million. FPI is required to have a diverse product line and offers more than 250 different products for sale, including mattresses, military clothing, sheets, towels, pajamas, gloves, electronic cable assemblies, helmets, printing services, signage, data input services, wood office furniture, systems furniture, metal lockers, pallet racking, and seating products. (Organizationally, these product lines are managed under several discrete divisions.) Its largest customer (approximately 50 percent of sales) is the Department of Defense. Other major customers include the General Services Administration, the Postal

Source: *Federal Prisons Journal*, 1(3) (Spring 1990): 11–15.

Service, the Veterans Administration, and the Social Security Administration.

FPI must in many ways operate like a business. Nevertheless, it is not "in business" to maximize profits, but to fulfill its correctional mission of employing and training inmates. In fact, as a correctional program, FPI has some built-in business inefficiencies not found in the private sector. For example, FPI follows Federal procurement regulations in its purchasing, which eliminates its buying flexibility.

Certain types of efficiencies would actually be counterproductive in terms of FPI's mission. For example, production must be labor-intensive so that as many inmates as possible can be put to work. Also, FPI uses an unskilled labor pool; its workers are subject to all sorts of interruptions and transfers for correctional purposes that are completely unrelated to business needs. Finally, FPI cannot control the size of its work force (the number of inmates that it receives) but must nevertheless keep them all busy.

Prison work must not be overly dependent on the vagaries of the market. Private business strives to be more efficient to increase market share. An overemphasis on this approach by FPI, on the other hand, could cause major changes in operations and lead to employing fewer inmates, reducing its training impact, and hiring inmates who already have good work skills—and thus are least in need of the experience.

It is sometimes thought that FPI prices are not competitive, since its products do not have to be competitively bid. Yet, by statute, FPI prices cannot exceed current market prices, and are therefore rigorously tested by customers. When FPI is not competitive in price, a waiver allows the contracting agency to procure the item from the private sector. In fact, in FY 1988, 2,500 contracts were waived in the Electronics Division alone.

A second misperception is that the low cost of inmate labor (an average of $1 per hour) gives FPI an unfair advantage in the selling price of products. However, FPI's labor costs (as a percentage of the selling price) are generally the same as those of most private operations manufacturing similar products, for several reasons. FPI focuses on labor-intensive operations to the greatest extent possible. There is a substantial training cost to develop inmates into useful employees. Finally, staff costs include prison security, a high ratio of "civilian foremen" to production inmates to ensure supervision and quality, and lost production time resulting from prison operations, such as counts, shakedowns, and searches of incoming and outgoing materials.

Because FPI has large total sales, it is often thought of as a single big business. However, it is more accurate to think of the corporation as more than 70 separate local operations with average sales of $4,500,000 per factory and employing fewer than 200 inmates per factory. These decentralized facilities operate like small businesses with regard to procurement of supplies and components.

There is also a perception that FPI is in direct competition with the private sector in its sales to the Federal Government. On the contrary, in many cases, FPI and private companies are partners in producing goods. FPI buys materials and component parts from domestic companies, and often adds to the available business of these firms; procurement from companies classified as "small business" can be between 25 and 50 percent of FPI's purchasing activity.

Occasionally, it is suggested that FPI should have to fully compete for its sales. In addition to its necessary role in correctional management, however, FPI is similar to other Federal programs that support industrial operations to employ the blind and other handicapped citizens. In such programs, employment is provided for a work force that needs training, work experience, and preparation for competing in (and contributing to) a mainstream work environment.

Product Development Guidelines

In early 1988, noting the tremendous growth that will occur over the next several years, FPI sought authority from Congress to borrow money from the U.S. Treasury for its capital expansion needs. Previously, FPI built and renovated factory operations out of current retained earnings. As a part of its deliberations regarding the FPI borrowing authority, and in an effort to ensure proper consideration of FPI's impact on the private sector, Congress required FPI to adhere to stringent product development guidelines.

Essentially, these guidelines require that, prior to adding any new product lines or significantly expanding a current product line, FPI must publish its intent to do so in the *Commerce Business Daily*, as well as notify affected trade associations. In addition, FPI must complete a thorough market analysis—determining the available market, identifying the intended portion of that market that FPI would anticipate producing, and estimating the impact on private industries of FPI's entrance into the market. The guidelines contain a provision for negotiating a reasonable market share. If the negotiation is not successful, a hearing is held before the FPI Board of Directors (appointed by the President). The Board makes the final determination whether FPI should be allowed to produce a product.

In summary, FPI is critical to the successful operation of Federal prisons. While it is important that FPI maintain its "program" emphasis, it must also maintain its ability to manufacture high-quality products at a competitive price.

Issues and Options for Future Growth

When thinking about the period of explosive growth the Federal Prison System will undergo over the next few years, a number of issues arise:

How can FPI expand to support a growing Federal Bureau of Prisons, yet be sensitive to the concerns of the private business community?

Even with the relatively small percentage of the Government market represented by FPI sales, is there a negative impact on the private sector?

How can FPI grow, yet maintain its emphasis as a correctional program?

Are there markets outside the Federal Government that could provide FPI with growth potential, while not raising serious concerns for private business or labor?

FPI's traditional market is the Federal Government; it is a mandatory source if its products meet the buyer's specifications for price, quality, and delivery. While there are often products for which FPI is the sole source within the Government, there are usually many vendors selling similar products outside the Government. To look at the growth demands on FPI, several options can be explored for their potential in meeting FPI growth needs.

Continued traditional Federal market—In this case, all growth in sales and inmate employment would continue in the future as in the past. An issue recently before Congress was whether FPI should maintain its mandatory source status in sales to the Federal Government. The Department of Justice argued that industrial operations are critical to the operation of Federal prisons; that recent statutory changes will send more offenders to Federal prisons and therefore require more work opportunities; that the newly enacted product development guidelines are designed to meet the private sector's concerns; and that the mandatory source is necessary to maintain FPI's program (rather than business) emphasis, and ensure enough work to avoid inmate idleness.

Without a mandatory source provision, the argument continues, FPI would lose significant sales because the mandatory source acts as an offset to the "stigma" of prison-made goods, the cost of operating within a prison environment, and the high training costs of inmate workers.

The benefits of using its traditional market to meet FPI growth needs include an assurance of a level of sales to maintain required inmate employment. FPI is familiar with the Federal market and need not incur business development costs to seek new markets, while the mandatory source requirements allow FPI to maintain its program emphasis.

However, this approach does little to reduce the concern of the private sector regarding FPI's growth within the Federal market, and its use of the mandatory source status to generate sales.

Subcontracting to prime Federal Government contractors—FPI is exploring the idea of subcontracting with private companies who sell to the Government. For example, FPI could provide the labor for assembling component parts, thereby marketing its labor, space, and work force to add value to a Government product that will be sold by a private firm.

In this situation, FPI would not use its mandatory source, but would compete in price, quality, and delivery. It is uncertain how much potential this market has, particularly since the prime contractor would be required to segregate all FPI products for Government use from the products for the nongovernment market.

There are many benefits to subcontracting. FPI would not be directly competing with the private sector. Many companies have moved their labor-intensive operations offshore to reduce costs. In many cases, FPI can compete with such offshore labor. If FPI can search out these opportunities, it represents a winning situation for all concerned.

Subcontracting also forges partnerships between FPI and the private sector, which may result in expanded, mutually beneficial programs. Contracting companies might consider released inmates for employment, since these workers would be familiar with the companies' products and procedures.

The disadvantages of this option include a concern on the part of the labor movement that "captive labor" would displace private sector employees. With stipulations that the focus be on assembly operations and component sales that have already moved offshore, some of this concern may be reduced; however, it must be addressed.

Marketing FPI products offshore—Another option is to allow FPI to export products (to either public or private markets). This certainly increases the available market for FPI-produced goods; however, there are many disadvantages to this approach. The export of products is dependent on the exchange rate of the dollar. From 1973 through 1985, the dollar appreciated and increased the foreign currency price of U.S. exports, thereby reducing foreign demand. From 1985–1988, the dollar depreciated in the world market and made U.S. exports more attractive. FPI goods, like other exports, would be forced to react to such world dollar variances.

There are other potential drawbacks. FPI is not familiar with marketing products offshore. While this expertise could be developed, it would increase sales costs. In addition, FPI may have trouble being competitive in price. Much of the current U.S. export business involves non-labor-intensive products, in which high technology or advanced manufacturing processes foster offshore demand. FPI's low-cost labor may not be that much of an advantage. (It should be noted that both of these last options would require changing FPI's enabling legislation.)

Subcontracting to prime contractors with an open market— Under this option, FPI would market itself as a subcontractor to private sector companies, offering assembly or component parts for their manufactured goods, similar to the subcontracting option mentioned earlier. The difference is that there would be no requirement for the finished products to be sold to the Federal Government.

The benefits are similar to some of those noted earlier. FPI would develop partnerships with the private sector, and dependence on mandatory sales to the Government would be reduced. FPI would have an accessible expanded market, would not compete for sales with the private sector, and would provide low-cost labor perhaps not available domestically. However, as with the other subcontracting option, there may be concerns about displacement of services and component goods offered by companies using domestic labor.

*Competing in a totally open market—*This is the most extreme option for FPI growth. Under this option, FPI could sell products to anyone. Almost two-thirds of State prison industries have an unrestricted market; to date these prison industries have not been seen as a serious threat to U.S. business.

The benefits are obvious. It creates a much larger market and provides the greatest opportunity for FPI to meet its growth needs without competing with the private sector for the Government market.

The danger is that FPI would have to be much more price-, and therefore cost-reduction, oriented. As mentioned, the program aspects of FPI have built-in inefficiencies that require some assurance of sales. To be truly competitive in an open market would mean making decisions that are more business- and efficiency-oriented, and possibly changing the makeup of operations to a degree that would undermine the original mission of FPI.

Conclusion

FPI is facing tremendous growth needs. It will be difficult to grow at the rate required, to find adequate markets for goods, to fund required capital expansion, and to keep FPI solvent during the process. Nevertheless, FPI is critical to the operation of safe, orderly prisons; it must be successful in this endeavor. As a correctional program, FPI must employ and train inmates, while being sensitive to the concerns of private industry.

This article has suggested some options to balance FPI growth with private sector concerns. The mandatory source provision for sales to the Federal Government must be maintained to ensure FPI a sufficient level of business to keep inmates employed. However, developing new markets without the use of a mandatory source would reduce the need for FPI growth to focus on its traditional Government market.

For the future, if mandatory source protection were maintained for sales to the Government, if product development guidelines were used for expanding sales in that market, and if other markets were opened without mandatory source protection, FPI would have an opportunity to meet its growth needs. Additionally, the private sector would be less affected by such growth, and perhaps would even benefit from partnerships with FPI.

28

The Post-Release Employment Project
Prison Work Has Measurable Effects on Post-Release Success

William G. Saylor
Gerald G. Gaes

An argument for continuing or even expanding industrial work opportunities in prisons is that such programs are needed to cope effectively with inmate idleness and that they help ensure the orderly running of correctional institutions. Advocates also suggest that such programs may give participants a better chance of remaining law-abiding after their release from prison.

The Post-Release Employment Project (PREP), a study by the Bureau of Prisons' Office of Research and Evaluation (ORE), seems to support the notion that prison work and training programs have a significant positive impact on participants. Initial PREP results indicate that inmates who receive training and work experience during their incarceration are less likely to receive misconduct reports in prison, more likely to be employed during their halfway house stay and after release, and less likely to recidivate than similar inmates who are not trained or employed during their imprisonment.

PREP was designed to answer fundamental questions about the effect of prison vocational training and work experience on offenders' behavior when they are released to the community. This article provides an overview of the PREP study and discusses the

Source: *Federal Prisons Journal*, 2(4) (Winter 1992): 33–36.

effect that such training and employment had on inmates during their time in prison, in halfway houses, and after release.

Some Basics about the Study

PREP is primarily an analysis of the differences between Federal offenders who received training and work experience (the study group) and similar offenders who did not participate in these activities (the comparison group). The study and comparison groups were also contrasted with a "baseline" group of offenders who represented all other inmates released in the same time frame as the study and comparison offenders.

While the study and comparison groups were similar in terms of expected length of stay, individuals in these groups were much more likely to have a longer expected length of stay than inmates in the baseline group.[1] In addition, the conviction offense for study and comparison groups tended to be more serious than for the baseline group.

These differences are especially significant because they underscore the fact that PREP study group participants were by no means those individuals who seemed most predisposed to succeed in either a prison program or in the community after release. (See note 2 at the end of this article for additional information on methodology.)

Institutional Adjustment

While PREP does not directly explore whether prison employment and job training programs help ensure the orderly running of correctional institutions, it asks a related and more specific question: Do inmates working in prison industries or participating in vocational training show better institutional adjustment than their matched comparison counterparts?

Initial PREP results suggest that program participants did show better institutional adjustment:

- Study group participants were less likely to have a misconduct report within their last year of incarceration.
- When they did have a misconduct report, it was less likely to have been for serious misconduct.
- Participants were rated by their unit teams to have a higher level of responsibility than their comparison counterparts. An inmate's level of responsibility refers to his/her level of dependability,

financial responsibility, and the nature of his/her interaction with staff and other inmates.

Halfway House Outcomes

The Bureau of Prisons contracts with halfway houses to provide qualifying inmates an opportunity, prior to the end of their imprisonment, to work in the community. This is also the first opportunity to recidivate. Although most study offenders were released through a halfway house, many of the comparison inmates were released directly to community supervision.

Almost the same proportion of study (83.9 percent) and comparison (83.3 percent) inmates successfully completed their halfway house stay. On average, study inmates spent 98.0 days in the halfway house environment prior to their release to community supervision, while comparison inmates spent 93.5 days. Study group members were 24.4 percent more likely than comparison group members to obtain a full-time job (of some duration) at some point during their halfway house stay. Of the 3,070 study inmates released through a halfway house, 86.5 percent obtained a full-time job, while only 62.1 percent of the 1,043 comparison inmates released through a halfway house had worked at a full-time job.

Study group members were also 7.7 percent more likely to obtain day labor employment (e.g., a 1-day job performing unskilled labor at a construction site). Nevertheless, both study and comparison group members who obtained employment spent the same proportion of their entire halfway house stay on their job (on average, about 4.1 and 1.5 days per week on full-time and day labor jobs respectively).

In summary, at the point of halfway house release, both study and comparison offenders were equally likely to have successfully completed their halfway house stay, although study inmates were far more likely to have obtained a full-time or day labor job.

Post-Release Outcome

Once released to community supervision, study and comparison group members were followed by making phone calls to their supervising probation officers. Followup occurred at 6- and 12-month intervals. However, monthly information was collected over the entire interval.

Figure 1[3] (see note 5) shows the 6- and 12-month dispositions for study and comparison group members. At both the 6- and 12-month

Figure 1 (see note 5)

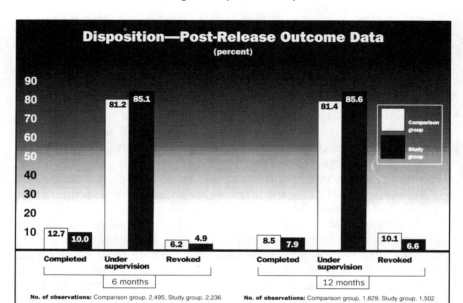

followup points, study group offenders were less likely to have been revoked from parole supervision.[4] Although the magnitude of difference may seem small, the differences are both statistically significant and substantively meaningful. At the 12-month time period, 10.1 percent of comparison offenders had been revoked, while only 6.6 percent of study offenders had been revoked. In other recidivism studies conducted by the Bureau, about 20 percent of released inmates were revoked or rearrested within a year of their release. In 1980, the percentage was 19.4; in 1982, 23.9; and in 1987, 19.2.

Although not depicted in Figure 1, study and comparison groups were statistically indistinguishable in their reason (parole violation vs. new offense) for being revoked at both the 6- and 12-month junctures. Nevertheless, the predominant reason for revocation during each 6-month period (60–70 percent) for both groups was a parole violation rather than a new offense.

The differences among study, comparison, and baseline groups indicate several important conclusions:

• Due to the research design and the matching methodology, there are characteristics of both study and comparison offenders that decrease each group's likelihood of recidivating.

- UNICOR work experience and vocational training further increase the likelihood of post-release success.
- Had we compared the study group to the general population (i.e., the baseline group), even with statistical controls, it is likely we would have exaggerated the differences between offenders who participated in work and vocational training and those who did not.

Table 1 (see note 6) shows the proportion of study and comparison group offenders who were employed during the followup period in any given month. It also shows the average wages earned in each month, as well as the 6- and 12-month totals. Although not indicated in Table 1, there is tremendous variability in post-release wages, which is probably why most comparisons did not reach statistical significance. The table shows that study group offenders were more likely to be employed in any of the 12 months following their release to the community. At the end of 12 months, study group inmates had averaged about $200 more in wages than comparison group offenders. Although this result was not statistically significant, it seems to be a pattern worthy of continued observation.

Table 1 (see note 6)

Employment—Post-Release Outcome Data

| Month | Percentage of offenders employed | | Average wages earned | |
	Comparison group	Study group	Comparison group	Study group
1	65.6	74.7	$ 668.25	$ 723.57
2	65.5	75.1	693.45	737.17
3	65.8	74.2	703.32	727.80 *
4	64.7	72.8	701.09	733.82 *
5	63.7	71.1	693.12	720.77 *
6	61.1	68.6	676.35	701.29 *
No. observations	(2,506)	(2,253)	(2,506)	(2,253)
Months 1-6 ($)			$4,135.59	$4,344.42 *
7	71.8	79.2	851.02	846.10 *
8	70.7	77.1	835.92	845.98 *
9	68.8	76.1	828.03	833.50 *
10	66.7	74.3	815.57	822.21 *
11	64.9	72.9	793.06	822.97 *
12	63.1	71.7	769.45	820.97 *
No. observations	(1,831)	(1,503)	(1,831)	(1,503)
Months 7-12 ($)			$4,893.06	$4,991.72 *
Months 1-12 ($)			$9,665.88	$9,862.82 *

*No statistically significant difference for these comparisons.

In summary, inmates who participated in UNICOR work and other vocational programming during their imprisonment showed better institutional adjustment, were less likely to be revoked at the end of their first year back in the community, were more likely to be employed in the halfway house and community, and earned slightly more money in the community than inmates who had similar background characteristics but who did not participate in work and vocational training programs.

Future Analyses and Reports

The analyses discussed in this report represent only the most fundamental differences between study and comparison offenders. Future analyses will address mobility issues—the impact of prison work and vocational training on changes in occupations before, during, and after release from prison. We will also analyze specific occupational work and training effects to the extent the data allow. Every inmate's job or vocational training was classified according to the Department of Labor's Dictionary of Occupational Titles (DOT). These DOT codes will allow us to look at broad, as well as more refined, classes of occupations and their impact on post-release outcome.

Additionally, work evaluations conducted by the inmates' supervisors and ratings of the inmates' performance in vocational training courses were collected on study inmates while they were in prison. This performance information will allow us to examine whether the intensity of an inmate's work or training performance affects post-release success.

We have also collected economic climate data. Data such as unemployment statistics, industrial sector information, and information on the demographic characteristics of the areas to which inmates were released will allow us to statistically control for differences in economic and labor market conditions and to examine the relative impact of these economic climate data in relation to work and vocational training.

It is likely that the economic climate of an area is an important determinant of an offender's community employment. We are well aware that many ex-offenders not only must overcome low skill levels, but also the conditions that compound the already formidable challenge of finding and keeping a job, given the stigma of past incarceration.

In this context, these economic climate data will not only provide statistical controls, but may be valuable in helping us to assess the value of specific skills acquisition.

Notes

[1] Actual time served was computed for the study and comparison groups and, as one would expect, based on the projected length of incarceration, the study group served more time than did the comparison group. On average, study group inmates served about 6 months longer than comparison group inmates.

[2] Preparation for the Post-Release Employment Project began in 1983. Data collection on post-release outcomes for more than 7,000 inmates continued, for the most part, into early 1987, although some data came in as late as October 1987.

Throughout the duration of this project, in which study and comparison inmates were released from the Bureau (1984 through 1986), about 35 percent of inmates in institutions with Federal Prison Industries (UNICOR) operations were employed by UNICOR. Currently, 32 percent of inmates in such institutions are employed by UNICOR. We do not know whether there is an optimal level of UNICOR employment in an institution. Increasing or decreasing the percentage of inmates employed in prison industries may or may not increase the positive effects of employment. Consequently, the conclusions of this study could be influenced by the proportion of inmates employed by UNICOR.

Unlike most studies of prison vocational training or work experience, PREP is a prospective, longitudinal study. Study inmates were identified by case management staff at the institution over a period of several years.

Inmates were selected for the study group prior to their release if they had participated in industrial work for at least 6 months or had successfully completed vocational instruction. The study group was composed primarily of inmates with UNICOR work experience—57 percent had exclusively UNICOR work experience, while 19 percent had a combination of UNICOR work experience and vocational training, or apprenticeship training. The remaining 24 percent were involved in some combination of vocational or apprenticeship training. The comparison group was chosen to be as much like the study group as possible. A comparison observation was selected specifically for each study group member from a cohort of individuals who were released during the same calendar quarter. Each pairing was based on an exact match of gender and individual security level and on the closest possible match in criminal, educational, and employment histories and characteristics of the current offense.

[3] All of the results in Figure 1 are statistically significant. In Table 1, contrasts are statistically significant unless indicated with an "*." Statistical tests in Figure 1 and the employment data for Table 1 are chi-square tests for differences in proportions. The statistical tests for employment wages in Table 1 were based on t-tests of differences in group means. We have also noted in each table the different number of observations. Not all information was collected or available on all observations in this study. Furthermore, as the study progressed through the post-release outcome stages, inmates would be revoked, or otherwise drop out of the study (e.g., successfully complete their period of supervision).

[4] Study group members who participated exclusively in UNICOR were also less likely to have their supervision revoked than were comparison group offenders.

[5] *(Figure 1):* The data in Figure 1 show that about 600–700 fewer inmates from each group were represented in the 12-month followup than in the 6-month followup. The reason for this is that when the PREP study was terminated, there were about that number of offenders still in the "pipeline" for whom no 12-month outcome data was collected.

[6] *(Table 1):* The increase in the percentage employed between months 6 and 7 for both groups is a statistical artifact. This is because the percentages are based on the number of observations still under supervision at the end of each 6-month interval. However, this does not influence the monthly comparisons between the two groups.

For the same reason, the average wages diminish over each 6-month interval. This is because the wages earned during the month (the numerator) are zero for any individual who was unemployed during a month and consequently earned no money, while the number of observations (the denominator) used to calculate the average is determined by the observations still under supervision at the end of each 6-month interval.

Although some individuals retained a job over the entire observation period and may have maintained, or even increased, their remuneration, the average wage for the group declined due to the increase in the number of individuals who became unemployed for some period of time and therefore earned zero dollars for those months.

29

We Must Educate Prisoners

Raymond Bell

Almost two decades ago, a cartoon appeared in the *Philadelphia Inquirer* that depicted a prison guard talking to his warden and saying, "I don't know what things are coming to, Warden. Sixty percent of the inmates in this prison can't write a decent extortion note!" As we approach a new century, the prison population has grown at an alarming rate, but the educational level is still as woeful as it was 20 years ago.

Prisons are a growth industry, with 182 under construction. When completed, they will add some 67,350 beds to the current capacity at a cost of $2,800,000,000. Even given the proposed new construction that is on the drawing boards and will provide 89,000 more beds, the jails, prison, and juvenile treatment centers of this country will be bursting at the seams.

In spite of what is written in the press about Ivan Boesky and Michael Milken, the average inmate in the nation's correctional facilities is functionally illiterate, probably has a learning disability, never had a steady job, was a juvenile delinquent, used drugs and alcohol, and came from a dysfunctional home in which he or she was abused physically and/or sexually. They are products of an educational system that has failed to prepare them to be able to contribute to society. If an individual does not have the skills, values, and abilities to earn a living legally and acceptably, he or she most certainly will turn to illegal pursuits.

The findings of various research studies regarding such inmates' backgrounds—academic, vocational, and social—are consistent over time. It is clear that prisoners come from a culturally and

Reprinted from *USA Today Magazine*, January, copyright 1993 by the Society for the Advancement of Education.

educationally deprived environment. Academically, the average inmate has not attended school beyond the 10th grade, and, although the time in attendance appears to be on the increase, achievement has remained constant at just below the seventh-grade level. Of greater concern, perhaps, is that this lack of academic performance can be attributed to the fact that at least half of them have a specific learning disability, usually associated with visual or auditory perception, especially the latter.

The distribution of intelligence among prison populations shows the average IQ to be 86. That is 14 points, or one standard deviation, under the national mean. Approximately 15% of inmates score below 75 on the Wechsler Scale of Adult Intelligence-Revised. A score of 75 generally is considered to be the cutoff for identifying those who may be mentally retarded. This would suggest a substantially higher percentage of moderately retarded individuals in prisons than in the general population. Moreover, 70% of inmates never have had any formal preparation in a skill, trade, or profession. A similar percentage have no consistent work history prior to incarceration. More than two-thirds come from broken or dysfunctional homes in which stability, discipline, and moral development were inconsistent at best. About 70% of adult prisoners have been involved with the juvenile justice system, which has had questionable success in rehabilitation.

Drug and alcohol abuse among this population is well-documented. Also telling is the extent to which these prisoners, especially females, have been victims of physical and/or sexual abuse both as children and adults. In the process of collecting data for a national study, researchers found that *every one* of the records of the 178 female subjects—drawn at random from inmates in Louisiana, Pennsylvania, and Washington—showed such abuse!

Almost 60% of those in the nation's correctional facilities come from minority groups. This, coupled with the recent finding that 25% of all young black men either are in prison or on probation, raises serious questions about the socioeconomic conditions in general, as well as the quality and availability of education and the application of justice, in minority communities.

The problem, then, is what can be done to teach prisoners to be productive citizens when they are released? In spite of new and tougher laws and determinate sentencing guidelines, about 87% of prisoners will return to crime. As a Baltimore bumper sticker proclaimed, "Today's Inmate Is Tomorrow's Neighbor!"

Inmates present educators with a series of problems. For prisoners, the words "education" and "school" conjure up failure, embarrassment, frustration, and rejection. They have learned to hide their deficiencies behind a series of barriers, masks, and coping mechanisms. They are street-wise, suspicious, and tough.

At the same time, educators must cope with the unique ethos within the correctional facility. By definition, prisons are places that are secure. The conflict between this role and the treatment function is constant and real. The work of teachers in such a setting is extremely draining. Correctional officers usually lack enthusiasm for anything that threatens routine security. When it comes to free educational opportunities for felons, their attitudes become distinctly cool. Adding to this conflict is the fact that many prisons are at least 100% above capacity. It is ironic, perhaps, that most wardens or superintendents heartily support educational programs not as treatment, but, rather, as a *control* system—"It keeps the inmates busy." Educational programming has become less and less of a priority in the budgeting process as the need for more cells and increasing security staff grows. Classrooms become occupied by bunks, and teaching slots get converted into security positions. The need to run the institution and feed, clothe, and house the inmates takes precedence.

The inmate subculture, too, is not conducive to learning. Attendance at school is not held in high esteem in the peer group. Classroom time may mean sacrificing income from a prison job, losing a recreational opportunity, or missing a family or lawyer visit. On the other hand, participation in an educational program, even when substantial accomplishment can be demonstrated, may have no impact on the time served. There are many disincentives to participating in education. It is to the credit of some states—Virginia and Ohio, for example—that, in spite of great fiscal stresses, they are requiring uneducated inmates to attend school.

If these educational needs are to be addressed, it is apparent that the means of instruction, the quality of the delivery system, and the sophistication of the diagnostic-remedial process must be substantially different from, and better than, those that already have failed on the outside. It cannot be a case of relying on "the prescription as before."

It is of little use to require child-like rote work of the public school or to offer vocational instruction in barber shops or auto-mechanical training on 1967 Chevrolets. Such programs certainly will keep inmates busy, but won't return them to society as productive, willing citizens. Neither will courses in psychology, law, or history taught to functionally illiterate inmates. The overwhelming number of inmates require classes that lead to demonstrable skills in literacy and numeracy taught in the context of a marketable vocation that can be parlayed into a job in the specific community to which he or she returns. These courses need to be structured, self-paced, and highly individualized.

Interactive video and microcomputers offer tremendous opportunities for instructional systems that not only overcome the embarrassment of the learning-deficient inmate, but also present alternative means to overcome auditory or visual difficulties. This joint adult basic education-vocational instruction should be offered in conjunction with specific social education curriculum focusing on increasing self-image and decision-making skills.

Education has been considered a secondary level add-on instead of the keystone to a successful treatment and rehabilitation program, especially in juvenile institutions. The critical time for inmates is just prior to and immediately after release. These periods necessitate much more attention, resources, and personnel than historically has been the case. More attention could be paid to the lessons learned by the military. The Defense Department has extensive experience in training learning-deficient individuals using structured, multi-media delivery systems that focus on basic academic and vocational skills. Further, it is vital to address the special requirements of women and non-English-speaking and mentally retarded inmates, particularly in highly utilitarian vocational education areas.

One additional source of frustration for correctional educators is the lack of a single, unified budget source. Administrators must cobble together financing from a remarkable array of sources, both public and private. It is not out of the ordinary to have funding from multiple programs in state and Federal Departments of Education, Labor, Justice, and Veterans Affairs. Each has its own fiscal priority, application process, evaluation criteria, deadlines, and administrative and eligibility requirements. It is not unique, either, to have several agencies and individuals, within the same facility, responsible for administering the same program.

An Agenda

It is obvious that the particular problems associated with the education of these populations cannot be addressed easily or readily. The problems are intertwined too intricately with social ills in the U.S. and, if the recent problems facing prison authorities in France and Britain are any example, around the world. State and Federal agencies and legislatures ultimately responsible might consider these points, however.

First, the specific standards and programs that apply to the treatment and education of individuals incarcerated in juvenile and adult facilities ought to be amended to address more fully the needs for adequate and sophisticated diagnosis and treatment for varying learning deficiencies and disabilities. It is necessary for the level of sophistication of professional preparation of teachers and counselors in such facilities to be increased and improved substantially. The needs of this unique population are much more complex, and must be addressed in such a peculiar environment, that the traditional professional preparation programs probably do not give the necessary level of skill and array of techniques.

Second, the demonstrated area of focus for programming is upon meeting the basic educational needs of the vast majority of inmates. These include increased emphasis upon functional literacy and numeracy skills in the context of vocational and social education in the most meaningful and practical sense. These recommendations require an increased expenditure for education. This is in complete contradiction to the trends in almost all state systems for increased security, not for treatment and education. Politicians will not go easily against such trends, being more willing to accept expediency than fact. It also is true that the process of alienation and recidivism of delinquents and prisoners is inescapable unless substantial changes occur in the number, quality, and degree of relevance and sophistication of educational opportunities.

Third, specific screening procedures should be instituted at intake into the criminal justice system to attend to inmates' particular sensory and neurological impairments. These have to be standardized and a common system of reporting and centralized record-keeping created. This particularly is needed in the array of agencies that cater to the juvenile offender. Additional emphasis, already beginning to emerge, ought to continue on drug and alcohol abuse treatment, prevention, and intervention. The public schools have a significant role to play in halting the vicious cycle that leads to prison. They should be encouraged to react more quickly to identify and treat the learning-deficient, abused, at-risk youth.

Fourth, the effectiveness of the juvenile system long has been in question. The evidence presented here indicates, yet again, that the longer an individual is in contact with the criminal justice system, the more violent and hardened he or she becomes. Correctional institutions often appear to be "schools for crime." Until diagnosis and treatment for juveniles in such facilities improve, rehabilitation will continue to be a myth. For the past decade, studies and commission reports repeatedly have called for more equitable, effective, and rigorous education at all levels of the nation. Such improvements are needed in America's prisons as well as its schools and universities.

The characteristics and the learning problems of the inmate population have been known for at least two decades. Apparently, society must be reminded that, in this situation, doing the same thing over and over again and expecting different results is insanity.

30

Electronic Monitors

Annesley K. Schmidt

Electronic monitors are a new telemetry device designed to verify that an offender is at a specified location during specified times. This technological option is stimulating a great deal of interest from jurisdictions considering the approach and from manufacturers entering the market. While the concept of electronic monitoring has been discussed in the literature and small experimental efforts have been undertaken since the sixties, the earliest of the currently operating programs only started in December 1984.[1]

In the short time since that first program began in Palm Beach County Florida, many jurisdictions have considered whether to develop monitoring programs and some have ordered equipment. Programs have been established in locations as diverse as Kenton County, Kentucky and Clackamus County, Oregon and by organizations as diverse as the Administrative Office of the Courts in New Jersey and the Utah Department of Corrections.

As the National Institute of Justice (NIJ) has monitored these developments, we have found that the growth of programs has coincided with the entry of manufacturers into this field. The accompanying table provides a list of the manufacturers who are known to us. They have come to our attention through responses to a solicitation in the *Commerce Business Daily* for manufacturers willing to participate in the NIJ-sponsored equipment testing program at the Law Enforcement Standards Laboratory of the National Bureau of Standards. We also learned of manufacturers when they responded to requests for bids made by jurisdictions

Source: *Federal Probation*, 50(2) (June 1986), pp. 56–59.

seeking to purchase equipment, when they requested information from us, and by word of mouth. The list reflects information current as of the date it was prepared. However, given the rate of development thus far, additional manufacturers may have entered the field.

As shown on the table, there are four basic technologies presently available; two use the telephone at the monitored location and two do not. Each of the technologies reflects a different approach to the problem of monitoring offenders in the community. In fact, even products within the same general technological group have important differences. These differences, and the cost and desirability of particular features, are a small part of the decisions that must be made when establishing a monitoring program.

The technology is so new and the research is, thus far, so limited that there are many questions about monitors of all kinds, on all levels. Some of these questions are: Should equipment be purchased? Can it be used legally? On whom should it be used? Will the community accept it? Will monitors provide the community with additional protection? The National Institute of Justice, through its Fiscal Year 1986 Solicited Research Programs, is seeking to support experimental projects that will provide some answers to some of these and other important questions. In the meantime, programmatic and technological questions remain.

Programmatic Questions

Monitors, at least in theory, could be used on any number of offender groups. They could be used on sentenced or unsentenced offenders. They could be used before sentencing, immediately after sentencing, or at a later point in the sentence when problems appear. They could be used to monitor house arrest, as an alternative to jail, as part of an intensive supervision program, or in the context of a work release program. All of these program possibilities have been discussed, and most of them are presently operational. However, we do not yet know if monitors are effective in these program applications much less where they are most effective.

We also do not know which offenders should be the focus of the program. There are clearly some offenders that nobody wants in the community, such as those who are violent. These offenders should go to prison. However, there are other offenders who are not so clearly dangerous and are not so obviously candidates for confinement. Can they be punished or deterred by other means? Can they be monitored in the community? Should they be monitored in the community? We do not know. Whether particular

Electronic Monitoring Equipment

(Purpose: To monitor an offender's presence in a given environment where the offender is required to remain)

Devices that use a telephone at the monitored location		Devices that do not use a telephone	
Continuously signaling	Programmed contact	Continuously signaling	Radio signaling
A miniaturized **transmitter** is strapped to the offender and it broadcasts an encoded signal at regular intervals over a range.	A **computer** is programmed to call the offender during the hours being monitored either randomly or at specifically selected times. It prepares reports on the results of the calls.	A **transmitter** is strapped to the offender which sends out a constant signal.	The **link** is a small transmitter worn by the offender.
A **receiver-dialer**, located in the offender's home, detects signals from the transmitter and reports to a central computer when it stops receiving the signal from the transmitter and when it starts receiving the signal again; it also provides periodic checks.	Strapped on the offender's arm is a **wristlet**, a black plastic module.	A **portable receiver**, in the car of the officer who is monitoring the offender, is tuned to receive the signal from the specific transmitter when the officer drives within one block of the offender's home.	The **locator unit**, placed in the offender's home or other approved location, receives the signal from the link, records it and relays the information by radio signals to the local area monitor.
A central **computer** or **receiver** accepts reports from the receiver-dialer over the telephone lines, compares them with the offender's curfew schedule, and alerts correctional officials to unauthorized absences.	When the computer calls, the wristlet is inserted into a **verifier box** connected to the telephone to verify that the call is being answered by the offender being monitored.	Manufacturer/Distributor:	The **local area monitor** is a microcomputer and information management system. This equipment is placed with the network manager (the leader of a small group of people who supervise the offender and encourage him to succeed). It receives information from the offender and coordinates communications among the network members. Each local network can handle 15 to 25 people.
Manufacturers/Distributors:	Manufacturer/Distributor:	**Cost-Effective Monitoring System.** Dr. Walter W. McMahon, 2207 Grange Circle, Urbana, IL 61801. Telephone Day 217-333-4579 or Evening 217-367-3990.	If required, a **central base station** can be added to provide increased security and back-up functions.
CSD Home Escort. Corrections Systems, Control Data Corporation, 7600 France Avenue, Edina, MN 55435. Telephone 612-921-6835.	**On Guard System.** Digital Products Corporation, 4021 Northeast 5th Terrace, Ft. Lauderdale, FL 33334. Telephone 305-564-0521.		Manufacturer/Distributor:
Supervisor. CONTRAC, Controlled Activities Corp., 93351 Overseas Highway, Tavernier, FL 33070. Telephone 305-852-9507.	The computer functions similarly to that described above, calling the offender and preparing reports on the results of the call.		**LENS System.** Life Sciences Research Group, 515 Fargo Street, Thousand Oaks, CA 91360. Telephone 805-492-4406.
In-House Arrest System. Correctional Services Inc., P.O. Box 2941, West Palm Beach, FL 33402. Telephone 305-683-7166.	However, **voice verification** technology assures that the telephone is answered by the offender being monitored.		
Contac. Computrac Systems, Inc., 420 East South Temple, Suite 340, Salt Lake City, UT 84111. Telephone 801-531-0500.	Manufacturer/Distributor:		
Prisoner Monitoring System. Controlec, Inc., Box 48132, Niles, IL 60648. Telephone 312-966-8435.	**Provotron.** VoxTron Systems Inc., 190 Seguin St., New Braunfels, TX 78130. Telephone 512-629-4807.		
ASC II b. * Advanced Signal Concepts, P.O. Box 1856, Clewiston, FL 33440. Telephone 813-983-2073.			
Home Incarceration Unit. * American Security Communications, P.O. Box 5238, Norman, OK 73070. Telephone 405-360-6605.			

* This device can transmit to the central unit over either telephone lines or long-range wireless repeater system.

types or groups of offenders can be monitored in a given community will depend, in part, on what that community, its judges, and its elected and political officials consider acceptable and appropriate punishment. For example, in some communities there may be strong pressure to jail drunk drivers; other communities may be satisfied if drunk drivers are required to stay home during their nonworking hours with monitors used to assure that they do so.

Another consideration related to who can and should be monitored in the community may depend on the type of equipment selected and the structure of the program in which it is used. Some equipment monitors the offender continually while others do so only intermittently. Some devices send a signal if tampered with and some do not, so that removal of or damage to the equipment is only detected with visual inspection. And, if the equipment indicates that the offender is not where he is supposed to be or that some other problem has occurred, has the program been designed so that there will be an immediate response or does the program staff review these indicators on weekdays during the day? A few present programs have the base computer located in a facility that is staffed 24-hours a day, 7 days a week. They then know immediately that a problem has occurred and can send staff to the offender's house to check and, if necessary, attempt to locate him. In other programs, the print-out is reviewed in the morning, and offenders are contacted to explain abnormalities found the previous night.

Next, how long *will* the offenders be monitored by the equipment? Here again the equipment is too new and the experience too limited to provide an answer. Officials at Pride, Inc. in West Palm Beach, Florida believe that offenders can tolerate the monitors for about 90 to 120 days. After that, they feel, offenders begin to chafe under the restriction. And, how long *should* they be kept on the equipment? This question must be answered in the context of why the program is being operated. The answer would be quite different if the goal is retribution as opposed to fulfilling the requirement of the law. In Palm Beach County, it has been decided that 3 days on the monitor is the equivalent of 1 day in jail to fulfill the required mandatory sentence for a second conviction for driving while intoxicated. For other offenses, the proscribed sentence is a range, and, therefore, the appropriate time on the monitor is not so clear.

Can electronic monitors solve or alleviate prison and jail crowding? The answer to this question is probably "no" for a variety of reasons. First, in addition to issues related to what a community can, will, and should be expected to tolerate, it should be reiterated that monitors are technological devices potentially useful in a variety of program contexts. The population selected as the focus of monitoring programs may or may not be one that might otherwise be sent to jail or prison if monitors were not available. Second, consideration needs to be given to the likely impact on the total problem. In a thousand-man jail, the release of 20 monitored inmates would reduce the population by only 2 percent. One hundred monitored inmates would have to be released before the population would be affected by 10 percent. In a smaller jail, more impact would be achieved by a system with a capacity for monitoring 20 inmates, the typical size of the initial equipment purchase being made. In the prison systems of many states with much larger populations, more monitored inmates would have to be released before a significant reduction in population could occur. Furthermore, the cost of a monitoring program cannot be directly compared to per diem costs of incarceration. The largest component of per diem costs is staff salaries. Therefore, until the number of released inmates is large enough to affect staffing of the facility, the only savings achieved are in marginal categories such as food.

The inverse to the question about jail crowding is the question of net-widening. Will offenders be sanctioned who otherwise would not be? Will offenders be more severely sanctioned? These issues deserve attention. If offenders are being monitored who would not otherwise have been incarcerated, the cost benefit equation on the use of the equipment is changed. If, on the other hand, offenders are monitored who might otherwise receive probation with little direct supervision, the question becomes "Is the community being better protected?" At present, the answer to that question is also unknown.

Taken together, the questions of reducing prison population and net-widening lead to the more basic question: Why is a monitoring program being established? Any jurisdiction establishing a program should be able to answer this. Clearly here are a wide variety of possible reasons. Reduction of prison or jail population is only one. Net-widening is a possibility but is more likely an unintended byproduct. Another possible answer is to better protect citizens from those offenders already in the community on some form of release. If the question cannot be answered, then the situation is equipment in search of a program, perhaps the most inappropriate way for program development to proceed.

Whatever the rationale for the monitoring program, another issue that must be considered is the legality of the use of monitors. However, it should be noted that there are no known test cases. Furthermore, the question of legality obviously would differ in each jurisdiction depending on statute and appellate decisions.

Another question is: "How much will it cost?" The answer of course depends on the type of equipment, the number of units, and whether the equipment is purchased or leased. In addition, there may be telephone charges and personnel costs. The In-House Arrest Work Release Program of the Sheriff's Stockade in Palm Beach County Florida charges participants in the voluntary program $9 per day.[2] Within the first 14 months of program operation, the program's investment in equipment had been returned by offender fees. However, if the initial amount invested is more or less, if fees are charged at a lower or higher rate or not at all, or if the equipment is in use a greater or lesser proportion of the time, then the payback period will change.

Existing programs using monitors in the community function as part of the criminal justice system. Therefore, they require the cooperation of the courts and probation and parole, at a minimum. Additionally, many times, they also may involve the sheriff, other law enforcement agencies, and others. As with any multi-agency effort, the lines of responsibility must be clear and the cooperation between them developed. For example, if the results of the monitoring are to be reviewed around the clock, then the base is optimally located where 24-hour staffing is already present. This facility might be a jail operated by the sheriff. The program, on the other hand, is being operated by the probation office. In this case, the division of responsibilities and expectations should be specified, preferably in writing.

Technological Questions

The questions above can be viewed at a theoretical, philosophical, or program planning level. However, there are also questions or potential problems that should be considered related to the functioning of the equipment itself. These questions emanate from the preliminary results of a study conducted at the Law Enforcement Standards Laboratory of the National Bureau of Standards supported by the National Institute of Justice. Information also has been gained from the experience of some of the monitoring programs. It should be noted that the comments are preliminary and often reflect results of testing of what is now the *previous* generation of equipment, since the technology itself is developing so rapidly.

One problem found was telephone line compatibility. Telephone lines carry electric current, and the characteristics of the current can vary with different telephone systems. Additionally, some telephone exchanges use very modern switching equipment and can handle pulses such as those from touchtone phones. Others use older equipment that may have trouble handling the electronic signals transmitted by some of the monitoring systems. Whether this is a problem can only be determined specifically through a test of the local system and local exchanges and/or consultation with the local telephone company.

Another problem that appears remediable and has been addressed by some manufacturers is the effects of weather conditions. During wind storms and thunderstorms, both electric lines and telephone lines are whipped around and may come into contact with other lines. This may lead to arcing of the power and power surges. In the same way that most users of home computers have surge protectors on the incoming power lines, these monitoring devices may have surge protectors placed on the incoming electrical and telephone lines. It appears that most manufacturers have installed surge protectors on their current equipment. In addition, uninterruptable power supplies are also provided by some manufacturers to guarantee power to the system even during power outages.

Many devices use radio frequency signals for communication between components of the system. In some locations, radio landing beacons from airports and radio station broadcasts can interfere with the functioning of the device. Whether this is a problem is dependent on the other radio transmissions in the area where the equipment is being used and the radio frequency that the device uses.

Another potential problem noted is the effect of iron and steel which may block signal transmission or create an electromagnetic field. This can occur in steel trailers or in stucco houses. It can also occur in houses which have large appliances such as refrigerators and cast iron bathroom fixtures. In some places, the problems can often be dealt with by moving the receiving equipment. In other settings, it may limit the offender's mobility to less than had been expected. At least one manufacturer provides repeater stations within the house to forward and amplify the signal.

These are some of the technological problems that have come to light and many of them have been solved. In other cases, ways to avoid them and minimize their effects have been noted. It is not surprising that they have developed, given the newness of the technologies. It would also not be surprising if additional problems come to light as broader experience with these devices is gained. It seems reasonable to assume that manufacturers will seek to solve any future problems as they have in the past.

In summary, monitors are new technological devices that offer exciting possibilities for controlling offenders in the community. However, there are still many unknowns, many issues which should be considered by those establishing programs and many questions yet to be asked and answered.

Notes

[1] Ralph K. Switzgebel, "Electronic Alternatives to Imprisonment," *Lex et Scientia*, 5(3), July-September 1968, 99–104.

Daniel Ford and A. K. Schmidt, "Electronically Monitored Home Confinement," *NIJ Reports*, SNI 194, November 1985, 2–6.

[2] Lt. Eugene D. Garcia, personal communication and "In-House Arrest Work Release Program," report of the Sheriff's Stockade, Palm Beach County, FL, February 15, 1986.

31

Shock Incarceration
Rehabilitation or Retribution?

Doris Layton Mackenzie
Larry A. Gould
Lisa M. Riechers
James W. Shaw

Shock incarceration is a relatively new type of alternative to standard prison incarceration. The specific components of shock incarceration programs vary. The similarity among all programs is the short period of imprisonment in a military "boot camp" type program involving participation in military drills, rigorous exercise and maintenance of living quarters. Programs differ, however, in whether activities such as work, community service, education or counseling are also incorporated in the schedule of activities. In addition, some jurisdictions stress the need for intensive supervision upon release if the behavioral changes brought about by the shock incarceration are to be continued on the outside.

The major incentive for developing shock incarceration programs appears to be the need for cost-effective methods of reducing overcrowding in prisons (Parent, 1988). Many people also feel that the enhanced discipline addresses a common problem of offenders and will, therefore, have rehabilitative benefits. After a national survey of shock incarceration programs, Parent (1988) stated that these programs have strong face validity to the public and to criminal justice personnel. In his opinion this may account for their ready acceptance. Proponents of these programs argue that the

Reprinted by permission from the *Journal of Offender Counseling, Services & Rehabilitation*, 14(2) (1989): 25–40. © 1990 by The Haworth Press, Inc.: Binghamton, NY.

short-term, demanding and rigorous boot camp component of the programs will be rehabilitative and deter future criminal behavior.

In the past there have been programs, called shock probation, which required offenders to spend a short period of time in prison (Vito, 1984; Parent, 1988). The major difference between the earlier shock probation programs and shock incarceration is the required participation in the drills and physical training that are components of the recent programs.

The earliest shock incarceration programs began in 1983 in Georgia and Oklahoma (Parent, 1988).[1] Since then another five states have started shock incarceration programs, five are developing programs and nine are seriously considering initiating such programs. Thus it is probable that in the next few years over 40 percent of the state correctional jurisdictions will have some type of shock incarceration program.

Of the seven state jurisdictions which presently have programs, most are designed for the young, non-violent, first offender who has a short sentence. In most jurisdictions offenders must volunteer, and additionally, they must not have any physical or mental impairment which would prohibit full participation in the program. There are large differences in the programs in terms of who controls placement and release decisions (judge, department of corrections or parole board). Jurisdictions also vary in whether, upon release, the offender receives intensive parole supervision.

To our knowledge there have been few formal evaluations of the shock incarceration programs. There are some early results from Georgia's Special Alternative Incarceration Program (SAIP) and from Oklahoma's Regimented Inmate Discipline Program (RID). During 1984, 260 offenders entered Georgia's SAIP and 92 percent of them successfully completed the program (Flowers, 1986). Of those who completed the program, 21.3 percent returned to prison within one year of program completion. This return rate was lower than the rate for those released from diversion centers (23.4 percent), higher than the rate for those on intensive probation supervision (18.8 percent) and much higher than those on regular probation supervision (7.5 percent).

One thing that must be kept in mind in comparing Georgia's program with other shock incarceration programs is the fact that in Georgia the "fundamental program concept is that a brief period of incarceration under harsh physical conditions, strenuous manual labor and exercise within a secured environment will 'shock' the younger and less seriously criminally oriented offender out of a future life of crime" (Flowers, 1986, p3). Thus the emphasis may be directed more towards a punishment model than are other shock incarceration programs that involve counseling, problem-solving or other treatments. SAIP was designed based in part on the earlier shock probation models.

In contrast to Georgia's shock incarceration program, treatment and individualized rehabilitation plans are an important ingredient of Oklahoma's RID program. In fact the program is part of the Nonviolent Intermediate Offender (NIO) program which is designed to be a method of planning rehabilitation programs for youthful offenders convicted of nonviolent crimes.

A study of 403 males, who completed the RID program between March 1984 and March 1985, revealed that 63 (15.7 percent) had been reincarcerated before March 1986 (Oklahoma Department of Corrections, 1986). The authors report this reincarceration rate is lower than the rate (45 to 77 percent) for the general population. However, it is difficult to make a meaningful comparison because the RID offenders are a carefully selected group who are most likely very different from the general population offender.

Components of Successful Rehabilitation Programs

In recent reviews of the literature on correctional rehabilitation it has been argued, contrary to a commonly expressed opinion, that there *is* empirical evidence of successful rehabilitation in some programs (Gendreau and Ross, 1987; Sechrest, White and Brown, 1979; Cullen and Gendreau, in press). However, rather than broad generalizations about types of programs (e.g., shock incarceration, intensive supervision, education) these reviewers suggest that it is necessary to consider the principles and strategies which have been associated with successful programs. That is, a program which incorporates anti-criminal modeling or problem solving, two principles that appear to be associated with successful correctional programs, should be more successful than one which does not incorporate these elements.

Early shock probation programs were attempts at getting tough and were designed to inculcate fear in offenders so they would be deterred from future criminal behavior (Vito, 1984; Vito and Allen, 1981). Such negative reinforcement does not appear to have strong support as a successful method of rehabilitation (Gendreau and Ross, 1981). Although such programs may help by reducing overcrowding in the short run, there is little evidence of a reduction in recidivism. Thus the impact on overcrowding may be relatively short lived.

There is little evidence that the "getting tough" element of shock incarceration will, by itself, lead to behavioral change. This would just be another type of punishment; and there is little research support for the effectiveness of punishment alone (Gendreau and Ross, 1987). However, voluntary participation in a "tough" program may be a test of commitment to change and other components (e.g., self-confidence) that may be indicative of success. Some of the other elements which have been identified as components of successful correctional rehabilitation programs are: formal rules, anticriminal modeling and reinforcement, problem solving, use of community resources, quality of interpersonal relationships, relapse prevention and self-efficacy, and therapeutic integrity (Gendreau and Ross, 1987; Cullen and Gendreau, in press; Andrews and Kiessling, 1980; Gendreau and Ross, 1983). Within the military framework of shock incarceration any or all of these elements could be present, although it is extremely difficult to tell to what degree or intensity they exist.

The goal of this paper is to describe the development and implementation of shock incarceration in one jurisdiction, Louisiana. In particular the elements of the program will be examined in terms of the principles which have been found to exist in successful rehabilitation programs according to recent reviews of the literature. This is part of a comprehensive evaluation of shock incarceration in Louisiana. The data reported are from correctional records and interviews with correctional personnel.

Louisiana's IMPACT Program

Shock incarceration programs differ so widely at this point in time that any evaluation of them must begin with a description of the specific components of the program. Louisiana's Intensive Motivational Program of Alternative Correctional Treatment (IMPACT) is a two-phase shock incarceration program begun in 1987 by the Louisiana Department of Public Safety and Corrections (LDPSC). In the first phase of IMPACT offenders are incarcerated for 90 to 180 days in a rigorous boot camp type atmosphere (LDPSC, 1987). Following this period of incarceration offenders are placed under intensive parole supervision for the second phase of the program.

At the system level, the IMPACT program was designed to be an alternative for youthful first offenders, to help alleviate overcrowding, to promote a positive image of corrections, and to improve public relations. In regard to the individual, LDPSC (1987) states that IMPACT was designed to teach the offender responsibility, respect for self and others, and self confidence. Other stated goals of the program are to reduce recidivism, improve skills in everyday living and to generally improve the lives of the participants.

Selecting Offenders for IMPACT

To be legally eligible for the program offenders must be parole eligible, this must be their first felony conviction, they must have a sentence of seven years or less and they must volunteer. Furthermore, they must be recommended by (1) the Division of Probation and Parole, (2) the sentencing court and (3) a classification committee at the LDPSC diagnostic center. To be admitted to IMPACT the offender must receive a positive recommendation from all three evaluators (e.g., probation and parole agent, judge, and classification committee).

The law also states that offenders who are selected for the program must be those who are "particularly likely to respond affirmatively to participation" (LDPSC, 1987). As a consequence of this requirement a list of characteristics or disqualifiers have been developed to be used by the three groups who are required to make recommendations about the program. During the first year of operation this list of disqualifiers was gradually lengthened. At the end of 1987 the following characteristics were considered viable reasons for excluding an offender from the program: pending charges; sex offense; felony DWI; mental or physical health problem; over age 40; pattern of assaultive behavior; assaultive escape; overt homosexuality; no acceptable residence identified for the intensive supervision phase of the program.

An important rationale for the three-group recommendation process was to insure that offenders who were sent to IMPACT would be drawn from the population of offenders who would normally be sent to prison, not from those who would normally be given probation. Therefore, if for some reason the offender is disqualified at the diagnostic center, he or she is sent to the general prison population to serve time until the date of parole eligibility.

By the fall of 1987 (approximately October) 327 offenders had arrived at the LDPSC diagnostic center with recommendations for IMPACT from the judge and from the Division of Probation and Parole. The classification committee at the diagnostic center recommended IMPACT for 230 (or 70.3 percent) of these offenders. The remaining 97 offenders (29.7 percent) were excluded from (never entered) the program and almost all went into the general population. Thirty-two (33 percent) of the 97 offenders were excluded because they did not volunteer, 23 (23.7 percent) because of a medical or psychological condition, and 21 (21.6 percent) because of an assaultive history. The reasons the remaining 21 (21.6 percent) were excluded varied widely (sexual conduct, pending charges, not first offense, etc.).

Graduation or Dismissal from IMPACT

Once an offender enters the program there are rigorous requirements which must be satisfactorily completed to move through
stages of the boot camp. Along with military training, the incarceration phase of IMPACT involves treatment programs such as
ventilation therapy, reeducative therapy, substance abuse
education, and prerelease education.

Offenders may be returned to general population after they enter
the IMPACT program if they fail to receive satisfactory evaluations
within the 180 days, if they commit some serious rule infraction
(assault, escape, etc.), if a medical or psychological condition is
identified, or if a pending change is uncovered. Furthermore, at any
time inmates may decide that they no longer wish to participate.
In all of the above cases the offender would be returned to general
population to await the regular parole hearing.

The first class of IMPACT inmates entered the program on
February 8, 1987. By the end of December 1987, there were
approximately 15 classes of entrants with an average of 18.3
offenders in each, for a total of 274 IMPACT entrants. Of these
entrants, 117 offenders had completed the incarceration phase of
the program and were paroled. Parole had been revoked for
technical violations for nine (7.7 percent) of the parolees. Fifty four
offenders were still in the program at the end of the year. The
remaining 103 offenders (37.6 percent) left the program before
completing the incarceration phase. Those who were admitted to
IMPACT and then left before completing the incarceration phase
left for the following reasons: medical (n = 9), voluntary (n = 63),
disciplinary (n = 17), other (n = 14).

Overall the average offender who entered IMPACT was a male
23.3 years old with a sentence of 3.7 years. Only 12 women entered.
More blacks (58.4 percent) than whites (41.6 percent) entered. A
little less than one-half of the entrants entered as probation violators
and the others entered with a new crime. Most of those who entered
were convicted of burglary or theft (63.1 percent) or drugs (22.1
percent).

Once an offender has completed between 90 and 180 days in
IMPACT with satisfactory performance evaluations, institutional
staff prepare a final report describing adjustment and progress. The
parole board is responsible for release decisions. Once paroled the
offender graduates from IMPACT and is released to the intensive
parole phase of the program. This is a three-stage program involving
less restrictions as offenders earn their way out of each stage.

IMPACT to General Population

An examination of the percent of the entrants to IMPACT who left the program and the number of offenders who were rejected at the diagnostic center suggests that a high percentage of the offenders recommended for IMPACT by the judge went to general population. At the time of sentencing, the judge may have expected the offender to have an alternative to standard prison (e.g. IMPACT) but, for many, this is not what happened. Thirty percent of the offenders who arrived at the diagnostic center with recommendations from the sentencing judge never entered IMPACT. Another 35 percent of the inmates who entered IMPACT did not complete the program. Using the data from both the entrants to IMPACT and the recommended IMPACT candidates, estimates can be made about the number of dropouts. Of the offenders who arrive at the diagnostic center with the judge's recommendation approximately 30 percent are excluded prior to entry to IMPACT. Of the remaining, another 35 percent will leave IMPACT before completing the incarceration phase. This means 54 percent of the total offenders recommended for IMPACT by the judge will go into the general prison population instead of being released after 90 to 180 days in IMPACT. An estimated 46 percent of the offenders who leave IMPACT before completing the incarceration phase, will either refuse to volunteer for IMPACT or will voluntarily ask to leave the program. The other 54 percent will leave for other reasons.

Selection and Dismissal Issues

A large number of the inmates recommended for IMPACT do not enter the program and still others do not complete the program. Personnel in the Division of Probation and Parole report some frustration with the large number of inmates who are dropped at diagnostic center before entering IMPACT. According to probation and parole staff some judges are frustrated because the offenders they recommend for IMPACT are rejected at the diagnostic center. Everyone seems to understand a medical or psychological condition may be a legitimate reason for denying an offender access to the program. Less agreed upon are the denials due to a past history of violence. However, the specific reasons for denial of an individual may not always be known by those outside the diagnostic center. Judges and probation and parole staff may believe an inmate has been denied entry to IMPACT when actually the offender failed to volunteer or asked to be dropped from the program.

Probation and parole staff believe that their experience in

supervising offenders on the street, makes them good judges of who will perform well on parole. Therefore, in their opinion, they should have a major role in deciding who should enter IMPACT. On the other hand, personnel at the diagnostic center believe that they must make decisions very carefully and conservatively, first because any serious offense by an IMPACT offender may destroy the program. And, second, offenders must see the reward of early release at the end of the incarceration phase of the program. It is assumed that early release must be assured for the offenders who take part in the program. If the offenders who enter IMPACT are not the type who will be released by the parole board then inmates will no longer feel assured that they will be released if they successfully complete the program. For this reason, the diagnostic staff try to anticipate the decisions of the parole board and omit offenders who are traditionally denied parole at the first hearing. This issue came to the forefront when one offender who satisfactorily completed IMPACT was denied parole (eventually after serving a short additional time he was paroled). Subsequent to this case, the disqualifier list was developed. The list was created and added to when various actors complained that they were uncertain about how and why decisions were made excluding some offenders from the program. There are a variety of opinions about whether the disqualifiers are valid reasons for disqualifying a person from the program. But in all cases someone in the decision making chain believes that such a characteristic is indicative of a person who is not "particularly likely to respond affirmatively to participation," a legal requirement for selecting offenders for the program.

A large proportion of those who do not enter the program or who drop out do so voluntarily. LDPSC staff feel strongly that the program should be voluntary and, therefore, offenders are permitted to voluntarily drop out at any time. In their opinion this shows that an offender who remains is sincerely committed to change. There is some concern, however, about the large number of voluntary dropouts early in the program. Once they are sent to the general population they are not permitted to return to IMPACT.

In summary, there is some debate about the offenders who are most apt to benefit from IMPACT, how to identify these offenders and who can best identify them. The offenders who are selected appear to be relatively low-risk offenders. The high number of voluntary dropouts suggests a relatively rigorous program.

Staff and Inmate Interaction

The attitude of the staff toward inmates was examined. In particular we were interested in whether the drill instructors (DIs) saw their task as one of instilling obedience and respect for authority, and maintaining control, or whether they attempted to influence the offenders in other ways. The question was whether staff viewed themselves also as models, counselors, and as agents of behavior change through positive reinforcement and support.

In general, the philosophy of the program seems to be that the drill instructors, who work most closely with the inmates, are supposed to be authority figures who are also models and provide a supportive environment conducive to growth and change. For example, offenders are rewarded for good behavior by moving to more advanced squads or to higher positions within squads. They also earn privileges such as time to watch TV, visits and use of the canteen.

The DIs work closely with the squads. They march, exercise or run with the participants. The program is arranged so that early during training the control and authority of the DIs is emphasized. During this period military bearing, courtesy, drills and ceremony, and physical training are the major focus.

"Even though its framework is military, institutional IMPACT is more than a boot camp for criminal offenders" (LDPSC, 1987, p6). This becomes particularly salient after the offender moves out of the beginners squad. The DIs hold courses for the more advanced squads in which concepts and information related to work and work behaviors are discussed. To emphasize the supportive role of the staff, the parole agents pick up the offenders when they leave the institutional phase and take them home.

In summary, those who are assigned the task of setting the rules do not appear to see their job as only authority and control. They also take steps to be supportive and helpful in other areas.

Authority and Abuse.   The emphasis from the administration is on both the supportive and authoritative position of the drill instructors. As is obvious, in programs such as this the line between abuse and authority (and control) is hard to define. It was reported that some correctional officers had difficulty changing from their traditional role of control to a role incorporating both the control and supportive guidance which they are expected to assume in this program. The administration is well aware of the need to carefully watch for signs of abuse. Overzealous control-oriented DIs have been removed from the program.

Facility Location.   The program is located within a larger mixed (medium/maximum) security facility surrounded by the general population. At first glance this appears to be a disadvantage. However, several important advantages have been identified. One advantage in having the program located within a large facility is that the program has close scrutiny from various personnel within (various administrators) and outside of the Department (visitors, news media). This is helpful in guarding against abuse.

A second important advantage in the location is the fact that staff can be easily rotated into and out of the program. One reason this is needed is if a correctional officer has difficulty in making the change to the DI job and appears to be having trouble in the roles expected (counselor, model or teacher) or if a DI's performance appears to be crossing the line from control/authority to abuse. In such cases staff can quickly be reassigned to another area of the prison. A second advantage in being able to rotate staff into and out of the program is burnout. Because the program is located in a large facility, staff who burn out or who might be abusive can be easily rotated.

Burnout.   There does appear to be a high burnout rate for DIs (one estimate was that DIs have, on the average, spent only 6 months in the program). Burnout might also be expected for the parole agents. They work in pairs and have a 50 per pair caseload. According to the administration, many of the "best" agents have volunteered to work with IMPACT offenders. A new title has been given to those taking this assignment. Newly hired agents in these positions receive higher pay. However, the type and amount of work is heavy—for example, agents are required to write narratives for every contact made with the offender and they are required to make at least four face-to-face contacts per week in the first phase of intensive incarceration.

Rehabilitative Components

This examination of the IMPACT program did not suggest that either negative reinforcement (punishment) nor just a busier program were the major goals or organizing principles of the program. IMPACT does appear to include many of the elements that have been associated with successful rehabilitation in the opinion of several authors who have reviewed the correctional rehabilitation literature (Gendreau and Ross, 1987; Cullen and Gendreau, in press). Based on these reviews, we examined possible rehabilitative elements: rules and authority; anticriminal modeling and reinforcement; problem solving; use of community resources; interpersonal relationships; and an overall therapeutic integrity.

The most outstanding aspect of IMPACT, of course, is the approach to formal rules and authority (e.g., enforced contingencies), one characteristic that has been found to be associated with rehabilitation. This is a highly visible component of the IMPACT program. The high number of those dropping out or being forced to drop the program attests to the enforcement and, also, the rigor of the rules. For those who are able to complete the program it would appear that their belief in their own ability to control events (or a sense of responsibility) would be increased because the program is difficult and they were able to complete it.

Other factors that have been associated with successful rehabilitation programs are anticriminal modeling and reinforcement. Again there is evidence that these are components of IMPACT. The DIs do participate in the drills and physical exercise that are required of the offenders. Time and activities are carefully controlled in the program, for example, the first squad is only permitted to watch the evening news on TV (which could be considered a prosocial activity) during the early weeks of the program. Group support and working together is encouraged during military drill and also in group counseling sessions. Furthermore the DIs encourage "positive thinking."

Many of the aspects of successful behavior modification programs are incorporated in the design of IMPACT. Most of the target behaviors (drill, attention to detail, hygiene, attitude, communication and physical training) are clearly defined and prosocial (Gendreau and Ross, 1983). The offender's peer group is involved in a positive way and it is the offender's choice as to whether to become involved in the program.

Problem solving is another component that has been associated with rehabilitation. This component is less obvious in the IMPACT schedule. It may be somewhat addressed during the pre-release and group counseling sessions. During the intensive supervision phase offenders are required to work (or show evidence of an intensive job search), complete community service, go to school, and keep to an early evening curfew among other requirements. Many of these would require problem solving skills. For example how to schedule one's time to arrive at work at the required hour, how to get a job, etc. are problems that must be solved, and the parole agent is there to assist the offender. Thus, problem solving is done in an applied setting.

The two phase structure of the program does make maximum use of community resources with some obvious advantages. For one, the intensive supervision on the street enables the parole agent to advise the offender about the availability and use of resources in the community. The parolee who has an alcohol problem can join AA and work with other nonoffenders (possibly better models). The offender learns to compete for resources with the help of the parole agent. Since resources in the community can be made available to everyone, the IMPACT program is more "acceptable" than other prison programs which are frequently criticized on the basis of why "excellent, costly" programs should be made available to offenders rather than to nonoffenders on the outside. This attitude almost always limits what is available to offenders in prison. Thus, maximizing the parolees' use of community programs means that better programs may be available to them outside the prison than would be possible within prison. Theoretically the offender has learned basic skills of living and how to follow rules while in the incarceration phase of IMPACT. Now, on the outside, with the help of the agent, the offender has the skills necessary to attend school or keep a job if he or she has the ability.

The quality of interpersonal relationships is another factor which has been associated with successful rehabilitation. This also seems to be an aspect of the IMPACT program. Offenders are encouraged to cooperate and work as a team with members of their squads. The DIs report that they often receive letters from graduates of the program thanking them for their help and support. The parole agents report that they now feel as if they are really doing something in assisting the IMPACT graduates on parole. However, the depth and consistency of this is difficult to objectively evaluate. At the least the philosophy of the program leans towards encouraging quality interpersonal relationships.

Therapeutic integrity or "to what extent do treatment personnel actually adhere to the principles and employ the techniques of the therapy they purport to provide? To what extent are the treatment staff competent? How hard do they work? How much is treatment diluted in the correctional environment so that it becomes treatment in name only?" (Gendreau and Ross, 1979, p467) might be considered the underlying requirement of any successful program. There is some evidence that the program has therapeutic integrity. For example, the high burnout rate of staff suggests that they are committed to the program and work hard. The program is so all encompassing that it does not appear to be diluted in the prison environment. Neither does it appear to be treatment in name only, there is definitely something going on or so many offenders would not leave the program and choose to spend a longer period of time in general population in prison. The extensive narratives written about the parolees by the parole agents during the intensive incarceration phase suggests the treatment is not diluted during this phase either.

There are some specific aspects of the program which should be examined for therapeutic integrity. For example, how strong the problem solving training is in the program, the quality of interpersonal relationships, and anticriminal modeling may all be more or less strongly evident. If these are to be incorporated into the program as important therapeutic elements it may be advantageous to initiate more formal staff training in these areas. This might also help reduce staff burnout, and the ability of staff to successfully act as DIs without abusiveness. To this same end, extra duty pay for staff when they are involved with the program may be a reasonable method of getting staff to volunteer for the program.

In summary, this paper has reviewed Louisiana's shock incarceration program and examined the components of the program in regard to rehabilitative potential. One of the major goals of the program is to foster prosocial changes in participants. The findings suggest that the term "shock incarceration" alone does not give enough information about the elements of a program to determine whether it includes components which might be expected to result in prosocial changes in the inmates. The examination of Louisiana's program suggests that many elements associated with successful rehabilitation are incorporated in IMPACT. Particularly important may be the intensity of the program, its volunteer nature and the two-phase (incarceration and intensive parole supervision) structure. The danger is that the punishment and retribution aspects of shock incarceration are emphasized and the possible rehabilitative components go unrecognized. Such an occurrence might lead to a rejection of such programs before their potential has been explored.

Note

[1] The comparisons with programs in other jurisdictions is taken from Parent's 1988 address to the American Correctional Association based on his National Institute of Justice, U.S. Department of Justice funded research project.

References

Andrews, D. A. and J. J. Kiessling. 1980. Program Structure and Effective Correctional Practices: A Summary of the CAVIC Research. In R. R. Ross and P. Gendreau (eds.), *Effective Correctional Treatment*. Toronto: Butterworths.

Cullen, F. T. and P. Gendreau. (In Press). The Effectiveness of Correctional Rehabilitation: Reconsidering the "Nothing Works" Debate. In L. I. Goodstein and D. L. MacKenzie (eds.), *The American Prison: Issues in Research and Policy*. New York: Plenum Publishing Co.

Flowers, G. T. 1986. An Evaluation of the Use and Performance of Special Alternative Incarceration in Georgia. Georgia Department of Corrections. Atlanta, Georgia. (Unpublished manuscript)

Gendreau, P. and R. R. Ross. 1987. Revivification of Rehabilitation: Evidence From the 1980s. *Justice Quarterly*, 4:349–407.

Gendreau, P. and R. R. Ross. 1983. Success in Corrections: Program and Principles. In R. Corrado, M. Leblanc and J. Trepanier (eds.), *Issues in Juvenile Justice*. Toronto: Butterworths.

Gendreau, P. and R. R. Ross. 1981. Correctional Potency: Treatment and Deterrence on Trial. In R. Roesch and R. R. Corrado (eds.), *Evaluation in Criminal Justice Policy*. Beverly Hills: Sage Publishing.

Gendreau, P. and R. R. Ross. 1979. Effective Correctional Treatment: Bibliotheraphy for Cynics. *Crime and Delinquency*, 25:463–489.

Louisiana Department of Public Safety and Corrections. 1987. *IMPACT: Purposes, Policies and Procedures*. Baton Rouge, LA.

Oklahoma Department of Corrections. 1986. *Oklahoma's Nonviolent Intermediate Offender Program: Its First Year of Operation*. Unpublished manuscript.

Parent, D. 1988. Shock Incarceration Programs. Address to the American Correctional Association Winter Conference, Phoenix, AZ.

Sechrest, L., S. O. White and G. D. Brown (eds.). 1979. *The Rehabilitation of Criminal Offenders*. Washington, DC: National Academy of Sciences.

Vito, G. F. 1984. Developments in Shock Probation: A Review of Research Findings and Policy Implications. *Federal Probation*. 48:22–27.

Vito, G. F. and H. E. Allen. 1981. Shock Probation in Ohio: A Comparison of Outcomes. *International Journal of Offender Therapy and Comparative Criminology*, 25:70–76.

32

Privatization in Corrections

Donald B. Walker

Proposals to increase private sector involvement in the delivery of services in the correctional field is a topic creating considerable controversy among correctional professionals. As noted by Levinson, "Correctional agencies have shown an increasing interest in the use of the private sector as a service provider" (Levinson, 1984:42). However the reliance on the private sector or "the privatization of corrections" as this process has come to be labelled presents different strengths and weaknesses depending on the definition of the concept.

In its broader sense, *privatization* involves "turning to the private sector for new ideas and possibly untapped expertise" (Travis, et al., 1985:11). In a narrower sense it is used to mean "a process where government relies on private corporations to construct and manage prisons and jails for an agreed fee" (Allen and Simonsen, 1986:479). Obviously the private sector has been providing resources for both adult and juvenile corrections for several decades.

Examples of this type of involvement range from foster care of adjudicated delinquents to the private operation of food services in adult correctional facilities. On the other hand, contracting with the private sector for the construction and operation of primary facilities is a relatively recent development. While the use of the private sector for the provision of selective services is not without its problems, it is the suggestion made by some correctional professionals that government turn to private enterprise for institutional operation which had created the most controversy.

The Problem: The recommendation that corrections should become more closely dependent on private enterprise is a consequence of a number of factors affecting contemporary corrections. First, the shift in correctional philosophy from the "medical model of individualized treatment" to the "just desserts model of equality of punishment" has produced higher rates of commitment coupled with longer institutional sentences.

Second, the overall conservative political climate has resulted in calls for the harsher treatment of offenders. The combined consequences of these factors has been a tremendous increase in the demand for prison and jail space coupled with escalating costs for services. For example, in 1982, the Ohio General Assembly authorized the expenditure of $600 million for new prison construction. Since that time, the state has constructed 14 new prisons adding 9,000 additional bed spaces to the prison system. Despite this increase in capacity, the system is 5,800 inmates over capacity. Even though new construction will continue, the gap between capacity and actual inmate population is projected to remain at the 5,800 figure at least through the mid-1990s. Unfortunately, Ohio is not unique as most states continue to experience serious problems of overcrowding despite ambitious prison construction programs.

A third factor, increasing reluctance of the taxpayer to pay for the increased need for correctional services has created a serious dilemma for government officials—how to support an increasing correctional clientele with dwindling public resources. Finally, one might argue that the overall political climate in recent years which has favored private enterprise generally makes the private sector a logical arena for hard pressed government officials to seek out as a resource for the solution to their problems. In short, "where demand for a service outstrips supply and where prices seem unreasonably high, conditions are ripe for competition and for the emergence of new sources of supply" (Logan and Rausch, 1985:303).

Private Enterprise and Corrections: As noted previously, private sector involvement in the correctional field is not a new phenomenon. Even the private control of correctional facilities has its traditional counterpart in the private operation of early jails which were operated by publicly appointed jailers on a fee for service basis. "The managers of early detention facilities charged their inmates for food and clothing, provided substandard service, and were all too often open to bribery and graft" (Travis, et al., 1985:12). Private enterprise and prison industry also has its historical antecedents in the convict lease system, Southern chain gangs, and the contract labor system. For a partial understanding of the heated debate created by the current call for increasing *privatization*, one need only be reminded that correctional reforms which led to placing institutional corrections wholly within the public sector rested in part on the appalling conditions and the corruption created by these early examples of private enterprise.

Both adult and juvenile corrections have historically and are currently contracting with the private sector for the provision of services. Examples of these services include medical, mental health, and food services for both adults and juveniles; private foster care and privately operated non-profit institutions such as Boystown, George Jr. Republic, and Boys Village for juveniles; and community halfway houses and work release programs for adult offenders. According to a recently completed study (Camp and Camp, 1984), on the average states have 82 contracts for services with the private sector and spend approximately $200 million annually for contracted services (Levinson, 1984:42). Privately run facilities for juveniles do operate in Florida and Pennsylvania while the federal government has private contracts for the operation of facilities for illegal aliens in Texas, California, Arizona and Colorado.

Contracting for Service: Reliance on the private sector to provide goods or resources for correctional clientele rests on two basic assumptions. First, that these resources already exist outside of the correctional field and secondly, that contracting for these resources is more economical and advantageous than is duplicating the services and providing them by correctional agencies. As Dell'Apa, et al., point out: "Services needed by the offender to make it in society are available in the community service network rather than in the criminal justice system." (Dell'Apa, et al., 1976:38). Further "to be sure, there is ample evidence that certain government services can be provided in a more effective and efficient fashion by private companies" (Travis, et al., 1985:11).

One might analyze service brokerage into three levels of service delivery: community field service, community residential service, and institutional service. The first type refers to those services which might be provided totally within the community by already existing private agencies. In this instance, correctional clientele are referred to private agencies for mental health, job training, substance abuse counseling or educational services. The referring agency (e.g., adult probation department, juvenile court, state parole agency or state department of corrections) enters into a contractual arrangement with the private service provider to accept a certain number of referrals per contract term and to provide specified services. The clients in this type of arrangement would be primarily adult and juvenile probationers and parolees. Community residential services would involve contracting with private corporations for the complete operation of a residential facility for correctional clientele. Examples of this type of *privatization* would include the operation of halfway houses, group homes, pre-release centers, or jails within the community. Finally contracting for institutional services is something quite different. Privatization in this sense means the complete operation of a correctional facility by a private corporation. In this approach, the total responsibility for care and custody of inmates on a long-term basis would be in the hands of a private corporation whose primary goal would be the profit motive. It is this latter proposal which has created the most heated controversy in contemporary corrections. As Mullen notes "Few proposals in the field of corrections have stimulated as sharply divided opinions as the prospect of contracting with the private sector for the management of prison and jail facilities" (Mullen, 1984:1). The reliance on the private sector for the provision of resources at any level presents both advantages and disadvantages for correctional professionals. The remainder of the paper will focus on these issues in each of the three forms of privatization previously proposed.

Community Field Service: The provision of specific services to correctional agencies on a contracted for basis is the form of *privatization* which has the longest history, is the most widespread, and causes the least concern. The agencies responding to the Camp survey referred to previously reported an average of 63 contracts per agency. Typically, vendors provide health care, mental health service, counseling, or educational programs on a fee per client basis.

There are a number of advantages cited in this approach. First, is cost-effectiveness. Already existing agencies with specialized personnel whose total operation is designed to provide a specific service (e.g., health care provider, psychiatric clinic) can provide this service at a lower cost than can a public agency which must necessarily hire its own specialized personnel. A second advantage is the provision of specialized services. Typically entry level positions in community corrections are staffed by persons having only a baccalaureate degree. As a consequence, they are not prepared by either experience or education to provide more specialized services required by clients. Further, the typical approach to service delivery is casework in which the caseworker attempts to be all things to his/her clients. Allen, et al., describes this method as follows:

> Casework is so extensively used in probation and parole
> supervision that it is considered the "norm" as a service
> provision strategy. It basically follows the medical model of
> corrections in which the supervising officer, through a one-to-
> one relationship, diagnoses the offender, formulates a treatment
> strategy, implements that strategy and, finally, evaluates the
> offender in light of the treatment (Allen, et al., 1985:174).

Given the educational level of most correctional caseworkers, the
heavy caseloads, and limited resources, service delivery to clients
is usually of the most elementary variety. Dell'Apa, et al., comment:

> . . . corrections programs insisting upon therapeutic intervention
> generally hire staff having a bachelor's degree or less . . . The
> bachelor level of study, however, is a long way from the training
> required of a "qualified therapist" (Dell'Apa, et al., 1976:37).

The utilization of community resources through contracting with
the private sector presents a very different service delivery
strategy—brokerage. Allen, et al., point out that:

> almost diametrically opposed to the casework approach is the
> brokerage approach, in which the supervising officer is not
> concerned primarily with understanding or changing the
> behavior of the offender, but rather with assessing the concrete
> needs of the individual and arranging for the probation or
> parolee to receive services that directly address those needs
> (Allen, et al., 1985:175).

The brokerage approach, therefore, has the advantage of
providing the correctional client with specialized services while at
the same time making use of the skills which entry level
practitioners have or can develop within a shorter period of time.
The brokerage approach also has the advantage of more efficient
delivery of services. Within the brokerage approach, the supervising
officer becomes a manager of existing resources, assessing the
needs of offenders and then arranging appropriate referrals for
services from contracted agencies.

For example, the Summit County Juvenile Court maintains a
contract with Phoenix Program which is an alternative school
program for students who have had serious behavior problems in
the Akron City schools. To illustrate the brokerage approach,
assume that a youngster is referred to the Juvenile Court on a
delinquency charge. Following a finding of delinquency, the
youngster is placed on probation. At some point during the period
of probation, the youngster is expelled from the Akron City schools
for school misconduct. In a situation such as this, the supervising
officer would assess the needs of the youngster to continue his/her
education and the ability of the youth to benefit from an alternative

school program such as Phoenix. If both conditions were positive, i.e., the child must continue schooling and could benefit from Phoenix Program, then the supervising officer would contact Phoenix Program and make arrangements for the youngster to be enrolled.

On their part, Phoenix Program has contracted with the Summit County Juvenile Court to provide an 18-week program consisting of educational, vocational, and counseling components including remedial reading and math skills to a certain number of probationers at a cost per student basis. If the court has not exceeded the yearly quota of students, (Phoenix Program has similar contracts with other agencies—most notably Department of Youth Services), the student would be accepted. The court would be billed on a per diem basis for each day the student attended to a maximum of 18 weeks. The child would continue to live at home, be under the supervision of the probation officer, and attend Phoenix Program as an alternative to the regular school system. If the student successfully completes the program, he/she is then eligible to re-enroll in the Akron City School system.

Even though this form of *privatization* is the least controversial, it is not entirely without its problems. Three general areas of concern can be identified: contract performance, employee relations, and cost-benefit. The provision of services under the contract implies obligations on the part of both parties—the referring agency and the service provider. Since the referring agency is ultimately responsible for the quality of service provided to the client, the agency must develop plans for monitoring and evaluating the service. Prior to this phase, the obligations of each party must be carefully outlined in the contract and some agreed upon definition of quality must be developed. The formulation of a clear and well-defined contract coupled with a sound plan for monitoring and evaluating the vendor is no easy task.

Making the plans operational may be even more difficult. Presumably the tasks of monitoring and evaluating the services provided to the correctional clientele will fall on the personnel of the correctional agency. If the original assumption is correct, that these personnel are not equipped by education or training to provide specialized services, are they any better prepared to evaluate the quality of services provided by others? Further one must assume that these personnel will continue to have some responsibility for monitoring the correctional clients even though referrals will have been made to outside vendors for the provision of specific services. In short, brokerage seems to add an additional dimension to the role of the correctional professional—the need to monitor contract performance by private vendors. We have merely substituted the monitoring function for the direct service delivery function. While the quality of provided services *may* be enhanced, this benefit cannot be taken for granted. Given continuing heavy caseloads, will correctional personnel be able to provide more than a perfunctory monitoring of vendor services just as at present the heavy burdens of probation and parole officers too often lead to the perfunctory provision of services? This problem is one of more than academic interest since it relates to the issue of accountability. Who do we hold accountable if a client fails to receive contracted for services and consequently commits further serious criminal acts—the private vendor for failing to provide the service or the public agency for failing to properly monitor the contract?

A second problem that the brokerage approach creates lies in the arena of the professional correctional personnel. Dell'Apa, et al., who strongly favor an expanding brokerage model for community corrections (although not necessarily through private vendors) point out that staff resistance is a significant problem which must be overcome because

> the notion of the probation or parole agent acting as a broker of services was a complete reversal of traditional roles; the idea of a probation or parole officer assuming change agent responsibility in the area of community development was considered a major issue regarding job enlargement (Dell'Apa, et al., 1976:40).

In short, the traditional professional role concept of the probation or parole agent is that of a caseworker rather than service broker. At the heart of the caseworker approach is the relationship between the supervising officer and the client. The correctional professional is viewed as the primary change agent in the casework approach. In the brokerage approach, however, the correctional professional becomes a resource manager rather than change agent. One can identify a basic dichotomy in the self-images of community corrections professionals, i.e. treatment/surveillance role conception. To the extent that the correctional professional identifies his/her role as that of change agent, one could anticipate increased staff resistance to the brokerage model. While those professionals who identify their roles as primarily that of surveillance and enforcement may be less resistant to brokerage, it cannot be assumed that they are more capable of monitoring and evaluating services provided by others. As Dell'Apa, notes:

> Whether the worker's self-image is that of a control agent, advocate, or counselor, the CRMT (Community Resources Management Team) will have to assume an additional role that of manager of community services (Dell'Apa, et al., 1976:41).

From all of this emerges an interesting dilemma, namely, that the professional with a casework self-image may be professionally best prepared to monitor and evaluate brokerage services but will be most resistant to change while the professional with a control agent self-image may be least prepared to evaluate brokered services but most open to change. While staff resistance to a brokerage model continues to be a potential problem, one might argue that as caseloads continue to escalate and resources lag behind, correctional professionals regardless of their self-image will be increasingly open to a shift to a brokerage model. In any event, an agency moving into increased service contracting is likely to face significant staff retraining needs.

These first two problems—contract performance and staff resistance—lead to the third problem—cost-benefit analysis. When the need for clearcut contract development, close monitoring of contract performance, and the evaluation of service quality is coupled with staff retraining, it may well be that service delivery cost will be greater not less. Agencies which realize cost savings may in fact do so by eliminating staff and/or engaging in superficial monitoring of service delivery.

Community Residential Service: A second form of private sector involvement is community residential service. Some examples of this type of contracting are pre-release centers, halfway houses and group homes for both adult and juvenile offenders. Contracting for community residential services by correctional agencies also has a long history and is still widely practiced. According to Mullen, twenty-eight states use pre-release, work-release, or halfway house facilities contracted with the private sector. California, Massachusetts, Michigan, New York, Ohio, Texas, and Washington have the most contracts for adult secondary facilities. Contracts with juvenile corrections is even more widely utilized (Mullen, 1984:4). Since this approach to privatization involves secondary placements in non-secure facilities, it has been successful and uncontroversial. The level of service provided is basically custodial rather than treatment oriented.

The principle rationale for private contracting of community residential services is cost effectiveness. The argument is that the "free market" provides incentives to reduce costs below that of publicly funded bureaucracies which are then translated into savings for the taxpayer. Support for this contention exists since public corrections agencies generally report that private contracting does result in lower costs. Seventy-four percent of the agencies reporting in the Camp survey did indicate a savings over public cost (Camp and Camp, 1984).

Another advantage which the private sector offers is flexibility. Flexibility becomes significant at the local level because it implies that private contractors are not constrained by jurisdictional boundaries. A privately operated group home, halfway house, or restitution center could service multiple juvenile or adult courts, again translating into staff savings while still providing community based sentencing alternatives for each of the courts involved.

Even though the history of private involvement in community residential services is generally a positive one, certain problems cannot be overlooked. Correctional agencies must face the problem of monitoring contracts and measuring the quality of services provided. These problems become particularly salient when one is reminded of the difficulties which have plagued the fields of mental health and gerontology following the deinstitutional movement. Scandalous conditions affecting the health and safety of residents in private nursing facilities for the aged and in privately operated group homes for the mentally retarded and mentally ill have been uncovered from coast to coast. These conditions are created by private entrepreneurs seeking to maximize profit by minimizing cost. Although one might argue that mentally ill, mentally retarded, and aged clients are far more vulnerable given their lack of autonomy than is the typical correctional client, the profit motive giving rise to these conditions is still present. Although the risk for poor quality of care in the correctional field may be less, the need for close monitoring of private vendors, especially in juvenile corrections, is still present.

Institutional Service: The provision of total institutional service by private contractors is the most recent form of privatization. Since the brokerage of specified community services and the provision of secondary community facilities by the private sector has proven generally successful, the suggestion is now being made by some correctional professionals that the management of secure primary correctional facilities be relegated to the private sector. Although the prospect of better quality institutions at a lower cost is an attractive argument, it is proving to be the most controversial form of privatization.

Presently the market for primary facility management is only in the beginning stages. Illegal aliens are being detained in privately operated facilities under contracts from the Immigration and Naturalization Service in Arizona, California, Colorado, Nevada and Texas. Serious juvenile offenders are also being held in secure facilities by private vendors in California, Florida, and Pennsylvania. In addition, adults are being held in a number of privately operated jail facilities in several states. The nation's only private prison was opened in 1986 in Marion, Kentucky. This institution is a 300-bed minimum security facility operated by the U.S. Corrections Corporation. Although the Corrections Corporation of America made an unsuccessful bid to take over the entire operation of Tennessee's prison system, further proposals for privately operated facilities at the local level are under consideration. Since interest in further expansion of private contracting is being given serious consideration at all levels—federal, state, and local—a careful examination of the issues is crucial.

Certainly the cost factor is the primary impetus for further private expansion. Logan and Rausch comment: "it is the overcrowding problem, and the vast sums of money presumably required for its solution, that have recently and rather suddenly caught the attention of the private sector" (Logan and Rausch, 1985:306). Private entrepreneurs are of the opinion that they can operate prison facilities as effectively as the public sector but with greater efficiency. Increased efficiency means lower cost for the public but still allows a margin of profit for themselves. These same authors, utilizing a number of arguments conclude: "initial empirical data, reports of correctional administrators, and *a priori* arguments derived from general considerations of public versus private services can all be used to support the proposition that commercial prisons could save taxpayers money" (Logan and Rausch, 1985:313).

On the other hand, Travis, et al., call for caution regarding the conclusion that private contracting for private facility operation will necessarily prove cheaper. They point out that the cost-benefit factor will be related to the type of contract utilized:

> a public utilities or "pentagon" model reimbursement where
> a contractor receives cost plus a profit percentage would not
> necessarily provide an incentive to contain cost of service—a per
> client charge may result in cost-overruns or even bankruptcy
> should the initial estimate prove wrong (Travis, et al., 1985:14).

Further, the cost analysis is beyond the direct control of the contracting agency. In monitoring cost, the contracting agency is dependent on reports provided by the vendor. Continuing "horror stories" from the Government Accounting Office of widespread abuses in government contracting in other areas of the private sector does not provide a sound basis for assuming that correctional contracting will be free of such abuses. The cost per inmate form of contract raises additional questions to be discussed later.

Another argument which is advanced for private contracting is flexibility. According to privatization advocates, flexibility in the private sector provides a number of advantages. First, the private vendor is not bound by bureaucratic "red tape" and hence is able to respond faster to changing demands. Concrete evidence of quick response by private contractors does exist to support this contention. The RCA Corporation set up and began operating the Weaversville Intensive Treatment Unit in Pennsylvania for hard core delinquents in ten days time. A facility under contract with INS for housing illegal aliens was built and operating in seven months. Other contractors claim to be able to place secure facilities "on-line" in six months time (Logan and Rausch, 1985:314).

These examples compare to the estimated three- to five-year time frame within the public sector. Most of the time savings is related to public financing (budget approval, funding appropriations, and bond issues) and site acquisition which is less burdensome for private entrepreneurs. Rapid response is especially attractive in times of severe prison overcrowding and continued population expansion. Mullen notes: "Most observers would agree that contracting offers public agencies the ability to respond to immediate needs with greater flexibility and speed than is typically possible under government operation" (Mullen, 1984:6).

Thus one area of flexibility is rapid response. A second area of flexibility is geographic. Private contractors are not constrained by jurisdictional boundaries hence regional facilities shared by several public agencies become much more feasible. Regionalization and shared facilities is a salient argument at the local level. A third advantage of flexibility is in programming. Program flexibility could provide both experimentation within private facilities and the development of specialized facilities. A private contractor might experiment with new and unique programs within a facility without being forced into long-term commitment to staff and material as public institutions generally would be. Since staff in public institutions are, for the most part, hired under civil service protection or long-range contracts, public institutions must proceed slowly in implementing innovative programs which may not prove worthwhile.

On the other hand, since private vendors would presumably hire personnel in the same manner as private corporations, they could more easily institute innovative programs and adapt personnel needs to the success or failure of these programs. The concept of flexibility therefore, applies to both programming and staffing. Flexibility also provides the opportunity for private vendors to respond to the needs of special offender populations. The development of specialized facilities would then provide alternative placements for current public institutions housing offenders with special needs within a general population. Flexibility in the private sector, presumably, would allow private contractors to expand or contract space in specialized facilities according to market demand.

If market demand for specialized housing should decrease, for example, a private facility operated by a private corporation might be more quickly converted to some other use or even closed than could a public facility controlled by a government bureaucracy.

In summary the element of flexibility in private contracting provides additional features which may prove attractive to governmental units considering moving towards private facility management. Flexibility implies more rapid response to changing population needs, the option for shared facilities through regionalization, experimentation in programming and specialization in facility development to meet the needs of special offender populations.

However just as the cost-benefit factor contains problems which must be considered, so does the element of flexibility.While rapid response to increasing offender populations means increasing the ability of government units to meet current needs, it also implies the reduction of public facilities and staff which may prove detrimental in the future. As Mullen notes:

> The possible cost may, however, be constraints on the government's ability to change course over the long term. . . . Contracting also means reducing the public sector's own facility management capabilities making it more difficult to revert to public management or limiting the personnel pool available to meet future corrections management needs (Mullen, 1984:6).

The same objection could be raised with regard to specialized institutions within the private sector. If public sector staff and institutions are reduced or eliminated in favor of private contracting, what happens if these private facilities for special needs offenders prove unprofitable or if there is a shift in demand for specialized facilities? Should that occur, it may be very costly and time consuming for government units to "get back in business."

Flexibility in programming which might lead to experimentation in innovative correctional approaches is really nothing more than a theoretical possibility. It rests on the assumption that the private sector can attract and retain quality professional staff. At the same time, flexibility implies some degree of employee insecurity; thus the two concepts may be incompatible and even self-defeating.

Finally, the idea of regionalization and shared facilities is likely to meet with staff resistance and management disputes over control. At this point, the issue of "turf consciousness" arises. Will local correctional managers relinquish control over budget and staff? Will employees in local public facilities step aside as they see their jobs threatened by private contracting? While cost benefits might be real and efficiency increased, local governments are likely to face serious opposition from staff and management in the form of political manipulation and lobbying. To underscore this issue, the National Sheriff's Association has already gone on record as formally opposing private jail operations. While this opposition may well be based on real concern for inmate welfare, the political element cannot be ignored.

Further Issues and Concerns: Thus far, we have set forth those issues and concerns which seem to arise from the apparent advantages of flexibility and cost benefits of total institutional management of correctional facilities by private entrepreneurs. There are a number of other issues, however, which are more generally related to this concept of *privatization*.

One fundamental issue is that of public responsibility for social defense. We take it for granted that the apprehension and conviction of offenders is a public responsibility, hence, the notion that convicted offenders should be the responsibility of private entrepreneurs motivated by profit seems contradictory and, to some, even repugnant. Ultimately the care, protection, and welfare of convicted offenders remains a public responsibility which cannot be delegated to private vendors. As Travis, et al., notes: "Social defense is a legitimate concern of government, that the rights individual offenders must be protected, and that the government ultimately accountable for crime control, among others, are no less important today" (Travis, et al., 1985:12).

Historically the care of offenders was placed in the private sector with privately operated jails and convict labor. The profit motive produced such abominable conditions and exploitation that public agencies assured responsibility. The present day movement to "re-privatize" primary facility management appears to assume that modern entrepreneurs are somehow more benevolent and humanistic so that the exploitation of the past will not reoccur. Travis, et al., commenting on this issue note "when we consider privatizing institutional corrections today the danger is that we may ignore the lessons of history" (Travis, et al., 1985:12).

A second issue of primary facility management is created by the form of contract utilized. If the private vendor enters into a per client charge basis (the most likely contract form), then the profit margin and even the continued operation of the private facility is related to population size. The profit motive may then become a substitute for individual inmate welfare leading to the retention of inmates beyond the point necessary either for their own well-being or public protection. As Travis, et al., point out "the profit motive could serve as an inhibitor to release of inmates and as an incentive to institutionalization" (Travis, et al., 1985:14). Not only does this create a risk for individual inmates but it could have a powerful effect on future correctional philosophy. Widespread development of private corporations dependant on "the prison business" has the potential for the development of a powerful lobby with a heavy stake in maintaining high prison populations, increasing utilization of institutional commitments as opposed to alternative dispositions, and continuing pressures for a conservative correctional philosophy on public officials. Who will ultimately be responsible for determining the release date for convicted offenders?

A third issue surrounds that of authority. In order to enter into contracts for primary facility operation by private vendors, most governmental units will need to pass enabling legislation. The key issue here is the extent to which previously assumed public responsibility can be delegated to the private sector. The delegation of authority to the private vendor involves the welfare of the inmate, the security of other inmates, and ultimately the public safety. Intimately involved in these problems are questions of the quality of medical care, food, housing, individual rights, population management, security and even the use of deadly force. While the question of the right of public agencies to contract for services from private vendors is certainly clear, the legal obligations and ultimate accountability for the actions of private corporations in managing primary facilities appear to be beyond the authority of government to delegate. In short, do governmental units really wish to be held accountable for the actions of employees over which they have little or no direct control?

Summary and Conclusion: This paper has addressed many of the positive and negative features of the present movement towards increasing the involvement of the private sector in the field of corrections. It was pointed out that corrections has long relied on private vendors to provide specific correctional services and even to provide secondary community care facilities. However, the new meaning given to the concept *privatization* creates additional issues of far-reaching consequences requiring careful deliberation.

The primary impetus for any form of *privatization* still revolves around arguments of cost benefit and efficiency. However, even this approach referred to as community field service is not without problems. Public agencies are still left with the task of clearly defining contractual obligations and then monitoring contract performance. Any concerted effort toward a shift from the traditional casework model toward a more fully developed brokerage model is likely to increase the problems of contract monitoring and, at the same time, to encounter problems of staff resistance.

The continued utilization of community residential services as secondary care facilities also appears assured. However, increased involvement with the private sector brings with it further issues. The need or careful and continued monitoring of the quality of care provided is obvious. As private sector involvement increases, this problem simply becomes larger and more crucial. Additionally private expansion in community residential services will encounter problems of "turf consciousness" by correctional administrators and staff resistance by public employees.

The expansion of *privatization* to include the provision of primary care facilities by private vendors presents even more critical issues requiring careful thought and deliberation. Philosophically, one might raise serious questions relative to the propriety of delegating the care and control of convicted offenders to profit seeking corporations. Since social defense is considered a fundamental role of government, this objection requires serious debate. On the more practical level, the promises of cost savings and flexibility remain unproven. While privately run institutions may prove cheaper, they may become so only at the expense of the offenders being housed. Profits may be realized only at the sacrifice of decent conditions of incarceration. While the private sector may provide greater flexibility in programming or in institutional specialization, they may create conditions such as loss of skilled personnel or the closing of specialized public facilities which will prove detrimental to the public sector of the corrections field in the long run. Finally, questions regarding accountability for quality care, security and control must be resolved. Even though the private sector seems to be an easy and attractive solution to current problems of over-crowding and financing when the complexity of issues involved are clearly outlined, this form of *privatization* may not prove to be the panacea which it now seems to be for some advocates.

References

Allen, Harry E., Eskridge, Chris W., Latessa, Edward J., and Vito, Gennaro (1985). *Probation and Parole in America*. New York: The Free Press.

Allen, Harry E. and Simonsen, Clifford E. (1986). *Corrections in America*, 4th. ed. New York: The Macmillan Publishing Co.

Camp, George and Camp, Camille, (1984). *Private Sector Involvement in Prison Services and Operations*. South Salem, NY: National Institute of Corrections.

Dell'Apa, Frank, Adams, W. Tom, Jorgensen, James D., and Sigurdson, Herbert R. (1976). "Advocacy Brokerage, Community: The ABC's of Probation and Parole." *Federal Probation* (December) 37–44.

Levinson, Robert B. (1984). "The Private Sector and Corrections." *Corrections Today* (August) 42–46.

Logan, Charles H. and Rausch, Sharla P. (1985). "Punish and Profit: The Emergence of Private Enterprise Prisons." *Justice Quarterly* 2(3) (September) 303–318.

Mullen, Joan (1984). "Corrections and the Private Sector." *National Institute of Justice Research in Brief* (October) 1–7.

Travis, Lawrence F, Latessa, Edward J. Jr., and Vito, Gennaro F. (1985). "Private Enterprise and Institutional Corrections: A Call for Caution." *Federal Probation* (December) 11–16.

33

Privatization in Juvenile Services
Competition Promotes Quality

Edward J. Loughran

The Massachusetts Department of Youth Services (DYS), the state's juvenile correctional agency, is notorious for being the first state agency to close all its large juvenile institutions and attempt a deinstitutionalized approach to reform. DYS Commissioner Jerome Miller took the quantum leap in 1970 when he emptied the Institute of Juvenile Guidance—a fortress-like building that had been opened in 1954 to house young people diagnosed as psychoneurotics, pre-psychotics, sexual deviants, habitual delinquents, custodial problems, and suffering from character disorders.

Encountering virtually no reprisals for this dramatic step, Miller dismantled the remaining "training schools" (as the institutions were called) during the next two years, leaving hundreds of delinquent youths free. The abrupt abandoning of this 125-year-old system of institutionalization signaled reform in the administration of justice for juveniles throughout the United States.

One observer who witnessed the closing of the Lyman School in 1973 described the scene like this:

> Jerome Miller hops off the first of several school buses that have just pulled through the gate. Like a commissar bent on dismantling one of the dreaded symbols of the "ancien régime," Miller strides into the administration building unannounced, determined to create history. "You can have the buildings," he tells the motley collection of political hangers-on who pass for the staff of the school, "but I'm taking the kids."

Reprinted by permission of the American Correctional Association from *Corrections Today*, 50(6) (Oct. 1988), pp. 78–87.

What followed in Massachusetts was the beginning of a balanced system of juvenile facilities, one in which privatization has played and continues to play a major role. As soon as the decision was made to replace reform schools with smaller, treatment-oriented programs, the state went in search of professional help from private providers to house and care for the recently liberated youths.

Initially, DYS turned to traditional child welfare agencies, such as the New England Home for Little Wanderers and Catholic Charities, since the majority of the programs needed did not exist prior to closing the institutions.

At that time, existing legislation permitted the department to purchase services and programs from nonprofit agencies. Before long, new alternatives to incarceration sprang up everywhere, albeit in a haphazard and uneven way. Still, they were considered far better than the institutions they had replaced. DYS was open to any ideas that would replace "bricks and mortar" with real people interested in caring for troubled kids.

The RFK Action Corps

The department found such a group in 1969 when it encountered a handful of young professionals who had cut their political teeth in the civil rights and anti-war movements and had labored in the field operations of the short-lived presidential campaign of Robert F. Kennedy. Still grieving over his loss, the group often gathered in the watering holes on historic Beacon Hill to comfort one another and speak of past glories. The sad talk gave way to ideas about how best to memorialize their slain leader.

They transformed their anger and sadness into political action and created a living memorial to their friend and mentor—an organization made up of people who would take care of children in trouble. The nonprofit Robert F. Kennedy Action Corps (RFK) was thus born.

RFK began contracting with various state agencies to care for neglected and abused children in Massachusetts. Today, as it begins its 20th year, the RFK Action Corps runs five DYS secure treatment units and four additional programs for the commonwealth's social service agency. It has more than 300 employees and an operating budget of $5 million.

Around the time that the RFK Action Corps was born, the Community Aftercare Program Inc., (CAP) entered the market. Now called the KEY program, CAP consisted of two brothers, Scott and Bill Wolfe. The Wolfes, one at Harvard, the other at Clark University, formed CAP with a vital idea and Harvard Business School methods to implement it.

Both had volunteered at institutions soon after Jerome Miller became DYS commissioner. Aware that DYS facilities were soon to be closed, the Wolfes believed they could supervise many of the youths at home and do it more cheaply and effectively than the state. Only juveniles whose crimes were not considered a threat to public safety were allowed to remain at home, albeit under intense supervision.

The concept was simple enough: Hire young college graduates, give them an opportunity to make a difference, and don't overwhelm them with unmanageable caseloads. CAP workers oversaw seven youths at a time, supervising, tutoring, and assisting in job placement. The worker was responsible for making personal contact with each youth and his family at least three times a week, as well as phoning school officials and employers to ensure attendance.

The intensive supervision came to be known as Outreach and Tracking and represents the most successful model of diversity and innovation in Massachusetts' era of deinstitutionalization. Eligible youths are managed in a less restrictive and more productive environment than the training schools. Today, DYS spends $2 million on private agencies to supervise 280 youths in Outreach and Tracking programs.

Decentralization

Shortly before the state institutions closed, DYS decentralized its service-delivery system and created seven (now five) regional offices. This enabled local administrators to work with providers to develop small residential group homes (10–15 beds), foster care, and alternative schools that would care for the youths.

The market response for community-based services produced a vast array of entrepreneurs offering more than 200 kinds of programs. Rather than using the same approach to reform with all youths (as was the case in the training schools), these new private providers offered services tailored to the individual needs of each teenager.

The introduction of the private sector into all aspects of juvenile justice nurtured experimentation. Privatization's survival depended on transforming a movement into a system.

Typically, contracts with new providers were based on trust, and handshakes rather than formal contractual agreements were the order of the day. After deinstitutionalization the emphasis of juvenile justice in Massachusetts shifted from territorial issues to finding the right programs to meet the needs of the kids. Little thought was given to bureaucratic requirements or expectations on either side of the bargaining table. Once a youth entered a vendor's program it wasn't clear who had ultimate decision-making responsibility—the department or the vendor.

Soon, DYS realized that such an informal purchase of service systems involving millions of dollars invited fiscal and programmatic mischief. New programs were springing up overnight, and the department felt pressure to place as many youths as possible in them.

By the mid-70s, DYS managers turned their energies toward the development of uniform contracting procedures and monitoring protocols that would guarantee a reasonable return on their investment. A contract unit was established within DYS' Central Administrative Office. Today, this unit executes each contract under general purchasing guidelines established by the state.

Program monitoring consists of a number of informal reviews at the regional and central office levels. DYS staff from the commissioner to caseworkers frequently visit programs during business and nonbusiness hours. Total access to contracted programs by the department prevents what otherwise might become an isolated and autonomous program. Fiscal oversight, monthly and quarterly reports, and in-depth program reviews are essential to ensuring mutual satisfaction. Periodic audits of private agencies are conducted by the state auditor and the Executive Office of Human Services, the umbrella agency for DYS.

Needs assessments of the youths to be served are conducted annually and determine both the retention of existing programs and the development of new ones. The department routinely disseminates Requests for Proposals (RFP), inviting responses from interested vendors. A contract review committee, composed of a contract officer and field staff, is assembled for each review. Their task is to evaluate written proposals, hear oral presentations, negotiate mutual obligations and cost agreements, and finally to make a recommendation. Contracts are rebid on a three-year basis, subject to the department's annual budget allocation.

Today, DYS allocates 60.7 percent of its $51.6 million annual budget to Purchase of Service programs. Forty-five private agencies account for 70 individual contracts, including secure treatment facilities, group homes, alternative schools, outreach and tracking programs, psychological assessments, and health services.

Eighteen years have passed since DYS pioneered privatization within human services in Massachusetts. In the budget for fiscal year 1988, human service agencies such as the departments of

Mental Health, Mental Retardation, Public Health, Correction, Social Services, and Welfare spent $500 million for contracted services.

Privatization Today

Privatization in Massachusetts is characterized by four factors: diversity, flexibility, cost-effectiveness, and competition.

Diversity. Opening the rehabilitative process to competitive market forces has yielded an abundance of approaches to treating juveniles. Experimentation allowed program models such as Outreach and Tracking, Tracking Plus (a short-term residential backup to Outreach and Tracking), and residential programs to take root and become integral parts of the reintegration process.

The private sector has developed expertise in both outreach and service delivery. Unlike the state bureaucracy, the private provider is better positioned to involve the community as full partners in youth rehabilitation. Their boards of directors—chosen from among business, religious, academic, and political leaders—have a stake in the program's performance.

Flexibility. Tenured staff, complex organizational subsystems, and sheer size made modifying or replacing large institutions a difficult effort. Today, DYS enjoys a high degree of flexibility in meeting both its legal responsibilities and the ever-changing needs of youths in the state's juvenile justice system.

If a provider is not performing up to acceptable standards, the state can serve notice and rebid the contract. In fact, either party can end the contractual arrangement for any reason with appropriate notification.

The problems and needs presented by today's young offenders are substantially different from those presented by delinquents of 20 years ago. Increases in the numbers of juvenile sex offenders, emotionally disturbed delinquents, violent offenders, and drug- and alcohol-dependent youths all require specialized responses. Purchase of service accounts permit the state to redirect funding to new programs rather than trying to alter already existing programs in the state bureaucracy.

Cost-Effectiveness. The programs that have replaced the institutions in Massachusetts are not necessarily less costly than their counterparts elsewhere. It is dangerous to view deinstitutionalization and privatization solely in terms of money spent. Quality programs, whether they exist in institutions or in the community, will be expensive if they are adequately staffed and resourced. However, the move away from large state-operated institutions to small, privately managed programs has produced efficiencies that were not possible when all the youths committed to DYS were sent to five large training schools.

By their nature, institutions create specialized maintenance subsystems in order to remain operational. They become increasingly costly and inefficient because most of the daily business in institutions becomes control and population management.

Today, the department uses a variety of programs that provide appropriate levels of security and programming as determined by the risks and needs presented by the youths in each program.

Competition. For 125 years, Massachusetts committed itself to a single system of intervention with young offenders. This state-operated approach was virtually assured of funding from year to year and had little if any incentive to be creative or innovative. Privatization introduced an essential element. By regularly re-bidding contracts, a competitive spirit is maintained that ensures the development of new and varied approaches to combating juvenile crime.

Adolescence is a state of "incompleteness" in the development of a life. Teenagers are still evolving emotionally, sexually, and psychologically. The juvenile court and its separate justice system was created in recognition of a youth's ability to change.

Having abandoned large training schools in favor of a community-based, contract-for-services approach, DYS committed itself to a policy that takes reasonable risks with the majority of young offenders, but yields a greater return. The state-run training schools took a low-risk approach and received equally low returns on their investment.

Experimentation with alternatives to institutions permitted DYS to discover what works best for whom and under what conditions. Today, it continues to take risks because tangible, positive outcomes result. The risks are appropriately managed by having more than 50 private programs to choose from, each with its own characteristics and strengths. Unlike the training school systems, DYS can now opt for another program at any point.

As our experience in community-based care increases and we incorporate new changes to better address the true needs of today's youth, privatization plays a key role in enabling us to combine order and stability with progress and change.